Palgrave Studies in European Union Politics

Edited by: **Michelle Egan,** American University, USA, **Neill Nugent,** Manchester Metropolitan University,UK and **William Paterson OBE,** University of Aston, UK.

Editorial Board: **Christopher Hill,** Cambridge, UK, **Simon Hix,** London School of Economics, UK, **Mark Pollack,** Temple University, USA, **Kalypso Nicolaïdis,** Oxford, UK, **Morten Egeberg,** University of Oslo, Norway, **Amy Verdun,** University of Victoria, Canada, **Claudio M. Radaelli,** University of Exeter, UK, **Frank Schimmelfennig,** Swiss Federal Institute of Technology, Switzerland

Following the sustained success of the acclaimed *European Union Series,* which essentially publishes research-based textbooks, *Palgrave Studies in European Union Politics* publishes cutting-edge research-driven monographs.

The remit of the series is broadly defined, both in terms of subject and academic discipline. All topics of significance concerning the nature and operation of the European Union potentially fall within the scope of the series. The series is multidisciplinary to reflect the growing importance of the EU as a political, economic and social phenomenon.

Titles include:
Ian Bache and Andrew Jordan (*editors*)
THE EUROPEANIZATION OF BRITISH POLITICS

Richard Balme and Brian Bridges (*editors*)
EUROPE-ASIA RELATIONS
Building Multilateralisms

Thierry Balzacq (*editor*)
THE EXTERNAL DIMENSION OF EU JUSTICE AND HOME AFFAIRS
Governance, Neighbours, Security

Michael Baun and Dan Marek (*editors*)
EU COHESION POLICY AFTER ENLARGEMENT

Derek Beach and Colette Mazzucelli (*editors*)
LEADERSHIP IN THE BIG BANGS OF EUROPEAN INTEGRATION

Tanja A. Börzel (*editor*)
COPING WITH ACCESSION TO THE EUROPEAN UNION
New Modes of Environmental Governance

Milena Büchs
NEW GOVERNANCE IN EUROPEAN SOCIAL POLICY
The Open Method of Coordination

Kenneth Dyson and Angelos Sepos (*editors*)
WHICH EUROPE?
The Politics of Differentiated Integration

Michelle Egan, Neill Nugent, William E. Paterson (*editors*)
RESEARCH AGENDAS IN EU STUDIES
Stalking the Elephant

Kevin Featherstone and Dimitris Papadimitriou
THE LIMITS OF EUROPEANIZATION
Reform Capacity and Policy Conflict in Greece

Stefan Gänzle and Allen G. Sens (*editors*)
THE CHANGING POLITICS OF EUROPEAN SECURITY
Europe Alone?

Heather Grabbe
THE EU'S TRANSFORMATIVE POWER

Eva Gross
THE EUROPEANIZATION OF NATIONAL FOREIGN POLICY
Continuity and Change in European Crisis Management

Hussein Kassim and Handley Stevens
AIR TRANSPORT AND THE EUROPEAN UNION
Europeanization and Its Limits

Robert Kissack
PURSUING EFFECTIVE MULTILATERALISM
The European Union, International Organizations and the Politics of Decision Making

Katie Verlin Laatikainen and Karen E. Smith (*editors*)
THE EUROPEAN UNION AND THE UNITED NATIONS
Intersecting Multilateralisms

Esra LaGro and Knud Erik Jørgensen (*editors*)
TURKEY AND THE EUROPEAN UNION
Prospects for a Difficult Encounter

Ingo Linsenmann, Christoph O. Meyer and Wolfgang T. Wessels (*editors*)
ECONOMIC GOVERNMENT OF THE EU
A Balance Sheet of New Modes of Policy Coordination

Hartmut Mayer and Henri Vogt (*editors*)
A RESPONSIBLE EUROPE?
Ethical Foundations of EU External Affairs

Philomena Murray (*editor*)
EUROPE AND ASIA
Regions in Flux

Costanza Musu
EUROPEAN UNION POLICY TOWARDS THE ARAB-ISRAELI PEACE PROCESS
The Quicksands of Politics

Daniel Naurin and Helen Wallace (*editors*)
UNVEILING THE COUNCIL OF THE EUROPEAN UNION
Games Governments Play in Brussels

David Phinnemore and Alex Warleigh-Lack
REFLECTIONS ON EUROPEAN INTEGRATION
50 Years of the Treaty of Rome

Sebastiaan Princen
AGENDA-SETTING IN THE EUROPEAN UNION

Asle Toje
AFTER THE POST-COLD WAR
The European Union as a Small Power

Richard G. Whitman, Stefan Wolff (*editors*)
THE EUROPEAN NEIGHBOURHOOD POLICY IN PERSPECTIVE
Context, Implementation and Impact

Palgrave Studies in European Union Politics
Series Standing Order ISBN 978-1-4039-9511-7 (hardback) and
ISBN 978-1-4039-9512-4 (paperback)

You can receive future titles in this series as they are published by placing a standing order. Please contact your bookseller or, in case of difficulty, write to us at the address below with your name and address, the title of the series and one of the ISBNs quoted above.

Customer Services Department, Macmillan Distribution Ltd, Houndmills, Basingstoke, Hampshire RG21 6XS, UK.

Which Europe?

The Politics of Differentiated Integration

Edited by

Kenneth Dyson
Research Professor, School of European Studies, Cardiff University, UK

Angelos Sepos
Lecturer in European Politics, School of Social Sciences, University of Manchester, UK

First published 2010 by
PALGRAVE MACMILLAN

Palgrave Macmillan in the UK is an imprint of Macmillan Publishers Limited,
registered in England, company number 785998, of Houndmills, Basingstoke,
Hampshire RG21 6XS.

Palgrave Macmillan in the US is a division of St Martin's Press LLC,
175 Fifth Avenue, New York, NY 10010.

Palgrave Macmillan is the global academic imprint of the above companies
and has companies and representatives throughout the world.

Palgrave® and Macmillan® are registered trademarks in the United States,
the United Kingdom, Europe and other countries.

ISBN 978–0–230–55377–4   hardback

This book is printed on paper suitable for recycling and made from fully
managed and sustained forest sources. Logging, pulping and manufacturing
processes are expected to conform to the environmental regulations of the
country of origin.

A catalogue record for this book is available from the British Library.

A catalog record for this book is available from the Library of Congress.

10 9 8 7 6 5 4 3 2 1
19 18 17 16 15 14 13 12 11 10

Printed and bound in Great Britain by
CPI Antony Rowe, Chippenham and Eastbourne

Contents

Preface and Acknowledgements

The model of unitary integration has dominated thinking about post-1945 European integration. Its power as a persuasive narrative derives from its combination of normative and causal beliefs that support and give coherence to the European project of 'ever closer union'. In normative terms the unitary principle rests on the political ideal of European solidarity through ensuring the equality of Member States in sharing common rights and obligations. The corollary is a unitary legal order embracing all states and their peoples. The unitary principle also reflects the economic values of efficiency and growth through exploiting large, continent-wide market scale. The corollary is that customs union, common external trade policy and, above all, the single market, with a 'level playing field' ensured by competition policy, become core to unitary integration. In this perspective differentiation is a temporary and highly constrained phenomenon, essentially an epiphenomenon.

In practice, this model has only ever applied with major reservations. Most basically, the Community-building process began with only six Member States, a mini-Europe. Even as the Community expanded in membership, the Cold War set boundaries to the process. There were 'multiple Europes' before the geostrategic parameters shifted decisively in 1989–90. Not least, 'economic' Europe and 'defence' Europe assumed different institutional forms (notably the European Economic Community and NATO) with non-identical memberships. 'Multiple Europes' survived the end of the Cold War. However, once its barriers were removed, more and more of European space became enclosed within the European Union. By 2007 it had grown to 27 members. In consequence, the unitary principle was territorially extended across Europe. Nevertheless, successive enlargements, before and after the end of the Cold War, acted as catalysts for renewed debates about the principle of differentiated integration. Greater diversity in membership, not least in levels of economic development and in institutional capacity, raised questions about the unitary principle. At the same time, extension of the scope of EU policies, along with 'deepening' of the integration process through institutional and procedural reforms, also posed challenges to the unitary principle. The combination of *enlargement*, increasing *scope* of policies and institutional *deepening* served to give a new saliency to the model (or rather models) of differentiated integration. Correspondingly, territory, function and temporality seemed of increasing relevance for understanding the complex and evolving balance between the unitary and differentiation principles.

This volume seeks to catalogue differentiated integration in Europe and to offer a set of partly complementary and partly competing explanations for this complex and multi-faceted phenomenon. Though its central disciplinary basis remains political science and international relations, the perspectives offered reach across disciplines into economics, geography, history and sociology. The volume does not seek to advocate a single unifying theory of differentiated

vii

integration. Its objective is to get readers to think theoretically about the phenom-enon by providing a range of tools for this purpose. Its other objective is empirical: to provide an inventory. The resulting picture is by no means complete. The very fact that such a wide ranging set of chapters contains gaps – for instance, territorially, the three Benelux states and, functionally, aspects of the single market – is testament to its sheer scale. In making necessary decisions about exclusion, we have sought to capture the 'wider' Europe beyond the conventional 'old' EEC We have also taken account of what the authors of the 'function' chapters – as subject experts – chose to select.

The idea for this volume was conceived by the editors during one of the research activities of the EU Consent Network of Excellence, coordinated by Professor Wolfgang Wessels of the University of Cologne, and was significantly shaped by the debates that took place within the network. This volume has benefited ines-timably from the British Academy Small Research Grant that made possible the organization of a three-day workshop at Cardiff University in September 2008. At this workshop the first drafts of the chapters were presented, with contribu-tors acting as discussants for each other's papers. The resulting debates enabled the editors to provide detailed guidance to authors. We are enormously grateful to authors for the good-natured way in which they dealt with the comments of discussants and editors. It must be stressed that the editors sought to organize a learning process amongst authors, not to advocate a single best approach. The main unifying theme was the political nature of differentiated integration.

The project also benefited from the earlier smaller workshop of the 'theory chapter' authors, held at the European University Institute in Florence in May 2008. We are very grateful to Professor Michael Keating for making the necessary arrangements. Last, but not least, we would like to thank two members of staff in the School of European Studies at Cardiff University: Dr Katja Seidel for organiz-ing the workshop; and Mary Raschella for handling the financial matters. Both Katja and Mary lightened our loads enormously.

In the final analysis, though, the quality of this volume owes so much to the authors of the theory, policy and territory chapters. It has been a pleasure as well as a source of intellectual profit to work with them.

Kenneth Dyson
Angelos Sepos

July 2009

Notes on Contributors

Kenneth Dyson is Research Professor in the School of European Studies at Cardiff University, Wales, a Fellow of the British Academy, an Academician of the Learned Societies of the Social Sciences, and Fellow of the Royal Historical Society. He has written extensively on European macro-economic governance and policies, including *Elusive Union: The Process of Economic and Monetary Union* (Longman, 1994), *The Road to Maastricht: Negotiating Economic and Monetary Union* (with Kevin Featherstone) (Oxford University Press, 1999), *The Politics of the Euro Zone* (Oxford University Press, 2000), *European States and the Euro* (Oxford University Press, 2002) and *Enlarging the Euro Area: External Empowerment and Domestic Transformation in East Central Europe* (Oxford University Press, 2006). His most recent edited books are *The Euro at 10* (Oxford University Press, 2008) and (with Martin Marcussen) *Central Banks in the Age of the Euro* (Oxford University Press, 2009). Also, he was adviser to the BBC2 series 'The Money Changers – The Struggle for the Euro'. He is co-editor of the 2010 special issue of *German Politics* on 'Grand Coalitions in German Politics'. His *State Tradition in Western Europe* is being reissued in the ECPR Classics series. He was DAAD Distinguished Visiting Professor at the Free University of Berlin. *dysonkh@cardiff.ac.uk*

Angelos Sepos is Lecturer in European Politics in the School of Social Sciences at the University of Manchester. After completing his PhD at Cambridge University, he was a Jean Monnet Fellow at the European University Institute and a Lecturer in European Politics at the University of Cyprus and Newcastle University. He is the author of *The Europeanization of Cyprus: Polity, Policies and Politics* (Palgrave Macmillan, 2008) and has also published work in journals and edited volumes on federalism, European public policy/public administration, Europeanization, differentiated integration and EU-Member States relations, particularly on Cyprus. *angelos.sepos@manchester.ac.uk*

Daniele Caramani is Professor of Comparative Politics at the University of St Gallen, Switzerland. On the topic of the chapter in this book, he has co-edited with Yves Mény *Challenges to Consensual Politics: Democracy, Identity, and Populist Protest in the Alpine Region* (P.I.E.-Peter Lang, 2005). He is also the author of *The Nationalization of Politics* (Cambridge University Press, 2004) for which he received the Stein Rokkan Prize, and is the editor of the textbook *Comparative Politics* (Oxford University Press, 2008). *daniele.caramani@unisg.ch*

Alistair Cole is Professor of European Politics at Cardiff University, a post he has held since 1999. His research interest lies in the sphere of contemporary and comparative European politics and policy, with special (but not exclusive) reference to France, Franco-German relations and Franco-British comparisons. He has published extensively in this field, with five monographs to his credit and articles in many of the leading political science and area studies journals. His most recent publication is *Governing and Governance in France* (Cambridge University Press, 2008). *colea@cf.ac.uk*

Tom Dyson is an Alexander von Humboldt Foundation Research Fellow at the Chair of German and European Politics at the University of Potsdam on a two-year sabbatical from the University of Surrey's Department of Political, International and Policy Studies, where he holds a lectureship in international security. Dr Dyson has published articles on post-Cold War European defence reform in *Defence Studies, Security Studies* and *European Security* and is the author of *The Politics of German Defence and Security: Policy Leadership and Military Reform in the Post-Cold War Era* (Berghahn, 2007) and of *Neoclassical Realism and Defence Reform in Post-Cold War Europe* (Palgrave Macmillan, 2010). *t.dyson@surrey.ac.uk*

Spyros Economides is Senior Lecturer in International Relations and European Politics in the European Institute at the London School of Economics, and Director of its research unit on South East Europe, 'LSEE'. He has been a Research Associate at the International Institute for Strategic Studies in London and Specialist Adviser to the House of Lords EU Committee in its report, 'Responding to the Balkan Challenge: The Role of EU Aid'. His publications include: *UN Interventionism: 1991–2004* (edited with Mats Berdal, Cambridge University Press, 2007); and *The Economic Factor in International Relations* (with Peter Wilson, I.B. Tauris, 2001). He is currently writing on the EU's Balkan experience since 1991. *s.economides@lse.ac.uk*

Geoffrey Edwards is Reader in European Studies in the Department of Politics and International Studies in the University of Cambridge and a Fellow of Pembroke College, Cambridge, where he is also a graduate Tutor. He holds a Jean Monnet chair in Political Science. His research interests are the institutional development of the EU and, in particular, the EU's foreign, security and defence policies on which he has written extensively. *gre1000@cam.ac.uk*

Paul Furlong is Professor of European Studies at Cardiff University and Head of the Cardiff School of European Studies. He has written widely on Italian politics, especially Italian political economy, and on European integration. He is currently working on a study of the political thought of Julius Evola. *furlongp@cardiff.ac.uk*

Andrew Gamble is Professor of Politics and a Fellow of Queens' College at the University of Cambridge. He is joint editor of *The Political Quarterly* and a Fellow of the British Academy. He has published widely on British politics, public policy, and political economy. In 2005 he was awarded the PSA Isaiah Berlin prize for Lifetime Contribution to Political Studies. His books include *Between Europe and America: The Future of British Politics* (Palgrave Macmillan, 2003) and *The Spectre at the Feast: Capitalist Crisis and the Politics of Recession* (Palgrave Macmillan, 2009). *amg59@cam.ac.uk*

Klaus H. Goetz holds the Chair in German and European Politics and Government at the University of Potsdam, Germany. He previously taught at the LSE and has held Visiting Professorships at Humboldt University of Berlin, the University of Tokyo and the Institute of Advanced Studies, Vienna. He is currently working on a research project on the temporality of EU governance, which is funded by the German Research Foundation. His most recent publication is a special issue of the *Journal of European Public Policy*, Vol. 16, No. 2, 2009, on the EU timescape. Since 2000, he has been co-editor of *West European Politics*. *khgoetz@uni-potsdam.de*

Béla Greskovits is Professor, PhD, at the Department of International Relations and European Studies, Central European University, Budapest, Hungary. His research interests are the political economy of east-central European capitalism, comparative democratization, and social protest. He has taught courses on the above at the Central European University, Harvard University and Cornell University. He is currently working on a book (co-authored with Dorothee Bohle) on *Capitalist Diversity on Europe's Periphery*. He is author of *The Political Economy of Protest and Patience. East European and Latin American Transformations Compared* (Central European University Press, 1998). His most recent articles have appeared in *Studies in Comparative and International Development, Labor History, Orbis, West European Politics, Competition and Change,* and *Journal of Democracy*. *greskovi@ceu.hu*

Paul M. Heywood is Sir Francis Hill Professor of European Politics at the University of Nottingham, and Adjunct Professor at Hunan University, China, where he is also Senior Adviser to the Anti-Corruption Research Centre. His main areas of research interest include democratization and political change in Europe; state capacity and the policy process; and political corruption. His principal focus has been on contemporary Spain and Western Europe, but he has also worked on central and eastern Europe, Asia and the countries of the former Soviet Union. *paul.heywood@nottingham.ac.uk*

David Howarth is a Senior Lecturer and Jean Monnet Chair in Politics and International Relations at the University of Edinburgh. He works on the political economy of European integration, Economic and Monetary Union, the European Central Bank, French political economy and France and European integration. He has written over four dozen articles, book chapters and books on these subjects. *d.howarth@ed.ac.uk*

Michael Keating is Professor of Politics at the European University Institute in Florence, and at the University of Aberdeen. Between 1988 and 1999 he was Professor of Political Science at the University of Western Ontario and before that was Senior Lecturer at the University of Strathclyde. He has taught in England, France, the United States and Spain. Dr Keating is author of numerous books and articles on European politics, nationalism, regionalism and public policy. His most recent book is *The Independence of Scotland* (Oxford University Press, 2009).

A second edition of his *The Government of Scotland* will be published by Edinburgh University Press in 2010. *keating@eui.eu*

Alkuin Kölliker is a Scientific Adviser at the Swiss State Secretariat for Economic Affairs and works in the field of regulatory impact assessment (RIA). He holds a degree in Economics from the University of Bern and a PhD in Political Science from the European University Institute in Florence. Previously, he was as a research fellow at the Max Planck Institute for Research on Collective Good in Bonn and an assistant professor at the University of Bielefeld. His publications focus on international collective action and include *Flexibility and European Unification: The Logic of Differentiated Integration* (Rowman & Littlefield, 2006). *alkuin.koelliker@ gmx.ch*

Marko Lehti is Senior Research Fellow at Tampere Peace Research Institute at the University of Tampere and Academic Director of the Baltic Sea Region Studies Master's Programme at the University of Turku, Finland. Publications include: *Contested and Shared Places of Memory: History and Politics in North Eastern Europe* (edited with Jörg Hackmann, Routledge, 2009), *The Struggle for the West: Divided and Contested Legacy of the West* (edited with Christopher Browning, Routledge, 2009), *The Baltic as a Multicultural World: Sea, Region and Peoples* (editor, BWV, 2005), *Post-Cold War Identity Politics. Northern and Baltic Experiences* (edited with David Smith, Frank Cass, 2003), *A Baltic League as a Construct of the New Europe. Envisioning a Baltic Region and Small State Sovereignty in the Aftermath of the First World War* (Peter Lang, 1999). *marko.lehti@uta.fi*

Lauren McLaren is Associate Professor of Politics and former Director of the Centre for the Study of European Governance at Nottingham University. Her publications include *Constructing Democracy in Southern Europe: A Comparative Analysis of Democratic Consolidation in Italy, Spain and Turkey* (Routledge, 2008), *Identity, Interests, and Opposition to European Integration* (Palgrave Macmillan, 2006), and articles on public opinion on immigration in Europe and attitudes to European integration in the *Journal of Politics*, the *European Journal of Political Research, Social Forces, European Union Politics*, and *Political Studies*. *lauren.mclaren@ nottingham.ac.uk*

Lee Miles is Professor of Political Science in the Department of Political and Historical Studies and Senior EU Academic Adviser at Karlstad University, Sweden. He is also Professor of Politics, Jean Monnet Chair in European Union Government and Politics and Co-Director of the Europe in the World Centre (EWC) at the University of Liverpool, UK. Dr Miles has written extensively on contemporary Nordic politics, and has a particular interest in researching Nordic relations with the European Union. Relevant publications include, for example, *Fusing with Europe? Sweden in the European Union* (Ashgate, 2005). From 2010 to 2012 he is also co-editor of the prestigious international relations journal, *Cooperation and Conflict* (published by SAGE). *l.s.miles@liverpool.ac.uk*

Jörg Monar, Dr.phil., Dr.rer.pol, is Director of Political and Administrative Studies at the College of Europe (Bruges) and Professor of Contemporary European Studies at the Sussex European Institute (University of Sussex). He was previously Professor and Director of the SECURINT project at the Université Robert Schuman (Strasbourg) and Professor of Politics and Director of CEPI at the University of Leicester. He is also Joint (founding) Editor of the *European Foreign Affairs Review* (Alphen), Member of the Board of the Institut für Europäische Politik (Berlin) and on the editorial/advisory board of *Comparative European Politics* (Basingstoke/New York), *Nowa Europa* (Warsaw), *Integration* (Berlin) and *Études Européennes* (Strasbourg). *jmonar@coleurop.be*

Nick Parsons is Reader in French at the School of European Studies, Cardiff University. He has published extensively on employment policy and industrial relations in Britain, France and Europe, as well as on French politics and society. His recent books are *French Industrial Relations in the New World Economy* (Palgrave, 2005) and (co-edited with Yuan Zhigang) *Economic Globalisation and Employment Policy* (Beijing, 2005). *parsonsn@Cardiff.ac.uk*

Philippe Pochet, a Political Scientist, is General Director of the European Trade Union Institute (ETUI). He lectures at the Université Catholique de Louvain (UCL). His main fields of research are European monetary integration, the social dimension and employment policies. His recent publications include *Social Pact in Europe* (co-edited with D. Natali and M. Keune, ETUI, 2009) and *The OMC in Action* (with J. Zeitlin, P.I.E.-Peter Lang, 2005). *ppochet@etui.org*

Jiří Přibáň is Professor of Law at Cardiff Law School, Cardiff University, and specializes in social theory of law, legal philosophy and theory of constitutionalism, European law and human rights. He is author and editor of a number of books in English and Czech, especially *Legal Symbolism* (2007), *Dissidents of Law* (2001), *Liquid Society and Its Law* (edited in 2007), *Systems of Justice in Transition* (edited with P. Roberts and J. Young in 2003), *Law's New Boundaries* (edited with D. Nelken in 2001) and *The Rule of Law in Central Europe* (edited with J. Young in 1999). He has been visiting professor and scholar, for instance, at UC Berkeley, Stanford University, New York University, the European University Institute, the Royal Flemish Academy, the University of Pretoria, and the University of New South Wales. He regularly contributes to Czech TV, radio and newspapers. *priban@cardiff.ac.uk*

Rüdiger Wurzel is Reader and Jean Monnet Chair in European Union Studies at the University of Hull where he is Director of the Centre for European Union Studies (CEUS). He has completed successfully a large number of externally funded research projects and published widely on issues of European environmental policy, EU and German politics and new modes of governance. His recent publications include *The Politics of Emissions Trading in Britain and Germany* (Anglo-German Foundation, 2008) and *Environmental Policy-Making in Britain, Germany and the European Union. The Europeanisation of Air and Water Pollution Control* (Manchester University Press, 2006). *r.k.wurzel@hull.ac.uk*

Anthony R. Zito is Reader in Politics at Newcastle University and is currently Politics Research Director and Co-Director of the Jean Monnet Centre at Newcastle University. His broad research interests focus on the European Union decision-making process, policy-making processes and expert networks. Dr Zito was a 2007 Leverhulme Fellow, conducting a comparative analysis of EU and United States environmental agencies. He has authored *Creating Environmental Policy in the European Union* (Palgrave, 2000) and articles in *Political Studies, Public Administration, Governance,* the *Journal of European Public Policy* and other journals, focusing on the EU policy process and environmental actors and policy-making. *a.r.zito@ncl.ac.uk*

Tables

Figure

Part I The Context of Differentiated Integration

1

Differentiation as Design Principle and as Tool in the Political Management of European Integration

Kenneth Dyson and Angelos Sepos

The Euro Area, 'Schengen' Europe, 'social' Europe, and the European Security and Defence Policy (ESDP) represent the visible tip of an iceberg of differentiated integration that has grown up within the European Union (EU). Differentiated integration is one instrument for addressing a classic political problem of collective action: that in many circumstances an outcome that is clearly to the advantage of most or all concerned is blocked by the fact that one or more find better reason to veto the proposal. In this respect it belongs alongside two other instruments: 'issue-linkage' and side payments, both of which have been traditional instruments to facilitate integration in Europe by buying off opposition. For reasons outlined in this chapter, differentiation has been increasingly used in European integration. This book uncovers and analyses its incidence in functional and territorial terms and examines the value of competing explanations of differentiated integration.

Aims, concepts and approach

This book has three main aims. Firstly, it seeks to fathom the uncharted depths of differentiated integration, to cast a searchlight into its murky complexities. This aim shapes the structure of the book, with its chapters dealing with various core functional fields and with key spatial clusters. In this way it is possible to plot the complexity of differentiated integration on a territorial as well as functional basis.

Secondly, the book addresses a set of themes about the politics of differentiated integration as a design principle and as a tool of political management that cut across the different chapters and that have more general implications for European integration.

Thirdly, and more challengingly, the book seeks to understand and explain the phenomenon of differentiated integration. This aim raises a series of difficulties that editors and contributors have struggled to manage. Understanding differentiated integration requires some boundary-setting to prevent concept-stretching. 'Integration' is not 'cooperation', arguably not even 'union', and it is not 'Europeanization'. Cooperation refers to working together without merging, let alone transferring, sovereignty. Europeanization refers to the effects of

European integration on the Member States, as opposed to how and why they play a role in integration.

However, though we must retain clear distinct conceptual boundaries, the phenomena of integration, cooperation and Europeanization are closely intertwined. Differential Europeanization of domestic economic and monetary policies as a consequence of Exchange Rate Mechanism (ERM) membership, especially in the 'hard' ERM, affected both the political will and the state capacity to gain entry to the Euro Area. Similarly, earlier differential cooperation on reducing border controls under the Schengen treaties formed the basis for later differential integration in internal security policies. Cooperation, integration and union can be conceptualized as a ladder. Boundary-setting is in fact not clear in some of the key concepts grouped under differentiated integration, like 'enhanced cooperation' and Europe *à la carte*.

Differentiated integration remains a concept 'replete with terminological and semantic confusion' (Edwards and Phillipart, 1997: 1). In the words of Stubb (1996), it suffers from 'semantic indigestion' (which since then has probably worsened). The subject seems prone to scholasticism, with endless verbal variations, subtle analytical refinements and internal quarrels that threaten inward-looking academic debates, intellectual confusion and exhaustion. The vocabulary proliferates: enhanced cooperation, permanent structured cooperation, flexibility, core Europe, two- or multi-tier Europe, two- or multi-speed Europe, concentric circles, avant-garde, pioneer group, variably geometry, *à la carte*. Whilst concepts like variable geometry, multi-speed and *à la carte* offer subtle analytical refinements, they lack sufficient properties of precision, internal coherence and distinctiveness to offer much value-added in clarifying the empirical complexity.

The challenge is how to make the concept serviceable and flexible for interdisciplinary research without over-stretching it. The definition that we proffer seeks to bring together the two main ways of thinking about differentiated integration: in functionally based policy terms and in territorially based constructions of identity. However, the definition retains a commitment to the more 'classical' institutional–legal perspective focusing on different rights and obligations and on differentiation amongst states and sub-state units:

> *Differentiated integration is the process whereby European states, or sub-state units, opt to move at different speeds and/or towards different objectives with regard to common policies. It involves adopting different formal and informal arrangements (hard and soft), inside or outside the EU treaty framework (membership and accession differentiation, alongside various differentiated forms of economic, trade and security relations). In this way relevant actors come to assume different rights and obligations and to share a distinct attitude towards the integration process – what it is appropriate to do together, and who belongs with whom.*

Though structurally embedded, states remain key units of analysis. This choice can be justified as states remain the main arenas for political contest about participating in differentiated integration, about its legitimation and about its appropriate forms – delegation, sharing of competences or cooperation.

At the same time, key 'drivers' of differentiated integration extend beyond the institutional–legal realm. They include functional specificity and spatial 'rescaling'. Functions migrate away from states, at different rates and in different ways. Similarly, new digital information and communication technologies create 'virtual' spaces, as in financial markets and central banking. The result is a complex and problematic territorial uncoupling of politics and policies that offers new and varying opportunities for differentiated integration (for instance, in financial market regulation and supervision and in monetary policies). Another key 'driver' is differences in the timing of EU accession in relation to the growth of the *acquis*. Norms and habits of solidarity are stronger amongst the original 'Six' EEC founding members because they have constructed the *acquis* from the outset and had time to adjust to it (though they are still differential in its application). Hence the 'Six' participate most actively in differentiated integration (for example, in the Euro Area, Schengen Area and ESDP). This pattern of participation makes them *de facto* a 'deeper core community' even in the absence of a formally instituted core Europe. Functional specificity, complex spatial 'rescaling' and differences in accession timing also suggest challenges to traditional 'state clustering' like Mediterranean, Nordic and Central European Europe.

In its efforts to understand and explain differentiated integration this book is not founded on the hard rock of a unified conceptual framework but in the wet marshes of multi-disciplinary perspectives. More precisely, each contributor has been given latitude to find their own most appropriate hard rock from which to tackle their particular topic. This approach does not stem from editorial laziness. It represents in part a shared sceptical empiricism that prefers to work from the particularities of the case to see if patterns can be discerned and generalizations can be drawn. It also recognizes the character of the phenomenon under investigation. Differentiated integration is a complex, multi-dimensional phenomenon that requires a cross-disciplinary approach. Though the team shares a solid grounding in Political Science and International Relations, its members work in different cross-disciplinary combinations. The disciplines on which they draw involve very different characteristic epistemologies, conceptual frameworks and theories, not to mention underlying ontologies. Some are constructivists, others realists, often in ways that say much about the sector involved (compare foreign policy and defence policy). The editorial decision has been to work with this diversity and to mould it lightly together both around a shared vocabulary of function, space and time as the core coordinates of differentiated integration and around a set of shared political questions and political themes.

In thinking about integration and differentiation we need to remember that they are not mutually exclusive, one-way processes. They are dynamically interrelated. Each frames the context of the other. We are investigating an attribute of integration, something that describes integration more fully. If integration suggests some European-level 'universality', the particularities of differentiation may prove complementary rather than competing with integration. On the one hand,

*transit'nal
or temp'l
transit'nal?*

changes in the 'governing scope', the 'deepening' and 'geographic scope' may act as catalysts for greater differentiation. On the other hand, differentiation has effects on European integration that also need to be investigated. Does it prove to be temporary/transitional or semi-permanent, notably after EU enlargement and after monetary union? This complex mix of complementarity and competition, of universality and particularity, must somehow be captured in how we think about and theorize differentiated integration. It is, at least in part, implicit in our focus on how EU broadening of scope, 'deepening' and 'widening' relate to differentiated integration.

We have avoided the search to impose a single, unified conceptual framework and to seek out simple cause–effect relations as too restrictive and rigid. We wish to capture the complexity and the richness of the forces shaping differentiated integration, and how it in turn is exerting its own effects. In particular, we do not see it as a simple epiphenomenon of enlargement. After all, differentiated integration comes sometimes before and at other times after enlargement. Moreover, function, space and time are properties as well as 'drivers' of differentiated integration. Contributors have, accordingly, been asked to examine the relationships of six key variables to differentiated integration: function, space and time; and EU broadening, 'deepening' and 'widening'.

Questions and structure

Alongside the chapter on law and the three framework chapters on function, territory and time, this chapter spells out the key factors shaping differentiated integration. They form the context for the later functional and territorial chapters. It should be stressed that the functions and territories have not been chosen on the assumption that they contain and help explain a high level of differentiated integration. Rather they show that evidence on differentiated integration is variable across functions and territories. It is interesting to ask why it is more weakly developed in some contexts than in others, for instance in the Balkans than in the Baltic.

Authors have been asked to consider:

- The context by highlighting the relevant historical factors and legacies and the relevant external pressures and leverage.
- The 'what' and the 'when' by mapping out the forms of differentiated integration in their area. How much differentiated integration exists, in what forms and at which levels? How has it evolved over time?
- The 'why' by trying to explain the form, scope and timing of differentiated integration, drawing as they see appropriate on the common reference points and language in the three theory chapters on function, territory and time. Why is it more prevalent in some contexts than others? We left it to the professional judgement of each author to assess which theories are more relevant to her/his functional or territorial area. However, we expected them to clarify the political context of differentiated integration with reference to the properties of policy areas (function), territories and time periods.

- The 'how' and the 'who' by examining the salient geo-strategic, politico-economic, socio-cultural and legal–institutional processes involved and the actors (supranational, state and sub-state) driving the process. We leave it to the professional judgement of each author to assess which processes are most 'salient' in their area and to justify her/his choice.
- One or more of the following key questions, as relevant, in their conclusion: 1) how differentiated integration relates to changes in EU broadening, 'deepening' and 'widening'; 2) whether and how differentiated integration has been used as a tool to strengthen regional identities; and 3) the growing political problem of misfit between functional migration to new spatial scales and the capacity of states and even of the EU (is differentiated integration 'rescuing' states and the EU?).

Differentiated integration as politics and history

This introduction focuses on the politics of differentiated integration in Europe. In addition to spelling out the design and structure of the volume, it analyses what different social science disciplines and what 'grand' theories of integration have had to say about the politics of differentiated integration. Along with law (see Chapter 2 by Přibáň), politics offers a macro-framework that helps us to understand how function, territory and time shape the scope and character of differentiated integration. It is important to analyse not just how much differentiated integration there is (scope) but also the ideological polarization (character) that it involves. In focusing on its political properties and drivers, the introduction raises some key questions: 1) How is differentiated integration affecting regional identity formation?; 2) Is differentiated integration 'rescuing' both states and the EU by making it possible to more effectively manage complex trans-national spaces? Alternatively, is it producing 'disintegration', measured, for instance, by declining support for EU membership or accession?; and 3) More generally, what are the implications of differentiated integration for integration theory and for the politics of European integration?

There is a broad historical context that gives a new saliency to the politics of differentiated integration. On the one hand, the principle of unitary integration – of all Member States sharing the same rights and obligations – has dominated the post-1945 integration process at the level of European Community building (though not on the larger pan-European level). The dominance of this principle owes much to the core belief in the mutual gains from continent-wide market scale for efficiency, growth and employment and fear of exclusion from these gains (Milward, 1984). The unitary principle is expressed in the core Community-building projects of the customs union, external trade policy, the European single market and competition policy. This belief in market scale explains the opposition of German Federal Economics Minister Ludwig Erhard to the original Community-building proposals; they represented a 'little' Europe. As this core of projects of unitary integration broadened, they offered two further attractions

(Majone, 2009). First, they offered opportunities for package deals that held the Community together in complex negotiating games. Second, Member State governments could use this complex core for 'blame avoidance' at the domestic level. In this historical context, differentiation has tended to be seen as provisional and temporary, as tightly constrained, in large part because gains were understood to be mutual and incentives to free-ride limited. Domestic elites also became socialized into, and internalized, these negotiating forums and their repeated, 'nested' games.

On the other hand, though this historical context remains influential, three factors – widening scope of integration, 'deepening' of integration, and successive waves of enlargement of membership – have been associated with an increased resort to differentiated integration in the European Community (EC), renamed the European Union (EU) in the Treaty on European Union of 1993. Differentiation has been used in part as a design principle, recognizing asymmetry in gains and costs from integration and thus increasing collective action problems in unitary integration. Above all, it has served as an increasingly attractive tool in the pragmatic political management of European integration.

Notable high points in debate about differentiation were in 1974–6, occasioned especially by UK entry and the British attempt to renegotiate membership; 1980–5, occasioned by the British government's insistence on a budget rebate, Greek entry and anticipation of Portuguese and Spanish entry (strengthening the Mediterranean dimension); 1994–5, occasioned by anticipated problems with the Maastricht road map to monetary union; 2000–1, when the opportunity offered by the new monetary union was to be followed by new risks associated with the forthcoming 'big bang' enlargement to post-communist states in central and east Europe; and 2003-4, occasioned by the divisions sparked by the Iraq 2 War and unilateral American action, supported by Britain, Italy, Spain and many new EU Member States. In various ways these events produced debates about core and periphery, about how to maintain momentum in integration, and about exclusion.

The increase in debate about, and resort to use of, differentiated integration is a response to the collective action problems thrown up by a series of complex and difficult challenges. They include integrating in new policy sectors in which costs and gains are distributed asymmetrically and attractive possibilities are offered to 'outsiders' to free-ride (like monetary policy); renewed political ambition to deepen European unification (notably from the Franco-German 'motor' and the 'Six' founder Members in the wake of German unification); the greater heterogeneity in membership, in disparities of income, and in economic and geo-strategic interests and cultural identities (especially after British and Danish membership in 1973 and, later, central and east European enlargement in 2004 and 2007); more variation in political will and institutional and economic capability to integrate amongst Member States (the UK and Germany contrasting in political will, new Member States differing from [most] older Member States in institutional and economic capability); and, not least, the often divisive impact of geo-strategic events and developments (like Iraq 2 in 2003, US Defence Secretary Ronald Rumsfeld's critique of the 'old' Europe, and debate about the need for a 'counterweight' to US power).

In particular, successive waves of enlargement faced the higher entry hurdles of a much larger *acquis communautaire*. Hence increased use was made of transition arrangements and derogations for new Member States. In addition, the enlargement process threw up new issues of 'accession', 'partnership' and 'trade' differentiation. What relationships should non-EU members have with the EU? The consequence of these developments was frustration and impatience of 'leader' Member States with the high barriers imposed by EU Council voting rules and the potential drag effect of 'laggards' on maintaining momentum in integration. In this changing context differentiation has been seen as enabling integration, whereas insistence on the unitary principle threatens to block integration.

This chapter focuses on the political dimension of differentiated integration. A central theme is the difference between the *potential* for differentiation (as suggested by changes in the properties of functions and by spatial 'rescaling') and how it is *used in practice* by institutionally located actors. This difference reflects two factors. First, there is the effect of the 'shadow' of differentiation (see Chapter 3 by Kölliker). The threat of differentiation may be used to deter potential 'outs' from risking costs of exclusion, thereby producing a solution consistent with the principle of unitary integration. Secondly, those who perceive net gains from differentiation may be deterred by Treaty restraints on imposing negative externalities on 'outs', especially in relation to the *acquis communautaire* (including the single market).

Whichever factor is at work, this difference between actual and potential differentiation shows its use as a political tool for managing integration in the presence of diversity of interests, of institutional capacities and of identities. Its use recognizes the mismatch between, on the one hand, ambitions for integration and, on the other, threats of institutional deadlock in Council, the opportunities offered to partisan veto players by tough Council voting rules, and the distinctiveness of preferences, institutional capacities and identities. Differentiation is a key instrument – alongside 'issue-linkage' and side payments – for overcoming collective action problems. However, precisely because it involves the internalization of constraints and the veiled use of threats, traces of its use may be difficult to find.

Differentiated integration is also a tool for anticipating, and coping with, uncertainty and risk. For 'insiders' its attraction is dependent on reducing potential negative internal effects by avoiding 'free-riding' on the part of 'outsiders' – the so-called 'leakage' of benefits. For example, the risk that benefits could flow to 'outsiders' pursuing tax competition has held back the use of the 'enhanced cooperation' procedure over the common consolidated corporate tax base (CCCTB). Ideally, differentiated integration is about creating mutual gains so that 'outsiders' have an incentive to join. This strategy has proved easier, though by no means unproblematic, in Euro Area entry, especially for small states that have most to gain from eliminating exchange-rate risk and uncertainty and the risks of dependence on illiquid domestic financial markets. For 'outsiders' political strategies focus on avoiding negative externalities from differentiated integration and hence costly asymmetric effects from non-participation, like trade diversion to the 'insiders' or wider loss of political influence. This strategy informed UK policy in mitigating the costs of staying out of the Euro Area by exploiting 'issue-linkage' to the European internal market and the principle of the integrity of the *acquis communautaire*. The risk to the position of the City of London in future euro-denominated wholesale financial markets was negated by ensuring equal access to the euro payment and settlement system (TARGET). Similarly, the new Euro Group was denied any formal decision-making authority.

Hence, in thinking and theorizing about differentiated integration, we need to recognize its use as a political tool for managing not just diversity and institutional deadlock but also uncertainty and risk, alongside other instruments like issue-linkage and side-payments. We also need to think about differentiated integration historically as well as politically. It is an old state-building phenomenon that predates 'European' integration and frames current attitudes to participation in Europe-wide differentiated integration. The integration of states was itself in part a process of differentiation, in which in various contrasting ways functional and territorial distinctiveness was recognized and historical legacies incorporated (even if in abridged forms). Differentiation was, and remains, internal to states as well as to European integration. Differentiated integration is an old story of how processes of integration within states are closely enmeshed with those across and above states. It is also bound up with the historical legacies of the collapse of Empires (like the Hapsburg, Romanov and Ottoman in 1917–18 and the Soviet in 1989–91), as well as of states (like Yugoslavia). These critical historical junctures were independently important in shaping attitudes to differentiated integration, for instance in the Balkans, the Baltic and central Europe.

In this volume we are dealing with differentiated integration on a European scale, understood as across and above states, as shaped by distinctive historical contexts of state-building, and as not just confined to the EU. The character of integration 'below states' lives in an important symbiotic relationship with differentiated integration, acting as a catalyst for it, accommodating it or resisting it. The state-building experience poses the prospect that longer-term historical traditions are re-emerging in the context of differentiated integration, for instance in the Baltic. This re-emergence of historical traditions may be apparent in the different ways that domestic elites frame Europe rather than just in the way that Europe impacts on them, for instance in the UK debate about the 'Anglo-sphere' or in debates about Nordic identity.

Central political themes

Put at its simplest, differentiated integration occurs within the EU when the 'unitary' principle in European integration proves impossible to sustain. It becomes impossible to sustain when, for various combinations of will and capability to integrate, European states are not all prepared to assume the same responsibilities and obligations in sharing or transferring competences, either in principle or at the same time. Differentiated integration is likely to become an increasingly important design principle and tool of political management because of the increasing variety of interests, identities and discourses, the growing differences

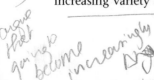

in economic structures and in geo-strategic positions, and the contrasts in the resources on which states can draw. This point applies both within the EU and on a wider European level. Indeed, on the macro-European level, differentiated integration has been long established as the central design principle and tool of management. The EU functions as 'core Europe', its gravitational pull exemplified in the attractions of accession negotiations. The EU context is the central reference point of this book because it functions as 'core' Europe on the macro-level and because its internal emphasis on legal uniformity (see Chapter 2) and the integrity of the *acquis* make differentiation problematic within the EU. At the same time we should also recognize that differentiated integration exists in other regional organizations. Thus in the Association of South East Asian Nations (ASEAN), Japan acts as the leading or vanguard state in this 'flying geese' formation; the US plays a similar role in the North American Free Trade Area (NAFTA); whilst Brazil and Venezuela compete for such a role in Mercosur and other associated organizations such as the Bolivarian Alliance for the Americas.

This book is bound together by a set of interrelated themes that recur in differentiated integration. These themes highlight the key political properties and drivers of differentiated integration, illuminate its central tensions and paradoxes, and provide the context for the key questions outlined in the next section.

Between historical significance and banality

A recurrent theme in differentiated integration is the contrast between historical significance and banality. Measured in terms of the political and policy 'deepening' and successive enlargements, European integration around the EU has been an enormous success story. A striking aspect of this success story has been the proliferation of various forms of differentiated integration, both internal and external to the EU. On the surface they include such examples as the Franco-German 'motor', the Euro Area, the 'Schengen' Area, the Bologna Process, the European Space Agency (with Ariane), EADS (including Airbus), and various derogations (for instance, on freedom of movement of workers) and 'opt-outs' (for instance, over working time). However, while these high-profile outlines are widely known, there is an uncharted depth of projects of differentiated integration, ranging from EU Battle Groups and 'Big Three' *directoires*, through the TARGET euro payment and settlement system, to the G6 police and intelligence cooperation agreement.

Between union, integration and cooperation

This uncharted depth highlights a second theme in differentiated integration: the grey areas between 'union', 'integration' and 'cooperation'. Union involves the transfer of competence, as in monetary union; integration characterizes the sharing of competences, as in environmental policies, while cooperation retains formal competence at the domestic level. 'Soft' differentiation in the form of cooperation has proliferated, for instance in industrial policies and in defence, where intergovernmental forms of cross-national action predominate. Cooperation falls short of pooling and sharing sovereignty and keeps clear of supra-national institutions like the European Commission, Parliament and Court of Justice. It is often seen as a way of 'learning by doing', a 'training ground' for later integration, as, for instance, with the Franco-German Brigade, the Schengen Treaty or the Prüm Treaty. In short, 'soft' differentiation is a step on the ladder towards integration and union. It may, however, be seen as an alternative to integration, an intergovernmental Europe of cooperation *à la carte*, which can be voluntarily joined and left on a 'pick and choose' basis (as in defence and industry policies).

Theory and practice

A third theme is the contrast between differentiation as a neat construct of how Europe should and might be integrated and the messy, convoluted empirical reality of differentiated integration. As a construct, it is about 'who belongs together' (identity) and 'who has power' (domination), two dimensions that readily fuse in discourse about differentiation. In its sense of 'identity' differentiated integration conveys a notion of solidarity based on shared principles (like the Copenhagen principles of 1993) and culture (like a 'stability culture' in the case of the Euro Area). It defines 'us' and 'them'.

In its sense of 'power' it is associated with four types of discourse. First, there is the discourse of giving leadership and direction to the integration process, typically sought by the bigger, 'stronger' and 'founder' Member States. They aspire to form 'pioneer groups', an *avant garde* or a *directoire*. They are inspired by a sense of similar geo-strategic and/or economic interests. Secondly, some Member States seek to be part of the European 'top league'. This aspiration is typical amongst medium-sized states, which might settle on 'two-speed' Europe as second best but above all fear being excluded from a 'core Europe'. Thirdly, there is the discourse of threats of domination and division, usually perceived by smaller and 'weaker' states. They embrace either the principle that 'all should move together at the same speed' or the utilitarian argument that generous side payments should be made for allowing others to proceed at greater speed. Finally, there is a discourse favouring the maximum freedom of manoeuvre for Member States within the integration process, in the form of a flexible and voluntary 'Europe *à la carte*'. This discourse is especially favoured by Member States such as the UK, whose will to integrate is very limited and conditional.

This variegated discourse mirrors the use of differentiation as a tool in the pursuit of state interests in securing their power and influence within Europe. Power and its use are never far beneath the surface of the discourse of differentiated integration. It is about who sets the European agenda, drives the process, and gets their way. However, the most ambitious of these constructs – a 'core Europe' – has proved difficult to realize. The key reasons include the legal doctrines on which the EU is based (notably of uniformity and of the integrity of the *acquis*); the structure of political power that is defined by stringent EU voting rules and the increasing number of small and medium-sized states in the EU; and, in some instances, fears that within a single market 'outsiders' could 'free-ride' to become the main gainers (for example, in tax policy, social policy or even financial regulation and supervision). The hurdles to 'enhanced cooperation' in the EU framework since the 1997 Amsterdam Treaty have deterred states from using this formal route.

Most of all, advocates of 'core Europe' are deterred by fear that they could foment a divisive debate about domination.

D) Transparency and accountability

A fourth theme is the way in which this messy, untidy and evolving reality has contributed to making for a European integration process that lacks both transparency and democratic accountability. The scale and nature of differentiated integration is barely comprehensible to political elites, never mind European publics. In consequence, the growth of differentiated integration has exacerbated some of the key political problems of the EU, especially critiques of its democratic 'deficit'. These problems of transparency and accountability derive in part from sheer organizational complexity, with differentiated integration sometimes within and sometimes outside the EU framework, or having special relationships to the EU that keep the European Commission, the European Parliament and the European Court of Justice (ECJ) at a distance. They are also cognitive and reflect the way in which debates within individual policy areas are often arcane, esoteric and secretive. Differentiated arrangements in defence, internal security and monetary policies are cloaked in professional mystique. In a context that marries organizational complexity with cognitive difficulties, transparency and accountability present serious problems. Differentiated integration is part and parcel of a larger problem of 'hollowing out' democratic governance that is as much an attribute of individual states as of the EU and the wider Europe. It does not seem to be part of its solution.

E) Disintegration or rescue?

A fifth theme is the tension between disintegration and rescue. The risk of disintegration can be measured by declining public support for the integration process and by elite–mass public conflict over European integration. It arises, for instance, with respect to whether Europeans learn to 'love the euro' (Dyson, 2008: 3–6). Conversely, differentiated integration can serve as a tool for 'rescuing' the integration process and the EU from the increasing weight of complexity and heterogeneity that it must bear. It can also serve as a tool to rescue Member States and thus strengthen their commitment to the integration process, through, for instance, removing threats from exchange-rate crisis or from competitive devaluation in a monetary union. This is yet another manifestation of a larger problem of tension between democratic engagement and the more efficient management of complex trans-national spaces, for instance with globally organized financial markets. Differentiated integration has had a recurring appeal to those seeking to unlock blockage in moving forward with European unification on terms that strengthen the capabilities of Member States to deliver improved policy outcomes.

F) Boundaries and spaces

The sixth theme involves the relationship between differentiated integration and traditional notions about boundaries and spaces in Europe. These notions encompass not simply state boundaries and sub-state regions and cities. They also include constructions of trans-national spaces like the Anglo-sphere, Central

Europe, the Baltic, the Nordic area, the Balkans, the Mediterranean, even a Franco-German Carolingian Europe. Differentiated integration offers a tool to articulate and reinforce these traditional 'state clusters'. For instance, EU accession served as a catalyst for strengthening Balkan, Baltic and Visegrád spaces. Conversely, European integration (in both its differentiated and unitary forms) can undermine the coherence of trans-national spaces and, as in central Europe, turn Member States into rivals. The Euro Area, for instance, slices through the Visegrád and Nordic 'clusters' (with Slovakia and Finland members). More paradoxically, the Euro Area incorporates the EU Mediterranean space, while simultaneously subjecting it to pressures to adopt a Germanic 'stability culture'. In so many ways differentiated integration escapes the boundaries of traditional, seemingly cohesive cross-national political spaces like central Europe.

(G) Symbolism, substance and rivalry

A seventh, related theme is the tension between the symbolic uses of differentiated integration and its substance. Differentiated integration is often used to appease past enmities and heal historical wounds or alternatively to express shared identity against an 'other'. An obvious example of the former is the Franco-German relationship, along with the Franco-German-Polish 'Weimar Triangle'. Many other examples can be found at the level of inter-regional cooperation, for instance in Alpine Europe. Baltic cooperation is very much a statement of independence from over-mighty Russia.

However, as many of the chapters show, these cases of differentiated integration often lack real substantive depth. They are pre-eminently declaratory. In this respect the legacies of past wars and empires put a heavy imprint on differentiated integration. At the same time inter-regional cooperation may act as a smokescreen, behind which rivalry for foreign investment and EU funding continues unabated. Rivalry may indeed intensify as European market integration deepens. This paradox of declaratory solidarity and practical rivalry runs through differentiated integration.

(H) Broadening, deepening and widening

An eighth theme is the close, symbiotic relationship between, on the one hand, differentiated integration and, on the other, the broadening of the EU's policy scope, 'deepening' of the integration process in institutional and procedural terms, and 'widening' of membership. In particular, the rise in intellectual and political attention to differentiated integration correlates with periodic anticipation of the difficulties associated with waves of EU enlargement. Cyclical attention peaked with enlargement to Denmark, Ireland and the UK in 1973 (for example, Brandt, 1974; Tindemans, 1975; Dahrendorf, 1979); again, with enlargement to Greece in 1981 and then to Spain and Portugal in 1986 (for example, Barre, 1980; French Planning Commission, 1980; Ehlermann, 1984; Grabitz, 1984; Tugendhat, 1984; Wallace and Ridley, 1985); the imminent move to monetary union (Schäuble and Lamers, 1994; Balladur, 1994a, 1994b); and, above all, the prospective 'big bang' enlargement of 2004 to east central Europe and in 2003 the divisions revealed by the Iraq invasion (Schneider and Cederman, 1994; Dewatripont et al., 1995;

Curtin, 1995; Edwards and Philippart, 1997; Stubb, 1996, 2002; Gstöhl, 1996; Ehlermann, 1998; Giscard d'Estaing and Schmidt, 2000; Fischer, 2000; Chirac, 2000; Delors, 2001; Warleigh, 2002; Wallace and Wallace, 1995; De Witte, 2004; Sarkozy, 2005; Kölliker, 2006b; Verhofstadt, 2006a, 2006b; Andersen and Sitter, 2006; De Neve, 2007). In these contexts differentiation offers a tool for flexibly managing increased diversity in the context of Council voting rules that impede agreement.

However, the linkage to widening is by no means simple and one-way. Enlargement has acted as a catalyst for debates about differentiated integration to the extent that it has produced greater heterogeneity of structures (with 'strong' and 'weak' states), more varied political interests, and differences of political will, and, not least, of capabilities to integrate. At the same time, enlargement has also been bound up with debates about a parallel EU 'deepening' to retain the coherence and momentum of European integration in the face of greater diversity and complexity of interests and capabilities. This 'deepening', in turn, opens up differences of will and capability to integrate more closely. It highlights the fundamentally contested nature of the integration process, with claims for 'opt-outs' – especially in new policy areas like social policy, defence and monetary policy – and granting of derogations, especially for new Member States. The context of the Schäuble/Lamers paper on 'core' Europe of 1994 was not so much 'widening' as contested 'deepening'. In contrast, the ideas of former Commission President Jacques Delors and of former French President Valery Giscard d'Estaing and former German Chancellor Helmut Schmidt about a 'core' Europe in 1999–2000 were more inspired by the combination of the birth of the Euro Area with prospective eastern enlargement.

Furthermore, as the need for deepening and widening is intrinsically linked with the global role, ambitions and weight of the EU in the world, it is no wonder that differentiated integration has been a key political tool in this process. The 'Mediterranean Union', the various peace-keeping and peace-making initiatives in Africa, South East Asia, the Balkans and the Caucasus, the preferential trade agreements of European powers with their former colonies in Africa and Latin America and energy agreements in the European neighbourhood and the developing world, suggest that differentiated integration may be increasingly used by certain Member States as a way to enhance national and EU power in the world, often with imperial tendencies and characteristics. In this sense, the way differentiated integration is used – and by whom – is critical as it has important consequences to the recipients of the EU's power projection in these parts of the world. Ultimately, it relates to the fundamental questions of *what is* the Union, as well as the associated questions of *what it does* and *what it should do* in the world, for example, whether the EU is a 'force for good', for progress and development, or a force of subtle – or perhaps not so subtle – exploitation that evokes memories of the recent imperial past of the continent.

In short, there is a complex, symbiotic relationship between deepening, widening and differentiation. Differentiation has grown with increasing heterogeneity of structures, will and capabilities and as the political ambition to deepen European unification has grown. At the same time, as noted in Chapter 2, it is channelled in particular ways by core legal doctrines on which the EU is founded, as well as the high barriers of voting rules and of relatively more smaller states. Its use as a design principle and as a tool of political management is legally and politically constrained.

The 'level of analysis' issue

The ninth theme is the 'level of analysis' aspect of differentiated integration. From the perspective of the governance of the European continent as a whole, the EU itself is a form of differentiated integration. It is in effect a 'core' Europe that serves as a pole of attraction to outsiders and that defines different modes of integration into its affairs (from trade, through broader cooperation, to more intense association agreements including the European Economic Area) (Schmitter, 1996). Europe comprises an overlapping system of regimes for the governance of such policy areas as security and defence (the North Atlantic Treaty Organization [NATO] and the Organization for Security and Cooperation in Europe [OSCE]), human rights (Council of Europe) and reconstruction and development (European Bank for Reconstruction and Development [EBRD], the World Bank, the International Monetary Fund [IMF] and the World Trade Organization [WTO]). These regimes have been created (like the EBRD) and transformed (like NATO, OSCE and the Council of Europe) in response to developments, notably the opportunities opened by the end of the Cold War. Some transcend Europe, notably the IMF, the World Bank and the WTO.

On this wider level of analysis, Europe comprises a complex, evolving network of differentiated integration that includes but extends beyond the EU. The EU remains central in this European architecture of differentiated integration because of its unique combination of policy scope, political ambition to deepen integration, and supra-national institutional capacity to articulate common interests. At the same time it is important to avoid the dangers of a too 'EU-centric' view of differentiated integration and to look beyond the EU 'across' states (both inside the EU and, as appropriate to European governance, outside). On this macro-level of analysis, the contested nature of Europe's borders comes to the fore, especially in sensitive relations to Russia, Ukraine, Moldova, Georgia and Turkey to the east. This contest goes beyond the question of where the EU borders should lie to questions about which borders should take priority and how these borders should be managed.

Institutional venue-hopping

The final, tenth, theme revolves around the macro-European and global levels and the way in which complex variegated governance mechanisms on these levels lead to 'institutional venue-hopping' by domestic policy-makers. Their attention shifts across venues depending on two main criteria of appropriateness: the relevance of particular venues to problem-solving; and the potential that individual venues offer to assert influence on outcomes. This behaviour is very apparent in European macro-economic governance, especially by President Nicolas Sarkozy during the French EU Presidency in the second half of 2008 when, after the collapse of the financial firm Lehman Brothers, the full force of the global economic crisis struck. He shifted venues from the European members of G7, the European members of G20, the Heads of State and Government of the Euro Area (convened for the first time), and the European Council. Depending on issue salience, macro-economic policy-makers hop between the IMF, the Bank for International Settlements (BIS), G20, G10, G7/8, the Organization for Economic Cooperation and Development (OECD), the EU institutions and the Euro Area institutions. These venues comprise different groupings of European states for different purposes, typically shifting to global forums as financial stability issues become salient. Presence within these venues, like G7/8, or weight within them, like the IMF, translates into intra-European influence.

The value of 'grand' theories in explaining differentiated integration

'Grand' theories of (European) integration, whether with a rationalist or constructivist root, have problems comprehensively explaining differentiated integration. Thus federalism, and its principle of 'unity in diversity', may explain the recurring emergence of differentiated integration. However, it fails to account for the institutional asymmetry and fragmentation (that is, non-federalist elements) that characterize this form of integration. This problem is common to Monnet's (1978) piecemeal functionalist approach to the construction of a federal Europe, to Spinelli's (1944 and 1972) vision of an immediate shift of political power to the European level, and to the 'Europe of the Regions' paradigm (Le Gales and Lequesne, 1997; Jeffery, 1997).

Neo-functionalism (Haas, 1958, 1975; Lindberg, 1963) and its notion of *'engrenage'*, that is, the process of a 'functional and political spill-over based on underlying and unanticipated interdependencies', may explain why states participating in an integration scheme may seek to deepen integration in a particular policy area and/or seek to expand in a related area. But it does not explain why spill-over affects only a group of states and certain policy areas (that is, an incomplete *engrenage*). Also it fails to explain why supranational actors, with their 'mediating' and 'policy entrepreneurship' roles, as well as concerned organized interests, are unable to achieve a common position between the diverging interests of states and prevent permanent schisms in the integrative structure. In other words, there is no explanation of why the integration process has 'gone awry' (Lindberg and Scheingold, 1971). Moreover, neo-functionalism does not explain why different forms of differentiated integration are more prevalent in certain policy areas than others (for example, multi-speed in economic and financial affairs; variable geometry in defence issues). This failure is related to the weakness of neo-functionalism in explaining European integration in the second pillar, as opposed to the first pillar. Finally, neo-functionalism does not take into account the exogenous forces that induce and shape forms of differentiated integration.

Transanctionalism (Deutsch, 1957), and its emphasis on 'amalgamated' and 'pluralistic' security communities 'integrated within a territory' and sharing a

18   *Which Europe?*

'sense of community', might explain differentiation as a result of transaction flows being very low. However, it cannot explain why in an increasingly interdependent Europe, with high and increasing transaction flows in the internal market and in other policy areas, differentiation occurs.

Inter-governmentalism (Hoffman, 1966) and its liberal variant (Moravcsik, 1993), with their notion that 'national preferences' are driving the integration process, can explain why a group of states may want to integrate further in a policy area of their interest (such as monetary affairs or defence) and how other states may want to block that process which they perceive to be against their interests. But it does not explain why in the process of intergovernmental bargaining the 'threat of alternative coalitions and exclusion' by the initiating members does not create enough 'negative policy externalities' so that 'recalcitrant members' would be motivated to participate in such initiatives (Moravcsik, 1993: 502–3).

Neo-institutionalism (March and Olsen, 1984; Scharpf, 1988; Hall and Taylor, 1996; Pierson, 1996), in its rational and historical variants, would argue that differentiated integration is initiated by powerful institutions such as the Commission and the European Court of Justice in order to further integration within the integrative structure and 'delegitimize' cooperation outside the *acquis*. It does not explain, however, why this institutionalization and constitutionalization of flexibility has failed to prevent states from pursuing integration outside the *acquis*, or why flexibility outside the integrative structures is increasingly gaining legitimacy. These inadequacies are partly related to the fact this approach is mostly concerned with looking at institutions as intervening variables of European integration and less so with what drives this process.

Constructivism or sociological institutionalism (Checkel, 1999; Christiansen et al., 1999; Risse, 2004) would argue, from an ontological perspective, that differentiated integration is a result of the existence of distinct identities in Europe that create the need for an institutional clustering of states – on the basis of their common identity – inside or outside the *acquis*. They cannot explain, however, why socialization and norm transfer have not been sufficient in creating shared interests that would prevent states from seeking differentiated integration inside or outside the *acquis*. Nor does it explain why certain forms of differentiated integration have been accepted more than others in the social discourse.

Governance approaches (Rhodes, 1996; Jachtenfuchs and Kohler-Koch, 2004) take a variety of forms: multi-level governance (Marks et al., 1996; Hooghe and Marks, 2001), policy networks (Eising and Kohler-Koch, 1999; Peterson, 2004), Europeanization (Ladrech, 1994; Muller, 1995; Radaelli, 2000, 2004; Goetz and Hix, 2000; Héritier, 2001; Caporaso et al., 2001; Knill, 2001; Stone Sweet et al., 2001; Featherstone and Radaelli, 2003; Olsen, 2002; Dyson and Goetz, 2003a, 2003b; Goetz, 2006; Vink and Graziano, 2006) and regulatory governance (Majone, 1994). They argue that differentiated integration conforms to their vision of a multi-level polity characterized by complexity, variability, fluidity, unpredictability and multiple actors. At the same time, the very ambiguity and the conceptual 'under-specificity' that characterizes this approach – which is not a theory of integration – limits its value in comprehensively explaining the origin and nature of differentiated integration.

Comparative Politics approaches (Hix, 1994) include cooperative federalism or consociationalism (Taylor, 1991; Chryssochoou, 1994) and share the view that EU politics is not inherently different from the practice of government in other democratic systems (such as federal Germany and Switzerland). They argue that differentiated integration exists within these political systems and societies in the form of 'institutional asymmetry' and 'segmental autonomy' as well as 'territorial, linguistic and religious cleavages'. However, these approaches have problems explaining the unequal distribution of power among Member States (or constitutive units) that results from differentiated integration arrangements. They also have difficulties with the notion that a state can pursue differentiated arrangements outside the *acquis*, thus defecting from the integrative (federal or consociational) structure of the Union. Also, these approaches cannot explain the origin and nature of differentiated integration, that is, what drives this process; they are mostly concerned with the politics of this process.

In conclusion, if, as Schmitter (2004: 47) argues, 'any comprehensive theory of (European) integration should also be a theory of disintegration', one can argue that the theoretical soundness of grand theories is problematic in so far as they do not explain why some states are excluded – willingly or unwillingly – from formal arrangements within the integrative structure, or why they pursue integration outside this structure. In other words, these theories have problems in explaining the 'disintegrative' element that characterizes differentiated integration. One of the aims of this book is to explore to what extent the notion of differentiated integration can be a basis for a new theoretical approach in integration studies.

Disciplinary perspectives: different dimensions of differentiated integration

In addressing the politics of differentiated integration, the value of 'grand' theories of integration is limited. What light then can different social science disciplines shed on this phenomenon? The book seeks an approach that is inclusive in accommodating different disciplinary perspectives on differentiation. These disciplinary perspectives vary in the significance that they attach to differentiated integration as a material phenomenon – notably its geo-strategic and its politico-economic dimensions – and as ideational – notably its institutional–legal and socio-cultural dimensions. In recognition of its multi-disciplinary character, we asked authors to reflect on these four different dimensions of differentiated integration. At the same time the centrality of political science has led us to adopt an institutional conception of differentiated integration, though one that stresses its informal as well as formal aspects, its extra-EU as well as EU contexts. The geo-strategic, politico-economic and socio-cultural dimensions clarify the context and shaping influences on its institutional forms.

The two dimensions of geo-strategy and political economy highlight the impacts on differentiated integration of external European and extra-European pressures and leverage, notably the roles of globalized financial markets and of 'hegemony'. Structural power figures prominently. The socio-cultural dimension focuses more on historical legacies and memories. In addition, the three dimensions highlight the influence of different sets of opportunities for, and constraints on, actors in pursuing differentiated integration as a political strategy. They include diversity of strategic capacity and vulnerability, of economic strength and risk, of identities and of institutional agility and resilience, and identity.

Institutional–legal forms

Differentiated integration involves different patterns of membership in European integration in terms of 'sharing' or 'delegating' competences or of cooperating in their exercise. It rests on varied sets of formal and informal rules on how decisions are to be taken, on who is to take them, and on when and under what conditions others can enter. The stress is on functional, spatial and temporal variations in the rights and obligations attached to membership. Our reason for defining differentiated integration in these terms and centring this dimension of the phenomenon reflects in part the political science roots of the book. Above all, however, it has the advantage of specificity and clear empirical referents, enabling change to be measured using institutional indicators of who participates in what (for instance, in ERM II, the Euro Area, Schengen Area, the Charter of Fundamental Rights, social policy, and ESDP).

In the literature differentiated integration is associated with a set of concepts that characterize different formal institutional properties: the 'two-speed' Europe of the Tindemans Report (1976), in which a group of states move ahead faster but remains open to joining by others and assists their preparations for entry (as with the ERM and EMU); the 'variable geometry' of the French Planning Commission (1980), in which the EU gives the 'green light' for those who have the will and capability to develop new areas (as in industrial collaboration); and the *à la carte* Europe of Dahrendorf (1979), which stresses an even higher degree of voluntary intergovernmental cooperation on a 'pick-and-choose' basis, outside the core EU policy areas (as with the Schengen Treaty before 1997).

These various concepts illustrate different design principles for the EU polity. A 'multi-speed' Europe of temporary derogations and transitional arrangements equates with belief in the core legal principle of the coherence and uniformity of EU law and the integrity of the *acquis*. In this way differentiation is confined to new policy areas and to new Member States and is no more than a short- to medium-term device to protect forward momentum in unitary integration. In contrast, ideas of core Europe, two-tier Europe, *directoire*, variable geometry and *à la carte* Europe embody an alternative design principle: a shift to a more permanent set of differentiated arrangements that live in tension if not conflict with traditional legal principles.

In practice, differentiated integration is poised delicately and uncomfortably between these two positions. The explanation is to be found in problems of institutional design in overcoming collective action problems. In many cases differentiated integration has exhibited a lack of centripetal pull on 'outs', who saw opportunities for free-riding and for securing the same gains by not cooperating (on which see Chapter 15 by Dyson on macro-economic policy). The utilitarian principle is very evident. Hence differentiated integration is associated with an image of stratagems and tactical manoeuvrings.

B) The geo-strategic dimension

This dimension characterizes differentiated integration in terms of variations in susceptibilities to external pressures, threats and leverage. There are differences in scale of exposure to the presence of an inwardly troubled and territorially assertive Russia to the east and of the sources of uncertainty, risk and instability associated with the Caucasus, Central Asia, the Middle East, North Africa and the eastern Mediterranean. Variation in strategic vulnerability reflects hard factors of geography. It is expressed in different historical constructions of threats to security in Europe, whether from over-mighty Russia, an unstable European 'neighbourhood' or the wider international system. Geo-strategic interests underpin contested notions of European 'borders', about where they lie and how 'hard' they should be, especially in relation to Turkey and Ukraine. In addition, geo-strategic interest mirrors asymmetries in the material capabilities of states, notably dependence on the United States for collective European defence and to mount 'out-of-area' crisis management operations. Strategic vulnerability combines with weak material capabilities to create a strongly 'Atlanticist' outlook in east central Europe and the Baltic states towards the organization of European defence.

This geo-strategic dimension informs in various ways the chapters on external and internal security, dealing with the post-Cold War context, the 'war on terror' and 'zones of instability' on Europe's borders. It also overlaps into other functional areas (like industrial policy) and territorial areas, like the Balkans, the Baltic and the Mediterranean. In terms of differentiated integration it has most clearly shaped the contested concepts of a *directoire* and of a 'two-tier' Europe, according to which the most powerful European states – Britain, France and Germany – should work closely together to develop joint policies, for instance in relation to Iran and Israel/Palestine, and project European influence in international affairs.

C) The politico-economic dimension

This dimension focuses on the creation of trans-national economic spaces that lead to an informal integration of economic activities across borders. These trans-national spaces involve 'agglomeration' processes in production and services as scarce professional skills cluster together, whether in manufacturing or services, and as favourable 'time zones' are exploited, notably in financial services. They also derive from so-called 'gravity' effects in investment and trade flows, based on geographical proximity to large, rich markets, low transportation costs and trade agreements (Krugman, 1991). In terms of 'gravity', Germany and the former 'D-Mark Zone' (of states that were until 1999 locked in the 'hard' Exchange Rate Mechanism [ERM] with the D-Mark as anchor currency) emerge as the core in the EU. On a macro-European level, the EU itself is the centre of gravity, far eclipsing the Commonwealth of Independent States (CIS) grouped around Russia.

Integration in the CIS offers much less economic value-added than integration in the EU. A key manifestation of this 'gravity' effect is supposed to be the so-called 'Blue Banana', which stretches from southern England, through Benelux and northern and eastern France, down the Rhine into southern Germany and Switzerland, branching into northern Italy and Spanish Catalonia.

In this perspective the economic geography of Europe is defined in terms of one or more spatial hierarchies (depending on what is being measured). Based on trade it is possible to produce a 'gravity index' that illustrates the centre–periphery character of Europe as defined by GDP per capita (Gros and Steinherr, 2004: 329–37). It is also possible to identify an inner 'optimal currency area' within the Euro Area, represented by those states that were part of the former 'hard' ERM. This area shares higher levels of intra-industry trade and more correlated business cycles. It also benefits disproportionately from the trade-creation effects of the euro (Baldwin, 2006a, 2006b). Again, Germany heads the hierarchy – and, though held back by southern Italy, the rest of the original Six founder members, plus Austria.

In politico-economic terms Europe is informally differentiated into a London-centred 'financial market' Europe and a Frankfurt-centred 'monetary policy' Europe. Financial stability is firmly anchored in the IMF in Washington DC and the BIS in Basle. In other words, related but different functions in European macro-economic governance involve different institutional venues and groupings of states: financial market regulation, the EU as part of the single market *acquis communautaire*; monetary policy, the ESCB; and financial stability, global institutions.

In this perspective the key measures of differentiation are not so much formal institutions like the Euro Area as transaction indicators like financial flows, investment, trade and business cycles. They point to informal processes of integration that create the material basis or 'drivers' that underpin more formal integration, for instance in cross-national industrial collaborations and in differentiated integration in European monetary policy. Another indicator is trans-national networks, for instance in high-speed train infrastructure, opening up new economic 'hubs'.

Politico-economic analysis also draws out the element of politics in time. In one version, 'politics in time' takes the form of historical 'path dependence' in patterns of economic activity, linked to old trading routes connecting cities (like the Hanseatic League, especially in the Baltic or north–south routes across the Alps). In another, the focus is on different time periods: the pre-1973 US-dollar-based Bretton Woods system of capital controls, the post-Bretton Woods era of floating exchange rates and liberalized capital movements, and the post-1990s emerging discourse of 'globalization' and of the historic shift in international economic power from the Atlantic economy to Asia, notably China and India. Differentiated integration is pictured as caught up in much larger historical–economic processes and international economic developments. The effect is to carve out different opportunities and constraints within which cities, regions and states can pursue differentiated integration.

The socio-cultural dimension

This dimension characterizes differentiated integration as a phenomenon of socialization, 'belonging' and 'identity', with 'insiders' and 'outsiders', on the basis of attributed cultural affinities or differences, characteristically 'the Other'. In these ways intellectual and political elites construct European integration in different ways, often reflecting differences in historical experiences of state-building and nation-building. In more modern terms they also mirror differences in the timing of accession: the 'old' EU members versus the 'new' members. In this regard particular and differing patterns can be found between the original 'Six' founders; the post-dictatorship Mediterranean states, the Nordic states; and the post-communist states. Their elites behave differently in constituting new European scales of action. Key indicators are attitude data on identity and on political support for European integration.

In socio-cultural analysis the focus is on the 'shadows of history' and on the role of differentiated integration in exorcising the ghosts of the past, especially war. Differentiated integration is bound up in elite discourses of historical legitimation that resort to historical memory in order to create 'imaginative spaces'. Examples include 'Carolingian' Europe to give meaning to the Franco-German 'motor' of European integration, or the 'Anglo-sphere', 'Baltic Europe' and 'Central Europe' to summon up historical memories in the service of national self-redefinition. These concepts evoke different subjective conceptions of space and time, of the 'proper' space (*Eigenraum*) and 'proper' time (*Eigenzeit*) in which European integration should proceed.

Conclusion

In designing this book we have sought to be inclusive in four senses. Firstly, the volume covers the varied range of individual functional and territorial aspects of differentiated integration. Secondly, its authors represent a number of relevant disciplines – Comparative Politics, Comparative Political Economy, International Relations, Law, and Strategic Studies – alongside various strands of European integration theory. Thirdly, the book spans the various relevant levels of analysis – global, European, state and sub-state. Finally, it allows for different and contending ontological positions (materialist, constructivist and 'critical') and epistemologies.

The reconciliation of parsimony and inclusiveness has proved a persistent difficulty in social science research. The difficulty increases with the ambition of the research questions. Given the context mapped out above, it was agreed not to ask contributors to test a single, comprehensive and systematic analytical framework (for instance, one derived from public goods theory). Instead, in the interests of manageability, the book focuses on a narrow range of research questions about the political management of differentiated integration and on a conceptual definition that highlights its politico-institutional character. At the same time we embed this stress on the politics of differentiated integration in a set of analytical dimensions that draw attention to the multi-disciplinary character of its study and in a body of shared languages (functional, spatial and temporal) in terms of which the phenomenon can be discussed in more interdisciplinary terms and from which authors, and ultimately readers, can select *à la carte*.

2
Legal Flexibility, Governance and Differentiated Integration: On Functional Differentiation of EU Law and Politics

Jiří Přibáň

The growing systemic complexity of European political institutions, laws and administrative regulations has led to the creation of new political concepts, metaphors and legal fictions. Their purpose is to grasp internal tensions, structural irritations and systemic paradoxes within the European Union and thus respond to its recent developments. The Union currently represents *the unity of conceptual contradictions*. Apart from the slogan 'widening is deepening', introduced in the 1990s, and the self-description of the EU as 'unity in diversity', political concepts, such as 'polity without statehood' and 'differentiated integration', have been adopted to describe current paradoxes of European politics and law.

Using the systems theory epistemology, the contemporary EU can be described as a social system differentiated into subsystems of law, politics, economy, education and so on. Each of these subsystems operates by producing meaning structures that further differentiate the initial situation, increase the systems' complexity, and thus constitute self-reproduction through internal varieties of meaning production. What looks like an incomprehensible plethora of *ad hoc* rules, fluid institutional settings and contingent decisions turns out to be the complexity of operations guaranteeing the external and internal differentiation, self-reproduction and self-regulation of both European law and politics.

The EU is functionally differentiated into social subsystems, each of them constituted and reproduced by its specific modes of internal differentiation. Its polity is defined by a process of *social differentiation* which is communicated within the political system through the notion of *differentiated integration* and within the legal system through the equivalent notion of *flexibility clauses*. Long before their institutionalization by the Maastricht and the Amsterdam Treaties, and the most recent provisions incorporated in the Treaty of Lisbon, mechanisms of differentiated integration had been affecting the European unification processes (Hanf, 2001: 3–26). The historical circumstances of differentiated integration, its juridification in the body of EU law, and the political implications of this illustrate not only the level of external differentiation and self-reference of European law and politics systems but also their capacity and modes of internal differentiation.

This chapter focuses on the construction of the EU polity by differentiated integration as a form of European governance that is legally channelled through the

EU flexibility clauses. The concept of differentiated integration illustrates the growing social differentiation of the EU and shows that the process of European integration proceeds alongside the process of European fragmentation. Furthermore, the accommodation of differentiated integration in the body of European law reveals semantic differences and the extent of systemic differentiation and self-reference in the systems of EU law and politics. Using the example of differentiated integration, the chapter describes the EU political system as internally differentiated between European governance and Member State governments. Although the Union transgresses its nation-state segmentation, the notions of statehood and democratic legitimacy continue to inform both the legal and political semantics of the EU. The chapter argues that, contrary to the theories of political and legal monism, the EU's further integration will not result in the establishment of statehood accompanied by the constitutional supremacy of EU laws, legitimized by a European democratic polity of strong common bonds and one collective identity. This polity, rather, is signified by processes of fragmentation, pluralization and functional differentiation of the EU and the evolving self-reference of the EU's legal and political systems. The democratic deficit associated by reliance on instrumental legitimation, justified by outcomes, cannot be closed by calls for symbolic constitutional legitimation through democratic values as commonly imagined by normative social and political theories. The split between legitimation by outcomes and legitimation by values, the most recent example of which is the Lisbon Treaty, illustrates, rather, the level of EU functional differentiation and the impossibility of fostering the ultimate construction of a normatively integrated and culturally united European polity. It reveals a much more profound social dynamics of differentiation at the level of emerging European society.

The emergence and juridification of the EU's differentiated integration

Although the process of differentiated integration has been part of European integration since the 1950s, its importance has grown with recent developments within and outside the EU. The ambitions of some European countries for progressive unification, especially the establishment of a currency union (the Euro Area) and the abolition of border controls (the Schengen Zone), were not welcomed by all EU Member States at the time. Instead of a common integration trajectory, accompanied by temporary opt-outs by individual countries in specific areas, the very process of integration started to be associated with the need for institutional and organizational flexibility in the 1990s. Reflecting these changes, the concept of differentiated integration has become part of the EU-related political and academic discourse during the last two decades. It has evolved from political debates on the speed, direction and purpose of European integration, especially the ambitious calls for a 'hard core' of Member States willing and capable of closer political integration.[1] The idea was originally promoted by countries such as Germany and France that favoured progressive integration and called for a core group of Member States that would not be held back by other Member States reluctant to join the ever-closer Union project (Lamers, 2000: 104–16; Levy, Pensky and Torpey, 2005). In their view, the rigidity of integration of all Member States in all areas at the same time should be abandoned in favour of an 'avant-garde' integration of the willing states which would operate as a source of inspiration for the rest of the EU.

Nevertheless, the principle of flexibility, which would legally operationalize the political possibility of differentiated integration of the EU, was finally incorporated in the Amsterdam Treaty as a functional response to what Ralf Dahrendorf (1979) had described as a 'remarkable institutional failure' in the process of further European integration. After initially negative responses to the prospect of a two-tier EU, divided into a hard core and potentially ever more hostile peripheries, the political, juridical and academic vocabulary resorted to the use of 'differentiated integration' and, later on, more politically correct and less controversial concepts of 'flexible integration', 'closer cooperation' or 'enhanced cooperation' (Stubb, 2002: 43). While the political language and legal concepts of the Amsterdam Treaty, the Nice Treaty and, most recently, the Lisbon Treaty refer to closer, enhanced cooperation, academic language has become saturated with writing on differentiated integration, flexible integration, multi-level integration and so on (see, for instance, Den Boer et al., 1998; Monar, 1997, 1998; Neunreither and Wiener, 2000; Tuytschaever, 1999; Westlake, 1998).

Differentiated integration was gradually transformed from familiar political practice within EU institutions into a rule of intergovernmental negotiations and a guiding European treaty principle (Shaw, 1998; Shaw and Wiener, 2000). After the enactment of the Amsterdam and Nice treaties incorporating the principle of flexibility and differentiated integration, the EU emerged as a supranational body integrating its Member States well beyond the framework of international law but granting them a sufficient level of national sovereignty to decide whether they chose to opt in or out of specific integration policies (Usher, 2002). In fact, the Maastricht Treaty on European Union had already effectively established a 'multi-speed Europe' by enacting Economic and Monetary Union (EMU) and the Schengen Zone. The institutionalization of differentiated integration in the Amsterdam Treaty subsequently enabled the Member States to develop progressive forms of multi-level integration under conditions defined by the legal language of the Treaty (Pernice, 2002). In other words:

> ... while Maastricht showed that unwilling member states cannot be forced to integrate, Amsterdam made clear that the reluctant countries cannot keep the others from further deepening. After the accession of three neutral countries in 1995 and in view of the long, heterogeneous queue of candidates, the Treaties finally acknowledged Europe's diversity. (Gstöhl, 2000: 42–3)

The original institutionalization of differentiated integration in the Amsterdam Treaty, ratified in 1999, and subsequent amendments in the Nice Treaty, ratified three years later, was primarily a response to growing political differences about the speed and scale and also the purpose, direction and limits of EU integration

(Gaja, 1998). However, recent EU enlargement processes and accession talks multiplied these differences and proved that differentiated integration was the only realistic way of dealing with economic, political, administrative, legal and international differences in Europe (Cameron, 2004). Issues of cultural diversity, economic or legal compatibility, and political heterogeneity became much more pressing after two unprecedented enlargements – the first, in 2004, opening the EU to ten new accession states, eight of which were post-communist democracies from the former Soviet bloc (the Czech Republic, Estonia, Hungary, Latvia, Lithuania, Poland, Slovakia and Slovenia) plus two others (Cyprus and Malta), and the second, in 2007, admitting Bulgaria and Romania despite their economic underdevelopment and significantly lower level of democratic and administrative accountability, even in comparison to the other post-communist states admitted in 2004 (Delhey, 2007).

Differentiated integration was an intrinsic part of the Copenhagen conditionality process which was inspired by the Maastricht Treaty and significantly affected economic, political and international developments in candidate states, especially in the early stages of accession talks (Haughton, 2007). Successive enlargement processes show that the flexibility clauses are not only internal legal measures facilitating the political opt-outs of Member States refusing to join specific EU policies. They also provide an operational framework for integrating candidate states without imperilling the existing state of European integration and the efficiency of different policies, such as the single monetary policy, free movement of labour, immigration, agriculture subsidies and so on. The example of the EMU, and the commitment of all new Member States to adopt the euro, reveals the 'integrative virtues' of the flexibility principle. While respecting the existing economic and monetary differences and structural imbalances of the EU (Martin, 2002), the EMU's differentiated integration model also operates as a convergence model setting up criteria for new Member States wishing to join the Euro Area (Allemand, 2005: 614). Apart from channelling progressive cooperation within the EU, differentiated integration has thus been an answer to the Union's enlargement ambitions that does not put existing integration policies at risk and invites new Member States to join under the existing criteria.

The internalization of differentiated integration by the EU legal system

From the legal perspective, the concept of differentiated integration may read like an anomaly (Walker, 1998: 375–8). Legality is commonly associated with the general application of rules, unity of legal authority and equal treatment of all subjects. The rule of law-based EU presumes the uniform interpretation and application of European laws. All powers conferred by Member States and remedies facilitated by European institutions are expected to be governed by generally applicable and enforceable legal rules. It is therefore not surprising that EU legal bodies have been hostile to the flexibility principle and differentiated integration and that, for instance, 'the Court of Justice has shown a disinclination to allow the presence of differentiated or partial arrangements to undermine the coherence and uniformity of the legal order it has created' (Shaw and Wiener, 2000: 86).

From the very beginning, the unification of Europe has been progressing as a continuous process of legalizing integration by enacting a series of European treaties and cultivating the growing body of the *acquis communautaire* (Armstrong, 1998). Since the Treaty of Rome in 1957, European integration has been based on the principle of legal unification beyond the common practices and limits of international law. Juridification has been another name for unification. It means that the actions of both Member States and EU institutions can be generally scrutinized and equally challenged by all legal subjects. Consequently, any legalization of the differentiation principle raises the problem of the universality of European legality.

Hence the policy of differentiated integration can only be legalized by European treaties as a legal exception in the form of the *flexibility clauses* that are typical of international law rather than of the hybrid transnational EU legal system. In this manner, legal provisions related to opt-outs from a particular EU policy need to restate that provisions, measures and decisions related to that policy area shall not affect the competences, rights and obligations of [non-participating] states.[2]

Different levels of commitment for different groups of states have often been considered merely a temporary side-effect of an otherwise strong and centripetal integration policy of *one* Union to rule *all* Member States by the same system of law. European opt-out legislation, such as the British and Danish protocols on stage three of EMU (Beaumont and Walker, 1999), had not been intended as a blueprint for the Union's official legal design, drawn according to the principle of differentiated integration. The intention was to resolve problems in specific policy areas arising from further unification that was not completely endorsed by all Member States at the same time. According to the persistent logic of progressive integration, these exemptions were negotiated as temporary measures to provide unwilling Member States with more time to adjust and accept new integration policies before adopting them like the rest of the Union's Member States (De Schutter, 2005). The original function of the flexibility clauses was to contribute to the final achievement of one overarching integration pattern facilitated by the body of European laws. However, the indefinite design and persistence of some clauses, such as the Irish and UK opt-outs from the Schengen Zone or the UK opt-outs from the Union's protection of social rights, have gradually weakened the original idea of flexibility as a transitional measure and made it an intrinsic feature of European legal integration (De Witte, 2005). The most recent examples of this development may be found in the Lisbon Treaty, such as its *Protocol on the Application of the Charter of Fundamental Rights of the European Union to Poland and to the United Kingdom* which explicitly guarantees the supremacy of the United Kingdom and Poland's national law as regards justiciability of rights recognized by the Charter.

The Union's 'betweenness' and legal pluralism

The EU flexibility clauses reaffirm the political and legal sovereignty and right of Member States to either stay out of a specific EU integration domain or join it after political deliberation and decision-making at national level in the future. The clauses are expected to outline the legally tolerable differences of integration (Walker, 2000). They contribute to the 'betweenness' (Laffan, 1998: 236) of the Union, struggling to accommodate national governments and European governance, international diplomacy and transnational politics, markets and social welfare, constitutional rights and jurisdictional limitations, and so on (Carter and Scott, 1998).

For legal scholars, officials and judges, the 'betweenness' of the Union represents a set of challenges associated with its 'non-state' pluralistic character, especially the absence of supreme legal authority and the impossibility of logically establishing the normative hierarchy of EU and national legal systems (Curtin, 1993). Despite numerous efforts by the European Court of Justice (ECJ) to pursue the vision of EU law as superior to the Member States' legal systems, national institutions, especially constitutional and supreme courts, persist in preserving the supremacy of national constitutions and their jurisdiction as final guardians of citizens' rights and freedoms.

The Union involves a number of integrative aspects that are impossible to conceptualize within common frameworks of national or international law and cannot be grasped by the jurisprudential concept of legal monism. It does not have a supreme legislative body and its laws are enacted by different institutions and legitimized by cooperative dynamics between specific EU bodies and the national political bodies of its Member States (Majone, 1994: 18). Though it has indisputably transformed the nation-state institutions of its members (Goldmann, 2001), the EU is not a state with a monopoly on political violence, and its ability to enforce laws is based on the Member States' commitment to uphold EU laws and administrative or judicial decisions.

Flexibility, rather than uniformity, has become a defining feature of the EU's constitutional system (de Búrca and Scott, 2000). Even strong advocates of European federal statehood, such as Mancini (1998) or von Bogdandy (1999), admit the plurality of the EU's institutional framework and its polycentric and fragmented forms of integration. Despite the discourse of supranational federalism, the heterarchy of EU regulations indicates that any form of progressive integration necessarily leads to the growing diffusion of the political authority and jurisdiction of EU bodies. The process of political integration increases the complexity of the legal system and thus inevitably contributes to the simultaneous process of transnational (both European and global) legal *fragmentation* (Fischer-Lescano and Teubner, 2004). The whole development looks like another strain on the EU's institutional framework and 'a Pandora's box with a high degree of uncertainty as to how, where and when the flexibility clauses will be used' (Stubb, 2002: 143).

It is relatively easy for the European legal system to operationalize differentiated integration by enacting the flexibility clauses that are politically negotiated by the Member States. Its operation has to conform to the Union's objectives, and its approval by the European Commission is conditional on the fact that these same objectives cannot be achieved by the Union as a whole. The clauses do not create a jurisdictional crisis or paralysis. In fact, they enhance the operational complexity of the European legal system and thus strengthen EU legal semantics (Leibfried and Pierson, 1995). By incorporating the flexibility clauses in EU treaties, the legal institutionalization of differentiated integration primarily minimizes the risk of the pursuit of progressive integration by individual Member States outside the treaty framework. Legal techniques formulate specific opt-outs by individual Member States and thus preserve the unity of EU legal integration. The acceptable level of differentiated integration is fully determined within the system of EU treaties and other legal documents.

Thus the European legal system allows the Member States to exercise their sovereignty even in the highly integrated and sovereignty-limiting institutional setting of the EU (Walker, 1998). Legal provisions guarantee the current political dynamics of the Union. The principle of legally predefined differentiation empowers the willing Member States to enhance their mutual cooperation, while guaranteeing the benefits of the existing levels of integration to all members of the Union (Tuytschaever, 1999).

Differentiated integration is based on the functionality of specific arrangements for cooperation and mutual coordination among varying sets of participating countries (Streeck, 1996: 70). The Union's complexity, polycentric structure and functionally differentiated pluralism represents a departure from the nation-state and its sovereignty as a unified system of representative authority in full territorial and political control (Bellamy and Castiglione, 1997). Its framework rules out the possibility of a new political centre or authoritative hierarchy. Instead, its internal dynamic is that of a 'self-regulated pluralistic society' (Chryssochoou, 2001: 27).

Within the context of EU law, this pluralism is typified by the absence of the ultimate rule of recognition and of the clear normative hierarchy of a legal system. The EU legal system is permanently challenged by the supremacy question and controversies arising between EU and national legal systems. However, there are no simple doctrinal answers because both European and national laws are equally valid within the EU. This level of legal differentiation and pluralism has been operationalized by EU lawyers and judges and turned into complex doctrines of the EU's divided constitutional sovereignty, judicial cooperation between EU and national courts, and European legal pluralism (Barber, 2006).

EU law can strengthen national law and vice-versa, and practical legal solutions can reinforce institutions of both Member States and the EU (Jacobs, 2007: 63). The fact that it is difference rather than unity that enhances the operation of the EU legal system rules out the unitary or one-dimensional approach to constitutional and legal sovereignty of both Member States and the EU (Walker, 2003: 26–7). The state of legal pluralism, flexibility clauses, diffusion and differentiated legal norms is the basic condition of the EU legal system.

Differentiated integration as part of European governance

The flexibility clauses that have been enacted by the European treaties as a new EU policy can be treated as enhancements of the operability of the European legal system. In other words, the clauses are not a threat to current European integration but its very expression at a time of growing complexity in the Union's political, legal, economic and civil society settlements. They enhance the level of autonomy and self-regulation of the EU's legal system, contribute to legal self-reference, and mark further differentiation in the legal system and the governance-based system of European politics. They are at the same time an instrument of politics and its legal restraint (Luhmann, 2004: 365). Correspondingly, the differentiation and growing separation of European law and politics leads to their growing interdependence.

Therefore, the legislation of differentiated integration needs to be contextualized as part of the more general process of the *juridification of politics* that is typical of functionally differentiated modern societies. However, this process is inseparable from the associated process of the political *instrumentalization of law,* which is, for instance, detectable in the use of European treaties for the purpose of further political integration. The processes of political instrumentalization of law and the legal limitation of political power coexist as typical of mutually differentiated systems of politics and law.

The political process of differentiated integration and the legal mechanism of flexibility clauses reveal both the high level of interdependence of European law and politics and their clear differentiation into two separate systems. European politics determines which laws become valid, but European laws are preconditions of the making of European politics. Despite the structural absence of political statehood, and the lack of political legitimation in terms of democratic government and opposition, the European political system has enough operative power to portray and represent itself in a 'rule-of-law-like' formula based on the tautology that 'the rule and the law are the same' (Luhmann, 2004: 370–1). This level of functional differentiation in European politics would be impossible without the operative power of European legality which has been a grand instrument for the realization of EU political goals.

The differentiated integration of the EU operates as 'integrated differentiation'. The EU internalizes both the supremacy of European laws and the constitutional sovereignty of its Member States. It is a system of multi-level interdependence between national and European institutions. While Member State national governments do not wish to constitute a European statehood, the EU's constitutional domain – as a self-referential system of laws significantly limiting national jurisdictions – has been established for several decades. The system of national negotiations and intergovernmental conferences transfers traditional nation-state powers to the Union, whilst also enhancing the autonomy of negotiating Member State governments (Moravcsik, 1993: 507). Sovereignty is 'pooled' between national and European bodies, and no European institution can claim supreme legislative authority. The ever closer Union is re-conceptualized as an 'ever closer fusion' (Wessels, 1997: 274).

Instead of replicating democratic sovereignty-building at EU level, recent political and legal developments show both the power of the Union to functionally differentiate further, without the recursive discourse of democratic statehood and legitimacy, and the limits to that power (Cram, 1994). The Union's evolution 'from policy to polity' and the constitution of 'politics like any other' (Chryssochoou, 2001: 96) indicate the emergence of a European political system with autonomous institutions and a structure independent of national politics. The system and its polity-formation role (Rhodes and Mazey, 1995) are 'an exercise in enlarging the operation of social engineering while creating new structures of opportunity above the state level, without conforming to the contours of a system-wide hierarchy that is typical of the component polities' (Chryssochoou, 2001: 97).

Modern political societies are associated with the simultaneous social processes of the 'positivization' of law, which means the loss of the transcendental legitimacy of legality, and the democratization of politics, which provides the constitutional rule of law with democratic legitimacy (Luhmann, 2004: 365). However, EU politics is different from national politics because it is based on multiple arenas of economic, administrative and technical governance rather than a democratically legitimate system of accountable government and legality operating at nation-state level.

Governance generally means the capacity of social networks to enhance their interaction and to organize themselves into a self-referential system which, unlike conventional political hierarchies, permanently negotiates shared goals, purposes and general rules of governing (Jessop, 2003). It has no sovereign authority (Kooiman, 1993), represents an alternative to both spontaneous market regulations and organizational hierarchies of political government, and reflects significant recent changes in the political system, methods and processes of governing. Practicality dominates over ideology, self-organizing networks over state bureaucratic authority (Rhodes, 1996).

Governance as a system for making and implementing collectively binding decisions is not limited to the EU's political decision-making and administration. It is not simply an alternative concept to democratic government but is, rather, adopted by national governments to devolve decision-making and hopefully deliver more efficient and better quality public services. Thus governance emerges at national, sub-national (state, regional and local) and transnational (global, European) levels (Peters and Pierre, 2004). It is focused on performance indicators and legitimized by outcomes rather than by democratic procedures and deliberations. Its structure is polycentric, involves a multiplicity of binding decisions and governing agencies, and contributes to 'the hollowing out of the state' (Rhodes, 1994) because individual networks of governance successfully preserve their autonomy and self-regulation and resist any attempts at centralized guidance.

At national level, governance involves a number of non-governmental institutions, thereby enhancing the management capacities of society through different kinds of expert knowledge. Its purpose is to minimize inefficiency in governmental administration and welfare distribution. However, the emphasis on instrumental rationality and legitimation by expertise makes governance a challenge to the political authority of democratically elected legislative and administrative bodies. At transnational level, this challenge is either successfully suppressed by transnational organizations, or made part of complex relations between those organizations and their members – states as democratically constituted entities.

Transnational governance thus expands and accelerates the general tendency of governance networks towards self-regulation without government and towards power beyond the state and its legal system (Djelic and Sahlin-Andersson, 2006).

EU history illustrates how strong governance-driven legitimation by efficiency and expert knowledge can, up to a certain point, successfully neutralize even genuine calls for institutional democratization and political reform (Zürn and Joerges, 2005). The EU's political system is a system of *governance* which is structurally differentiated from democratically formed and legitimized Member State *governments*. Indeed, European governance includes national governments and their specific governance networks. However, the duality of democratic government and administrative governance, which is typical of national political systems, does not exist at the European level. European governance without government is self-regulatory and operates beyond the constraints of the government-based political systems of Member States.

The Union of European *governance* and national *governments*: on functions and segments of the European political system

The difference between the legal semantics of the flexibility clauses and the political semantics of differentiated integration shows how European legality and politics have managed to benefit systemically from being insulated from each other's interventions. After outlining the legal semantics of the flexibility clauses and the general operation of EU legality, it is important to examine what constitutes the self-referential system of European politics and how the policy of differentiated integration contributes to it and to the construction of the European polity.

The structural difference between EU governance and Member State governments informs all major debates regarding the paradigmatic shift and the experimental character of European integration (Laffan et al., 1999). This difference also explains why the policy of differentiated integration has been facilitating EU integration while granting the organizational autonomy of Member States and making national political operations part of European politics. By incorporating national governments as its segments, the European political system enhances its operability.

European governance is an example of *negotiated governance* that has been agreed by the national governments of Member States. While the Union has been changing its political and institutional shape, individual states have continued to exercise their state sovereignty, externally and internally. Some, like the United Kingdom, Spain and Belgium, have even radically transformed their constitutional settlements. The processes of decentralization, devolution, federalization and other forms of constitutional engineering have affected both the Union and its Member States in the last two decades. However, these processes can hardly be interpreted as justifying further European integration and leading to the general transformation of state sovereignty (Taylor, 1996) because Member State governments, irrespective of national constitutional transformations and settlements, continue to exercise their power at EU level and thus secure their national interests within the general system of European governance.

Differences in the bargaining power of national governments profoundly influence the operative power of European institutions (Moravcsik, 1993). However, this paradox of Member State governments communicating their goals through the channels of EU governance has actually been a source of the Union's growing operational capacity, resulting in the emergence of the European self-referential political system. National interests get reformulated as European interests and, as such, are subsequently pursued and protected by EU institutions, irrespective of their country of origin.

The Union has transgressed, and yet not made completely redundant, one of the main structural limitations of modernity – the organization of societies into nation-states, relying on political semantics of popular sovereignty, democratic legitimacy, citizenship and civil rights, and the like. The complex political dynamics of the EU are also illustrated in much more technical and legalistic contexts, such as the controversial subsidiarity principle which 'can, on the one hand, suggest a desire to reduce EU-level intervention into national policy, or, on the other hand, the normatively more attractive and positive desire to enhance self-government and to involve those most directly affected by decision-making as fully as possible in the process' (de Búrca, 2001: 133). National societies, politically represented by the state organization, keep their importance in the highly integrated EU (Marks et al., 1996). The question of to what extent the Union's institutional framework can replicate the system of democratic decision-making and legitimacy typical of its Member States remains a major source of political controversies, disputes, optimistic projects and sceptical remarks (Weale, 1995). The nation-state's democratic legitimacy and accountability function as a source of the *politicization* of otherwise depoliticized technocratic and instrumental European governance (Přibáň, 2007: 116–28).

Turning fear of a democratic deficit into political desire: the Treaty of Lisbon

The dissociation of territorial state constituencies and of the functional competences that enhance the differentiation of the social subsystems of the EU strengthens the operational autonomy of European governance. The policy of differentiated integration contributes to the stabilization of this autonomy by turning national governments into segments of the EU's self-referential political system. However, the system of European governance, like any political system of collectively binding decisions, is split between its internal 'system effectiveness' and the more general demand of democratic participation in the processes of decision-making (Dahl, 1994). While some theories claim that governance in general can neutralize the systemic tension between effectiveness and democratic participation or representation because it channels multiple interests through its internal networks and processes the most suitable and effective policy outputs (Ruzza, 2004), the policy of differentiated integration driven by the Union's nation-state segmentation persuasively shows that the question of democratic legitimacy cannot be neutralized by the system of supranational governance legitimized by its outcomes. The project of ever-closer European integration rather translates this question to the supranational settings of EU politics by anxiously asking whether there is a European *demos* or, at least, the European public sphere normatively justifying the emergence of European democratic *polity*. These questions are increasingly raised by both European and Member State political and legal institutions in their decision-making and reasoning.

Within the context of European governance, the tension between instrumental *legitimation by outcomes* (based on policy effectiveness) and symbolic *legitimation by values* (based on democratic representation and participation) (Scharpf, 1999) has always been articulated through the often-criticized 'democratic deficit' and 'common benefit' discourses (Majone, 1998). In the 1990s, the 'permissive consensus' between the citizens of EU countries and the 'Eurocratic' élite administrative decisions was gradually replaced by a 'constraining dissensus' regarding the future direction and legal or constitutional settlement of European integration (Tsakatika, 2007: 31). In these circumstances, differentiated integration became a response to the democratic deficit and growing systemic tensions between European governance and Member State governments. Apart from keeping the enlarging EU governable in all major areas, differentiated integration was thus expected to enhance the Union's legitimacy (Shaw, 1998).

The European Commission sought to link the concept of governance to the new polity emerging within the EU (Sweet and Sandholtz, 1998; Craig and Harlow, 1998). It introduced into 1990s European public debate the political themes of 'who is actually governed by EU governance, how, in whose name, and to what end' (Banchoff and Smith, 1999). At the most basic level, democratic procedures and institutions have been a precondition of EU membership and thus are embedded in nation-states – as segments of the EU political system. However, the EU's burden of a governing bureaucracy without democratic accountability highlights the Union's traditionally ambivalent relationship to popular politics. This ambivalence is 'a testimony not just to the élite character of the EU's invention and development, but also to the fears of an incursionary democratic politics of Europe (whether regressive or emancipatory)' (Clarke, 2005: 28).

The persistence of the democratic legitimation and/or deficit arguments shows that the modern notion of democratic statehood cannot be easily sidelined by governance theories. It also reflects the semantic (both legal and political) importance of popular state sovereignty, even in the globalized, post-sovereign and post-national EU constellation.

In the modern democratic polity, power circulates between the people, party politics, administration and public opinion as communicated through mass media (Luhmann, 2002: 258). While the principle of popular sovereignty – sovereignty 'by the people' – provides the system with democratic legitimacy, political parties struggle to win power by winning a majority of the votes 'of the people'. In this way they form a government administering specific policies 'for the people' that can be recursively evaluated by the public, affect political preferences, and thus contribute to the future processes of political majority-building. This power circulation obviously does not exist in the European Union. The EU political system circulates power by the self-referential operation of its administrative organization. Though state organization is missing, alternative forms of governing and processes of decision-making are no less powerful. In the absence of EU democratic government, good governance is considered a major force integrating the emerging European polity (Riekmann et al., 2005).

According to this view, the form of European governance determines the form of the European polity (Lindberg and Scheingold, 1970). EU treaties and political documents thus interpret the obligation of good governance as a commitment to the enhancement of the democratic legitimacy of EU political decision-making. The substantive objectives of good governance, legitimized by instrumental efficiency, are increasingly intertwined with the procedural objectives of decision-making ultimately legitimized by democratic principles and values (Joerges and Dehousse, 2002).

Drawing on calls for strengthening the democratic legitimacy commitment incorporated in the Treaty of Amsterdam and the Treaty of Nice (Kohler-Koch and Rittberger, 2007), the Lisbon 'Reform' Treaty subsequently attempted to turn the EU's biggest fear, the democratic deficit, into a strong political desire. It opened by making an explicit link between the Union's legitimacy and democracy:

> DESIRING to enhance further the democratic and efficient functioning of the institutions so as to enable them better to carry out, within a single institutional framework, the tasks entrusted to them.[3]

The legal provisions of the Treaty expose the Union much more to the discourse of democratic legitimation and/or of its absence. The legalism of the EU treaty incorporates the need to democratize European governance and its global dissemination by promoting multilateralism in international relations (Article 21, Title V). Moving beyond the narrow criterion of efficiency, it associates good governance with political participation, openness and the public accountability of EU institutions.

The political semantics of good governance dominates Title II of the Lisbon Treaty, entitled 'Provisions on Democratic Principles', which legislates for the principle of representative democracy and its application at EU level (especially Article 10 and Article 11). Indeed, the Lisbon Treaty strengthens the overall political tendency to increased majoritarianism in the EU's decision-making and further limits the once-prevailing veto power of individual states. The danger of decision-making paralysis stemming from the veto power is lessened at the expense of protecting the political interests of individual states. However, the incorporated principle of active involvement by national parliaments in EU politics confirms the operative condition and capacity of the EU to combine governance with the democratic governments of Member States and to continue regulating it by means of the EU legal principles of subsidiarity and proportionality (MacCormick, 1997).

Concluding remarks on the administrative state of the EU

The Lisbon Treaty reveals the Union as stretched between instrumental and democratic legitimacy. The famous formula of 'things administering themselves' in modern political societies applies to European governance in the form of objective directives and decrees, which lack democratically legitimized authority. Administrative decrees and practices are primarily motivated by instrumental reasoning and organizational purposes.

The current state of the EU mirrors earlier social developments within the nation-state more than a century ago when the bureaucracy became the most important legitimizing element of the political will, the concept of legitimacy by legality drew on the rationality of bureaucratic order, and the bureaucracy was considered the superior partner transforming 'the law of the parliamentary legislative state into the measures of the administrative state' (Schmitt, 2004: 14). The EU, which emerged as a supranational organization actively endorsed by democratically elected national governments, represents the bureaucratically administered state relying on efficient measures and regulatory 'necessities'. It has been supported by Member State governments in order to supplement their democratic legitimacy with further components of efficiency and legitimation by 'common benefit'. However, progressive political integration has put the instrumental rationality of the Union in question, and the call for democratic legitimation and democratization of the Union's polity-building and constitution-making has become a recurring theme of the European political system, most recently manifested during the drafting of the Lisbon Treaty.

The Union's differentiated integration operates as integrated differentiation. The policy of differentiated integration legally channelled through the EU flexibility clauses shows both the growing differentiation of the EU's political and legal systems and the internal political differentiation of European governance and Member State governments. This functional and systemic differentiation of the EU indicates that any form of future progressive integration will result in the growing diffusion and fragmentation of the political authority and jurisdiction of EU bodies. However, it also indicates that any theoretical and political conceptualizations attempting to link European governance to the European polity or polity-building, characteristic of European federalists and advocates of the 'ever-closer' Union, will only increase reliance on the discourse of democratic legitimacy, reveal the scale of the EU's democratic deficit, and thus highlight the current incommensurability and impossibility of reconciling instrumental legitimation through efficiency with symbolic legitimation based on democratic values.

Notes

1. The term was coined by two top German conservative politicians, Karl Lamers and Wolfgang Schäuble, in their paper presented to the Christian Democratic Union/Christian Social Union Parliamentary Party in the Lower House of Parliament of Germany in September 1994 (Schäuble and Lamers, 1994; Booker and North, 2005: 380–5).
2. See, for instance, Protocol No. 4 on the position of the United Kingdom and Ireland annexed to the (Amsterdam) Treaty on European Union and to the Treaty establishing European Community (signed in Amsterdam on 2 October 1997). The Protocol guarantees opt-outs of both countries from the Schengen-related *acquis* (for further details, see Griller et al., 2000: 514–18).

3. In the text approved at the Intergovernmental Conference in Brussels in December 2007, there is an explicit remark tracing this commitment back to the Treaty of Amsterdam and the Treaty of Nice: 'Desiring to complete the process started by the Treaty of Amsterdam and by the Treaty of Nice with a view to enhancing the efficiency and democratic legitimacy of the Union and to improving the coherence of its action ...'.

3
The Functional Dimension

Alkuin Kölliker

Introduction

This chapter explores properties of the functional dimension of politics that may help to understand the dynamics of differentiated integration in the context of the European Union. In other words, it investigates the role that differentiation plays in the institutional deepening, functional extension, territorial enlargement and progress over time of EU-related cooperation among European countries. Differentiation may simultaneously play a role as an aspect of integration itself (differentiation as a property of integration), as an outcome of integration (differentiation as a dependent variable), or as a driver of integration (differentiation as an explanatory variable).[1] Together with the two following chapters, this chapter provides questions, concepts and some theoretical insights that might enter into a dialogue with, inspire or guide empirical research on the role of function, space and time in differentiated European integration.

The chapter is structured as follows: Section 2 specifies some questions that are important for understanding the role of the functional dimension of differentiated European integration. Section 3 then clarifies the concept of differentiation as used in this chapter and highlights some important distinctions concerning various dimensions of differentiation. Section 4 identifies three scholarly fields in which answers to the identified questions may be found. Sections 5 to 7 briefly investigate these fields, looking at theories of European integration and international relations, comparative politics and policy analysis, and public goods theory, respectively. The section on public goods theory presents a partial theory of differentiated integration. Section 8 presents some conclusions about the different types of differentiation that can be drawn from this theory. The concluding section summarizes the theoretical observations from the various areas. It also includes some reflections on the three 'key political questions' about differentiated integration that have been identified in Chapter 1.

Questions about the functional dimension

General questions about differentiation and integration. The fundamental question in this volume concerns the relationship between differentiation and the progress (or stagnation) of European integration over time, space and function. A comprehensive answer needs to be based, first of all, on an appropriate definition of the relevant basic concept, including differentiation and relevant sub-types of differentiation. It also requires a description of actual differentiated arrangements created in the EU context across time, space and functions (that is, differentiation as a property of integration). On this basis, two key questions can then be addressed: first, under which circumstances – relating to specific properties of the spatial, functional and temporal dimensions – are different types of differentiation used (that is, differentiation as an outcome of integration)? And, second, what are the effects – in particular on the progress of integration over space, function and time – of the use of different types of differentiation (that is, differentiation as a driver of integration)? Whereas differentiation is the dependent variable in the first question, it is an explanatory variable in the second. These questions can be asked for individual arrangements, for groups of arrangements, and even for the totality of differentiated arrangements in the EU context. It may also be important to take into account how differentiated arrangements influence each other, as well as the use of alternative instruments to overcome deadlock in EU decision-making (for example, issue-linkage and side payments).

Specific questions on the role of the functional dimension. All these general questions on the relationship between differentiation and integration are also relevant when considering the functional dimension. Therefore, the basic question is: How do aspects of the functional dimension influence differentiation 1) as a property; 2) as an outcome; and 3) as a driver of integration? Or it can be posed in three more specific questions: first, how can the functional dimension help to describe (different types of) differentiated integration? Second, how can properties of the functional dimension help explain the use of (different types of) differentiated integration? And, finally, how can the functional dimension contribute to explaining the effects of (different types of) differentiated integration?

Taking into account anticipated effects of differentiation. Whenever actors use differentiation as an instrument to achieve specific objectives, their motivations are closely connected to the expected effects of differentiation. Hence, in order to understand its use, it is necessary (but not sufficient) to clarify what motivates actors. In order to understand both the motivation for, and the use of, differentiation, it is necessary to know what actors expect from differentiation. It is necessary, in other words, to know the effects of differentiated integration as anticipated by decision-makers.

Types of differentiation in the EU context

Definition of differentiation. In this chapter differentiation primarily means legal differentiation. Legal differentiation in the EU context means that, for a certain time (whether limited or not), EU Member States may have different rights and obligations (ranging from full participation to complete absence) in regard to specific EU policies. Legal differentiation may be linked with differences concerning the polity, economy, society or geography of countries or groups of countries. These differences matter either as potential causes or as potential effects of legal differentiation. The focus on legal differentiation does not mean the exclusion of economic and societal differentiation when it helps understanding of the causes and effects of legal differentiation.

Distinguishing types of differentiated integration. Progress in understanding the nature, causes and effects of differentiated integration in the EU and beyond has so far been hampered by the lack of solid and broadly agreed conceptual bases. For the time being, the 'semantic indigestion' bemoaned by Alexander Stubb (1995) still appears to prevail.[2] However, differentiation cannot be properly analysed without taking into account major differences between the various differentiated arrangements that actually exist. While a generalization may be correct for one type of differentiation, it is more often than not wrong or misleading for other types of differentiation. Differentiated arrangements can be distinguished along various dimensions. Combining clearly defined dimensions in a comprehensive and transparent manner would lead to a useful multi-dimensional typology of differentiated integration. In turn, it would allow for much more precise questions and answers about differentiated integration in Europe.

Basic distinctions in differentiated arrangements. The scope of this chapter does not allow for developing and presenting a stringent, multi-dimensional categorization of differentiated integration. In its absence it is still useful, as a first step, to take into account several individual dimensions along which differentiated arrangements can be distinguished. Table 3.1 identifies six dimensions, selected on the basis of their presumed importance, along which differentiated arrangements can be distinguished. It provides a brief explanation and an example for each of the various types.

Table 3.1 Types of differentiation

Distinction concerning differentiation	Explanation	Examples
1a – actual*	Differentiation is actually applied.	Monetary union
1b – potential ('shadow of differentiation')	Differentiation is merely a possibility in legal/political terms, but not (yet) actually applied.	Treaty of Amsterdam clauses on closer cooperation
2a – inside EU law*	Differentiated arrangement is based on EC/EU law.	Monetary union
2b – outside EU law	Differentiated arrangement is based on traditional international law instead of EC/EU law.	Schengen Agreement (1985) Prüm Treaty (2005)

(*continued*)

Table 3.1   Continued

Distinction concerning differentiation	Explanation	Examples
3a – inside EU borders*	Creates differentiation between EU Member States (some Member States participate, others do not).	Monetary union
3b – outside EU borders	Refers to extension of EU-related policies beyond EU borders. Creates differentiation between EU non-Member States (some non-members participate, others do not).	European Economic Area (EU Member States, Norway, Iceland, Liechtenstein)
4a – broad issues	Differentiated arrangement includes one or several broad issue areas.	Schengen Agreement
4b – narrow issues	Differentiation is limited to one narrow issue or issue area.	Eurocorps
5a – due to unwillingness of 'outs' ('*à la carte*')	Differentiation is motivated by the (subjective) initial unwillingness of certain countries to participate.	Non-participation of UK in monetary union
5b – due to unwillingness of 'ins' ('*directoire*')	Differentiation is motivated by the (subjective) unwillingness of initial participants to let other countries participate.	Meetings of 'G6' interior ministers (Germany, France, UK, Italy, Spain, Poland)
5c – due to inability of 'outs'	Differentiation is motivated by the (objective) inability of non-participants to participate.	Exclusion of new EU members from monetary union (2004)
5d – due to inability of 'ins'	Differentiation is motivated by the (objective) inability of participants to let other countries participate.	(Probably no clear example yet; 'empty' category? Links, for example, to 'absorbtion capacity'.)
6a – temporary ('transitory period')	Differentiated arrangement whereby 'outs' participate after a pre-determined time period.	Transitory period for free movement of persons concerning Eastern enlargement countries
6b – conditional ('different speeds')	Differentiated arrangement whereby 'outs' participate if and when specific, objective, pre-determined conditions are fulfilled.	Participation of EU countries in monetary union based on the 'Maastricht criteria' (except UK, DK; see below)
6c – permanent ('variable geometry')	Differentiated arrangement whereby no pre-determined conditions or time limits apply. Non-participation of 'outs' may be permanent.	Non-participation of EU countries with a derogation from monetary union (UK, DK)

* Arrangements combining types 1a, 2a and 3a (creating actual differentiation based on EC/EU law inside EU borders) represent differentiation in a narrow sense and belong to the 'classical' examples of differentiation within the EU. If arrangements combining types 1b, 2b and 3b are included, it is preferable to speak of differentiation in a larger sense, or differentiation 'in the EU context'.

Theoretical approaches and the functional dimension of differentiated integration

The three dimensions of legal differentiation. Legal differentiation as defined above explicitly refers to all three dimensions of differentiation investigated in this volume. It has a spatial dimension (participating Member States), a functional dimension (issue areas included) and a temporal dimension (time periods during which differentiation applies). As understood in the EU context, legal differentiation necessarily and primarily refers to differentiation along the territorial dimension. A differentiated arrangement includes some countries while excluding others. It is therefore only natural to turn toward the properties of countries – in political, economic, social and geographical terms – in search of factors explaining differentiation (see Chapter 4 by Michael Keating). But differentiated arrangements also have a temporal dimension. They develop over time, add new participants and sometimes end up with full participation, thus terminating differentiation in regard to that specific arrangement. Last but not least, all differentiated arrangements in the EU context also have a functional dimension. Individual arrangements cover some issue areas, but not others. Hence it is equally important to turn to the functional dimension in search of factors explaining why and how differentiation is used in some issue areas, but not – or differently – in others. The following three paragraphs briefly introduce three areas of political science and beyond in which concepts and hypotheses may be found or newly generated that have the potential to illuminate the use of differentiated integration from a functional perspective. Sections 4 to 6 provide some more details on all three of these areas.

Theories of integration and international relations. Among the various theories of integration and of international relations, only functionalism and neo-functionalism address systematically the functional dimension. However, relevant concepts and insights may be found in other approaches, such as Moravcsik's 'liberal intergovernmentalism', and in the distinction between 'high politics' and 'low politics'.

Comparative politics and policy analysis. Students of comparative politics examine actors, institutions and policies across different political systems. The study of policies and thus of the functional dimension is younger than the study of institutions and the interplay of actors. It has, nevertheless, generated a number of concepts and hypotheses that could be useful when trying to understand the functional dimension of differentiated European integration. Section 5 briefly explores the potential of Lowi's distinction between 'regulatory', 'distributive' and 'redistributive' policies; the concepts of 'policy networks' and 'advocacy coalitions' as used by Adrienne Héritier and Paul Sabatier, respectively; and the concept of policy cycles involving specific stages of the policy process.

Public goods theory. Section 6 focuses on public goods theory and a (partial) 'theory of differentiated integration' that has been formulated on this basis. Theories about public goods and externalities originate in economic theory. They have turned out to be useful for the study of differentiation. EU policies can be seen as goods collectively produced by EU Member States. In previous contributions (see Kölliker, 2001, 2006b) I have shown how the dynamics of differentiated integration differs depending on the types of goods and externalities that different policies generate. Section 6 presents the main characteristics and insights of this 'differentiated integration theory'.

Theories of European integration and international relations

Functionalism and neo-functionalism. From their inception in the second half of the 19th century, international organizations have been organized predominantly around specific functions. The creation of the three European Communities in the 1950s followed the logic of 'functionalism' as conceptualized and favoured by David Mitrany (1943, 1948, 1966). Functionalism was an integral part of Jean Monnet's doctrine of European unification. In the form of 'neo-functionalism', the normative and descriptive concept of functionalism was complemented by a causal theory with elements of prediction. Neo-functionalism as developed by Haas (1958) explained how integration in one policy area could spill over into other policy areas (see Schmitter, 2005 for an evaluation of Haas's legacy).

Possible insights into differentiated integration. Like other theorists of European integration, neo-functionalists paid little attention to differentiation when it started to become more important from the mid-1980s onwards. Yet neo-functionalist insights can be potentially very useful when applied to differentiated integration. For instance, neo-functionalists would expect a differentiated arrangement in one policy area to generate spillover effects and incentives to create corresponding differentiated arrangements in other policy areas. In some cases, spillover effects may not affect all the participating countries. In other cases, non-participating countries may be affected by 'externalities' (or 'geographical spillover'; see the next paragraph). In these cases, it could be expected that the participation in new differentiated arrangements resulting from spillover effects may differ from the original arrangement. One example is the spillover effects from the abolition of internal border controls on the surveillance of Europe's maritime frontiers.[3]

Other theories of European integration and international relations. Other theories of European integration and international relations give somewhat less attention to the functional dimension. This is the case for intergovernmentalism, as advocated by Stanley Hoffmann (1966), and also for the various institutionalist approaches (rational choice institutionalism, historical institutionalism, sociological institutionalism) that came to dominate European integration theory in the 1990s (see Pollack, 2004). When developing his liberal intergovernmentalist approach, Moravcsik (1991, 1993) observed that the threat of a two-tier Europe – potential differentiation as defined in Section 3 – could be used to convince reluctant countries to participate in new EU policies. Moravcsik already noticed that the threat of exclusion could only be used in the case of policies creating negative externalities for non-participants. In this context, he used the term 'geographical spillover'.

'High politics', 'low politics' and differentiation. International relations theory refers to the functional dimension in distinguishing 'high politics' from 'low politics'. Stable and far-reaching international cooperation is supposed to be difficult in areas involving national security ('high politics'). Conversely, it is considered more likely in areas such as economic, social and environmental policies ('low politics'). The potential implications of this distinction for differentiated European integration are not obvious. But one theoretical implication could be as follows: first, it would mean that we observe more genuine integration in 'low politics' issues (inside the EC pillar), and less far-reaching international cooperation in 'high politics' issues (in the other two EU pillars and outside EU law). The history and pre-history of the three EU pillars does not make this hypothesis seem entirely implausible. Second, we can observe empirically that differentiated integration is less constrained, the more we move from the EC pillar of the EU to the second pillar, the third pillar, and beyond (cooperation outside EU law). These two observations lead to the conclusion that differentiation is more widespread in the area of 'high EU politics' than in the area of 'low EU politics'.[4]

Comparative politics and policy analysis

Regulatory, distributive and redistributive policies. The often-used distinction between regulative, distributive and redistributive policies goes back to Theodore Lowi (1964, 1972). He suggested that these three types of policies lead to different kinds and intensities of political conflicts, and hence that 'policies determine politics'. Giandomenico Majone (1994) used this distinction to characterize the EU as a 'regulatory state'. While this observation is broadly correct, the EU also includes areas in which it distributes publicly provided goods or redistributes resources. The 'Galilei' project for Europe's own global positioning system serves as an example of a distributive policy, while the European structural funds redistribute money within the EU.

Redistributive policies and differentiated integration. When we consider the policy areas in which differentiation has been used, it is striking that differentiation appears to have been virtually absent in the case of redistributive policies. Can we conclude that, although redistributive policies tend to be highly contested, differentiation is not an appropriate tool to overcome deadlock in this case, because opt-outs for the rich countries would render redistributive policies pointless? Though it is tempting to think so, further investigation is needed.

Different motives for unwillingness to participate in differentiated integration. Another observation could be that, in the case of distributive policies, unwillingness to participate and opt-outs tend to arise from the burden on the Member States that are supposed to contribute to the production of the good. In the case of regulatory policies, by contrast, unwillingness and opt-outs tend to be motivated by the burden

on the addressees of regulation and their worries about competitiveness. While distributive policies lead mainly to direct costs for the public sector, which produces a publicly provided good, regulatory policies principally generate indirect compliance costs
for the addressees in the private sector, who have to comply with the regulations.

Policy networks and advocacy coalition. The development of differentiated arrangements in the EU, just like national and European policies more generally, may be
driven (or hampered) by specific policy networks and advocacy coalitions (Héritier,
1993; Sabatier, 1993, 1998, 1999). Börzel (1997) explored the relevance of the concept
of policy networks for studying European politics, while Radaelli (1999) applied an
advocacy coalition approach for investigating the issue of tax harmonization within
the EU. It would be interesting to investigate if and how these concepts, as well as the
insights they have generated, can be applied to the establishment of differentiated
arrangements in the EU context. One of the key questions is whether and how policy
networks and advocacy coalitions can influence the application of differentiation in
specific policy areas and the participation of countries in these arrangements.

The policy cycle and its influence. The concept of policy cycles (including stages such
as problem definition, agenda-setting, policy formulation, policy implementation
and policy evaluation) is of particular interest because it clearly refers both to
the functional and to the temporal dimensions of politics. It may thus provide a
bridge between this chapter and Chapter 5 in this volume on the temporal dimension by Klaus Goetz. In empirical case studies, the notion of policy cycles could
help explain both in which policy areas and when differentiated integration takes
place. The existence of separate policy cycles in different issue-areas, each with its
own dynamic and timing, could provide an additional framework for investigating and explaining why differentiated arrangements are established at a specific
point in time in some issue-areas, but not in others, and why some countries participate, but not others. Peter de Leon (in Sabatier, 1999) provided an overview of
the stages approach to the policy process. However, the 'stages heuristic' has been
criticized by Sabatier (1999: 6–7) for not being a causal theory, as well as for being
descriptively inaccurate, legalistic and simplistic.

Public goods and differentiated integration theory

Differentiation is an instrument for overcoming deadlock in EU decision-making,
which often results from the unanimity requirement (especially at the treaty level).
It has not only the static effect of letting some Member States establish closer cooperation but also the dynamic effect of drawing initially unwilling countries into the
cooperative arrangements. But why do countries that prefer the previous situation
(*status quo ante*) to joining a new cooperative arrangement end up participating
in some of these arrangements, but not in others? Public goods theory provides
concepts and insights that help answer this question (Kölliker, 2001, 2006b). It can
explain why differentiated integration tends to create centripetal effects on initially
unwilling outsiders in some issue areas, and centrifugal effects in others.

Positive and negative internal and external effects. Cooperative arrangements (whether differentiated or not) exist because they are supposed to generate positive effects for the participant countries. But alongside these 'positive internal effects', cooperative arrangements also generate 'negative internal effects' on the participating countries, such as the financial costs of the arrangements and negative side-effects. However, many effects of cooperative arrangements go beyond the formal boundaries of the arrangement. As a result, non-participating countries may benefit from positive external effects (or 'positive externalities') and suffer from negative external effects (or 'negative externalities'). Different patterns of positive and negative, internal and external effects lead to different incentives for 'initially willing' countries to establish differentiated arrangements, and for 'initially unwilling' countries to participate therein.

Basic concepts of public goods theory. What explains these patterns of positive and negative internal and external effects? And how exactly do these patterns affect the incentives for establishing and participating in differentiated arrangements? If we apply the logic of public goods theory, international collective action in the framework of cooperative arrangements produces specific international collective goods, that is, positive effects that are produced collectively and valued individually by countries. Public goods theory distinguishes two essential properties of goods, namely, the degree to which there is excludability and rivalry in regard to the consumption of the good.[5] If free-riding on specific goods is impossible, those goods are 'excludable' goods. To the extent that non-participant countries can free-ride on goods, they are 'non-excludable'. If additional consumers diminish the utility that other consumers can draw from a given unit of the good, consumption is 'rival'; if utility remains constant, consumption is 'neutral'; and, if utility even increases, consumption is 'complementary'. The distinction between excludable and non-excludable goods, on the one hand, and between goods with rival, neutral and complementary consumption, on the other hand, leads to a typology of six types of goods. Table 3.2 gives an overview of the six types of goods resulting from this two-dimensional classification. For each of the six categories of goods it provides examples drawn from both everyday life and from the context of EU policies (for detailed explanations of the examples see Kölliker 2006b: 56–60). In Chapter 15 of this volume, Kenneth Dyson uses the terminology of public goods theory in discussing the effects of EMU, notably in the section 'The Limited, Non-linear Evolution of Differentiated Integration'.

The impact on differentiated arrangements. The incentives for countries both to establish and to participate in differentiated arrangements are influenced by the character of issues and issue-areas in terms of public goods theory. Other things being equal, the incentives for countries to collectively produce an international good are relatively favourable if a good is excludable and if there is no rivalry in consumption. The strongest incentives can be found if consumption is not just neutral, but complementary (excludable network good). The weakest incentives exist, by contrast, if a good is characterized by both excludability and rivalry in consumption (common pool resource). The six types of goods can be ranked

Table 3.2   Classification of goods in public goods theory

		Excludability	
		High	**Low**
Consumption	Rival	Private goods • Food • Cohesion Funds	Common pool resources • Sea fish • Mobile tax base
	Neutral	Toll goods • Bridge • Free movement of persons	Public goods • Lighthouse • Peace-keeping
	Complementary	Excludable network goods • Computer software • Schengen Information System	Non-excludable network goods • Language • Technical standards

Source: Kölliker, 2006b: 58 (with minor adaptations).

according to the incentives that they give initially unwilling countries to eventually participate (in other words, their 'centripetal effects').

Ranking types of goods according to their centripetal effect. Excludable network goods (characterized by excludability and complementary consumption) develop the strongest centripetal effects.[6] They are followed by toll goods (characterized by excludability and neutral consumption). Private goods (characterized by excludability and rival consumption) follow next, ranking somewhere in the middle. Non-excludable network goods (combining non-excludability and complementary consumption) and public goods (combining non-excludability and neutral consumption) share the same ranking and develop even weaker centripetal effects. However, due to the phenomenon of 'leakage', whereby the benefits of cooperation may 'leak' from the participants to the free-riding non-participants, it is the common pool resources (combining non-excludability and rivalry in consumption) that develop the weakest centripetal (or the strongest centrifugal) effects.[7]

The role of negative externalities. So far, the analysis has focused on the positive effects of cooperation and on excludability and rivalry in regard to the goods produced. In the framework of a rational choice analysis, however, negative externalities must necessarily (that is, as a necessary but not sufficient condition) be present if initially unwilling countries, other things being equal, end up participating voluntarily in a differentiated arrangement. An initially unwilling country prefers the *status quo ante* – without the proposed arrangement – to participating and being affected by the arrangement's positive and negative internal effects. Other things being equal, this preference will not change when the arrangement becomes operational. In the case of non-excludable goods, positive externalities for free-riders even reinforce the incentives to stay outside. What may alter the attitude of initially unwilling non-participants, however, are negative effects. If non-participants are excluded from the positive effects of an arrangement, but not from the negative ones, this provides additional incentives to participate.

But even in the case of non-excludable goods generating positive externalities, negative externalities can give otherwise unwilling countries the necessary additional incentives to participate. For this to be the case, negative effects must be worse for the non-participants than for the participants. In other words, negative external effects must be more significant than negative internal effects.[8]

Conclusions. The incentives for initially willing countries to establish a differentiated arrangement are basically intact in the case of excludable goods, while they are weakened by free-riding in the case of non-excludable goods. Due to the phenomenon of 'leakage', the incentives for establishing differentiated arrangements are particularly weak in the case of common pool resources. Initially unwilling countries are most likely to participate in arrangements producing excludable goods, but participation hinges on the existence of negative externalities generated by those arrangements. Rivalry in consumption may also play a significant role. To the extent that rivalry in consumption is limited, additional participants lower the costs per country that is necessary to generate a specific level of utility for each of the participant countries.[9] In the case of toll goods, participation becomes therefore more attractive as the number of participants increases (as long as there is no congestion). This effect is even stronger in the case of excludable network goods. In the case of private goods, the incentives to participate are independent of the number of participants. If consumption is fully rival, the cost-benefit ratio remains stable when new participants join in.[10]

Implications for the use of differentiated integration

What are the implications of differentiated integration theory for the use of various types of differentiation? A number of observations may help in clarifying the circumstances under which different types of differentiation are used, as well as the reasons and consequences of the application of differentiation.[11]

Differentiation inside/outside EU borders. The theoretical observations presented in the previous section are basically applicable to differentiated arrangements both within and beyond EU borders. In fact, it might be easier to observe the centripetal or centrifugal effects of specific cooperative arrangements on countries outside the EU. Inside EU borders, differentiation remains an instrument of last resort, to be used when other instruments to overcome deadlock, such as issue-linkage, have proved ineffective. By contrast, when non-EU members adopt EU policies, a differentiated participation is the rule rather than the exception.

Differentiation inside/outside EU law. In the case of differentiation within EU law, it is much less likely that the 'ins' can impose negative externalities on the 'outs' than in the case of differentiation outside EU law. Přibáň (in Chapter 2) shows that this is due to the law, processes and organs of the EU.[12] Yet the participation of initially unwilling countries depends on the existence of negative externalities. If differentiated integration outside EU law has been popular among integration-minded EU members, it was probably not least because it allowed them to pursue integration regardless of negative externalities, without the assent of other members, and with the additional advantage that negative externalities might convince initially unwilling countries to eventually participate.

Actual/potential differentiation. The mere potential to use differentiation in a given area may have strong but not easily observable effects. Anticipating negative externalities and centripetal effects, initially unwilling countries may decide to participate in a cooperative arrangement from the very beginning, thereby making the actual application of differentiation superfluous. In such cases, the 'shadow of differentiation' might further integration without creating actual legal fragmentation at any given point in time. The anticipation of effects plays a decisive role in this mechanism, and it is worth noting that uncertainty tends to be much greater when evaluating future effects, rather than present or past ones. An important example of the effects of potential differentiation could be the signing of the Single European Act in 1986 by the UK despite certain misgivings about the treaty. Previously, other members had openly discussed the possibility of moving ahead without the UK.

Differentiation motivated by unwillingness/inability. Differentiated integration theory is limited to differentiation that is motivated by unwillingness rather than inability and focuses on the unwillingness of 'outs' rather than 'ins'. The theoretical conclusions concerning the eventual participation of initially unwilling countries have been presented in the previous section. However, some conclusions can also be drawn about the incentives and hence the willingness of 'ins' to include the 'outs' (see also Kölliker 2006a: 227–8, 230). Due to 'leaking' benefits of cooperation, the 'ins' have the strongest incentives to include the 'outs' when cooperation concerns a common pool resource (a situation that involves regulatory competition; see endnote 7). In the case of private goods, the 'ins' tend to be indifferent about the participation of 'outs', because the average costs per unit of consumption remain stable as the number of participants increases. For the remaining four types of goods, these costs diminish, which leads to certain incentives for allowing 'outs' to participate. These incentives differ for the four types and are less strong than in the case of common pool resources.

Conclusion

Properties relating to the functional dimension of politics (political issues, issue areas, policies) are as important for understanding differentiated integration as they are for understanding integration more generally. Relevant concepts and hypotheses can be found in, or derived from, theories of European integration and international relations, the field of comparative politics, and theories of collective action, such as public goods theory.

Neo-functionalism. Among the theories of European integration, neo-functionalism has the closest links to the functional dimension of politics. Moreover, it makes explicit – though not easily testable – statements on how integration may spread from one issue to another. Neo-functionalism can and should be specified to be applied to differentiated integration, thereby generating not only insights into the functional dimension of differentiated integration but also refinements to neo-functionalist theory itself. While neo-functionalism and rational choice institution-alism have very different roots, the obvious conceptual bridge between (functional) 'spillovers' and (territorial) 'externalities' should be broadened by taking both func-tional and territorial (and possibly also inter-temporal) spillovers/externalities into account in each of the two approaches. This would make neo-functionalism more applicable to the territorial enlargement of differentiated arrangements, and rational choice approaches more applicable to the functional expansion of cooperation into new areas. Inter-temporal spillovers/externalities (the future effects of present coop-eration arrangements, whether within or beyond their functional and territorial boundaries) have a potential to illuminate how cooperation develops over time, the third dimension on which this volume focuses (see Chapter 5 by Goetz).

Other theories of European integration and international relations. Other theories of European integration and international relations have less to say about the func-tional dimension of politics. But a closer look at inter-governmentalism, liberal inter-governmentalism, and the various types of institutionalisms that have been applied in the context of European integration (rational, historical, sociological) might lead to concepts and hypotheses that are relevant to studying differentiated integration from a functional perspective. One example is the somewhat rough, but potentially useful, hypothesis of increased differentiation in 'high politics' areas, and more circumscribed differentiation in 'low politics' areas.

Comparative politics and policy analysis. Concepts from comparative politics – especially from policy analysis, the sub-field focusing on the functional dimen-sion of politics – may equally be useful. An example is the distinction between distributive, redistributive and regulatory policies, which helps understanding why differentiation is not used in certain fields. Where solidarity is the very essence of a policy, as in redistributive policies, differentiation would make the whole policy pointless. Redistributive policies tend therefore to be established within non-differentiated arrangements – or not at all. Opt-out and opt-in preferences by countries may differ in a generalizable fashion for distributive and regulatory policies, as participation entails different categories of costs (direct financial public sector costs versus indirect compliance costs in the private sector).

Public goods and differentiated integration theory. Theories of collective action, in par-ticular the theory of public goods and externalities, have a great potential for help-ing to understand the dynamic of differentiated European integration. The (partial) theory of differentiated integration that has been briefly introduced in this chapter suggests that the centripetal and centrifugal effects of differentiated arrangements on initially unwilling outsiders are closely related to the types of goods and the negative externalities generated. The incentives of the initial participants to first establish and later expand differentiated arrangements are equally related to the types of goods and externalities involved.

Conclusions about 'key political questions'. The introductory chapter to this volume proposed three key questions about differentiated integration. The first concerns the relationship between differentiation and groups of European countries that share certain properties and in some cases sub-regional cooperation arrangements ('state clusters'). The second question is about the relationship between differentiation and integration. The third question relates to the nature of differentiation and its deeper political implications. All three of these questions would need to be clarified and specified to be applied to the functional aspects of differentiated integration. There is not nearly enough room here to do this and appropriately explore potential answers. Instead, I will present a small number of necessarily incomplete and preliminary observations, which are not necessarily limited to the functional aspects.

Relationship with 'clusters' of European countries. How does differentiated integration, as opposed to EU-wide unitary integration, affect sub-regional groups of countries – and how do these sub-groups affect the dynamic of differentiated integration? If participation in differentiated arrangements reflects the patterns of such sub-regional groups, and if differentiation persists for longer periods of time, the perception of included or excluded groups as such might be reinforced. In this context, it would also be interesting to investigate empirically to what extent pre-existing sub-regional cooperation arrangements (Nordic Passport Union, Benelux, Belgium–Luxembourg Economic Union) have influenced the dynamic of differentiated integration by making it harder to include one group member while excluding another. Examples include the participation of Belgium as a founding member of the Euro Area despite difficulties in complying with the Maastricht deficit criteria, and the Schengen participation of Iceland, a non-EU country.

Relationship with integration/disintegration. In almost all cases, differentiation in the EU context has led to further integration (opting for new obligations) rather than disintegration (opting out of already existing obligations). Differentiated arrangements and their underlying doctrine have hence favoured integration, not disintegration. The real question is about the price in terms of legal fragmentation. If a differentiated arrangement develops centripetal effects on initially unwilling outsiders, they tend to ultimately join, thereby ending legal fragmentation. Otherwise, fragmentation within the EU increases with every arrangement that is unable to attract initially unwilling outsiders.

Political implications. The political implications of differentiated integration are potentially far-reaching.[13] However, differentiation is still the exception, an instrument of last resort to overcome deadlock in unanimous EU decision-making. If differentiation was the rule, allowing Member States to opt in and out of new and existing policies at will, the EU would no longer be a European federation in the making. It would be a novel type of polity for which no blueprints exist at the national level, or indeed at any level of governance. It would be faced with unprecedented challenges concerning the increased complexity, and the ensuing lack of transparency, democratic control, legitimacy and solidarity within its polity.

Already the existing differentiated arrangements raise questions in this regard, but to a much more limited extent than a fully differentiated polity.

Notes

1. For an analysis of differentiation as a property as well as a driver of integration see the contribution to this volume by Klaus Goetz (Chapter 5).
2. For an early and convincing example for the classification of differentiated arrangements, see Grabitz (1984).
3. Concerning international cooperation within and outside the EU law in this area, see, for instance: European Security and Defence Assembly/Assembly of WEU, Report on the surveillance of Europe's maritime frontiers, Document A/1986, 3 December 2007 (www.assembly-weu.org/en/documents/sessions_ordinaires/rpt/2007/1986.php#P88_1353). This issue has links to the Schengen Agreement in the functional dimension, and the Mediterranean, the Nordic and the Baltic regions in the spatial dimension; see the respective contributions by Marko Lehti (Chapter 9), Paul Haywood/Lauren McLaren (Chapter 12), Lee Miles (Chapter 13) and Jörg Monar (Chapter 19) in this book.
4. See in this context the contribution by Angelos Sepos on foreign and security policies in Chapter 21 of this volume, which mentions numerous differentiated arrangements in this area.
5. The foundations of the economic theory of public goods have been laid by Samuelson (1954). Cornes and Sandler (1996) have published an authoritative overview of public goods theory.
6. The Schengen Information System is an international collective good that comes very close to being an excludable network good. Non-participating countries can be excluded, while the system grows more useful as more countries participate, feeding information already collected at the national level into the European system – at minor additional costs.
7. Interestingly, it can be shown that regulatory competition must necessarily develop around some kind of common pool resource. There must be a rival and non-excludable resource for which different jurisdictions compete. Differentiated integration is therefore much more difficult in areas involving strong regulatory competition. The clearest and most important example here is the difficult taxation of mobile factors such as capital, which involves intense competition between jurisdictions.
8. One example of negative externalities discussed in the literature on international trade is the phenomenon of trade diversion, which means that the members of a free trade arrangement start to trade more products among themselves rather than with henceforward disadvantaged third countries.
9. The higher the number of cars using a specific toll bridge (the archetypical toll good), the lower are the shared costs for each car. The utility for each car remains stable (up to the point where too many cars lead to congestion).
10. The total cost for the provision of the good and the aggregate utility for all consumers increase in parallel as more countries participate, leaving the costs per participant and per unit of consumption unchanged.
11. One aspect that is neglected here are the (institutional) preferences of different types of countries (for example, 'ins' or 'outs') for the application of various types of differentiation, the circumstances allowing countries to impose these preferences on other countries, and the compromise solutions that might emerge in the case of deadlock.
12. The Amsterdam Treaty, for instance, provided that closer cooperation may not affect the 'interests of those Member States which do not participate therein' (Art. 43.1(f) of the EU Treaty; Amsterdam version). The Nice Treaty later removed the reference to the interests on non-participant Member States. See Kölliker (2006b: 247–8).
13. For a closer investigation of the impact of differentiation on the EU system of governance, see Philippart and Sie Dhian Ho (2000).

4
The Spatial Dimension

Michael Keating

Territorial differentiation

European integration has differentiated effects on the spatial articulation of economic, social and cultural systems and on political institutions. Territories are opened up and boundaries shifted, while new spaces are created, above, below and across states. Territory is unbundled as systems are rescaling at different levels. The result is neither de-territorialization nor a new spatial hierarchy, but a differentiated and asymmetrical order. Yet EU institutions are still largely based on a dual structure of Union and state, with differentiation applied only at the state level.

Space and the social sciences

The social sciences have found it difficult to conceptualize territory or to incorporate it into their schemes of analysis. There has been a prevailing view that somehow territory and function are alternative principles of social and political organization and that, as the one strengthens, the other must weaken. A recurrent modernization paradigm has predicted the eclipse of territory and compression of space in the process of universalism. If a particular place showed distinctive characteristics, whether of political behaviour, economic prosperity or social cohesion, this must be because of the coincidence in space of functional variables that owed nothing to space itself. So territory could always be reduced to something else and could not itself explain anything.

There are in fact two versions of this integration paradigm. One is universalist, predicated on global integration and the dissolution of borders with the 'end of territory' literature (Badie, 1995). The globalization excitement of the 1990s has now been dampened by the resilience of the nation-state. The second one concerns the construction of nation-states as bounded systems, within (but not between) which territorial differentiation disappears. The key dimensions are geo-strategic; economic; cultural; social; and political–institutional. States are first constructed by rulers for the purposes of aggrandizement and defence and internal order imposed. Markets develop within these boundaries to create national economies.

Cultural integration is fostered both by market exchange and by nation-building policies pursued by state elites. Social solidarity emerges from shared identity and as a balance to the inegalitarian effects of the market. Political institutions, parties and systems of representation and accountability follow the same boundaries. So political incorporation, bureaucratic subordination, the extension of the impersonal market and cultural assimilation go together in a mutually reinforcing process (Deutsch, 1966) and create conterminous boundaries for states, economic systems, culture, solidarity and political mobilization.

If globalization theory is regularly refuted by the persistence of states, so state integration theories also need to be modified. Since the 1970s, there has been a wave of work showing how, within nation-states, territorial differentiation persists and how states need to engage in continuous policies for territorial management (Rokkan and Urwin, 1982, 1983; Keating, 1988, 1998). Territory and function are not necessarily competing principles of social organization, but are in constant interaction. Nor can these processes be confined within state boundaries. Stein Rokkan never completed his 'conceptual map of Europe' but, showing how territory interacts with function on a European scale, he opened up new ways of thinking not only about the European past but also about the emerging European order.

Theories of European integration owe much to these two models of development. For some, Europe is a form of universalism (or 'globalization') superseding the nation-state in recognition of its deficiencies and historical record and dissolving territorial particularisms. For others, European integration is a new form of polity-building, the creation of a new territorial order with new boundaries. The Cold War shifted geo-politics to a new level, pitting the Euro-Atlantic alliance against the Soviet Union but suppressing conflict within it. Functionalism and neo-functionalism postulate an interdependence of the strategic, economic, political and (sometimes) cultural dimensions of polity-building and the effective elimination of spatial particularities, to create a new and higher polity. Yet, as in the nation-state, integration does not always suppress territorial distinctiveness, but can generate new forms of territorial politics, giving rise to new strategies of territorial management.

Both Europe-as-globalization and Europe-as-polity-building thus create new spatial cleavages. It would be a serious analytical error to view these new forms of territorial differentiation as necessarily based on state boundaries, so that spatial differentiation becomes merely inter-state differentiation or at best differentiation among groups or families of states. Nor is it the case, as Přibáň seems to suggest (in Chapter 2), that internal devolution does not affect the relationship of states with the EU. Rather, integration is transforming the link between function and space by creating new spaces at the supranational level (above the state); the sub-state level; and the trans-national level (across states). Yet while there are strong functional drivers for territorial differentiation across European space, the institutional design of the EU does not give much scope for its expression. On the contrary, it stresses uniformity of policies and regulation and has failed to develop effective mechanisms for the expression of territorial pluralism.

The new territorial politics

Developments in social science since the 1980s have restored territory to a central place in analysis and questioned the assumptions of universalizing theory (Brenner et al., 2003; Keating, 1988, 1998; Paasi, 2002; Pike, 2007). Space is seen not just as a topographical delineation, but as a container for social, economic and political processes. Spatial differentiation may represent no more than the uneven distribution of functional or socio-economic variables. It may also, however, represent the interaction of those variables to produce more than the sum of the whole. Territorial distinctiveness is not to be seen as a remnant of the past as in traditional approaches (and still largely in Rokkan). Rather, territory is invented and reinvented under the impact of social, economic and political change. We are seeing not a de-territorialization of economy, society and polity, but rather a re-territorialization, at new spatial levels, above, below and across states, a differentiation of spatial scales for different functional systems, and a series of efforts to re-integrate them through politics.

European integration, in its institutional dimension, represents both boundary-removal in Europe and boundary-imposition at the borders of Europe. In the functional dimension, matters are more complicated, since the European project encourages the emergence and re-emergence of identities and functional systems at multiple levels. Unlike in the old nation-state, these are not coterminous. This disaggregates state systems of policy-making and provides possibilities for partial exit for functional interests that are able to operate at other spatial levels (Bartolini, 2005). European integration thus provokes new forms of territorial differentiation. Where this corresponds to state boundaries and institutions, it has produced opt-outs, re-nationalization, or intergovernmentalization of policy-making, as charted in other chapters. Other differences, however, arise at the sub-state or trans-national levels. These in turn could be regulated by a greater uniformity across Europe, a Europeanization of policy fields and a more *communautaire* mode of policy-making. Alternatively, Europe itself could develop in a differentiated way, recognizing territorial diversity. All of these patterns can, in practice, be observed.

The elements for understanding the new territorial politics are the same as in the classic model of state and nation-building: geo-strategic, economic, cultural, social and political–institutional. These may coincide to create new spaces, or be differentiated, giving rise to a complexity that calls for a differentiated response.

Geo-strategic differentiation: the marches of Europe

Within western Europe since the Second World War and now more recently across the enlarged European Union, there has been no major international security question, and geo-strategic questions have lost their salience. This does not mean that state borders have disappeared but that, having lost their original rationale, they have been transformed, serving other functions and increasingly penetrated.

Enlargement of the EU and the end of the Cold War have posed the geo-political question of the territorial limits to the European project and where and how it ends. Within the EU there has been a zone of stability that has allowed a degree of institutional experimentation and differentiation and some discursive ambivalence that has permitted otherwise conflicting sovereignty claims to co-exist in practice. At the border, however, are zones of instability, in the Balkans, the Caucasus, eastern Europe, the Middle East and North Africa as well as the difficult question of Turkey. The model of stabilization pursued thus far has relied heavily on the promise of incorporation into the European project and conditionality as a guarantor of good behaviour. Membership can be achieved by meeting the accession criteria laid down by the EU and NATO, and adopting the *acquis*. As Geoffrey Edwards (2008) shows, the alternative mechanism, through the European Neighbourhood Policy, is seen as second-best.

This model is already showing its limits in the Balkans. The only real incentive to cooperate in Bosnia, Serbia and Kosovo is the promise of EU membership, but if this is postponed too long these countries risk turning away, with the threat of destabilization. Beyond the Balkans, the question is posed of just how far can Europe expand. At present there is a hard border, with incorporating member-ship on this side and exclusion on the other. Yet Europe, like other expanding dominions, will always have its marches, or borderlands. It may be then that neighbouring territories will be included for some purposes and excluded for oth-ers. Already, there is some differentiation in security, with the Organization for Security and Co-operation in Europe operating at the widest level, while NATO groups a smaller number of Euro-Asian countries together with the United States and Canada. The EU's own foreign and defence effort forms a more integrated body of activity. Neighbouring states are brought into the single market, even adopting large parts of the *acquis* in order to gain trading concessions, without full membership. The political and institutional aspects of European integration, including control over the policy process, are reserved for the full members.

Economic differentiation

The original vision for European union assumed that spatial economic dispari-ties would diminish with the single market and mobility of labour and capital. Later it was recognized that integration could itself exacerbate disparities, as better-endowed regions could attract more investment and build up cumulative advantages. This underlay a centre–periphery vision, in which wealth would be concentrated in the 'golden triangle', formed by the Ruhr, south-east England and the Paris region, a metaphor later replaced by the 'blue banana'. Since the 1990s, it has been recognized that matters are more complicated and favoured meta-phors have included the mosaic, in which islands of prosperity and deprivation are scattered across Europe and in which deprivation can be found even within wealthy metropoles like Greater London.

Economic development can no longer be understood within the context of the nation-state. It responds to global imperatives and is regulated at both global and

European levels. At the same time, it increasingly responds to local factors, including the institutions and social networks of local societies (Cooke and Morgan, 1998; Scott, 1998; Storper, 1997). Some authors write of localities not as places but as systems of production with their own internal logic (Crouch et al., 2001). Some versions of this new economic sociology stay close to the neo-classical paradigm, seeing spatial proximity merely as a means of increasing knowledge, stimulating innovation and reducing uncertainty and transaction costs. This explains the paradox that the sectors that rely most on high technology and communication, such as financial services and information technology, show some of the highest tendencies to spatial concentration. Other observers draw more attention to local and regional norms and culture in the building of systems of collective action (Keating et al., 2003). From the constitution of localities and regions as systems of production it is a short step towards presenting them as being in competition for investment, technology, innovation and markets. This has given rise to a panoply of policies based on regional competitiveness and, at the local level, a certain neo-mercantilism as though the gains of one region must be at the expense of others. Traditional regional policies based on integration of regions as complementary elements in national economies (spatial Keynesianism) has given way to the promotion of regional competitiveness in European and global markets.

This has led to a differentiation of economic development policies but, as Dyson notes, the Single Market is undifferentiated. Competition policies now penetrate down to the local level, limiting the discretion of regional governments in taxation, industrial policy and, in some ways, welfare spending. Indeed the Commission has been in many ways less tolerant of intra-state than of inter-state differentiation in state aids and tax competition. On the other hand, there are odd occasions when European integration exists in the absence of state uniformity, such as the provision whereby English students pay fees at Scottish universities but, under EU law, those from other Member States pay the same as Scottish students, which currently means they pay nothing.

While one element of spatial development policy focuses on territorial competition (see also Greskovits, Chapter 10 this volume) which implies disparities and difference, another element is concerned with management and cohesion. National anti-disparity policies are tightly constrained in the name of competition policy. On the other hand, since the mid-1970s the European Commission has sought to redress this by an active regional policy, taking over from Member States the responsibility for spatial regulation. This is expressed in the commitment in the Lisbon Treaty to the new principle of territorial cohesion alongside economic and social cohesion. As a concomitant, it has sought dialogue with regional governments and interests and promoted partnership among levels of government and between public and private sectors. It was not doing this in order to undermine the nation-state or to create a new political order, but rather as an inherent element of development policy as it has been elaborated since the 1950s.

It has succeeded only in part as control of regional policy through regional and later structural funds has been contested among the Commission, Member States and regions. Until the reforms of 1988, states ensured that regional funds were little more than an intergovernmental compensation mechanism (Hooghe and Keating, 1994). In order to keep all states on board, everybody had to get something, even the richest members. Gradually, the Commission succeeded in getting common criteria for eligibility and a single European map of assisted areas, but Member States shared responsibility for designing this and controlled much of the implementation. Over time the Commission also succeeded in targeting resources better on the poorer regions but could never promote the idea of focusing all the moneys on the deprived, since this would undermine the idea of a common European spatial policy operating continent-wide, as well as weakening support for it in the contributing countries. Enlargement was a critical challenge since there was an obvious policy case (supported by Britain and in part by Germany) for concentrating all the money on the new Member States and re-nationalizing policy in the EU15. This, however, would have represented too much differentiation and a deepening of the Old Europe–New Europe cleavage, so about half of the money now goes to the new Member States and the rest, in the form of new policy instruments, to the older ones. Formal asymmetry has thus been avoided.

National/cultural differentiation

The concept of the nation-state is deeply problematic. For some scholars, the term means no more than the sovereign state, as a subject of international order, although in this case the prefix 'nation' does not seem to add anything. For others it implies that states are or should be nations, of integrated political communities with a single focus of loyalty. While this is true of some parts of Europe, it is certainly not of others.

In one way, European integration may exacerbate the nationalities question, that is, the problem of reconciling states with national claims. There is a spatial rescaling of concerns about culture and identity, with the revival of local particularisms as the European project challenges the monopoly of the state in the definition of political identities and provides new opportunity structures and a new discursive space for representing the nation (Keating, 2004). By providing security and guaranteeing market access, it lowers the threshold and costs for secession. On the other hand, it may moderate nationalist claims, by positing new forms of self-determination short of statehood (McGarry and Keating, 2006). Europe transforms the meaning of sovereignty and detaches it from an exclusive connection with the state. The idea of shared sovereignty, reaching from the European down to the sub-state level, permits a recognition of self-determination claims that fall short of secession (Keating, 2001). Rights have been delinked from citizenship and taken to the European level (through the Council of Europe's European Charter of Human Rights and Fundamental Freedoms), allowing more asymmetry within states. Nationalist movements have responded widely to this by playing down aspirations to statehood and supporting European integration (Keating, 2004). Yet they have done so in different ways, creating further differentiation across the continent.

In the multi-national states of western Europe, there has been a tendency for nationality movements to territorialize their claims and to merge with the themes of the new regionalism in order to explore possibilities for forging an economic, political and social project in the new European space. States have responded to both sorts of pressure, to varying degrees, with political devolution. So Spain has conceded self-government to the historic nationalities while extending similar possibilities for devolution to the other regions. Belgium has conceded self-government for Flanders, where language issues were predominant, and in Wallonia, where the main grievance is economic, and completed it with autonomy for the Brussels region. In the United Kingdom, there are different arrangements for Scotland, Wales and Northern Ireland, while England still comes directly under the central state. As Gamble notes in Chapter 7, political movements in the four parts of the UK and in Ireland are adapting differently to the challenge of Europe, leading to a loosening of the formal British union and the functional ties with Ireland.

In central and eastern Europe the problematic is more often framed as that of national minorities or minority rights. These are not always territorially concentrated and have not been mobilized around new regionalist themes to the extent that is the case in western Europe. New Member States are reluctant to concede regional devolution and strong fear of separatism and irredentism. European institutions such as the European Union, the Council of Europe and the Organization for Security and Co-operation in Europe have been reluctant to intervene within states to impose specific forms of government. There is an emerging European regime for minority rights, carried and developed by these organizations rather than codified in law. It includes the Council of Europe's Framework Convention on the Protection of National Minorities and requirements in the EU's Copenhagen Criteria for accession that minorities be protected. This, however, has not been incorporated into the *acquis*, in order to avoid its application in the older Member States. The implication is that there will be minority protection provisions in central and eastern Europe but not in the established states in the west, producing a new form of differentiation.

Differentiating welfare

The welfare state rests upon three premises. The first is national identity, which underpins solidarity and social citizenship (Marshall, 1992; McEwen and Moreno, 2005). The second is the existence of strong boundaries, enclosing polities, economies, cultural identities and institutions of representation, so forcing capital and labour to cooperate and turning politics inwards. The third is risk-pooling over wide areas. All three are challenged by trans-national integration. National identity cannot be located uniquely at the state level. Market regulation is migrating to the European level, while market-making in the form of economic development is increasingly local, while the state remains responsible for welfare. This encourages 'partial exit' (Bartolini, 2005) of actors and venue-shopping for the scale at which they will get best treatment. In particular, capital no longer needs to commit itself to a territory or engage in social compromise. Risk-pooling at the state level appeared rational when the future balance of risks was unknown, and territorial redistribution within national markets was rational when the wealthy regions knew that the money would come back in the form of orders for their goods. In the trans-national market, there are long-term disparities as some regions are more competitive, and political and business leaders there complain that redistribution hampers their competitiveness within the wider market. This may provoke two reactions. One is the 'revolt of the rich' as wealthy regions de-solidarize with their poorer compatriots, as we have seen in Italy, Spain, Belgium and Germany. The other is the 'race to the bottom' as poorer states and regions cut taxes and social overheads in order to attract footloose investors. The response has not been to take the welfare state role up to the European level, as Europe lacks the sense of solidarity or fiscal capacity for this. Some gestures are made to the European social model and the structural funds provide some form of redistribution, albeit on a territorial rather than an inter-personal basis. Welfare states remain, however, nationally and increasingly regionally differentiated as regional and local governments experiment with new forms of social intervention underpinned by their own resources and territorial solidarities (Ferrera, 2006; Keating, 2007).

The Single Market has impinged on public services in many ways, restricting the rights of national governments to subsidize services or privilege state monopolies. It has opened various rights to non-citizens. In practice this has created a complex tangle of welfare and service entitlements which challenge the old singular conception of social citizenship. Occasionally European law may create more uniformity at the European level than exists within the state, as in the position of university fees in Scotland, payable by English students but not by other Europeans.

Political–institutional differentiation and the Europe of the regions

On the political–institutional dimension, we are seeing the emergence of institutions at new spatial levels, above and below the state. The most striking is the rise of the 'meso' or regional level (Sharpe, 1993). All the large European states and some of the smaller ones now have such a level of government in order to capture and regulate the functional systems that exist or at least can be managed at this level, as well as to recognize the politicization of cultural and identity differentiation.

There is a link between the infra-national and supra-national levels of restructuring. Some responsibilities devolved under state provisions to regions and localities are also Europeanized. Yet in principle, it is Member States that are represented in the main decision-making instances of the EU, notably the Council of Ministers. Local and regional governments implement European laws and directives but national governments are responsible for the fulfilment. This all leads to the re-entry of central governments into devolved responsibility and potentially to a recentralization at state level. Regional and local governments also articulate distinct social and economic demands in European matters, differentiating their interests from the rest of the state. Competition policies since the 1980s, seeking a single European market, have trespassed on local and regional prerogatives, re-imposing centralization in the face of state decentralization. This poses the question of the representation of territorial governments and interests in the European institutional structure.

In the early days of the European project, there was more opposition at the periphery, a tendency still visible in the Nordic countries, where the remoter regions depend on state transfer mechanisms. Elsewhere, however, peripheral regions have abandoned Euro-scepticism to seek opportunities in the Single Market and embrace supra-nationalism as a means of escaping the domination of local hegemons – Ireland and Scotland are examples.

At one time there was much talk of a Europe of the Regions or three-tiered federalism. This proved impossible because of resistance from states to but also because of the heterogeneity of territorial institutions and interests. Spatial levels range from the very local to the large regions. The status and powers of sub-state governments differ enormously, from constituent units of federal system to weak municipalities. The political significance of territories differs, from stateless nations to mere administrative divisions. So again there is a tension between the pressures for a uniform European system of representation and regulation and a very diverse reality.

Regions have gained some concessions on representation in Europe, notably in the Maastricht Treaty on European Union. A Committee of the Regions (CoR) was set up with consultative powers. Yet the CoR experiences great difficulty in finding common ground among its constituent members. The large and powerful regions have consistently sought a differentiated status in recognition of their constitutional importance and the fact that, in many matters (such as the transposition of directive), they play a role closer to that of Member States than of municipal governments. The latter refuse to concede the distinction, especially in those states where no regional level exists. A group of Regions with Legislative Powers (RegLeg) was set up around the Convention on the Future of Europe but made little impact in view of the hostility both of municipalities and of Member States.

Another concession allows regions to participate in the Council of Ministers where regional government has a ministerial structure and national law allows it. So far this possibility has been used by Germany, Austria, Belgium, Spain, the United Kingdom and Italy but in very different ways. Only in Germany and Belgium do regions have a right to participate, as opposed to being invited by the state. In Germany the Länder must agree on a common position and designate one of their number to participate, using the voting mechanisms of the Bundesrat. This ensures that it is the Länder as a whole and not individual Länder that have the influence. In Belgium the system gives more weight to individual regions and language communities, since the agreement of all affected governments is required. Yet if this is lacking, the only option is that Belgium should abstain in the Council. Participation in the Council of Ministers is, then, a mechanism for ensuring that regional interests are heard at European level but it is still the Member States who are represented, so this provides no real way in which individual regions can differentiate themselves.

In preparation for the enlargement of 2004, the Commission appeared to be promoting the idea of regional government, loosely drawing on western European examples. This was part of state modernization and embodied in the structural funds and modern regional policy, with its emphasis on local initiative and decentralization. Around 2000, however, it underwent a U-turn and insisted that structural funds should be centralized and concentrated on hard infrastructure (Hughes et al., 2003, 2004; Keating, 2003). One reason was the need to spend all the funds rapidly in the two years remaining of the current funding programme. Another was distrust of the underdeveloped and possibly corrupt and clientelistic structures of power at local and regional level. The result was a reinforcement of centralized states in central and eastern Europe while western Europe continued to decentralize, a measure of differentiation that is likely to be of continued importance.

Trans-national spaces

European integration is also helping the creation or re-emergence of spaces previously divided by state borders. It is striking how the 'blue banana' invented by French economists recalls the commercial routes and arc of prosperity of the early modern period, as well as Rokkan's 'shatter belt' of cultural communities surviving between the French and German nation-building projects, site of the failed Lotharingian or Burgundian state-building project. Across the former Habsburg domains there has been an effort to reinstate transport and trading routes broken by the emergence of nation-states after the First World War and the Cold War after 1945.

EU regional policy has placed a lot of emphasis on cross-border cooperation. The idea is rooted in comparative advantage theory, promoting the best use of resources in a complementary fashion within a territorial space. There is also a neo-functionalist logic, that increasing transactions will lessen antagonism and promote integration. In some cases, the idea is to bring together national minorities divided by borders in new forms of cooperation, so as to lessen secessionist or irredentist movements such as in Northern Ireland, the Tirol and the Basque Country. One precondition is, ironically, the mutual acceptance of the state border so that functional partnership will not be seen as a precursor for political integration. The Hungarian status law of 2001, extending some citizenship rights to ethnic Hungarian citizens of neighbouring countries, by contrast, aroused strong opposition because of the political context (Kemp, 2006). The opening of frontiers has very complex effects, resulting in the transformation of some boundaries and the reinforcement of others. The creation of a single Basque space spanning France and Spain runs up against the fact that Basqueness itself has been constructed differently in different parts of a region that is itself almost impossible to define (Keating and Bray, 2010). Practical obstacles are still legion, including national controls, differences in the powers of local and regional governments, inter-territorial competition for investment and the fact that politicians are still answerable to domestic constituencies.

Another form of trans-national space is the supra-national European region. At the very beginning of the integration process, the Benelux countries sought unity in a trans-national space with common economic interests, some cultural and linguistic affinities (and linguistic boundaries that crossed rather than encompassed states) and a common past. The concept of the Nordic countries, however, has perhaps been more hindered than helped by Europe, since Norway remains outside the Union and other functions that could be furthered by regional coop-eration are taken now to the European (EU or EEA) level. The Northern Ireland peace process owes little directly to the EU but it has provided a context in which questions of sovereignty can be put in abeyance and co-operation promoted (McGarry, 2006). Out of this has arisen the notion of 'the islands'[1], institution-alized in the British Irish Council (colloquially the Council of the Isles). The concept of Central Europe or *Mitteleuropa* has been pressed into service again, but comprises so many meanings, political and geographic, as to be completely overloaded; Greskovits in Chapter 10 shows how it has been instrumentalized. Yet these imaginative spaces, especially where they have some historical reso-nance, are used by politicians to sustain visions of Europe going beyond both the symmetrical vision of Europe and the intergovernmental one.

How much differentiation?

There have thus been important spatial restructurings in Europe. Some of these are the product of global changes representing the erosion of boundaries and forms of universalism. Others are the product of European integration, which is both a move towards universalism, and a new territorial polity. Yet this new polity is not a territorially uniform one, nor even one hierarchically organized such that territories are nested neatly within each other. Geo-strategic change has transformed borders within Europe, allowing more differentiation but has posed new questions about the borders of Europe itself. Economic change has created complex new forms, no longer corresponding to state borders and greater territo-rial differentiation. Cultures and identities are being made and remade in the new conditions, at various levels. Welfare and social policies are being reshaped more slowly, and may be delinking from the system of economic regulation and from affective communities of identity. Political institutions are adapting in varied ways, with a tendency for the emergence of new, intermediate or 'meso' levels of government, but in a very diverse way between and even within states. These new governments are positioning themselves within the new European economic and social spaces, both as economic competitors and as policy influencers within the European policy process.

Yet there is no new spatial hierarchy to replace the old vision of states. Geo-strategic, economic, cultural, social, political and institutional spaces do not necessarily coincide with each other. New spaces are being carved out at differ-ent levels. There is the state level, the sub-state level, the supra-national level represented by the European Union, and the trans-national level represented by cross-border and inter-regional governmental or functional cooperation. Yet it has proved rather difficult for the EU to accept territorial differentiation, if we mean by this more than national opt-out from sectoral policies. Economic policies have been formulated within a pan-European perspective and even the regional policy has to be framed so as to apply across the territory and not just to parts of it. Yet economic development itself is increasingly local and regional. Welfare states remain national, although there is some territorial differentiation encouraged by the opening of markets and trans-national packages of entitlements linking European, state and regional levels. The Europe of the Regions movement, aimed at recognition of territorial and institutional diversity, has been frustrated by an insistence that no regions can gain a special status, an insistence that has held back both regions and municipalities from finding a space in the institutions. National minorities policies have de facto been differentiated in western and east-central Europe but formally there is no such distinction recognized in the treaties or in law. Finally, at the borders the EU has given the choice of integration within the *acquis* or exclusion, depriving itself of other instruments to manage its border-lands and neighbouring territories.

There are a number of perspectives on the effects of this spatial rescaling and ways of reconceptualizing it. Some scholars emphasize the disaggregation of functional systems, particularly the separation of market-making and regulation from market-correction, so undermining the old welfare state bargain and the failure to bring these together at the European level (see, for example, Bartolini, 2005). The literature on the 'new regionalism' (Keating, 1998) draws attention to the constitution of new scales of action and the possibilities for reintegrating economic promotion, social cohesion and culture, albeit in more loosely bounded systems. Some of this literature in the 1990s was exuberantly optimistic, seeing in the regional level a new way of reconciling economic competitive and social inclusion. Accounts now are more balanced, drawing attention to the different experiences of different regions. In some cases, such as Scotland or Catalonia, there is a coincidence of the functional, cultural, historical and institutional meanings of space, allowing new systems of collective action and social compromise to emerge, linked both to state and European levels. Flanders represents a case in which strong cultural and institutional elements have been used to create a region out of historically very disparate territories. In these cases, we are seeing a re-politicization of regions and strong form of polity-building. If 'governance' is seen as a system of pluralist order in the absence of traditional political government, then we see here a move from governance to government. In other cases, the territory is contested, as in Northern Ireland or the Basque Country. There is thus strong political differentiation as well as the potential for economic and public service differentiation as some regions gain from their superior levels of organization and institutionalization, while others are marginalized (Keating et al., 2003).

Further widening and deepening of the EU can only reinforce these tendencies. Southern and eastern enlargement has widened economic disparities and, as it is unlikely that transfers to the east will be a large as those to the south in the 1990s, eastern regions will be reliant more on their own resources. Those closer to the west are already doing better (as are national capitals) while those further east are peripheralized in all senses. Enlargement brings in more difficult nationality questions (notably in the Balkans) while nationalists in Scotland, Flanders or Catalonia ask why very small southern and eastern states should be recognized as full members while they have to make do with regional status. Deepening of the European project will increase the number of policy fields in which European and regional competences overlap, provoking demands for a more effective territorial input into the EU and a recognition of territorial diversity. It will also reduce the relevance of the state level for places with nationalist movements, potentially increasing secessionist demands. For individual nations like Scotland, this might make for a peaceful resumption of statehood within a broader union, but the dynamic effects could be highly destabilizing as other nationality movements seek to imitate them. At the other extreme are places like Kosovo, recognized by most EU members as a sovereign state but in practice an international protectorate with no prospects of viability on its own.

Differentiated Europe

Some observers continue to regard Europe primarily as an inter-governmental organization, to be understood using the concepts and theories of international relations. Others see it as a form of globalization and universalism. Others again view it as a new form of polity, meaning usually a type of state, albeit federal or composite rather than unitary. What all these visions have in common is a model of territorial integration largely derived from modernization and diffusion theory. Inter-governmentalists insist on the continuing importance of state boundaries enclosing political, economic and cultural spaces, with primacy granted to the institutions of the state and other territories contained within it. Globalists tend to suppress territory. European federalists see the EU as a territorially layered system with a hierarchy of tiers, each nested in the one above. A centre–periphery perspective, drawing on the work of Rokkan, would see an integrated core surrounded by less tightly connected peripheries. None does justice to the complexity of spatial rescaling and the new connections between space, function, identity and representation. More recently, scholars have introduced the analogy of empire (Colomer, 2006; Zielonka, 2006). This gives us better leverage on the issue of differentiation than analogies with states of whatever sort. Stripped of the colonial connotations that it acquired during the 19th century, an empire is a form of polity in which the various parts have different relationships with the centre. This is the historic European conception of empire. There is the possibility of cultural pluralism, but also of common citizenship, a single market and some common institutions. The borders of historic empires were not typically sealed, but rather porous, with imperial authority gradually fading out rather than coming to an abrupt halt. Empires did not historically adapt well to the challenges of democratization and their legacy is difficult to rehabilitate in eastern and central Europe; and it would be an anachronism to go back to pre-modern forms of political regulation. Yet the underlying principles of diversity and differentiation might provide a guide to the emerging differentiated Europe.

Note

1.   The old expression British Isles has been abandoned in the face of Irish objections but the Irish version, 'these islands', hardly helps to locate them in European space.

5
The Temporal Dimension

Klaus H. Goetz

Why time matters

Debate surrounding the phenomenon of differentiated integration is replete with time-centred images and metaphors. In Stubb's (1996) categorization, time is one of the three main variables of differentiated integration, the other being 'space' and 'matter'; more recent contributions employ similar distinctions (Andersen and Sitter, 2006; De Neve, 2006). Discussions of temporal differentiation include frequent references to multi-speed Europe, vanguards and laggards, and major examples of differentiation include transition periods, temporary derogations, phasing-in and phasing-out arrangements or differential timing in the full adoption of the euro (Stubb, 1996; see also Dyson, 2009a).

If we try to think systematically about the nature of the linkages between time and differentiated integration, at least two facets deserve exploration: the temporal properties of differentiated integration; and the analytical status of time in explanatory accounts of differentiated integration.

Time as a property of differentiated integration

The first basic question here is: What do we know about differentiation *by means of time*? Sequencing – notably the order in which Member States assume policy commitments and integrate into EU-wide institutional arrangements – is of central importance here. Who advances first, which Member States are the followers (or laggards)? Other temporal categories to consider include timing and speed. For example, are there consistent differences amongst the Member States when it comes to the timing of the transposition of EU directives? Do some Member States implement judgements of the European Court of Justice consistently more speedily than others?

The second basic question, which, unlike the first, has rarely been asked, is: What do we know about temporal, spatial and functional differentiation *in time*? For example, *when* have flexible arrangements been introduced and terminated? Are there distinct *sequences* that can be identified, for example, between formal treaty reforms and a prior or subsequent spread of differentiated arrangements? What can we say about the *speed* with which such arrangements have tended to be introduced or abolished? Answers to the latter question help us to judge whether differentiation is a short-term expediency or part of longer-term political strategies. And what can we say about the *duration* of differentiated arrangements? Are they a transitional phenomenon? Or do we need to agree with Přibáň (Chapter 2 in this volume), who argues that 'the indefinite design and persistence of some clauses, such as the Irish and UK opt-outs from the Schengen Zone or the UK opt-outs from the Union's protection of social rights, have gradually weakened the original idea of flexibility as a transitional measure and made it an intrinsic feature of European legal integration'?

Time as part of an explanation of differentiated integration

When it comes to exploring how time may promote, facilitate or impede differentiated integration, two main questions will be explored. First, what is the explanatory status of time in integration theories and accounts of 'clustered Europeanization' (Goetz, 2006, 2007)? Second, how do the 'EU timescape' (Goetz, 2009; Goetz and Meyer-Sahling, 2009) and the opportunities for the tactical and strategic use of time that the EU political system affords matter for differentiated integration?

The remainder of this chapter explores the questions and arguments just outlined in more depth. The basic point it makes is twofold: that 'taking time seriously' helps us to understand the possibilities of, and limitations to, temporal differentiation as a political strategy; and that time is critical in shaping differentiation, be it spatial (Keating, Chapter 4 in this volume), functional (Kölliker, Chapter 3 in this volume) or temporal. The chapter certainly raises more questions than it answers. But it contends that the questions about time are worth asking and that paying greater attention to the temporality of European integration promises considerable advances in our understanding of the dynamics of the European project.

How time matters

Most political scientists would readily agree that the manner in which time is arranged in a political system – for example, the length of electoral mandates or the rules that govern the timing of elections – is vital to understanding how democracies work. Yet, the link between time and politics is rarely systematically explored. In their 'invitation' from the late 1990s to concentrate research on political time, Schedler and Santiso (1998) suggest two broad perspectives: time as a horizon and time as a resource. The first is concerned with the time horizons within which political systems operate, 'their past, their present, their future' (1998: 6). The latter perspective revolves around the implications of the scarcity of time in democratic politics: time as a valuable resource (and constraint). Under this rubric, students of politics have studied time rules, which 'define the temporal structures or the timetables of democratic politics, its time budgets, its points of initiation and termination, its pace, its sequences, and its cycles' (1998: 8); time strategies of how to manage temporal constraints; time discourses about the 'rights' and 'wrongs' of temporal decisions (1998: 12f); and 'time traces', that is, the manner in which the *'passage of time* leaves its own imprint on certain structures and processes'

(1998: 13, emphasis in the original). More recently, with explicit reference to political time in the EU, Goetz and Meyer-Sahling (2009) have distinguished between a polity dimension of political time: the length of mandates, time budgets and time horizons; a politics dimension, which is concerned with rules relating to timing, sequencing, speed and duration in political decision-making; and a policy dimension, which concerns temporal policy features such as the intertemporal distribution of costs and benefits in major EU policies.

In the present context, three of these takes on time merit brief elaboration. In each case, we can distinguish further between temporal properties – time as part of the 'dependent variable' – and time as an explanation – that is, time as part of the 'independent variable'. First, there is the *passage of time*. It is arguably the most fundamental way in which time matters. Where time is treated as a 'dependent variable', this perspective is especially concerned with identifying phases, stages, eras, epochs or cycles of political development. The analytical impetus is to try to bring order to the seemingly incessant flow of time by 'parcelling up' historical time, as when, for example, analysts seek to distinguish between 'peaks' and 'troughs' (Ginsburg, 2007) in European integration or distinctive 'phases' in policy development (for example, see Wurzel and Zito, Chapter 18 in this volume). Where time is treated as independent variable, analysts are essentially concerned about the 'weight of history', that is, the impact of the past upon the present and the future. Such arguments come in many guises, as, for example, in historical–institutionalist analyses, with their emphasis on long-term processes and associated 'slow-moving causal processes', such as cumulative causes, threshold effects, causal chains, cumulative outcomes, structural effects or path dependencies and feedback loops (Pierson, 2004: 79ff); constructivist accounts that emphasise the importance of 'time-consuming' processes underlying political change, such as learning, socialization or routinization; or rationalist explanations of decision-taking that highlight the importance of reiteration. Closely associated with such an agenda is the search for specific historical moments – temporal locations in time–that possess explanatory power, such as 'critical junctures' or, say, specific Intergovernmental Conferences.

Second, *the time budgets and time horizons* of actors matter. As a dependent variable, the inherent limitation to time budgets and time horizons is fundamental to democratic politics. Democratic politics is, by definition, about power *pro tempore* (Linz, 1998). Hence, it is seen to matter for the distribution of power whether the presidency of the European Council rotates every six months or whether a president is elected for a period of 30 months (as introduced by the Lisbon Treaty). But time budgets and time horizons are also frequently employed in explanatory accounts of political developments, whether it is in work on political business cycles, which has noted the link between electoral rules, resultant time budgets and time horizons of political decision-makers, on the one hand, and the 'opportunistic' timing of economic policy tools, on the other (for a review of much of this work see Drazen, 2001); research on time pressures and their impact on political negotiations (Conceição-Heldt, 2009); or in historical–institutionalist accounts of integration which emphasize the explanatory power of actors' differential time horizons (Pierson 1996, 2004; see also below).

Third, *time rules* matter as they influence timing – when something happens; sequence – in what order things happen; speed – how fast things happen; and duration – for how long things happen. They provide both important points of reference in describing political phenomena and, in particular, in explanations of politics. As regards the latter, political time is often understood as a resource (and a constraint) in decision-making. What is critical in this respect is the malleability and manipulability of time. For example, the careful timing of initiatives, delay or acceleration can be used in the pursuit of substantive objectives. From this perspective, time is fundamentally about the discretion to make temporal choices in order to gain an advantage in political processes. Clearly, such an instrumental view of time is closely connected to an interest in (temporal) differentiation as a political strategy.

Temporal properties of differentiated integration

After this brief survey of why time matters and how it matters, let us now turn to the temporal properties of differentiated integration. As regards differentiation *by means of time*, the policy dimension is the one most frequently discussed. Its practical importance has lately been underlined in the context of the EU enlargements of 2005 and 2007. As part of the enlargement negotiations, a host of temporary derogations of varying lengths were agreed, which covered chapters such as the free movement of goods, the freedom of movement of persons, the freedom of movement of services, and agriculture. There were also provisions regarding the phasing in of policy measures, notably as regards the phasing in of EU agricultural direct payments between 2004 and 2013; and transitional arrangements such as the 'transition facility', that is, post-accession financial assistance to the new Member States that could not benefit from the Structural Funds for the period of 2004–6.

Policy differentiation through temporary derogations, the adoption of transitional measures, and phasing-in arrangements that apply unequally to different Member States is at the heart of temporal differentiation, but the latter can also be observed at the level of decision-making procedures and institutions. Decision-making for dossiers relating to EMU and the euro constitute a major example. Thus, Member States whose currency is the euro meet in the informal, but highly influential, body of the Eurogroup to deal with issues relating to EMU (Puetter, 2006). The countries that have not secured a permanent opt-out (unlike Denmark and the UK) are, in principle, only temporarily excluded from this club. When the Ecofin Council, in which, of course, all Member States are represented, deals with EMU and euro dossiers, the temporary non-members and the permanent opt-outs do not take part in the vote. Temporally differentiated policy is thus associated with differentiation in procedures and institutions (Dyson, 2009).

In addition, we need to consider temporal, spatial and functional differentiation *in time*, especially if we wish to get a better understanding of how differentiated integration has been used as a political strategy within the context of progressive EU deepening, widening and enlargement. The following questions are especially relevant: First, *when* have flexible arrangements been introduced, extended, shortened or terminated? This question relates, for example, to the timing of differentiated arrangements relative to stages of the integration process; relative to treaty reforms, enlargements and major extensions of the *acquis*; or relative to major socio-economic developments. Second, are there distinct *sequences* in the introduction or termination of differentiated arrangements? For example, are there typical sequences that lead from policy to decision-making to institutional differentiation? A third temporal consideration relates to the *speed* with which such arrangements have been introduced or abolished. Can one identify phases of acceleration or slowing down in the introduction of differentiating measures? Are decisions on differentiation taken in an *ad hoc* manner or are they product of careful deliberations? In others words, are they a short-term expediency or employed strategically? Finally, what do we know about the *duration* of differentiated arrangements? Is there really a gradual shift towards open-ended differentiation, so that what used to be seen as a temporary exception to the rule becomes a long-term norm, making an eventual move towards uniformity in institutions, procedures and policies increasingly less likely?

Questions relating to differentiation *by means of time* and *in time* ultimately aim at situating the phenomenon within the broader development of integration and Europeanization. Is differentiation by *means of time* a price that has to be paid where commonly applicable standards cannot – yet – be reached? Or is it an important resource that allows integration to progress through pace-setting vanguards? Does an examination of – temporal, spatial and functional – differentiation *in time* suggest that it is becoming more common, more profound, more permanent and more formalized? And if so, why might this be the case? Such questions can only begin to be answered satisfactorily if one turns to integration and Europeanization theory. In so doing, we will, again, foreground the role of time.

How time shapes differentiated integration

The general question of how time promotes, facilitates or impedes differentiated integration raises a broad range of issues. Two preliminary remarks help to frame the discussion. First, in trying to understand how 'time matters', we need to engage with all three of the time dimensions introduced above, the passage of time; time budgets and time horizons; and time rules and their use. For example, the passage of time plays a critical role in neo-functionalist accounts of integration with their emphasis on spillovers; time horizons of actors are central to both historical–institutionalist explanations of integration and liberal intergovernmentalist accounts that stress uncertainty about the future and the need for credible commitments; and time rules help explain the dynamics of EU treaty negotiations and their outcomes.

Second, both integration and Europeanization theories are relevant. The former has a long pedigree, is aimed at a fairly clear explanandum and can be characterized with reference to recognized schools of thought. The latter is of more recent origin, its explanandum is often loosely defined as change and continuity in the political systems of EU Member States and countries seeking EU accession in response to (the prospect of) membership, and existing theoretical accounts are less developed, so that 'there remains plenty of mileage in theorizing Europeanization' (Bulmer, 2007: 57). Yet, both complement each other when it comes to explaining the developmental dynamics of differentiated integration and the specific forms – temporal, spatial and functional – that it takes.

Time in integration theory

At first sight, theories of European integration may appear to give little consideration to the role of time in integration, let alone *differentiated* integration. The lengthy subject indexes of major textbooks on integration theory do not contain entries on 'time' (Chryssochoou, 2009; Rosamond, 2000; Wiener and Diez, 2009), nor do collections of readings on the subject (Nelsen and Stubb, 2003; O'Neill, 1996). One might therefore be tempted to conclude that integration theory has little more to say on time and integration than that the latter is a historical process which takes place over time and that time is needed whether it is for functional and political spillovers to occur, as in neo-functionalism; lock-ins and path dependencies to unfold, as in historical institutionalism; or norm diffusion, socialization and identity-building to develop, as stressed in constructivist accounts.

However, such an easy dismissal would be fundamentally misplaced. Let us first consider neo-functionalism and 'neo-neofunctionalism' (Schmitter, 2004). Both passage of time and time rules feature prominently in its explanatory account. To begin with, neo-neofunctionalism sets out to be a 'transformative theory', which assumes that 'both actors and the "games they play" will change significantly in the course of the integration process' (ibid.: 47). Perhaps more importantly, Schmitter (2004), building on work first published more than 30 years previously, has sought to elucidate the temporal logic that underlies functional spillovers in economic–social integration and the spillover of the latter into political integration. In so doing, he puts emphasis on the fundamental importance of cycles, including 'initiation cycles', 'priming cycles' and 'transforming cycles'. While initiation cycles constitute the start of the integration process, priming cycles are about changes that 'define the context of a crisis that is compelling actors to change their strategies' (ibid.: 61), including differences in relative size and power of states; in rates of transaction; in members' internal pluralism; in elite value complementarity; and in extra-regional dependence (ibid.). During a 'transformative cycle', a qualitative transformation takes place: the Member States 'will have exhausted the potentialities inherent in functionally integrating their economies and dedicate more and more of their efforts to functionally integrating their polities' (ibid.: 65–6). Writing in 2004, Schmitter suggested that it was 'debatable' whether the EU had yet entered such a transformative cycle.

In the context of our present interest in differentiated integration, it is especially relevant to note that the idea of a cyclical development is closely linked to notions of asynchronic change in the key variables that drive actors to alter their strategies, that is, issues of timing, sequence, speed and duration. Thus, Schmitter hypothesises that during priming cycles, asynchrony in rates of change at the national level sets up – due to their differing marginal impacts – asynchrony in rates of regional change. This, in turn, enhances the probability that less convergent, and possibly divergent, actor strategies will be promoted and this makes the adoption of a joint policy vector more and more difficult. (ibid.: 64)

Several implications flow from these suggestions. First, if it makes sense to think of European integration as a process with pronounced cyclical elements, then it might also be instructive to explore evidence for cycles of differentiated integration and for distinct phases within such cycles. Second, in thinking about such phases, it might be useful to engage with the idea of 'interstitial institutional change', as developed by Farrell and Héritier (2007). The decisive point here is to understand the dynamics of informal differentiation on the one hand, and formal differentiation on the other. A 'cycle of differentiation' could be expected to come to an end when the possibilities for informal differentiation within a given Treaty framework are exhausted and Treaty revisions are required to either consolidate differentiation or move towards uniform integration. Third, the notion of asynchronic development in national conditions that shape integration – both within and across states – might help us to account for both the emergence of demands for differentiation and the durability or transience of the latter.

Time is, of course, also of central theoretical status in historical institutionalism. The *locus classicus* is Pierson's (1996) historical institutionalist analysis of the 'path to European integration', but others, notably Bulmer (1998) and Armstrong and Bulmer (1998) have also applied insights from this approach to explaining EU governance. As Pollack notes in the context of his discussion of the 'new institutionalism' and European integration, this approach emphasizes

> *inertia*, or *lock-ins*, whereby existing institutions may remain in equilibrium for extended periods despite considerable political change; *a critical role for timing and sequencing*, in which relatively small and contingent events that occur at *critical junctures* early in a sequence shape (that is, provide the institutional context for) events that occur later; and *path-dependence*, in which early choices provide incentives for actors to perpetuate institutional and policy choices inherited from the past. (Pollack, 2004: 140, emphases in the original)

The central substantive argument put forward by Pierson is that the historical development of European integration is characterized by the recurrent opening up of gaps in Member State control 'over the evolution of European institutions and policies'; during those gaps, actors other than the Member States, in particular the supra-national actors, gain in influence. This is a process that the Member States find very difficult to reverse, because supra-national actors will try to fight any such reversal; because of institutional barriers to reforms that would reassert control; and because of sunk costs and the rising price of exit (Pierson, 1996). When 'European integration is examined over time, the gaps in member-state control appear far more prominent than they do in intergovernmentalist accounts'.

Crucial to the opening up of these gaps is that domestic political decision-makers tend to have short time horizons: 'long-term institutional consequences are often the by-products of actions taken for short-term political reasons' (ibid.).

Pierson's account can be read to imply distinct patterns of differentiated integration: we would expect differentiated integration to flourish during phases of strong Member State control, but become less prominent during 'gaps', when supra-national actors may assert themselves. Moreover, the historical institutionalist account provides a potential explanation for *why* we can expect such a patterning *over* time, which is itself grounded in temporal considerations, namely the differences between short-term time horizons of state actors and the long-term, often unintended, consequences of their actions.

Turning to liberal intergovernmentalism, it may at first appear largely insensitive to time in its explanatory account of the integration trajectory. Liberal intergovernmentalism, as exemplified by Moravcsik's (1998) work, first treats time as the specific historical circumstances in which intergovernmental negotiations take place. EU integration can 'best be explained as a series of rational choices made by national leaders' (ibid.: 18). These choices are thought to respond to 'constraints and opportunities stemming from economic interests of powerful domestic constituents, the relative power of each state in the international system, and the role of international institutions in bolstering the credibility of interstate commitments' (ibid.). Clearly, all three of these factors can change over time but, in the eyes of its critics, liberal intergovernmentalism in its ontology is reproductive 'since the key assumptions are that dominant actors remain sovereign national states pursuing their unitary national interests and controlling the pace and outcomes through periodic revisions of their mutual treaty obligations' (Schmitter, 2004: 47).

However, liberal intergovernmentalism is time-sensitive in another respect. The passage of time may not transform the game being played, and time rules are not accorded a central role in its analysis of inter-state bargaining processes. Time horizons, however, are crucial in explaining decisions on 'institutional choice', that is, the pooling and delegation of sovereignty, in that these decisions are motivated by a desire for 'credible commitments'. Thus, the theory of credible commitments posits that delegation and pooling are

> designed to precommit governments to a stream of future decisions by removing them from unilateral control of individual governments [...] Governments are likely to accept pooling or delegation as a means to assure that other governments will accept agreed legislation and enforcement, to signal their own credibility, or to lock in future decisions against domestic opposition. (Moravcsik, 1998: 73)

Credible commitments as a way to 'control' the future are, accordingly, central to Moravcsik's account of the trajectory of European integration, and differentiated integration – in addition to reflecting economic interests and the power of Member States – needs to be understood as a result of calculations about the future. Temporal, spatial and functional differentiation may, therefore, be seen to reflect differences amongst the Member States in the willingness or capacity both to signal credibility and to lock in future decisions. As Moravscik himself highlights, 'the credibility explanation predicts that delegation and pooling will vary by issue and by country' (1998: 75).

Time in Europeanization theory

Compared to integration theory, theoretical accounts of Europeanization are of more recent origin. They are principally grounded in different variants of the new institutionalism – rational choice, historical and sociological (Bulmer, 2007), but, although all three are, in principle, suited to incorporating time in their explanatory schemes of processes and patterns of Europeanization, temporal categories do not feature prominently in leading accounts. In his discussion of 'key problems' in the theorization of Europeanization, Bulmer (2007: 53) highlights the 'under-representation of the classic HI [historical institutionalist] themes of time, timing and tempo'. Similarly, Goetz and Meyer-Sahling (2008), reviewing the literature on the Europeanization of national parliaments and executives, suggest that foregrounding time in causal accounts of Europeanization could help to make sense of cross-temporal, cross-sectoral and cross-country patterns that might otherwise remain difficult to explain.

One attempt to engage with this challenge is the analysis of 'clustered Europeanization' (Goetz, 2006, 2007). Its basic empirical contention is as follows: comparative analysis suggests that there exist several regional groupings – 'worlds' or 'clusters' – of Europeanization. These multi-country clusters exhibit, on the one hand, high levels of intra-regional commonality and, on the other, significant inter-regional differences in both the substance and prevalent modes of Europeanization. Crucially, in the present context, this clustering is thought to have been promoted by the interaction of two 'distant' explanatory variables: territory and temporality. Territory influences Europeanization primarily through 'families of nation' and centre–periphery structures in an expanding European political space (Goetz, 2007). Which 'family of nation' a country belongs to and where it is located in the European political, socio-economic and cultural space matters for Europeanization. Temporality is thought to affect Europeanization primarily through passage of time; through the timing of accession in relation to domestic political and economic development and to the phase of European integration; and through the speed and duration of the accession process.

To be sure, territory and temporality are not understood as alternatives to the dominant explanations of Europeanization, which stress the importance of domestic variables – be they concerned with institutions, interests, ideas or identities – and the role of integration-related variables (such as, for example, in arguments about differences in the capacity of Member States to 'upload' their preferences to the European level and their impact on patterns of 'downloading'). Rather, it is suggested that once territory and temporality are considered systematically, it becomes clear that they promote clustering in the more 'proximate' domestic and integration-related variables. This clustering of proximate explanatory variables in turn promotes clustered Europeanization.

The empirical argument then runs as follows: successive enlargements have followed a fairly clear regional pattern, integrating groups of countries that already shared many important political, socio-economic and cultural characteristics. Europeanization is likely to have reinforced this distinctness (see Heywood and McLaren, Chapter 12 in this volume, for an opposing view). First, Europeanization interacted strongly with democratization and socio-economic modernization in some cases (notably southern Europe), but did not do so in others (notably the Nordic countries). Put differently, while in some cases democratic political consolidation and socio-economic modernization preceded integration – Nordic enlargement is a case in point – in the southern and central and eastern European enlargements integration coincided with democratization and modernization. Second, regionally based, multi-country groupings joined the EU at distinct phases of European integration. Third, the speed and duration of the accession process differed from one enlargement to the next.

What is the relevance of these arguments for differentiated integration? Several points deserve highlighting. First, the 'relative time of accession' is likely to matter when it comes to pressures for, and resistance against, policy, decision-making and institutional arrangements that imply territorial, functional and temporal differentiation. Where democracy and market economy precede the quest for accession, demands for transitional arrangements, temporary derogations and the phasing in of policies are likely to be much less pressing than where they coincide. But to the extent that demands for differentiation are made by consolidated democracies, they are likely to favour permanence – in the sense of opt-outs – rather than temporary measures, since 'misfits' will be more deeply embedded in their policy and institutional traditions than is the case in 'transitional' political systems.

Second, open-ended 'temporary' arrangements – that is, those which are regarded as temporary in principle, but without a fixed end-date – are likely to be increasingly difficult to abolish as time goes on and national interest coalitions form around them. This observation applies, in particular, in the case of fully consolidated democracies. Third, insistence on the full adoption of the *acquis* at the time of accession in the case of non-consolidated democracies may come at the cost of 'shallow institutionalisation' that follows a 'logic of reversibility' (Goetz, 2005; Dimitrov et al., 2006). Thus, post-accession gaps in policy practices and institutional arrangements are more likely to open up where the instruments of formal temporal differentiation have not been used. Finally, and perhaps most importantly, the clustered Europeanization thesis underlines the close interaction between time and territory in shaping pressures for formal and informal differentiation.

The EU timescape and time as a resource

Another fruitful way to think about the impact of time on differentiated integration may be opened up by paying attention to the specificities of the EU timescape (Meyer-Sahling and Goetz, 2009), the opportunities for the use of time that the EU political system affords, and how these might promote spatial, functional and also temporal differentiation.[1] Political timescapes reflect the manner in which time is institutionalised in a political system along the polity, politics and policy dimensions. They are concerned, in particular, with the term lengths of political and senior administrative officeholders, their time budgets and time horizons; the formal and informal rules that govern the timing, sequence, speed and duration of political decision-making processes; and the temporal properties of public policies

The analysis of the EU timescape is still in its infant stages, but several of its features are worth highlighting in the present context (for extended discussions see Goetz, 2009; Goetz and Meyer-Sahling, 2009; Meyer-Sahling and Goetz, 2009). First, there is no dominant political time-setter in the EU and no dominant institutional and policy cycle that is comparable to the electoral cycle in national politics. Second, there are strong elements of ongoingness to the EU's workings, and the Commission, in particular, can often afford to take 'the long view'. Third, the EU's *Eigenzeit* ('own time') is fragile and sensitive to external influences, the most important of which are the political and, in particular, electoral calendars of the major Member States. Fourth, there is intense intra-institutional and inter-institutional bargaining over institutional and policy timetables. The latter, especially with long time horizons and fixed dates and sequences, assume a crucial role as commitment and compliance tools, as the example of enlargement governance highlights (Avery, 2009). Finally, despite frequent recourse to governing by timetable, the ability of the EU to realise its temporal preferences *vis-à-vis* the Member States is limited as is its ability to restrict *de facto* temporal differentiation – whether it concerns the speed with which different Member States move towards the goals of the Lisbon agenda, reduce or increase national public debt, or transpose EU directives.

These salient features of the EU timescape are likely to have important consequences for differentiation. To begin with, the absence of a dominant time-setter and of a dominant cycle means that the EU timescape is capable of accommodating a considerable degree of both temporal and functional differentiation. While in domestic contexts, elections largely set a common clock for national policy-makers, in the EU key institutions run on different clocks and different policy areas develop distinct *Eigenzeiten* (see K. Dyson, 2008, 2009a). This can make mobilization in time and synchronization across institutions and policies very arduous; but is also reduces the need for inter-sectoral coordination and the need to fit policy, decision-making and institutional schedules within a strongly cyclical political calendar. The manner in which political time is institutionalized in the EU is well suited to heterotemporality, that is, the co-existence of multiple political times in its institutions, decision-making procedures and policy development.

The emphasis on ongoingness is visible, for example, in the practice that legislation still pending at the end of one parliamentary term is carried over into the newly elected European Parliament; the 'discontinuity principle' practised in most national legislatures is effectively suspended. Ongoingness tends to increase the time budgets of key actors – notably the Commission and the European

Parliament – and, by implication, their time horizons. It is precisely this ability to 'take the long view' which helps to promote the acceptance of 'provisional' solutions in the form of *à la carte* participation or differences in the timing, speed and sequences that Member States follow in the pursuit of common goals. In a political system in which time horizons are extended, it is more acceptable to wait for 'eventual participation' than where the time budgets and time horizons of the key actors are strongly bounded by elections (see Kölliker, 2006b, who discusses the calculations surrounding 'eventual participation').

It is also worth noting that although EU political time reaches deeply into the institutional timetables of the Member States, notably of executives (Ekengren, 2002), the EU is as much a 'time-taker' from the Member States as it is a 'time-setter' for them. For example, despite a highly developed system of surveillance of the Member States' budgets and an elaborate system of time rules designed to ensure compliance with the Stability and Growth Pact, national political calendars have repeatedly proved more powerful than the clocks of the Pact (Dyson, 2009a). Cross-country differences in compliance with transposition deadlines and, in particular, questions over timely substantive implementation also underline the limitations to EU control over political time in the Member States. For example, in their work on labour law directives in both old and new Member States, Falkner et al. (2005) identified three 'worlds of compliance', consisting of a 'world of law observance', a 'world of domestic politics', and a 'world of neglect'. In their most recent work, Falkner and her co-authors add a fourth 'world of dead letters' (Falkner et al., 2008). What these and many other findings on transposition and implementation indicate is that there is a great deal of *de facto* differentiation that the Commission is either unable or unwilling to contain.

If, in Moravscik's terms, decisions on pooling and delegation at Inter-governmental Conferences are about future commitments, then elaborate time-tables constitute the daily currency of pre-commitments in the EU. 'Governing by timetable' helps to ensure commitment under conditions of frequently changing actor constellations; but is also helps to keep temporal differentiation manageable, in that differences in the timing, sequence, speed and duration of Member State commitments are made transparent and predictable.

Conclusion: taking time seriously

Why is it important to focus on time in discussions of differentiated integration and what are the key questions to be raised? The *topos* of a multi-speed Europe long predates the foundation of the European Communities and it has always played on the intimate connection of space and time, as in discussions of the 'slow South' and the 'faster North'. As Eder (2004: 101) points outs, the European project may well promote such asynchronicities, but, at the same time, it needs to maintain a semblance of synchrony amongst the Member States:

> This is the point of the famous formula of a Europe *à plusieurs vitesses*. The synchronization of rates of change are coordinated by forming classes of fast

and slow countries. This is based on the presupposition that all will arrive at the same goal, but some will simply arrive later and be excluded from some of the advantages of those who are faster.

Temporal differences are, thus, a fundamental condition of the project of European integration.

As the contributions to this volume show, the EU possesses a rich repertoire of responses to deal with such temporal differences. They range from formal insistence on temporal differentiation, as in the rules governing the convergence criteria that must be met before a country's admittance to the Euro area (Dyson, 2009a; Dyson, Chapter 15 in this volume); to formal acceptance of differentiation, as in temporary derogations; to tacit (or perhaps even unreflected) toleration of differences in policy timing, sequences, speed and duration (as research on transposition and compliance would suggest; see Howarth, Chapter 16 in this volume); to policies that are aimed at accelerating rates of change so that countries can 'catch up' and asynchrony is reduced – enlargement policy offers many examples (Avery, 2009). In between, a great deal of political and administrative effort is expended on containing temporal differentiation and on minimizing its effects on the smooth working of the EU institutions. Hence the propensity to 'govern by timetable'.

The EU timescape – at the level of institutions, decision-making procedures and policies – certainly offers a favourable environment for asynchronic integration. The heterotemporality fostered by the absence of a dominant time-setter and the lengthening of time horizons that the lessening of the constraints typically associated with electorally bounded time afford make it possible to tolerate temporal–spatial and temporal–functional differences within the EU that would be difficult to accommodate within the confines of democratic nation-states. However, a combination of two trends might endanger these favourable conditions in the longer term. There are, first, indications that EU time is becoming increasingly electorally bounded, as the powers of the directly elected European Parliament increase and the other institutions, notably the Commission, become increasingly sensitive to the electorally constrained time of the legislature. Under such conditions, 'playing the long game' becomes more difficult and the tolerance for 'slow movers' can be expected to decrease. Second, Member State resistance to EU time-setting may also be expected to increase. Wayne Hope (2009: 62–3) raises the prospect of a temporal clash between the trans-national or supra-national sphere of policy-making and national politics:

As the upper reaches of the nation state conform to the temporal urgency of institutionalized supranational decision making, the marginalized national polity is answerable to the slower temporal rhythms of representative assembly, the election cycle, public policy formation and civil society.

Thus, the EU's capacity to tolerate temporal differentiation may decline just when the need to respond to the *Eigenzeiten* of its members becomes more acute.

Note

1. I am aware of the potential for confusion and circularity in argument that may arise from the presence of time both in the 'independent variable' – here, the specific character of the EU timescape – and the 'dependent variable' – here, differentiated integration, which includes, but is not, of course, restricted to, temporal differentiation. However, the key characteristics of the EU timescape I wish to highlight are different from the temporal properties of differentiated integration.

Part II Territorial Manifestations of Differentiated Integration

6
Alpine Europe

Daniele Caramani

Introduction: differential integration at the 'heart of Europe'

The *Financial Times* suggests drawing on a map a circle of 200km radius centred on Lucerne, Switzerland, to identify the Alpine Ring. This Ring is characterized – according to the columnist – by a Protestant working craftsmanship, conservative principles, family businesses and small and medium enterprises based on the hard work of the middle classes (*Mittelstand*).[1] This chapter examines such aspects in a region that lies right at the heart of Europe. The Alpine region plays an important role in the context of European integration. The Alps have for centuries been a strategic geo-economic node of the European 'city-belt' and the peasant communities there have been controlling the most important passes in the south–north trade routes. Up to the present, most negotiations between Alpine regions and the European Union (EU) concern transport policies, be it rail or road.

The Alpine region is important for European integration for other reasons, too. Because of a delayed process of state formation, with shifting boundaries until recently, and an incomplete process of nation-building leaving numerous ethnic, linguistic and religious minorities scattered along national borders, this area presents a unique level of cultural diversity in Western Europe.[2] This diversity leads to a specific vision of how the EU should define itself (*demos*), but also because it has led to specific institutions – namely, consociational, multi-level, decentralized ones in which consensus and accommodation cultures play a crucial role. Finally, Alpine Europe is Eurosceptic. In recent decades movements and parties have developed precisely as a defensive reaction to the threats that integration poses to its wealth and natural resources, its identities, as well as its political traditions. Be it the *Schweizerische Volkspartei* (SVP), Haider's *Freiheitliche Partei Österreichs* (FPÖ) or Italy's *Lega Nord*, we find a strong populist reaction in Alpine Europe.

These common elements make 'Alpine Europe' a well-defined area, in spite of internal differences, across national borders, making it a 'family of regions'. This has attracted the attention of both policy-makers and scholars.[3] In this chapter 'Alpine Europe' is defined as a transnational region covering the area which was first defined by the EU's INTERREG IIIb 'Alpine Space Programme' – Switzerland,

Austria, Slovenia, Northern Italy, South Germany and South-East France.[4] To what extent and in which respect is there a specificity of Alpine Europe in its integration to the EU? 'Which' and 'how much' differentiation is there? And what are the historical, cultural and geo-economic factors that account for it? The contention of this chapter is *not* that there is a differentiated integration that distinguishes the Alpine region (since it is part of larger states with different histories of integration) but rather that there are distinct elements determined by the geo-economic, cultural and institutional specificities of this area. This chapter thus attempts to establish 'what explains' the distinctiveness of this region, through three sets of explanatory factors:

- First, *structural* factors such as geo-economic and geopolitical location, economic activities and social composition;
- Second, *cultural* factors such as attitudes, identities and definitions of *demos* (insiders and outsiders), ethno-linguistic and religious diversity, as well as patterns of trust.
- Third, *institutional* factors such as decentralized, multi-level structures, neo-corporatist arrangements and consociational decision-making practices.

In line with the general framework of the book set out in Chapter 1 of this book, these factors are used as *intervening variables* that help explain why, under the pressure of 'deepening and widening' of European integration, the Alpine area (*space*) resists integration and delays it (*time*) focusing on policy areas such as transportation, environment, energy and immigration (*function*). These factors are defined as intervening variables as they account for the differentiated response from the Alpine region, as a 'cluster of Europeanization', to the deepening and widening of integration – that is, the two main *independent variables*.

The chapter starts by showing how commonalities have resulted in cross-border cooperation and EU initiatives to define an Alpine Euro-Region. Then, the chapter analyses how the structural, cultural and institutional intervening variables work in creating an Alpine vision of Europe. In doing this, the question of which 'activators' are at the origin of the resistance to integration is addressed, namely strong populist parties. The conclusion stresses how the distinctiveness of the Alps has the potential to develop into a European-wide cleavage.

Alpine Europe: a region in the making?

The geopolitical and geo-economic position of the Alps

Since the times of the Roman Empire the Alpine region has had a long-standing central position within the European network of trade routes. Its pivotal position was strengthened with the dissolution of the Roman Empire, when it became crucial to control the mountain passes between the maritime and commercial Italian cities and the flourishing North (the Flemish cities and the Hanseatic League).

As in the rest of the European city-belt (Rokkan, 1981), this area was characterized by political fragmentation that hindered the emergence of a centre able to unify vast territories. State formation in these areas was delayed until the late 19th and early 20th centuries with recurrent border modifications even after the First World War (including frequent transfers of territories and policies of assimilation). Furthermore, the entire Alpine arc (from Nice and Savoy in France to Istria), until the Second World War, suffered from unstable borders.

In addition, cultural fragmentation led to multi-lingual and religiously mixed nations and, consequently, to 'incomplete' nation-building along the Alpine relieves.[5] The morphology of this region has reinforced local cultural specificities. Both Germany and Switzerland have been religiously diverse since the Reformation and the religious wars in the 17th century. Furthermore, the linguistic diversity has survived in a number of regions: French in the *Suisse romande*, Italian in the canton Ticino (and, partly, in the Grisons where *Reto-Romanisch* is also spoken), German in the Italian province of South Tyrol, French in Valle d'Aosta, and *Ladino* in parts of Italy, as well as Italian in parts of Slovenia and Mediterranean France.

Transnational cooperation in the Alpine region

Common history, shared strategic interests and similar geo-economic position make it possible to speak of Alpine Europe as of a transnational region. Sometimes spurred by political affinity, the regional and national governments have initiated various forms of collaboration between the Alpine regions of neighbouring countries. The last decades have witnessed an increasing number of initiatives across borders, between both local governments and political parties (for example, the right-wing political movement *Alpi-Adria* created in Italy by former members of the *Lega Nord* but with links to Bavaria and Austria).

The transnational character of the Alpine region appears in a number of formal agreements. As early as 1963 there were initiatives for cooperation in the region of Basle – the 'Regio Basiliensis' – that brings together French, German and Swiss surrounding localities. This developed in a more extended network of collaboration and working groups such as the 'Regio TriRhena' around the Rhine valley (a Europe-Region funded by EU's INTERREG IIIb Programme). These are examples of early cross-border functional networks of which more followed in the subsequent years, such as the 'Alp-Adria Working Group' in 1978 to deal with matters such as transport, environment and research, or the 'Working Community of the Western Alps' (COTRAO).[6] This working group was founded in 1982 by a number of German *Länder*, Italian regions and Swiss cantons with an emphasis on functional cooperation in fields such as transportation, culture and natural preservation. In 1999 the six standing committees on which COTRAO was based were abolished and replaced by working groups based on specific and non-permanent tasks (Keating, 2005: 67).

In all these cases collaboration is not limited to functional sectors, but is extended to overcome past divisions and to work on the co-existence of different cultures, ethnic identities and languages. Although one of the issues that started the collaboration was settlements of border issues between Italy, Yugoslavia and Austria, the organization was careful not to touch upon sensitive issues of nationality and ethnicity and rather depicted Europe – as well as historical–geographical references such as *Mitteleuropa* – as solutions to overcome past divisions and recover some of the common history overshadowed by 19th-century nationalism. For example, after the treaty between Italy and Austria in 1993, and after Austrian EU accession in 1995, cooperation developed between the Austrian Tyrol and the two autonomous provinces of Bolzano/Bozen and Trento in Italy. In 1998 they created a 'Euro-Region' and have a joint office in Brussels.

The existence of a transnational character of the Alpine region has encouraged the EU to develop an Alpine 'vision' – particularly after the accession of Austria in 1995 and the beginning of the negotiations for accession with Slovenia. As for the local programmes mentioned above, this process was initiated by policy considerations determined by the geo-economic and communication centrality of the Alps in Europe. The 'Alpine Convention' was signed in 1995 between the European Commission and the various states around the Alps, including both EU Member States and non-EU countries (Switzerland).[7] In 2001 the 'Alpine Space Programme' was launched under the INTERREG IIIb Community Initiative funded by the European Regional Development Fund (ERDF). The INTERREG IIIb Programme ran from 2000 to 2006,[8] and has since then been upgraded to 'European Territorial Cooperation' programme (Objective 3 of the Regional Policy) for the Structural Fund period 2007–13. Figure 6.1 depicts the geographical area covered by the Alpine Space Programme. The Alpine Space Programme is one of 14 such programmes through which the ERDF aims at increasing cross-border cooperation and breaking competitiveness.

Even though the Alpine sub-national regions belong to countries with very different levels of integration, a cluster with well-defined areas of collaboration is indeed emerging. Yet, as Keating notes, '[t]he Alpine region has [...] not developed those middle-range transnational spaces that could lift questions out of the local context while not taking them all the way to Europe. There is nothing like the Nordic area or the British Isles' (2005: 67). How, then, is the Alpine region different?

Explaining differential integration in the Alps

The preliminary working hypothesis on which this book is based sees two fundamental dimensions of integration as the main causes of differential integration. Both are relevant in the Alpine case as both are perceived as 'threats':

- *Deepening* (centre-building, standardization – the *removal of internal boundaries*): Threatens autonomy in a number of policy fields (such as fiscal competition in the Swiss cantons) and increases the distance between citizens and elites.
- *Widening* (penetration – the *extension of external boundaries*): Threatens labour markets (for example, outsourcing in Central and Eastern Europe and immigrant competition for low-paid work in local markets) and identity and moral standards (immigration).

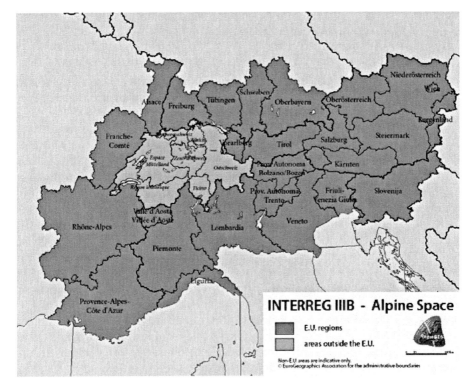

Figure 6.1 Area of the 'Alpine Space Programme'
Source: EU Community Initiative 'Alpine Space Programme' (www.alpinespace.org).

The defensive elements of the Alpine political culture *react* to these threats posed by deepening and widening. In this process the European supra-national state replaces the nation-state as the main source of threat to the Alpine region. The result is a differentiated attitude and relationship towards the EU from the Alpine areas. As Chapter 1 in this volume makes clear, part of the definition of 'differentiated integration' is the idea that European integration takes place at different paces in specific Member States or trans-national regions. The Alpine region is a case of *resistance to integration*, as well as one of *'variable geometry'* in that it focuses precisely on specific functional areas through a 'pragmatic process of seeking out opportunities' as Dyson and Sepos point out in their opening chapter to this book.[9] This resistance to integration and the Alpine Eurosceptic attitude is rooted in socio-economic structures, shared historical memories and institutions. These are the 'intervening variables' that help explain the *differential of attitudes towards the EU* in Alpine Europe. This differential attitude is the consequence of the geo-economic and geo-political position of the Alps in Europe described above. First, the survival of what one may call 'pre-industrial' factors in the political space: ruralism, regionalism and religiosity. Second, a specific political culture. And third, consociational multi-level democracy. These are all common elements of the Alpine regions that create its distinctiveness from others in its relationship to the EU.

Structural factors: ruralism, regionalism, religiosity

Rural–urban, ethno-linguistic (more general centre–periphery oppositions) and religious cleavages were expressed in the political sphere with the mobilization of mass electorates. In the Alps there is a comparatively strong presence of peasants' organizations and farmers' parties representing the *Mittelstand* and small and medium enterprises. Urban sites developed at the fringes of the Alps and gave rise to the opposition between urban/industrial centres on the foothills and the more rural areas in the Alpine valleys. Because of the geological morphology, Atlantic capitalism in the 16th century and the rise of overseas empires, and the commercial decline of northern Italy, Alpine areas remained based on agricultural and pastoral economy.[10] As in the Scandinavian countries, peasants' political organizations were movements for the defence of small or medium units of production. Their development very much depended on the market relationship between the towns and the countryside. This type of small farming economy is exposed to the uncertainties of the free market economy and to the threat of lower trade tariffs.

As far as regionalism is concerned, the entire Alpine arc is characterized by, first, *regional autonomy* – in spite of different types of states and contrasting experiences of national integration: cases of delayed federalization within former loose confederations (Germany and Switzerland); cases of strong centre formation (the French 'Napoleonian' model, also adopted by Italy); cases of break-up of multinational empires (Austria and Slovenia) – and, second, *parties for territorial and cultural defence* against attempts at fiscal and military penetration by the emerging nation-states' centre, and attempts at cultural standardization. In addition, Germany and Switzerland are – together with the Netherlands and Northern Ireland – the only religiously mixed cases in western Europe. Consequently, the Alpine region appears as a culturally fragmented area, both religiously and linguistically, with strong centre–periphery tensions.

Cultural factors: identity, trust, ethics

What are the consequences of the specific processes of state formation and political structuring that depended upon the political culture of the Alpine region? Table 6.1 sketches the argument from left to right. Starting with the first column on the left, political cultures are defined as sets of values and beliefs about social constructs. This follows the classical definition involving cognitive, affective and evaluational orientations towards three main elements of the political system (Almond and Verba, 1963).

The second column of Table 6.1 identifies the distinctive characters of the Alpine political culture. If one were to identify a common denominator for the different defining elements of this political culture, it would be the idea of a *threat from 'outside'*. The Alpine political culture is mainly a defensive set of attitudes which are reflected in the relationship with the 'outside environment'. The geographical–spatial

Table 6.1 The Alpine political culture and its impact on anti-Europeanism

Dimensions of political culture	'Alpine' cultural characters	Sources/ perception of external threats	Defensive political expression	Sceptical relationship to EU integration
Orientations Attitudes, values, beliefs	*Traditions* Religiosity, nature, work ethics	*Modernization* Secularization and urbanization	*Preservation* Family structure and social role	*Rural–urban cleavage* CAP
Preferences, priorities, policies		Financial capitalism, globalization, unemployment	Protectionism, SME, locals first	Transportation policies
			Environment	Natural resources
Community/ identity	*Ethnic*	*Civic*	*Retrenchment*	*Cultural cleavages*
Definition of group: us vs. them, insiders vs. outsiders	*'Volk', 'Gemeinschaft', 'Heimat'*	Assimilationist model, supra-national integration and 'Americanization'	Differentialist model (anti-immigration), 'true' identities: ethnicity, language, religion	Ethno-linguistic: "Europe of the Regions/People" Religion vs. secularization External borders
			Populism	*Left–right cleavage*
Institutions/ personnel	*Distrust*	*Distance*		
Expectations and evaluations about political system: degree of support	Distrust in elites: efficiency and honesty	Geographical and social remoteness: partitocracy, corporatism, coalitions, *Verflechtung*	Anti-party and anti-establishment discourse: electoral support from 'losers' of integration	Democratic deficit, welfare state, liberalization and privatization

Source: Adapted from Caramani (2005: 93).

dimension of 'closure' (communication networks) has been emphasized above. This idea of closure, however, can be extended to the aspect of a defence of communitarian identities, religiosity and traditions against the secularization of urban centres, the ecological preservation of the landscapes, and economic (agricultural) protectionism against the free market. These dimensions of *distance, closure* and *distinctiveness* mark the Alpine political culture.

Orientations involve, first, *nature* as a distinctive element of Alpine political cultures. The natural heritage is seen to be in danger and in need of being defended. Policy issues which are concerned with this goal of the protection of the resources of nature are not limited to environmental policy. Transportation policy (the *Transit* across Alpine passes and tunnels) has become a major issue both in domestic political discourse and in bi-lateral and multi-lateral international negotiations.[11] The low level of agricultural production and the high quality of its natural products makes this type of activity vulnerable to external effects (climatic and economic) and leads to considerable calls for protectionism. Second, one of the more recurrent themes of this culture is that of *work ethics*. Physical hard work is considered to be one of its characteristic features of the *Mittelstand*. There is a strong emphasis on the real or material economy of artisans, peasants and shopkeepers, in opposition to immaterial or virtual international finance. As Betz notes, '[w]hat makes Alpine populism distinct is its pronounced "producerist" bent, together with an equally pronounced emphasis on the entrepreneurial virtues characteristic of the *Mittelstand'* (Betz, 2005). The equation between identity and work appears in opposition to immigrants from Third World countries or Southern European countries (in Austria, Germany or Switzerland), but also in opposition to national sub-groups (as in the case of Southerners in Italy).

As far as identity is concerned, processes of supra-national integration have led to a defensive attitude in search for secure roots in a world that looks uncertain. Identity in the Alpine region can be illustrated through three German words: *Volk, Gemeinschaft* and *Heimat*. The relationship between individuals, territory and community is, again, defined in *natural* terms: *Volk* is a natural entity that embodies the primordiality of the community. *Gemeinschaft* is considered as being under threat because of the processes of economic modernization and a form of state-building that is transforming communities into *Gesellschaften*. On the one hand, the *Gemeinschaft* aspect is opposed to the idea of the atomized society that formed during the Industrial Revolution. This leads to the rediscovery of traditional forms of social organization, ethnic identities, family and religious affiliations. On the other hand, the *Gemeinschaft* aspect is opposed to the legalistic, universalistic and political construct of citizenship (Brubaker, 1992; Habermas, 1992).[12] Third, the idea of protecting the *Heimat* reappears. This protectionism results in anti-immigration views. Clearly, the definition of identity is related to the issue of nature. Ethnic communities and the *Heimat* are seen as *natural* things, and not as social constructs. Or, to use the oxymoron already used elsewhere, they become 'natural cultures' (Caramani, 2005).

The last dimension consists of attitudes towards institutions and authorities. The political system is often seen as corrupt and distant, and its personnel are criticized for not maintaining high standards of political morality. The centre–periphery and rural–urban cleavages deepen the distance with the administration and the headquarters of political actors. Furthermore, the monetary wealth gained through the culture of 'hard and honest work' has to be defended against 'those in power'. This results in general anti-state and anti-establishment pro-positions.

In conclusion, the perception of a threat to economic prosperity, social traditions, group identity and the ecological equilibrium, all of which are seen to originate from the *external* (national or international) environment, is typical of this political culture. The response to this threat is a retrenchment back to 'natural' (that is, pre-industrial and pre-state) social schemes*.

Institutional factors: consociationalism, neo-corporatism, decentralization

The third consequence of the processes of state formation and nation-building in the Alpine area is the development of patterns of consociational decision-making and of negotiation democracies. In the Alpine region consensual accommodation between segments of the society, neo-corporatist agreements between government, associations and trade unions, the existence of multiple levels of government (*Politikverflechtung*), as well as the practice of governmental coalitions, have created a *Konkordanz* or *Proporz* type of democracy.

Consociational, negotiation or accommodation democracies and corporatist agreements develop in response to the great social, territorial and cultural heterogeneity of the population described above, as well as to the external threats to which small countries are confronted in the international economy (Katzenstein, 1985). Political accommodation, neo-corporatist agreements and *Konkordanz* between parties is a process that takes place at the top of the stratification of societies, rather than at the level of the masses.[13] In addition the political cartelization of decision-making processes is paralleled by a multi-layered structure with several levels of government and strong regional autonomy (to which the EU adds a further level). We find federal structures in Austria, Germany and Switzerland, all countries which belong to the *Mitteleuropean* tradition of decentralized political systems, communal liberties and multi-ethnic societies (a tradition that can also be found in the 'pan-European' thinking that is typical of Central Europe; see Vidman and Delanty, 2008). The northern regions in Italy and Slovenia (both long under the Hapsburg Empire) also belong to this tradition, in which – in spite of the centralized nature of the Italian state – one finds autonomous provinces (such as those of Bolzano/Bozen and Trento), and regions with special status.[14]

The 'activators': populist parties in the Alps

In line with the general scheme depicted in the introduction to this volume, this section asks: who are the actors that help drive the process of resistence to integration in Alpine Europe? The most important 'activators' are populist and regionalist parties that gained weight in the last decade. The expression of the political *Verdrossenheit* and the reaction to immobile negotiation and consociational democracies which has emerged from segmented societies has taken the form of right-wing populist

*(On the role of external threats, see Hooghe and Mazka, 2008; McLaren, 2004)

and protest parties. There is a crucial link between consensual and negotiation democracy (caused by the territorially and culturally segmented nature of this region and the 'smallness' in the world economy) and the populist reaction (Checkel and Katzenstein, 2009).

The argument is not that populist parties do not exist outside the Alpine region, but rather that they are linked to geopolitical and geo-economic, historical, socio-economic and cultural conditions that make the populist response more accentuated and acute. More than anywhere else populist parties in the Alpine arc have been able to consolidate their electorates, with a surprising electoral stability in the last 10 years, and to influence the configuration of national political systems, as the *Lega Nord* did in Italy, the FPÖ in Austria, the SVP in Switzerland and the CSU in Germany.

In recent years identity and political traditions have not only been challenged in the usual arena of the nation-state, but have also been increasingly challenged in the way these elements are transposed and used in the construction of a supra-national political system – in other words, against the EU and the *current type of integration* (Hooghe and Mazka, 2008; Kriesi, 2009; Kriesi et al., 2008). Many of the 'threats' are increasingly perceived as originating from the EU rather than from the nation-state: cultural standardization, the artificial and impersonal character of citizenship, distant bureaucracy, and open immigration from non-Christian populations through the blurring of borders. This leads not only to a sceptical view of European integration but also to an *alternative conception of Europe*.

What strategies did these parties follow in order to activate the differential vision of integration? Five points seem particularly relevant:

- First, stressing *populist attitudes*, including the accusation of the distance between the people and the elites (also economic elites and religious institutions) stressing distrust in the political system and, more particularly, party politics (Bornschier, 2010).
- Second, using elements of *protest*.[15] One of the common elements of the cases considered here is the relationship to a   political system which is seen as immobile and unable to renew itself (Scharpf, 2009).[16] In the Alpine region the lack of dynamics in the political system is strengthened by the consociational, negotiational and multi-layered nature of the system.
- Third, the emphasis on *protection and defence*. There is a strong emphasis on the threat from outside. Immigration is perceived as affecting only the ordinary people and not the élites.[17] Furthermore, the Alpine areas and their political parties are not assimilationists; instead, they are differentialists (Brubaker, 1992). Party programmes include a 'national preference' (be it nationally or regionally defined) as far as the labour market is concerned.[18]
- Fourth, *electoral support* stems from 'losers of modernity' (Betz, 1998; Kriesi et al., 2008): small entrepreneurs, non-qualified independent workers, workers in small-sized firms, small farmers, shopkeepers and the like. These sectors are subjected to the uncertainties of integration more than others. The on-going change is seen as a bigger challenge for rural and remote areas, which are confronted with the opening up of society, than for urban centres, which have

always been at the centre of exchange networks. The geography of electoral support, in most of the cases, follows the rural–urban pattern. Several of the Alpine populist parties have agrarian origins.

• Fifth, the political culture is expressed by elements of strong *leadership*. The emphasis on the natural character of the community finds its expression in the role of the (almost) life-time leaders who embody the values of the community (see Holmes, 2009).

The Alpine relationship to the EU

In the initial phase of EU integration regions saw great opportunities for economic and institutional development in the emerging decentralized setting of the EU.[19] In a second phase, many regionalist parties turned against integration, in some cases virulently (Jolly, 2007). However, instead of being merely and negatively 'anti-European', these parties put forward an alternative conception of Europe and integration based on ethnic and religious identity, rather than on artificial and impersonal citizenship, with more subsidiarity and federalism in place of the current centralization and cultural standardization, with more power for 'small people' against lobbies at EU level (Marks et al., 2002). The resulting image proposed by the parties that activate it is one that can be summarized in the following four points.

1. *A Europe of the Peoples and Regions* – On-going standardization and homogenization processes are perceived as a major threat to regional identities. Furthermore, the impersonal and bureaucratic character of the new Europe leads to an artificial and impersonal citizenship. In contrast, the regionalist and populist parties of the Alpine region advocate a Europe of the People (originally, a leftist slogan), based on the 'true' ethnic identities of European populations. The threat of an external 'civic' idea of citizenship had originated from the nation-state. Today, this threat is increasingly perceived as coming from the EU. The reaction includes a return to the 'natural' elements of identity and to closure. In addition, there is the rejection of the impersonal and bureaucratic character of the new Europe.[20] One of the common elements in this vision of the organization of Europe is the federal legacy of *Mitteleuropean* political thinking.[21] This is, for example, expressed in the clear proposals for Alpine federalism (as in the case of the *Ligue Savoisienne*), and for broader systems of regional autonomies based on the model of federal states. The European federative model – the *Europe of the Regions* on the model of the Swiss Confederation – should replace the current centralized model as a parallel process to the creation of a *Europe of the Peoples* replacing the abstract character of European identity (Mayer and Palmowski, 2004).

2. *A Christian Europe* – The accent on the identity of Europe is put on the variety of its 'peoples' but also on its unity under a classic and Christian history (Byrnes and Katzenstein, 2006). This element stresses the fundamental unity of European culture. This is a horizontal/geographical demarcation that appears

in debates about European identity (such as the debate around a Christian mention in the Constitutional Treaty put to vote in 2005). This issue becomes more critical in rounds of enlargement when external boundaries are redefined. The debate about the accession of Turkey is one example (Schoen, 2008).[22]

3. *A Democratic Europe* – In its critique directed against the abstract type of EU citizenship, the lack of democratic elements is also stressed. The themes against the consociational and the elitist character of national decision-making are thus increasingly used to criticize the *modus operandi* of the EU (Fossum, 2001; Eriksen and Fossum, 2007). Europeanization constitutes an additional factor that increases the multi-level character of institutions, which aggravates problems of accountability. The strong influence of lobbies and interest groups in 'Brussels' is seen as an usurpation of popular sovereignty in that lobbies and interest groups are beyond any and all democratic control (Lord and Magnette, 2004).[23] Feelings of disempowerment are reinforced by the perception that the process of European integration has weakened the influence of voters at the level of local and national parliaments, with elected bodies increasingly losing their autonomy and capacity to steer the economy. The local and national democratic circuits are being curtailed by the loss of competences and autonomy through integration while, at the European level, the reduced role of the European Parliament, the consociational and negotiational nature of decision-making, and the role of neo-corporatist practices through lobbies and interest groups, all serve to increase the feelings of democratic deficit and dispossession.[24]

4. *A Fortress Europe* – The defensive and protectionist character of the Alpine attitude determined by the structural, cultural and institutional specificities of the area ultimately leads to closure. This corresponds to the idea of 'Fortress Europe' built on the assertion of the specific values of European culture as opposed to other cultures, the necessity to preserve ethnic integrity in Europe, and the stress on the internal regional plurality of peoples and cultures in Europe (Castiglione, 2009). Economically there is also a clear perception of the threat stemming from international competition and the opening up of markets which have been well protected from external influences for a long time.

Summing up, this view of Europe is not simply a sceptical one, but also a view which represents an *alternative* form of integration. Europe itself is seen as a natural entity, both geographically and in its ethnic pluralism, which is based on specific Western and Christian values, and whose identity is today threatened from outside. Against centralizing tendencies, these movements oppose stronger elements of subsidiarity and federalism. Europe must replace the former protectionist role of the nation-state. Finally, these movements propose a more democratic Europe with direct participation countering the influence of technocrats and lobbies. Thus, rather than being merely anti-European, these movements are against the currently dominant idea of Europe, and propose a different, more pan-European or *Mitteleuropean* idea of Europe.

Conclusion: towards a centre–periphery cleavage in Europe?

Alpine Europe does not present a homogeneous cluster of differentiated integration. The countries to which the various sub-national regions in the Alps belong to have divergent national histories of integration from which they cannot escape. Yet the Alpine transnational region presents a homogeneous cluster of attitudes towards, and visions of, Europe. This contrasts with the predominant mode of integration. A diversity of the views concerning the type of integration (as opposed to the pro/anti-European dichotomy) relates to questions of 'which Europe?' (Jachtenfuchs et al., 1998). Highlighting the different perceptions of Europe also means contrasting completely different ideas of states, political systems and communities/citizenships. European territories differ not only with regard to national cultures and ethnic, linguistic and religious identities, but also in types of state traditions and citizenship, which entail both political nations based on a legalistic notion of citizenship, as well as universalistic values and ethnic nations (Smith, 1986).

To what extent does this alternative image of European integration *cut across or overlap* with other oppositions in the European cleavage constellation?[25] The first question concerns the 'renaissance' of a territorial dimension in Europe (Kohler-Koch, 1998). For a long time, the literature has argued that processes of socio-economic modernization in Western societies have led to the integration of peripheral cultural identities and economic areas within broader political contexts and markets. Theories of state formation and nation-building, as well as of the hegemony of the left–right cleavage and class alignments, seemed to indicate the disappearance of the territorial and cultural dimension (Caramani, 2004). Yet the disappearance of pre-industrial cleavages and territoriality cannot be taken for granted at the EU level. The survival of old identities and the emergence of new ones can lead to the reappearance of a territorial dimension at European level. Conflicts could emerge with regard to the levels of economic subsidies, the degree of regional autonomy in the new constitutional framework, and subsidiarity. The territorial dimension over the type of European integration cuts across the left–right dimension. It has been argued that the developing European electorate and party system will strongly depend on whether or not the left–right dimension imposes itself on the 'sovereignty dimension' (Bartolini, 2002).[26] Also, sub- and transnational regions may join the sovereign nation-state in resisting EU centre formation.

The centre–periphery dimension entails strong *cultural* connotations. First, ethno-linguistic identities might play an important role in matters of local or regional identity, in contrast with the above-mentioned abstract and universalistic conception of citizenship (at national and at European level). Second, religious contrasts might, on the one hand, focus on religious vs secularized orientations within the EU and, on the other, focus on the common religious heritage of European versus 'neighbouring civilizations' such as Turkey. In both cases, this has a strong implication for the definition of a European identity, be it assimilationist or differentialist (with consequences for immigration and free movement policies).

Concerning the first cleavage produced by the Industrial Revolution – the *rural–urban* dimension – as a further functional dimension of differentiation, Schmitter (2000) points to agriculture – a cleavage that has disappeared, or has been incorporated in other alignments, in national cleavage landscapes – but which is re-emerging at EU level as a consequence of the important resources for the Common Agricultural Policy controlled by the EU and through alliances of 'integration losers'. Contrasts focus here on the support for specific economic activities, such as the Common Agricultural Policy and small and medium-sized enterprises. Furthermore, protectionist attitudes may contrast with liberalization and privatizing policies in the form of anti-redistribution positions, 'locals first' in the labour market and maintenance of local wealth (taxation, ecological resources, control of transportation axes).

How do these dimensions relate to the *left–right* opposition? Here, the cleavage constituted by an alternative political culture and vision of European integration cuts across, rather than overlaps with, the left–right dimension. The development of a critical image of European integration takes place in an alliance of integration losers at the extremes of the left–right spectrum (Schmitter, 2000: 68; Kriesi, 2009; Kriesi et al., 2008). This alliance is composed of the extremes of the political spectrum (extreme left-wing and extreme neo-populist right-wing parties). Contrasts not only concern the strong critique in terms of the democratic deficit of the EU, which relates to the anti-party and anti-lobby distrust towards élite institutions and bureaucracies, but also concern the defence of welfare protection whose cuts (necessary because of policies of deficit reduction, low inflation and monetary stability) affect the weaker strata of the population.

In conclusion, the specificities of this area do lead to an alternative vision of European integration. This alternative image represents a challenge – which is mainly activated by regionalist and populist right-wing parties – both at national and EU levels, as well as a new cleavage. This new cleavage interacts with other industrial and pre-industrial cleavages. *It overlaps with the main pre-industrial cleavages* – centre–periphery, rural–urban, ethno-linguistic and religious – *and cuts across the most important industrial cleavage* – namely, the left–right dimension. The existence of such a cleavage might also have an impact on the institutional framework, and not only the policies, of the EU, with a strong regional component. It becomes clear that conceptualizing sub- and transnational regions is much more than an area-restricted analysis.

Notes

1. 'Survive the Credit Crisis the Alpine Way', *Financial Times* (Comment) by P. Marsh (29 January 2009).
2. Indeed political systems like Switzerland's have frequently been used as possible models for European institutions. For an empirical assessment see Hug and Sciarini (1995).
3. Two volumes have stressed the analytical relevance, as well as the socio-economic and political relevance, of this region. See Ihl et al. (2003) and Caramani and Mény (2005). For a historical overview see Viazzo (1990). In Garmisch-Partenkirchen, Germany, an Alpine Research Institute was created in 1994.

4. As far as Bavaria is concerned, this is restricted to its southern and mostly Catholic areas between the Danube and the Alps.
5. This delay most notably concerns the two large cultural areas of Italy and Germany which achieved national political unity in 1861 and 1871. Switzerland, too, was transformed from a lose *Staatenbund* to a sovereign *Bundesstaat* in 1848/1874. State formation in Austria and Slovenia is, on the other hand, the result of the break-up of multinational empires.
6. The original members of the 'Alp-Adria Working Group' were Friuli–Venezia–Giulia, Trentino–Alto Adige, Carinthia, Upper Austria, Steiemark, Slovenia and Croatia. Later, they were joined by Salzburg, Bavaria and Lombardy and, in 1986, by Ticino and two Hungarian regions.
7. Liechtenstein and the Principality of Monaco are also part of the Alpine Convention. Liechtenstein is also part of the 'Alpine Space Programme'.
8. The cooperation area includes the Alpine core areas, the surrounding foothills and low-lands (the 'peri-Alpine belt') as well as coastal areas of the Adriatic and Ligurian Seas and the great river valleys (Danube, Po, Adige, Rhône and Rhine). Most of the regions are based on the NUTS II classification. For Germany it includes the four *Regierungsbezirke* of Upper Bavaria and Swabia (Bavaria) and Tübingen and Freiburg (Baden-Württemberg). For Italy the regions are Friuli–Venezia–Giulia, Veneto, Lombardia, Valle d'Aosta, Piemonte, Liguria and the two autonomous provinces of Bolzano/Bozen and Trento. In France the regions are Rhône-Alpes, Alsace, Franche-Comté and Provence–Alpes–Côte d'Azur. For Austria and Switzerland the entire country is part of the programme (the regions are *Länder* and *Grosregionen* respectively). Slovenia is also part but is not divided into regions.
9. Defining differentiated integration as a 'dependent variable' faces a methodological dif-ficulty in a chapter about a transnational region. European integration is negotiated and decided by *national* governments and not by regional ones. In the Alpine case, whereas Switzerland, Austria and Slovenia are part as whole countries of this region, for France, Germany and Italy only regions are part of it. Their nature and degree of integration therefore depends (also or mainly) on the will of the rest of the countries they belong to. Whereas France, Germany and Italy were the three major founding members of the EU in 1957, Austria and Slovenia joined much later, and Switzerland never did and instead negotiated a number of bilateral agreements in subsequent rounds.
10. The largest of these is the *Schweizerische Bauern-, Gewerbe- und Bürgerpartei* – today *Schweizerische Volkspartei* (SVP). In Germany strong agrarian parties developed in Bavaria, in particular the *Bayerischer Bauernbund* in alliance with the *Deutscher Wirtschaftsbund für Stadt und Land* during the Weimar Republic (later *Deutsche Bauernpartei*). In Austria, the various regional agrarian parties unified in the *Landbund für Österreich* in 1922. In Italy, the *Partito Agrario* (*Partito dei Contadini d'Italia* after the Second World War) was strong in Piemonte.
11. There has even been an attempt to make transportation issues part of package deals. For example, there was the opinion in Austria that the Austrian Chancellor should have signed the enlargement treaty of the EU only if the EU solved the *Transitproblem* accord-ing to the Austrian wishes. The same issue often arises in direct democracy consultations concerning European integration in Switzerland.
12. See also the distinction between 'new' and 'old' regionalism in Keating (2005).
13. The terms were coined back in 1967 by Lehmbruch. In 1996 he speaks of these democ-racies as *korporative Verhandlungsdemokratien* (corporative negotiation democracies). On consensual democracy see Lijphart (1984) and Powell (2000). The elements of negotiation democracy are outlined in Czada (2003): 1) *Konkordanz* between parties; 2) a federal struc-ture; and 3) corporatist agreements between sectoral organizations and the government.
14. Three of the five regions with special status in Italy are located along the Alps: Trentino-Alto Adige, Friuli–Venezia–Giulia and Valle d'Aosta.
15. See, for example, Betz (1998). There is however an ambiguity with the participa-tion of these parties in governmental coalitions: the FPÖ has been in coalition with the ÖVP, the *Lega Nord* is part of the Berlusconi government, the SVP is part of the

'magic formula' in Switzerland, and the CSU is part of the government alliance with the CDU.

16. This is the thesis of Taggart (1996), according to which populism in Western Europe has been favoured by the long social-democrat hegemony and by neo-corporatist practices and the consociational style of democracy (see also Papadopoulos, 1992). This also has close links with the discussion about the 'democratic deficit' at EU level (see below). The Italian term *immobilismo* also denotes the incapability of the political system to change and renew itself.

17. This type of discourse is often shaped by frequent references to the founding mythology, for example, Giussano da Pontida in the case of the *Lega Nord* or Wilhelm Tell in the case of the SVP, similar to other populist parties (such as the French *Front National* and Jeanne d'Arc).

18. This happens to different degrees. While the *Lega Nord* and the FPÖ are quite clear about it (the FPÖ initiated a referendum *Österreich zuerst* and the *Lega Nord* made similar proposals concerning the labour market in Italy), the CSU is less explicit.

19. Brubaker (1996) develops and defines the concept of 'structure of incentives' for the mobilization of cultural and territorial differences within the fluid institutional framework of the new Europe more precisely.

20. For example, the leader of the *Lega Nord* has repeatedly criticized the European super-state guided by non-elected technocrats. He spoke of a Stalinist super-state and of a 'Western Soviet Union' and called for resistance against Jacobin Europe (Caramani, 2002: 136–9). In Austria, the anti-European stance of the leader of the FPÖ on the occasion of the accession of Austria to the EU led to the split of the *Liberales Forum*. The Bavarian CSU also regularly expresses its criticism of Brussels. The then Bavarian Prime Minister Edmund Stoiber was explicitly opposed to the Maastricht process and the common European currency.

21. This tradition goes back to the pan-European thinking typical of Germanic Central Europe which was represented by thinkers of the Hapsburg Empire (who are often mentioned in the public discourses), such as József Eötvös, František Palacký, Carlo Cattaneo, Karl Renner and others. On this tradition of thinking, see Batt (2003).

22. The accent on Christian values also entails a critique of the consumerism and individualism of modern industrial and urban societies, as well as of aggressive capitalism and international finance (especially in the current financial crisis).

23. More generally, these critiques are extended to all supra-national and international organizations, such as the UN, the WTO, the World Bank and the IMF. The scepticism toward international organization is notably strong in Switzerland which has a long tradition of isolationism. In the 1986 referendum, the Swiss voted against joining the United Nations. In the 1990s, this was followed by a number of other referenda on the European Economic Space (1992) or bilateral agreements with the EU (on Swiss isolationism, see Kobach, 1997).

24. Examples of the virulent attacks by the *Lega Nord* towards the EU and its fundamentally non-democratic, technocratic, and Jacobine nature as a 'super-state' can be found in Caramani (2002). Anti-European positions were also frequent in the FPÖ and the CSU (against the Treaty of Maastricht and the European common currency).

25. The theoretical approach taken here is a 'historical sociology' one (Bartolini, 2007; Rokkan, 1999) or a 'sociological institutionalist' one (Checkel, 1999; Christiansen et al., 1999). It is what the introduction to this volume labels a 'comparative politics approach' which is particularly important because – among the various theories of integration – it is the one that looks inside states.

26. According to Marks and Steenbergen (2002), the interaction between cleavage 'residues' from the 19th and 20th centuries – especially the left–right dimension – and the pro- vs anti-European dimension will also determine the nature and shape of the European-wide party system.

7
'Anglo-America' and Atlantic Europe

Andrew Gamble

The United Kingdom and the Republic of Ireland share the same group of islands off the European mainland, and for several centuries they formed a single state, following the conquest of Ireland by England. Most of Ireland broke away from British rule in 1921, but six counties in the North remained part of the United Kingdom. The relationship between the two countries has been profoundly shaped firstly by the period of colonial rule and its legacies, secondly by the strong cultural and economic ties between the two countries, and thirdly by their dual membership of the wider Anglosphere and the European Union. Ireland was distinctive from England, Scotland and Wales from the 16th century because of its Catholicism, although it shared particularly with Scotland and Wales a Celtic heritage.

The Anglo-Irish bilateral relationship and differentiated integration

The dependence of the Irish economy on the British economy after independence remained very strong, which limited the opportunities for Irish development, and encouraged the development of clientelistic political relationships more common in Southern Europe. Ireland was keen to join the European Community at the same time as Britain to boost its opportunities for economic development, so De Gaulle's veto on Britain was also a veto on Ireland. The two countries eventually joined the EU together in 1973, but their attitude to the EU has been very different. The Irish, until recently, have been enthusiastic members, seeing European integration as a way to build state capacity, using European cohesion funds to strengthen Irish identity and the Irish economy. Ireland was seen as strongly pro-European, and one of the main beneficiaries from the EU, so the rejection by the Irish of first the Nice Treaty in 2001 and then of the revised constitutional treaty in 2008 came as a surprise.

The ambivalent attitudes displayed by British governments, many parts of the British political class, and the British electorate to the project of European integration has been much discussed (George, 1994). The British have insisted on more opt-outs from European treaties than any other Member State, apart from Denmark, and they have lagged behind throughout the process of European integration. The European Commission at each stage had to accommodate the preferences of the British because of the priority attached to keeping Britain within the Union, and this has been one of the main ways by which differentiated integration has developed.

Britain chose not to participate in the original discussions which established the Common Market, which meant that it did not finally join until 17 years after the signing of the Treaty of Rome. The retrospective referendum in 1975 held to ratify membership was comfortably won, but did not signal a consensus on membership or any great desire to make it work. Part of the British political class on both left and right has remained opposed to the principle of membership, and wider scepticism about the benefits of membership has always been strong, magnified by a generally hostile press (Baker and Seawright, 1998). British governments have generally been cautious about committing themselves to further integration, most evident in the refusal to join the ERM when it was first launched, and in the opt-outs on European and monetary union and the social chapter that were negotiated in the Maastricht Treaty. Further opt-outs were needed at the time of the Amsterdam Treaty, which incorporated the Schengen Agreement into Community law, and the Lisbon Treaty, concerning the Charter of Fundamental Rights.

British political leaders have generally preferred a decentralized, patchwork Europe, based on bilateral deals, a minimum of common rules and common commitments, and tolerance of anomalies and asymmetries. They have wanted a Europe based on mutual accommodation between sovereign nation-states, with only a supporting role for the supra-national institutions. This has drawn them to ideas of a multi-speed Europe, variable geometry, and *à la carte* Europe, returning the initiative in European affairs to nation-states and taking it away from the supra-national institutions such as the Commission and the European Court.

This approach has meant that the British have given strong support to the widening of the Union, particularly the inclusion of new members following the collapse of communism in eastern and central Europe, and they have been keen advocates of Turkey's candidature. The British are noticeably cooler and more resistant to the process of deeper European integration, certainly when compared with the other major Member States, and also when compared with Ireland, which is more comfortable with deeper integration and less so with enlargement. Britain's failure to join the euro and the strength of popular opposition to the Lisbon treaty are recent examples of British ambivalence. But the British record is not uniformly negative. Britain took the lead in pressing for the single market, and has been a strong backer of the Lisbon process, as well as of initiatives like the Bologna process.

The mainstream view in Britain and in Ireland across all parties favours an EU which permits differentiated integration in specific functional areas rather than a universal integration obliging all participants to operate the same rules and principles in identical ways. This chapter will examine the three dimensions of differentiated integration laid out in the Introduction to this volume – functional, spatial and temporal – and how they relate to developments in Britain and Ireland.

Atlantic Europe: the spatial dimension

The British stance of appearing apart from Europe is bound up with its relationship with the United States and the wider English-speaking world. There have been a number of terms for this, including Greater Britain, the English-speaking Union, Anglo-America, and most recently the Anglosphere (Bell, 2007; Gamble, 2003; Bennett, 2004). The existence of this trans-national space has allowed the British for 350 years to imagine themselves as both part of Europe and not part of Europe, and to define their identity in part against Europe. Other European nations – France, Spain, Portugal and the Netherlands – also established large overseas empires, which were important in the construction of their own national identities and their relationship to Europe. But what marks out the British experience is that one of its colonies, the United States, became in the 20th century the world hegemon, eventually overshadowing not just Britain but the whole of Europe. It intervened decisively twice on Britain's side in the two world wars in the 20th century, and in doing so succeeded Britain as the leading world power and guarantor of a liberal world order.

The United States became a magnet for all European peoples, not just British, and its original identity as 'Anglo-America' has weakened (Kaufmann, 2004). Americans with English, Irish, Welsh or Scottish roots are a steadily declining proportion of the US population. But throughout the 20th century and up to the present there has been a persistent special relationship between Britain and the United States, which is not just a security and defence relationship, but also a relationship of political economy, of ideology and culture, and of political and legal institutions. The reality of this special relationship has always been much debated (Dumbrell, 2001) and it has certainly waxed and waned. Viewed from outside the partnership has a solid substance, captured in the German notion current in the late 19th and early 20th centuries of 'Anglosaxondom'. De Gaulle's main reason for vetoing British entry into the Common Market in 1961 was that he feared Britain would not give priority to its membership of the European Communities, but to its relationship with the United States. He doubted that Britain would ever consider itself primarily a European power, and this for him disqualified Britain from membership of the new Europe (Lacouture, 1991).

The correctness of this view of Britain has often seemed confirmed by the actions of British governments and by prevailing currents of thought and opinion in Britain. Examples would include the enthusiasm with which British political leaders, notably Margaret Thatcher and Tony Blair, supported the United States and its increasingly unilateralist foreign policy, or by the rise of the discourses of neo-liberalism and globalization to frame policy choices in the past 30 years, or by the institutions of a specific Anglo-American or Anglo-Saxon capitalism. In all these ways the British have often set themselves apart from the European majority, and many British Eurosceptics have come to pose the choice for Britain as precisely a choice between belonging to an Atlantic sphere or a European sphere (Redwood, 2001). Europe and America in this discourse become two ideal types, and Britain is regarded as belonging fundamentally to the world of Anglo-America and the Anglosphere rather than to that of the European Union. The anxiety for Eurosceptics is that having signed the Treaties, Britain, whether it likes it or not, is subject to legal and institutional processes which are gradually transforming all the Member States, and making them recognizably more European, tying them into a European space.

The Union and the Isles

The attitudes of the British towards differentiated integration have therefore always been powerfully shaped by their perception of also being part of the trans-national space of Anglo-America. A further complication is the relationship between the states and peoples which inhabit the collection of islands off the western coast of the European landmass. There are four nations, but currently only two states. For just over 200 years, between 1707 and 1922, there was only one state, England having succeeded in its aim of subjugating or incorporating all the other nations into a single state ruled from London (Davies, 1999). Irish independence did not immediately have consequences for the rest of the United Kingdom, but in the past 30 years the multi-national Union which underpins the United Kingdom has again become unstable, and has led to debate about the possibility of a further breakup of the Union (Johnson, 2004; Heffer, 2006; Fry, 2006).

The dynamics of the relationships between the different parts of the United Kingdom, and between the United Kingdom and Ireland, are important for understanding both British and Irish attitudes to differentiated integration in the EU. When there was a single Union covering the Isles, there were always great differences in the way the different regions were integrated into the economy, the culture and the state. Nonetheless there were enough common features as well as dependencies and interdependencies which made the Isles a unity. One of the most interesting of these is the extent to which the four nations of the Isles can be considered part of the Anglosphere and Anglo-America. For the Irish to be named part of anything 'Anglo' is unacceptable, just as they reject the term 'British Isles'. It is a long time since anyone thought of the Irish as West Britons. Yet the use of English as the main language, and common cultural and institutional traditions, do give Ireland special affinities to the nations in the United Kingdom and to the wider Anglosphere. The substantial differences between Ireland and the UK show the extent and limits of spatial differentiated integration in this part of the EU; at the same time being fellow members of the EU has been one of the most important factors in transforming the relationships between Ireland and the UK as well as loosening the ties between the nations still inside the Union. The existence of a new larger Union in Europe has facilitated the rethinking of the British Union.

The creation of devolved administrations in Edinburgh and Cardiff and the prospect of further devolution in the future, or even independence, suggest possible spatial reconfigurations. Wales and Scotland might form a bloc with the Irish, defining themselves against England, and sharing more in common with other small states within the EU framework; or they might continue to form a distinct Anglosphere grouping within the EU. There are different strategies which might be pursued, and the case of Ireland sends out ambiguous signals. Is Ireland to be considered part of the Anglosphere as American neo-conservatives contend (Bennett, 1994), or is it now primarily part of the new European Union? During the boom of the 1990s many in Ireland assumed it was the latter. But the loss of the referendum on the Lisbon Treaty in 2008, following the earlier rejection of the Nice Treaty in 2001, and the economic crash in 2008 have raised doubts about how Ireland really sees itself.

Atlantic Europe: the functional dimension

Three cases will be used to illustrate the functional dimension, each one showing a differing response from Britain and Ireland. In the first case, foreign and defence policy, Britain has pursued limited differential integration, while Ireland has held back; in the second case, on borders, the UK and Ireland have maintained their own common policy and refused to integrate with the Schengen countries; in the third case, the euro, Ireland has joined the eurozone while Britain has not. In each of these cases the European initiative can be seen as providing a public good. For foreign and defence policy, Ireland has been mainly a free-rider both on NATO and on EU projects, while the same has been true of Britain in relation to EMU. Britain has benefited greatly from the positive policy externalities due to the financial stability of the eurozone, its major market, by keeping the flexibility to control its own interest rates and its own currency. Ireland did not have that flexibility in the downturn in 2008.

Foreign and defence policy

The development of a common foreign and security policy, originally the second pillar of the Maastricht Treaty, has been the policy area where supra-national coordination has been most difficult to obtain, because several states, including Britain, refuse to cede sovereignty in this area. Britain and Ireland have quite different reasons for seeking to limit the development of a common foreign and security policy. British governments fear that their freedom of action, and in particular their freedom to cooperate with the United States in foreign and defence policy, would be constrained by the need to seek a European consensus. Ireland has a policy of strict neutrality, so a common foreign and security policy risks breaking that neutrality by associating them with interventionist policies abroad.

This contrast is reflected in attitudes towards NATO. Britain continues to regard NATO as the foundation of both British and European defence, and has always argued that giving top priority to NATO is essential to keeping the United States committed to the defence of Europe. Britain has therefore tended to oppose the emergence of any European capability which has been separate from NATO. There have been some exceptions to this, such as the cooperation between France and Britain announced by Blair and Chirac at the St Malo Conference in 1998. This opened the way to the development of the European Security and Defence Policy (ESDP) and the emergence of strategic planning capability and even the deployment of some European forces. Britain consistently opposed the French desire for a European force that would be separate from the United States and NATO and would allow Europe to chart an independent path. The French vision articulated by Dominique de Villepin during the Iraq war that there should be a number of regional poles contrasted sharply with Tony Blair's view that there should be only one pole, the United States, and that Europe should develop its military and strategic capabilities not to challenge the United States but to be a more effective support to American policies in the world (Riddell, 2003).

The St Malo summit, coming as it did at the beginning of the Blair premiership, seemed to promise much closer Franco/British cooperation on defence matters, and for a time it did so, leading to fears among British Atlanticists that Blair was undermining the Atlantic Alliance. Military cooperation was always a prime example of functional differentiated integration since many members of the EU did not want to be significantly involved in it if it meant a commitment to the deployment of military force. But the progress was much less than hoped because of the major foreign policy crisis which developed over the Iraq war, with Britain, Spain and Italy strongly supporting the United States, and France and Germany strongly opposed. The issue was complicated by the fact that while most public opinion in 'old Europe' was strongly against the war, several governments still aligned themselves with the USA, while in 'new Europe' many of the new and aspirant members from east and central Europe were strongly pro-American.

Any ESDP needed British and French cooperation to be successful since these two countries had the most significant military capabilities in Europe, and the political will to use them. But the possibility of progress was constantly hampered by the disagreement between France and Britain over the role of the United States, and whether Europe should be its partner or rival. It was also severely impeded by those states who either had neutralism written into their constitutions, like Ireland and Austria, or were wary of any intervention involving military force.

The election of Barack Obama as US President in 2008 and the decision by France to rejoin the command structure of NATO raised hopes for a new phase of cooperation on ESDP, anchored in the British view that the primary purpose of ESDP is to complement and support NATO and the Atlantic Alliance, not replace them. This may permit greater differentiated integration in this area to emerge in the future.

Earlier initiatives that followed the same pattern include the Western European Union, which was first set up by the Treaty of Brussels in 1948 and existed as a form of differentiated integration to a large extent separate from EU structures. By 1954 the member countries included France, the UK and Germany. The core members were all eventually members of both NATO and the EU. Some other countries such as Ireland, Austria and Sweden had observer status but did not possess voting rights. Under the Treaty of Amsterdam it was envisaged that the WEU might form the core of an independent European defence capability, but after 2000 it became subsumed under the ESDP.

The advantages of European collaboration in the defence and security fields, including defence procurement and space programmes, have always been evident and new initiatives are launched from time to time. These include the European Space Agency, and various technology projects, such as Galileo and Ariane. The United Kingdom has been involved in all these, but its commitment has often been lower than some other states, notably France. The tendency of the UK to look west to the United States has limited the enthusiasm of British governments to invest heavily in European programmes.

The reason why the existence of Anglo-America constantly hampers European cooperation is because ever since their wartime alliance with the United States the British have given priority to their strong working relationships with the Americans in the defence, intelligence and diplomatic communities. The links with European countries are not so great. This is why the British can so often appear as an arm of US policy. Peter Riddell has observed that British foreign policy conducted by every post-war British government, with the possible exception of that of Edward Heath, has given priority to maintaining insider influence in Washington (Riddell, 2003; Hitchens, 2004). This has meant that public disagreements with the Americans are kept to a minimum. It has been extremely rare for British leaders to criticize American policy or dissent from it, particularly in recent years. Both Thatcher and Blair as a result were accused of being poodles to the Americans, but their policies did not arise from weakness but out of a calculation that this was the way to exert most influence and safeguard Britain's most enduring interests, and also out of a conviction that the only way to maintain the security of the West was to accept US leadership.

Justice and human affairs

The justice and human affairs pillar in the Maastricht Treaty originally included items such as asylum, external borders, immigration, and police and judicial cooperation. Some of these were transferred to the first pillar following the Treaty of Amsterdam, and all have now been consolidated in the Lisbon Treaty, although given the Irish rejection this has yet to come into force. In general the British have been keen to promote police and judicial cooperation across Europe, and the third pillar has suited British interests well because decisions have been taken by qualified majority voting in the Council of Ministers, allowing the six largest states to dominate and accommodate each others' interests. The security threat after 9/11 has made such cooperation still more urgent and desirable, especially to governments which acknowledge a significant terrorist threat. Integration here has been pushed ahead through the inter-governmental mechanism of the Council of Ministers.

The British have been much less keen to become involved in common European policies on borders, immigration and asylum. They were not willing to sign the Schengen Agreement, which abolished border controls between its signatories, and when Schengen was incorporated in the Amsterdam Treaty, Britain and Ireland both opted out of its provisions. Britain refused to abandon controls over its borders, and insisted on its right to police them. This power was regarded in Britain as one of the most important functions of the nation-state, and could not be abandoned given the level of public anxiety about immigration. In practical terms refusing to accept Schengen made little practical difference, since the number of immigrants, particularly from other EU countries and the new entrants, rose to record levels in the early years of the 21st century (Geddes, 2002). Under EU law Britain could not refuse to admit EU citizens. But the symbolism of Britain still being in charge of its borders was deemed essential in British domestic politics.

The position in Ireland was rather different. The Irish would almost certainly have signed the Schengen Agreement, but they were constrained by the Common Travel Area they enjoyed with the UK. Although Ireland had formally separated from the UK in 1922, the UK continued to treat Irish citizens as though they were British citizens. This has led to many anomalies, some of which have been removed by later legislation, but some of which persist. One of the benefits of the continuing close relationship was the maintenance of a Common Travel Area between the two countries which was like a mini-Schengen Agreement. It meant there were no border or immigration controls between the two countries, but this required that Ireland implement British immigration policy – in effect the two states continued to operate a common border – and as far as UK law was concerned Ireland continued to be treated as though it were part of the United Kingdom. Apart from the free movement of British and Irish citizens within the whole area of Ireland and the United Kingdom, the particular benefit as far as the Irish were concerned was the open border with Northern Ireland. The disadvantage was that whenever the United Kingdom changed its immigration policy Ireland had to follow suit if it wished to preserve the Common Travel Area. Ireland could have signed the Schengen Agreement and abolished border controls with the rest of the EU, but this would have meant abandoning the Common Travel Area with the UK. Maintaining the Common Travel Area has so far been of greater importance to Ireland. There are suggestions that this may change in the future, particularly if the UK creates electronic borders, but so far Irish politicians have denied that there are plans to abolish the Common Travel Area, in part because of fears that a border might then be imposed between the South and the North.

The Common Travel Area is an example of differentiated integration, in which Ireland continues to function as though it were part of the United Kingdom, rather than part of the European Union. This particular pattern, and the opt-out associated with it, will persist as long as Britain stays outside the Schengen Agreement, and given the sensitivity of immigration and asylum in UK domestic politics, this is unlikely to change. It is also an example of how the common law traditions of the two countries still bind them together.

Monetary policy

A very different picture presents itself on monetary policy. Here Ireland has broken away from its former dependence on Britain, and joined the euro. This was a remarkably bold political decision, given the dependence of the Irish economy on both the British economy and the US economy. Ireland is relatively less well integrated into the eurozone, and some economists doubted the wisdom of Ireland being part of the eurozone at all, given the nature of its economy, and the fact that its economic cycle seemed more aligned with the cycle in the UK and the

US than with the rest of the eurozone (Thom, 2002). These economists agreed that Ireland should no longer tie their currency to the British pound, accepting the monetary policy laid down by the Bank of England and the British Treasury. Instead they favoured Ireland pursuing an independent course, setting interest rates and conducting its monetary policy in accordance with what seemed best for the Irish economy. The Irish had joined the ERM at the beginning, but had found the constraints it imposed increasingly hard to handle in the 1990s, and had been forced to devalue the Irish pound by 10 per cent in 1993. Despite this experience, Irish politicians had no hesitation in committing Ireland to join the euro in the first wave, although, as economists pointed out, within the euro no devaluations were possible, and the Irish government would have to live with whatever interest rate the ECB decided was best for the whole eurozone. The government chose not to dwell on the problems this might cause one day for the Irish economy.

The Irish hoped that Britain would not exercise its opt-out agreed at Maastricht, and would join the euro, if not in the first wave, then subsequently. The UK was such an important market for Ireland that a common currency would be desirable, not to mention the fact that if the UK remained outside the eurozone there would be a potential new source of division with Northern Ireland. John Major's Conservative government contained several ministers, including the Deputy Prime Minister, Michael Heseltine, and the Chancellor, Kenneth Clarke, who were strong supporters of Britain joining the euro without a referendum, in the same way that the Thatcher government had eventually joined the ERM. But in the 1992–7 Parliament the Conservative Party was in a state of civil war over Europe and the Maastricht Treaty in particular, and John Major was not strong enough to deliver his party and government to early euro entry. Instead he played for time and promised a referendum, which the Labour opposition matched. Once in government Labour gave priority to establishing its reputation for economic competence and fiscal prudence, and Gordon Brown as Chancellor decided that the political risks of early euro entry were too high. Tony Blair wanted to take the political risk because it would commit Britain to be a full player in Europe, and end Britain's detachment. But he could not convince his Chancellor and the moment when a referendum might have been held and won slipped away (Gamble and Kelly, 2002).

For Britain as for Ireland the economic argument for being part of the eurozone was never as strong as the political argument. The British and Irish economies have similar economic cycles, a much greater dependence on trade with the United States than is common with other European economies, a financial structure which is prone to financial bubbles, particularly in housing, and high levels of personal debt. This is linked as well to institutional and ideological traits which make the British and Irish economies resemble both each other and the United States more than they do other European economies. In political economy terms these are recognisably the same type of capitalism, distinct from the Nordic model or the German or French model (Coates, 2000).

The Irish boom of the 1990s, the phenomenon of the Celtic Tiger (Kirby, 2002; Cassidy, 2002; O'Hearn, 2001), illustrates this well. An economy which under

British rule had remained underdeveloped, and had been primarily a source of primary products and simple manufactures, with a very high rate of emigration, had continued to languish in the decades following independence, despite the adoption of highly protectionist and interventionist economic policies. What transformed Ireland's position was membership of the EU, although not immediately. When Ireland joined in 1973 Irish GDP was generally below 70 per cent of the EU average. As recently as 1986 it was only 64 per cent. Twenty years later Ireland had closed the gap and was bidding to become one of the richest economies in the EU. The transformation was achieved from the end of the 1980s onwards, when Ireland adopted a new strategy aimed at attracting inward investment, particularly from the United States. The strategy involved very low business tax rates (10 per cent) across the board, specific location incentives and subsidies. The relative strength of the Irish trade unions, compared with the strength of the unions in the US and the post-Thatcher UK, meant that this aspect of the neo-liberal model was not present in Ireland. In its place the Irish government developed a social partnership policy, which involved corporatist involvement of the unions in a wage strategy which prevented wage demands from threatening corporate profits and growth (Kirby, 2002).

The results were dramatic. Ireland achieved consistently high growth rates through the 1990s, and unemployment was drastically reduced. Critics argued that Ireland was a one-off, since it was attracting a huge proportion of the available US investment in the IT sector, which was attracted to Ireland because of its low taxes, business-friendly environment, access to the European Union, stable industrial relations, plentiful supply of labour, and subsequently membership of the eurozone. There was less evidence of a permanent improvement in the productivity or the number of indigenous Irish manufacturing enterprises, leading to fears that the inward investment boom might stop as suddenly as it had started, leaving Ireland with relatively little to fall back on. The advantage Ireland derived from its low tax policies became a target in the EU debate on tax harmonization, with even signs that Britain was keen to see some restraints imposed because of the relocation of businesses to Ireland.

The 2008 crash transformed the economic policy landscape. But before it struck there was no doubting the success of the Irish economy, in marked contrast to the sluggish performance of most other European economies. The IMF and OECD and the business press held up Ireland as an example of what could be achieved by a small country willing to accept the constraints and opportunities of globalization.

The British economic miracle was much more muted than the Irish, but it had some of the same features, particularly a reliance on inward investment, and a neo-liberal strategy to adjust the economy and society to the perceived threats and challenges of globalization. Like the Irish economy the British economy enjoyed uninterrupted growth in the 1990s, the longest boom in British economic history, but which finally ended in 2008. The British and Irish achievements were both hailed as examples of the success of Anglo-Saxon or Anglo-American capitalism. The model that had been regarded as lagging in the 1980s now seemed to lead the field. The British in particular sought to export their model to the rest of the EU, and had some success, particularly in the adoption of the Lisbon agenda in 2001.

As the example of the Lisbon agenda shows, the notion that there are radically different models of capitalism in the EU has to be treated with care. Although there is no likelihood of a convergence on to a common set of institutions and practices, the power of neo-liberal ideas is very strong, and the EU has adopted a neo-liberal rhetoric, although the willingness of its members to implement neo-liberal reforms remains patchy (Haller, 2008). What is noticeable within neo-liberal discourse is that there are significant differences in policy options, even within the Anglo-Saxon countries. Most actual national political economies are in any case hybrids, so that different sectors may be more strongly associated with one particular model of capitalism than others. Nevertheless the distinction between liberal market economies and coordinated market economies (Hall and Soskice, 2001) remains a useful one, as does the earlier distinction between different worlds of welfare capitalism (Esping-Andersen, 1990). A further important distinction is between the role which financial and capital markets play in national economies, and with them the proneness of economies to financial bubbles and financial instabilities. All of these characteristics can be observed in Ireland and the United Kingdom, and they are characteristics they share with the United States. The main differences in the Irish case, as already discussed, are its industrial relations system, and its membership of the eurozone.

Anglosphere Europe: the temporal dimension

The temporal dimension of differentiated integration in relation to Britain and Ireland is intertwined with the other dimensions. The timing of the decision by Britain to apply for membership of the EU affected the outcome, and delayed British and Irish entry until the 1970s. Had Britain been part of the original negotiations to set up the European Community, a very different Europe might have emerged. The failure to integrate Britain at the outset had a major long-term impact on the European project because of Britain's size and importance, and it made differentiated integration as the solution to the problems of such a diverse union more likely.

Temporal issues are also involved in many of the specific functional areas. A series of contingencies, such as the forced departure of sterling from the ERM in 1992, and the decision by first John Major (for internal party reasons) and then Tony Blair (for electoral reasons) to promise a referendum before Britain adopted the euro, ruled out Britain's entry in the first wave. If Britain had remained in the ERM it would almost certainly have adopted the euro.

Defence and security issues have been powerfully affected by the temporal dimension. There was little prospect of much serious European cooperation on defence outside NATO while the Cold War was still going on. But once the Cold War was over, a very different conjuncture emerged, one in which, with the demise of the Soviet Union, a more active and independent European force became thinkable. But how far this would develop was always dependent on the strength of the Franco-German relationship, as Alastair Cole points out in Chapter 11 of this volume. The Anglo-French relationship tended to be strong when the Franco-German relationship was weak and weak when it was strong. The terrorist attacks of 9/11 also changed everything by creating a new security emergency which the United States responded to in a way which was to divide its allies, and particularly its European allies.

The most important impact of the temporal dimension, however, lies in its interaction with the spatial dimension. The temporalities associated with the Anglosphere, with Anglo-Irish relations and with the relations of Britain to the rest of Europe are exceedingly complex, but structure all the attempts to secure greater integration in Europe, and help explain why differentiated integration has been increasingly the way in which the project has developed.

The notion of the Anglosphere popularized by American neo-conservatives (Bennett, 2004) treats the English-speaking countries as a network Commonwealth, which share common language, common traditions, common institutions and common values. The countries of the Anglosphere are more like one another, it is claimed, than they are like any other group of countries, and this implies that they should act to strengthen the links between them. The kind of capitalism the Anglosphere countries have developed is said to be distinctive (and successful) because of the strong emphasis placed on civil society rather than on the state, which contributes to a climate of enterprise, high levels of trust, individual dynamism and creativity. This kind of capitalism is flexible, innovative and characterized by greater degree of inequality than in the more solidaristic European capitalisms. Welfare expenditures are relatively low, and greater emphasis is placed on individual self-reliance, although there is a social minimum. The state plays at best an enabling role.

In terms of differentiated integration in the EU, the notion of the Anglosphere in part reflects certain patterns, particularly in the area of political economy and the model of capitalism established in both Ireland and the United Kingdom. But it works much less well for security matters, where the positions of the United Kingdom and Ireland are radically different. Irish neutralism stems from the history of its relationship with the United Kingdom, and even when the United States replaced Britain as the leading world power, it did not change Irish attitudes. Despite the very close links between Ireland and America, there is no likelihood of the Irish becoming partners in American-led military interventions.

If Scotland were to become independent at some point in the future, this would impart a further dynamic to relationships of differentiated integration in this region. One consequence would be the amount of integration/disintegration with the former territory of the United Kingdom, and a second would be the amount of integration/disintegration with the rest of the EU. As can be seen in relation to Ireland, the resulting pattern could be quite complex, reflecting different arrangements in political economy, justice and home affairs, and external security in the separate nation-states. But as the result of the Irish referendum on the Lisbon Treaty showed, there is no automatic majority support for further integration in the EU in any of the potential states in Atlantic Europe. For this group of countries, the present strong current of Euroscepticism will both encourage further differentiated integration in the EU, and further cooperation with the other English-speaking nations.

As far as Britain and Ireland are concerned, differentiated integration has strengthened the existing bond between these two states, but weakened it in others. Differentiated integration has given opportunities to Ireland which it did not previously have to escape from dependence on Britain and forge new links and networks. In other respects Ireland has converged still more closely with Britain, and diverges from the rest of the EU, for example, in its embrace of an extreme version of the financial growth model pioneered in the Anglosphere. Britain was always wary of further steps to deepen European integration, and by securing opt-outs for some crucial policies, Britain was one of the key architects of differentiated integration. It became clear the Union could not move as one in some areas. Britain's position was complicated, however, because it was willing to participate in differentiated integration in some areas, particularly security and defence. The more that differentiated integration proceeds the harder it becomes to present the EU as a common project. The awkwardness was apparent at the G20 summit in April 2009 with Britain, France, Germany and Italy all claiming their seats as independent players, alongside a separate seat for the EU. The conspicuous lack of a common will or leadership should make the EU a less frightening phenomenon to Eurosceptics, but there is not much sign of it yet. The effects of differentiated integration on the politics of European integration are that the Union will become increasingly diffuse, yet still able to mount concerted action in particular areas. Differentiated integration means that in some areas very deep integration can occur. In present circumstances Britain and Ireland will be involved in a few of these areas but not the majority.

8
Balkan Europe

Spyros Economides

Introduction

Most studies of differentiated integration are confined within the framework of the European Union. The EU/Balkan relationship allows for the possibility that differentiated integration can apply to a set of links between the EU and a cluster of external states.

If differentiated integration has any relevance to the EU/Balkan relationship three key points need to be made. First, differentiated integration in the Balkans results from the interests and policy preferences of existing EU members. Balkan states, if given the option, would choose immediate and full membership of the EU, but they would not willingly adopt polices of differentiated integration. The range and depth of EU involvement in the Balkans has been such since 1991 that, arguably, there has been an *imposition* of differentiated integration on the region by the EU. If differentiated integration shows how European states pursue integration at different speeds, in the case of the Balkans it shows how European states opt *for other (non-EU) states* to integrate at different speeds.

Second, if differentiated integration in the Balkans is cast in the context of enlargement, we have to emphasize the essentially political nature of this process: there is very little that is technical or functional in the EU's decisions to treat the Balkans through a process of differentiated integration. Differentiated integration is a direct manifestation of political strategies for managing a range of so-called Balkan problems – ethnic rivalries, irredentism, separatism, war, democratization, institution-building. This complex set of problems in the Balkans, in conjunction with the range of interests of EU members and the lack of applicable instruments in the EU, is the cause of differentiated integration.

Third is the EU's insistence on treating the Balkans as a region. There are historical and psychological reasons why this is the case: some of them emanate from Yugoslavia's wars of disintegration, others from the more distant past; some are real, others perceived. Differentiated integration in this regionalist context has two implications: 1) The Balkans are treated differently from other European regions in the course of European enlargement; 2) Although there is a great raft of regionalism embedded in the EU's Balkan policies, the EU differentiates between parts of the Balkans in terms of integration.

This chapter initially looks at the context of the EU/Balkan relationship and traces the origins of the need for a policy of differentiated integration. The chapter will also consider the EU/Balkan relationship through the context of widening and examine the actual policies of the EU towards the region, focusing on the Stability Pact for South Eastern Europe (SP), now transformed into the Regional Co-operation Council (RCC), the Stabilisation and Association Process (SAP), and ultimately the enlargement process proper. There seems to be no better evidence of differentiated integration than this mix of policies which draw individual members of the Balkans towards the EU at different speeds. The regionalism element will also be examined to evaluate to what extent a functional form of integration has taken root in the Balkans. Is this regional approach realistic and does it serve the interests of the EU rather than those of Balkan states? The conclusion is that differentiated integration is at play in the Balkans, especially in temporal and spatial terms, but that the concept of differentiated integration can only be valid if it is agreed that the process can take place beyond the borders of the EU.

Context

EU Balkan policy is framed by two essential spatial questions. What is the Balkans? Where do we want our own (EU) territorial limits to be? These questions are important for two reasons. First, the EU formulates policies which address Balkan states as a territorial cluster and urges these states to adopt regional cooperation as a key step in their 'European perspective', while simultaneously differentiating between states in their approach to candidacy or prospective membership of the EU. Second, differentiated integration also results from an upsurge in the debate within the EU on the limits of EU enlargement. If indeed the EU is trying to build states in the Balkans, tie them together regionally and transcend ethnic and national rifts to bring them closer to the European mainstream, these are being undermined by European hostility to further enlargement.

What has to be addressed is how exactly the Balkans have been viewed in terms of identity and territory by Europe and what effect that this will have on the further widening and deepening of the European project. This is crucial in establishing how and why differentiated integration is occurring in the Balkans and whether the region is treated in a radically different way to other aspiring members of the EU.

Contemporary definitions of 'the Balkans' have changed, especially because of the relationship with the EU. The consensus is that the 'modern Balkans' are made up of Albania, Bulgaria, Greece, Romania, Turkey and Yugoslavia (and its successor states). When Yugoslavia disintegrated, the most northern constituent republics, Slovenia and Croatia, attempted to distance themselves as rapidly as possible from the Balkans, appropriating a Central European, 'Habsburg' heritage. Nevertheless, they still have a deep Balkan heritage as well as being part of the Balkan politico-economic nexus. It is also noteworthy that many Balkan states share a

Mediterranean background as well, and this is not limited to the obvious cases of Greece or Turkey. Croatia is just as much a Mediterranean state as Albania.

Ideationally, the Balkans have proved an easy target for western Europe. From the assassination of Archduke Franz Ferdinand to the violent collapse of Yugoslavia, modern Balkan history is easily condemnable. The phrases 'Balkan powder keg' or 'cockpit of Europe's wars' are readily trotted out, almost caricaturing the region. The long-term western perception of the Balkans is not only of a troubled region but also an alien one. An imposter in Europe's midst; geographically in Europe but in attitudes and actions not of Europe. Some dispute this strongly, arguing that in fact what has been created in western minds is 'an imagined Balkans' (Todorova, 1997). What is real is that the Balkans, and its inhabitants, stir up set, negative reactions in European circles, and the events of the 1990s reinforced them.

This is underlined by the religious dimension of the Balkans' topography; a meeting place not only of Christianity and Islam, but also of 'western' and 'eastern' Christianity, Roman Catholicism and Orthodoxy. It is not accidental that Samuel Huntington drew his civilizational 'fault line' through the heart of the Balkans, distinguishing east from west. The resulting assumption is that eastern Christianity, whose adherents include Serbs, Bulgarians, Greeks and others, is civilizationally almost as distant from, if not incompatible with, western Christianity, as is Islam.

How does this translate into a contemporary understanding of what the Balkans are and what impact it has had on EU policies towards the region? In other words, to what extent have these negative attitudes, built on a series of historical perceptions, influenced how the EU had involved itself in the Balkans?[1] Clearly, the answer is enormously complex, especially as a result of the breakdown of Yugoslavia, the most recent 'round' in the development of the Balkans' international personality.

As federal Yugoslavia descended into bloody conflict, Europe was going through a different and equally radical transformation. In the East, the collapse of communism and the path towards democratization was in the main peacefully conducted (and celebrated as such). Significant change was also occurring in the West: the European project continued apace with the finalization of the Maastricht Treaty and the creation of the EU. In grand terms this was the re-creation of Europe, not only a spatial or territorial re-creation, but also a cultural and ideological one. On the surface of it, the nation-state was also being overwhelmed by this tide of change. The European project, in its universalist mode,[2] was rendering the nation-state unimportant if not redundant. The end of communism did lead to the re-assertion of ethnic identity and nationalism in some states. But this bowed to the power of democratic values and systems (and the reconstitution of a European space seemingly built on these).

Simultaneously, this euphoria – and self-satisfaction – was undermined by a European war being waged in a space bordering both East and West Europe. It was difficult to understand how this could be. The easy retort was to return to the explanation of the 'imagined Balkans'; a stereotyped response explaining away Yugoslavia's wars based on old assumptions about a very 'un-European' part of the continent (Kaplan, 1993). Consequently, Europe's attitudes to the Balkans were conditioned by the reactions to Yugoslavia's wars of dissolution.

'The Balkans' became a catch-all, pejorative term for a region whose core was at war. As conflict engulfed Yugoslavia, the rest of the region was perceived to be heading the same way, supposedly wrought by the same age-old animosities. The war in Yugoslavia was seen as a Balkan war (Glenny, 1993)

The main reason for the conflation of Yugoslavia and the Balkans was the lack of a distinction made between the geo-strategic threats or consequences of Yugoslavia's disintegration and the socio-cultural issues underpinning potential regional unrest. The mainstream view had it that Yugoslavia's wars – and hence the essence of Balkan politics – were a nationalist struggle (an anachronism in the world of advanced European integration). Two points arise here. First, Yugoslavia's problems at this level were not the problems of the Balkans as a whole. Romania and Bulgaria, for example, were not held captive by ethnic issues in the same way as Yugoslavia's republics, nor were their own potential flashpoints considered as volatile. Second, there is a convincing argument that Yugoslavia's demise was not attributable to a simple formula of ethnic rivalries, but a much more subtle and complex interplay of economic, political and constitutional issues at work in a specific domestic and international context (Woodward, 1995)

Therefore, from 1991, the causes and consequences of Yugoslavia's breakdown were considered Balkan problems and a de facto negative perception of the region was born. Unable to reach consensus on what action to take, and lacking strong instruments of persuasion and coercion, the EU settled for a policy of containment of war, refugees and economic migrants, spanning the whole region. Containment became the dominant EU policy towards the Balkans until well into the second half of the decade. Arguably, this began a particular policy of differentiated integration, one of keeping the Balkan states out of the EU (unlike the Central and Eastern European [CEE] states which were being drawn in much more quickly). It was only after the end of the war in Bosnia, that Balkan states – Slovenia, Romania and Bulgaria – entered into association agreements with the EU, and subsequently began accession negotiations. What bound the Balkans together was an external perception of what they shared in common, rather than an internally generated belief in common interests and goals based on geographical and cultural bonds.

The second aspect of this regionalism was the realization in western European circles that the term 'the Balkans' had taken on such negative connotations that it had become unhelpful. Consequently, the term Southeastern Europe (SEE) supplanted 'the Balkans' in EU terminology. In this new regional context, the EU found it easier to initiate separate sets of relations with separate states and groups of states in the region. The 'Eastern Balkans', that is Romania and Bulgaria, were granted their own distinct route to EU membership: they applied for EU membership in December 1995, the Luxembourg European Council of December 1997 issued a favourable *avis* and negotiations for full membership began in early 2000.[3] Slovenia too had followed a different path and its approaches to the EU were viewed much more favourably both because of its ability to meet accession criteria and the *acquis* but also because of strong support from within the EU (Gow and Carmichael, 2000).[4]

In fact, what we had progressively from the late 1990s was a shrinking region, being broken down into more basic elements. By the end of the Kosovo crisis we moved from a general Balkan region, or that of SEE, to a very specific *policy-relevant* region known as the Western Balkans (WB). The formulaic, 'the WB is the states of former Yugoslavia minus Slovenia and plus Albania' became a mantra among EU officials. In reality, the WB became *the Balkans* in terms of the EU and of our interest in differentiated integration (Delevic, 2007).

Therefore in spatial terms, the 'region' we are dealing with is a state cluster known as the WB, created from the remnants of federal Yugoslavia and united under this rubric of WB to differentiate it from Romania, Bulgaria and Slovenia which progressed to EU membership more rapidly (if not always smoothly in the case of the first two). The logic of the cluster is that these are 'problem' states with a long way to go before making a realistic application for EU membership. Different states in the WB are on different trajectories to EU membership and a variety of initiatives implemented by the EU are at play with respect to the WB. A key initiative is the EU's Regional Approach, pushing the WB states into forms of regional cooperation, to be met if they wish to pursue deeper, contractual relations with the EU. So the WB is not a region which shares natural characteristics either in terms of identity, culture or politico-economic development. Albania is different to Croatia which is different to FYROM (Macedonia). What binds these states together are: geographical proximity; a common and troubled recent history; late post-communist politico-economic development; and, most importantly, the EU policy of grouping them together. Territorially the EU defines the WB partly on the grounds of location and proximity but mainly on the basis of a troubled recent past. There may be economies of scope to be gained by regional economic initiatives, even though this is in question (Delevic, 2007: 13–14) but the regionalism promoted by the EU is based primarily on getting 'hostile' states to cooperate (while their entry to the EU is delayed for a variety of reasons).

This leads to the second spatial issue: Where does enlargement stop? This is crucial for spatially differentiated integration with respect to the Balkans. The WB countries have for some time seen both the EU accession of other SEE states, and the EU's insistence on regional cooperation, as indications that their prospects of accession are dim. Is the insistence on regional cooperation a means by which to speed up the move towards the EU or for constructing a form of regional integration which will act as a substitute for EU enlargement (albeit with preferential sectoral agreements with the EU)? These fears multiply as the EU proposes a series of new contractual arrangements for the WB, short of accession agreements.

For at least two reasons EU enlargement to the WB is caught up with wider debates on Europe's geographical and political limits. The perceived limits of the WB's 'Europeanness' as embodied in, for example, Serbia's difficult relationship with the EU over the International Criminal Tribunal for the former Yugoslavia (ICTY) and Kosovo, acts as a brake on the whole region's EU future. Similarly, the debate on Turkey's European credentials both in terms of geography/religion/

culture and the institutional politico-economic implications of it joining the EU, have entangled the WB in their web (witness Croatia's accession negotiations). In other words, the WB states stress that while they are considered geographically European, confirmed by the EU through the 'European perspective', they are often marginalized because their behaviour is considered 'un-European'. Turkey, by comparison, offers a different dilemma. For the WB this is immensely frustrating. Geographically it is European, it ostensibly has a European future in EU terms, yet is sidelined by a European fixation with the future of Turkey. They might well conclude that who joins the EU depends on what the interests of the existing members are and not on the credentials of the applicants. The limits of Europe, in other words, are highly political and politicized; our understanding of geography is flexible.

Therefore, the spatial dimension of differentiated integration is influenced by two features, one relating to our understanding of the Balkans and another to our vision of the territorial limits of European integration. What there was of the Balkans has been shrinking. What remains is a rump SEE commonly referred to as the WB which is the locus of the EU's policies of differentiated integration. In the next section I will highlight how the Balkans have shrunk as a result of EU policies, examine policies developed by the EU for the SEE and WB, and argue that indeed the temporal aspect of differentiated integration is a key feature of EU policy in the region.

From Southeastern Europe to the Western Balkans

Perhaps there have been too many EU policies towards the Balkans since the mid-1990s. These initiatives have had three primary objectives: reconstruction, state- and institution-building, and EU membership itself. Ostensibly, the Commission has applied a variety of tools in implementing these initiatives with a view to promoting membership of the EU for all SEE states. In practice, these initiatives have been at play simultaneously. While some states such as Romania, Bulgaria and Slovenia have achieved membership through a traditional route, other Balkans states are faced with the prospect of a variety of different agreements prior to reaching the 'Holy Grail' of entry negotiations.

For the WB states, for example, European Partnerships and Stabilisation and Association Agreements (SAA) are stepping stones on the path to potential candidacy of the EU. The EU has differentiated between these states and others in SEE. This results in a form of spatial differentiated integration, where the WB is lagging behind other parts of SEE in accession terms. A new territorial cluster – a European space – has been created as a result and it is the object of substantial EU policy. This has also created a specific timeline or temporal differentiated integration terms, where some states are moving towards potential EU accession more rapidly than others.

On the surface, this supports Goetz's observation about temporally differentiated integration which 'differs from "variable geometry" and an *á la carte approach* in that it does not question common objectives' (Chapter 5 in this volume): it allows some to move ahead more quickly than others while goals remain the same. The common goal is EU membership – all SEE states want this. This, we are constantly reminded by the Commission, is the stated intention of the EU (Thessaloniki Agenda, 2003). The most often used analogy to describe the process of enlargement to WB is that of a 'regatta not a convoy' (*The Economist*, 2006): there is a defined finishing line towards which all are striving but some will get there sooner than others. What is not developed in this analogy is the fact that some of the contestants in the regatta may fall foul of the rules or run into inclement weather, or more importantly that the rules of the regatta may change or further legs be added, lengthening the run to the finishing line. Many see this as the evolving EU policy towards WB. While some states progress to EU membership through the established route of Europe Agreements and accession negotiations, the WB states are asked to negotiate and adhere to a series of 'pre-agreements', before contemplating applying for full membership. Some see this as a case of obstructionist tactics, others as a more permanent obstacle to EU membership. Either way it enhances the notion of spatially differentiated integration and creates a parallel process of temporally defined differentiated integration.

Objectives, policies and instruments

Objectives

EU policy towards SEE has had three major objectives: reconstruction; state and institution-building; and EU membership. Logically, states would sequentially move through these three phases and become full members of the Union. In SEE, these three processes have been occurring simultaneously since the mid-1990s. Before analysing and illustrating the policies used to achieve these objectives – and their timing – we briefly need to explain these three processes.

Reconstruction in the Balkan context is fundamentally important for two obvious reasons. The first is shared by all post-communist states in Europe; the reconstruction of devastated economies was an attempt to provide basic economic remedies to long-term economic ills, and foundations for the process of transition. Additionally, the starting threshold of SEE economic development was substantially lower than the CEE countries. But SEE also had to contend with the consequences of war in Yugoslavia. Reconstruction was both physical and 'economic'. Funds were devoted to the physical reconstruction of infrastructure and plant destroyed during Yugoslavia's wars or of the decayed and degraded infrastructure that had proved impossible to repair because of war. The physical effects of Yugoslavia's wars were also felt regionally as intra-regional trade ceased; routine maintenance of infrastructure proved difficult and international trade embargoes and sanctions affected all states in the region. The most relevant of the EU's initiatives in this field was the SP.

State and institution-building, in this context, refers to something different than preparation for entry negotiations. One could term it democratization, where the state is readied politically and institutionally for the process of candidacy – let alone accession – to begin. Whether it be reform of the judicial system in Croatia, the handing over of indicted war criminals to ICTY in Serbia, or the reduction of corruption/criminality (an ongoing issue in Romania and Bulgaria), these are normative and functional issues to be dealt with before EU membership is considered. This is not 'a new form of polity-building' through European integration (see Chapter 4 in this volume by Keating) but the establishment – and acceptance – of ground rules and institutions for integration to ensue. Therefore, this is democratization as an ideal, rather than democratization for the purposes of immediate accession to the EU. A good example of the tool used to promote this policy is that of the SAA, which holds out as an incentive for reform the possibility of candidacy for membership, as well as significant economic assistance, but no guarantees and much conditionality.

Lastly, we have the actual accession or EU membership, from which Slovenia, Romania and Bulgaria have benefited. This is the easiest to define, and illustrate. Certain states were deemed ready for accession negotiations and ultimately membership by the EU. Having fulfilled the required criteria and adopted the *acquis* they were inducted into the club. For Slovenia, this was a relatively swift process, for Romania and Bulgaria rather more drawn out. What is more relevant here is why these states were propelled down a different path from others in SEE and what this tells us about differentiated integration.

Policies and instruments

The SP was agreed at the Cologne European Council in June 1999 and launched, symbolically, in Sarajevo at the end of July. An EU initiative, it drew together 28 states and 17 International Financial Institutions (IFIs) and international organizations, to 'develop a shared strategy for stability and growth of the region ... and to accelerate democratic and economic development in the region' (SCSP Constituent Document, 1999).[5] It was the first time in a decade that the EU had launched a proactive policy towards the Balkans, meaning to provide a focal point for its strategy towards the region. The regional approach was a key element, focusing on the SEE as a whole, including Romania and Bulgaria. While the initial objectives of the Pact were laudably high, including democratization, human rights and security issues, as well as providing the region with an interim stepping stone on the path towards 'Euro-Atlantic integration', its activities concentrated on reconstruction and the jump-starting of economic development. The first donor conference, held by the SP in March 2000, launched the 'Quick Start' programme, inviting donors to concentrate their funding on 35 schemes, mostly infrastructure projects. It was in this policy area that the SP would concentrate most of its activities.

The other relevant key policy of the Pact is that, through the SP, countries 'commit[ed] themselves to bilateral and regional cooperation among themselves to advance their integration, on an individual basis, into Euro-Atlantic structures' (SCSP Constituent Document, 1999). This was a clear indication that participation in this EU regional initiative was considered an important step towards EU integration for all SEE states (each at their own speed).

The end of the Kosovo intervention in June 1999 allowed the EU to launch a proactive, civilian, policy towards SEE (Friis and Murphy, 2000). This brought into sharp relief the fact that progress towards EU membership by SEE states could only be achieved if staggered and it would be a lengthy – and costly – process. Romania and Bulgaria, although Pact members, pursued their own path to membership and only participated in the hope of securing early accession. The SP thus became the initial forum for the EU's attempts to deal with the economic and political reconstruction and development of the WB. While the situation in Kosovo was still tense and Milosevic remained in power in Serbia, little could be done to put the EU–Balkan relationship on a sounder footing. Other WB states would either refuse to participate while Milosevic was still in power or, as with Croatia, believed they were being held back under the SP (which did not offer them enough in their transition process). In short, the policy of reconstructing and sparking the economic recovery and development of SEE on a regional basis, and thus promoting its European perspective, was weakened by Balkan politics, and by the built-in proviso that each state could pursue its European future at its own pace. When Milosevic fell from power in October 2000, the SP was displaced, not replaced, by a new programme, the SAP – which was more binding and dealt with issues far beyond those tackled in the SP. While it had a significant regional dimension to it, its essence was a prospective contractual relationship between the EU and individual WB states. The Balkans would now shrink from SEE to WB.

The SAP was instituted at the Zagreb summit in November 2000 and built on the EU's Regional Approach of 1997, a declaratory policy in the aftermath of Yugoslavia's wars that laid the groundwork for further initiatives. Apart from regional cooperation, the other two stated aims of the SAP are 'stabilisation and a swift transition to a market economy', and 'the promotion ... of the prospect of EU accession'. The SAP was to move beyond reconstruction and target the WB states for a specific kind of *partnership* with the EU. The EU would offer increasingly closer ties backed up by substantial financial and technical support, and preferential agreements, with the 'prospect of EU accession' as a non-binding possibility. In return, the WB would conduct extensive reforms, fulfil conditionalities, participate in regional cooperation and conform to European and international standards of behaviour. The contractual agreement at the heart of the arrangement was the Stabilisation and Association Agreement (SAA). To help achieve an SAA, the EU was committed to financial assistance to the WB through the CARDS programme,[6] while preferential trade agreements would flow from the signing of an SAA.

The first two signatories of SAAs were FYROM and Croatia in April and October 2001, respectively.[7] While the WB appreciated the novelty of the EU's policy, the SAP was seen mainly as a source of financial assistance and predominantly as a substitute to the 'Europe Agreements' (Phinnemore, 2003). Some saw the SAP as a way of short-circuiting the accession process but it became clear that expectations were not being met as states like Bosnia, Serbia and Albania were nowhere near signing SAAs, and indeed that the SAP was designed as precursor to the accession process rather than as a substitute.

The EU, spurred on by the Greek presidency of 2003 and 'Big Bang' enlargement, moved to add definition to the SAP, 'enrich' it in the language of the Commission, and introduce new instruments (an indication that the EU was increasingly concerned with the inability of certain WB states to progress along the SAP). While the Thessaloniki Agenda added depth and new tools to the SAP, by reinforcing the region's 'European perspective', adding an EU–WB consultative forum and beefing up financial assistance through a new Instrument for Pre-Accession Assistance (IPA), it did nothing to prevent a process of differentiated integration. In one sense differentiated integration was taking place as FYROM and Croatia moved ahead of the rest of the WB pack by becoming candidate countries. In another sense the remaining WB countries perceived that the new 'Europe Partnerships', a new step in the SAP created by Thessaloniki, were a further obstacle rather than boost to their European prospects. This was differentiated integration of a different sort; not only were some WB countries moving ahead, others were seemingly being obstructed from the EU.

More recently, Albania, Bosnia and Herzegovina, Montenegro and Serbia have all signed SAAs and even Kosovo has established an 'SAP-Tracking mechanism'. Differentiated integration is an obvious phenomenon in this process. Either it occurs by design, where countries such as Croatia move ahead with their reform processes and fulfil the conditions set out by the EU through the SAP, or it does not occur at all, either by design or by default. In the first case, Serbia was prevented from signing an SAA primarily because of its unwillingness to meet basic conditions set by the EU (the arrest and extradition of Karadzic and Mladic to ICTY). In the second case, Albania for many years simply could not meet the criteria set out by the EU.

The Accession process is the most obvious of the policies which the EU has employed in the region, but it is not a regional policy. While the EU held out the prospect of candidate status to all SEE countries, encouraging regional cooperation as a pre-condition, enlargement has taken place on a piecemeal basis (and it has worn away the Balkans and hence regionalism with it). Slovenia's accession, in 2003, is a well-documented process. As a result it was not inclined, or forced, to participate in regional initiatives to the extent that others have been. Slovenia applied for membership and was granted candidate status in 1997 and began entry negotiations in 1998. Romania and Bulgaria, although never required to participate in the SAP, were full members of the SP and played a full role in the EU's regional initiatives. Croatia has been a candidate country since June 2004 and began its accession negotiations in October 2005.[8] Similarly, FYROM was granted candidate status in December 2005 but the EU has been unwilling to begin accession negotiations. Therefore, we have various tiers of countries enjoying different levels of contractual relationships with the EU, occurring in different timeframes. There is clear evidence that spatially and temporally differentiated integration is taking place in the Balkan context with different parts of the region moving closer to EU membership at different paces. The region is being redefined by the polices of the EU and the 'regatta' towards accession. SEE has become the WB – which could be eroded in the near future – yet the EU insists on treating it as a region by promoting regional cooperation as a key facet of the 'European perspective'. It seems that the Balkans is no longer a region in spatial or temporal terms – at least not in its relations with the EU. What remains to be seen is whether through regional cooperation, as demanded by the EU, there is any form of functional integration which gives the region meaning.

Regionalism

SEE has been the object of a bewildering variety of regional initiatives since the mid-1990s. The Royaumont Process, the Southeast Europe Cooperation Initiative (SECI) and the South East European Cooperation Process (SEECP) are three examples. In addition, various SEE states participate in the Central European Free Trade Area (CEFTA), the Central European Initiative (CEI), Black Sea Economic Cooperation (BSEC) and the rather more obscure Adriatic–Ionian Initiative, all of which extend beyond the region.

Of relevance to us, we also have the EU-sponsored or -inspired regional initiatives stemming from the Regional Approach of 1997, stating that Balkan peace and stability could only be achieved with extensive regional cooperation. It was a political scheme which was subsequently developed into the SP and became a cornerstone of the SAP. In the latter, regional cooperation became a necessity for SEE and particularly the WB.

By laying down regional cooperation as a principle of relations with the EU, the aim is 'to encourage the countries of the region to behave towards each other and work with each other in a manner comparable to the relationships that now exist between EU Member States' (Regional Approach, 1997). The most publicized and well-funded of these areas of regional cooperation is trade where the EU has encouraged free trade agreements between countries in the region, and applied Autonomous Trade Measures allowing freer access to the EU market. There has been greater success in areas where third (regional) parties have taken a greater stake and invested heavily in the market.

This is not solely a state-driven process. In the financial sector, numerous Greek banks have invested heavily in the retail sector in the WB. The most active has been the National Bank of Greece , which apart from its extensive retail network operation, has acquired majority stakes in banks in Bulgaria, FYROM, Romania and, most recently, Vojvodjanska Bank, which is Serbia's sixth largest. In the field of telecoms, and especially mobile telephony, Austrian telecoms firm Mobilkom has invested heavily in Serbia, becoming the third largest operator there, as well as developing significant interests elsewhere in the region. In the energy sector, a diverse range of EU-based companies are actively engaged in the SEE market. A most interesting and less reported case is that of investment in nuclear energy. Discussions on the energy sector tend to focus on pipeline diplomacy and the possible routes for these conduits bringing Russian oil and gas to the EU market. But for regional electricity power generation, alternative sources of energy such as nuclear are key for the longer term. A good example is that of RWE Power AG, a German company – part of a bigger British-owned group – which has invested heavily in nuclear plants in Bulgaria and Romania. It has taken a 49 per cent stake in the Belene nuclear plant in Bulgaria, worth almost €2 billion, while in Romania it is part of a six-member consortium which has agreed to invest €2.5 billion to add two additional units to the existing Cernavoda nuclear facility.

The EU and especially the Commission react favourably to this activity, considering it a keystone of the policy of enhanced regional cooperation and the stabilizing benefits this brings. The Commission's own activities in the investment sphere, as part of enlargement policy, are focused on cooperation with IFIs such as the EBRD (European Bank for Development and Reconstruction) and the EIB (European Investment Bank). The Commission has also promised the creation of a WB Investment Framework, to be in place by 2010, targeting small and medium-sized enterprises (SMEs). And of course the Commission places great emphasis on the work of the RCC, the successor to the SP, as the hub of much regional activity.

But the Commission is also reluctant or unable to do much more about his particular form of soft power. It channels its own funding activities towards the region through the IPA and attempts to smooth private initiative and the enhancement of market-based economies by highlighting the conditionalities relating to freedom of movement of people, goods, capital and services. Therefore, while it is certainly in the interest of the EU's WB policies to encourage private investment in the region, private investors in the region are often seen as either national champions representing individual EU Member States or indeed simply private enterprises. They certainly are not seen as representatives of the EU with an impact on the prospects of enhanced regional cooperation or enlargement to the region.

The EU's insistence on regional cooperation is undermined by a number of factors. First is that by paying lip service to this aspect of EU conditionality and participating in as wide a range of regional initiatives as possible, states claim compliance with the EU's expectations. Second, in real terms, it is difficult to see where the economics of regional cooperation are going to be successful. Third, while trade creation is a basic feature of regional cooperation and integration policies, the idea that individual WB states will join the EU when and if they can – and ahead of others – is a great incentive for trade diversion. Fourth, some countries believe that regional cooperation is a drag on their European prospects and that they are better off without it. There is also the widespread belief that the EU is fostering regional cooperation as a precursor to a formalized regional integration organization which would substitute for the EU.

While attempting to create a spirit of unity, and in more practical terms a regional market and trade interdependence, the overriding idea that EU accession can be achieved (and probably will be achieved) on a solitary basis is detrimental to regional cooperation.

Conclusion

This chapter has attempted to show that differentiated integration is at work in the Balkans and has had to contend with two main questions. First, can the concept of differentiated integration be applied to a group, or 'cluster', of states which are not EU members? Second, is there is a state cluster known as 'the Balkans', or a common understanding of what this consists of?

There is a strong case that differentiated integration is at play in the relationship between the EU and the Balkans, especially in temporal and spatial terms. Different states, at different times, have entered into binding and deep-rooted contractual agreements with the EU which are all intended to enhance their 'European perspective' (potentially leading to EU membership). Objectives are seemingly common, there is a sequencing of commitments, and territorially there is an intention to prepare states so that boundaries can be redrawn and they can be included within them.

Functionally differentiated integration as a concept faces a greater challenge because the Balkans are not part of the EU. Variable geometry and *á la carte* choices are not readily available to the Balkan states and as such their fate is decided by the existing membership and not by their own choices (apart from the fact that they have the choice to opt out of membership as a whole). *They have a set menu with no choice.* The problems encountered in this dimension of differentiated integration is that serious doubts are raised among the aspiring members of the EU in the Balkans as to whether they are really wanted as members, and whether indeed they should pursue membership of an institution which treats them in a less than equitable manner. Why is it that some states are fast-tracked to EU membership and others made to jump through a series of extra hoops before they can join the accession process? The answer is clearly political, but the result is accordingly functional. The consensus among Balkan states on the prospects of EU membership is not always as favourable as many EU policy-makers would like it to be. Consequently, the functional impact of differentiated integration is that, even though it attempts to create regional coherence if not unity, it often pits state against state in regional terms, and perhaps against the EU itself.

The case of differentiated integration with respect to the Balkans is further confused by the vagueness of the geographical region under examination. The Balkans have in fact shrunk as countries join the EU, and what is left, apart from the grander descriptive term of SEE, is a highly *policy-relevant* region known as the WB. This is now the Balkans; it is the creation of the EU and is what provokes attempts at regional cooperation both internally and externally. Whether it is a region, or can sustain meaningful regional cooperation in real terms is doubtful. In spatial or territorial terms, differentiated integration aims to reinforce a new state cluster – the WB – in its path towards closer ties and potential membership of the EU. Nevertheless, this form of differentiated integration has effectively dissolved 'the Balkans' or SEE as a relevant state cluster, by plotting out and accommodating different accession trajectories for different states in the broader region. Perhaps the ultimate sign of success in the EU's policy of differentiated integration will be if and when the WB is also dissolved as its constituent states join the Union.

Ultimately, it is the politics, and strategic issues, that matter. In regional terms, WB governments and peoples make decisions about how they wish to relate to the EU, and whether they want to and can meet the conditions that will lead to EU accession. The biggest political decisions, nevertheless, are made by the existing

EU members, according to their interests. It is their decisions about enlarging the Union which ultimately make differentiated integration a useful tool in examining the EU–Balkan relationship.

Notes

1. This should help us understand the roots of differentiated integration by the EU towards the region as a whole and not necessarily between states in the region.
2. See Chapter 4 by Keating.
3. This is illustrative of the politics of the decision. The lag between the favourable *avis* and the start of negotiations is attributable to the fact that while for political and strategic reasons the EU wished to encourage Romania and Bulgaria, in real terms these countries could not meet the accession criteria in the short term.
4. Despite strong Italian objections.
5. As an EU initiative, the SP Special Co-ordinator was appointed by the EU, and the Commission played the leading role in developing strategy and coordinating fundraising.
6. Community Assistance for Reconstruction, Development and Stabilisation. CARDS pledged €4.6 billion between 2000 and 2006 to achieve its objectives.
7. In both cases they took a long time to come into force, FYROM in 2004 and Croatia in 2005.
8. The delay in Croatia's accession negotiations was due to the condition laid down by the EU that the talks would not commence until General Ante Gotovina, indicted by ICTY, was in custody.

9
Baltic Europe

Marko Lehti

The Baltic Region in the EU

The notion of the Baltic region has a double meaning. On the one hand, it refers to the three Baltic States (Estonia, Latvia and Lithuania), which gained their membership in the European Union in 2004. On the other hand, it refers to the whole Baltic Sea Area (BSA), including also Finland, Sweden, Denmark and parts of Germany, Poland and Russia. These two Baltic regions are often overlapping, and their logic is often but not necessarily congruent. This chapter examines the role of both Baltic regions in recent EU development. However, only the Baltic States' political goals with regard to the EU are closely scrutinized (Lee Miles, in Chapter 13 of this volume, deals with the Nordic countries).

The Baltic Sea has been recently referred to both as the 'Mediterranean of the North' and as a model region. The first term reminds us that the 'cradle of Europe' is to be found not just in the Mediterranean but also in the North, which has its own rich cultural heritage. The comparison of the Baltic Sea to the Mediterranean aims to offer a counterbalance to French-led political efforts to launch the Mediterranean Union (see Chapter 12 in this volume by Heywood and McLaren). However, comparisons between these two regional processes may not be fair, given the higher political visibility, and particularly the financial strength, of the Mediterranean region. Nevertheless, the Baltic Sea Region can be described as a 'region of best practice' and a model for others (Henningsen, 2008).

In the European North, a process described as 'the regionalist revolt' took place in the 1990s (Joenniemi, 2003: 226; also Wæver, 1997). Northern Europe was portrayed as representing a true experimental area of regionalization in the European framework and a prime example of a 'Europe of Regions'. In the early 1990s the Baltic Sea-based cooperation opened up intensive regionalization and networking across the boundaries of the old Iron Curtain. Even if the whole process had been initiated by the Scandinavians and northern Germans, it was the re-emergence of the three small Baltic States that provided the dynamic for this regionalization. Their re-emergence created a new opportunity for regionalization. At the time, Baltic-based regionalization was seen necessary to counterbalance central and western European integration and thus prevent further marginalization of northern Europe (Lehti, 2003: 22–4). The initial region-building efforts of the Baltic Sea area were not integrated into the EU; instead, Baltic institutions and networks were built more or less as a parallel system. The Nordic enlargement of the EU in 1995, with the accession of Finland and Sweden, soon brought the EU into more central position. Finally, a decade later, the Baltic States' and Poland's membership in the EU transformed the Baltic Sea into almost an inland sea of the EU, with small but important Russian enclaves of Kaliningrad and St Petersburg. Since the 2004 wave of enlargement, the Baltic Sea Area cooperation can no longer develop as a parallel system because the EU 'has become a northern European power' that sets the framework for regional cooperation (Aalto, 2006: 1).

The countries around the Baltic Sea rim are far from being homogenous in regard to their history and to their economic and security position within the EU. Within the whole Baltic Sea Area, countries play distinctive roles. The Nordic states are often labelled 'reluctant Europeans', while the Balts and Finns have aimed to be 'model pupils' of the EU. Similarly the Balts are seen by many as 'poor East European cousins', while the Nordics are regarded as the most prosperous and welfare-conscious states of the EU. These divisions are important, because other European countries, and, in particular, the old EU Member States, grant different roles to Nordic and Baltic states, setting different criteria and requirements for them. Nordics are allowed to remain reluctant Europeans and have certain exemptions from unitary integration (Browning, 2007; Trägårdh, 2002), while the Balts are expected to be merely invisible model pupils (Kuus, 2007; Lehti, 2007). This distinction sets a clear framework for the development of differentiated integration in the Baltic Sea Area as well as among its states.

Membership of the tiny Baltic States (and other new eastern European countries) has, however, already drastically changed the EU. According to Delanty and Rumford (2005: 49), 'enlargement is not just about getting bigger but is about transformation'. Thus, new Member States, including the small Baltic states, reshaped the EU despite the western European understanding of enlargement as assimilation or integration of former 'eastern lands' into a sphere of 'western civilization'. Still, bringing together countries with different historical trajectories can have a deeper influence. Following Delanty and Rumford, Europe '... is no longer based on a singular, western modernity, but multiple modernities'. Europe is becoming more poly-centric, with more than one centre and also more than one historical origin. Even so, the old members acted as if enlargement was merely a process of assimilation to western European standards rather than a real change (Kuus, 2004). This chapter argues that the tension that arises from the emergence of a new poly-centric Europe with different historical memories constitutes a major challenge and an unpredictable dynamic for the future shape of the EU.

This chapter first examines the Baltic States' challenge for the EU. How do they envisage Europe, and what kind of politics have they have adopted to shape Europe? The second part focuses on scrutinizing the integrity of the small Baltic region within the EU context. It focuses on the whole Baltic Sea Area and questions whether the 'European North' is a particular case in the European integration process.

The Baltic States: challenge from the margin

For the three Baltic States – Estonia, Latvia and Lithuania – EU membership was the fulfilment of long-term dreams. It was seen as a seal of their belonging to the West and a proof of a successful escape from the Russian sphere, that is, 'Eastern-ness'. Furthermore, membership symbolized the ultimate transformation from the abnormality related to the Soviet past to a state of normality (Stukuls Eglitis, 2002: 8–10). The route from one union to another, from a Soviet republic to an EU country, took only just over a decade, and one does not expect any other former Soviet republics to follow the same path in the near future. The EU membership of the Baltic States can be regarded as representing the end of a decade-long transition period. Still, the perception of 'backward eastern Europeans' has not vanished in the minds of western Europeans. As Merje Kuus (2004: 484) argues, even after eastern enlargement the division between European 'Europe' and not yet fully European 'eastern Europe' still remains.

The Baltic story of 'returning to Europe' is thus an indisputable success story. It represented the fulfilment of a decade-long political struggle and of the dominating driving force in Baltic foreign policies. After 2004 the solutions to political problems were no longer as simple and obvious as they were in the 'heroic age' of struggle towards the West (Goble, 2005: 19–20). Thus, the 'return to Europe' has been followed by scepticism and challenge towards the 'old Europe'. Europe and the West are no longer idealized. Instead, major questions have arisen about the possibilities for contributing to Europe and about what an ideal Europe would look like from a Baltic perspective. More particularly, the Balts' conceptualization of Europe has three major pillars. Firstly, it believes in neo-liberal economic logic and emphasizes the strengthening of the competitiveness of the European economy. Secondly, it strongly emphasizes traditional security politics. Russia is seen as the 'Other' against which Europe has to stand united. Russia is viewed as only understanding the language of power. Hence Europe needs to flex its muscles towards its eastern neighbour, which in turn necessitates the EU's close cooperation and dependence on the USA. The third pillar underlines the moral commitment to continue enlargement, particularly eastwards. If the first pillar crumbles, as it did with the global financial crisis after 2007, the two remaining pillars may gain more importance in the near future.

A major challenge for the Baltic States is their marginal status and how to make their voice heard within the EU. Among the smaller Member States in the EU, their combined population is 7 million, which represents only 1.4 per cent of the total EU population. In economic terms, their share is even smaller – only 0.6 per cent of the EU's gross GDP. Furthermore, they are located on the northeastern border of the EU, distant from the traditional power centres. Are these new EU members constrained to be peripheral, invisible, powerless and small? How can they influence EU developments, and do their opinions and policies matter? Following Christopher Browning's (2006) formulation, the question is not how small they are but how smart they could be.

Too often small states are seen as lacking voice and capacity to shape broader European developments. Being understood as marginal, peripheral or remote should not be equated with a lack of subjectivity or capacity to influence, as Browning (2006) argues. Margins can often bite back. Not all small states are located on the margins, and not all margins constitute just small states. However, in the case of the three Baltic States these two phenomena are clearly congruent, setting limits to their influence within the EU.

Traditional Realist and Neo-realist readings comprehend smallness as equivalent to lack of power and equate smallness with weakness. They perceive that small states need to accept their smallness and powerlessness and merely concentrate on securing their sovereignty in a world of power and political struggles. Possible alternative tactics would be an alliance with a great power or trying to remain as invisible as possible. In contrast to the Realist interpretation, liberal institutional theories emphasize how small states can also escape power struggles by joining security communities like the EU in which realist power is weakened because of the existence of 'a dense network of norms of acceptable behaviour' (Browning, 2006: 670–4). Mutual trust for peaceful changes prevails within security communities. However, the problem with sub-regional communities is whether dependable expectations exist between members and non-members (Möller, 2007: 34).

Small states, such as the Baltics, are seen as strong supporters of international institutions, which provide opportunities for manoeuvre and influence. For example, the Estonian Ambassador Margus Laidre stated that 'for small countries it is crucial to be visible in the ever changing world' and that the EU 'gives a place in the sun to Europe's smaller and middle-sized nations'.[1] But how does a state achieve influence and power within a security community? Do small states need to be salient? Salience is not the only alternative. There are other ways in which small states can be smart. It is necessary to recognize that smallness is relative. It is not only a question of being small. Far more important is how states cope with smallness and marginality. This chapter argues that being smart is associated with identity politics. Taking Europe for granted or having one's own vision of European development, based on different understandings of identity, can contribute to different kind of policies. It is a matter of how Europe is written into national identity and how it is possible to cope with marginality. The search for self-esteem, subjectivity and acceptance dominates the political discourse of small states.

In another perspective there are two available alternative policies. A state can seek to escape from marginality towards the centre by seeking recognition from the centre: or to embrace marginality in order to find uniqueness and use marginality as a source of strong self-esteem (Browning and Lehti, 2007). Visibility and goals to secure influence are different in each case. The first is based on approval of existing policies, avoiding of controversies and a tactic of being present where decisions are made. In the second case, the goals of the centre are challenged, openly or covertly. The margin is then presented as a home of reforms and necessary change through a combination of both identity and political tactics.

Membership in western organizations was for more than a decade a driving force of Baltic foreign and identity politics. They aimed in all possible ways to promote their belonging to the West. This desperate escape from 'Eastern-ness' was associated with an escape from marginality. Thus models and guidance from

Brussels were accepted without hesitation. The Baltic States have generally been regarded – both during and after their membership negotiations – as quick learners and model pupils in their relations with the EU. According to Kuus (2007: 104–13), this does not mean that the Balts unconditionally tried to imitate western Europeans but merely that they quickly learned what western Europeans wanted to hear and how they were expected to behave. In small, marginal countries like the Baltic States it is common for a few diplomats or politicians or artists to come to represent the whole nation to foreign observers. However, beneath this image of 'good Estonians' (or Latvians or Lithuanians) the gradual strengthening of Euroscepticism and challenge to 'old Europeans' remains less well-known.

Since accession, there has been an identity shift from 'escape from marginality' to 'escape to marginality' in Baltic politics. Baltic politicians have for some time reminded domestic and foreign publics about the growth rates of their economy and depicted themselves as quick learners of market economics. Recently, it has been pointed out that the Balts are more efficient and more successful in implementing reforms than the old established states and thus have something to teach other Europeans.[2] The Balts, and the Estonians in particular, have found a strong self-esteem based on their economic success story. The economic miracle has constituted a source of national pride that needs to be secured so that national sovereignty can survive and flourish.

The Balts are no longer simply emulating 'western' Europeans but have come to argue that in certain key 'progressive' sectors they are actually ahead of many western states. According to Kristina Ojuland, the former Estonian foreign minister, the Balts see themselves as the 'Tigers of Europe', a term that refers to the Asian examples of South Korea, Taiwan, Hong Kong and Singapore and, more recently, the EU's own 'Celtic Tiger', Ireland.[3] The Balts are claiming to be pacesetters in comparison to the 'old Europe' of France and Germany, which is presented as the stagnating part of the continent, and which, some argue, is responsible for the shrinking role of the EU in the global markets (Varbalane, 2005).

However, this 'tiny tiger-hood' has not found major expression in the Balts' EU policy so far, except in resisting deepening integration in social issues and taxation, which has been seen as a threat to the economic miracle.[4] It has remained more or less as a narrative challenging the 'old Europe', abandoning the 'model-pupil' role and placing their nations among the pacesetters of Europe. In these narratives, the Balts managed to contribute to shaping Europe with a unique voice as well as challenging existing policies of the EU core. However, significantly, by the end of 2008, the deep global financial and economic crisis hit hard all three Baltic States, inflicting pain on their economies. It had significant negative effects on their self-confidence, with their collapsing economies denting national pride.

Despite the increased security with EU and NATO memberships, the primary foreign-policy interests of these new Member States still lie in the East (Ilves, 2005: 197). The EU–Russian border is still a key issue that very much defines and determines the limits on and possibilities of their influence within the wider EU. Being on that border can be a source of power and influence for the Baltic States. It can also shackle policy options. In the Balts' geopolitical visions, Russia was securitized at the very beginning of independence and seen as a main threat to Baltic sovereignty. Thus the only remaining option was desperately to seek recognition from western powers for one's own European-ness and Western-ness. Estonian foreign minister Jüri Luik mapped Estonia in 1994 as located between 'the devil and the deep blue sea' (Smith, 2003a). Over a decade later and after receiving membership in the EU and NATO the same logic can be still recognized in the Balts' geopolitical rhetoric (Lamoreaux and Galbreath, 2008).

This emphasis on the Baltic States' fundamental differences from Russia places them on the western side of the 'civilizational' fault line. 'Through the reification of differences, the civilizational narrative generates the notion that Estonia is fundamentally insecure because it is located on a putative civilizational boundary' (Kuus, 2007: 55). The Russian–Georgian War in August 2008 was taken very seriously in the Baltic States and was interpreted as marking the termination of the era of idealism after the end of Cold War and the return of power struggle between liberal democracies and authoritarian capitalist countries. Thus, the border is imagined now more as geo-political, and mistrust has increased towards the EU core that is blamed for being too pro-Russian while the stronger involvement of the USA is called for to safeguard security.[5] According to Bugajski and Teleki (2005: 100): 'For the Baltic countries, in particular, if Russia continues to act assertively under President Vladimir Putin's authoritarianism while the EU's security and foreign policy is perceived to be lacking muscle, it seems implausible that pro-Washington positions will weaken in Tallinn, Riga, or Vilnius'. Hence, when Europe was split into pro- and anti-American positions, the Balts did not hesitate to declare their loyalty to the USA (Lehti, 2007).

After becoming EU Member States, the Balts emphatically tried to influence the formulation of the EU's Russian policy and introduced more sceptical views towards Russia (Mälksoo 2006: 282–6). An excellent example of the Balts' power to influence the EU's Russian policy is Lithuania's active campaign to introduce stricter criteria into EU–Russia partnership negotiations during the spring of 2008. Deadlock was finally resolved by introducing Lithuanian provisions into the EU mandate. These criteria include three issues: the Druzhba pipeline; the Medininkai massacre; and the frozen conflicts of Georgia and Moldova.[6] The Druzhba (literally 'friendship') pipeline is the world's longest oil pipeline, stretching from southeast Russia to points in Ukraine, Hungary, Poland and Germany. The pipeline had a branch supplying Lithuanian Mazeikiai Oil but this supply was suspended in July 2006 after the company was sold to the Poles and Lithuanians for political reasons. The so-called Medininkai massacre took place in 1991 when the Soviet OMON (Special Purpose Police Squad) attacked a Lithuanian customs post and seven officers were killed. Lithuania claims that Russia is hiding criminals and demands that those responsible for the murders face Lithuanian justice. The Georgia/South Ossetia dispute was transformed in 2008 from a frozen peace to a hot conflict. These three issues are highly sensitive. Equally, the Russian side will have little willingness to compromise. Thus, the presence of these issues on the EU agenda provides Lithuania with the right to use the veto in the Russian–EU partnership negotiation.

In conclusion, the Baltic States have remained entangled with Russia so that their security-political interests overrun EU communality. Because of this dominance of security politics the Baltic States have remained more or less one-issue countries in their relations with the EU, focused on the Russian question. The Baltic–Russian relationship is far from normal, and issues easily escalate if they touch in one way or another on the Soviet legacy. It is easy to agree with Mouritzen (2006) that past geopolitics dominate and have set a barrier for changes in the Baltics.

The presence of the Soviet legacy can also be noticed in the increasing expressions of solidarity with other post-Soviet republics, in particular with Ukraine and Georgia, and in calls for a stronger eastern dimension of the EU (Ilves 2005: 201).[7] According to the Estonian foreign minister, Urmas Paet, in June 2005: 'The European Union itself must be prepared to accept new members. The membership perspective is a strong motivation for countries in the process of carrying out market economy and democratic reforms. This, in turn, promotes the spreading and deepening of stability and security in Europe.'[8] Estonia's President Ilves accused the 'old Europe' of being arrogant towards the countries in the east: 'We have a responsibility to defend and help those who today risk their lives in the name of democracy and freedom.' European interests lie in the East, and closing the EU is not the solution. Ilves describes the division within Europe between the old and new members, accusing the former of being selfish and patronizing towards the new members, who seemingly have the moral backbone to give direction to Europe and constitute a true Europe.[9]

Strong expressions of solidarity with other post-Soviet states challenge the dominant interpretation of the general goals of the European Neighbourhood Policy (ENP). After the eastern enlargement the EU has sought to create a more standardized and unambiguous policy towards all neighbours,[10] which obviously limits regional freedom to define alternative policies within and across the EU's external border. The driving force is the need to control and prevent further enlargement and instead set final borders for the EU. For this purpose it is important to restrain hopes in several eastern European countries like Ukraine or Moldova regarding their EU membership in the near future. Instead Brussels would like to see the emergence of a 'ring of friends' around its external borders that are bound to the EU but are not in the waiting room for full membership. Thus, the main function of the ENP is to determine who remains permanently outside the EU and how relations with close outsiders will be organized (Browning and Joenniemi, 2007). Interestingly, in their public statements Baltic politicians gave their full support to the ENP. But at the same time they stated that for them this policy was a step towards full membership in the EU.[11] Their perspective brings them closer to the USA, which also calls for a 'wider Europe' that extends beyond the borders of the EU. Encouraged by Washington, the Baltic governments also actively adopted missionary aims, for example, educating young Georgian, Moldovan and Ukrainian diplomats and officers. While Estonia promoted projects with Georgia and Lithuania, and Latvia concentrated on Ukraine and Moldova, all three also supported Armenia and Azerbaijan (Lamoreaux and Galbreath, 2008: 8; Lehti, 2007).[12] In other words, they have shown to their 'eastern' neighbours how to behave and act as 'western', which is a prerequisite for acceptance to the EU and NATO. If one considers that the original aim of the ENP was to set closure on enlargement, it can be argued that the Balts' way of talking about the ENP is redefining the whole policy and challenging the western European interpretation of it.

The Baltic region in a Europe of competing regions

How well integrated is the group of the three Baltic States within the EU framework? Even if outsiders are used to labelling Estonia, Latvia and Lithuania as a core *Baltic*, the notion remains problematic. The Baltic States returned to wider attention only in the late 1980s as a result of their 'singing revolution'. Baltic solidarity was then strong, expressed in a series of joint demonstrations, in particular the human chain from Tallinn to Vilnius in 1989 on the 50th anniversary of the Molotov–Ribbentrop treaty, which expressed a feeling of common interests and shared position. The joint institutions of the Baltic Council and the Baltic Assembly were created immediately after regaining independence, bringing together the Baltic governments and parliaments (Jurkynas, 2007: 58–61). However, solidarity soon started to fade away. By the late 1990s the notion of 'the Baltic' had changed; indeed the term was rarely used in public and was even seen as representing something shameful. Its usage was seen to express a continuation of 'Easternization' by signifying those post-Soviet countries in transition at a time when the Balts were desperately trying to distance themselves from the Soviet legacy and trying to envisage a dividing-line of civilizations on the Baltic–Russian border (Lehti, 2006: 70–3).

EU accession in 2004 changed completely the previous constellation and dynamism of the region. From the Balts' perspective, the previous struggle for membership was replaced by efforts to cope with day-to-day EU politics. The significance of the Baltic region is now broadly recognized, and the notion of 'the Baltic' is no longer regarded as synonymous with something shameful within the three Baltic States. Rather, it is being seen as a potential resource. Estonian foreign minister Urmas Paet concluded that there is a new momentum for the Baltic group after the fulfilment of EU and NATO memberships. There are, in his view, again common interests among all three Baltic States within a common framework.[13] The Baltic label is now seen to be a flexible signifier that complements Estonian, Latvian or Lithuanian European identity rather than challenging it, as was previously thought.

In 2005 old political structures of mutual cooperation were renewed. The status of the Baltic Council of Ministers was amended. Besides yearly foreign minister meetings, five committees of senior officials prepare questions raised at the trilateral, regional and European levels (Jurkynas 2007: 139–45). The Baltic Council of Ministers has been transformed into a major institution. The heads of the Baltic States are also more willing to issue joint political statements and communiqués, for example on the eve of the Iraq war, or in support of Georgia in its conflict with Russia.[14]

So far major common interests within the EU have been seen as lying in energy security, referring mainly to reliability of energy production and supply and, at least from the Estonian perspective, in 'cooperation in the fight against cyber crime'.[15] Energy issues are closely linked to Russia and thus highly securitized. So far the Baltic States have not managed to constitute a single energy market or join with the Nordic region. Perhaps the most crucial single issue concerns the resistance to the Nord Stream gas pipeline under the Baltic Sea, connecting Russia to Germany but bypassing the Baltic States (Nielsen, 2007: 123–4).

For the Baltic States, cooperation with the Nordic countries has traditionally been an important option. In the early phase, Estonians in particular used to describe their country as Nordic (Lehti, 2006: 73–5).[16] However, the Nordic core remained exclusive, even if it opened up eastwards (Smith, 2003b: 62). From the Nordic perspective, Estonia has not become Nordic. Even though it may be approached as Nordic, and has become a close partner with Nordic countries, it remains a Baltic partner. Indeed, there emerged in the 1990s a new Baltic–Nordic linkage. The Baltic States were seen to belong to the Nordic 'near abroad', and the Nordics were seen to have a moral obligation to assist and give patronage to the Baltics (Lehti, 2003: 24–7). Besides creating a Nordic–Baltic communality, 'Nordic multilateral integration' has also been presented as helping prepare the Baltic States for EU membership (Bergman, 2006: 87).

Following EU membership, the Balts no longer want to become Nordic. Rather, the Nordic and Baltic States are perceived as having 'different societal histories' and differences in economic development. At the same time they are also seen as having 'common political and cultural traits', suggesting that they may also have common interests in the EU.[17] The original so-called 'five plus three' Nordic and Baltic cooperation model was renamed in 2000 as 'NB8'. There are regular meetings and discussions at the highest political level. After the granting of the Baltic States' EU membership, Nordic and Baltic ministers have held their mutual meetings before the European Council (Jurkynas 2007: 149–50). However, while the contents of meetings have been substantial, they have not generated a strong and coherent group identity.

The EU is seen more and more as a platform for competing and allying regions. In this framework, the image of the Baltic group has been strengthened, but questions remain about with whom the Balts should cooperate. As the Latvian Foreign Minister Maris Riekstins has emphasized: '... the success of today's Europe lies within its regions but the Nordics are not any more seen as the only partner.'[18] Baltic and Nordic interests still differ on many issues and in particular on security politics. This lack of common ground contributed to statements such as that from the Estonian Foreign Minister Paet who called for closer cooperation with the Visegrád group and with Benelux in the EU.[19] However, initiatives for regional integration between the Baltic and Visegrád countries, launched by Poland in 2002, remained inactive (Jurkynas 2007: 154). According to this new logic, the Balts perceive that, as small and marginal states, they should look after their interests against established European big powers by forming their own regional groupings and cooperating with them.

The emerging Baltic Sea Area

Since 2004 the integration of the Baltic Sea Area into the EU-based system has been the major challenge. Is there an emerging Baltic Sea Area group in the EU, contrasting itself to the Mediterranean group? Or do diverse interests and identities among Baltic Sea States hinder the emergence of a new regional grouping? At the moment, the EU is shaping its strategy for the Baltic Sea Area, but the major question is, in which terms, if any, the integration process there differs from other regions. Nonetheless, the Russian position in Baltic Sea Area cooperation constitutes a major challenge and problem. How is it possible to engage Russia in Baltic Sea Area-based cooperation that is shaped within the EU framework? Conversely, how it is possible to avoid the exclusion of Russia from Baltic cooperation?

If the three Baltic States are in total small and peripheral, the Baltic Sea Area looks quite different. It is the home to 57.5 million people, and its annual GDP is about €1450 billion. These figures do not include the whole of Germany, Russia and Poland but only those regions having a Baltic connection. The Baltic Sea Area has an economy about 60 per cent the size of Germany and 90 per cent of California (SRR, 2008: 5–7). Its economic dynamic represents 6 per cent of the world figure and is much larger than its share of population. Furthermore, the geographic location of the Baltic Sea Area provides 'a balance of positive and negative influences for prosperity ... It is located at the periphery of the European market, one of the largest markets in the global economy providing many opportunities for trade and investment' (SRR, 2008: 48). The Baltic Sea Area countries are seen to have a well-diversified industrial structure and fully developed trade, service and information centres. What is even more important is that the Baltic Sea Area can be described as a true 'knowledge-based' society (Henningsen, 2008). But the question remains whether the Baltic Sea Area really constitutes an integrated sub-region, or whether it is more a 'paper tiger' promoted as a competitive and dynamic economic area by organizations such as the Baltic Development Forum. As Browning and Joenniemi (2004: 248) argue, the Baltic Sea Area is still more an emerging region than a region in reality.

The Baltic Sea Area is a prime example of the so-called 'new regionalism' that 'is not confined merely to formal inter-state regional organisations and institutions, but is characterised by multidimensionality, complexity, fluidity and non-conformity and by the fact that it involves a variety of state and non-state actors that often come together in rather informal ways' (Paasi, 2009: 127). Multidimensionality has been a characteristic of the Baltic Sea Area from the very beginning. In the very early phase, the activities of non-governmental organizations (NGOs), academics, as well as several sub-state actors, were crucial, even if the nation-state was still the main actor in the establishment of the Council of the Baltic Sea States (CBSS) in 1992. The Baltic Sea Area remained a fluid and vague entity which was open to the contribution of various stakeholders. By the late 1990s when the Baltic Sea Area partly lost its political agenda and disappeared from government officials' speeches, this multi-dimensionality sustained its activity in other sectors such as higher education. With the EU Strategy for the Baltic Sea Region, the Baltic Sea Area seems to be returning to the political agenda, but in a new form.

The major problem in earlier region-building initiatives of the Baltic Sea States arose from attempts to present an exaggerated notion of homogeneity and uniformity and a picture of a historical region returning to and/or taking centre stage in Europe. In practice, the area was a long way from such uniformity, given the existence of dividing factors like the unequal distribution of wealth, different levels of corruption, diverging security interests, divisive energy issues and differing commitment to the welfare state. For example, the Nordic countries constitute 73 per cent of the total GDP of the Baltic Sea Area (SRR, 2008: 7). Security interests of Baltic and Nordic countries also diverge. While the Balts favour a return of geopolitics and struggle for power, the Nordics are decreasing their defence budgets and prioritizing the tackling of environmental problems over traditional security threats. Also, in energy security, the Nord Stream project for an underwater gas pipeline connecting Russia and Germany has generated varying responses and anxieties within the Baltic and in Nordic countries. From the Baltic perspective, it is pictured as a new Molotov–Ribbentrop treaty, dividing the Baltic Sea, whereas the Nordics have been more concerned about the deleterious environmental effects (Zwitserloot, 2008; Oviir, 2008; Nõlvak, 2008; Haavisto, 2008; Hautala, 2007). More generally, the term Baltic Sea Area '... continues to suffer from considerable East-West disparities', and polarization '... between metropolitan regions and the more peripheral and less densely populated' areas is increasing (Damsgaard, 2008). Two areas that most unite the Baltic Sea countries are economic growth and concerns about the sea – it remains to be seen if that will be enough.

Baltic Sea cooperation originated from the early 1990s, following an intensive and innovative period of regional cooperation. The Baltic Sea Area was presented then as potentially a leading European region. It aimed to avert marginalization as well as help integrate the Baltic States into the democratic Nordic area (Lehti, 2003: 21–34). The dynamic of 1990s Baltic cooperation contributed to the foundation of numerous Baltic Sea Area-based organizations and networks (Suominen et al., 2000). The CBSS remained a prime symbol of institutionalized Baltic space. However, the function and rationale of this organization remained vague. Although the European Commission became a member of the CBSS, it has not integrated well into the new EU-led Northern Europe. This lack of integration is primarily because it was created before the EU's Nordic and Eastern enlargements and merely constitutes a parallel system that is integrated into the EU.

The political motivation for investing in Baltic Sea cooperation slowly lost its momentum and faded away in the mid-1990s. The Balts and Nordics have long had a different understanding of a shared Baltic identity (Lehti, 2003b; Aalto, 2004). In recent years it is possible to recognize clear signs that a visionary type of thinking is returning to promote the Baltic Sea Area. The Baltic Sea Area has become again politically attractive, as Latvian Foreign Minister Artis Pabriks' eloquent description of the Baltic Area in December 2007 shows:

Finally, I return to one of our common goals – *regional identity of the Baltic Sea region,* which should be recognized, strengthened and used for our own common good. We don't look alike, we don't speak one language, we don't live in one country and we don't have a joint team in [the] world ice hockey championship. But we share the Baltic Sea, a common history, values and spirit of dynamism, skillfulness and creativity. However, what is more important – *we share the same dreams about our region's future: to be competitive, stable, advanced and always a developing region."*[20]

Pabriks was adapting the 'Baltic Tiger' narrative about innovation and competitiveness to the Baltic region as a whole and making the growth of the region a necessity for the development of its individual states.

The recently revived Baltic Sea Area is now attached to the EU and its institutions. The most recent development has been the so-called EU Strategy for the Baltic Sea Area that was planned to be accepted during the Swedish chairmanship of the EU in the second half of 2009. The origins of the recent initiative can be dated back to discussions and lobbying conducted by members of the European Parliament and the Swedish government. A Baltic Strategy Working Group of seven MEPs presented to the President of the European Commission, José Manuel Barroso, a memorandum on Europe's strategy for the Baltic Sea Area. It defined the goal as combining the EU institutions and the existing Baltic Sea organizations in order to develop a more secure, stable and competitive region. Apart from the traditional economic, cultural, educational and security questions, environmental issues were also highly prioritized (Beazley, 2007).[21] Another major advocate was the Swedish government, which promoted the programme in order to highlight its leadership role. For example, the Swedish Minister for EU Affairs, Cecilia Malmström, declared in December 2007 that: ' ... the Baltic area should be Europe's strongest area of growth, and ... we should use all the opportunities to strengthen the cooperation.' The goal would be 'deeper integration and creating a more sustainable region'.[22]

The goals of the EU Strategy have been presented as four-fold: to make the Baltic Sea Area environmentally sustainable, prosperous, accessible and secure (Barroso, 2008). It is still too early to analyse practical influences on the development of the Baltic Sea Area. What is striking is the process itself and how its goals are prioritized. The European Commission adopted an active and consultative role in the process. Several stakeholders' meetings were organized:

> In total 109 authorities, institutions or individuals responded to the consultation and presented their views. Out of these, 8 were Member States (every Member State presented a position paper), 3 non-Member States (Russia, Belarus, Norway), 31 were regional and local authorities, 48 were inter-governmental and non-governmental bodies, 19 were representatives from the private sector out of which 2 were experts/researchers and 3 were individuals. (SRR, 2008: 87)[23]

The Strategy aims to present the Baltic Sea Area as a model case. Instead of emphasizing the strategy either as the Commission's policy or the region's strategy, the process is presented as a multi-dimensional process, involving in the early phase the Commission, Member State, regional and local governments, NGOs, business and the academic sector. This tactic fits well with the nature of the Baltic Sea Area, which emerged initially as a bottom-up initiative, later hijacked by the states and then left again to NGOs. The strategy can be seen as an effort to combine existing activities and to create an intermediate level between the EU and its Member States, without founding any new institutions. 'The EU Baltic Strategy is starting to become the crystallization point for many regional institutions to see their part in the overall agenda and collaborate with partners in pursing specific themes' (SRR, 2008: 30).

Also, in many respects, the Strategy is experimental within the EU context. It would be the first regional-based programme that is focused solely in EU territory. Previous regional approaches, like the Northern Dimension or the Barcelona Process, were created for managing cooperation and interaction across EU borders with third-party countries. Thus, the Strategy is attempting to develop a 'transnational area of enhanced cooperation and governance' and a new level of governance between the nation-state and the supra-national community. If this experiment proves to be successful, there would probably be similar initiatives in other areas such as the Danube (Schymik and Krumrey, 2009).

The prioritization of environmental issues in the action plan is also exceptional. The Baltic Sea is one of the most polluted in the world, and environmental awareness is becoming a key dynamic in regional cooperation. Again, there is a natural continuity in this strategy since the Baltic Sea Area began in 1974 as a single convention by the then seven Baltic coastal states for cooperation. In the light of political changes, and developments in international environmental and maritime law, a new convention was signed in 1992 (coming into force in 2000, known as HELCOM) by all states bordering on the Baltic Sea and the European Community. The new convention covers the whole sea area, including inland waters, the sea itself and the sea-bed (SRR, 2008: 93–5).[24] The pollution of the sea has also been an issue in the Northern Dimension policy, and indeed the most concrete achievements of the Northern Dimension are linked with environmental cooperation. The Northern Dimension Environmental Partnership (NDEP) was founded in 2002.[25] Its main achievement in the environmental sector was the opening up of the St Petersburg Southwest Wastewater Treatment Plant in September 2005. NDEP is also participating in the construction of the St Petersburg Flood Protection Barrier. With the EU Strategy for the Baltic Sea Region, environmental issues rose to the level of high politics. In particular, Sweden and Finland prioritized the goal of achieving a more environmentally sustainable sea, a goal that is seen as a crucial precondition for the success of the area (see, for example, Lehtomäki, 2008; Luoto, 2008; Carlgren, 2008). The strategy of environmental integration is a step on to a new level. The Baltic Sea Area is arguably forging ahead of other regions in this sector.

This strategy has generated a new kind of activity and dynamism around the Baltic Sea Area – which had been stagnating since the late 1990s – and has brought it into the political spotlight again. Some major remaining questions revolve around the role of Russia in this strategy, since, so far, it has been excluded. The Northern Dimension policy remains reserved for external relations. Its framework agreement from 2006 was signed by the EU, Russia, Norway and Iceland (Lehtinen, 2008). However, how the EU Strategy and the Northern Dimension fit together remains an open question.

To summarize, the promotion of the Baltic Sea Area has intensified in the past few years. Several action plans have been published with the aim of increasing innovation and competitiveness in the region.[26] This promotion has been successful, and the image of the Baltic Sea Area as an exceptional region has been widely accepted. For example, the Vice-President of the European Commission, Günter Verheugen, defined the Baltic Sea Area 'as one of the most dynamic parts of Europe. It is a region of high growth rates and an example of economic dynamism and reform' (Verheugen, 2007). In regards to differentiated integration, the Baltic Sea Area can serve as the model region in certain sectors such as the environment and conservation of the sea as well as promotion of a 'knowledge-based' society. The latter is promoted with the use of EU funding in higher education, the private sector and regional governments – although these areas received only minor attention in the Commission's most recent Action Plan. This neglect by the Commission could pose a risk to the whole strategy because the Baltic Sea Area's real strength has been its 'knowledge-based society', while both institutionalization and networking have been most active in this sector. Furthermore, there remain divergences on many issues, for example in the energy sector, and a major challenge is to increase mutual trust among Baltic Sea countries as well as to include Russia in the process.

Conclusion

The eastern enlargement of the EU in 2004 significantly changed the previous constellation and dynamism of the Baltic region. The Baltic Sea Area has become more closely and intensively framed within the EU framework. Cooperative activity is, in one way or another, dependent on what is happening and has been decided in Brussels and elsewhere within the EU (Hubel, 2004). The Baltic States and Finland have been seen as model actors in terms of adapting to EU regulations. At the same time the Baltic region has differentiated itself from certain spheres of European integration. A prerequisite for this differentiation has been an identity-based political shift from Baltic States' efforts to escape from marginality in search of recognition, to having their own vision of Europe. However, the states' newly achieved pride following this shift was seriously compromised by the post-2007 financial and economic crisis. The three Baltic States have their own views about managing the Schengen border by aiming, on the one hand, to keep the door open for Ukraine, Georgia and Moldova but, on the other, promoting a harsher policy towards Russia. Also, disappointment and distrust towards the 'old Europe' has increased since EU accession, in particular after the Russian–Georgian War confirmed the need to rely more on the USA and to affiliate regional groupings in the EU.

The Baltic Sea Area is an interesting case of differentiated integration. It is a region that has the potential to become a model region though, given the fallout from the financial and economic crisis, this is still too early to assess. Ideally, the Baltic Sea Area will open a new era in which the EU Commission will generate cooperation with state and non-state actors and thus in practice contribute to a certain form of well-controlled regional differentiation. Whether this experiment will be successful in the 'European North' remains to be seen.

Notes

1. Ambassador Margus Laidre's lecture 'Remembering the Future', 23 January 2008, at: www.vm.ee/eng/kat_140/9235.html?arhiiv_kuup=kuup_2008 (accessed 6 June 2009).
2. Kristina Ojuland, 'Tiny Tigers Will Always Be Tigers', Berlin, 15–16 November 2002; Ojuland, 'An EU of 25 and Estonia's Role in It', Brussels, 23 October 2002; both at Estonian Ministry of Foreign Affairs: www.vm.ee. See also Vaira Vīke-Freiberga, 'Latvia's Contribution to a New Europe' Vienna, 18 June 2001; Indulis Bērziņš, 'Latvia for Europe and Europe for Latvia', London 14–15 February 2002, both at Ministry of Foreign Affairs of the Republic of Latvia: www.am.gov.lv (accessed 2 January 2007).
3. Ojuland, 'Tiny Tigers Will Always Be Tigers', op. cit.
4. Joint article by Prime Ministers Juhan Parts and Tony Blair, 'An Enlarged Europe Needs Competition', at: www.valitsus.ee (accessed 6 June 2009). About criticism see, for example, Goble, 2005: 12.
5. President Ilves: 'NATO in Estonia, Estonia in NATO. Our Common Security in the 21st Century', Helsinki 1 December 2008, at: www.president.ee (accessed 9 March 2009).
6. 'Lithuania refused to give a "green light" to EU–Russia negotiations', 30 April 2008; 'Lithuania pursuing Poland's support on its EU-Russia talks veto', 7 May 2008; 'EU Ministers agree to include Lithuania-proposed provisions in talks with Russia', 12 May 2008; 'Lithuania not going to back down on fundamental issues over EU–Russia talks', 16 May 2008; 'Saeima Foreign Affairs Committee supports Lithuania's position in EU talks with Russia', 16 May 2008: all at: www.euro.lt (accessed 27 August 2008).
7. Joint Communiqué of the Meeting of the Presidents of Estonia, Latvia, Lithuania and Poland, Vilnius, 6 November 2006, at: www.am.gov.lv/en/policy/4595/Joint-communique 06112006/ (accessed 2 January 2007).
8. Urmas Paet, 'Main Guidelines of Estonia's Foreign Policy', 7 June 2005, at: www.vm.ee/eng/kat_140/5487.html?arhiiv_kuup=kuup_2005 (accessed 2 January 2007).
9. President Ilves at the Riikikogu Conference, 30 October 2006, at: www.president.ee/en/duties/?gid=83450 (accessed 2 January 2007).
10. Algeria, Armenia, Azerbaijan, Belarus, Egypt, Georgia, Israel, Jordan, Lebanon, Libya, Moldova, Morocco, the Palestinian Authority, Syria, Tunisia and Ukraine.
11. See, for example, 'Remarks by Estonian Foreign Minister Mr Urmas Paet: European Neighbourhood Policy – towards a Europe of Common Values', 23 November 2007, at: www.vm.ee; 'Opening remarks by H. E. Mr Maris Riekstins at the conference "The Baltic States and the EU Neighbourhood Policy"', 23 November 2007, at: www.am.lv (accessed 27 August 2008).
12. 'Report by Foreign Minister of Estonia Urmas Paet on the activities of the Baltic Council of Ministers in 2005', 25 November 2005, at: www.vm.ee/eng/kat_140/7138.html?arhiiv_kuup=kuup_2005 (accessed 2 January 2007).
13. 'Report by Foreign Minister of Estonia Urmas Paet on the activities of the Baltic Council of Ministers in 2005, Baltic Council, Tallinn', 25 November 2005, at: www.vm.ee/eng/kat_140/7138.html?arhiiv_kuup=kuup_2005 (accessed 2 January 2007).
14. For example, 'Declaration of Presidents of the Baltic States', 10 August 2008, at: www.am.gov.lv (accessed 24 November 2008).

15. 'Address by Estonian Foreign Minister Urmas Paet to the 13th Baltic Council of Ministers', 23 November 2007, at: www.vm.ee (accessed 27 August 2008).
16. T.H. Ilves: 'Estonia as a Nordic country'; speech at the Swedish Institute of Foreign Affairs 14 December 1999, at: www.vm.ee (accessed 2 January 2007).
17. Baltic Cooperation: Estonia, Latvia and Lithuania, memorandum, 25 September 2005; Urmas Paet: 'Future Cooperation Trends of the Baltic and Nordic Countries', 28 April 2005, both at: www.wm.ee (accessed 2 January 2007).
18. Opening speech by H.E. Maris Riekstins, Minister of Foreign Affairs of Latvia, at the seminar 'Baltic Sea Region in Europe', Stockholm, 17 January 2008, at: www.am.gov.lv (accessed 26 August 2008).
19. 'Address by Estonian Foreign Minister Urmas Paet to the 13th Baltic Council of Ministers', 23 November 2007, at: www.vm.ee (accessed 27 August 2008).
20. 'Intervention by His Excellency Mr Artis Pabriks, Latvia Foreign Minister and the CBSS Chairman at the 16th Baltic Sea Parliamentary Conference', 27 August 2007, at: www.am.gov.lv (accessed 27 August 2008).
21. 'Europe's Strategy for the Baltic Sea Region', written by Baltic Strategy Working Group, given by the President of the European Commission José Manuel Barroso, 15 November 2006.
22. 'An EU Strategy for the Baltic Sea Region', speech by Cecilia Malmström at a discussion with the Baltic Intergroup, European Parliament, Strasbourg, 12 Dec 2007, at: www.sweden.gov.se (accessed 6 June 2009).
23. See EU, 'Strategy for the Baltic Sea Region, Regional Policy – Inforegio', at: ec.europa.eu/regional_policy/cooperation/baltic/ (accessed 8 April 2009).
24. For information on HELCOM, see www.helcom.fi/helcom/en_GB/aboutus/ (accessed 8 April 2009).
25. See www.ndep.org
26. A good example is the Baltic Metropoles Network (BaltMET) and its action plan; see www.baltmet.org/pub/ (accessed 9 April 2009).

10
Central Europe

Béla Greskovits

The Visegrád group founded by Czechoslovakia, Hungary and Poland in 1991 represents a specific spatial cluster within the EU. Its political economy is characterized by three main features, which provide the functional focus of the chapter. First, the region's integration into the Single Market converged on a foreign-led export-oriented model underpinned by adequate infrastructure development, generous incentive packages, and investment promotion agencies to attract transnational corporations (TNCs). Second, over the early 1990s and mid-2000s the Visegrád states kept in place relatively generous systems of social welfare uniquely geared towards the elderly 'non-productive' groups of society. Although the adopted industrial and social policies have not been without success, they are at odds with the Lisbon agenda that gives preference to alternative ways of combining economic competitiveness with social inclusion. Finally, the simultaneous pursuit of the above costly and contradictory agendas made the coordination of fiscal and monetary policies difficult. Hence the third peculiar aspect of the Visegrád path lies in contested and ineffective institutions of macro-economic coordination. Accordingly, on the temporal dimension of membership integration the region is differentiated by delays in the implementation of the Lisbon agenda and, with the exception of Slovakia, lagging compliance with the Maastricht criteria of macro-economic convergence, which led to repeated postponement of eurozone entry. After substantiating in some detail the peculiarity of the Visegrád path, section two asks about the logics of its emergence.

Explanations are sought at three levels – national, supra-national and regional – and in the interplay among their political processes (see Keating, Chapter 4 in this volume). After the influence of domestic politics and the EU are touched upon, the chapter's main task is to establish the impact of the intermediate *regional* context. Does the Visegrád group form a region characterized by shared attitudes to European integration and institutions of regional cooperation? What are the particular mechanisms through which regionalization has left its mark on these countries' common features?

The proposed answer is that although the Visegrád group can indeed be viewed as a region, its logic of regionalization is unusual in the sense that nation-states' competition has been more influential in reproducing its attributes than their

cooperation. Hence the chapter's central contention: the Visegrád group constitutes a *region of rivals*, while its countries *cooperate only occasionally* and in special
circumstances. To understand the conditions of cooperation and the motifs and
forms of competition time, both historical *longue durée* and the shorter horizons
of transformation and Europeanization, must be factored in (see Goetz, Chapter 5
in this volume). Section three briefly revisits the historical contexts within which
these states and their predecessors cooperated or competed with each other, or
rather walked their own way.

Section four argues that in the aftermath of exceptional cooperative efforts
characterizing the early transformation years, state and private actors' rivalry
in the emerging Visegrád growth pole of foreign-controlled export industries
became the dominant force of differentiation in the context of Europeanization.
In particular, the chapter identifies two types of competitive regional logics.
The first denotes *rivalry among peer nations* and is rooted in historically shaped
national and ethnic identitities. The second falls closer to a *marketing logic* and
stems from these states' efforts to differentiate their locations from those of
their neighbours to attract foreign direct investment (FDI) more effectively.
The chapter concludes with a summary of the findings and a brief reflection on
how state rivalry tends to undermine the region's willingness and capacity to
combat collectively the devastating impact of the current global financial and
economic crisis.

Domestic and supra-national political factors of the Visegrád states' similarities

Simultaneous pursuit of conflicting and costly social objectives financed by a
handful of taxpayers and social security contributors leading to recurrent fiscal
instability is the simplified summary of the features making for the distinctiveness
of the Visegrád group's integration pattern. As Bohle and Greskovits (2007) established, no other new Member State of the EU has opted for as generous industrial
policy regimes and welfare states as the Visegrád countries have. During the first
half of the 1990s, industrial firms and banks were granted time and financial
resources to weather the hard times, restructure activities and find new outlets for
their products. From the late 1990s, the earlier *ad hoc* rescue measures have been
replaced by proactive and more institutionalized intervention geared towards
attracting TNCs, which are increasingly recognized as the main agents of export-
oriented reindustrialization. Subsidies, cash grants, tax incentives, cheap credit
and special privatization techniques have been adopted and large infrastructure
development projects initiated region-wide to 'pamper in their infancy' and later
help the growth of transnational export industries. It is striking to recognize the
region's success in eliciting the involvement of powerful change agents of the
global economy. By 2007, the region's inward foreign direct investment (FDI)
stock far exceeded that of Brazil, Mexico and Russia, and equalled that of Africa
(UNDP, 2008). FDI poured into the physical and human capital-intensive complex
industries and turned the Visegrád countries into major producers and exporters

of goods in which many of the advanced economies of continental Europe specialize: cars, machinery and equipment, electronics and chemicals.

At the same time, the Visegrád countries spent little on R&D, and generally neglected assistance to small and medium-size domestic firms. Until the early 2000s lack of finance impaired the expansion of new private firms, as foreign bank subsidiaries preferred financing large TNC- and state-owned enterprises to the riskier business of small-scale lending, while the financial and production-related services tailored to small firms' needs developed slowly. In the absence of adequate industrial policies it was, arguably, the post-socialist states' incapacity and/or unwillingness to enforce tax and social security payments to regulate employment standards in the grey economy that rescued the *petit bourgeoisie* from region-wide extinction. Combined with other factors, the above policies, which allowed businesses to escape fiscal contributions either legally (due to official incentive schemes) or illegally (due to authorities' tolerance of evasion), undermined the financial basis of generous social policies.

Notwithstanding financial constraints, as late as in the early 2000s and beyond social spending remained remarkably high in the Visegrád area. Overall, these welfare states have had a fair record in maintaining a degree of social cohesion, as in light of measures of poverty risk or relative income shares around the mid-2000s the Visegrád newcomers did not suffer from significantly larger poverty or inequality than many old EU Member States (EUROSTAT, n.d.). Nevertheless, the structure, main target groups and impact of social policies have been unique.

On the one hand, the Visegrád states' social contract envisages protection from decline in social hierarchy due to material deprivation and status loss. Protection has been granted primarily to those who had acquired a fair social status through work in socialist times. These vulnerable and politically vocal groups have been appeased by encompassing schemes of public healthcare and liberalized access to disability pensions and early retirement resulting in 'abnormal' (under-age) pensioner booms (Vanhuysse, 2007). These systems' way of redistributing risk of impoverishment across age groups is unique. While children and youth run the highest risk of becoming poor, the Visegrád populations' at-risk-of-poverty rate gradually declines with aging, and reaches its bottom in the oldest generations.[1] To be sure, it is not the generosity of pensions *per se* that saves the elderly from high risk of impoverishment. Rather, early retirement offers a degree of material security, which allows reintegration into formal or informal markets – whether by running family businesses or moonlighting – from relatively safe positions (Szalai, 2007). On the other hand, under the above social contract the most vulnerable unemployed and partly Roma dependants of the welfare state are pushed to the sidelines – witness the meagre spending on active and passive labour-market policies and the failure of Roma integration programmes region-wide.

As to the sustainability of the Visegrád group's social budgets, the essence of their problem is well captured by Rhodes' contention: 'If you want to have a large and sustainable welfare state, you have to be able to pay for it' (2002: 309). The same applies to generous public aid granted to 'sunset' or 'sunrise' industries and services. As collection of social-security contributions and taxes in the necessary amount and structure has been a serious challenge for the Visegrád states, their social protection systems have been on the verge of bankruptcy, and their state households and budgets in high debt and deficit. While over the hard times of transformation welfare expenditures and widely tolerated non-contribution of fiscal revenues kept disruptive social protest and political radicalism at bay, the coexistence of large public households and a large informal economy eventually threatened to trap the Visegrád states in a vicious circle. Rampant evasion of tax and social-security payments spurred legal workers and firms (which found their own tax burdens climbing as so many opted out around them) to begin looking for ways to avoid their own obligations (Rhodes and Keune 2006: 284).

These symptoms shed light on a grave coordination problem and the related political features of the Visegrád states' integration path. As argued by Katzenstein, '[f]iscal effectiveness can be interpreted as an indirect, economic-outcome measure of the coordination of diverging political objectives across different policy sectors' (1985: 93). In the western European small states democratic corporatist institutions delivered, on a permanent basis, the balancing acts required for the efficient coordination of partly conflicting social objectives. Since democratic corporatism has not sunk deep roots in the Visegrád area, the task of balancing among the costs of social welfare and industrial policies and the requirements of macro-economic stability has been *largely left to the process of democratic competition*. How have democratic politics shaped the Visegrád integration path?

Crucial initial choices to generate consent and legitimacy through mitigating the social and economic costs of transformation locked political parties into a peculiar pattern of democratic competition that reproduced pensioner-biased welfarism, foreign-biased industry protectionism, fiscal overspending – and generally the dominance of short-term political motifs behind policy decisions. Aware of the popularity of social programmes and pensioners' voting power, and knowing the crucial importance of attracting FDI, centrist parties went into debt to keep up spending on welfare and industry despite negative macro-economic consequences. However, as the social programmes provided were insufficient relative to needs, during elections citizens kept punishing incumbents, who they saw as responsible for their grievances. In consequence, centre-right and centre-left forces alternated in power with generally meagre chances for a second term in government.

As to the supra-national dimension of the Visegrád states' policy convergence, the EU has, of course, become increasingly important as an agenda-setter and a constraint on deviant stances. In this regard, it is important to note that by the time of EU enlargement and beyond, the above aspects of the Visegrád political economies ran counter to the Lisbon approach to competitiveness and social cohesion, as well as to the Maastricht criteria of macro-economic convergence. The Lisbon Review of members' performance gives preference to market-enhancing competition policy over excessive state aid, assistance to new domestic start-ups over subsidies to huge foreign firms, and reformed social policies to reintegrate people into the workforce rather than pension-dominated welfare provisions. On these dimensions the Visegrád group ranks behind most of the old and even some of the new EU Member States (Blanke and Lopez-Claros, 2004). Furthermore, apart from exceptional short periods of good performance, the Visegrád countries have been laggards in meeting the Maastricht convergence criteria, and, save for Slovakia, have had to give up their earlier hopes of a fast-track eurozone entry.

Interestingly, the lapses of compliance with the Lisbon and Maastricht requirements common to the majority of Visegrád countries have not led to their coordinated search for remedies. These states have failed in effectively pressuring the EU to adjust the Lisbon or Maastricht agendas to better fit their specific situation of late development, foreign-led economic restructuring, and need for fast catching-up growth and political stability. Neither have they intensified collective efforts to beef up R&D, higher education, infrastructure development, or better exploit the developmental potential of cross-border Euroregions.

At a first glance, the absence of collaboration might not be all that surprising. Analysing the dynamics of regional cooperation after socialism, Bunce noted that 'inter-state cooperation is the exception, not the rule, in international politics. States do not tend to form cooperative linkages with each other because there is an appeal and a logic to "going it alone"' (1998: 245–6). As argued above, 'going it alone' certainly had its political appeal and logic in the Visegrád democracies' domestic arenas.

Equally important is the fact that the EU's approach to the Visegrád countries' regionalization was ambivalent. On the one hand, as demonstrated below, from the early 1990s the EU has promoted certain forms of regional cooperation. On the other hand, during the crucial accession negotiations the EU has opted for a strict case-by-case approach rather than attributing any importance to membership in the Visegrád group or the Central European Free Trade Area (CEFTA) from the viewpoint of full membership (Bohle, 2006). Moreover, while after accession the short-term logic of democratic competition has remained a driving force of differentiation, the EU's reluctance to provide incentives for compliance or seriously sanction temporary divergence has been permissive thereof. Even concerning macro-economic convergence, where the EU pressed harder for compliance than in case of the Lisbon agenda, let alone the European Social Model, after enlargement it had no more effective sanctions at its disposal than shaming and forcing weak performers to 'revise and resubmit' their convergence programmes. Importantly, international financial actors continued to feel relatively sure that the Visegrád countries were still on a path towards qualifying for full membership in EMU. In consequence, before autumn 2008 they made no moves to punish these states despite the fact that Hungary, for instance, has been plagued by permanent fiscal instability.

That said, from a culturalist viewpoint, shared identity, geo-strategic position and common attitudes towards European integration should have resulted in substantially more cooperation among the Visegrád states in the above or in other matters crucial for upgrading their membership status and reputation within the EU. After all, as Love notes, throughout centuries, 'for the region's leaders and intellectuals ... progress was a road, rough but not impassable, leading to Europe, the First World' (Love, 1996: 5–6). Similarly, many ordinary Visegrád-country citizens shared the view of the EU as a place abundant in all those properties that their region lacked: an efficient economy, a generous public welfare system, political freedom and respected national sovereignty. Last but not least, the region has not lacked the ideational and organizational conditions for more effective and frequent cooperation.

To understand the outcome, three important peculiarities must be considered. First, these countries have had a far more contradictory, ambivalent and frequently strained relationship with western culture and the international community than is the case with any other European region. Ironically, while sizable local elite groups have for long been western-oriented, they *never fully trusted* the West. Indeed, a common *fil rouge* woven through the region's history is the feeling of repeated betrayal by western, in particular European, powers. Examples abound, as each country can tell about its painful experience (Bibó, 1986). Second, the region's own history can equally justify mistrust and trust among its Member States. Finally, similarities can breed competition and cooperation alike – depending on the context. A brief detour to history will help to illuminate the salience of these factors.

Past regional experiences

Simply put, the Visegrád area's history is no less replete with externally imposed but locally resented frameworks and processes of regional cooperation than with episodes of failed bottom-up initiatives to that end, which were routinely frustrated by the ruling empires and quasi-empires: the Austro-Hungarian monarchy and the Soviet Union. Thus, Keating is right in pointing out that acting as 'empire' the EU might invoke a legacy that 'is difficult to rehabilitate in eastern and central Europe' (Keating, Chapter 4 in this volume).

Kende's study provides a perceptive overview of the *longue durée* of failed bottom-up attempts, from the ideas to transform the Habsburg Empire into a 'Confederation of the Peoples of the Danube Valley', to the various plans to integrate Czechoslovakia with Poland, or Romania with Hungary or Bulgaria, proposed after the Second World War by a few conservative or communist leaders and blocked, in the latter cases, by Stalin. Kende asserts that despite their popularity in intellectual circles, the plans of confederation and integration had been sentenced to failure by their neglect of existing power relations and by the fact that they 'never could rely on broad popular support, and were rather incompatible with economic "interests" (or rather aspirations)' (Kende, 1990: 10).

Indeed, whatever economic cooperation among the industrialized and agrarian lands of the Habsburg Empire occurred, it took place in the context of fierce political competition among Hungarians, Czechs, Slovaks and Romanians and other peoples. Initially, their rivalry had centred on achieving cultural autonomy or enhanced political status and power within the Monarchy. By the end of Empire, aspirations for independence pitted these nations and ethnic groups against each other. As is well-known, both sides had aligned with the Axis or Allied powers to change or maintain the status quo, which was altered during and restored again after the Second World War. As the post-Second World War settlement established the new states of Czechoslovakia, Romania and Yugoslavia incorporating two-thirds of Hungary's former territory and a (dominantly non-Hungarian) half of its population, the hitherto ethnic-based rivalry turned into inter-state hostility between the loser and the winners. In light of their abundant legacies of rivalry and hostility, it is hardly surprising that after their forced incorporation into the military and economic bodies of the Soviet bloc, the Warsaw Treaty Organization and the Council for Mutual Economic Assistance (CMEA), the satellite states found it difficult to reinvent themselves as brothers-in-arms.

While outright hostility was kept at bay by the Soviet interest in keeping order in its 'backyard', the satellite communist elites' mutual suspicions about each others' revisionism or anti-Soviet nationalism helped the Kremlin to resort to techniques of divide and rule. Indeed, up to the end of the socialist system, domestic political processes and events had been remarkably out of phase with those of neighbours. During the Polish and Hungarian revolutions of 1956, Czechoslovakia had been among the advocates of hard-line remedies for the system's crises. A decade later, in 1968, military troops of the then reform-socialist Hungary and Poland joined the Soviet Army to crush the Prague Spring attempt to adopt 'socialism with a human face'. In 1981, General Wojcziech Jaruzelski's dictatorship, which outlawed Solidarity and cracked down on unruly Poles with martial law, received support from both Gustáv Husák's pacified Czechoslovakia and János Kádár's 'cheerful barrack of the camp', Hungary.

As far as economic issues are concerned, a different dynamic pattern had been set in motion by Soviet-type central planning and its consequence, the shortage economy. Evidently, economic competition among the satellites could be marginal at best. At the same time, inability to elicit their cooperation had been a major weakness of the CMEA. All in all, autarky prevailed over collaboration, import-substitution over export-orientation, and all-encompassing production profiles over specialization in selected production segments or niches. The almost identical evolving economic structures originated in socialist development strategists' undifferentiated preference for heavy industries, such as metallurgy, basic chemicals, and heavy machinery and equipment.

Irony of ironies, the autarkic logic remained appealing during the 1970s and 1980s, when the oil-price hikes, *détente*, growing awareness of a West–East technological divide and welfare considerations all forced the CMEA to encourage a new division of labour based on specialization, transfer of technology and know-how, and intra-industry trade to advance towards complementary rather than structurally similar profiles (Tardos, 1980). The satellite economies did make some attempts to specialize: for example, Hungary in production of buses and pharmaceuticals, Czechoslovakia and Poland automobiles and heavy chemicals, and all three countries in varied branches of consumer electronics and computers. Yet these efforts were permanently hampered by the shortage syndrome that characterized the regional as much as the domestic economies. At the regional level, the syndrome manifested itself in insatiable demand for imported inputs, long delivery times, poor quality and lack of product differentiation, consumer services and other features, which have all been analysed in detail by Kornai (1992).

In consequence, individual countries remained interested in 'going it alone' and keeping up parallel industrial structures and the longest possible supplier chains within their own economic space, in order to minimize dependence on unreliable, low-quality and shortage-prone intra-industry trade with their neighbours. They were no less reluctant to share with their neighbours the western licences, technology and know-how that they had either purchased for hard currency or accessed through smuggling and industrial espionage. Despite the efforts towards specialization and cooperation through intra-industry trade, CMEA trade largely remained the same as it ever was: exchange of finished manufacturing products among the smaller Member States, and manufacturing goods and foodstuffs for resources between the latter and the Soviet Union.

While thus national autarky was the quintessential legacy of the socialist system, its collapse heralded a heyday of regional cooperation – albeit more in political than economic matters. Three, respectively ideational, political and economic manifestations, all dating to the first heroic period of systemic change, deserve to be mentioned: the revival of the Central European idea, the Visegrád Declaration and the founding of the Central European Free Trade Area (CEFTA). The ideological and political initiatives reflected these states' own aspirations, whereas the new framework of regional economic cooperation was encouraged by the EU, and only reluctantly adopted by the post-socialist countries.

The idea of Central Europe's cultural, political and economic distinctiveness was revived by dissident artists and public intellectuals, such as the Czech novelist Milan Kundera and Poland's Nobel Prize-winning poet Czeslaw Milosz. The theme was subsequently picked up by US political strategists, prominently Zbigniew Brzezinski, and the region's political leaders, such as Václav Havel. The long historical roots of (East-)Central European exceptionalism had been revealed by the influential study of the Hungarian historian Szücs about Europe's three historical regions. In his view, while East-Central Europe's history had for long been shaped by western influences, eastern and southeastern Europe's path radically diverged as it had been mainly influenced by the Byzantine Empire (1981).

Most important for this chapter's focus is the political career of the idea. As socialism collapsed, the notion of Central Europe's 'westernness' was adopted to justify demands for preferential treatment on the part of the West. In particular, the new elites used historicized regionalism as the ideological cornerstone of their strategies of differentiated (in the sense of fast and full) EU integration (Todorova, 1997). In some ways, the western-rim countries' differentiation from the rest of the 'East' had preceded and predicted similar discursive and policy efforts of local elites and the EU to redefine Bulgaria, Romania and, lately, Croatia as parts of Europe rather than the dramatically 'shrinking Balkans' (see Economides, Chapter 8 in this volume, and Dimitrova, 2008).

Alas, once its intellectuals and politicians reinvented Central Europe as a historical region, western leaders who in the early 1990s were still ambivalent about EU enlargement bought into the idea and suggested that Czechoslovakia, Hungary and Poland practise their regionalism and try and cooperate with each other before rushing to join the EU. So they did. Led by shared interests in building democratic capitalism, security, stability and a 'return to Europe' and concerned over the possibility of economic and political pressures from the teetering Soviet Union, in 1991 the three countries expressed their commitment to cooperation in the Visegrád Declaration (Bunce, 1998: 251–2).

However, while the fora and areas of cooperation were specified, the Visegrád group has never developed an institutional framework for regional cooperation. Rather 'it is based solely on the principle of periodical meetings of its representatives at various levels (from Prime Ministers and Presidents to expert consultations). An official meeting of Prime Ministers takes place on an annual basis. Between these summits, one of the V4 countries holds presidency, the part of which is the responsibility for drafting a one-year plan of action.'[2]

The plans of action are further concretized via the meetings of Visegrád state officials and bodies: that is, occasional meetings of various ministers; State Secretaries of Foreign Affairs (twice a year); ambassadors (four times a year); coordinators (twice a year); and expert groups. These meetings' agendas are crowded with tasks of enhancing cooperation in border and immigration affairs, security and defence, energy, transport, telecommunications and culture. It is beyond this chapter's scope and its author's competence to review, let alone assess, all these initiatives (see Chapters 16–22 of this volume). However, the actual achievements seem to have been subject to constraints both before and after EU accession.

Before 2004, Visegrád-area politicians shared a suspicion that the EU had a hidden agenda to use them as a buffer region outside its boundaries and promote their regionalism as a substitute for membership. Czech Premier Václav Klaus formulated this fear most clearly when he rejected 'any concept of the group as a poor man's club and buffer zone to keep the Balkans and the former Soviet Union at a safe distance from Western Europe' (RFE/RL Daily Report, no. 57, 24 March 1993, cited by Todorova 1997: 159).

Such concerns had been reinforced by the EU's insistence on the importance of economic rather than merely sluggish political cooperation for a true revival of the historical region. Thus, even if in 1992 each member of the Visegrád group signed the CEFTA that established the region as a free trade area and 'became the *only* regional institution that the Visegrád group has in fact constructed' (Bunce, 1998: 260), they did so without much enthusiasm. One rationale behind the CEFTA was that the bilateral Europe Agreements 'gave more tariff advantages in trade with the EC than the "Most Favoured Nation" framework' under which the Visegrád group's members traded with each other, and the new agreement merely ensured equal treatment for them on the regional market (Dimitrova, 1999: 4). However, even if 'CEFTA was a way to avoid the overreaction in trade reorientation, the members did not seem to perceive it as such; rather, they had to be urged' by the EU (ibid.). Furthermore, the further institutional development of regional economic cooperation has been minimal, not least because of the Visegrád states' fear that overdoing regionalization would give 'the EU an excuse to put off the question of full membership of the central European countries' (Bunce, 1998: 260).

However, there have been deeper structural obstacles to state-led economic regionalization. Due to their inheritance of almost identical rather than complementary economic and industrial structures, the Visegrád economies did not have much to trade with each other to begin with. Indeed, their modest initial shares in regional markets dropped still further as the recession following CMEA's breakdown and the Europe Agreements diverted their trade to western European markets. All in all, the revival of regional trade and the thorough integration of the Visegrád group's economic space did not happen before TNCs incorporated the region's main assets, privatized firms, skilled labour and relevant infrastructure into their global and European cross-border systems of production, commerce and finance.

State competition within the transnational economic cluster

With the benefit of hindsight it is clear that the exceptional collaborative efforts of the heroic period, including, ironically, the tacit cooperation in cutting back on the EU's over-zealous efforts to craft a Visegrád region, left behind their own legacy that proved to be important for the means and mechanisms of regionalization a decade later. Through their newly accumulated experience in effective collective action while leaving the East and returning to Europe, the Visegrád states learned to consider one another as *peer nations*, whose moves in economic policy or political strategy deserved serious attention and scrutiny for their potential impact on other states within the region. Although this new experience fell short of ending their historically engrained rivalry, in all likelihood it enhanced their interest in each other, and thereby laid the groundwork for the ensuing peculiar pattern of regional economic integration. Two logics of state action, both competitive rather than cooperative, paved the way towards that outcome.

Paradoxically, the socialist legacy of highly similar industrial structures, initially so disadvantageous for a fast reinvigoration of regional trade, proved to be an advantage as it provided the essential foundations for the Visegrád economies' rapid foreign-led and export-oriented reindustrialization. The inherited fairly complex industries helped the Visegrád group to attract transnational manufacturing investors, whose first locational choices in the post-socialist East critically hinged upon the relative abundance of adequate human capital.

To account for TNCs' original motivation to invest in the region, Greskovits (2005) adopted Vernon's product cycle theory which contends that 'investment will go first to those countries whose supply structures (proxied by factors of production) are most similar to those in the home country, and later to countries whose supply structures are less similar' (Vernon, 1971; Kurth, 1979: 3–4). Accordingly, in the 1990s the Visegrád countries that had been relatively large automobile, machinery or electronics producers and exporters under socialism could rightly expect much higher inflows of automotive or electronics FDI than the others where such industries would have to be built from scratch. At this point, it is useful to recall that while by the 1980s the small CMEA Member States increased their physical and human capital-intensive exports to their mainly east European foreign markets, exports from the Soviet Union became largely resource-based.

To be sure, the evolving foreign-invested and controlled systems of production did not have much of a true national character. Rather, by the early 2000s, the clustering of complex industries brought about the tight cross-border integration of the Czech Republic, south-western Poland, the north-west of the Slovak Republic and north-western Hungary that further enhanced the attraction of the fast-emerging regional economy. In 2006, the region had more than five per cent of the EU's entire inward FDI stock. Remarkably, in 2002–6, more than one-fifth of the EU's total number of greenfield foreign investment projects were initiated in the Visegrád cluster (UNDP, 2007). In 2007 one in six of all European cars was produced in the area, and the region's share in European car production was expected to climb to well above 20 per cent in the coming years (Heimer, 2008).

However, this kind of regionalization has not advanced through inter-state cooperation but rather its reverse: cut-throat rivalry. Perhaps more than the TNCs themselves, which by the beginning of the new millennium could produce efficiently virtually anywhere within the cluster, the Visegrád states, and especially the ambitious latecomer Slovak Republic, have cared a great deal about whether a new car-assembly or electronics transplant operated on their own, or on their neighbours', territory. They have had two separate, equally powerful motifs and strategies to compete.

On the one hand, precisely because the essential locational advantages orienting foreign investors have been rather similar across the whole cluster, increasingly the Visegrád states have borrowed elements of the marketing strategies of competing private firms, and integrated them into their own policies to boost FDI. Acting like firms, these states went far in 'differentiating their products', namely those of their own locations 'on sale', from those offered by their regional competitors (Kolesár, 2006; Trnik, 2007).

This said, however, the Visegrád states have not merely adopted the strategies of private businesses. They also tried to mobilize broad popular support for their efforts to out-compete peer nations, by conscious appeals to historically rooted national identity and pride. Politicians and the national media attributed massive greenfield projects a symbolic meaning, and interpreted the outcome of cross-regional competition for FDI as the national victory of, say, 'the tiger of the Tatra mountains' Slovakia over the 'Pannonian puma' Hungary (to cite only two of the many exotic terms adopted), or vice versa. The resulting 'bidding war' of tax incentives, targeted subsidy-packages and auxiliary infrastructure investment magnified the overall cost of complex FDI inflows and exacerbated the competitive disadvantages of countries outside the cluster, especially if they were structurally handicapped too.

In sum, within the emerging trans-national regional economy, the Visegrád countries could not any longer follow the logic of 'going it alone'. Rather, both the logic of rivalry among peer nations and the marketing logic of product differentiation forced them to take cognizance of their counterparts' policies and be responsive to them. Through the implied multi-dimensional and frequent interaction mobilizing interest no less than identity, state rivalry contributed to the emergence of the Visegrád regional economy. In addition, the regional logics of competition have been underpinned by supra-national and trans-national pressures too.

On the one hand, international political economy accounts stress that '[s]ince the 1980s, the European mode of integration has aimed at enhancing competitiveness at all levels of European societies, [and thus] the EU has developed into an interface that enhances regime competition between different national systems of governance' (Bohle, 2006: 65). On the other hand, TNCs have tried to exploit state competition for their own competitive strategies. They adopted various techniques and methods to keep in motion the Visegrád regions' incentive-driven 'race to the top' (Kolesár 2006).

As Ziltener argues, 'Most of the burden of the adaptation process to this new competitive environment rests upon the nation state and national institutions' (2000: 88–96). In the Visegrád area this seems to be the case indeed. The self-propelling logics of regional competition accelerated the convergence of national industrial policies on generous incentives to foreign capital, led to costly infrastructure development projects geared towards the needs of the expanding cluster, and provoked recurrent cycles of competition through lowered taxes and social-security payments. Such changes, in turn, deepened the fiscal crisis of the welfare state that justified the attempts at public sector reform and retrenchment, to which citizens responded with increasing social and electoral protest.

Conclusions

Eventually the competitive pressures paved the way for *intra-regional differentiation*. Latecomer Slovakia took the lead in welfare retrenchment, encompassing reform of its public sector and, fulfilling all entry conditions, being allowed to introduce the euro in 2009. In contrast, over 2000–6 Hungary increased its welfare expenditure dramatically, delayed the reform of its public sector, failed to comply with any of the Maastricht convergence criteria, and had to repeatedly postpone euro entry. Today Slovakia weathers the global financial and economic crisis from a safer position than Hungary, which from autumn 2008 has had to face savage speculative attacks against its national currency, runs on its transnational banks, massive capital flight, recession of its foreign-controlled industries, rising unemployment and foreign debt, and all in all became one of the 'hotspots' of the crisis. Unsurprisingly, the crisis has reinforced the whole syndrome of Visegrád states' competition.

Apparently not bothered by his words' inevitable negative reception in Hungary, Slovak Premier Robert Fico did not shy away from displaying *Schadenfreude* over the troubles of his country's once formidable rival:

> Today we can clearly see the difference between Slovakia and crisis-ridden Hungary. We observe from a secure position the struggle of our Hungarian friends, who messed up everything from economic to social and financial

policies, as no one else in the world did. Slovakia will combat the crisis, while Hungary currently lacks the needed capacities.[3]

As if in response, Hungary's new government's Premier Gordon Bajnai tried to justify his programme of draconic fiscal austerity in spring 2009 by claiming that, 'it will depend on our present decisions whether in future new jobs will be created in Slovakia or Romania, or here in Hungary'.[4]

More importantly, when in March 2009 Bajnai's predecessor Ferenc Gyurcsány tried to convince EU leaders of the necessity of a special rescue package for the new members, other Visegrád statesmen (and even Bulgaria) backed off from supporting the plan on the grounds that despite the crisis their own economies were still better off than that of Hungary. Moreover, when questioning the necessity and wisdom of a regional approach to new members' problems, German Chancellor Angela Merkel could aptly refer to Slovak, Czech and Polish views on the Visegrád group's internal differentiation, and suggest that, on these grounds, the case-by-case approach ought to be the preferred response.

This chapter has argued that the Visegrád countries have largely failed to act collectively in order to settle their difficulties of compliance with key EU agendas or combat economic and financial problems which eventually, of course, affect them all. But if these states have been reluctant to effectively cooperate in such crucial matters, then how accurate is it to view them as constituent parts of a region? The proposed answer is that although the Visegrád space is more than a pure geographic term or a convenient organizing myth, the primary driving forces of its regionalization are not shared identity, attitudes to the EU, or common interest in integration but rivalry among peer nations that frequently tend to act as competing private businesses. As state competition within the trans-national economic cluster contributed to reproducing the distinctive functional features of foreign industry protectionism, welfarism under stress and fiscal overspending, the region emerged as a new and salient political level, the processes and pressures of which shaped its differentiated integration path as much as factors traced to the national or EU levels did. All this implies that by exploring the varied logics of regional rivalry, respectively stemming from democracy, national identity and a trans-national regional economy, we should arrive at a more accurate account of differentiated integration than we would achieve by focusing merely on national or supra-national politics, or on the shared attitudes and forms of cooperation that make a region.

Is the Visegrád states' differentiated integration breaking down or reinforcing traditional state clusters? It seems to do both simultaneously. On the one hand, as argued above, the Visegrád economic space is no longer parcelled out among nation-states but became a trans-national space interwoven by foreign-controlled systems of production, commerce and finance, where national borders do not limit cross-border transactions and movement of capital and labour. On the other hand, TNCs rely heavily on these nation-states for incentive packages, infrastructure and welfare systems to reproduce their skilled and healthy labour forces and control the social damage caused by capital mobility. Will the differentiated integration have an effect on the politics of EU integration? One consequence might be that the peculiar driving forces of the differentiated Visegrád path have made it easier for EU bodies to deal with these states either on a case-by-case basis or as one region – depending on the EU's own, or its more powerful and coopera-tive members', interests.

Notes

1. Author's calculation based on EUROSTAT (n.d.).
2. www.visegradgroup.eu/main.php?folder
3. *Népszabadság*, 22 November 2008, accessed online at: http://nol.hu
4. *Népszabadság*, 4 April 2009, accessed online at: http://nol.hu

11
Franco-German Europe

Alistair Cole

The Franco-German relationship can lay a strong claim to be the principal bilateral relationship within the European Union. To reason in terms of a Franco-German Europe makes no sense unless these two powerful states are identified as forming a core cluster, irrespective of precise legal arrangements. In the case of France and Germany, core Europe might refer both to the formal bilateral alliance between the two leading continental European EU states (the introductory section) or to the role of the Franco-German relationship in providing a form of leadership of the (differentiated) European integration project (the main body of this chapter). In their own right, France and Germany have staked a claim to leadership based on the fact that they were founder-members, repositories of historical memory and chief actors of the symbolism of post-war reconciliation (Hendriks and Morgan, 2001; Webber, 1999). The strongest confirmation of Franco-German leadership, however, is one where formal differentiated integration ought not to be necessary. Explicit calls for *avant-garde* action by France and Germany are, more often than not, signs of weakness, of an inability to co-steer the European ship. Somewhat paradoxically, the prospect of a core Europe can reveal a hollow core.

The Franco-German bilateral relationship and differentiated integration

There is a need for conceptual clarity about a Franco-German Europe and differentiated integration. The existence of a formal bilateral, treaty-based agreement between two EU Member States is arguably the original form of differentiated integration outside of the Community institutions. Most observers of Franco-German relations insist upon the high degree of institutionalization of their bilateral relationship (Schild, 2002). The two countries are bound by a far-reaching treaty signed in 1963 and strengthened in 2003 (Vailliant, 2002; Defrance and Pfeil, 2005). Writers in the neo-Realist tradition sometimes specifically identify the Franco-German relationship as a directorate leading the European Union (Baun, 1994; Chang, 1999; Pedersen, 1998). This leadership claim has depended, in part, upon the relationships maintained between individual French and German political leaders, whose propensity to drive forward an integrationist agenda has been variable. For most of the Gaullist period (1958–69) France looked to tie in Germany, but was unwilling to go beyond an asymmetrical bilateral relationship, conceived of as a directorate (*directoire*). In de Gaulle's vision, France would lead Europe in privileged alliance with Germany on the basis of close intergovernmental cooperation. The directorate was conceived of by de Gaulle as a direct challenge to multilateral supra-nationalism and in particular to the Monnet method of staged progress towards supra-national leadership of the EU. From the German perspective, France was often an awkward partner after de Gaulle's return to power in 1958. The General's dual veto of British entry into the EC, in 1963 and 1967, embarrassed the Federal Republic. De Gaulle's empty chair policy of 1965, leading to the Luxembourg compromise of 1966, directly challenged the community mode of governance favoured by the Germans (Henig, 1997). The Gaullist rhetoric of European autonomy was unacceptable in most respects to the semi-sovereign, pro-Atlanticist Federal Republic under Erhard or Kiesinger.

De Gaulle's successor, Pompidou, and German Chancellor Brandt distrusted each other, the former focused upon facilitating British entry into the EEC, the latter preoccupied with *ostpolitik*. President Giscard d'Estaing and Chancellor Schmidt were the first leadership couple since de Gaulle and Adenauer to enjoy a relationship based on mutual confidence. Giscard d'Estaing and Schmidt together piloted two major decisions whose effect was to enhance European integration: the creation of the European Council in 1974 and of the European Monetary System (EMS) in 1979. The integrationist tempo was further accelerated under President Mitterrand and Chancellor Kohl: the internal market and the Single European Act (1986), moves towards economic and monetary union and closer defence and security collaboration in the Maastricht Treaty (1992) were all directly associated with Kohl and Mitterrand, though other actors were also important. The leadership couple of Jacques Chirac and Gerhard Schröder defended established positions, rather than launching new ideas. Both men were instinctively 'nationals' and neither felt a personal imperative to promote European integration. Today, neither the current Chancellor, Angela Merkel, nor the French President Nicolas Sarkozy are unconditional supporters of an exclusive Franco-German relationship.

The claim that the Franco-German relationship itself is a form of differentiated integration is a powerful one. Whether or not we accept the neo-Realist framing of France and Germany as forming a *directoire*, many of the most important decisions in the history of the European Union are of French or Franco-German origin. When they have produced common initiatives, as over the single market, EMU or CAP reform, they have operated as a very persuasive and powerful political force. Franco-German leadership has been most effective when France and Germany have been encouraged by other states to be proactive. Historically, the Franco-German relationship has performed a powerful agenda-setting role, especially in treaty negotiations and major decisions such as budgetary reforms. Franco-German bargains are one important variable for understanding EU constitutive politics; analysis of the Maastricht and Amsterdam Treaty negotiations highlighted the powerful agenda-setting role of France and Germany

(Cole, 2001; Mazzucelli, 1997). So, the influence of the Franco-German relation-ship should not be underestimated and continues to provide one version of the leadership of the EU.

A Franco-German Europe? Alternative visions of differentiated integration

The debate over a European core has regularly resurfaced at critical junctures in the development of the European Union. The most celebrated German proposals for a 'hard core' came in the form of the Schäuble-Lamers CDU paper of 1994 (drawn up by Wolfgang Schäuble, a close aide of Helmut Kohl), an explicit attempt to theorize a multi-speed Europe. The CDU paper called for the adoption of a federal European constitution, a speeding up of EMU and the creation of a European defence com-munity. At the heart of the proposals lay the creation of a hard core of five Member States, consisting of Germany, France and the Benelux countries. The hard core would push ahead with a single currency and a single CFSP, allowing other states to catch up when and if they were able. The Schäuble-Lamers paper also advocated widening the Community to include the central and eastern European countries by the year 2000. Reconciling widening and deepening required the emergence of a hard core (Janning, 1996). These proposals provoked a strong reaction in several European capitals, with excluded founding-member country Italy especially out-raged. France strongly opposed the idea of a two-speed EMU: she had consistently espoused the cause of a broadly based economic and monetary union and feared being submerged in a Germanic sphere of influence, especially in the monetary domain. The 1994 'hard core' episode laid bare the ambiguities of the Franco-German relationship more generally. French Premier Edouard Balladur advanced the concept of 'variable geometry' shortly after, whereby the degree of integration should be dependent upon the qualities of the issue-area involved. The French view was close to the 'strengthened cooperation' procedure eventually adopted in the Amsterdam summit, strengthened at Nice and again in the Lisbon Treaty. 'Strengthened cooperation' falls far short of a hard core.

Proposals for differentiated integration have tended to follow national prefer-ences; a form of enhanced federalism for Germany, a strengthened inter-government-alism for France. These contrasting styles were illustrated by rival speeches by Joshka Fischer and Jacques Chirac in spring 2000. In May 2000, German Foreign Minister Fischer gave his vision of a European Federation in a speech to the Humboldt University, calling for the creation of a 'federalist centre of gravity' of the most integrationist states. In his speech to the Bundestag in June 2000, Chirac called for a pioneer group, which should come into existence from 2001. This pioneer group would be called upon to cooperate over economic policy coordination, defence and crime, all areas where states should perform the lead role. The pioneer group would be an inter-governmental structure from which the Commission would be excluded. No new treaty would be needed, though Chirac agreed with Fischer's call for a new European constitution. French institutional and policy preferences would best be served by such a pioneer group with a base in the treaties (the enhanced co-operation procedure defined at Amsterdam, refined at Nice), but with minimal interference from the Commission.

French and German leaders have tended to advocate inner cores when Europe has not been working well. Notions of inner cores inevitably strengthen inter-governmental conceptions of European integration; hence they arouse German suspicions, provoke the hostility of the Commission and the anxiety of potentially excluded members. The smaller EU countries are generally opposed to notions of the 'pioneer group', 'core Europe' 'federalist centre of gravity' or other formulations. They still look to the Commission and the community method to safeguard their interests. The Commission itself is very suspicious of forms of enhanced cooperation amongst the stronger Member States. The Commission's role as defender of the European general interest has led it to attempt to protect the smaller Member States, to resist any attempts at hegemony or *directoire* strategies. A Franco-German Union would be a very narrow conception of European unification, especially for Germany (Garton-Ash, 1994). Apart, perhaps, from the Gaullist period, French and German leaders have preferred to develop their bilateral relations within a wider European context (Markovits and Reich, 1997). Following the framework of analysis set out by Dyson and Sepos in Chapter 1 of this volume, the main body of the chapter will now consider in turn the functional, spatial and temporal dimensions of Franco-German relations and differentiated integration.

A Franco-German Europe: the functional dimension

In the following section, several core functional areas are considered that each differ in their potential for differentiated integration. Though other areas might have enriched even further our understanding and enabled more fine-grained comparisons, the constraints of space prevented consideration of areas such as immigration, Schengen or legal integration. The following examples include a sufficient variety of different types of issue-area to enable fairly robust conclusions to be drawn. The CAP offers a good example of *not* favouring differentiated integration, but of mobilizing community resources in the interests of one lobby. The example of the Growth and Stability Pact, on the other hand, demonstrates how arrangements initially conceived in terms of differentiated integration rebounded against Germany. The case of industrial and economic policy challenges any coherent notion of a Franco-German form of differentiated integration in this domain. The most sophisticated forms of differentiated integration in defence and foreign policy have not been driven by France and Germany acting alone.

The CAP: an undifferentiated core

The Common Agricultural Policy was based on a founding Franco-German agreement, whereby France agreed to lift tariff barriers on German industrial goods in return for a system of price support for its farmers. Respecting the CAP has been an important element of the Franco-German compact, though narrow French and German interests diverge in relation to the common policy. Recent evidence demonstrates how important the CAP is as a concrete symbol of Franco-German collaboration. Throughout the 1990s, there was profound disagreement between France and Germany over financing the CAP, with Germany reluctant to continue to subsidize a policy that mainly benefits French farmers. Yet the CAP forms part of the initial bargain between France and Germany, and Germany feels duty-bound to respect France's position. After years of public recriminations, France and Germany came to a bilateral agreement over CAP reform in October 2002 that was subsequently presented to the other Member States for ratification. The agreement on agriculture was a classic Franco-German bargain. The UK Prime Minister Tony Blair was excluded, and had not foreseen this renewed Franco-German strategy. The European Commission was also ignored, with neither France nor Germany referring to the conclusions of a report published months before by the Agriculture Commissioner Junckler. This episode demonstrated that the Franco-German relationship remains a very powerful defensive coalition when it can reach agreement on issues that otherwise endanger the functioning of the EU. Agreement on agriculture on French terms was essential to allow enlargement to take place: hence side payments and issue linkage, not differentiated integration, were the key drivers.

EMU: an expansive core?

The case of EMU is highly relevant, not just for the principle of differentiated integration that it embodies, but for the opposing French and German perspectives in terms of formulation, decision-making and implementation. In their research on monetary union, Dyson and Featherstone (1999) identify two rival advocacy coalitions – the 'monetarists' and the 'economists' – divided on the proper relationship between economic convergence and monetary union. The dominant coalition was the 'economist' one. It was represented by German, British, Dutch and Danish governments and their central banks. This advocacy coalition envisaged monetary union as being the end result of a long process towards economic convergence. The 'economist' coalition was opposed by the 'monetarist' one. This consisted of a group of states led by France (including Italy and Belgium) and supported by the Delors Commission. The monetarist coalition argued that the creation of a new monetary institution would itself force a process of economic convergence. This belief was consistent with the traditional Community method approach, based on elite socialization into EC institutional structures, the assumption of passive approval and progress through tight deadlines. The preference of the monetarist coalition was for a large number of states to be able to progress to EMU, rather than a narrow core. A hard-core EMU would be little more than a deutschmark zone and would entrench German hegemony.

In the case of EMU, Germany was the herald of differentiated integration. All German actors (in the Chancellery, the Finance Ministry, the Bundesbank) were inflexible in insisting that the single currency was implemented according to German rules and that Member States had to earn the right to form part of single currency zone. By insisting upon the Stability Pact (which became the Growth and Stability Pact [GSP] after the 1997 Amsterdam summit) Germany was able to introduce tough convergence criteria to accompany the implementation of the single currency. In practice, neither Germany nor France have been able to respect the tough criteria written into the Growth and Stability Pact that were intended to ensure the compliance of 'weak' states such as Italy and Greece. France and Germany defended their short-term national interests when they jointly buried the original Growth and Stability Pact in November 2003. It is striking how France and Germany continue to defend distinct positions in relation to the governance of the eurozone economies and the single currency. We would reject the hypothesis of a Franco-German Europe in this domain. Successive French presidents since Mitterrand (including Sarkozy) have called for an 'economic government' of the eurozone that successive German chancellors (including Merkel) have rejected.

An industrial core: protecting European capacities?

There is something counter-intuitive about setting a Franco-German Europe at the centre of differentiated integration in the economic and industrial policy sectors. The two nations have distinctive economic policy traditions (German ordo-liberalism, French *dirigisme*) that are opposed in key respects (Cole, 2001; Smith, 2005). German and French firms sometimes cooperate, sometimes not. Much closer relationships exist elsewhere – such as between German and Austrian companies, for example. In areas of recent market liberalization, France and Germany have often been at loggerheads. In telecommunications, an early alliance between France Télécom and Deutsche Telekom collapsed amidst bitter recriminations in 1999. In energy, regionally based German energy firms (RTE, E.ON) have opposed the acquisitive tastes of the French energy giants EDF and GDF (though the French and German governments share a common view on resisting the separation of energy production and distribution). In the automobile sector, there has been stiff industrial competition, for example between Renault and Volkswagen. In financial services, the proposed creation of the London/Frankfurt *bürse* in the late 1990s was perceived as a slight not just by the Paris stock exchange, but more generally by the French government. The Paris-based Euronext exchange ultimately preferred to be taken over by the NYSE (in 2006), rather than allying with the Frankfurt exchange. In transport, the rivalry between the French Alsthom and the German Siemens for building high-speed train links spans the globe.

Only in sectors such as aerospace and defence, where public procurement policies are of primordial importance, have French and German companies responded to political pressures to merge or collaborate. For years, France, Germany, Britain and Spain cooperated in the Airbus consortium, a rare example of European industrial cooperation and technology-sharing. Formal cooperation was taken a step further with the creation of the Franco–German–Spanish aerospace company EADS (the European Aeronautic Defence and Space Company) in 1999. EADS has been successful industrially, but remains tainted by its political origins, notably the shareholders' pact signed in 1999 which insisted on a balance between French and German shareholders. Both French and German governments have been openly interventionist in defending their national interests within EADS, and each has suspected the other of seeking to obtain a technological edge. In the area of defence procurement, there are examples of Franco-German industrial cooperation (Eurocopter), but equally significant, the Eurofighter alliance (UK, Germany, Italy, Spain) and the French Dassault company (makers of the current Rafale) are in open competition for the production of the next generation of fighter aircraft. From this overview we conclude that private or non-state actors have performed a relatively minor role in promoting Franco-German cooperation.

Defence and foreign policy: whose core Europe?

There is a long history of institutional collaboration and cooperation, but also of mutual misunderstanding, on defence issues. The 1963 Treaty called for 'a convergence of strategic and tactical doctrines' to allow for a common defence identity to be developed. The lower house of the German parliament, the Bundestag, insisted on introducing a preamble which referred to the strategic defence community with the United States and to the need to associate the UK. De Gaulle's partial withdrawal from NATO in 1966 and the pro-US stance of the Federal Republic limited convergence and cooperation in this sphere. From these modest beginnings, France and Germany have worked hard on strategic issues. In 1987, French and German troops held joint military manoeuvres for the first time and, in 1988, the two governments created the Franco-German brigade, eventually subsumed under the Eurocorps. In 1988, on the 25th anniversary of the Elysée treaty, France and Germany announced the creation of a number of new instruments that were annexed as protocols to the Treaty; the Security and Defence Council was the first and foremost amongst these. The French were the driving force behind this process of institutional creation. France was also the main instigator of the common foreign and security policy, fronted by France and supported by Germany at the Maastricht and Amsterdam summits.

German unification changed the terms of reference of the debate and redistributed the cards within the Franco-German alliance. Not only had Germany become the main economic player, it had recovered sovereignty in its foreign and security policy. Over the 1990s, Germany began to play a much more active role on the international arena: notably in the Middle East, the Balkans and Afghanistan. For its part, France lost its status as victor. Moreover, its nuclear arsenal has become a less valuable resource. After the Cold War, France moved much closer to the idea of European defence. Under pressure from France, the West European Union (WEO) was finally integrated into the EU in 1997. In 1998, with the St Malo process, integration went a step further (Marsh and Mackenstein, 2005). The St Malo process launched the European Security and Defence Policy (ESDP), which involves developing an autonomous EU capacity that can be called upon by the Union in those instances where NATO is not involved. The St Malo process was an inter-governmental Franco-British initiative, subsequently extended to include the Germans (Cole, 2001). In this precise case, the Franco-German relationship did not lead the European Union, and nor was Franco-German collaboration essential to the pursuit of the policy, but Britain and France both wanted Germany to be closely associated with it. The Iraq War of 2003 produced a more genuine convergence between France and Germany in favour of a European defence identity (Roger-Lacan, 2003). Germany has moved closer to France in relation to the CFSP/ESDP and France and Germany have cooperated closely within NATO (for example, by rejecting Georgian and Ukrainian membership in 2008).

Consideration of this broad functional spectrum demonstrates that differentiated integration is 'second best', a high-risk strategy with unintended consequences. The public goods approach developed by Kölliker in Chapter 3 of this volume contains some useful insights into why this is the case. In the opinion of Kölliker, 'differentiation inside EU borders tends to be used as an instrument of last resort, when other instruments to overcome deadlock, such as issue-linkage, are exhausted'. In its own terms of reference, the Franco-German relationship has been at its most effective not when advocating forms of differentiated integration, but when proposing leadership solutions that bridge the broad range of geographical, sectoral and political interests within the EU. Kölliker also argues that 'integration-minded EU Member States have often preferred differentiation outside EU law'; such a strategy underpins both the classic *directoire* approach and the very idea of a Franco-German intergovernmental compact as a form of leadership of the European Integration project. Most convincing of all, using the metaphor of the 'shadow of differentiation', the cases of France and Germany confirm that differentiation can be used as a strategy for exclusion, or for potential exclusion. Insofar as France and Germany are involved in all areas of differentiated integration that one might conceive of, however, the distinction in terms of the functional properties of issue-areas is less pertinent than it might be in other areas covered by this book. The functional properties of goods weigh less heavily in strategies of differentiated integration than issue-linkage, side payments, or quite simply the exercise of joint leadership. These various examples demonstrate that, even when the core Europe strategy is tempting, it is difficult to operationalize and is potentially counterproductive, a point that becomes clearer when considering the spatial dimension.

A Franco-German Europe: the spatial dimension

In Chapter 4 of the current volume, Michael Keating elucidates the multiple forms that constructions of space and territory can assume: from sub-state identity construction to the EU as a new empire, thorough re-scaling, economic differentiation and the hollowing out of the state. The framing of territory can also have a temporal dimension; historical memory is used as a resource to be mobilized in support of contemporary European maps. Advocates of a tight Franco-German alliance occasionally refer still to the Carolingian empire of Charlemagne (742–814) which covered much of contemporary France and Germany (Leenhardt and Picht, 1997). In the context of the present discussion, however, we limit our discussion to the spatial dimensions and utilities of the Franco-German relationship as it relates to the leadership of the European integration project. Quite apart from the internal dynamics of their own relationship, France and Germany usually speak for broader functional and spatial coalitions of interest throughout the EU. France has often emerged as the principal spokesperson for southern European interests, notably in *agriculture and international trade negotiations*. France was also closely aligned with the southern European states in advocating a broadly based euro. Germany has tended rather to be aligned with the northern free-trade states.

Germany has also been a fundamental reference for many of the new 'Accession 8' democracies of central and eastern Europe. Though Germany has been anxious to maintain France as a friendly ally to its west, she has also looked to anchor the A8 countries to the European Union; moving too close to France can be interpreted in terms of neglect by these new Member States.

These distinctive roles challenge the reality of a Franco-German axis at the heart of European integration. Empirical evidence casts doubt upon the Franco-German axis. Selck and Kaeding (2004), for instance, reject the hypothesis that there is a Franco-German axis in Council proceedings. Based on mapping votes under qualified majority voting (QMV) in Council from January 1999 to December 2000, they argue that the UK was the most likely to see its preferences taken up in EU legislation; and that the UK and Germany were likely to be much closer than France and Germany. For its part, France headed up a Mediterranean axis and its closest ally in Council meetings was Italy. The brokerage roles performed by Germany, France and, to a lesser degree, the UK in practice act as a counterweight to the temptation for differentiated integration. Taking into account all territorial interests within the EU tends to produce lowest common denominator agreements, a case well illustrated both with the history of 'widening' and enlargement and the recent attempt to create a Mediterranean Union.

Widening ...

Initially conceived as an ever-closer union of six Member States, the EU expanded to include 27 by 2007. More often than not, enlargement has constituted an area of Franco-German discord. Successive enlargements were initially opposed by French governments, for whom a broader Community threatened vital national interests and who called for deepening before widening. De Gaulle's double veto of British membership of the EU in 1963 and 1967 caused serious frictions between the two countries. In 1969 French President Pompidou finally agreed to British entry. At each successive enlargement, French vital interests were initially felt to be threatened. In the case of Greece (1981) and Spain and Portugal (1986) the French feared the direct economic challenge to French farmers through increased competition for CAP resources. President Mitterrand was also originally hostile to opening up the EU to the former EFTA countries (Austria, Sweden, Finland) in 1995. France and Germany adopted rather different attitudes towards the 2004 enlargement. France was reluctant to agree to a rapid enlargement; Germany saw it as a means of embedding stability and creating a buffer zone around Germany itself (Martens, 2002; Stark, 2006). The Federal Republic drew from its collective memory the belief that she had a historic responsibility to promote the broadest possible historical reconciliation. More than any other country, Germany had a strong interest in regional stability. Any failure of democracy in the former Communist countries would create incalculable problems of economic and political dislocation on Germany's doorstep. On each occasion, French attitudes eventually shifted under the pressure from Germany.

Far from promoting a core Europe, Germany and France have put into operation a wider Europe over which they (collectively) have less and less control.

Successive enlargements of the Union have diluted Franco-German influence. The 1995 enlargement introduced into the EU two Scandinavian states and Austria, who were much less deferential to either France or Germany. The 2004 and 2007 enlargements introduced 12 new members, 10 of which were former Communist regimes. A number of these new countries looked to the United States as a safeguard against Russia, and also to a lesser degree against Germany. The new entrants are much less sensitive to the idea that Franco-German leadership of the EU is a legitimate aspiration, or that they should exercise a subordinate role. They are deeply resistant both to the operation of any large country *directoire* and to foreign policy initiatives that threaten US security guarantees and are too accommodating with Russia. As far as the new Member States are concerned, the Franco-German relationship is a hangover from the Cold War period, rather than a powerful symbolic affirmation of European reconciliation.

... and stretching

France's view of itself as the natural leader of Mediterranean Europe was revived under President Sarkozy with the episode of the Mediterranean Union, which offers an excellent case study of the limits both of differentiated integration and the continuing brokerage role of the Franco-German relationship.[1] French President Sarkozy announced in October 2007 his intention to launch the 'Mediterranean Union', initially conceived as a new organization outside the existing EU that would bring together only those 12 states bordering the Mediterranean. The MU was designed to provide for functional cooperation amongst Mediterranean-rim states in areas such as energy, transport, pollution and the law of the sea. The French President argued that there was a need to direct resources towards the Mediterranean-rim countries in order to stabilize the EU in its existing borders and minimize future security threats.

The Sarkozy project faced three overwhelming obstacles. The first of these came from the European Commission; the proposed MU ignored the existing 'Barcelona process' and the EuroMed dialogue that had been launched in 1995. Second, the MU was interpreted as a manoeuvre to prevent Turkey from ever acceding to the status of a full member of the EU and to scupper negotiations in course since 2005.[2] Third, crucially, Germany was opposed to this attempt to set Mediterranean Europe against northern, central and eastern Europe. Germany insisted that EU resources could only be committed to the project if all 27 existing EU states were invited to join the organization. The German Chancellor Angela Merkel made it clear that Germany would block the project of the MU as it then stood. The MU caused a deep rift in the relationship and tensions were palpable between Sarkozy and Merkel. Beyond the dynamics of the Franco-German relationship, the MU episode lay at the heart of reflections on differentiated integration. Merkel rejected the idea of creating a new structure outside of the existing treaties. There was stiff opposition from the Commission as well, which regarded it as a means of preventing Turkish entry and because it ignored the Barcelona process. The Germans only agreed once it was acknowledged that the EU Commission would be the driving force in the MU and once Sarkozy had amended his project to ensure that all EU states could participate. In the event, the MU was the first major initiative of the 2008 French EU Presidency. President Sarkozy of France scored a major diplomatic victory when he managed to attract representatives of 44 countries to Paris for the 12–13 July summit which launched the renamed Union for the Mediterranean (UFM).

The two cases considered above demonstrate that the core brokerage roles performed by France and Germany are not readily compatible with forms of geographically or spatially differentiated integration. The spatial context itself is heavily influenced by the changing temporal dynamics of European integration.

A Franco-German Europe: the temporal dimension

In Chapter 5 of this volume, Klaus Goetz theorizes upon the temporal dimension in a sophisticated and original way. Time is fundamental to understanding the Franco-German relationship in key respects. The temporal dimension is suggestive of models of 'clustered Europeanization' (Goetz's term), where there are inter-regional commonalities amongst families of nations, but also inter-regional differences in the integration experience according to waves of entering the EU. As founder-members present throughout all phases of the integration process, France and Germany would form part of almost any mental map of a core Europe. They arguably have more institutional, symbolic, economic and political leadership resources at their disposal than any other grouping within the EU. As the most significant founding fathers of the EU, France and Germany arguably count more than others. Their union symbolizes reconciliation, solidarity and peace – these are precious qualities within the context of European history. As the two most powerful founder Member States they were initially in a powerful position to control the speed and duration of the integration process. The two countries have been influential in shaping the *acquis*, in part because they are founder-members, in part because Franco-German bargains were especially influential in explaining evolution at the early stages of the EU and in the core decisions over the single European Act and Maastricht.

But time has also altered the capacity of the Franco-German relationship to exercise coherent political leadership of the European integration project. The institutional, symbolic, economic and political leadership resources of the Franco-German relationship have all diminished with the ebb of the integrationist tide since the early 1990s. Germany has been focused on the core business of managing unification and integrating the former East German *länder*. France has been struggling to come to terms with its role in a post-Cold War world and an enlarged European Union. Time has also altered the equilibrium within the Franco-German relationship, substantially modified by the impact of German unification, which upset the delicate equilibrium based on trading German economic resources and French political prestige.

Like the European integration project itself, the Franco-German relationship has evolved over time. The post-war Franco-German relationship initially survived and prospered because, in the context of the Cold War, it fulfilled specific functions. It allowed France to exercise a heavyweight role within the European Union, while facilitating Germany's re-admission into the international concert of nations. There were fundamental complementarities in strategic and economic terms. In the Cold War period, France and Germany were forced together in the defence of western Europe against the threat of Soviet aggression. Ultimately protected by US strategic leadership, France and Germany were able to channel their energies into the development of the European Union. Franco-German cooperation in the 1960s was, in the end, undermined by disagreements about the basic Gaullist premise of enhanced European autonomy and about distancing the Franco-German relationship from the United States. Closer collaboration from the early 1970s to the early 1990s was closely interwoven with the turn of domestic and global events: the ending of the Bretton Woods fixed parities system in 1971 promoted closer monetary collaboration; tighter economic interdependency amongst the leading European nations provided the stimulus for the Single European Act; the gradual recognition of the need to develop European capacity in security and defence or space technology drove the development of common policies in these areas. If Maastricht represented the height of the integrationist agenda, the period since 1991 has been one of finishing off the business of Maastricht and tidying up the treaties. Since 1991, the main imperative has been to integrate the new democracies of central and eastern Europe (accomplished in 2004 and 2007) and to provide a stable framework for political and market governance across the continent.

Temporal variables are important not just in understanding the weight of past decisions and the impact of critical junctures, but also in accounting for the diminishing returns of specific spatial alliances and styles. Narrow interstate bargains are much less likely to be acceptable or practical in the 2000s – in the context of an enlarged EU in which supra-national community institutions escape from tight Member State control – than they were in the 1960s or 1970s. When France and Germany have attempted to impose their leadership without the agreement of other states they have generally failed. As demonstrated at Amsterdam in 1997, or in the negotiations over the constitutional treaty, the Franco-German relationship must negotiate when confronted with the determined defence of established interests on behalf of other EU coalitions, such as the 'cohesion group' countries, the Benelux states, or Spain and Poland. Even before the most recent enlargement, the Franco-German relationship had had to cope with the emergence of new players. Spain has emerged as an important country in its own right and as a powerful and ambitious spokesperson for the 'cohesion fund' countries; this was demonstrated at the Amsterdam summit, during the Agenda 2000 negotiations and in the constitutional treaty negotiations of 2003–4. British influence increased after the election of the Blair government in 1997. In certain spheres, such as defence and security policy, Britain has assumed a leading role. The Benelux states have always been influential, not least because of their activism within the Commission and their over-representation in the Council (on a population basis). Even small countries such as Denmark or Ireland can place obstacles in the way of Franco-German grand strategy; this was the lesson to be drawn from the 1992 Danish referendum on the Maastricht Treaty or the Irish 2008 referendum on the Lisbon Treaty. The countries of central and eastern Europe have stoutly defended their interests. Poland (along with Spain, another rising force) held up the conclusion of the constitutional treaty negotiations for several months. The support of the central and eastern Europeans for the Anglo-American position over Iraq prevented France, Germany and Belgium fronting a European consensus against the war.

The Franco-German *directoire* was historically bounded, at best an idiosyncratic strategy in the political context of the 1960s and 1970s, but an unrealistic one after the end of the Cold War. Tight bilateral Franco-German cooperation might be framed today in terms of the broader needs of European integration, but it has little currency as an alternative to the existing European architecture. Though French and German politicians have periodically entertained notions of 'core Europe', they have rarely done so in harmony or at the same *time*. France has traditionally feared being left alone with Germany and has feared being swallowed up in a 'hard core' entity. As French influence has diminished, however, ideas of Franco-German Union have found more favour with Paris. In 2003 Dominique de Villepin, then French Foreign Affairs Minister, floated the idea of creating a Franco-German Union and he did so again as Prime Minister in 2005. The Germans rejected France's overtures without undue ceremony in 2003 and again in 2005. Germany has no interest in joining in a Franco-German union outside of the treaties.

There is a weak correlation between moves to enhanced differentiation and the role of France and Germany acting in concert. In their self-appointed role as the *avant garde*, France and Germany have, on occasion, held forth the prospect of exclusion from 'core Europe' in order to influence the behaviour of other Member States. Differentiated integration has formed one strategy for driving through change, embraced by either France (CFSP) or Germany (EMU) or, occasionally, by both of them (EMS, Schengen). As a general rule, however, strategies for differentiated integration have not been driven by France and Germany acting in tandem and exclusively. When one partner has advocated a strategy based on differentiated integration, the other has not always followed. 'Core Europe' strategies are not only divisive, but also difficult to implement. When either France or Germany have sought to negotiate opt-outs (from provisions of the takeover directive for France, or the free movement of A8 labour for Germany, France and others), they have acted in their own national interest, rather than as part of a self-conscious leadership alliance.

From this brief overview, Franco-German relations have always been highly complex, but the claim to exercise leadership has diminished with time (McCarthy, 1993; Soutou, 1996). Since the 1995, 2004 and 2007 enlargements, the direction of change is towards a rather weaker steering role for the Franco-German relationship across the whole dimension of EU policy. There are specific dangers for Germany in maintaining too close a relationship with France, especially one based on perceptions of a *directoire* or a core Europe. Principles of differentiation are difficult to accept for most of the smaller and medium-sized states whose faith in the community method remains intact. A France-first strategy of the type engaged by Schröder had as a consequence a lessening of credibility with the central and eastern European states. For its part, France has called for a Franco-German political union at its periods of greatest weakness, most notably after the rejection by French voters of the constitutional treaty in 2005. If the capacity of France and Germany to steer Europe has diminished, however, it is unlikely that any other coalition will provide an alternative overarching leadership. There is no Anglo-Italian, Anglo-Spanish, Anglo-Hispanic-Polish alternative to the Franco-German relationship. France and Germany remain the most important alliance grouping within the EU, even if their influence has become more defensive and their ability to impose decisions has diminished.

Conclusion

Intuitively, there is a neat causal linkage between the challenge of deepening, widening and the adoption of strategies of differentiated integration. In the specific case of Franco-German relations, however, core Europe strategies have foundered upon misunderstandings, mutual suspicions of motives and distinct institutional preferences. A core Europe strategy is tempting and can act as a useful discursive device. But it is difficult to operationalize and potentially counterproductive. Moreover, the brokerage roles performed by Germany and France in practice act as a counterweight to the temptation for differentiated integration. The principal role of these two leading continental European states is to bridge rival political and spatial coalitions. Though the temptation for differentiation can be very powerful – as in the case of the Mediterranean Union – the logic of integration usually precludes this. Indeed, the history of a range of policy sectors and issue-areas is one of the undifferentiating of differential forms of integration. Hence, the euro has expanded to 16 members and will undoubtedly encompass more; Schengen now forms part of the *acquis* (except for the specific case of Ireland and the UK); Denmark is seeking to renounce its opt-outs; and even the UK has opted in to some aspects of Schengen. Taking into account all territorial interests within the EU tends to produce a pressure for all Member States to share common goods. Differentiated integration is not the core business of the Franco-German 'regime'.

Notes

1. The title 'Mediterranean Union' gave way, under pressure from Germany and the European Commission, to the Union for the Mediterranean.
2. Opinion on Turkey cut across simple divisions between France and Germany. There was much opposition within France and Germany to entering into accession negotiations (begun in October 2005). Though French public opinion was hostile to Turkish entry, former President Chirac was supportive of Turkey becoming the first Muslim country in the EU. German parties and politicians were, likewise, divided, the SPD in favour, the CDU opposed. Since 2007, both Sarkozy and German Chancellor Merkel have been opposed to full Turkish membership, but accession negotiations are continuing.

12
Mediterranean Europe

Paul M. Heywood and Lauren McLaren[1]

Introduction

Conventionally, in the context of the European Union, 'Mediterranean Europe' has been taken to refer to those countries which stretch from the Iberian peninsula to the Aegean Sea: that is, Cyprus, Greece, Italy, Malta, Portugal and Spain (with Turkey potentially included as an aspirant Member State) – and these are the countries on which this chapter concentrates. However, recent literature increasingly suggests that generalizations about these countries in relation to European integration have largely been – if not wholly rejected – at least called into question. For example, Nugent (2001) has pointed out that 'Mediterranean Europe' does not have a particularly strong tendency of 'voting together' and does not constitute a so-called 'voting bloc' within the EU, as evidenced for instance by the diverse voting behaviour of Spain and Portugal. While there are patterns of certain countries in the region working (and voting) together, as with Greece and Cyprus and the so-called 'two Greeces problem', such coordinated action is not a region-wide 'Mediterranean' phenomenon.

Indeed, a new perception of the 'Mediterranean' has emerged in recent years through regional initiatives such as the Euro-Mediterranean Dialogue and Partnership (1995), the European Neighbourhood Policy (2004) and the twin French initiatives, the Mediterranean Union (2007) and the revised Union for the Mediterranean (2008). When exploring differentiated European integration in 'Mediterranean Europe', it should be noted that in the EU literature as well as in practice the term 'Mediterranean' is increasingly used with reference to initiatives such as these. Thus, 'Mediterranean' now generally refers to the Euro-Mediterranean Partnership (EMP) countries, rather than just the EU Member States listed above, and Turkey (see, for example, Boening 2007, 2008; Tassinari 2006; and Chapter 14 by Edwards in this volume).[2] Recent discussions of initiatives such as President Sarkozy's Mediterranean Union, proposed in October 2007 in a speech in Tangiers, further underlines that the term 'Mediterranean' in today's Europe could be seen as referring to another region altogether than the countries which form the main focus of this chapter.[3]

This is not to suggest that there are no identifiable clusters or patterns in relation to European integration amongst the countries considered here, but rather that these often take a different shape than might be suggested by the 'Mediterranean Europe' label. In spatial terms, an alternative cluster to Mediterranean Europe could encompass southern Europe (including the Balkans), although Italy – obviously both southern European and Mediterranean – is also a member of the Central European Initiative. (For further discussion of the complexities involved in European spatial mapping, see Chapter 14 by Edwards in this volume.)

In regard to functional integration, rather than look at Mediterranean Europe as a whole, it might be more appropriate to focus on clusters of smaller and larger Member States. Thus, Cyprus and Malta could be grouped together with, for example, the Baltic States, whose processes of European integration are arguably characterized by factors of size (see Chapter 1 by Dyson and Sepos in this volume). The 2000 Nice Summit provides an example in which significant cleavages were evident between small and large EU Member States.[4]

From a temporal perspective, differentiated integration within the region might be better captured by clustering Member States according to the timing of their EU accession, widely seen in the literature as exercising a significant impact on the nature of a country's integration process. Thus, Italy would stand somewhat apart from Greece, Portugal and Spain on the one hand, and Cyprus and Malta on the other.

While it is generally accepted that EU accession and the process of further European integration significantly influences the domestic political systems of new Member States, it is also the case that before formal accession, the very prospect of EU membership can affect processes of European integration. For example, Agapiou-Josephides (2003: 240) argues that 'Over the last ten years, the EU has undoubtedly proven to be the single most important driving force for Cyprus's socio-political, economic and institutional modernisation; hundreds of new laws have been adopted, numerous new institutions have been set up and a great number of structures in the public and private field have been adapted to the country's accession perspective.' Aydin and Keyman (2004) support this argument by suggesting that European integration and the prospect of EU membership has led to a transformation of Turkish democracy. In particular, they stress the 'substantial improvements' with regard to the role of the military in politics, respect for human rights, protection of minorities and reform of the judicial system. In legislative and institutional terms much has been achieved, although with regard to implementation a lot still remains to be done.

Table 12.1 Differentiated temporal integration

	EU accession	Euro accession
Italy	1957	1999
Greece	1981	2001
Portugal	1986	1999
Spain	1986	1999
Cyprus	2004	2008
Malta	2004	2008
Turkey	–	–

In the rest of this chapter, we explore differentiated functional integration across Italy, Greece, Spain, Portugal, Malta, Cyprus and Turkey with reference to five policy dimensions: economic; social; environmental; foreign policy and security and defence; and Schengen and free movement. Given the importance of economic integration to so much of what the European Union is designed to achieve, particular attention is paid to that dimension. The chapter argues that, while important commonalities do exist across the region, integration along these five dimensions also varies considerably across what is understood, for the purpose of this volume, as 'Mediterranean Europe'. Ultimately, although there may be some common characteristics across the countries in the region, in terms of EU integration other factors play a more important explanatory role in accounting for differentiation.

Economic integration and 'Euro' Europe

There are significant differences in the relative economic size of the Mediterranean countries within the EU, with Italy and Spain amongst the five large Member States (those with more than 5 per cent share of the total EU27 GDP), Greece and Portugal amongst the 11 medium-sized states (1–5 per cent of total EU27 GDP) and Cyprus and Malta occupying two of the last three places amongst the small states (less than 1 per cent of total EU27 GDP). Turkey, meanwhile, would be at the lower end of the medium-sized states were it to join the European Union. As shown in Table 12.2, there are also some notable differences in terms of the contribution to gross value-added by the main components of GDP.

In Mediterranean Europe, economic (as well as political) development has been intimately tied to requirements imposed by the EU with regard to Economic and Monetary Union (EMU), the introduction of the euro, the and the wider process of closer economic integration in Europe. These requirements include substantial structural adjustments of trade relations, financial-market liberalization and the pursuit of disinflationary macroeconomic policies. Effectively, this policy agenda has been both reflected in and dictated by the Maastricht convergence criteria. The consequential negative impact on growth and employment rates across several of

Table 12.2   Gross value-added, per cent total 2006

	Agriculture	Industry	Service
Italy	2.1	26.8	71.1
Greece	3.7	24.3	72.0
Portugal	2.9	24.3	72.4
Spain	2.9	30.4	66.8
Cyprus	2.6	19.1	78.3
Malta	2.8	21.6	75.6
Turkey	10.5	25.9	63.6
EU	1.8	26.4	71.8

Source: Eurostat, *European Economic Statistics*, 2008, 162; figures for Turkey are for 2005 from the *OECD Factbook 2005*, available at: http://oberon.sourceoecd.org/ vl=2393008/cl=34/nw=1/rpsv/fact2005/

the countries in the region were in turn cushioned by the EU Structural Funds. Economic integration in Mediterranean Europe meant that the state authorities in these countries lost, in a relatively short timespan, their capacity to influence economic activity through traditional policy instruments such as state subsidies, tariffs, quotas, and interest and exchange rates. However, integration into the European (and global) market has arguably had major distributional effects, with both positive and negative repercussions. On the positive side, European integration (and internationalization) has liberalized markets, increased competition, increased transparency in policy-making and enhanced efficiency in administrative and regulatory regimes. On the negative side, it has contributed to an increase in unemployment, more unequal income distribution and weakened political integration (Katseli, 2001).

Even going back to the very early days of the European integration process, the creation of the Social Fund as part of the founding EEC treaty already signalled that Italy not only had the weakest economy of the six initial members, but anticipated difficulties in adapting to the trade liberalization which was a core principle of the EEC. In practice, the process of economic integration was never smooth in Italy: indeed, Sbragia (1992) outlined how the country was seen as an 'awkward partner' in Europe, out of step in terms of political and administrative structures with the other founding members. Giuliani (1999: 8) describes how various aspects of the Italian political system – famously characterized in terms of 'surviving without governing' (Di Palma, 1977) – were misaligned with the Brussels-based technocratic 'model'; lack of effective ministerial coordination, complex law-making processes, poor democratic scrutiny and an ineffective and inefficient administrative system, all rendering the adoption and implementation of EU legislation extraordinarily difficult in Italy. However, the single market programme and the negotiations over the emblematic Maastricht Treaty, which led to the creation of the euro and key changes in the operation of the EU's structural funds, placed enormous pressure on Italy's long-established politico-economic structure. The stimulus of the single currency, together with a historic failure either to exert sufficient influence on or derive sufficient benefit from structural funds, prompted a move towards greater institutionalization of Italy's approach to European integration (Sotiropoulos, 2006; Giuliani and Piattoni, 2006).

The first two Mediterranean enlargements of the EU were special, in the sense that these were the first cases in which new Member States were simultaneously seeking fully to secure their transitions to democratic rule. The Greek integration process had started in the early 1960s, but was interrupted during the dictatorship between 1967 to 1974. The return to democracy saw negotiations restarted and in 1981 Greece's entry into the Community symbolized that democracy in the country was considered safe (Katseli, 2001). When Spain and Portugal joined the EU in 1986, this too was consistent with the regionalization strategies of European corporations and compatible with the objectives of both national and European policy-makers, which gave impetus and depth to the European internal market. Not only did it enlarge the market, but these first Mediterranean enlargements also introduced significant labour-cost advantages for production, relative to the previous core European regions. At the domestic level, the larger market was complemented by a symbolic legitimization of the democratization processes, which had begun in the mid-1970s with the overthrow of the Caetano regime in Portugal and the death of Franco in Spain.

In all three countries, the process of economic integration was two-pronged. On the one hand, it proceeded through rapid liberalization of commodity markets, largely brought about through the dismantling of tariff and non-tariff trade barriers and the gradual deregulation and liberalization of the service sectors. After the implementation of the Single European Act (1987), the process was completed by the harmonization of taxation, public procurement, customs policies and the like. On the other hand, economic integration in these three countries was associated with the steady opening of capital accounts due to the adoption of Community directives for a freer regulatory framework (on both inflows and outflows). After the widening of the exchange rate band of the European Exchange Rate Mechanism (ERM) in 1993, short-term capital controls were also lifted. Spain, Portugal and Greece all faced the same policy challenge of fostering the necessary rapid structural changes in their productive and technological capacities without recourse to traditional policy tools to protect domestic production and employment. In doing so, they had to operate under constraints derived from their Community membership, which included the loss of autonomy in monetary and exchange rate policy, and a commitment drastically to reduce government deficits and public debt in order to comply with the Maastricht convergence criteria and the timetable for the creation of EMU by the end of the decade (Katseli, 2001).

In Spain, the Socialist PSOE administration of Felipe González used strong public support for EU membership as a rationale for pushing through far-reaching restructuring measures which would ultimately contribute to a dramatic improvement in Spain's overall economic position, although the short-term cost was very high in terms of unemployment. It also led to a breakdown in relations between the PSOE and the trade union movement (Closa and Heywood, 2004). Similarly, in Portugal 'the implementation of the necessary economic reforms associated with EC membership was also painful and caused economic and social problems' (Royo, 2004: 96). None the less, 'real' as opposed to 'nominal' or 'statistical' convergence with Europe's leading players became the watchword and principal commitment of governments in both Spain and Portugal, a position which was bolstered by a strong sense of common purpose with the EU Commission under Jacques Delors.

Despite these shared conditions of economic integration in Spain, Portugal and Greece, there were also important differences between them which affected their respective European paths. According to Katseli (2001), four characteristics are particularly important in this respect: relative size; distance from the industrial centre of the EU; the speed and sequencing of policy reforms (in relation to accession); and the quality of their administrative and political systems. Differentiated economic integration in Mediterranean Europe must thus be examined in the context not only of European (and global) market realities, but also in the context of the initial conditions and policy choices of each individual Member State. For example, Spain's size, its long industrial tradition and its proximity to the European core market made it a profitable location for foreign direct investment (FDI). The relative stability of the new political system and the relative efficiency of the administrative apparatus further provided a more conducive environment for growth and structural change than was the case in Portugal or Greece. Indeed, in Greece the implementation of reforms was particularly hindered by weak, inefficient bureaucratic structures, which meant the country failed to take advantage of structural funds to develop its economy to the same extent as its southern neighbours (see Hibou, 2005; Royo, 2004).

All three countries experienced a rapid and generalized deterioration in almost all sectors of economic activity following accession, as measured by their relative performance. Such deterioration indicates that – at least initially – their productive industrial structures had been severely distorted and were largely inefficient compared to the European core countries. The result was a sharp decline in structural competitiveness immediately after entry, especially in Spain and Greece, with a more mixed picture in Portugal. European integration in these three countries thus became identified with economic liberalization, which brought about a significant loss of structural competitiveness due to structural inefficiencies that characterized their productive systems – notably, small-sized firms, inflexible labour markets, lack of modern infrastructure, organizational inefficiencies (in both public and private sectors) and low levels of technical efficiency in production and distribution systems (Sapelli, 1995). These structural rigidities and the ensuing segmentation of financial and labour markets made domestic industrial structures vulnerable to external competitive pressures and gave rise to severe distortions and lack of flexibility following the post-1985 liberalization of commodity markets.

The enlargement of the Community and the adoption of the Single European Act in 1986 were accompanied by major reform and growth of the EU's Structural Funds (from 7.8 billion European currency units (ECU) in 1988 to 14.9 billion ECU in 1992), designed to reduce the costs of integration. The post-entry deterioration of the trade balance-to-GDP ratio continued up to 1992 in both Spain and Portugal and was reversed thereafter largely as a consequence of a real exchange rate adjustment. The pursuit of a more flexible exchange rate policy after 1992 improved competitiveness and trade performances in the Iberian Peninsula and reduced surpluses recorded in the basic balance. Structural adjustments in Spain, Portugal and Greece were underpinned and facilitated by substantial financing provided by the Community (through structural funds) and private capital inflows. Together, these helped ease the adjustment burden of economic integration in all three countries (Katseli, 2001) – but most especially in Spain, which was by some margin the major recipient of structural funds (Closa and Heywood, 2004: 186–214).

When the euro was launched on 1 January 1999, it became the official currency of Spain, Italy and Portugal (alongside eight other EU countries).[5] Greece joined the eurozone on 1 January 2001, and Cyprus and Malta followed suit on 1 January 2008. The integration of Cyprus and Malta into the eurozone was informed by the experience of other countries. According to the European Commission, the Cypriot and Maltese public administrations and enterprises had prepared themselves adequately and in good time for adoption of the euro (see also Cini, 2001;

Pace, 2006; Sepos, 2008). Experts from both countries participated in information and training events organized by the Commission, the European Central Bank and Europol to make them familiar with EU procedures and methods designed to protect the euro against counterfeiting. In line with a so-called 'big bang changeover scenario', all administrative and financial systems were running exclusively in their respective national currencies until 31 December 2007 and successfully changed over to the euro on 1 January 2008. This well-prepared and integrated approach to the changeover allowed for only a four-week dual circulation period before a complete integration of both countries into the Euro Area (European Commission, 2008b).

With the exception of Turkey, all of the Mediterranean European countries are now members of both the EMU and the eurozone. A number of differences have been evident since its creation across the eurozone as a whole, but also between the countries of Mediterranean Europe. In terms of growth, Italy and Portugal (along with Germany and the Netherlands) have consistently been below average, while Greece and Spain (along with Ireland, Luxembourg and Finland) have been above the average. The rest of the eurozone states grew by close to the average. These growth differences were narrowed somewhat by the 2006 improvements in the Italian economy (and the strengthening of the German economy that year). Italy and Spain (along with Luxembourg) failed positively to combine labour and capital in the productive process in an effective way. In effect, these countries experienced negative rates of total factor productivity (TFP), whereas the rest of the eurozone states had positive TFP rates.

In terms of inflation, similar differences have persisted. Greece, Spain, Italy and Portugal (alongside Ireland and Slovenia) consistently experienced inflation above the Euro Area average in the period 1999–2006. Differences in current account balances also widened significantly after 1999, the result of a sharp deterioration in current account deficits in Greece, Spain and Portugal (and, to a lesser degree, of markedly rising surpluses in Finland, Germany, Austria and the Netherlands). The external balance of countries already in deficit when EMU commenced failed to improve. Portugal, for instance, remained in deficit from 1996 onwards, recording a figure of close to 9 per cent of GDP in 2007. Likewise, the current account positions of Spain and Greece deteriorated during this period (by 6 per cent and 2.8 per cent respectively). Deeper financial integration in Europe thus played an important role in the widening diversity of current account positions within the Euro Area, allowing a cut in the risk premium and a loosening in credit constraints, which enlarged the borrowing capacity of the private sector in Greece, Spain and Portugal. As these countries have a lower per capita income than the Euro Area average, deepening financial integration has made it possible to meet potentially higher financing needs through additional foreign capital flows. A further explanatory factor for the diversity in current account positions relates to changes in competitiveness. In particular, poor levels of competitiveness in Spain and Portugal have been compounded by the sluggish response of wages to a slowdown in productivity (for a more detailed overview of country-specific experiences within the EMU, see European Commission, DG ECOFIN 2007).

The Mediterranean region has experienced extraordinarily high public fiscal imbalances, according to Tsarouhas and Bolukbasi (2006); however, the situation varies in each country. Greece, for example, has seen exceptionally high levels of debt and deficit, the result in part of policy decisions in the 1970s and 1980s which failed to control wage inflation. By contrast, in Spain, the question of economic stability became a policy priority during the early stages of democratization, and macro-economic considerations were thus included in collective bargaining negotiations which resulted in a series of relatively successful (albeit relatively one-sided) social bargains between 1977 and 1986. Although the consensus on which such agreements were established increasingly broke down after Spain joined the EU, significant industrial restructuring and agricultural reform had already taken place by then (Closa and Heywood, 2004: 19–30).

Turkey, although not a member of the EU, has increasingly been influenced by European economic integration. When the Customs Union with the EU came into effect on the 1 January 1996, Turkey abolished all duties and equivalent charges on imports of industrial goods from EU countries. The Customs Union covers an estimated 30 per cent of all goods produced in Turkey, covering everything except agriculture, services and public procurement. Under its terms, Turkey is required to abide by the relevant *acquis,* in relation, for example, to industrial standards, but without any reciprocal rights in relation to EU decision-making. In 1996 Turkey also started to harmonize its tariffs and equivalent charges on imports from third countries with the EU's Common External Tariff (CET). The CET implies that Turkey is obliged to provide preferential access to its markets for all countries to which the EU also grants preferential access. Such forms of integration with the EU have increasingly opened the Turkish economy. In return, Turkey benefits from broader access to EU markets and financial support, as well as the higher confidence of world markets that comes with its increased economic integration with the EU and its candidate-member status. Furthermore, FDI in Turkey mainly originates from EU countries (65 per cent in 2002) and 3 million Turkish workers are employed in other EU countries (Elveren and Kar, 2005).

According to Elveren and Kar (2005), the volume and range of products traded with EU Member States provide evidence of Turkey's high degree of economic integration with the Euro Area. Trade with the EU accounts for about 50 per cent of overall Turkish exports. In addition to the volume of trade, which has increased rapidly in recent years, Turkey's export structure has also changed radically: in the 1960s and 1970s, it mainly exported raw materials and agricultural products, whereas by the mid-2000s 80 per cent of exports were manufactured goods. Finally, in terms of macro-economic development, Turkey has been cooperating with the IMF to bridge the gap with the EU and meet the Maastricht convergence criteria with regard to inflation, interest rates, budget deficit and public debt (Elveren and Kar, 2005). It should be noted, however, that Turkish economic integration with Europe is still seen as comparatively limited, and – like Greece and Italy – this is often attributed to inefficient (and in some cases corrupt) bureaucratic structures (Ugur, 2001; Keyman and Duzgit, 2007).

Social Europe

The countries in Mediterranean Europe have generally been characterized by severe labour market rigidity, segmentation and very high levels of fragmentation in welfare provisions structured largely along occupational lines and employment status (Garcia and Karakatsanis, 2006). EU scholars have predicted that the continuing process of intensified economic integration (through the SEA, Maastricht and EMU) would transform European labour relations as a result of cross-country competition. In effect, a neo-liberalization of labour regulations through, for example, the decentralization of wage bargaining, more flexible labour markets via changes in legislation on hiring and firing, and a drop in unionization rates was expected. The Greek and Spanish experiences, however, do not fully support such expectations.

Although the rate of unionization has dropped in Greece since its peak in the early 1980s, union density in Spain increased from 1980 to 2000 (although it remained relatively low). With regard to labour market flexibility, both Greece and Spain liberalized their rigid frameworks for hiring and firing; however, whereas Spain has reformed its old system substantially, Greece has been much slower, despite significant pressure. Finally, Spain has decentralized wage bargaining, whereas Greece has not. Spain underwent a coordinated process of decentralizing its social pacts in the 1990s (Royo, 2002), whereas in Greece a mixture of social partnerships and legislative changes have led to a re-regulation of bargaining along more coordinated lines comparable to the 1980s.

If we turn to labour relations, social pacts in Spain and legislative changes combined with a different approach by the social partners in Greece have meant that labour has been able to participate in the process of restructuring and welfare reform in both countries. Participation in these terms means being able to influence policy outcomes and changes to labour regulation and welfare environment in ways that are conducive to the unions' agendas. An example of this was the Spanish reform of wage bargaining structures in 1997 – although, in periods of majority rule, core executive dominance has been the norm in Spain (Chari and Heywood, 2009). The Spanish and Greek cases thus underline the importance of domestic institutional arrangements in filtering the impact of European integration with regard to 'Social Europe' in the Mediterranean region.

Environmental Europe

Overall compliance levels with EU environmental law are not impressive, and the Mediterranean states in particular have had a reputation for being exceptional laggards in this regard. Their poor record has often been attributed to systemic deficiencies in political and administrative structures: explanations referring to the 'Mediterranean syndrome' or the 'Southern problem' reflect a perceived lack of administrative capacity, individualism, clientelism, corruption and fragmented, reactive and party-dominated legal processes which undermine the will and ability of these countries to comply with EU environmental regulations (see, for a more detailed discussion, La Spina and Sciortino, 1993; Pridham and Cini, 1994).

However, Börzel (2000) argues, in contrast, that there is no simple north–south divide with regard to compliance with EU environmental law. Instead, she demonstrates that compliance can vary not only across countries in the north and the south of Europe, but also across different policy areas.

Overall, Greece and Italy have low levels of compliance, while Portugal is among the leaders in environmental implementation and Spain's compliance record is in the middle between leaders and laggards. With regard to the transposition rate, Spain and Portugal (both 90 per cent) compare well to the UK (90 per cent), Luxembourg (91 per cent) and France (94 per cent) and find themselves not far behind the Netherlands (94 per cent) and Denmark (99 per cent), which top the list, while Greece (84 per cent) and Italy (75 per cent) are at the very bottom. Likewise, Greece and Italy account for the highest numbers of infringement proceedings, while Portugal is among the five countries with the lowest number of infringements. These are just some examples of the cross-national implementation variations, which cut across not only Mediterranean Europe, but also across the perceived north–south divide. Such findings challenge the received wisdom of a Mediterranean Syndrome reflecting poor implementation patterns in EU environmental integration (Börzel, 2000).

Based on the annual implementation reports of the Commission, there is actually a considerable difference in environmental compliance across the Mediterranean European Member States. Börzel (2000) suggests that this variation in compliance is better explained by the 'fit' of the policy with already existing domestic legal and administrative structures and domestic mobilization of actors putting pressure on the Member State authorities to comply with EU environmental law. Here Börzel argues that environmental leaders and laggards face similar problems when faced with a 'policy misfit'. Her comparative study of Germany and Spain[6] supports this argument, as in all cases of policy misfit between EU directives and domestic structures both countries were reluctant to introduce the necessary legal and administrative changes in order to ensure full transposition. Formal compliance, however, is increasingly less of a problem.

It is at the level of practical implementation and enforcement that most problems occur, and here Börzel highlights striking similarities in the implementation patterns of perceived environmental leaders and laggards. Although Germany does have a better compliance record than Spain, the difference is not the result of a general systemic Spanish incapacity to implement EU policies efficiently. On the contrary, Börzel argues that due to the regulatory competition in EU policy-making, politically less powerful countries with less advanced environmental policies (here she mentions Italy, Greece, Spain and Portugal) are more likely to experience policy misfits with EU environmental law than more influential EU Member States such as Germany and the UK, which are often more successful in exporting their advanced policies to the EU level. Börzel thus argues that it is the lower environmental starting point, the lesser bargaining power of the Mediterranean Member States in EU decision-making in this particular sphere, and the lower levels of resources, information, expertise and support for domestic environmental groups that together cause the variation in compliance, rather than a lack of will or ability of these countries to integrate effectively in 'Environmental Europe'. The variation in compliance is thus better explained by a domestic push-pull model[7] than a European north–south divide.

Foreign and Security Europe and Defence Europe

In the sphere of foreign, security and defence policy, there are significantly different levels of European integration across and within Mediterranean Europe. Cyprus and Malta, for example, are not members of NATO, which causes problems with regard to European Security and Defence Policy (ESDP) developments, such as intelligence-sharing. Furthermore, Malta's constitution prohibits membership of a military alliance and the presence of any foreign military base on Maltese soil. As former members of the Non-Aligned Movement, Cyprus and Malta also have particular commitments to development cooperation and strongly support decolonization and self-determination. On security issues in general, Cyprus and Malta are more likely, it seems, to adopt a posture similar to that of traditionally neutral Member States such as Sweden than that of the other countries in Mediterranean Europe (Bretherton and Vogler, 2007; see also Cini, 2001; Pace, 2006; Sepos, 2008).

Turkey, on the other hand, although not a member of the EU, has an important role in Foreign, Security and Defence Europe, and has strategic importance through its involvement in other organizations. Of particular note is Turkey's membership and strong position in NATO. Turkey is also becoming increasingly integrated into the EU's security and defence structures, where it participates actively in several ESDP missions. Furthermore, Turkey is perceived by many within the EU as an important asset for the revival of the Euro-Med Partnership and the regional constellation of the wider Mediterranean. It is also seen to have a potential role in resolving ongoing conflicts in the Middle East and in the South Caucasus on account of the Georgian and Abkhazian diaspora in Turkey and various agreements signed with Georgia and Azerbaijan. Finally, Turkey is playing an increasingly significant role with regard to energy security and the transit of oil and gas (Tassinari, 2006).

Differences in the level of security and defence integration of Malta and Cyprus on the one hand, and Turkey on the other, suggest that a functional rather than a spatial categorization might better explain differentiation. Spain and Italy, which are also active players within the emerging CFSP and ESDP structures, meanwhile have chosen to join Britain, France and Germany in enhanced cooperation on counter-terrorism issues, rather than seek to form any form of 'Mediterranean bloc', which again suggests that the integration patterns are better seen as functional rather than spatial (Tassinari, 2006).

Schengen Europe and Europe of Rights

Although freedom of movement is a fundamental principle of European integration, the right of Greek citizens to free movement within the EU was subject to significant restrictions during an initial transition period following its 1981 entry. Spanish and Portuguese accession in 1986 also saw a delay in the free movement of persons. Initially, the Iberian transition period for freedom of movement was seven years; however, as fears of mass immigration from these countries proved unfounded, the period was reduced to six years. Malta and Cyprus, on the other hand, enjoyed freedom of movement of persons within the EU even before their accession in 2004. In fact, Malta was concerned that large numbers of EU citizens might move into its territory after enlargement, and therefore it pushed for (and obtained) a 'safeguard mechanism to be adopted on the freedom of movement of workers taking into consideration the disruption of the labour market in Malta in the event of a high inflow of workers following access' (European Parliament, 2001). The rest of the 2004 accession countries, however, were subject to EU restrictions and transition periods with regard to freedom of movement, arising primarily from fears that their citizens would flood the labour markets of existing Member States (Maas, 2005). Turkish citizens currently do not have Schengen-based rights because the country is not a full EU Member State; even if it becomes one, Turkey is likely to experience a similar waiting period to other less economically developed Member States. However, all full EU members in the Mediterranean region currently enjoy and participate in Schengen arrangements.

Conclusion

EU membership has clearly had an impact on policies and political structures in all of the Mediterranean countries, although to varying degrees. The economies of the traditionally poorer members of this group of countries certainly improved after joining the EU, and traditionally laggard Member States like Italy managed to adapt their economic structures in line with stipulations laid down for EMU and the introduction of the euro. Greece, Spain and Portugal also managed to meet the convergence criteria. Moreover, new Member States Cyprus and Malta both met the criteria and implemented the required economic legislation quickly. Non-member Turkey has also seen marked integration of economic structures with the EU. Thus, on the surface, it appears that economic integration with the EU has advanced considerably across the Mediterranean countries.

However, this chapter has shown that some of the Member States – particularly Spain, Portugal, Malta and Cyprus – have been better at adopting and implementing economic legislation, adapting administrative structures, and ultimately establishing economic structures that are more in line with EU norms than others such as Italy and Greece (or, indeed, Turkey). Greece and Italy also have an overall low level of compliance in the area of environmental policy, while Portugal is among the leaders in environmental implementation and Spain's compliance record is somewhere between leaders and laggards. In the sphere of foreign, security and defence policy, there are also significantly different levels of European integration across and within Mediterranean Europe, partly resulting from non-participation in NATO on the part of Malta and Cyprus, but also connected to the pursuit of functional linkages across subsets of Member States, as noted above. One area in which all Mediterranean Member States participate fully, though, is in Schengen free movement regulations, although non-member Turkey still has no access to Schengen privileges.

New members Cyprus and Malta are noteworthy in having experienced a number of innovative features which were introduced into their political systems as a result of European integration. For example, bureaucratic structures were drastically reformed in the lead-up to EU membership. In addition, in Cyprus the relationships between the Parliament and the wider society, more transparent and participatory political processes, a more visible role for women and youth and an environment more conducive to future peace and cooperation among Greek Cypriots and Turkish Cypriots are emerging. Agapiou-Josephides (2003) argues that Cypriot political parties have viewed European integration as a potentially positive factor in the quest for internal reunification, which in turn, she argues, has affected cross-community (Greek–Turkish) and cross-partisan cooperation and support for European integration. In this sense, European integration might have helped internal Cypriot integration.

This brief review of the Mediterranean Member States and Turkey indicates that the so-called 'Mediterranean syndrome' is a somewhat inaccurate generalization, at least when it comes to European integration. Moreover, assumptions about the relationship between the length of time a country has been in the EU and the extent of its integration with Europe should also not be over-generalized. Specifically, we have found that despite initially small and relatively weak administrative structures in countries like Malta and Cyprus and despite the relatively short time these countries have been in the EU, they have both performed very well in terms of converging with the EU on the macro-economic level and in terms of adoption and implementation of the *acquis*. On the other hand, the longest-serving Member States of the EU within the Mediterranean group, Italy and Greece, continue to be amongst the least integrated with EU norms and structures, and Turkey – also with a very long association with the EU – has also struggled to adopt such norms and structures. Spain and Portugal, meanwhile, have witnessed far-reaching transformations in their economic structures which reflect a high degree of both real and nominal integration with the EU. A key explanation of their success has been the relative efficacy of their governmental structures, with powerful core executives supported by state bureaucracies which have become increasingly attuned to their role within Europe. In short, the policy areas reviewed in this chapter have illustrated the wide range of experiences of integration with Europe across the Mediterranean and have highlighted the need to consider factors other than just region in explaining differentiated integration in the EU.

Notes

1. The authors are grateful to Annemarie Rodt for essential research assistance in the course of preparing this chapter.
2. The EMP currently comprises the 27 EU Member States and 13 so-called Euro-Med Partners: Albania, Algeria, Egypt, Israel, Jordan, Lebanon, Libya, Mauritania, Morocco, the Palestinian Authority, Syria, Tunisia and Turkey (which is also an EU candidate country). See the European Commission, DG Relex, Euro-Med webpage at: http://ec.europa.eu/external_relations/euromed/index_en.htm

3. The MU/UFM was to bring together the 12 countries bordering the Mediterranean in a new organization to form part of the EU's near-neighbourhood policy. The new MU – separate from, but funded by, the EU – was intended to promote functional cooperation amongst the Mediterranean-rim states in areas such as energy, transport, pollution and the law of the sea. Its key purpose, according to Sarkozy, was to stabilize the EU within its existing borders and minimize future security threats. The Mediterranean Union was opposed by the Commission, which saw it as a competitor project to the existing EuroMed Dialogue and the Barcelona Process. Furthermore, it was seen as a manoeuvre to prevent the future full EU membership of Turkey. Germany was strongly opposed and threatened to block the initiative. Eventually a compromise for a Union for the Mediterranean was reached. The revised initiative included all 27 EU Member States and its principal objective was to improve relations between the EU and its neighbours in North Africa and the Middle East. For further information on these initiatives, see Chapter 11 by Cole in this volume; see also EURActiv, 'Summit Approves "Union for the Mediterranean"' (14 March 2008) at: www.euractiv.com/en/enlargement/summit-union-mediterranean/artcle-170976.
4. On small states and European integration see, for example, Goetschel (1998), Griffiths and Pharo (1995), Kelstrup (1993) and Thorhallsson (2001). For the specific case of Cyprus see Nugent (2001).
5. Belgium, Germany, Ireland, France, Luxembourg, the Netherlands, Austria and Finland.
6. The study investigated five areas of EU environmental policy; the Drinking Water Directive, the Directive on the Combatting of Air Pollution of Industrial Plants, the Large Combustion Plant Directive, the Access to Information Directive and the Environmental Impact Assessment.
7. The push-pull model is based on two propositions: 1) compliance problems arise when implementation of EU policies imposes considerable costs (material and political) on the public administrations of Member States; 2) pressure from below, where domestic actors may mobilize against ineffective implementation (pull), and from above, where the European Commission may introduce infringement proceedings (push), may both increase the effectiveness of implementing 'costly' EU policies. For further details see Börzel (2000).

13
Nordic Europe

Lee Miles

Introduction

In many ways, the Nordic region – here defined as 'Nordic Europe' – represents an exemplary example of a region with many homogenous and common features uniting its component states. Notable political scientists have quite regularly evaluated why the Nordic countries have been identified as a 'family of nations' (Castles, 1993) and have stressed their commonalities. They are, for example, usually categorized as mature liberal democracies, with advanced corporatist economies. Nevertheless, Nordic Europe, for all its internal cohesiveness, has also not been immune to processes of differentiation, and especially those influencing their relations with the evolving European Community/Union (EC/EU), where a diversity of approaches has been, and is, commonplace.

This chapter examines the complex interrelationship between the Nordic region – here understood to cover the territories of the five principal Nordic countries of Denmark, Finland, Iceland, Norway and Sweden and the European Community/European Union – with particular reference to their specific attitudes towards differentiated integration. In order to do this, differentiated integration is taken to be defined, as it is in the introduction to this volume, in a largely 'classical' institutional–legal way; namely as

> the process whereby European states, or sub-units, opt to move at different speeds and/or towards different objectives with regard to common policies, by adopting different formal and informal arrangements, whether inside or outside the EU treaty framework, and by assuming different rights and obligations.

The approach assumes that, alongside regional dynamics, the respective states remain the key units of analysis. One caveat is worth stipulating; namely that the primary focus of the evaluations are the Nordic political elites, and more specifically, the Nordic governments. This is important since distinguishing between 'states' and 'governments' in the EU context 'is not just a matter of splitting hairs' (Wallace, 2005: 28). A focus on national executives, and thereby governmental perspectives, is appropriate since they hold key positions in the decision-making and implementation of EU policies and thus influence the way in which Nordic states, whether as EU members or non-EU countries, shape EU policies and institutions and adapt to them (Börzel, 2005: 62).[1] This chapter conceptualizes the activities of governmental elites when formulating national EU policy. In particular, their perspectives towards the EU that influence policy design, policy negotiation, policy legitimization and policy implementation dimensions; and thus, as the central platform with which to understand the *policy positions* of Nordic governments towards European integration and how this may influence the conduct of Nordic policies towards the EU. It says much less about public views and discourses on European integration. Such a state-centric approach is not without its dangers or costs. By focusing on the actions and reactions of Nordic governments, this is not to dismiss the influences upon governments from other Nordic political elites, such as parliamentarians, corporate actors, non-governmental organizations (NGOs) and regional actors. These form the bed-rock for an intensive, yet often low-level 'cobweb' of contact and collaboration that became synonymous with Nordic Cooperation. In addition, this plethora of other Nordic actors may also have direct access to EU institutions, and thus offer divergent perspectives from that of the governing elite in EU circles and policy fora. However, the Nordic governments remain, for the most part, the dominant, if not exclusive, representatives of the national interest and thus governmental political elites have particular resonance.

This chapter has three tasks. First, to explore in detail why the Nordic region, and its component countries, are often portrayed as a relatively coherent area consisting of a 'family of nations' with a strong regional identity; and, more specifically, how this can be related to spatial and functional dimensions, as well as being rooted in a historical and political attachment to the 'Nordic model' and 'Nordic internationalism' and a general conceptualization of being on the periphery of Europe. The focus is very much then on the 'Nordic'. Second, the chapter also discusses that, in spite of this focus on the 'Nordic', there is also some deviation in the approaches of the Nordic governments, especially towards European integration. Moreover, alongside the growing differentiation within the Nordic countries that has challenged the validity of a 'Nordic model', differentiation integration has continued to be the norm even among the three Nordic EU members. A Nordic Europe has often been a differentiated one in practice, and this can be examined using spatial, temporal and functional dimensions. Third, the chapter concludes by arguing that, while it is accurate to regard Nordic Europe as a regional entity, it is also one part of Europe where differentiation is the norm, and where governments practise both formal and informal practices of differentiated integration. Nordic Europe is a place of differentiated Europeans, where differences in governmental approach, towards both full EU membership status and to further integration questions, continues to exist.

The Nordic Region: similarities and path dependencies

The political elites of the Nordic countries often share strong commonalities in approach and this substantially influences the conduct of their national politics.

From a comparative politics perspective, these countries are identified, and for a long time identified themselves, as social democratic polities, that have since the 1930s practised a particular form of welfare capitalism and implemented generous welfare state provision. Moreover, their political elites often stressed the constitutional prowess of the Nordic countries as liberal democracies that have balanced long traditions of open and transparent government alongside a commitment to constitutional and policy innovation, for example, in terms of gender equality. Hence, domestic discourses in these countries have, albeit to a limited extent, highlighted that national political elites were pursuing a distinctive, somewhat superior, form of domestic politics that was more social democratically inspired, more liberal and possibly more innovative than that usually found in 'continental Europe'.

Furthermore, the distinctiveness of Nordic national politics was complimented by broader, and equally strong, identifications of the region as a common *Norden* that translated into a commitment to 'Nordic internationalism'. The influence of these common attributes could be found within each respective country's foreign policy. Indeed, many have suggested that there has been a particular form of Nordic internationalism, rooted in active support for international institutions like the United Nations, strong advocacy of international development aid and for nuclear disarmament, as well as a forthright respect for international law, Hilson (2008: 186), for instance, claimed that 'what seems remarkable is the resilience and stability of *Norden* as a concept, and Bergman (2006) argues that the Nordic countries continue to practise a form of 'adjacent internationalism'. For some, such as Ingebritsen (2006), the Nordic countries were viewed, and perceived themselves as, 'a social laboratory' that affected both their national politics and their international relations, with Nordic elites acting as 'norm entrepreneurs' on the international stage.

The existence of a Nordic political discourse that stressed the characteristics of a Nordic model of (supposedly superior) good governance and welfare capitalism, complimented by healthy dose of Nordic internationalism which often sought to export the advantages of these aspects on the international stage, clearly had an influence upon views of the dominant political elites in the Nordic countries on matters of European integration. For many, the Nordic countries could be categorised as 'reluctant Europeans' (Miljan, 1977). For a long time, they were sceptical towards joining a supra-national organization that might impinge upon national sovereignty and were wary of any attempts at establishing a Federal Europe that might contradict or undermine their national pursuits of welfare capitalism. For a long time, they traditionally favoured inter-governmental forms of cooperation between sovereign states (Miljan, 1977; Gstöhl, 2002). None of the Nordic countries were, after all, founder members of the European Coal and Steel Community (ECSC), or of the European Economic Community (EEC) during the 1950s. Instead, Denmark, Norway and Sweden joined the intergovernmental European Free Trade Association (EFTA) in 1960, which established a free-trade area among its members, and was largely seen by Nordic political elites as merely an economic project (Egeberg, 2005) with limited political ambitions. It took until the early

1970s for the first of the Nordic countries (Denmark) to become a full member of the European Community (EC) and now European Union (EU).

Referring to Keating's spatial dimensions (see Chapter 4 in this volume), it could be argued that *national/cultural differentiation* (the concept and role of the nation-state), *differentiating welfare,* and *political-institutional differentiation,* were all features of how the Nordic countries set themselves apart from the rest of Europe. As regards *national/cultural differentiation,* then the fact that these countries are, in historical terms, Protestant Lutheran countries perched on the periphery of mainland Europe has perpetuated a self-image (that features in Nordic discourses on European integration) that these states are somehow different and also 'distant' from the largely Catholic continental Europe.

Highlighting Keating's emphasis on welfare dynamics, the dominance of social democratic-inspired discourses since the 1930s in most of the Nordic countries also meant that, within their discussions on European integration, there existed the prevailing idea that Nordic-style welfare states encompassed a stronger commitment towards innovative social justice based on universal and solidarity principles and thereby required national political elites to maintain control over national instruments. Nordic political elites often argued that welfare politics was in essence a much greater priority than mere European integration. Furthermore, it was often alleged that the development of Nordic-style generous welfare provision may be, at best, undermined by participation in supra-national European integration (Kuisma, 2007). In simple terms, Nordic discussions of welfare often led to the additional conclusion that continental-inspired European integration was 'too capitalist' for the Nordic countries since they were pursuing a fundamentally similar, yet slightly varied, model of economic development and welfare.

With reference to Keating's highlighting of political–institutional aspects, then the discourses among Nordic political elites often asserted that, alongside the commitments to welfare capitalism, there were similar ones towards innovative social engineering, such as pursuing highly progressive gender equality, that not only required retaining control over national policy instruments but also seemed to be based on more liberal and modernistic priorities than those usually pursued on mainland Europe. Hence, in general terms, there was a self-image perpetuated by Nordic political elites that the states of mainland Europe, as the masters of European integration, were also 'too conservative' compared to *Norden.* To draw on the words of Tage Erlander, the former Swedish Prime Minister, not only was European integration built upon different priorities but it was also driven by states in continental Europe that were 'too Catholic, too capitalist and too conservative', and thereby different from the Nordic countries.

Similarly, Nordic debates in the context of Nordic internationalism and security were not always conducive towards European integration. The spectre of non-alignment and neutrality was an important contextual issue. For Finland and Sweden at least, their continuing security policy doctrines of non-alignment (in peacetime) and neutrality (in wartime) in the post-war period ensured that full EEC/EC membership was highly problematic. Above all, their political elites argued that they needed to demonstrate freedom of action and independence in trade policy and thus participation in supra-national European integration, and more specifically, a Common Commercial Policy (CCP) governed by supra-national institutions was, for a long time, deemed incompatible with non-alignment. Across all five Nordic countries, it would also be accurate to state that Nordic security discourses were built upon the assertion that European security was fundamentally based in the post-war period on US participation.

Through the practice of Nordic internationalism, and more specifically Nordic Co-operation, in the form of the Nordic Passport Union and Nordic Labour Market, the Nordic countries were also some way near to establishing a *transnational space* that in some Nordic countries, such as Norway, has been articulated at various times as an alternative to full EU membership. Equally, and as Goetz argues (Chapter 5 of this volume), temporal issues may also be useful here – not least in seeing the Nordics as 'a family of nations' framed in a stable, largely peripheral territorial environment as a 'zone of peace' (Archer, 2006), that, in temporal terms, enjoyed a golden era during the majority of the post-war period, and perpetuating a self-image of the Nordic model that highlighted tensions with central aspects of European integration.

The prevalence and resonance of these features has waxed and waned across all the Nordic countries. As Egeberg (2005: 186) comments, the Nordic countries have been involved in the European integration process 'at different points in time and to different degrees'. Moreover, there have been notable changes in the form and content of Nordic politics since the 1990s that have challenged the salience of social-democratic-inspired discourses and the existence of a heavily social-democratic Nordic political culture. Yet, although Browning (2007) argues that Nordicity as a brand may be past its sell-by date, it can be argued that, at least in terms of European integration, debates around Nordic models and Nordic internationalism have powerful path dependencies. For Norway and Iceland, many of these discourses were strong enough to ensure that they have not been able to secure full membership status (yet). Ultimately for three of them, there were sufficient changes to enable them to become full members of the EC/EU (Denmark in 1973; Finland and Sweden in 1995). Yet, even today, 'Nordic' aspects feature strongly in domestic debates in the three Nordic members and explain why, at least in the realms of public discussions on European integration, there are still pronounced sections of the populations that feel reluctant about their respective countries' participation in European integration and why Nordic governments have faced major challenges when handling questions of European integration.

Differentiated integration as the norm

Any *prima facie* examination of the policy positions of the Nordic countries towards European integration highlights a remarkable degree of commonality in terms of their policy priorities towards European integration. Whether as full EU members or as non-EU states, commonalities towards European integration in policy terms are detectable to some degree. Again some of this is influenced by path dependencies arising from (past) debates on a Nordic model and the need for close economic relations with the EC/EU. During the early 1970s, for example, each of the Nordic countries (excluding Denmark, who joined the Community then) signed Free Trade Agreements with the European Community establishing a free-trade area and guaranteeing the Nordic countries access to Community markets. When these provisions ran out of steam in the early 1980s, the Nordic countries participated in discussions on establishing a European Economic Space (EES) between the EC and EFTA that eventually resulted in the 1992 European Economic Area (EEA) agreement. As signatories of the EEA, the Nordic countries accepted substantial parts of the EC *acquis* pertaining to the Single European Market. Since 1995, when the balance between Nordic EU members and non-members moved in favour of a majority inside the Union, similarities in terms of policy positions can also be readily found.

All of the Nordic countries, have, for example, remained steadfast opponents of the development of the Union into a Federal Europe and are generally cautious towards major institutional reform of the Union that may be regarded as a major step on the road towards this. For instance, although most of the political elites in the Nordic countries supported the processes leading to the 2004 Constitutional Treaty, and the later 2007 Lisbon Treaty, few were advocates of major EU institutional reform and all were keen to ensure that the rights of small states in EU decision-making were respected and protected. On the other hand, all of the Nordic countries are strong advocates of reforming the Union to enhance openness and transparency in the Union in order to ensure that the EU remains compatible with Nordic traditions of open government. In addition, the Nordic countries have been ardent proponents of the Union developing its environmental policy competencies at the EU level, particularly in order to tackle climate change. They have also regularly advocated the further enhancement of the Union's social dimension in order to ensure continuing compatibility between the Union's Single European Market principles of free movement with Nordic labour market rules. In the light of their Nordic internationalism, the five states have also welcomed the enhancement of the Union's role in external relations, and its crisis management capacities, that enable the Union to play a more prominent role in peace-making and peace-keeping. All the Nordic states – and particularly the three Nordic Member States – for example, were supporters of the strengthening of the Union's external relations capacities, such as reforms to create a permanent EU Council President as well as a High Representative with increased powers in foreign affairs as part of the 2007 Treaty of Lisbon. Above all, and especially in the case of the three EU members, the governments of the Nordic countries have been rather consistent supporters of further EU enlargement up to and beyond the EU27.

However, alongside and balancing such commonalities in the Nordic countries' perspectives towards European integration has been an equally discernible trend of deviation and diversity. In spite of talk about common Nordic approaches towards European integration, the picture has been one characterized as much by differentiated integration as common approaches. Moreover, this applies to a wide variety of Nordic perspectives towards European integration.

Such deviation can take the form of more formal kinds of differentiation among the Nordic countries. Firstly, and most obviously, this applies to the fundamental question of whether to seek full membership of the EU. Today, only three of the Nordic states are full EU members, and even then full accession was achieved at different times (Denmark, 1973 and Finland and Sweden, 1995) signalling the potential for differing temporal and spatial dimensions influencing Nordic governmental perspectives even on the fundamental question of full membership.

Furthermore, there are also notable divergences of perspective towards questions of further European integration, especially in 'flagship' policy fields such as EMU. Although several authors discussed the possibilities of cooperation between the Nordic EU and non-EU members producing a potential bloc within the EU (for instance, Miles, 1996), the reality has been somewhat different. Even among the three existing Nordic EU members, there have also been varying adaptation to, and participation in, flagship EU projects. Mouritzen and Wivel (2005) have argued that it may be wise to see European states in terms of being 'insiders', 'near-insiders' and 'outsiders' to the processes of European integration.

If this is taken at face value then it may be pertinent to comment upon the divergent experiences of the five Nordic states towards European integration. Turning to Denmark, although this Nordic state was one of the first to seek full membership status in the 1960s (its first application was submitted as early as 1961) and to become a full EU member (in 1973), Danish experiences of full membership have been somewhat turbulent, to say the least. Early on, the Danish people supported accession in the 1972 referendum with a vote of 63.4 per cent, but domestic support was largely secured on the grounds that the Community was to remain an essentially economic-orientated 'Common Market'. During the 1970s, successive Danish governments resisted any fundamental institutional reform and attained something of a reputation for being an awkward EEC member, although the Danes approved the 1986 Single European Act and supported the establishment of the Single European Market (SEM).

Continuing Danish concerns with participation in further integration were illustrated by the events surrounding the 1992 Treaty on European Union (TEU) ratification when the Danish public narrowly rejected the Treaty in an initial referendum in 1992, and again by the rejection of Danish adoption of the single currency in 2000. In the former case, this resulted in a national compromise between the national political parties, and four 'opt-outs' (from the EMU, CFSP, JHA pillars as well as from EU citizenship) were secured at the 1992 Edinburgh European Council summit. Not only did the securing of the four opt-outs enable the Danish population to approve the Treaty in 1993, but it also created a rather unusual domestic environment in which further European integration is debated in Denmark, and which constrained positions towards European integration. In many ways then, Denmark has, since the early 1990s, operated one of the most visible and formal forms of differentiation in the contemporary European Union. Two examples are illustrative. First, at various points since 2001, the Fogh Rasmussen Liberal government (2001–9) argued that the 'opt-outs' should be removed, even though this would probably have required a further referendum in Denmark just to abolish any of the opt-outs. Second, the continuing existence of the opt-outs has prompted some rather interesting foreign policy decisions; for instance, in the 1990s the Danes were forced to withdraw troops from peace-keeping missions in the Balkans when the command of those troops transferred from NATO to EU command and thus brought the issue of the CFSP opt-out into the Danish public eye.

Sweden and Finland, who both joined the Union in 1995, have also shown notable differentiation in terms of perspectives and participation in further European integration. At best, only Finland can be classified as being close to the core of EU activity (Mouritzen and Wivel, 2005) with the Finnish public generally being less sceptical as to the benefits of EU membership – seeing it as much as a vote for the West as for European integration itself. This facilitated a process whereby the vast majority of the mainstream Finnish political parties became relatively quickly reconciled to the question of continuing membership (most notably during the years of the Rainbow Coalition governments of 1995–2003), and then to Finnish participation in key flagship integration projects. The greater propensity for 'pro-European' positions to be found back home has permitted a generally higher level of EU activity among Finnish political elites, for example, in pushing forward policies such as the EU Northern Dimension. More specifically, Finland became a founder member of the Euro Area, with the euro enjoying quite high levels of support on the streets of Helsinki.

In contrast, Sweden's transition to full membership has not been as smooth, partly because the 1994 accession referendum was only narrowly approved and was significantly closer than in the Finnish case. The governing Social Democratic governments of 1994–2006 also suffered from internal disunity among the rank and file of the Social Democratic Party, and until 2009 the Left Party in Sweden was still canvassing for Swedish withdrawal from the Union. The Swedish party system has thus found it much more difficult to cope with the pressures of European integration issues than its Finnish counterpart. Hence, in spite of having no formal opt-outs as in the Danish case, the Swedes have still conducted differentiated integration, having decided not to join either the ERM2 or the third stage of EMU in 1999. Even after a successful first Swedish EU Council Presidency in 2001, the (then) Social Democratic government of Göran Persson was unable to convince the Swedish population of the benefits of adopting the single currency, and the Swedish public categorically rejected the euro in a public referendum in September 2003. Even today, Sweden remains outside the Euro Area and is not even a member of the ERM2; there is very little evidence of a likely change in that position in the near future.

Nevertheless, Sweden's position as a 'euro-outsider' (see Lindahl and Naurin, 2005) should not be taken as evidence of an overwhelmingly inter-governmental position on the part of the Swedes in recent years. At least since the country's full accession in 1995, the Swedish political elite can in fact be much more accurately described as 'selective supra-nationalists'; they have, for example, been at the forefront of promoting the development of a supra-national environmental policy. The Swedish case is very much a mixed perspective (see Miles, 2005). For example, in the case of the EU's evolving crisis management functions and the capacities of the CFSP and ESDP, the Swedes have resisted attempts to turn the EU into a formal defence alliance (akin to Article V of NATO), yet they have also remained very active proponents of the crisis management role of the EU and have not invoked non-alignment as a rationale for securing a formal opt-out in the CFSP domain, as Denmark did. Nevertheless, the pro-European non-socialist Alliance government (in office since 2006) has faced domestic opposition to European integration, and questions as to the compatibility of Swedish welfare and labour rights with European law came to the fore in the light of the Laval and Viking cases, which strengthened domestic concerns about some aspects of European integration. It seems likely then that Sweden will continue as a 'near core insider' but one where quite pronounced levels of informal differentiated integration are practised.

At face value, Norway and Iceland can be categorized as outsiders since neither has secured full membership status (yet). Given Icelandic sensitivities that EU accession might imply opening up the country's fiercely protected fishing grounds under the Common Fisheries Policy (CFP) as part of the obligations of being a full member, Icelandic governments have traditionally shied away from initiating extensive debates on EU questions, and thus the question of full membership has only featured intermittently in Icelandic domestic political debates. According to Thorhallson (2004), even participation in the 1992 EEA was controversial, requiring Iceland to negotiate a clause in the agreement banning foreign investment in its fishing industry. Nevertheless, this has not prevented Iceland from participating selectively in aspects of European integration and thus to have been a practitioner of differentiated integration when necessary and/or advisable. Iceland, for instance, became a signatory to the Schengen Agreement on policy and border control cooperation in order to handle the implications of having greater numbers of Nordic EU members in the Nordic Passport Union.

However, with the onset of the global financial crisis in 2008–9, which prompted the virtual collapse of the entire Icelandic banking sector, and which brought Iceland to the point of near-bankruptcy, discussions of European integration reappeared. Initially, the discussions in Iceland focused primarily on questions of whether to join the Euro Area and not on full membership itself, displaying, albeit to a limited extent, Nordic tendencies towards differentiated integration. However, when EMU participation was rejected by the European Union as not being viable without first securing EU full membership, the Icelandic government went on to submit a full membership application on 16 July 2009, with a target of full EU accession by 2012 subject to prior approval by national referendum. It remains to be seen whether this will be achieved.

For Norway, its status as an outsider has to be considerably qualified. Between 1961–72 and 1992–4, Norwegian governments strove for full membership and in both periods reached the point of signing accession treaties with the Community/ Union. However, deeply held domestic concerns about European integration have resulted in public rejections of proposed Norwegian full membership in two referenda (1972 and 1994) that formally ruled out full membership (Archer, 2005).

In general the Norwegian public, as well as some parts of the Norwegian political and economic establishment, have not been entirely convinced by the arguments supporting full EU membership.

However, despite of, and probably because of, the failure of these membership applications, the Norwegian political elite has taken a strategic view of enhancing Norway's associations with the EU. Put simply, they have become architects and practitioners of various forms of formal and informal differentiated integration short of full membership of the European Union. Sverdrup (1998), for instance, refers to Norway as a selective yet 'adaptive non-member' and certainly one that is involved in complex forms of formal and informal differentiated integration with the Union.

In formal terms, Norway's relationship with the Union is clearly differentiated. Norway was a signatory of the EEA and went on to join the Schengen Agreement to maximize Norwegian access to and participation in many aspects of the Single European Market and the 'four freedoms', and thus remains closely and formally tied to many policy-related aspects of the Union's deepening process. Norway is also a regular contributor to core EU policies, such as environmental policy, structural funds and research and development programmes, as well as having 'equal partner' status in some of the Union's flagship policies for the region, such as the EU Northern Dimension. It has also readily been co-opted into and developed substantial cooperation under the auspices of the CFSP. In terms of informal differentiated integration, the Norwegian political elites have developed very sophisticated ways to ensure their involvement in EU policy discussions. Norway is a major player in the Union and, as the works of Trondal (2000) and Egeberg and Trondal (1999) demonstrate, there are many instances where, in practice, Norwegian policy-makers are more fully integrated into EU policy processes than some full but reluctant EU Member States, such as the United Kingdom. If anything, Norway is probably closer to being a 'would-be insider' and has developed substantial strategies of association to reduce the impacts of non-membership. In many dimensions, Norway is integrated, and exhibits clearly clustered Europeanization.

Overall, the Nordic states are regular practitioners of formal and informal forms of differentiated integration, and there are major variations in approach among the Nordic countries towards differing EU policies, respective and irrespective of the membership–non-membership dichotomy.

Understanding differentiated integration in the Nordic countries

Spatial dimensions

Referring to the 'spatial dimensions' outlined by Michael Keating in Chapter 4, then several aspects of his spatial dimension of differentiated integration are helpful in explaining the differing perspectives of the Nordic countries on questions of European integration, and indeed, on EU membership itself.

First, they can be explained by *geo-strategic differentiation* – in particular, the influence of the Cold War and relations with the United States in shaping their perspectives on European integration. The fact that three of the Nordic states are members of NATO, and indeed place great emphasis on the transatlantic relationship, is an explanatory factor in understanding why Norway and Iceland have not secured EU membership. The primacy of NATO and transatlantic-based security has been a consistent and influential part of their elite and domestic debates on full EU membership, as well as, for a long time, it shaping Danish hesitancy towards a EU defence dimension. In the Finnish case, the close proximity of the USSR was a major influence on it not seeking NATO membership, while the post-1989 changes in Europe have largely been portrayed as a major rationale for Finland's enthusiastic accommodation with the EU. Furthermore, in more recent times, differences among the Nordic countries have emerged over the role of US hegemony in world politics and the required response from Nordic governments. Under the Liberal-led governments in Denmark (since 2001), for example, the country has been a staunch supporter of US involvement in the 'war on terror' and has been actively engaged in Iraq. In contrast, successive Swedish governments – in line with the last vestiges of non-alignment – were openly critical of US unilateralism in international affairs, and regularly questioned the implications of the Iraq war for the functioning of international institutions and international law.

Second, there is *economic differentiation* – best understood in the Nordic case as compatibilities between the Nordic model of welfare capitalism and the free market capitalist aspirations of the EC/EU. Here, it is important to recognize that these have been highly influential in shaping Nordic opposition first to membership, based around a belief in the superiority of the Nordic model, and then, with the model's gradual decline at the hands of economic recession and globalization, as a prism with which to view the possibilities of EU membership and further European integration. A closer accommodation with the EU reflects a growing, albeit limited, belief in the decline of the Nordic model. Most notably, it could be argued that the development of the Nordic model has roughly been in four phases, affecting Nordic perspectives on European integration: 1) the problems of the 1970s, when structural problems first appear, run alongside, but not necessarily relate to Danish accession; 2) the 1980s and the introduction of the SEM, prompting Nordic differentiated approaches towards accommodation through the EEA; 3) the early 1990s and the onset of severe economic recession, which severely affected Finland and Sweden and pushed forward arguments that EU accession could be a catalyst for a neo-liberal injection to modernize the Nordic model; and 4) the post-2000 period, where changes in government, particularly in Denmark, led to differing approaches towards the free-movement-of-labour question and CFSP orientations. Yet, again, however, there has been discernible economic differentiation, not least in the positions of Norway and Iceland, which have been influenced by substantially different economic fortunes in their leading sectors – namely fisheries and oil in the case of Norway and fisheries and now financial services in the case of Iceland.

Temporal dimensions

Equally, the temporal dimensions, articulated by Klaus Goetz in Chapter 5 of this volume, are of use in understanding the Nordic case. In the Nordic countries, there are notable cases of differentiated integration that can be partly explained by patterns of temporal differentiation. Three examples spring to mind. First, the fact that Denmark was first to become a member of the EC/EU (1973) and since then has held no fewer than six full referenda on EU questions provided regular opportunities for Danish debates on further integration to take place. Moreover, with the rejection of the Treaty of European Union (TEU) in a 1992 public referendum, this ultimately resulted in Denmark securing the four formal opt-outs from the TEU, and have meant that Danish debates on European integration have taken place in a different domestic setting compared to most other EU countries. It also required the other Nordic states to embark on differing forms of differentiated integration with the Union in order to take account of the variant membership of Denmark in the context of Nordic cooperation. Second, the achievement of full EU accession by Sweden and Finland was undertaken only shortly before the launch of the Third Stage of EMU and the evolution of the CFSP. This resulted in a very strong focus on these questions becoming a central aspect of the early years of their membership; it also made 'opt-outs' impossible even if they would have been wanted. In simple terms, Sweden and Finland never had access to, or the possibility of, securing the types of formal differentiation that Denmark has. Third, the decision by Norway to seek membership again in November 1992 was largely based on considerations of issues not of their own making; it was largely a reflection of changing conditions in the Nordic region brought on by alterations in Swedish and Finnish perspectives rather than fundamental changes in the rather rigid, domestic debates on European integration current in Norway. Hence, the Norwegian political elite had to develop and enhance already sophisticated forms of association with the Union once the public had again rejected full membership in 1994. The temporal processes of adaptation and Europeanization have been different across the Nordic countries, and this may explain the degree of differentiation in the approaches of Nordic governments towards some questions of European integration.

The emphasis on the relationship between time of accession and domestic developments is also significant and can explain the slower adaptation to EU membership in Sweden compared to Finland. The configuration of the respective party systems in the Nordic countries, timings of elections, and governmental choices as to whether or not to utilize referenda on EU proposals such as EMU, are influential factors that have shaped the differentiated approaches of Nordic governments towards aspects of European integration.

Functional dimensions

The observations on functional dimensions by Kölliker in Chapter 3 of this volume also have explanatory value. First, Kölliker highlights the need to understand the ramifications of *differentiation across EU borders*. In this context, the

Nordic governments adopted both formal and informal measures to take account of the differentiated status of the Nordic states in terms of EU membership. In particular, the Nordic governments needed to handle the political and economic challenges arising from the fact that one of the formal external borders of the Union has run directly across the Nordic region – between Norway and Sweden and Norway and Finland – since 1995. Indeed, Nordic Cooperation, and the Nordic Council as its most notable institutional manifestation, has remained a useful and long-established formal and informal framework for handling such challenges. Furthermore, the Nordic governments utilized the Schengen Agreement as a legal and institutional framework for handling the implications of this external border for the free movement of Nordic peoples and thus maintained the Nordic Passport Union, which has been operational since the 1950s.

Second, Kölliker stresses the need to understand the ramifications of *differentiation inside and outside the margins of EU law*. Reference could again be made to the Schengen example, where legal agreements have been used in innovative ways to pursue differentiated integration. However, Nordic approaches towards cooperative arrangements in the CFSP/ESDP structures and actions provide an even more pronounced example. Swedish and Finnish policy-makers have both officially retained their domestically popular policies of non-alignment and avoided NATO membership (which is unpopular among their publics), while still being highly active in CFSP crisis management functions through innovative use of the margins of EU law. By consistently stressing that the CFSP/ESDP does not yet contain collective defence assurances and thus is not a formal defence alliance, the Swedes and Finns have been able to be actively involved in the CFSP/ESDP, and have even been strident champions of the development of a civilian crisis management portfolio for the Union. They have, in essence, been able to use legal definitions to pursue an unofficial yet EU-compatible form of 'semi-alignment' (Miles, 2000).

Third, Kölliker emphasizes that it is important to take account of differences between actual and potential differentiation. This is particularly important in factoring in the limitations set in Nordic countries by Eurosceptic public opinion, which can often constrain the policy options of Nordic governments. Again, there is a need to highlight that even where formal differentiation has been secured this has not usually led to its full potential being used by respective Nordic governments in their dealings with the European Union. In the case of Denmark and its 'opt-outs', while the existence of these has been useful for Danish governments in managing domestic concerns over future participation in European integration, it is also clear that Danish governments over the past decade have been highly reluctant to invoke them at the EU level; indeed, the Danish Prime Minister, Fogh Rasmussen (2001–9), regularly expressed his wish to see them removed at the earliest politically viable opportunity.

Finally, attention needs to be paid to practical differentiation motivated, according to Kölliker, by *unwillingness and inability*. Although the lack of Norwegian membership may, at face value, indicate *public unwillingness* to become fully immersed in the EU through accession, Norwegian political elites have actively sought participation in EU policies in order to demonstrate their *willingness* for

Norway to be involved in European integration. It is necessary not just to talk about differentiated attitudes among the Nordic states, but also of differentiation based on differing levels of willingness and ability *within* the Nordic states, and particularly differentiation in elite versus public attitudes towards their country's participation in European integration.

Conclusion

This brief application of spatial, temporal and functional dimensions of European integration to case of Nordic Europe suggests that, in the words of the editors of this volume, there is indeed a time and a place for differentiated integration within the policies of the Nordic governments. If anything, this evaluation suggests that, for the most part, formal and informal differentiation acts as both a policy goal and a policy instrument used by Nordic governments when handling the pressures of European integration. Indeed, we can further conclude that a more detailed understanding of the complexities of differentiated integration provides a useful tool for understanding why the Nordic countries should be viewed as 'selective supra-nationalists' and not as ardent, inter-governmental-obsessed 'reluctant Europeans' (Miles, 2001). In reality, the actions of Nordic political elites suggest that they operate within a policy spectrum in which they pursue largely pro-supra-national, yet 'federo-sceptic' (Miles, 2005), solutions for European integration (to some extent irrespective of their status as EU or non-EU members), using the opportunities provided by, and through, informal and formal differentiated integration in an EU27 and beyond.

Note

1. There are influences upon governments from other Nordic political elites, such as parliamentarians and corporate actors, and also they, in a fusing EU, may have direct access to EU institutions. However, the Nordic governments remain, for the most part, the dominant, if not exclusive, representatives of the national interest and thus governmental political elites have particular resonance.

14
Europe's Neighbourhood and Transboundary Differentiation

Geoffrey Edwards

Introduction

The European Union has long sought to influence countries in its neighbourhood whether in the interests of stability, security or prosperity. If, during the Cold War, these efforts were largely directed towards members of EFTA and the countries of the Mediterranean, the Cold War's end brought about a profound transformation of the geopolitical landscape of Europe, with 10 central and eastern European states (CEECs) becoming EU members in 2004 and 2007. That enlargement not only extended the EU's borders with Russia but brought the EU to the shores of the Black Sea and created new or near neighbours in eastern Europe and in the southern Caucuses. The result has been tension between sometimes differing aims: managing the new borders in the interests of efficiency and effectiveness, especially to counter illegal migration and criminality; preventing new divisions between countries that had formerly been highly integrated within the former Soviet 'space'; and, at the same time, reconciling those seeking to fulfil their European vocation through future EU membership with an alternative path towards 'Europeanization'. All this had to be set against a widespread sense of 'enlargement fatigue' within many older Member States, compounded by the fact that Turkish and Croatian applications were already on the table, and seemingly confirmed in the negative responses to referendums in France and the Netherlands. It was a fatigue that was also symptomatic of deeper questions about the nature of the European construction, its identity and its borders.

But the result in 2004 was a new Neighbourhood Policy (ENP) which covered the countries of the Mediterranean as well as those of eastern Europe and the southern Caucasus. That the ENP should cover all three regions reflected the very different interests and concerns of old and new Member States. For the Mediterranean states, led by France and Spain, there was a determination to ensure balance between the demands of the now more strongly represented eastern Europe and those of the Mediterranean – particularly in view of the Barcelona Process's lack of success. For the new CEEC Member States, the ENP was an unsatisfactory first step that endangered the European perspective of the remaining countries of eastern Europe and the southern Caucasus. Such a perspective was regarded as vital given the difficulties and ambiguities in the positions of governments unwilling or unable to do much more than reiterate their European vocation, and a resurgent, dynamic Russia under President Putin.

The ENP soon ran into considerable criticism from both within and without the Union. The criticism made by the Ukrainian Ambassador to the EU, Roman Shpek, typified that of others when he declared in September 2007 that 'We cannot recognise the ENP as an adequate basis for Ukraine–EU relations, we can recognise only an instrument that will acknowledge that Ukraine is an integral part of Europe.' (Shpek, 2007). From within the Union, the Policy and its implementing Action Plans were not regarded as sufficient to protect and promote the concerns of the Mediterranean states, as was made clear by President Sarkozy in pursuing his Mediterranean Union initiative (see Chapter 12 in this volume). Nor was it regarded as enough for the new Member States of central and eastern Europe. While there had been a further development after the accession of Bulgaria and Romania with the Black Sea Synergy, which further encouraged what Emerson (2008a: 2) has described as 'technical regionalism' (with a focus on, in this instance, energy, environment and transport) with some 'security regionalism' (against trafficking and other international crime), a membership perspective was still missing. The Poles, allying themselves with the Swedes, then pushed for a new Eastern Partnership in May 2008 which, after some initial reluctance within the Commission, gained support at the European Council in December 2008. But the aim remained one of deepening relations between individual Neighbours and the Union without prejudice to their aspirations for future membership. As the Summit of EU and prospective eastern partners in May 2009 put it, the goal was 'to create the necessary conditions to accelerate political association and further economic integration' by bringing about political and socio-economic reforms that would facilitate 'approximation towards the European Union' (Council of the European Union, 2009).

In calling for such extensive cooperation, approximation and even integration within the framework of the Internal Market, it is not surprising that the ENP should be seen by some in terms of external governance (Lavenex, 2004). Even if results may have been patchy, 'legal' boundaries no longer appear to be quite coterminous with the Union's 'institutional' boundaries. Others have regarded the EU in its neighbourhood as a form of post-modern or liberal imperialism bringing about regime change which could lead to good governance in lasting form (Cooper, 2003), or neo-medieval imperialism (Zielonka, 2005), where the Union appears doomed for ever to enlarge to contain instability on its borders but with looser and more flexible forms of governance. Even more critically, Balzacq and others have regarded it as less an exercise in furthering partnership than attempting to extend an implicit tutelage (Balzacq, 2007).

Other perspectives have also been put forward – the literature on the ENP is now considerable[1] – many summarized by Janis Emmanouilidis in his policy paper for ELIAMEP 'Conceptualizing a Differentiated Europe' (2008: 40ff). Among these possible examples of transboundary differentiation, he includes: Association

Plus or 'deep free trade' put forward by Emerson et al. (2006); 'privileged partnerships' – frequently cited by German government and other sources as a way of dealing with Turkey (see, for example, zu Guttenberg 2004; Merkel 2006a); 'security partnerships' suggested by Grant (2006); other limited membership schemes; and a European Commonwealth (suggested, *inter alia*, by Palmer, 2008). He discusses the strengths and weaknesses and degrees of attractiveness of these various proposals – as do Bechev and Nicolaïdis in their report to the European Parliament of 2007, a report aptly entitled 'Integration without Accession'. They are concerned in particular to recognize the importance of status for those in the neighbourhood, so that any special relationship should not be seen as 'accession minus' but should emphasize inclusion:

> Organising fluidity in the Eurosphere ... would constitute a preventive strategy against extremism and terrorism, more effective than any crackdown in recent history. (Bechev and Nicolaïdis, 2007: 39)

Such fluidity, the mixed motives and different aims of the EU and its Member States towards the Neighbourhood that have combined some functional integration within a framework of political cooperation, has meant some blurring of the boundaries of the European Union (Grant 2006). This chapter therefore focuses on some of the different tensions that lie behind these different drivers for closer cooperation and the centripetal forces that continue to ensure the significance of 'borderdom', with particular attention to the position of the 'Eastern Neighbours'.

Geopolitics and the ENP

While some two years in gestation, the ENP appeared sometimes to be a hurriedly drafted policy that owed a great deal to the accession process of the CEECs. Indeed, some have argued that it owed too much to the process while lacking the crucial element that made the process successful: the prospect of membership (see, *inter alia*, Del Sarto and Schumacher, 2005). The policy was an inevitable compromise (Edwards, 2009). On the one hand, there were those, including the (Polish) Commissioner, Danuta Hübner, who were convinced that

> the Union must keep its doors open to European countries which are not yet members. There may be an alternative to membership, of course, which will satisfy some of these states, even though the experience of the European Economic Area does not bode well for alternatives. Excluding some countries by artificially drawing the 'frontiers of Europe' will only create frustration and problems for the future. I hardly dare mention the word Yalta in this context. (Hübner, 2006)

On the other hand, as the Director General for External Relations, Eneko Landaburu, declared, there *must* be alternatives to membership: Enlargement has been a key tool in projecting stability across our continent. But it is a reality that the EU cannot expand ad infinitum – everything has its limits. (Landaburu, 2006)

What was needed, he went on, was an effective policy in pursuit of 'our geostrategic interest in expanding the zone of prosperity, stability and security beyond our borders for our mutual benefit.' (ibid.). Those security interests had already been set out in the European Security Strategy of 2003 whereby:

Neighbours who are engaged in violent conflict, weak states where organised crime flourishes, dysfunctional societies or exploding population growth on its borders all pose problems for Europe. (Council of the European Union, 2003).

The primary aim, therefore, as the Commission President, Romano Prodi, had put it a little earlier, had to be 'to build a "ring of friends" on its future borders to the East and around the Mediterranean's shores to project stability even further' (Prodi, 2003). Key to reaching such common goals and dealing with 'common threats, such as crime, terrorism, illegal migration and environmental challenges' was the idea of 'sharing everything with the Union but institutions' (Prodi, 2002). The centrepiece was to be the EU's single market, and even if not the free movement of all factors of production, the aim was free trade, open investment policies and the approximation of legislation. And, he argued, the absence of completely free movement of people and labour should not prevent cultural exchanges or regional cooperation (ibid.).

The ENP was not therefore a policy of enlargement but was regarded, especially by its initiators, as a particularly novel approach that was designed to provide a 'new strategic framework and tools for engaging with these neighbours on wide-ranging issues which are of mutual importance and which can only be tackled together' (Landabaru, 2006). Indeed, the Director-General for External Relations (who, significantly, had formerly been Director General for Enlargement) went on to add:

In the same way that the EU is something beyond the nation-state, the ENP is an example of our foreign policy being more than traditional diplomacy or any repackaging of traditional relationships. It is certainly not 'old wine in new bottles' but, rather, a truly modern foreign policy, *harnessing and integrating instruments from across the spectrum* – from support for human rights to judicial reform to elections, support for institution-building, increased political dialogue and cooperation on crisis management ... (ibid., emphasis in original)

And the ENP has sought to be comprehensive in its approach, dealing with all three pillars of the Maastricht Treaty, from trade and economic development, energy and the environment, to CFSP issues, including cooperation of regional partners on EU conflict prevention policies or on weapons of mass destruction, and, of particular importance, JHA issues such as migration, organized crime and counter-terrorism.

The ENP and its Action Plans

Implementation of the ENP was to be through Action Plans negotiated individually by the EU with each participating state. So far, Plans have been signed with 12 of the 16 countries of the Mediterranean, eastern Europe and southern Caucasus – the exceptions being Belarus, Algeria, Libya and Syria. The Plans have been regarded as the central element of the ENP and set out not only an agenda of political and economic reforms but also the priorities to be pursued. Although the Plans are not legally binding, they complement the various other Association and Partnership and Cooperation agreements. The emphasis within the broad Neighbourhood Policy framework is, therefore, on differentiation – in terms, that is, of customized agreements that take account of differences. The President of the Commission put it thus:

> The ENP is not, and never has been, a one-size-fits-all policy. There are as many variations of ENP as there are partners. We cannot and do not wish to ignore the differences between our partners. (Barroso, 2007)

Given the range of political and economic models from Morocco to Belarus and on to Azerbaijan, such differentiation was a matter of common sense – even though themes such as democratization and economic liberalism, policy instruments such as conditionality, and policy options are common to all, regardless of the partner's European 'vocation'.

Even while customized, the Action Plans fit within an overall framework that owes much to the ideas and instruments that were seen as having been successful in the accession. Each Plan covers political dialogue and reform with the aim of strengthening the rule of law, democracy and respect for human rights, the promotion of (market-oriented) economic and social cooperation, cooperation in justice and home affairs, and cooperation on foreign policy objectives such as counter-terrorism.

The policy instruments of each Plan are also similar insofar as they rely heavily on regulatory incentives and capacity-building instruments (Balzacq, 2008). As in the accession process, benchmarking is seen as a key management strategy, that is, 'a permanent monitoring process designed to improve the performance of such programmes or policies according to identified best practices and on the basis of a number of pre-determined criteria and indicators' (Del Sarto et al., 2006: 18). It is a 'soft law' approach that for the EMP states meant a shift to 'positive' from 'negative' conditionality as it existed under the Barcelona Process (Del Sarto and Schumacher, 2005: 21). But for the other neighbours, it included the positive conditionality of the accession process without necessarily the prospect of accession.

The EU remains a powerful economic magnet for those in the Neighbourhood even though the real and potential costs of converging on the EU's *acquis* are significant. At the same time, as Gutu (2006) points out, the cost of noncompliance with the regulations underpinning the Internal Market, whether in terms of economic governance or product-related, may be high in terms of losing existing markets – Romania, say, in the case of Moldova – or expanding into new markets elsewhere within the EU or south-eastern Europe. But compliance can require huge investment and commitment to achieve as well as a healthy economy (Gutu, 2006: 22). Being aware of the issues involved is only half the battle – the Moldovan government recognized in 2004 that 'prospects for cooperation with the EU, including a possibility to enter into an FTA, will depend on Moldova's success in the development of the legal, economic, social and other systems according to the EU principles and standards.' (cited in Gutu, 2006: 21) Realizing the political commitment among the political elite, in cooperation with economic leaders through a consistently applied strategic programme in the face of political instability, has remained elusive, helping to engender a certain 'institutional laziness' (ibid.). But as Wolczuk has reported on Ukraine: 'The implementation of these reforms poses a formidable challenge for a country that has seen its state institutions and public standards deteriorate for over a decade since the collapse of communism' (Wolczuk, 2006: 8). The frequent declarations on how committed Ukraine is to future membership by its government and political and economic elites – who, as Schweickert suggests, simply 'do not accept the missing membership opportunity in the ENP' (2008: 36) – have raised expectations of an ambitious programme to fulfil requirements:

> Engaged in the power struggles, the Ukrainian leadership has little room for implementation of EU-style reforms. Indeed, it has not been the Ukrainian leadership that drives the implementation of the A[ction]P[lan] priorities, but business groups and 'EU-oriented' enclaves in the Ukrainian bureaucracy. (ibid.: 37)

However, without the mobilizing prospect of membership, those elites may well be as influenced by other factors, not least more short-term business interests, as well as wider considerations such as WTO (Jakubiak and Kolesnichenko, 2006) or even NATO membership.

They have also been faced with alternative initiatives and ideas emanating from Russia. The continuing presence of an alternative vision of economic – or even political – integration has inevitably complicated the position of leaders already engaged in difficult power struggles. Russia has, for example, looked for Ukrainian membership of a Common Economic Area with Russia, Belarus and Kazakhstan. Politically, too, Russia is directly or indirectly involved in most of the so-called 'frozen conflicts' in the Neighbourhood. Russia's role in such conflicts has been a cause not only of direct concern, as in the case of Georgia and South Ossetia and Abkhazia in 2008, but has been an additional factor in creating even stronger pressure among many of the newer EU Member States to enhance the bilateral relations with the EU. The EU's role in these conflicts has tended to be marginal – notwithstanding the role of President Sarkozy when President of the Council in negotiating a ceasefire with Russia and Georgia in 2008. The ENP, as Benita Ferrero-Waldner, Commissioner responsible for External Relations, remarked, is not in itself a conflict prevention or settlement mechanism. But through promoting democracy and regional cooperation, boosting national reform programmes and improving the socio-economic prospects of the region, it can contribute to a more positive climate for conflict settlement. (Ferrero-Waldner, 2006)

While the Action Plans have often referred to the frozen conflicts (as in those with Moldova, Armenia and Azerbaijan, and, indeed, the one with Israel), such political dialogues as have been encouraged have been dismissed, by Smith and Webber, for example, as 'missed opportunities and unrealized potential'. (2008: 94). As noted by Sushko (2006) and Wichmann (2007), the EU has tended to emphasize the more technical rather than political (or even ESDP) dimensions of such initiatives as the EU Border Assistance Mission to Moldova and Ukraine (EUBAM). This has led to a somewhat paradoxical situation in which the EU has been attempting de-politicize some border issues while at the same time securitizing them by emphasizing them as threats to EU internal security and taking them beyond ordinary political procedures.

Such a lack of consistency has been noted by many in terms of the EU in the ENP (see, *inter alia*, Del Sarto and Schumacher, 2005, 2008; Schwickert, 2008). The EU has, for example, sought to stress the extent and depth of the values shared between itself and its Member States and the ENP partners in terms of democratization, the rule of law and so on. However, in terms of Action Plan priorities, such values have tended to remain more declaratory than made substantial. Del Sarto et al. concluded that the Action Plans with five Mediterranean partner states in 2004

> show that, in contrast to the Commission's declarations, any clear identification of *specific key priorities* in the realm of democratisation and human rights is conspicuously lacking. In fact, the Action Plans' provisions on democracy and the rule of law, and the respect of human rights, are sketchy and ambiguous at best. (Del Sarto et al., 2006: 44)

The argument has been taken further by Richard Youngs, who has long plotted the EU's promotion of democracy in North Africa and elsewhere (see, for example, Youngs, 2002), who concluded in 2008:

> Although governance is considered a European strength, it is doubtful that EU governance projects have done much to assist democracy abroad. This may be because democracy itself is not the expressed goal of such projects. For example, European diplomats often say that strengthening border controls is their main governance priority. (Youngs, 2008: 167)

And it has indeed been the case that where the EU has been decidedly less vague on prioritization and processes has been in the area of Justice and Home Affairs. It is here where Rijpma and Cremosa have suggested that the EU has sought extra-territorialization, a process whereby the EU attempts 'to push back the EU's external borders or rather to police them at a distance in order to control unwanted migration flows' (2007; 10). As Wichmann (2007: 8–9) has pointed out, the EU and Ukraine JHA Action Plan adopted with Ukraine in 2001 and updated in 2006 contains a plethora of detailed measures, with some 99 objectives and 224 joint actions listed. As in the case of the EU itself through its Tampere and Hague Programmes, there is also an accompanying scoreboard to monitor progress. This is discussed at regular meetings between officials at all levels of seniority, as well as at ministerial level through JHA Troika meetings with Ukrainian ministers.

Within the overall framework of more effective border management, there has been a strong focus on visa facilitation and readmission agreements in an attempt to balance different and conflicting needs. On the one hand, visa controls and readmission agreements that allowed for the return of 'irregular' migrants and failed asylum-seekers were regarded as vital in protecting the EU from a politically unstable neighbourhood where law and order and the fight against international crime was problematic and when illegal immigration had become a highly sensitive domestic political issue. On the other hand, with the end of the Cold War, central and eastern European states had pursued a uniquely liberalized and open policy on movement of people; indeed it was regarded a critically important part of improving political relationships between governments given the mosaic of minorities within the region. As Apap et al. have written: 'The open-borders policy has affected thousands of ordinary citizens on both sides of the border, and has significantly contributed to efforts to overcome the historical legacy of mutual prejudice, stereotypes and resentment' (2001: 2). The enlargements of 2004 and 2007 meant that new Schengen restrictions had to be introduced, with the potential for political and economic dislocation and instability. Beginning with the negotiations with Ukraine and Russia, Trauner and Kruse show how the linkage between visas and readmission became a standard part of ENP 'mobility packages' (2008: 14). But they also point out the contradiction in seeking to exercise control while also trying to stabilize the region. But moving towards a clearer policy was seen in the EU as part of a recognition that the ENP needed to improve, with the German Presidency of 2006 taking a lead in trying to persuade the Neighbours of the EU's seriousness. Ideas of an 'ENP Plus' may have won widespread support, but the actual negotiation of agreements on facilitation has been a slow process.

Given the costs and difficulties of pursuing the priorities outlined in the Action Plans, the EU has offered a number of incentives in addition to those of a future, closer integration within the Internal Market. It has offered access to funding beyond that available under TACIS (for eastern European states) and MEDA (for the Mediterranean) through a 'flexible, policy-driven' new European Neighbourhood and Partnership Instrument. A new 'Governance Facility' was introduced in 2007 (described at the time by Emerson et al. as 'disappointingly small, becoming only a token gesture') to support those progressing particularly well in implementing their governance priorities (with funding in 2007, for example, going to Morocco and Ukraine). A Neighbourhood Investment Facility, a joint venture with Member States to leverage additional funding from other sources, was also set up to fund projects of common interest, particularly in energy, environment and transport. Access to programmes such as TAIEX, assistance that had helped the new Member States to transpose the *acquis* into national legislation, was also extended to the ENP partner.

Such assistance was seen as a vital element in capacity-building. Common in many assessments of the implementation of Action Plans was not simply political commitment but also the lack of expertise within government on how to bring about convergence. 'Twinning' was a policy used effectively in the accession process of the CEECs and was therefore continued in the interests of developing capacity within public administration to tackle the enormity of aligning with the *acquis*. Many projects are still at the developing stage (Zakonyi, 2007) but, as Wichmann points out, it is a practice more extensively carried within the ENP framework in the field of customs issues than JHA where the issues are often more politically sensitive (Wichmann 2007: 10)

Nonetheless, even within the wider JHA field there has been a growing range of informal as well as formal efforts at capacity-building. Wichmann, for example, reports on the unofficial network of counter-terrorist agencies and police cooperation (Wichmann 2007: 16–17). Closer cooperation on counter-terrorism has been a high priority for the EU and indeed proved one of the few agreements reached at the Barcelona meeting to celebrate the 10th anniversary of the Barcelona Process (Galli, 2008: 17). EUROPOL and Moldova signed an agreement in 2007 which aimed to enhance cooperation in the fight against drug-trafficking, money-laundering and illegal immigration. It focused particularly on the exchange of strategic and technical information and on the exchange visits of experts and police. FRONTEX, described by Jeandesboz as being 'at the heart of the drive for surveillance of the borders' of the EU or even 'beyond the geographical "external" borders' (2008: 4), has also established working relations with several of the Eastern Partners including Ukraine – with Operation Gordius a joint operation of several EU Member States with Moldova. Jeandesboz also reports that the Commission, in its evaluation report of 2008, was considering developing relations with Belarus despite strained relations over fundamental freedoms and human rights (ibid.: 16).

The combination of these various instruments – particularly conditionality with its continuous interaction through progress reports – and capacity-building and such ventures as twinning, were regarded as having been especially effective in the socialization of accession country elites. That process was regarded as an important component of the ENP (see, for example, Kelley, 2006). However, that again raises one of the key criticisms of the Neighbourhood Policy: the CEEC elites could, eventually, see full membership as the outcome an outcome denied to the Partners. Whereas for the CEECs, converging on the values, standards and practices of the EU was an integral part of manifesting their European 'vocation', for the Neighbours, there is a greater ambivalence over whether convergence is seen as a genuine public good involving shared values or whether it is more a question of strategic bargaining over costs and benefits when the benefits are themselves particularly uncertain.

The ENP as a framework for variable geometry

In seeking a policy that eschewed the prospect of membership but nonetheless sought transformation of the Neighbourhood towards European values and standards, the EU inevitably created division. So much of the conceptual and policy framework, instruments and institutional structure of the ENP reflected not only the processes and procedures that had led to the enlargements of 2004 and 2007 but also the EU's dominant position in the region. As a consequence, for some, the ENP was neither the 'result of a thorough assessment and evaluation with regard to previous policies', nor 'a more or less linear development of the EU's Mediterranean policy'. Rather it was a policy that was the result of 'internal dynamics that are linked to EU enlargement', even though it was meant to be addressing different priorities (Del Sarto and Schumacher, 2005: 25). Bicchi (2006: 287) characterized it as 'an unreflexive attempt to promote its own model *because institutions tend to export institutional isomorphism as a default option*' (italics in original), while Cremona and Hillion have suggested that asymmetries in the relationship began with the ENP's very title:

> The ENP is clearly and unambiguously an *EU policy* directed at its neighbours rather than the creation of something new (a space or an area) or a shared enterprise (a process or partnership). (2006: 11)

They, too, see the Action Plans as 'first and foremost a vehicle for the EU to *project* a corpus of norms and practices considered to be appropriate for political and economic reform' (ibid.).

The extent to which the Neighbours were actually involved in drawing up the Action Plans has inevitably varied both from country to country, issue-area to issue-area. On the basis of her interviews largely on JHA issues, Wichmann, for example, concluded that 'that both sides had a say in defining the priority actions in the Action Plans' (2008: 8), while Del Sarto et al., for all their criticisms, recognized that some governments had been able to defend at least some of their interests, thereby allowing the Commission to argue that this indicated at least some elements of 'co-ownership' and 'partnership'. (2006: 45). Kelley reinforces the point by reporting that some ENP Partner officials were in almost daily contact with Commission counterparts, adding:

> A Moldovan ENP official noted: 'it wasn't an easy negotiation process but we managed to make the functioning of the joint ownership principle declared as one of [the] core principles of the ENP. We can see an improvement in our communication with the Commission starting at the end of 2003 and we hope the further we will advance in the action plan implementation process the better our relationship will become. (Kelley 2006: 39)

Others have concluded, however, that the EU has largely determined the conditions and scope of the 'partnership'; 'Neighbours ... may be consulted, but planning and decision-making, as well the conditions for cooperation, are rarely a shared process' (Tassinari 2005: 5).

It is also clear that a 'more intense political dialogue between the EU and ENP partners does not immediately translate into economic and social realities' (Paczynski, 2009: 26). Such a translation depends on the clarity and coherence of the EU's proposals and the capacity and consent of the Partners to implement them. All the Member States may have shared the vision of 'an arc of well-governed states' to the east and south, involving 'stable and prosperous neighbours [who] will contribute to both our external and internal security' (Council of the European Union, 2003), but there remained differences. On some issues such as the Internal Market, with a strong lead from the Commission, there have been highly specific programmes that once achieved in effect the integration of the Neighbourhood economy into that of the Union. That functional integration is matched by what might be termed more variable 'intensive transgovernmental-ism' (Wallace, 2000) that goes beyond benchmarking in tackling issues relating to data exchange on migration, counter-terrorism and so on within a JHA frame-work – through a trans-nationalism in which the roles of government are highly asymmetrical.

But while the EU might have sought closer political dialogue, the proposals relating to democratization have tended to be vague both in terms of ends and means. Indeed, as others have pointed out, the involvement of autocratic or non-democratic governments in determining Plans promoting democracy and respect for human rights somewhat undermines the seriousness of the EU's commitment (see, for example, Del Sarto et al., 2006: 45). With only deliberately vague programmes, there have also been too few incentives for many in the Neighbourhood to converge on EU norms, particularly in the face of adverse economic and political conditions, even in Morocco and Ukraine which have seen large increases in political aid. Youngs cites a Dutch diplomat admitting that 'the European focus on state-building has put too much emphasis on effectiveness, too little on legitimacy' (Youngs 2008a: 168). Rather more has been left to other internal forces seeking change, not all of whom were recipients of EU assistance, or to other, more global, pressures for reform.

Even if it could also be argued that it is as yet too soon to say quite what the impact of the ENP has been, there has been an air of dissatisfaction about the ENP that has not been confined to those new Member States who have largely supported those in the East looking for a membership perspective. As the German Minister of State in the *Auswaertiges Amt*, Gernot Erler, declared in a speech at Georgetown in February 2007:

> Today the European Neighbourhood Policy is already playing an important role in transforming and modernizing our neighbouring regions and those of Russia. However, the EU can and must become even more assertive and effec-tive than it has so far been in terms of giving our partners a stronger impetus to embrace the process of reform. Not least, this will serve to counter the calls of certain ENP partners for an EU membership perspective with a substantive offer to deepen the partnership. (Erler, 2007)

On membership, the German government's position was clear and found favour in Paris, insofar as the German position on Turkey and the EU's borders appeared firm and not out of line with that of the French. As Angela Merkel had made clear, not all those who seek membership could necessarily be admitted. In May 2006, for example, she had argued in the Bundestag:

> As we cannot take on board all countries seeking membership, we will develop the neighbourhood policy. [...] I am firmly convinced that we cannot do this with trade-association agreements alone. We will have to offer these countries enhanced political cooperation, one which, however, must not necessarily mean full membership. I have mentioned the reasons why Europe must be effective. An entity that does not have borders cannot act coherently and with adequate structures. We must be aware of this and must therefore set out these borders. (Merkel, 2006b)

There were, however, differences with Paris over how the EU might become more assertive. The ENP, even if a part of a Europeanization process, was clearly not regarded as assertive enough of either French or European interests by President Sarkozy – or his predecessor, Jacques Chirac – to win back influence against increasing US interest (Schmid, 2005: 97; Lefebvre, 2004: 6). The incoming French President, Nicolas Sarkozy, had put forward a proposal for a Mediterranean Union in his election campaign, the grounds being, at least according to *Le Figaro*, that the future President believed firmly that 'the future of Europe and France is decided also, and perhaps first of all, in the Mediterranean' (*Le Figaro*, 10 July 2007). Similarly, the Spanish Prime Minister has also been seen as enthusiastic about reviving the Barcelona Process to offset the lack of Spanish foreign policy successes in the region (Barbé and Soler I Lecha, 2005: 91). In their joint statement of 20 December 2007, the French, Italian and Spanish leaders declared themselves 'Convinced that the Mediterranean, crucible of culture and civilisation, should resume its role as a zone of peace, prosperity and tolerance' and that they planned a union for the Mediterranean that 'would have a mission to reunite Europe and Africa around the countries along the Mediterranean rim and to set up a partnership on an equal footing between the countries' north and south of the sea (*France 24*, 2007). It became increasingly clear, however, that the initiative, whatever support it had among the Spanish and Italians, contained little in terms of detail. It was regarded with considerable hostility by other Member States, not least by the Czech Prime Minister, Mirek Topolanek, who questioned what exactly the role of the new Mediterranean setup was to be, suggesting that the French President was working above all to reach national goals (*EUObserver*, 2008)

Key was the response of Chancellor Merkel, not least because Germany then held the Presidency of the EU Council. Merkel was particularly concerned that the proposal would be divisive, declaring in the Bundestag:

> One thing is very important to me, however: there must always be general agreement for any group-specific cooperation. The closer cooperation of a

group of countries must on principle remain open to all; there must be no closed-shop Europe. If we bear this in mind, this working principle will take us forwards ... (Merkel, 2007)

The end result was, in effect, 'Barcelona Plus', an enhancement of the EMP (Emerson, 2008). One unresolved element was quite how membership and the proposed institutional structure, including joint Presidencies, would play out given the problems experienced within the EMP over Israeli participation. None-theless, a first meeting of the Union for the Mediterranean took place in Paris on 13 July 2008, co-chaired by the French and Egyptian Presidents.

Very much in response to the Sarkozy initiative, the Poles, together with the Swedes, submitted proposals for an Eastern Partnership to the EU in May 2008. While developing the Commission's own ideas about differentiation, the propos-als, in effect, challenged the basis of its ENP approach by further emphasizing the distinction between those who were potential European Member States and the countries of the Mediterranean. Given Polish pains to win support before launching the initiative (Cianciara, 2008), agreement was reached at the European Council of June 2008 to ask the Commission to examine possible modalities of more intensive regional cooperation both among the EU's eastern neighbours as well as between the EU and the region 'on the basis of differentiation and an individual approach, respecting the character of the ENP as a single and coherent policy framework' (European Council, 2008). The Russian invasion of Georgia in August 2008 and further gas-supply issues over the winter of 2008–9 only gave added impetus to the search for agreement.

The Prague Summit of May 2009 that brought together the 27 Member States with the six former Soviet states saw as its goal the creation of

> the necessary conditions to accelerate political association and further econom-ic integration between the European Union and interested partner countries [...] With this aim, the Eastern Partnership will seek to support political and socio-economic reforms of the partner countries, facilitating approximation towards the European Union. This serves the shared commitment to stability, security and prosperity ... (Council of the European Union, 2009)

But while there seemed to be a greater emphasis on institution-building, on greater potential socialization through a Parliamentary Assembly and on a civil society forum, there seemed to be little more funding and little given away by the EU in terms of any future membership. It may be too soon to declare the project 'still-born' (Shapovalova, 2009), but, as the Russian ambassador to the EU was reported as saying in relation to both the Union for the Mediterranean and the Eastern Partnership initiatives, 'They have one common problem – they don't have dedicated finances and support. Whatever isn't supported by a line in the budget usually doesn't fly very high' (Chizhov, 2009).

The Eastern Partnership, together with the Union for the Mediterranean, the ENP itself as well as the Black Sea Synergy and the Northern Dimension, not to mention the EEA, suggest that the EU has sought an almost bewildering array of means of meeting the geopolitical challenges of the Neighbourhood and the economic interdependence created by its regional dominance. The search clearly continues in view of the mixed success of the ENP and the disappointing beginning of the Mediterranean Union (the Eastern Partnership is too new to judge). But a number of motives appear to have underpinned EU policy. These include the need to create a stable and secure Neighbourhood; to have effective management of the borders given the political sensitivities surrounding migration, asylum-seeking, terrorism and organized crime; and to see democratic norms and economic liberalism accepted and promoted as core values. Equally important, however, has been the determination of the majority of EU Member States to ensure that membership has not been on the agenda. They have argued that the enlargements of 2004 and 2007 have needed to be consolidated, particularly at a time, if not of growing Euroscepticism, of at least widespread doubts about the nature and further construction of the EU. Tassinari has drawn an interesting conclusion when contrasting the accession negotiations and those on the ENP:

> In sum, when the EU talks membership to its neighbours, it is inclusive: it sets conditions, offers significant incentives and most of all signals the strength of its integration process. When Brussels talks partnership to its neighbours, it is exclusive: it is often ineffective, rather unattractive and unable to exert influence or to preserve security on the continent. (Tassinari, 2005: 5)

For those in the Neighbourhood looking for a European perspective, the ENP has therefore been regarded very much as a consolation prize rather than the positive, constructive policy they had hoped for. And the asymmetries in the relationship have been made starker when the EU has appeared to ignore or prevaricate on issues of particular concern such as visa facilitation or access of agricultural goods. And, for countries where there are internal divisions over any 'return to Europe', as in Ukraine, the lack of certainty – however distant they accept that actual membership might be – provides useful material for those looking towards Russia and its various political and economic initiatives as an alternative pole of attraction and support. That, in turn, reinforces the views of many of the newer Member States where there is, after all, a close identity with those who have also emerged from Soviet domination both in terms of the difficulties of transition to democratic, economically liberal states and in the sense that a resurgent Russia continues to be seen as the primary threat.

The result has been tension over quite how to manage the Neighbourhood; hence the proposals for the Black Sea Synergy, the Union for the Mediterranean and the Eastern Partnership. Member States still see added value in Europeanizing elements of their relationships with the countries of Mediterranean and/or among the Eastern Neighbours, but with very different priorities and perceptions that derive from past relationships and histories. And that lack of unity weakens the impact of the EU not least because the Neighbours have no certainty about the status to which they are aspiring. As a result, positive conditionality becomes a somewhat vague concept – even a dangerous one if it means opening up still-vulnerable markets to the full rigours of EU competition – while negative conditionality seems to have been unworkable, at least as far as Mediterranean states have been concerned. Amirah-Fernández and Youngs concluded:

> As a minimum, it is essential that European countries develop greater unity on this question amongst themselves. Otherwise, political difficulties will continue to arise every time the EU addresses local realities that provoke negative reactions in non-democratic governments and among conservative religious and nationalist sectors in the southern Mediterranean. So far, it has been the case of some Arab governments conditioning the EU more than vice versa, in what could be termed a 'reverse conditionality'. (Amirah Fernández and Youngs, 2006: 160)

And even for those who aspire to membership, uncertainties conspire with vested interests or the distractions of alternatives to make the process of Europeanization particularly patchy. There is, as Zielonka has pointed out, already enough diversity within the Union, exacerbated by the 2004 and 2007 enlargements with different types of political units, institutional arrangements and loyalties, multiple identities, economic heterogeneity and fuzzy borders – making it less a fortress Europe than 'a maze Europe' (Zielonka, 2006: 4)

But within that maze and mismatch of legal, economic and social borders that possibly make up a neo-medieval Empire, there remains so far a relatively fixed idea: whatever the pull of differing geopolitical interests, and the variety of trans-border arrangements, the political borders remain to be managed by the Union and not breached by individual states or groups. Chancellor Merkel was effective in insisting that the Union for the Mediterranean should be open to all Member States; there could not be discrete groups of states entering into exclusionary arrangements. But it was not only that the Member States should determine any enhanced cooperation together; for Chancellor Merkel and others, borders remain important to lend coherence and identity to Europe.

Note

1. The European Commission's own website has some 16 pages of books, articles and papers on the subject. See http://ec.europa.eu/world/enp/pdf/background_material.pdf (accessed 12 August 2009).

Part III Functional Manifestations of Differentiated Integration

15

'Euro' Europe: 'Fuzzy' Boundaries and 'Constrained' Differentiation in Macro-Economic Governance

Kenneth Dyson

European macro-economic governance comprises hybrid patterns of unitary and differentiated integration. This mixed character reflects its combination of sector-specific distinctiveness with internally variegated functional attributes. In consequence, it escapes easy categorization in terms of public goods theory, exhibits varying territorial forms, and changes dynamically over time. The sector-specific distinctiveness of European macro-economic governance is shaped by the nature of its expert elites, above all its central bankers, and by the post-Bretton Woods structural context of international capital liberalization, floating exchange rates, and global and volatile financial markets. Supported by the powerful theoretical backbone of monetary economics, with its primacy given to price stability and central bank independence, this context plays a constitutive role in the discursive commitment of the expert elites to 'globalization' and to policy 'credibility'. They tend to nest European macro-economic governance within this larger commitment. 'Globalization-centredness' and primacy to the single European market as the core project deeply condition attitudes to differentiated integration and to crisis management.

The internal variegation in European macro-economic governance reflects different factors: the varying EU and domestic constraints within which its expert elites operate (contrast, for instance, fiscal and monetary policies); the different historical paths of evolution of 'economic union' and 'monetary union', with broad-based EU market integration preceding monetary union; and, tying both these factors together, the greater willingness of some states to delegate sovereignty in monetary policy rather than in fiscal policy or in other aspects of economic union. Hence European macro-economic governance lacks full 'parallelism' of development in economic and in monetary union (EMU). The principle of parallelism had been originally envisaged in the Werner Report of 1970, and even – in a more attenuated form – by Jacques Delors when he chaired the Committee on Economic and Monetary Union in 1988–9 (Dyson and Featherstone, 1999).

The unitary principle triumphed in economic union, which involved relatively minor institutional adaptation in single market, competition and fiscal policies and in economic reforms through the post-2000 Lisbon process. Here the EU sought above all to capture mutual trade gains through continent-wide economic scale. Conversely, differentiated integration evolved in monetary union, where major supra-national institutional changes occurred. Here the gains of price stability could be captured not just inside the Euro Area but also outside – through domestic inflation targeting in the hands of an independent national central bank. A key difference was the insistence of the German Bundesbank on the principle of the 'indivisibility' of monetary policy in the Delors Report of 1989: monetary policy competence could not be shared between national central banks and a new European central bank without endangering stability (Dyson and Featherstone, 1999). This principle challenged the notion of national sovereignty more directly than proposals in economic union, with the exception of 'binding' rules for national fiscal policies. In the final stage, it meant the creation of a new, powerful supra-national institution, the European Central Bank (ECB) rather than more limited central bank coordination in a European Monetary Fund.

This difference in scale of challenge to national sovereignty from proposals to 'deepen' economic and monetary union led to internal variegation. European macro-economic governance incorporates several different components. Monetary union consists of an inner 'core' with a 'hard' boundary: surrounded by concentric circles in the various ways in which EU and non-EU central banks relate to the European System of Central Banks (ESCB). This complex differentiation in monetary governance contrasts with the dominance of the unitary principle in economic union: above all, in macro-economic policy coordination (the Broad Economic Policy Guidelines, BEPGs), the Lisbon agenda of economic reform, and the European single market. Financial market infrastructure and fiscal policy coordination represent a third, 'grey' hybrid area in which the unitary principle coexists with differentiated integration. Though they relate closely to monetary union, and thus engage the ECB, this area is also bound up respectively with the notion of a 'level playing field' in the European internal market and with macro-economic policy coordination and economic reform. To complicate European macro-economic governance further, the financial stability function and the evolving idea of macro-prudential supervision escape the spatial confines of Europe to the global level of the International Monetary Fund (IMF), G20 and G7/8, and the Bank for International Settlements (BIS). The result is the 'fuzzy' boundaries of European macro-economic governance.

Four factors contribute to these 'fuzzy' boundaries. First, contrasting EU Treaty- and law-based provisions mark out monetary union as special and, through the Maastricht convergence criteria for euro entry, provide it with tough entry and 'boundary-drawing' rules (Dyson and Quaglia, 2010). Second, the contrasting functional properties of its component issue areas are apparent in differences in mutual gains from integration and in scope for 'free riding'. Third, and very much related to this second factor, there are differences in the beliefs of political and expert elites about the appropriate spatial and temporal organization of macro-economic governance. Finally, the differences of interest between 'large' and 'small' states, and between 'success' and 'problem' states in economic performance, cut in complex ways across the simple division into euro 'insiders' and 'outsiders' (Dyson and Marcussen, 2010). There are 'success' euro outsiders, like Denmark and Sweden, and 'problem' euro insiders, like Greece and Portugal. The result is strong incentives to incorporate 'success' euro outsiders in European macro-economic integration, not least in the Lisbon process.

Hence, seen 'from within', European macro-economic governance has not evolved in a linear way, according to a single rule. It comprises a bundling of different activities: some involve varying rights and obligations of EU Member States, notably related to the single currency and monetary policy; whilst others – especially linked to the single European market – impose equal rights and obligations. Integration curves in different forms according to function, space and time.

The limited, non-linear evolution of differentiated integration

The centripetal effects of the Euro Area stem from the insurance gains of insulation from foreign-exchange market volatility and crisis (its 'shelter' function), access to large euro financial markets (its liquidity function), and the trade and investment gains from the removal of currency risk and reduced transaction costs (its 'trade gain' function). However, this 'pull' has not translated into either a uniform attraction for EU Member States or an incentive to build a narrower 'core Europe' club around 'economic government' by the Euro Group of 15 Euro Area finance ministers and by the Euro Area heads of state and government. The incentives for euro entry are stronger for small, open economies with weakly developed financial markets. In addition, the incentive to build a narrower 'core' Europe around the Euro Area has been trumped by the incentive to capture for all 27 EU Member States the collective benefits of the single market, of efficient and stable financial markets, of fiscal discipline and of the Lisbon economic reform strategy. Moreover, the perceived costs of exclusion from the single currency – negative externalities – have been reduced. Euro insiders and outsiders can access euro payment and settlement systems on equal terms, whilst – through presence in a Euro Area state – a bank that has its headquarters in an 'outsider' state can access the Eurosystem's relatively generous liquidity provision. Above all, through participating in the EU single market, states can capture many of the trade gains from the single currency without euro membership (Baldwin, 2006a, 2006b). In effect, there is a leakage of benefits from the Euro Area on which outsiders can free ride.

Remaining outside the Euro Area can be perceived as a net gain. Outsiders retain the flexibility – even if restricted – to use domestic interest-rate policy and the nominal exchange rate to speed and ease adjustment to asymmetric shocks (as Poland did in response to the 2008–9 crisis). Denmark's monetary policy is tightly tied to the ECB through a tight fluctuation band in the Exchange Rate Mechanism II (ERM II). However, by remaining a euro outsider, it retains the potential to free ride by an ERM exit in an emergency. In contrast, domestic adjustment processes to economic imbalances in the Euro Area prove long-term and protracted and take the form of politically painful cuts in wages and non-wage costs (as in Ireland in 2008–9). The result is a disincentive to euro entry for politicians, whose time horizons are defined by short-term electoral cycles and who are inclined to favour sharp, temporary shocks. Also, relatively weak economic growth performance of the Euro Area in the period 2001–5, and then the sharp economic contraction in 2008–9, reinforced the incentive to remain outside. This incentive was greater for new EU Member States in east-central Europe, for which the top priority was a 'catch-up' to average EU living standards through high economic growth.

The result is a paradox. The variable, but often weak, gravitational pull of the Euro Area cemented differentiation in monetary policies as more than just a short-term, transitional phenomenon. It also reduced the power of 'advanced' differentiated integration in monetary policy to shape the evolution of other functions of European macro-economic governance. Of course, this weak gravitational pull may prove temporary, should the relative economic performance of the Euro Area improve in a sustained manner and crises prove contagious amongst outsiders.

Hence, despite the single currency, the evolution of differentiation has remained limited and non-linear. This limitation reflects in part the concentration of legal authority in ECOFIN (the Council of Economic and Finance Ministers) rather than in the smaller Euro Group (of the ministers of the Member States whose currency is the euro). Despite its diminished efficacy as a deliberative body since the 2004 EU enlargement, ECOFIN jealously guarded its prerogatives. Consequently, the Lisbon Treaty in Articles 136–7 and Protocol 10 achieved only a modest strengthening of the Euro Group's role in 'enhanced dialogue'. Though confirming the informal nature of its meetings, the Euro Group was now enabled to adopt its own measures relating to fiscal policy coordination and to the economic policy guidelines.

In part, the limited and non-linear evolution of differentiated integration also reveals the fears of significant domestic political and expert elites about net negative economic and political costs for those taking part and net gains for those excluded. Examples include the reluctance to use new Treaty provision for 'enhanced cooperation' in such areas as corporate tax harmonization and employment policy. This unwillingness was pronounced amongst certain small states in the Euro Area, notably Ireland, which found more common ground with small states outside the Euro Area. As we see below, the 'size nexus' cuts across formal insider/outsider differentiation.

The rationale for treating the non-monetary functions of European macro-economic governance as Euro Area 'club goods' or 'private goods' proved weak in the context of the *acquis communautaire,* above all the EU internal market and competition policies. Even in monetary policy the 'public good' of price stability could be secured by means other than Euro Area entry (the main alternative being domestic central bank independence, inflation targeting and exchange-rate flexibility). Moreover, the benefits of extending efficient and stable financial markets to all the EU-27, and beyond to the European Economic Area (EEA), were overwhelming. A similar logic applied to the excessive deficit procedure in fiscal policies, the Lisbon process of structural reforms, and macro-economic coordination through the 'Integrated Guidelines'. Though the Lisbon Treaty opens up new legal provisions for more differentiated integration, the incentives for the Euro Group to use them are limited.

The hybrid nature of European macro-economic governance

European macro-economic governance has a curious hybrid character. At the macro-level, it represents a distinctive 'individualized' space–time nexus. The entrenched discourses of globalization and of sustainable growth and credible fiscal policies are 'domain-specific' in their characteristic conceptions of space (a strong extra-European focus) and time (linear) and of how they are best organized and used. On the micro-level, European macro-economic governance comprises a cluster of interrelated but differing individualized spaces and times. For instance, there is more contestation between cyclical and linear conceptions of time in fiscal than in monetary policy (Dyson, 2009a). This hybrid nature reflects the frame of reference.

Seen within the broad frame of reference of EU policies, European macro-economic governance appears to display some clear, simple patterns of its own. 'Space–time compression' takes on an unusually intensive, 'globalized' form (cf. Harvey, 1990). European macro-economic governance exhibits a highly developed spatial discourse of 'globalization' that also has a strong temporal dimension of a 'new age' to which economies must adapt. Its central angle of view is the global scale of financial markets, money and trade (with associated random cross-national 'contagion' risks). The focus is global-scale, GDP-based measures of economic performance and sovereign risk that yield comparative international 'league tables' and competitiveness indexes, from which the scale of challenges can be deduced. The discourse focuses variously on facing up to the European and state-level 'logic', or on insuring against the costs, of this global challenge.

Similarly, the temporal discourse of European macro-economic governance has a pronounced bias to long time horizons and firm time rules and to the strategic use of time as deadline to discipline Member States (cf. Schedler and Santiso, 1998; Schmitter and Santiso, 1998; Dyson, 2009a). This bias is grounded in part in a wider EU 'timescape' that seeks to escape the constraints of domestic electoral calendars (Goetz, 2007a). It also reflects practical, 'domain-specific' experience of the extreme randomness of the global, interconnected scale of the issues with which European macro-economic governance deals and the lessons derived from past financial crises (cf. Taleb, 2007: 31–5). In other words, spatial and temporal discourses are complementary. Both reflect the extreme vulnerability of the core issue areas of European macro-economic governance to international contagion from small, 'distant' events and the associated historical fractures that have shaped this policy domain. The sense of vulnerability was reinforced by the origins of the 2008–9 financial and economic crisis in the US sub-prime mortgage market.

Looked at 'from within', however, European macro-economic governance displays much greater internal differentiation in terms of how these broad spatial and temporal biases express themselves. This complexity derives from the mixed properties of its constituent issues areas: monetary policy, financial market infrastructure, fiscal policies, structural reform policies and macro-economic coordination. Outside monetary and associated financial market infrastructure policies, the political calculus of gain/loss is more complex and daunting both in 'deepening' integration in general and in pursuing differentiated integration. The political hesitations derive from the direct, specific and short-term costs of fiscal policy changes and economic reforms for politically significant party and electoral interests and the associated destabilizing risks of populist political mobilization. Political calculus in these issue areas has also to take into account variations over space and time in distributions of political, economic and social preferences within and across Member States. There are different preferences in work–life balance and in efficiency–equity trade-offs and in the intensity with which they are held. In addition, political calculus has to accommodate unsynchronized domestic electoral calendars across EU Member States (Dyson, 2009a). Electoral time rules offer short-term opportunities to express spatial variations in preferences that are difficult to reconcile and, in consequence, have the potential to affect the political rhythms of EU-level commitment and compliance in fiscal policies and structural reforms. Hence variations within European macro-economic governance reflect the different properties of issue-areas and different institutional opportunities and constraints for political elites to become engaged and to set parameters on expert problem-solving. Weakly shared incentives to 'deepen' integration translate into limited scope for differentiated integration.

This duality in the nature of European macro-economic governance, reflecting differences in the frame of reference, means that it is paradoxically both linear and asymmetrical, 'curving' in different shapes in space and time. As one shifts the frame, European macro-economic governance looks different. What we see, and how we go about explaining it, changes with the broadening or shrinking of the frame of reference.

The global and historical context of European macro-economic governance: 'constrained' differentiation

The 'domain-specificity' of European macro-economic governance has its origins in three related, global-scale structural transformations that can be traced back to the demise of the Bretton Woods system in 1971–3. They represent compound historical 'fractures', ushering in a highly contingent and unstable world of international capital mobility, exchange-rate volatility, financial market innovation, opacity and turbulence, and step-change in the incidence of banking crises. The characteristic spatial and temporal discourses of European macro-economic governance represent attempts to impose some order on this fragile world and to insure against its high randomness. They highlight the new post-1973 centrality of monetary policy and central bankers. These discourses also constrain differentiated integration.

First, the collapse of US leadership of the Bretton Woods system of managed exchange rates in 1973 through the dollar standard created a vacuum of 'hegemonic' monetary power in the international economic system. It also opened up new systemic opportunities to pursue EMU by giving centrality to European monetary integration as a 'new Bretton Woods for Europe' (Dyson, 2009b). Secondly, the post-Bretton Woods era of floating exchange rates and capital liberalization acted a catalyst for an unprecedented growth in the scale, volume, complexity and opacity of financial markets (Moran, 1991). This transformation made first

European steps in monetary integration highly vulnerable to destabilizing financial market crises, notably in 1982–3, 1987 and 1992–3 (Dyson, 1994). In the process the ERM evolved as differentiated integration. It had its core (those pursuing a 'hard-ERM' policy), a periphery with a broad fluctuation band, and others remaining outside. EU Member States sought protection by migrating either to full monetary union (11 Member States in 1999) or to floating and 'managed' floats (like Britain after 1992). Financial 'exuberance' and interconnected markets also increased vulnerability to contagious financial market instability and banking failure, exemplified in the US-centred equity crisis of 1987 and the US-centred credit and solvency crisis of 2007–8, above all after the Lehman Brothers collapse (cf. Kindleberger, 2005).

Thirdly, the socio-cultural context of European macro-economic governance was shaped by intense 'space–time compression'. It was facilitated by screen-based communication technologies like the internet, email and videoconferencing, as well as by easier travel (cf. Harvey, 1990). The density of interactions amongst officials increased at both EU and global levels, along with their sense of being a professional 'club' dedicated to economic and financial stability. Correspondingly, their assessment of the relevance of the domestic level to macro-economic governance diminished (Dyson and Quaglia, 2008).

This socio-cultural change reinforced the autonomy and sense of professional vocation and shared identity of the core EU-level bodies (besides the European Central Bank): the Economic and Financial Committee (EFC) and the Economic Policy Committee (EPC), which prepare the work of ECOFIN and the Euro Group. They provide the institutional node through which the business of European macro-economic governance flows: financial market regulation and supervision, fiscal policies, structural policies and economic policy coordination. This attitudinal change, reflecting 'space–time compression', reinforced expert incentives to value unitary over differentiated integration.

These three global-scale structural transformations underpinned the 'club-like' but internationally open character of the expert elites in central banking and finance ministries. It exemplified the slow, variable-speed convergence of their consensus-seeking behaviour around long-term 'stability-oriented' policies and the global 'competitiveness' agenda. It also reinforced their aversion to the risks of 'managed' exchange-rate regimes (like the ERM) in favour of either full European monetary union or (managed) floats. Free trade, exchange-rate regimes and autonomous monetary policies were seen as incompatible (the so-called 'trilemma'). Despite this incentive to migrate in one of two directions, and consequent differentiation in monetary policy, the context was a system of European macro-economic governance united around a high degree of paradigm consensus and reflected in a shared spatial and temporal discourse.

Correspondingly, other than for those with Treaty 'opt-outs', like Britain and Denmark on monetary union, the broad expectation was that differentiation would be no more than short-term and transitional. It would follow the pattern of derogations in single market measures. The net trade gains from the EU scale, as opposed to the Euro Area scale, acted as a further powerful disincentive to pursue ideas of differentiated integration in single market measures. In any case, other than temporary derogations, EU law did not provide opportunities for these ideas.

The Euro Area did not act as a catalyst for a 'core' Europe with its single monetary policy flanked by its own fiscal, business taxation, trade, labour mobility and financial market liberalization policies. Insiders faced the risk that the net gains from a single currency could be offset, even reversed, by the losses to participants from narrowing market scale and from enabling 'outsiders' to free ride. The calculus of potential net costs acted as a deterrent to differentiated integration in social and employment policies and in business tax harmonization. Any gains from preventing social and economic 'dumping' through harmonization would be threatened as the non-participants gained competitive cost advantages in a single market.

Financial stability highlights further the constraints on differentiated integration. Banking and financial market supervision remains firmly a national-level responsibility and exhibits cross-European institutional divergence, reflecting the persisting domestic differences in financial structures. On the other hand, financial stability is seen as primarily a global-level function, focused on the BIS, the IMF and the Financial Stability Forum. Thus the EU 'downloaded' the global standards of the BIS 'Basle II' rules on banking supervision. Only with the 2008–9 crisis did the EU begin to reflect seriously on an institutional template for banking and financial market supervision with the de Larosière report (2009). However, its proposals raised difficult issues about the relationship of the new EU-wide European Systemic Risk Council (ESRC) to the ECB and about the capacity of the three upgraded EU-wide regulatory agencies, including for banking, to commit national governments to fiscal bale-outs of insolvent banks. The preference remained for EU-wide 'soft' institutional mechanisms for coordination, symbolized in the idea of Colleges of Supervisors for cross-national banks, and for BIS, G7/8 and increasingly G20 action. Similarly, the G7 and the IMF were the central forums for coordinating financial market interventions by the ECB, the Bank of England, the Swiss National Bank and the US Federal Reserve in seeking to manage the credit crisis of 2007–8. This crisis highlighted differentiation in the form of the international coordination role assumed by the EU members of the G7 (Britain, France, Germany and Italy) and of the G20.

Though, in contrast to financial stability, monetary policy remains a national/ Euro Area responsibility, it too operates in a global context of consensus about the primacy of price stability. Price stability is understood as safeguarded by the medium-term orientation of monetary strategy (understood in the ECB as 18–24 months), by institutionalizing central bank independence, and by a framework of time rules that avoid short-term activism in interest-rate policy. The objective is locking in long-term market expectations of inflation so that they are consistent with the official definition of price stability. Though, as we shall see, there is no firm European consensus about how this shared monetary policy objective is best achieved, monetary policy rests on a powerful international foundation of shared theory. Its principal components are that: money is 'neutral' with respect to long-term growth and employment; inflation is a phenomenon of expectations so that credibility of commitments is the central policy requirement; there is a 'time-inconsistency' problem, which results from the expectation that politicians will renege on commitments to price stability when facing elections; and the solution lies in central bank independence and some clear medium-term policy rule (see generally, Dyson, 1994, 2000; more specifically, Alesina, 1987; Giavazzi and Pagano, 1988; Kydland and Prescott, 1977; Lucas, 1976; Rogoff, 1987).

Overall, the distinctive character of European macro-economic governance derives from a set of shared global-level structural transformations and the consequent intellectual privileging of monetary economics, central banking and trade theory. Their elaborate spatial and temporal discourses have focused on the global and EU levels and on long time horizons and clear time rules. The consequent disincentive to differentiated integration has been reinforced by the concentration of legal authority over non-monetary issues in ECOFIN and in the EFC and EPC as institutional nodes of coordination. The EFC and EPC have retained a strong professional identity as a 'club'.

However, as we see below, differing functional characteristics of issue-areas open up potentially enduring processes of differentiated integration. This inability to confine differentiated integration to a short-term phenomenon derives from the relatively low net cost and even potential net benefit of exclusion from the Euro Area and the single currency for at least some states. In consequence of the weak and varying centripetal effects of the Euro Area's monetary policy, short-term differentiation is likely to produce a paradox: both an increase in the number of participating states – from 11 in 1999 to 16 in 2009 – and a semi-permanent differentiation. Strikingly, the increase in numbers relates to small states with limited financial markets (Cyprus, Greece, Malta, Slovenia and Slovakia).

Functional properties, institutional constraints and the power of central bankers

Seen 'from within', European macro-economic governance exhibits a more complex variety of conceptualizations and practices of space and time. This variety has its roots in contrasting constraints and incentives to pursue differentiated integration. These constraints and incentives derive from differences in the functional characteristics of individual policy areas, in institutional opportunities and constraints, and in the autonomy of supra-national central bankers. The autonomy of the ECB matters for differentiated integration in European macro-economic governance because it acts as the inner guardian of tough conditionality in euro entry. Also, across a range of policy areas related to monetary policy, it is the leading advocate of the integrity of its own monetary policy and of the primacy of long time horizons, clear and firm time rules, and the use of strict timetables to coordinate expectations, discipline action and speed action. This advocacy has led the ECB to argue for a strengthening of the Euro Group in fiscal, structural reform and macro-economic coordination policies and of the European Commission in the excessive deficit procedure and in the Lisbon process. It also means that the ECB places great emphasis on the Eurosystem's role in the euro financial market infrastructure.

However, the scope for this advocacy role of the ECB to strengthen differentiated integration is conditioned by functional specificities and institutional opportunities and constraints. Thus the ECB has less scope in banking regulation and supervision and in building financial market infrastructure elements such as euro payment and settlement systems than in monetary policy. Its advocacy capacity – and that of the European Commission – is even lower in fiscal policy coordination and the Lisbon process. The result is the various individualized space–time configurations examined below.

Monetary governance: hard boundaries of union

Monetary policy is the prime formal institutional expression of differentiated integration in European macro-economic governance. It represents a 'Europe of concentric circles' in central banking, with hard boundaries around the 'inner core' of Eurosystem members (that is, the ECB and the national central banks of the Member States whose currency is the euro). Exclusive competence in Euro Area monetary policy-making is bestowed on the ECB, specifically its Governing Council, which comprises the six executive board members and the national central bank governors (16 in 2009).

Formally, all EU central banks form part of the European System of Central Banks (ESCB). As such, they share a commitment to a number of Treaty articles, including central bank independence and the non-monetary financing of budget deficits. They meet in the ECB General Council, which considers central banking issues of EU-wide interest, like financial stability and euro payment and settlement issues.

Within this very broad framework, different circles of ESCB members can be identified. A close 'outer circle' comprises those EU states that are ERM II members and in the 'waiting room' for euro entry. Their currencies are pegged to the euro and must abide by the Maastricht convergence criteria of no 'severe' tensions and no devaluation within two years within the 'normal' fluctuation band. The ERM II group can in turn be differentiated into those willing but unable to enter, like the Baltic States, and those, like Denmark, which are able but not willing. Beyond, there is another circle of those willing but not yet able to join ERM II, let alone the euro, such as the Czech Republic, Hungary and Poland.

The outer layers include the states that are candidates for EU accession and thus entry into the ESCB and hence intensely focused on compliance with the standards for ESCB membership. They include Croatia and Turkey. Another layer is states that are not EU-entry candidates but that have monetary and exchange-rate agreements with the Euro Area, like Monaco, San Marino and the Vatican (which have the euro as their official currency) or French territories which either use the euro or peg their currencies to it. The cases of Kosovo and Montenegro represent different cases of unilateral official 'euroisation' (of which the ECB and the European Commission officially disapprove of as inconsistent with the Treaty).

This formal distinction between circles of European monetary governance is complemented by the living reality of certain states that have become *de facto* 'semi-permanent' euro outsiders. In the case of Britain and Denmark this status is buttressed by formal Treaty 'opt-outs'. However, Sweden too is a 'semi-permanent' outsider even though formally it has a derogation. Formally, all other EU states have a derogation. However, it is conceivable that some of them may, like Sweden, become *de facto* 'semi-permanent' outsiders: whether participating in ERM II, like Denmark, or opting for domestic inflation-targeting monetary regimes and managed floats with independent central banks. This situation is likely where their policy-makers see the Maastricht convergence criteria as inappropriate for their domestic needs, especially 'real' convergence of living standards in east-central Europe.

In policing the inner hard boundaries of monetary union, the ECB acts as guardian of the 'tough' conditionality requirements for euro entry contained in the Maastricht convergence criteria. These criteria form the basis for autonomous ECB and European Commission (and with the Lisbon Treaty also Euro Group) recommendations on whether individual EU states qualify for euro entry. In 2006, for instance, Lithuania was deemed not to qualify.

A more difficult question involves internal differentiation within the Eurosystem and the power of the four main states in the Euro Area – France, Germany, Italy and Spain – inside the Eurosystem. Do they have the potential to form a *directoire?* There is clear evidence of internal differentiation as national central banks (NCBs) look for niche roles and jobs (see Dyson, 2009c). However, the claim of a *directoire* is more difficult to sustain. Since 1999, other than the short period before Jean-Claude Trichet took up post as President of the ECB, the 'big four' had eight out of (in 2009) 22 seats in the Governing Board, consequent on continuing to provide four of the six Executive Board members. Hence, in terms of national origin, they dominated the Executive Board and had a substantial one-third presence in the Governing Council. Conversely, there is no substantial evidence that, once in post, national origin matters. Monetary policy debate focuses on Euro Area data and analysis.

A second source of evidence comes from the so-called 'rotation' model for reform of voting rules in the Governing Council to adapt to Euro Area enlargement (the new rules are still to be put into practice). This model differentiates a group of 'large' states, measured by GDP and financial assets (for details see Dyson, 2008). The voting rights of their central bank governors rotate less frequently than those of smaller states. However, unlike in the US Federal Reserve, none of them is given a permanent voting right.

More practical evidence of internal differentiation stems from the emerging division of labour amongst national central banks in the Eurosystem. The common IT platform for the TARGET2 euro clearing and payment system was developed and is managed by the French, German and Italian central banks; while TARGET2-Securities (T2S) for settlement of securities transactions is being developed for operation by the French, German, Italian and Spanish central banks. Once again, however, the evidence is mixed. Other smaller NCBs are also developing niche, leading roles: for instance, the new Collateral Central Bank Management (CCCBM2) is being developed by the Belgian and Dutch central banks to increase the efficiency of the collateral management of Eurosystem central banks.

This analysis of the 'circles' of European monetary governance suggests three conclusions. First, claims about a *directoire* within the Eurosystem are difficult to sustain. Secondly, the net benefits for some EU states in non-participation in the euro imply that differentiation in monetary policy could prove long-term rather than transitional. This conclusion is qualified, as cost–benefit calculations can alter over time. More serious in this respect are the cases of Britain and Sweden, which carry painful negative memories of past failed ERM policies. Their ERM failures constituted domestic historical fractures in EU membership that cemented differentiated integration in monetary policy and acted as warnings to later ERM II aspirants. European monetary governance bears these marks of historical fractures and anticipated fears of future fractures.

Thirdly, as we see below, differentiation in monetary policy is not the 'inner circle' to which other functions – fiscal policies, structural reform policies, and macro-economic coordination – are gravitating, even for Euro Area members. In delivering the public good of price stability the ECB can make strong claims to institutional independence and speaking for the Euro Area. However, outside this narrow function, the ECB is reduced to playing a role as catalyst and coordinator (as in retail payment systems) or to exhortation (as in fiscal and structural reform policies). Because European macro-economic governance remains a domain of 'fuzzy' boundaries outside monetary policy, the Euro Group has not developed into an 'economic government'. Equally, the EU exhibits a lack of unified representation and voice in forums like the IMF, G7/8 and G20. 'Fuzziness' extends to international representation, with authority spread across the Commission, ECOFIN chair, Euro Group president, and president of the ECB.

Financial market infrastructure: 'fuzzy' boundaries

The development of a European financial market infrastructure of euro payment and settlement systems illustrates the 'fuzzy' boundary problem in European macro-economic governance. This boundary problem stems from the significance of the speed, cost and security of this infrastructure for the 'logics' of both the European single market programme and the Euro Area monetary policy. In other words, it spans the EU-27/EEA and the Euro-16. The ECB's capacity to shape integration in this policy area increased, the closer projects were to the integrity and efficacy of its monetary policy responsibility.

The Commission and the ECB exhibited differences in attitudes. The ECB preferred to accelerate the pace of change by prioritizing the Euro Area states over the rest of the EU and the EEA. It also sought to give a lead role to the biggest Eurosystem central banks (the French, German and Italian), in part because of their importance in euro settlement transactions and in part because of their greater experience and resources.

The 'fuzzy' boundaries of differentiated integration were apparent in TARGET (1999–) and TARGET2 (post-2007). These first- and second-generation systems were designed to enable banks to make electronic (primarily large-value) interbank and customer payments in euros, using central bank money and thereby eliminating credit risk and lowering systemic risk. On the one hand, TARGET was made available to banks within the EEA (31 states). This wide spatial scale reflected not least the significance of the British settlement system and British interests in protecting the position of the City of London. In 2007 TARGET was in use in 17 EU states, including Britain, Denmark, Estonia and Poland outside the Euro Area. On the other hand, the Eurosystem was the architect and overseer of TARGET, enforcing a set of core principles to ensure efficiency, safety and above all protection against systemic risk.

TARGET2 was a more centralized shared IT platform, seen as essential to the improved efficiency of the ECB monetary transmission mechanism. It was developed and managed by the French, German and Italian central banks. Again, with their leading role, it was phased in as a Single Shared Platform (SSP) between November 2007 and May 2008, with current TARGET countries including Euro Area members migrating in three 'country groups', plus Latvia and Lithuania. The remaining six EU states were expected to remain outside until euro entry. Notably, the Bank of England was not part of the migration to TARGET2.

TARGET2-Securities (T2S) and the Single Euro Payments Area (SEPA) were more problematic projects because they involved the difficult challenge of mobilizing the banking sector and corporate service-providers and users. T2S was seen as an attempt at role expansion by the Eurosystem and as such ran into controversy. The problem of getting market commitment to a timetable for the T2S proposal was that the ECB was not just acting as a catalyst in mobilizing market changes to promote financial integration and efficiency but also expanding its own tasks.

SEPA functioned much more on the 'fuzzy' boundaries of differentiated integration. This complex, ambitious project aimed to create a fully integrated market for cashless retail payment services in the Euro Area. It encompassed credit transfers, direct debits and credit cards with the aim of ensuring that euro payments were conducted on the same terms across borders as at the domestic level. The ECB was a catalyst at its launch in 2002 and a continuing champion, alongside the European Commission, in order to reap the full benefits of the new single currency. At the same time, SEPA had potentially major implications for the competitive position of EU banks in the single European financial market. Hence it fell within the remit of the single market principle of a 'level playing field'. In consequence, common SEPA instruments, standards and infrastructures for retail payments in euro were developed in the European Payments Council, which brings together banks and banking associations across the 31 states of the EEA. The ECB sought to 'assist' this process on a pan-European scale through ideas and organizational help and to set it in the context of the European Commission's programme for a single EU financial market and of the EU-scale Lisbon process. At the same time it saw SEPA as above all a project of importance for the Euro Area. In addition to acting as 'catalyst' for private-sector activities and as 'coordinator', the ECB defined 'high-level' requirements for safeguarding financial stability and ensuring smooth operation of payment systems.

The Stability and Growth Pact: the hybrid character of European macro-economic governance

Fiscal policy coordination through the Stability and Growth Pact (SGP) illustrates the hybrid character of European macro-economic governance. On the one hand, the SGP reflects a wider global-level and Europe-wide shift from Keynesian belief in discretionary fiscal fine-tuning, allocating primacy to annual budgets, to long-term fiscal rules and public expenditure reviews. Consequent credibility gains from commitment to fiscal policy rules are reflected in lower debt-servicing costs. This shift reflects the new belief in the centrality of the longer-term horizons of monetary policy rather than annual budgets in macro-economic governance. Hence EU states, whether Euro Area members or not, and including Britain, had a shared interest in embracing a set of fiscal rules and in demonstrating their compliance. There was an underlying collective incentive to comply, though it functioned differently. Euro Area states had the collective incentive to demonstrate their support for the single currency and to avoid loss of reputation and financial sanctions. In contrast, euro outsiders remained directly exposed to the penalties of financial market sanctions and immune from SGP sanctions (though not from withdrawal of Structural Funds).

On the other hand, EU-level fiscal policy coordination remained much more connected than Euro Area monetary policy to domestic electoral calendars and to annual national economic policy cycles through the central role of ECOFIN in the excessive deficit procedure. Hence time horizons for complying with commitments to fiscal consolidation under SGP rules were conditional, whilst annual budgets were often poorly synchronized with SGP review processes for domestic stability programmes.

The negotiation of the SGP in 1995–7 under German intellectual and political leadership was closely linked to differentiated integration. Chancellor Helmut Kohl linked the German 'Stability Pact' proposal politically to the creation of a 'larger' Euro Area that would incorporate all of the Six founder members, especially Belgium and Italy (whose debt levels far exceeded the Maastricht convergence criteria). It would reassure a deeply sceptical German public opinion that anything more than a small Euro Area could deliver a 'stability culture'. Secondly, the SGP retained the central purpose of 'flanking' and supporting the ECB monetary policy mandate. The 'corrective' arm of the SGP focused on the deficit rule of 3 per cent GDP, commencing with 'early warnings' and – only in the case of Euro Area members – leading ultimately to financial sanctions (though the accession states of 2004 and 2007 can be deprived of Structural Funds). EU Member States were committed to two different annual reporting processes: euro outsiders produce 'convergence' programmes, whilst euro insiders produce 'stability' programmes (Heipertz and Verdun, 2005).

Of note in this context of monetary union, the SGP crisis of November 2003 was generated amongst Euro Area Member States when the French, German and Italian governments rejected the economic and political costs of compliance as too high in a context of continuing economic stagnation. The subsequent review of procedures and rules fell short of being radical for four reasons: an enduring consensus amongst all EU states about the need for time rules to give credibility to the euro; a blocking coalition of small Euro Area states against radical reforms; the Treaty basis of the excessive deficit procedure; and the enduring support in German public opinion for its core values.

The ECB is not a signatory to the SGP and hence had no formal role in the 2005 reform. Its proposals focused on strengthening the 'preventive' arm in economic 'good times'; on retaining the current rules for the 'corrective' arm; and, above all, on implementation in 'a rigorous and consistent manner'. Not least, it sought a leading role from the Euro Group in offering a demonstration of sound fiscal policies. In these hopes the ECB was mostly disappointed.

'Lisbonizing' European economic policy coordination: soft boundaries

The central macro-economic and structural reform coordination mechanisms remained resolutely at EU, not Euro Area, level. Their central problems – synchronizing their different administrative 'clocks', focusing on a few clear priorities, and securing domestic implementation – reflected the underlying weaknesses of the European Commission and of the Euro Group. The challenge of synchronizing 'clocks' grew as the number of coordination mechanisms increased (cf. Eder, 2004; Ekengren, 2002). Initially, the multilateral surveillance on the basis of the Broad Economic Policy Guidelines (BEPGs) was seen as the pivot of a series of different processes, each with its own rules and forums: the SGP, employment policy (the Luxembourg process), structural reform policies (the Cardiff process), and the Macro-Economic Dialogue (the Cologne process). Opacity was not reduced when in 1999, reflecting a centre-left majority, the Cologne European Council tied the latter three processes into the European Employment Pact (as its 'three pillars'). The Lisbon strategy was added in 2000.

In the absence of precise prioritized objectives, clear 'road maps' and firm deadlines, economic policy coordination mechanisms were weak in mobilizing Member State governments. This weakness was most apparent in the Lisbon strategy. The Lisbon strategy reflected the ambitions of centre-left governments in 1999–2000 to place growth at the centre of EU policy. However, in place of initial discussions about committing to a 3 per cent annual growth objective, the Lisbon European Council in 2000 agreed to a target date of 2010 for transforming the EU into 'the most dynamic and competitive knowledge-based economy in the world, capable of sustainable economic growth with more and better jobs and greater social cohesion'. This ambitious and vague objective was to be achieved through the 'Open Method of Cooperation', notably reliance on 'benchmarking' and diffusing best practice. The lack of a precise 'road map', incorporating a few clear objectives tied to a timetable, reflected the unwillingness of Member State governments to be taken hostage to firm commitments. It resulted in the depressing conclusions of the 2004–5 mid-term review that the Lisbon strategy had failed to deliver sufficient structural reforms.

The re-launched Lisbon strategy of 2005 prompted the new Barroso Commission to give top priority to strengthening the Lisbon process, in effect to 'Lisbonizing' European economic policy coordination. The Commission de-emphasized the discredited 2010 objective in favour of focusing more precisely on growth and employment and of redesigning the governance framework. In redesigning the European economic governance framework, the 2005 review produced a closer synchronization of the various 'clocks' of European economic policy coordination: the BEPGs, the Employment Guidelines and the 'Cardiff process' (reforms to product and capital markets). Following the model of the BEPG reform in 2003, they were to be synchronized in a new three-year package, known as the 'Integrated Guidelines for Growth and Jobs' (Umbach, forthcoming). The Integrated Guidelines form the basis for three-year National Reform Programmes, which offer a more detailed road map of domestic structural reforms to product, services, labour and capital markets. They are coordinated by new high-level national Lisbon coordinators. In addition, the Guidelines provide the framework for a three-year EU-level Community Lisbon Programme. In 2007 they were updated into country-specific guidelines.

Again, as with the SGP, size seems to matter more than formal euro insider/outsider status in the scope and pace of domestic structural reforms (Duval and Elmeskov, 2006). Large states proved more reluctant reformers than small states. There was a plausible connection between the two stories of fiscal policy and economic reform. Inadequate room for fiscal manoeuvre under the 'corrective' arm of the SGP limited the capacity to accompany large-scale reforms with generous compensation for losers (cf. Delpla and Wyplosz, 2007). Ending pension, product-market or labour-market privileges poses serious domestic political issues of good faith in relation to losers. Domestic governments whose fiscal hands are tied are, in consequence, limited in capacity to engage in bold structural reforms. Hence, as with the SGP, it was unclear that the enhanced powers of the Euro Group in decisions about non-compliance with the Integrated Guidelines under the Lisbon Treaty would strengthen differentiated integration by bolstering political commitment and compliance in the Euro Area. The ECB was limited to exhortation on behalf of speedier, more comprehensive structural reforms.

Conclusions

The single most powerful historical factor shaping – and constraining – differentiated integration in European macro-economic governance appears to be shared beliefs in the values of market scale and of economic discipline. They take the form of a dominant spatial discourse of 'globalization' and its 'logic' and of the values of the single market in European integration, as well as a dominant temporal discourse of 'time consistency', 'credibility' and 'sustainability'. Cumulatively, they sharply constrain and relativize differentiation in European macro-economic governance. These discourses help explain the prevalence of 'fuzzy' and 'soft' boundaries over hard boundaries.

The bias towards 'fuzzy' boundaries is also rooted in the institutional linkage between EU-level authority over the single market (extending to the EEA) and ECB authority over Euro Area monetary policy. Financial market infrastructure is caught in this complex linkage. In fiscal policy and structural reforms the Euro Group has been deprived of independent authority to act, though the Lisbon Treaty strengthens its potential power. The will to act to carve out an independent Euro Area profile in fiscal and structural reform policies remains, however, questionable as long as the state 'size' issue remains so potent a differentiator of willingness to commit and comply. In short, differentiated integration in fiscal and structural reforms depends on changes of behaviour by France, Germany and Italy. 'Size' has the capacity to trump formal differentiation into euro insiders and outsiders as a determinant of behaviour.

The effects of differentiated integration in consequence of the creation of the Euro Area are complex and paradoxical. Firstly, in terms of traditional state 'clusters', the

Euro Area has served to reinforce the former 'D-Mark Zone' through its asymmetrical gains in trade effects and in business cycle synchronization (Baldwin, 2006a, 2006b). In consequence, the 'D-Mark Zone' can claim to be an 'optimum currency area' within the Euro Area. The problem is that its macro-economic performance in 1999–2005 was very weak. Moreover, on fiscal consolidation and economic reforms the 'D-Mark-Zone' cluster was divided between large and small states, with states like Austria and the Netherlands using OECD data to attack the complacency of the large states like France and Germany. 'Size' proved an independently potent factor. The Euro Area's lack of political solidarity was further evident in Dutch and French rejection of the Draft Constitutional Treaty in 2005, which in part at least was seen as helping strengthen political union as a parallel to monetary union.

At the same time, the fact that Euro Area has not been able to become an 'optimum currency area' in its own right illustrates its relative lack of effects on other state 'clusters'. It has had some effect in exposing Mediterranean states to a Germanic 'stability culture', not least through denial of the resort to devaluation as a domestic adjustment mechanism. However, the Euro Area periphery has been a source of problems, especially stemming from its declining competitiveness *vis-à-vis* the 'D-Mark-Zone' core. These problems have been exacerbated in some cases by asset price booms in housing and property markets consequent on low real interest rates after euro entry. Mediterranean state central bankers do not appear to depart from the shared central banking culture of the Eurosystem. They are, nevertheless, politically exposed at home as a consequence of the reform agendas that they espouse. Euro Area enlargement offers some further evidence of breaking down in traditional state 'clusters'. For instance, both Slovenia and Slovakia have joined, whereas the Baltic States, the Czech Republic, Hungary and Poland have pushed their projected entry dates further into the future. This evidence remains, however, not very convincing. Slovenia was always an 'outlier' case, escaping Yugoslav for an Alpine/Austrian identity; whilst Slovakia, a new state in 1993, sought to carve out an independent role. East-central Europe is more a region of rivals than partners. This rivalry has if anything been accentuated by euro entry.

Secondly, the Euro Area has served to rescue the European integration process from divisive ERM crises, like those of 1983, 1987, 1992 and 1993, which struck at the heart of the core Franco-German relationship. Rescuing this relationship from ERM crises was a central and successful purpose of the Euro Area. On the other hand, the evidence that the Euro Area has rescued the EU and Euro Area states by improving growth potential is at best mixed. Many states benefited from substantially lower real interest rates, triggering domestic booms. However, as in Ireland and Spain, these booms proved unsustainable and contributed to declining competitiveness and eventual financial and economic crisis. To add to problems, especially between 2001 and 2005, the German economy experienced protracted stagnation. In fact, this period hid a painful strengthening of the banking system (along with tight domestic credit) and prolonged radical restructuring in the export manufacturing sector that resulted in improved competitiveness. Though this German revival offered a positive message, official ECB and IMF calculations of the potential trend growth rate of the Euro Area (without accelerating inflation) remained constant and historically low. Hence it was difficult to build a persuasive narrative that the Euro Area had rescued the EU economy in order to strengthen its centripetal effects. It had removed internal vulnerability to exchange-rate crisis, but not accelerated growth. Moreover, the question remained unanswered of whether the source of vulnerability has shifted to cross-national banking crises in a more interlocked financial structure.

The final question relates to the implications for the politics of European integration. For the makers of European monetary union, the implications were clear: for the German Bundesbank, the need to accelerate European political union to parallel monetary union and to offer a protective umbrella of solidarity; for French policy-makers, the need to establish an 'economic government' to coordinate monetary with other policies. For some, like Schäuble and Lamers (1994) earlier and Verhofstadt (2006b) later, monetary union suggested a new historical opportunity to form a 'core' Europe. However, for the reasons given in this paper, the Euro Area has not formed the nucleus of a 'core' Europe in any of these senses. The German Bundesbank remained ambiguous and vague and unclear in its calls for political union, focusing eventually on protecting the Maastricht monetary constitution. Its former Chief Economist (then the ECB's first Chief Economist), Otmar Issing (2008), argued that all that monetary union required was supportive mechanisms to enforce fiscal discipline and flexible markets. In turn, German policy-makers have staunchly resisted calls for a European 'economic government' as inconsistent with the paramount principle of an independent ECB. Just how internally divided on political union the potential 'core' was became clear with the failed Dutch and French referenda of 2005, sinking the Constitutional Treaty, and the failed Irish referendum on the Lisbon Treaty in 2008. Consequently, monetary union had to rely on the resourcefulness of its central bankers. For them, political union was in any case a mixed blessing to the extent that it stimulated proposals that directly or indirectly challenged the independence of the ECB. For many of them monetary union had to be able to stand on its own legs. Political union was desirable, but only as long as it did not undermine the credibility of monetary policy.

The one 'hard' boundary remained euro entry, guarded by the ECB and the Commission. The 2008–9 crisis underlined that the main incentive for seeking membership was the Euro Area's shelter function. However, deepening Euro Area recession, exposure of its weakness in tackling its banking problems, and problems of domestic adjustment without exchange-rate and interest-rate policies in Ireland and Spain created centrifugal pressures. They were highly unlikely to lead to euro exits by states like Italy; the costs were prohibitive (see Eichengreen, 2007). This complex and changing mix of centripetal and centrifugal pressures meant a shifting configuration of pacesetters and laggards in euro entry. It also suggested that continuing risks and uncertainties surrounding euro entry would crystallize a group of semi-permanent outsiders.

16

'Industrial' Europe: The Softer Side of Differentiated Integration

David Howarth

Prior to considering differentiated integration in European Union industrial policy, it is first necessary to understand what this policy encompasses. EU industrial policy incorporates a range of policies that have a direct or indirect impact upon industry. The European Commission (2005) adopts an official definition of industrial policy that is narrow and focused upon manufacturing, effectively excluding service industries. In its view, industrial policy involves creating the conditions for manufacturing to thrive, complementing work at the Member State level. The EU's industrial policy officially includes seven cross-sector initiatives – on competitiveness, energy and the environment; intellectual property rights; better regulation; industrial research and innovation; market access; skills; and managing structural change – which is to benefit a wide range of industrial sectors. In addition, the Commission has introduced seven new initiatives targeted at specific sectors – pharmaceuticals, chemicals, space, defence, information and communication technologies, mechanical engineering, food, and the fashion and design industries.

EU industrial policy is officially geared towards proposing specific solutions to improve the competitiveness of European industry and prevent de-industrialization, notably 'in the light of increasingly strong competition from China and Asia' (Commission, 2005: 1). It is also 'an important step in the delivery of the new Lisbon "Partnership for Growth and Jobs"' (ibid.). The Lisbon Agenda focuses upon competitiveness, stimulating innovation and supporting small and medium-sized enterprises (SMEs) as part of the broader goals of transforming the EU into 'the most dynamic and competitive knowledge-based economy in the world ... by 2010'. EU industrial policy covers a range of internal market legislation that regulates the operation of industry, including health and safety legislation and environmental legislation (see Chapter 18 by Wurzel and Zito in this volume). It includes support for research and development (R&D) and, potentially, aid for 'declining industrial regions'. Not least, it incorporates the application of EU competition policy and the restrictions imposed through this policy on national industrial policies.

EU industrial policy differs from what is traditionally known as industrial policy, which encompasses everything that governments can do to influence industry, including financial and fiscal intervention. Until the 1980s, the concept of industrial policy was synonymous with market-distorting actions by national governments. EU state-aid rules had little practical effect upon national practices because the Commission was unable to control the sheer volume of subsidies and other assistance to companies. The EU itself possesses few policy instruments, a weak legal basis and little funding to intervene actively to promote particular industries outside of agriculture, coal and steel. The heyday of EU industrial interventionism was during the first half of the 1980s, when the Commission led schemes to cushion the restructuring of the steel industry by enforcing production quotas. The Single European Act's Article 130 (Articles 163–173 TEC) sanctioned new EU funding to subsidize cross-border R&D. There is also a legal basis for exemptions to the application of EU competition policy to allow for interventionist national industrial policies. Provisions in the Treaty of Rome (Articles 87–89 TEC) specify categories of national state aid to industry that are not incompatible with the common market (that is, those having a 'social character') or not necessarily incompatible (such as 'aid to promote the economic development of areas where the standard of living is abnormally low') and the possibility of creating new categories.

With the rise of economic liberalism and the decline (but not disappearance) of national interventionism, EU industrial policy was shaped by national preference for state withdrawal from the economy. The EU's less interventionist approach to industrial policy dates from the early 1990s and Martin Bangemann's takeover of the industrial policy portfolio. Bangemann (1992: 20) insisted that the 'old, sectoral industrial policy would be replaced by a modern, horizontal approach which would no longer support individual industrial [sectors] but competitiveness on a large scale'. This new policy corresponded to the reinforced application of EU competition policy rules. Nonetheless, in a limited range of areas, notably information technology, the Commission continued to push for major investment programmes. France and some other Member States also continued to demand a more active EU policy. Provisions were inserted into the Maastricht Treaty (now Article 173 Consolidated Version of the Treaty) pledging the EU and its Member States to ensure the 'conditions necessary for the competitiveness' of industry, to provide greater assistance to SMEs and to ensure improved industrial exploitation of the EU's research policies. Yet because these provisions outline a strategy more than they mandate a policy and require unanimity in the Council to adopt actions, strong constraints have been placed upon the potential development of EU-led interventionism (Peterson, 1996).

Differentiated integration in this policy area is the result of one or more of five factors: differences in ideology among Member States, domestic political circumstances, capacity (level of economic development), national economic structures, and technical preferences. There is a considerable degree of 'capitalist diversity' in the EU (Hancké et al., 2007; Wilks, 1996). Even among the 'Original Six' Member States there are important differences in approach to economic regulation, even if they all embrace the EU system (Gerber, 2000). Ideological difference may contribute to differentiation in that Member States where economic liberalism holds more sway in government circles will pursue different policies than those pursued by Member States where interventionist solutions to industrial problems are more acceptable. Different levels of economic development have repeatedly been used as a justification for temporary derogations for poorer Member States in the implementation of EU legislation. Justifications stemming from ideology, economic development and structures can result in differentiated participation in EU-led or other European R&D projects. Technical preference has been a cited reason for delays in certain national programmes of sector-based market liberalisation.

In several areas these five factors overlap, and assessing their relative importance is difficult. Thus in energy-market liberalization, ideology and domestic political opposition have had a potentially significant role. There is an entrenched scepticism in certain Member States about the desirability of liberalizing the production and supply of electricity and gas, on the grounds that these are public services which should be protected from market forces. Ideology is also likely to be of relevance with regard to national infringements of EU competition policy. However, the national rhetoric of protectionism versus liberalism does not correlate perfectly with the degree to which Member States abide by EU internal market and competition policy rules.

Differentiated integration in industrial policy areas is largely 'soft' and unofficial and comes in three forms: varying national participation in EU and other European projects; the discretion permitted in the implementation of EU legislation; and varying levels of compliance with EU legislation. Legally entrenched, multi-speed differentiation is present principally in terms of temporary derogation on a limited range of EU legislation. The explicit legal sanction of more permanent differentiation in industrial policy areas is rare. The permitted provision of state aid to poorer regions is, potentially, one example – to the extent that this permission contributes to differentiation in national practice. The penultimate section of this chapter presents one recent legislative development that effectively entrenches differentiation in energy markets and potentially undermines market integration in this sector.

It is necessary to draw a distinction between differentiated participation and differentiated integration. The former in, say, EU-led industrial initiatives and non-EU R&D and industrial projects does not necessarily result in differentiated integration. In some cases differentiated participation will reflect existing differentiated integration in linked areas (for example, defence industry cooperation). However, in others differentiated participation will simply reflect the reality of different national economic structures. Table 16.1 provides an overview of the various policy areas that can be considered to be part of industrial policy and the kinds of differentiated participation and integration that have arisen in these areas. Rather than consider each in turn, examples will be drawn to demonstrate different forms of 'soft' and 'hard' differentiation.

Non-EU projects and differentiation

European R&D programmes and industrial projects involving some or many (but not all) EU Member States potentially contribute to differentiated integration. These include the European Space Agency (ESA), ESPRIT, Eureka, JET, Airbus and Ariane. Differentiated participation reflects principally different levels of

Table 16.1   EU industrial policy and differentiated participation and integration

Area	Action	Differentiated participation and integration
Internal market legislation	Implementation of EU legislation (industrial standards; pollution; health and safety at work)	Varying respect for EU legislation; implementation delays; permitted temporary derogation for existing poorer Member States; permitted temporary derogation for the new 10 CEEC Member States in their terms of accession.
Competition policy	Implementation of EU rules and decisions on competition	1) Lighter application of state aid policy to eastern Europe (and other less prosperous areas of the EU); 2) varying application of EU public procurement rules; 3) EU competition policy decisions more rigorously enforced in some Member States; 4) different reinforcement of national competition authorities.
Energy markets	Implementation of EU directives	1) Certain Member States dragging their heels on liberalization; 2) EU legislation permitting three forms of unbundling network and supply aspects of energy.
Sectoral assistance	EU and/or Member States coordinated funding for specific industries; loans from the European Investment Bank	Different Member States' participation in funded sectors: notably, coal, steel, aerospace, armaments, ICT.
R&D	EU-funded projects and research centres	EU R&D spending is concentrated in particular countries (arguably those with more vibrant research environments). Four EU-funded research centres (Italy, Belgium, Germany, Netherlands).
Euratom research	EU-funded projects and coordinated national funding programmes	Not all Member States have nuclear energy programmes. All EU Member States are members of Euratom but there is differentiation in terms of participation in CERN and JET.
Involvement in specific EU and non-EU European research networks (such as ESPRIT and Eureka)	Coordinated national research programmes and funding; EU funding.	Different Member States' participation in research networks/funding programmes (Eureka, ESPRIT, etc.).

(continued)

Table 16.1 Continued

Area	Action	Differentiated participation and integration
Structural funding (notably, European Regional Development Fund [ERDF])	EU funding for regions in industrial decline	1) Member States with more poorer regions and older industrial regions experiencing restructuring benefit disproportionately from funds; 2) specific Community Initiatives, such as the RECHAR programme, benefit coal-producing industries and areas.
Cross-sectoral policy initiatives	Organization of fora and high-level groups (industry officials with – in several cases – government officials) to discuss challenges and required government support to economic sectors	Some Member States are more involved than others by virtue of the national presence of specific industrial sectors.

economic development and economic structures, but also, potentially, ideological difference. Wallace and Wallace (1995: 53) note that the term 'variable geometry' was originally used in the late 1970s in industrial policy where different Member States would participate in different consortia along functional lines, especially to enhance their technological capabilities. The term was used mainly because the Member States chose to invest in a policy outside regular Community action. However, the authors did not consider these projects – namely, JET, Eureka, Airbus and Ariane – to be significant examples of variable geometry because they were not 'Communitarized' and did not play a major part in the overall dynamics of European integration.[1] While this is a valid claim, the developing links between some of these projects and EU policies mean that they should be considered in terms of their potential contribution to differentiated integration.

Membership in Eureka (the European high technology research coordinating agency) has, over the more than two decades of its existence, differed from EU membership. Member State participation has varied over time depending on the projects funded. The creation of Eureka in 1985 reflects in part the ideological preference of French (notably Socialist-led) governments seeking to increase the effectiveness of state intervention through multi-national European coordination. However, while French governments (joined by the Commission) pushed for more EC R&D funding, Germany and the UK were more reluctant to expand the EC's budget (Peterson, 1993). Eureka was created as an intergovernmental framework for promoting cross-border collaboration in pre-competitive research and for keeping more funding at the national level rather than transferring it through the Commission and the EU Framework Programmes.

Eureka membership presently includes all the EU Member States, with the exception of Bulgaria which nonetheless possesses a national information point allowing it to participate in Eureka projects. There are an additional 13 non-EU members, including Russia and Turkey. Large amounts of public and private funding have been mobilized to support the R&D carried out within the Eureka framework. Although Eureka is not an EU programme, it has been closely linked with the EU and the objectives of the Lisbon Agenda. Most Eureka projects funded have tended to involve a limited number of big European firms (such as Thomson-SGS, Plessey, Siemens and Philips) and, despite efforts to include more SMEs, the large firms tend to dominate decision-making (Peterson, 1993). Most projects involve only a limited number of EU Member States, and the larger Member States will tend to be involved in funding more projects than others. Unlike Eureka, the European Strategic Programme for Information Technology (ESPRIT) was an EC/EU R&D programme and, from 1993, was managed by the Commission's Directorate-General for Industry. Operating from 1983–99, ESPRIT facilitated a diverse range of partnerships and joint ventures among representatives of government, industry, universities and research institutes, with differentiated levels of participation.

The impact of Eureka, ESPRIT and other R&D programmes upon European integration has been analysed in terms of rejecting the old strategies of national champions, promoting close cooperation among European firms, facilitating the adoption of common European standards (thus eliminating important non-tariff barriers), and laying the basis for a lobby pushing for European market integration (Sharp, 1990). Differentiated participation in these projects has also contributed to different influence in shaping certain aspects of European market integration, as well as reflecting differentiated integration into a European research community. However, differentiated participation has not contributed to differentiated integration *per se*.

There is considerable differentiation in the field of atomic energy research. All EU Member States are members of Euratom. However, seven EC/EU Member States have not in the past participated, or do not at present participate, in the principal centre for fundamental physics and computer science research, CERN, the European Organization for Nuclear Research. While the industrial applications of research at CERN may be limited, CERN itself has involved significant industrial collaboration, notably in the construction of the rapid particle accelerator. CERN was founded in 1954, and membership included all the Original Six in addition to several other European countries. Most, but not all, other European countries joined prior to their EC membership. Those Member States that have more developed programmes in atomic energy research are equally those with a greater presence at CERN, and national funding contributions (on a per capita basis) have varied considerably. In 2009 eight EU Member States were not members: Ireland, Romania, the three Baltic States, Malta, Cyprus and Slovenia.

Just under a third of the budget for the EC's Seventh Research Framework Programme – €2750 million for the period 2007–11 – is earmarked for research in the field of nuclear fission, to be carried out either by means of a programme of indirect actions or by the EU's Joint Research Centre (JRC), focusing on the safe exploitation and development of fission reactor systems, the management of radioactive waste, radiation protection and safety, and security related to non-proliferation. Nearly two-thirds of this funding will go towards research in the field of fusion energy, based on work taking place in the International Thermonuclear Experimental Reactor (ITER) project. This project in turn derives from previous work undertaken since the first EC research programme, which funded the establishment of the Joint European Torus (JET) at Culham, Oxfordshire. JET has frequently not involved all EU Member States. Since 2000, the European Fusion Development Agreement (EFDA) has directed the activities of JET. With the exception of Estonia, all EU Member States now participate in EFDA, although several still do not participate in JET research and development. Given the importance of nuclear research in terms of EU priorities, the differentiated participation of EU Member States in nuclear research projects can be said to contribute to differentiated integration.

The memberships of the European Space Agency (ESA) and EU have frequently not corresponded, and non-EU countries have also been members of the ESA. There is some 'multi-speed' differentiation in Member State participation. In order to participate in ESA procurements and most ESA programmes, a country must sign a European Cooperating State (ECS) Agreement as a first stage of membership. While the financial contribution of such a country increases, it is still much lower that that of a full Member State. The ECS Agreement is normally followed by a Plan for European Cooperating States (or PECS Charter), a five-year programme of basic research and development activities, aimed at improving a country's space industry capacity. At the end of the five-year period the country can either begin negotiations to become a full Member State in the ESA or an associated state or sign a new PECS Charter. Only one of the 12 newest EU Member States is at present a full member: the Czech Republic achieved this status at the start of 2009. Hungary, Poland, Estonia, Slovenia and Romania have signed ECS agreements, and Romania and Poland have signed the PECS Charter. Differing membership has an impact upon potential participation in the European space programme which covers all the activities and measures undertaken by the EU, ESA and national space organizations. The Ariane rocket system is manufactured under the authority of the ESA. While dominated by the French (the Centre National d'Études Spatiales) and the French company EADS Astrium, which is the prime contractor, a limited number of other EU Member States and companies based in these countries have been involved in Ariane R&D.

Airbus, one of the world's two main large commercial aircraft manufacturers, also involves the participation of only a small number of EU Member States. The bulk of Airbus staff are based at 16 sites in four EU Member States: Germany, France, the UK and Spain. The governments of these countries initially developed Airbus as a consortium of publicly and privately owned aerospace manufacturers to coordinate their R&D efforts. These companies were consolidated at the turn of the century, and since 2006 the French based-company EADS has owned the entire Airbus company.

Wallace and Wallace (1995: 54) specifically list two industrial policy areas where different levels of participation have had a more direct impact upon differentiated integration: the Trans-European Networks (the TENS) and the reconfiguration of the EU Member State defence industries. The TENS were created under provisions introduced in the Maastricht Treaty (Articles 154–156 TEC) and involve EU funding for major infrastructural projects to reinforce European market integration and contribute to European social and economic cohesion. The projects under development as TENS are, by their nature, selective in membership and in competition for limited resources. Differentiation has arisen through the selection of particular projects and particular countries or groups of countries. Defence is considered below in the context of bilateral and multilateral industrial cooperation because the various projects that have been developed involve only a small number of EU Member States.

The Commission's cross-sector policy initiatives do not create much scope for differentiated integration. However, the seven sector-specific initiatives or actions do create scope for differentiated participation of the Member States to the extent that some Member States are more involved than others by virtue of their presence in specific industrial sectors. The Steering Group of the Pharmaceuticals Forum, which held its first meeting in 2006, included representatives from only seven Member States (although to ensure fairness these were representatives from recent and forthcoming Council presidencies). The High-level Group on the Chemicals Industry (meeting from 2007–9) was more exclusive and involved government representatives from only eight Member States (principally the largest, and those with a significant manufacturing presence in this sector). The Task Force on the Competitiveness of Information and Communication Technologies (meeting from 2005–6) did not include national representatives *per se*. However, its participants came for the most part from major corporations and organizations, effectively excluding participants from the majority of Member States and almost all the newest Member States.

Bilateral and multilateral Member State industrial policy as differentiation

Non-EU, bilateral and multilateral industrial projects, funded by a limited number of national governments, are another form of differentiated participation. A large number of these projects have involved only France and Germany or have been led by these two countries. The impressive range of proposals over the past two decades suggests a Franco-German core in industrial policy. However, Cole (in Chapter 11 of this volume) demonstrates the failure of most of these initiatives, outside the realm of aerospace and defence where public procurement policies are of great importance. The recent collapse of the project to create a search engine, Quaero, is a good example of the limits of Franco-German bilateralism.

In defence procurement there are several examples of ongoing Franco-German cooperation.[2] The merger of Aerospatiale-Matra (France) and Daimler-Chrysler Aerospace (Germany) in 1992 led to the development of Eurocopter that in 2000 became a subsidiary of EADS. Eurocopter produced the Tiger multi-role attack helicopter that began production in March 2003 and will be capable of providing air-ground combat support. The Organization for Joint

Armament Cooperation (OCCAR) was established in 1996 to manage collaborative armaments programmes by France, Germany, Italy and the UK (joined by Belgium in 2003 and Spain in 2005). It has provided an important framework, enabling the cross-national coordination of procurement. Membership is open to other EU Member States and NATO members, which also have the option of participating in a procurement programme under a cooperative agreement (as is the case with the Netherlands, Luxembourg and Turkey). OCCAR has coordinated cooperation for several joint European ventures which reinforce the capacity of European states to undertake crisis-management operations within NATO/ESDP frameworks.

There are also several examples of projects not involving both France and Germany, undermining claims of a special relationship and a European 'core'. The Eurofighter alliance involves companies from the UK, Germany, Italy and Spain. The French-led 'nEUROn' UCAV (Unmanned Combat Aerial Vehicle) has, since 2005, involved the delegation of 50 per cent of the work to other European partners – Alenia (Italy); Saab (Sweden), Hellenic Aerospace Industry (Greece); EADS CASA (Spain) and UAG (Switzerland). The FSAF (Future Surface-to-Air Anti-Missile Family), launched in October 1998, resulted in the development by France and Italy of common surface-to-air ground and naval-based anti-missile systems. The project has been developed under the Anglo-Franco-Italian Eurosam (ES) venture, established by Aerospatiale, Alenia and Thompson CSF in June 1989. Such bilateral and multilateral defence industrial projects are allowed because Treaty of Rome provisions exempted the armaments sector from Internal Market rules (Article 296b TEC).

Wallace and Wallace (1995: 54) argue that the development of Eurocorps in the early 1990s would have industrial implications which, in turn, would 'bear on the debate about the "core" group for defence'. The subsequent development of ESDP in the 1990s and 2000s and industrial developments further suggest that certain Member States are more likely than others to be involved in bilateral and multilateral industrial projects linked to the construction of a European military capacity. However, given that the countries involved to date in these projects are diverse, it is problematic to talk of the reinforcement of a 'core'. Franco-German bilateralism in defence industry developments has been limited. There is potential relevance of varying participation in these projects to Member State participation in European military cooperation and the construction of ESDP. However, national economic capacity and industrial strategy – as in France's refusal to participate in the Eurofighter project – is of much greater relevance. The majority of EU Member States have not participated in these projects. The creation of the European Defence Agency (EDA) in 2004 (as called for under Article 28D of the Lisbon Treaty) has reinforced the contribution of differentiated participation in joint defence research and industrial projects to differentiated integration, to the extent that EDA-promoted projects become more closely tied to the construction of European military cooperation more broadly. Membership of the EDA is not a requirement for EU Member States, although all except Denmark – which has an opt-out on the Common Foreign and Security Policy – have chosen to join.

Article 28D2 of the Lisbon Treaty makes it clear that differentiated participation will shape the organization and activities of the Agency:

> The European Defence Agency shall be open to all Member States wishing to be part of it. The Council, acting by a qualified majority, shall adopt a decision defining the Agency's statute, seat and operational rules. That decision should take account of the level of effective participation in the Agency's activities. Specific groups shall be set up within the Agency bringing together Member States engaged in joint projects.

Temporary derogation as differentiation

Legal temporary derogation is provided for through specific legislative provisions and accession treaty provisions adopted with regard to the application of policies that have significant cost implications for industry. Present or future Member States argue that factors specific to their national industry (or broader economy) justify derogation. Notably, the poorer countries of central and eastern Europe have argued that many sectors of domestic industry were financially unable to comply with EU environmental and health and safety regulation. Thus, for example, the 2004 accession treaties permitted a delay until the end of 2005 for the implementation of EU health and safety legislation. To provide a more specific example, temporary derogations were granted to seven of the 10 2004 applicants permitting the delayed implementation of certain provisions of the directive relating to waste electrical and electronic equipment (2002/96/EC). Existing Member States have also benefited from specific provisions in EU legislation allowing for delayed implementation. The Packaging and Packaging Waste Directive 1994 (94/62/EC) allowed the then four poorest EU Member States (Spain, Portugal, Greece and Ireland) a delay to achieve the waste recovery and recycling targets. The 2004 amendment to the directive which established new targets granted a revised derogation to Ireland, Portugal and Greece.

Discretionary differentiation

Andersen and Sitter (2006: 313) widen the use of the term differentiated integration 'to capture both the formal and informal arrangements for policy opt-outs as well as the differences, or discretionary aspects, associated with putting EU policy into practice'. They emphasize, in effect, the heterogeneity of integration. Given that Member States implement directives differently, the result can be considerable intra-sector variation. Discretionary differentiation is particularly relevant with regard to the implementation of internal market, health and safety, and environmental legislation.

There are two main sources of this kind of differentiation. First, Member States can design directives to be less specific in order to allow for greater national margin of manoeuvre in implementation. Even those Member States without considerable reservations about a directive may take advantage of the scope for discretion written into a directive (Andersen and Sitter, 2006). When flexibility and voluntary measures replace strict requirements, the result is that states are effectively allowed – if not encouraged – to go their own way. Second, there are pressures for 'de-coupling' within Member States, notably from regional and local governments, and institutional resistance, which can prevent governments from implementing policies that they have agreed at the EU level. Thus national governments may be committed to a directive and its implementation, but local resistance will result in its distorted implementation. Differentiation via discretion should be distinguished from differentiation through non-compliance, although pushing the boundaries of discretion can result in non-compliance.

There are several forms of discretion found in EU legislation. In addition to deliberately vague wording, allowing for the continuation of national practice, there is discretion for national room to manoeuvre in the achievement of a broad goal (for example, sector-based liberalization). The liberalization of the telecommunications sector can be described as an example of multi-speed differentiation. EU directives allowed Member States to liberalize at their own pace. The Commission adopted a gradualist approach that allowed considerable margin of manoeuvre to Member States in terms of domestic organizational solutions and the timing of liberalization (Eyre and Sitter, 1999). However, in this sector a strong coalition of actors had incentives to pursue the goal of rapid liberalization in order to meet international market and technological challenges.

A third form of discretion allows exemptions from legislative requirements for specific reasons. One recent example is in the REACH directive which allows for the application of a 'socio-economic analysis' to permit derogation (Articles 62(5)(a) and 69(6)(b) and Annex XVI). To the extent that 'socio-economic analysis' might create a national bias (for example, allowing more flexible application of the rules in poorer Member States), the result is scope for more patterned and permanent differentiation.

Compliance and non-compliance as differentiation

EU industrial policy can be described as 'horizontal' to the extent that policy seeks to compensate for the failure of national governments to provide open competitive markets (Nicolaides, 1993; Peterson, 1996). EU competition policy is thus a core element of the EU's industrial policy. To the extent that levels of compliance by EU Member States with EU competition policy and internal market rules on the free movement of capital differ, there is persistent differentiation in industrial policy. Different national compliance levels can also reflect the persistence of different national forms of industrial policy, interventionism and protectionism. These forms include the provision of state aid, intervention in mergers, protection of sectors from foreign ownership (including the ownership of companies based in other EU Member States), and the maintenance of

Table 16.2   SEM implementation deficits, 2006

	Number of Directives not transposed after deadline	Commission Infringements proceedings
Austria	23	60
Belgium	32	59
Cyprus	17	16
Czech Republic	48	7
Denmark	8	29
Estonia	23	4
Finland	24	40
France	31	107
Germany	29	99
Greece	62	98
Hungary	18	11
Ireland	32	52
Italy	62	166
Latvia	25	8
Lithuania	19	4
Luxembourg	62	41
Malta	35	7
Netherlands	24	47
Poland	23	20
Portugal	60	61
Slovakia	23	5
Slovenia	20	1
Spain	28	114
Sweden	23	46
United Kingdom	21	61

Source: Adapted from European Commission Scorecard, April 2006.

state ownership. There are also substantial differences in terms of Member State responses to decisions on infringement by the Commission and rulings by the European Court of Justice.

'Infringement cases' in the above table include: 'cases where the transposition is presumed not to be in conformity with the directive it transposes or cases where Internal Market rules (both rules contained in the EC Treaty an in Internal Market directives) are presumed to be incorrectly applied and where a letter of formal notice has been sent to the Member State concerned.'

Although decreasing, the provision of state aid to industry – some of which contravenes EU rules – varies considerably from country to country. Table 16.4 categorizes state aid in terms of amounts provided. Sweden, Austria and Germany can be placed in the large-provider category, while the UK provides relatively little. In terms of state aid for companies as a percentage of GDP (excluding agriculture, fisheries and transport), only six Member States provide more than 0.6 per cent of GDP (notably, Germany, Austria and Sweden). Five provide less than 0.2 per cent of GDP (including the UK which provided 0.16 per cent in 2006). There are significant differences between Member States in the sectors to which they direct

Table 16.3   SEM implementation deficits, 2008

	Long-overdue transposition (2 years+)	Number of Directives not transposed after deadline (13 May 2008)	Commission Infringements proceedings (as of 1 May 2008)
Austria	3	20	54
Belgium	7	23	64
Bulgaria	N/A	0	14
Cyprus	3	29	18
Czech Republic	6	42	31
Denmark	2	11	25
Estonia	2	15	26
Finland	0	15	33
France	2	15	94
Germany	2	9	87
Greece	3	24	88
Hungary	1	16	26
Ireland	0	17	53
Italy	1	21	127
Latvia	0	10	28
Lithuania	1	10	18
Luxembourg	12	31	31
Malta	1	15	45
Netherlands	0	14	48
Poland	3	31	58
Portugal	2	32	68
Romania	N/A	7	9
Slovakia	0	6	22
Slovenia	2	11	23
Spain	2	14	108
Sweden	2	14	43
United Kingdom	1	15	57

Source: Adapted from European Commission Scorecard, April 2008.

state aid. However, prior to the international financial crisis and recession starting in 2008, the bulk of state aid in most Member States went to manufacturing (60 and 66 per cent in Italy and Germany, with far higher percentages in smaller Member States, including Sweden). In terms of aid to SMEs allowed under block exemptions, the amounts granted by Italy far exceed amounts granted by other Member States (in terms of spending as a percentage of GDP) and comprised 45 per cent of the total. As a percentage of GDP, Irish, Belgian and Czech state aid was particularly high. On pending recovery cases, Spain, Italy and Germany are the worst offenders (in terms of total number of cases), while the majority of Member States (including the UK) have had no cases brought against them.

Several EU Member States intervene regularly to encourage or block potential mergers and takeovers. France, Italy, Germany and Spain have engaged in interventionism on mergers with the aim of maintaining national ownership in particular

Table 16.4   State aid awarded in the EU Member States, 2006

	Total state aid for industry and services (= total state aid less agriculture, fisheries and transport) in € billion	Total state aid for industry and services (= total state aid less agriculture, fisheries and transport) as % of GDP
EU-25	66.7	0.42
EU-15	61.1	0.41
EU-10 (2004 enlargement Member States	5.6	0.52
Greater than 0.6% of GDP		
Malta	0.1	1.77
Sweden	3.5	0.94
Hungary	1.4	0.93
Portugal	1.5	0.91
Germany	20.2	0.69
Austria	2.3	0.60
Between 0.3% and 0.6% of GDP		
Czech Republic	0.8	0.51
Cyprus	0.1	0.48
Slovenia	0.3	0.48
Denmark	1.3	0.46
Slovakia	0.2	0.45
Poland	2.3	0.45
France	10.4	0.41
Spain	4.9	0.39
Finland	2.6	0.35
Below 0.3% of GDP		
Ireland	1.0	0.28
Belgium	1.2	0.28
Italy	5.5	0.26
Netherlands	1.9	0.24
Lithuania	0.1	0.23
United Kingdom	4.2	0.16
Latvia	0.3	0.15
Greece	0.6	0.15
Luxembourg	0.1	0.13
Estonia	0.1	0.08

sectors. Other Member States – notably the UK and the Netherlands – pursue a more *laissez-faire* position. Several Member States (but not all) have outlined a range of sectors that should be protected from foreign ownership. Several national governments maintain state ownership or control (through golden shares) of companies, which is not necessarily contrary to EU rules. Despite large privatization programmes over the past two decades, France and Italy in particular have significant state-owned sectors. The governments of both countries have delayed the privatization of state-owned former energy monopolies. National competition law (affecting the operation of companies which are located primarily in the national market and thus not subject to EU competition policy) continues to be distinct, which also reflects differing attitudes to the application of EU competition policy. Eyre and Lodge (2000) provide a detailed account of the Europeanization of competition law, describing the tension between convergence and divergence as countries have increasingly come to play a 'European melody', but with distinct 'national tunes'.

Since the launch of the Single Market Programme, the European Commission has sought to challenge public procurement by national governments that discriminate in favour of protected national firms and against foreign competitors. Total public procurement in the EU – that is, the purchases of goods, services and public works by governments and public utilities – was estimated at about 16 per cent of the EU's GDP or €1500 billion in 2002. Its importance varies significantly between Member States, ranging between 11 per cent and 20 per cent of GDP (see http://ec.europa.eu/internal_market/publicprocurement/index_en.htm). An evaluation of the public procurement market demonstrates persistent differentiation. Those Member States with relatively informal procurement legislation before the adoption of EU directives (notably Germany, the Netherlands and Denmark) and those which had more decentralized procurement practices (again Germany and the Netherlands) had more problems with compliance and more compliance costs. A list of infringement cases brought by the Commission against EU Member States for failing to follow public procurement rules demonstrates differentiation (Table 16.5). This list provides the best indication (albeit incomplete) of different government actions with regard to respecting EU public procurement rules. The trends seen in the implementation of EU competition and internal market policy rules apply. The Scandinavian countries are the most compliant, while Germany

Table 16.5 Infringement cases brought to the ECJ on public procurement rules (2000–8)

Member State	Number of cases brought to the ECJ
Germany	12
Italy	12
Spain	7
France	7
United Kingdom	4
Greece	4
Austria	3
Ireland	3
Portugal	2
Netherlands	1
Luxembourg	1
Sweden	1

Note: Member States with no infringement cases are not listed.
Source: http://ec.europa.eu/internal_market/publicprocurement/infringements_en.htm

and Italy have the greatest difficulty following EU rules, followed by Spain and France. Member States with strongly centralized procurement policies (like the UK or Portugal) are more likely to respect EU rules.

Differentiation has persisted in the energy sector despite the ongoing efforts of the European Commission and certain Member States to bring about liberalization (Andersen, 2001). Article 90 of the Treaty of Rome (now Article 86 TEC) equipped the Commission with the legal power unilaterally to break up national monopolies. Some Member States, notably the UK, supported the Commission's push for liberalization. Others, notably France and Germany, were sceptical of if not hostile to full liberalization and the unbundling of production and supply. As a result, some Member States have moved quickly towards liberalization, while others have dragged their heels. German and French governments stuck to the minimum requirements of the 1996 and 1998 directives to liberalize, respectively, the electricity and gas sectors (96/92/EC and 98/30/EC, revised in 2003), while EU-level legal action forced some action. In addition to ideological opposition to liberalization, there has been persistent domestic political opposition, with strong trade-union, party-political and public hostility – encouraged by the fear that gas and electricity prices would rise after liberalization. Third-party access to transmission networks for electricity and gas was blocked by several Member States through the discretion allowed in the 1998 directive: a combination of ambiguous wording and omissions. Member States were allowed to choose between regulated and negotiated third-party access, and to develop or maintain their national regulatory models. The Commission, encouraged by Britain and a minority of EU Member States, pushed for a complete unbundling of production and supply. In several Member States, public take-up of alternative energy providers has been minimal and market access restricted. Homogenous integration worked only with respect to limited policy initiatives in the energy sector such as price transparency for electricity and gas contracts.

Legislated differentiation

In January 2008 the European Commission proposed a new directive on unbundling energy production. Previously, the Commission had demanded that energy producers sell off transmission networks. Because this demand met the intransigent opposition of several Member States (the so-called Group of Eight: France, Germany, Austria, Bulgaria, Greece, Latvia, Luxembourg and Slovakia) and the EU continued to lack a clear legislative framework on energy, the Commission decided to change tack. Its proposed directive would effectively allow Member States that had not decoupled to avoid doing so. Energy companies would not have to sell grids and pipelines. However, they would face tougher regulation and a requirement for more independent management. The Commission proposed the establishment of an independent system operator (ISO). Big energy companies would retain ownership of the transmission lines, but pass managing control over networks to an entirely separate operator which would be required to have a different group of shareholders from the parent company.

This proposed compromise gesture was still rejected by the Group of Eight. In June 2008, Member State governments reached a compromise, agreeing to embed into EU law the right for individual governments to choose one of three different models of unbundling: full ownership unbundling, when a parent company sells its transmission networks to a different firm; the independent system operator (ISO) option proposed by the Commission in January that allows big energy companies to retain ownership of the transmission lines but requires them to transfer managing control over networks to an entirely separate operator (which would not share any shareholders with the parent company); and a third option (very close to the one preferred by the Group of Eight) – the creation of a so-called independent transmission operator (ITO) which permits a parent company to retain ownership of transmission networks which would be heavily supervised by a national regulator. Under this new third option, the directive imposes additional requirements upon the parent company and the ITO to reinforce the independence of the latter, including a mechanism preventing top management from moving freely between a company's production and transmission wings. Furthermore, the national regulator would examine the transmission operator's development and investment plans and could demand changes.

While the new directive will bring about a change in national practice in the eight Member States which have to date opposed unbundling, ongoing differentiation in the organization of national energy markets and regulation has been explicitly recognized. The result is the adoption of an unprecedented piece of EU legislation. Opponents of the directive have argued that it effectively endorses the practices in certain Member States which undermine full market liberalization and European market integration.

Conclusion

A complete study of differentiated integration in industrial policy would have to cover potentially all the policy areas mentioned in the introduction. Official opt-outs exist in none. On specific pieces of legislation or in particular policies, clauses may be inserted allowing for temporary derogation. These derogations are never intended to be permanent, even if they arguably demonstrate a *de facto* recognition that some Member States are not really expected by the others to implement the piece of legislation in the foreseeable future. Only very recently in EU history have legislative provisions been adopted – in the field of energy market liberalization – that officially recognize differentiation in the rules that govern the operation of an industrial sector.

Varying EU Member State participation in European R&D programmes and industrial projects can contribute to differentiated integration. However, the degree to which the two are linked must be seen as limited. Some differentiation can be detected in the context of bilateral and multilateral industrial initiatives developed by specific EU Member States. Even so, the contribution of this differentiation in participation to differentiated integration is unclear. Derogations and different levels of compliance (as measured by Commission notification, court cases brought against Member States and other statistics) demonstrate differentiated integration.

However, it is discretion allowed in the implementation of EU legislation that remains the greatest source of differentiation. An exhaustive study of differentiation through discretion is beyond the scope of this chapter. Further research is necessary to determine the extent to which this differentiation reflects a persistent ideological division in Europe about the meaning of market integration and the desirable nature of EU and national industrial policies, rather than temporary differences that better reflect different levels of economic development, economic structures and technical preferences.

Notes

1. Wallace and Wallace (1995: 53) write: 'The preoccupation belongs to the period in which the R&D and technology programmes of the EC were being developed, closely linked to groupings of countries and companies with a particular stake in specific high-tech industries. Current EU policy is more diffusely construed and the consortium principle of self-including groups of countries seems less pertinent, especially given the ambivalences of European industrial policy. Some elements of the discussion linger on in other frameworks, such as the European Space Agency or Eureka. Here we should note in passing that efforts to "communitarise" these consortia have not succeeded and thus that their patterns of varied participation impinge relatively little on the discussions within the EU as such.'
2. Information on bilateral and multilateral armaments projects has been drawn from T. Dyson, 'Differentiated Cooperation in Defence and Security Policy: Reformed Bandwagoning in the Context of Systemic Unipolarity', paper presented at the Workshop on Differentiated Integration, Cardiff, 10–12 September 2008.

17
'Social' Europe

Nick Parsons and Philippe Pochet

Despite talk of a European social model, the notion of 'social Europe' is a very nebulous one. Social protection is in many senses the poor relation of European integration, arriving late on the scene and advancing far less than, for example, economic integration (see Chapter 15 by Dyson and Chapter 16 by Howarth in this volume). This chapter will examine why, on the one hand, differentiated integration in this field has been limited and, on the other, the realm of social policy has not been a propitious one for integration at the European level. It begins with a brief presentation of the different periods and the main achievements in the history of social Europe, before examining the differentiated nature of social policy in the EU. The following sections explain the lack of integration in the social policy field in terms of spatial, temporal and functional variables.

A brief history of 'social Europe'

When the Treaty of Rome was signed in 1957, harmonization in the area of social policy was considered unnecessary as differences between welfare states and social provision were seen as sustainable within what was essentially a customs union. Responsibility for social policy was therefore left to national governments. The main policies were the granting of the right of free movement to workers and the establishment of the European Social Fund in the 1960s. Both aimed to increase internal mobility by achieving equality between EU and national workers within each national territory and not between countries. The next phase came in the context of economic crisis in the late 1970s, when efforts were made to promote the upwards harmonization of working conditions and living standards, particularly in the areas of gender equality, health and safety and collective redundancies (Pochet, 2005: 3–5). The third step was at the turn of the 1970s with the ideological victory of neo-liberal thinking and the political victory in the UK of the Thatcher administration and, later, other neo-liberal governments. At this time, the key topic was no longer social policy but employment. The explanations of the causes of high unemployment were considered to be the welfare state, because of its cost on labour, and regulation, due to the supposed rigidities it created. The consensus of the following years saw processes of deregulation and 'market-making' reforms at the national level.

The build-up to the Single European Market in the 1980s proved to be a turning point for 'social Europe', with European-level intervention increasing in the wake of the 1987 Single European Act (SEA). Until then, the main thrust of integration was economic, with social concerns very much secondary. However, in the wake of economic recession and, importantly, of negotiations over the creation of the Single European Market, European Commission President Jacques Delors attempted to get trade unions to sign up to greater economic integration through promoting the notion of a 'social dimension' to European integration. This firstly found concrete expression in the Social Action Programme, adopted by the Council in June 1984, before Delors raised the possibility of European-level collective agreements in the following year (Carley, 1993: 108). To promote social dialogue with the aim of harmonizing national social regulation, Delors brought together members of the Commission and the European social partners – UNICE (now Business Europe), ETUC and CEEP – to begin what became known as the Val Duchesse process. Over the next few years this resulted in a few vague joint Opinions, mainly on macro-economic policy and education/training, as the political debate was dominated by concerns over deregulation and social dumping. The background was increasing global economic competition, not only from the developed economies of the USA and Japan, but also from emerging ones in Brazil, Taiwan and Korea. In this context, the late 1980s and early 1990s witnessed little more than the definition of minimum social norms which found concrete expression in the 1989 Community Charter of the Fundamental Social Rights of Workers and its accompanying action programme. However, their impact was minimal and did not improve upon the rights enjoyed by workers in their national settings (Pochet, 2005: 5).

Despite these failings, the notion of the European social dialogue was given renewed vigour in the 1990s (Carley, 1993: 113–17). In 1991, the social partners jointly proposed that they should have the possibility of concluding an agreement on areas of social policy which would then be implemented by a directive from the Council or via collective agreements at national level. The proposal was taken up in the Social Protocol of the 1991 Maastricht Treaty on European Union, from which the British Conservative government opted out. The social partners adopted three collective agreements transformed into directives in the 1990s: on parental leave (1996), part-time work (1997) and fixed-term work (1999). However, this proved difficult to sustain. Firstly, the failure to conclude an agreement on temporary agency workers stopped the dynamic of signing an agreement every two years. Secondly, the Commission was less and less supportive of the trade unions, and, finally, the Commission was no longer threatening employers with legislation if they did not negotiate with the ETUC. The social partners then decided to follow a more autonomous path (possible in the Treaty) and adopted three autonomous agreements: on telework in 2002, stress at work in 2004, and harassment and violence at work in 2007. These have to be implemented through the national social partners according to their tradition.

The UK 'opt-out' from the Social Protocol of the Maastricht Treaty led to a confusing period of exclusion of the UK from European social policy based on the Social Protocol. As two legal bases with different implications coexisted, it was possible to develop an enhanced cooperation (without the UK) in this domain. For example, the 1996 Directive on European Work Councils was based on the Social Protocol and did not apply to the UK. On the other hand, the 1993 Working Time Directive and the 1992 Directive on Pregnant Workers and Workers Who Have Recently Given Birth were based on the health and safety provisions of the Treaty (which required qualified majority voting, QMV) and therefore applied to all Member States. This situation returned to normal when New Labour won the 1997 UK general election and accepted the integration of the Social Protocol into the Treaty of Amsterdam in the same year.

The Treaty of Amsterdam signalled, in addition to the possibility of European collective agreements and the end of the UK opt-out from European social policy, the introduction of other recent institutional developments at the EU level that can be seen as giving a stimulus to supra-national regulation of social policy. Firstly, the Treaty extended the use of QMV over certain areas of social policy. More importantly, an Employment Title was also incorporated into the Treaty, signalling a shift towards greater coordination, via the Open Method of Coordination (OMC), rather than the Community method of legal regulation, as a means of harmonizing social policy. In the context of EMU, OMC had already been applied to economic policy coordination, and – following employment – was extended to the areas of poverty and social exclusion and pensions (Pochet, 2005). The Social Protection Committee, set up by Ministers of Social Affairs in 2000, and the integrated open method of co-ordination for social protection from 2006, completed this architecture. In all these areas, through the establishment of benchmarks, guidelines and targets, OMC aimed at policy learning through sharing best practice and creating a normative pressure for convergence on outcomes of social policy. Thus, rather than focusing on a harmonization of the content of social policies and national institutions, the new instruments that have been developed at the EU level since the early 1990s aim at improving national social policies, while recognizing that this can be done in a variety of ways that accommodate national diversity in social models.

Differentiated integration in social policy

The period between the SEA and the Maastricht Treaty was crucial for differentiated integration in social policy, with tensions between two competing visions of European integration – the purely market-oriented approach, supported by the UK Conservative government, and the more political and social approach, supported by a coalition led by France. These tensions were resolved by the self-exclusion of the UK from European social policy. Many discussions took place on the implications of this exclusion. As a consequence, the Commission tried to use mainly the provisions of the Treaty (which applied to the UK) when dealing with social issues, interpreting health and safety in the broadest sense. As a result, the possibilities offered by the Social Protocol were not fully exploited. The main reason for this was that social policy was supposed to establish the basic rules of the (social) game in order to reduce economic competition and the risk of social dumping. However, if one important player is out of the game, then it distorts competition rules even more. The situation was summarized by the former British Prime Minister, John Major: 'They have the social regulations, and we have the jobs.'

There was an intense debate within trade union organizations at that time on the right strategy to follow. On the one hand, developing the social dimension without the UK would allow better directives in terms of content and would by-pass the veto due to the unanimity rule contained in the Treaty (with the exception of health and safety). On the other hand, the UK was not alone in its opposition to social Europe, so the result in terms of content was not guaranteed and could open the way for other opt-outs by other Member States. The risk was of a patchwork social Europe in the sense that some directives would only apply to a group of countries (Europe *à la carte*) and not to Europe as a whole. Finally, it was decided not to enter into a debate on enhanced cooperation in the social field but to privilege the conception of social protection as a public good which cannot be divided spatially.

Autonomous agreements constitute the second form of differentiated integration. These agreements between the social partners are a legal instrument based on the Maastricht Treaty. Implementation is left to the national organizations that have signed the agreement at EU level through their umbrella organizations, ETUC and Business Europe. What has emerged from the implementation process of the three agreements signed so far is great variation, with the use of law (some of the new Member States), national collective agreements, sector collective agreements, enterprise agreements or common guidelines (see Table 17.1 for the agreement on telework). Autonomous agreements will therefore be implemented very differently in different Member States because of different traditions, industrial relations structures and the involvement of national social partners. The result is a fragmentation of social Europe as not all workers are covered in the same way.

The same can even be said of EU directives, which may have a differential impact on countries, due to their industrial relations traditions, and even differentiate between groups of workers within a given territory. The 1996 Posted Workers Directive (PWD), for example, has very different implications for wages according to whether wages are subject to universally applicable national collective agreements or not. Thus, in countries with centralized collective bargaining structures, such as Austria, posted workers will benefit from collective agreements. In countries such as the UK, however, where bargaining takes place mainly at company level, posted workers only benefit from minimum wage legislation.

Furthermore, on 19 June 2008 the ECJ ruled, in Case 319/06 (Commission v Luxembourg), that Luxembourg had contravened EC Treaty Article 49 and failed to properly implement the PWD in setting certain requirements when a non-Luxembourg employer had workers within the Duchy. This included

Table 17.1 Instruments chosen to implement the Framework Agreement on Telework

Instruments chosen*		Countries
Collective agreements at national level	cross-industry	FR, BE, LU, GR[1,2] and IS[1]
	extended by decree/binding *erga omnes* binding on signatory parties and their members	IT
	sectoral	DK[3]
Agreements by social partners	recommendations to lower bargaining levels	FI and ES[2]
Guidelines, recommendations	addressed mainly to lower bargaining levels as well as companies and teleworkers	NL and SE[2]
	addressed mainly to individual companies and teleworkers	UK, IE[4], AT[5], LV[2] and NO[2]
Joint declarations		DE
Model agreements proposed by social partners		DE[5] and IE
Legislation	based on agreement between social partners	PL
	after consultation of social partners	HU, SK and CZ[6]
	no/little involvement of social partners	PT and SI[6]
no implementation yet/no information		CY, EE, LT, MT, BG and RO

Notes:
*This table does not cover sector-specific or regional agreements reported by social partners which relate to a small number of sectors or regions only and which have sometimes been adopted prior to/without any reference to the Framework Agreement (such as DE, ES and AT). Furthermore, it does not cover individual company agreements on telework reported by social partners and adopted prior to or as follow-up to the Framework Agreement (such as NL, DE and ES). Incomplete or example-based reporting of individual instruments and the difficulty of identifying them in all Member States could distort the overall presentation.

1. Legal status not fully certain.
2. Mainly based on literal translation/translation in annex, that is, little adaptation to national context.
3. Covers the industry, services, local, regional and national government sectors, is accompanied by guidelines and is supplemented by cross-industry agreement.
4. Implementation not finalized.
5. Unilateral instruments, that is, not jointly adopted.
6. Partial implementation only.

Source: European Commission (2008a).

requirements for a written contract of indefinite duration, compliance with collective agreements, the automatic indexation of wages to the cost of living, the provision of certain extensive and detailed information to the Luxembourg authorities, and for an agent to be in place within Luxembourg to ensure compliance. Such 'public order' legislation, applicable to all companies established in Luxembourg, was deemed excessive for the protection of posted workers and imposed an additional burden for undertakings established in another Member State that went beyond the Directive's requirements and dissuaded them from providing services. As a result, Luxembourg companies have to comply with such legislation, whereas posted workers from outside the Duchy do not benefit from the social protection accorded in this way (Parsons, 2009).

The third example of differentiation stems from the 'soft' law process. In recent years, European bodies have attempted to influence the intellectual process of redesigning social policy. Indeed, influencing national ideas in welfare policies has become one of the main targets of the EU, through the OMC. Since 1997, employment policies, under the Luxembourg process, and since 2000 social protection (especially policies dealing with pensions and social exclusion), under the Lisbon process, have been formally included in European competence under the specific procedure of the OMC. The arrival of employment and social policies on the European agenda and procedures can be understood as an unintended consequence (a spill-over effect) of European economic and monetary integration. While most of the literature on the spill-over of European economic integration on social policies foresaw a 'race to the bottom', very few predicted a competition over competences in social fields between different European organizations, leading to innovation in European social policy orientation and practices. In the field of employment policy, as well as in social protection, 'economically-oriented' actors tried to pre-empt the definition of policy design so that welfare reforms could conform to their own economic nostrums. 'Socially-oriented' actors reacted in alarm, lobbying national governments and promoting an alternative social policy orientation.

It is difficult to trace the potential impact of this soft method as it could have a voluntary impact (strategic use by the actors) or an uncontrolled impact (idea diffusion). Most analyses have tried to evaluate the learning effect, if any, and the instruments linked to it (exchange of good practice, peer review, employment committee, and so on). What emerges from the European Employment Strategy (EES) is a global message about change at national level, with two opposite directions for such change: on the one hand Denmark and the Netherlands, on the other the UK. It reinforces the discourse that the Southern and 'Bismarckian' models are in deep trouble. This discourse was already internally produced by senior academics (see Streeck, 2003, and Scharpf, 2000, for the German case) and supported by national 'modernizers' at political level. EU employment strategy was therefore part of a global paradigm shift. Ideas were uploaded to the EU level from diverse pressures and ideas developed at national level, which were not in line with the traditional approaches of the Bismarckian countries (Palier and Pochet, 2009; Palier, 2009).

On the impact at national level, Heidenreich and Bischoff (2007: 22) underline for Germany:

> In conclusion, on the one hand we have to acknowledge the fundamental autonomy of the national political arena. In comparison with the numerous veto players of the German system [...], the impact of European incentives, suggestions, obligations and constraints are relatively low. Effective change is only possible when the challenges are recognized as such by the domestic actors. On the other hand, within the small administrative and political elites which have finally designed the German labour market and social reforms, the cognitive impact [...] was considerable.

The same goes for the most comprehensive evaluation of the impact of Europe on French social policies. It appears clearly that the impact has been on new directions (employment rate in place of unemployment rate) (EGAS, 2006). The analysis of the interaction between French employment and pensions policies and the EES and OMC shows that if OMC does not dictate the orientation of French policies it provides national actors with European resources that might help them in their action at the national level (Barbier and Samba Sylla, 2001; Coron and Palier, 2002; Erhel et al., 2005). According to Mandin and Palier (2004) French political or administrative elites denied any direct impact but mentioned a 'leverage effect' (an expression used first by Coron and Palier, 2002) produced by the instruments developed within the OMC. The question was less whether they were 'implementing' OMC guidelines than whether these were useful to them in their interaction with other national actors. OMC thus becomes a supplementary resource for national actors rather than a non-negotiable external constraint, to be used as a lever to win or to legitimize certain reforms (for a detailed analysis of this 'leverage effect', see Coron and Palier, 2002; Erhel et al., 2005). The same conclusions are drawn by Obinger and Talos (2009) for the Austrian case; they underline the influence of the EES and OMC not on the details of the reforms but on their trajectory and goals. When we look in detail at the reforms (for example, activation policies), there are still considerable differences (see Barbier, 2006). The (new) vocabulary was particularly useful for 'modernizers' in the Bismarkian welfare states. Other welfare states began the process of reform before the EES and OMC, which therefore had an impact, but not on the broad directions.

The flexicurity debate illustrates an interesting evolution in thinking about convergence and diversity. As discussed above, it has been argued that the EES and OMC would lead to some convergence by benchmarking national performances (one best model) and/or by developing shared ideas. In the case of flexicurity, it was decided, after long debate in the Employment Committee, to propose (four) different pathways to accommodate national diversities, trajectories and political considerations. However, the Member States resisted being associated with a particular cluster and wanted to keep some room for manoeuvre in this complex debate. As a result, the pathways were presented in a rather abstract manner. Finally, the Council has also adopted 10 common principles that should guide national reforms. This episode shows us another route not yet fully exploited, based on the recognition of internal diversity and different policies to resolve national problems. Potentially, it opens the way to much more differentiated European social policies that would address national differences in a common general and loose framework.

Spatial explanations

As pointed out by Keating in Chapter 4, the spatial decoupling of economic regulation, which operates at the European level, and social regulation, operating at the national level, means that it is difficult to replicate at the European level the sort of social compromises that emerged in European nations in the aftermath of the Second World War. The only possibility for this development would have been at the beginning of EU construction when national welfare states were still under construction. However, this direction was not taken. Rather, the different social spaces were interlinked through Regulation 1407, which gives the same rights to EC migrants as to a national on the same territory. This Regulation created a bridge between the different systems but not any harmonization.

Given this, many commentators see economic pressures as leading to welfare-state retrenchment and a 'race to the bottom' in social protection, as each Member State has an incentive to offer the most advantageous conditions for capital investment in order to attract employment to its territory. EU-level fiscal and social policy harmonization would provide a potential insurance against this risk. The problem here, however, is that welfare states and redistributive social policies, such as publicly provided healthcare and education, depend on a mutual recognition and acceptance, amongst at least a majority of the members of a particular society, of the rights and obligations of membership, or citizenship, in the interests of social cohesion. This requires social solidarity, expressed institutionally in the acceptance of taxation to pay for public goods, including welfare benefits. Such solidarity is politically and culturally organized at the national level (Offe, 2000). In other words, in spatial terms, the boundaries of the welfare state are also mainly those of the nation-state.

Behind social solidarity and citizenship rights and obligations, and underpinning them, lies the notion of a *demos*, a people with a shared cultural and political identity that enables and legitimizes sacrifice on the part of some for the sake of others in the name of social cohesion. Again, and although contested in some states, the boundaries of such identities usually coincide with national borders, enabling redistribution legitimately to take place within these borders. Although some redistribution takes place at the European level through the Structural Funds and the like, without the construction of a European *demos* it is difficult to imagine the establishment of an integrated European welfare state, implying as it does a far greater cross-border transfer of funds than applies at present. Nevertheless, it cannot be said the EU has no influence at all. But its influence is mainly indirect through ECJ judgements and economic and monetary integration (Leibfried and Pierson, 1995; Ferrera, 2005; Pochet, 2009).

Indeed, given the difficulties, even impossibility, of harmonization on a pan-European scale, the coordination of social policies through the processes of OMC and social dialogue attempt to create a new social compromise based around competitiveness in a global economy. While social protection, employment and welfare policies remain within the domain of the nation-state, policy coordination provides a link to the larger spatial entity of the EU as a form of market regulation, while orienting national policies towards European economic competitiveness in the global economy. For Euro Area members, the convergence criteria for euro entry and the Stability and Growth Pact (SGP) re-establish the link between economic and social regulation by providing deficit and debt constraints on government welfare spending. In this sense, economic regulation and social regulation operate at different spatial levels but are linked in that they are also operating with reference to the wider spatial entity of the global economy. Thus, constraints on welfare spending by national governments are necessary in order to control inflation and thereby improve the competitiveness of the Euro Area economy on a global scale but are operationalized at the European level. For those countries not in the Euro Area, global economic pressures work in the same direction, with global financial markets playing the disciplining role of the ECB. Welfare reform and social policy, then, are nested within the wider constraints of global economic competition, whether this is mediated or not by the structures and institutions of Euro Area economic governance.

However, this opens up the question of the spatial dimensions within which different actors operate. Here competing logics can be seen to be at play. At the EU level, policy coordination through the OMC and social dialogue and its outputs in terms of joint agreements, texts, action programmes and so on can be seen to obey a 'solidarity' logic, insofar as it aims to protect or improve the lives of wage-earners on a pan-European basis. At the national level, however, governments and the social partners are more concerned with national competitiveness. National bargains, increasingly in the form of social pacts, can be seen to be based on a logic of competitiveness in order to maintain and attract investment and employment within the national territory. They may therefore engage in competitive underbidding as far as wages and social provision are concerned, according to the logic of the 'competition state' (Parsons, 2007). The strength and political will of national trade-union organizations is important here, but these are in retreat everywhere. The picture is further complicated by the increasing tendency of national bargains to be compatible with a decentralization of industrial relations by allowing for 'opt-out' or 'opening' clauses and for transnational companies to distance themselves from them and to apply their own 'coercive comparisons' across establishments in different countries in the name of competitiveness (Parsons and Pochet, 2009).

Coordination through the OMC and social dialogue are not, therefore, incompatible with great diversity in terms and conditions of employment or, indeed, in wider agreements on welfare provision and social protection. Furthermore, the impact of European-level collective agreements and guidelines depends upon effective implementation at the national level, and national trade-union strength will affect this. Such diversity, again, will only be increased by EU enlargement. In other words, enlargement to countries with weak social-partner organizations may mean that the 'delivery gap' is set to increase, particularly at the sector level where such weakness is most apparent.

Temporal explanations

The main point here is sequencing: moves towards economic integration preceded the initiatives to create a 'social dimension' to the European project. With the original EEC comprising six Bismarckian welfare states, and with globalization and responses to it not on the political agenda in a period of welfare expansion, the harmonization or reform of social policy was not a concern at the European level. In 1973, the entry of the UK, Ireland and Denmark added Anglo-Saxon and Scandinavian models to the Community, reinforcing welfare-state differentiation (Scharpf, 2002: 647) and making any putative harmonization more difficult and complex. Where regulation occurred, it tended to set minimum standards and to reinforce the 'market-making' aspects of European integration, rather than being 'market-correcting'. Indeed, measures that were taken to ensure a level playing field for economic competition conformed more closely to Majone's (1993) notion of the 'regulatory state', wherein regulation is designed to ensure the most efficient allocation of economic resources. In the 1980s, even Delors' promotion of 'social Europe' can be seen as a form of legitimizing discourse for, and a 'spill-over' from, economic integration and not something pursued as an intrinsic part of European integration in its own right. Meanwhile, prospects for integration in the social sphere appeared to recede as the 1981 and 1986 enlargements involving Greece, Spain and Portugal added the southern European social model into the Community, increasing diversity and complexity.

This diversity was reinforced with the 1995 enlargement to Sweden, Finland and Austria. The entry of these high-standard welfare states exacerbated fears of social dumping, but made harmonization even more problematic in that any upwards harmonization would have been impossible for poorer southern European states (Scharpf, 2002: 650). At the same time, the inclusion of richer countries that had developed welfare states soon showed that the neo-liberal road was not the only one. Indeed, it created an alternative paradigm, necessitating some European-level response. This response was to legislate in favour of minimum rights, to use the social dialogue to produce flexible policies that could respect national diversity, and to coordinate convergence in outcomes through target-setting using the OMC (Pochet, 2005: 8).

The 2004 enlargement again brought much more diversity within Europe, particularly for social policies. Though not all the new Member States were against the development of a European social dimension, most of them were. This enlargement also brought new structural problems, mainly for the social partners and in relation to the possibility of collective bargaining, because in many countries (the Baltic States, Hungary, Poland, Czech Republic) trade unions are weak. Collective bargaining in these countries is generally at plant level, and there is no mechanism for extending agreements to sector or national level. Welfare states were restructured, and often aspects of them (pensions and healthcare) were partly privatized.

Thus, the issue of labour-market policies, social protection and welfare became a major concern at the European level only after economic integration was well and truly advanced, as a result of the issue linkage involved. By this time, however, and despite an increasing awareness of the need for coordinated policies in the area in order to avoid the possibility of a race to the bottom, harmonization was never a realistic possibility. Part of the explanation lies in the great diversity of social models that were present in the EU by this time.

Functional explanations

A discourse centred on the need for the European economy to be competitive in global terms (for example in the Lisbon Agenda) along with the OMC has produced some trends towards convergence, such as in activation in welfare policies, pension reform, labour-market flexibility, an emphasis on supply-side measures such as training, and provisions for strengthening social dialogue at both company and national level. However, integration akin to that which has occurred in the economic sphere appears out of the question for the foreseeable future for several reasons related to the nature of social policy itself. We have already dealt with the idea that welfare states are mainly nationally bounded due to their relationship to citizenship and identities, rendering the type of cross-border sacrifices necessary for redistribution unlikely. This deficit in European integration is related not only to the spatial organization of social provision but also to its function of securing cohesion within an identifiable community.

This function of social provision in securing cohesion makes 'non-path dependent' change of the type necessary for any European harmonization or integration of Member States' social models problematic. Welfare states have grown and developed over the course of many decades, with two principal results for European integration. Firstly, the increasing role of government in social provision in the post-1945 period has resulted, in western Europe, in highly complex institutional arrangements with many policy interdependencies. Welfare reform is, consequently, a difficult and complex task at the national level, resulting in a certain level of institutional inertia. Secondly, social institutions embody social compromises, sometimes won as a result of considerable struggle, to which national populations are attached, particularly through the rights that these compromises accord them. Any reform of social provision that is perceived as downgrading such provision can therefore be expected to be hotly contested, with such political and/or popular opposition often related to client groups. Constraints on government spending through the SGP or wider global forces also mean that national governments have a limited margin for manoeuvre to compensate the 'losers' when engaging in welfare reform. Again, the consequence is institutional inertia or path-dependent reform. Therefore one can still differentiate between the different 'welfare families' within the European Union.

A further functional explanation for the difficulty of social policy integration is derived from public goods theory (see Kölliker, Chapter 3 in this volume). In a context of European integration, welfare, social protection and labour-market policies and institutions can be considered as common pool resources. Given constraints on public spending, public expenditure in these areas has finite limits, and an integrated European welfare state would therefore be characterized by rivalry in consumption in that an increase in spending in one country (as a result of an asymmetric shock causing a hike in unemployment, for example) would risk a decrease in others. In a national context, governments could, of course, borrow more money to pay for such an increase, but would then run the risk of fuelling inflation, losing competitiveness and provoking further unemployment, and could be subject to the disciplining effects of the SGP and/or global financial markets.

In this sense, the question of issue-linkage with European economic integration and, more widely, economic globalization, means that welfare, social protection and labour-market policies and institutions are also characterized by non-excludability, for two reasons. Firstly, although welfare provision and social protection have traditionally been seen as rights associated with national citizenship, the free movement of labour has weakened this link. This means that there is a risk of 'welfare tourism' or, more accurately, welfare migration, as high-standard welfare states could be expected to attract the unemployed from lower-standard welfare states, other things being equal. Secondly, for given levels of productivity, high-standard welfare states imply additional costs for industry and can be undercut by lower levels of provision and social protection in other countries. Following the logic of regime competition theories, the latter could then attract investment and create employment by undercutting the former, in effect free-riding on more advanced welfare states by exporting unemployment to these countries. While the above provides incentives for an upwards harmonization among advanced welfare states characterized by high levels of social protection, it also offers less advanced welfare states an incentive to reject such harmonization.

The centripetal effects on unwilling non-participants in an integrated welfare state are therefore weak as the positive internal effects may leak to free-riders outside as positive external effects. This outcome is not confined to EU countries either, but can also be seen to benefit emerging economies in a context of increasing global economic interdependencies. Furthermore, even among countries with high levels of social protection and welfare provision, it only needs one country to break ranks and downgrade provision for others to have increased incentives to follow suit. Governments, in particular, having lost the capacity for economic regulation, particularly in the Euro Area, have a vested interest in maintaining control over the levers of the social dimensions of national economic management.

Conclusion

The realm of social policy has been resistant to harmonization at the European level for several reasons. We have analysed these in terms of space, time and function.

In reality, these explanations are not as easily disaggregated as suggested above, and are all related to the characteristics of the functional issue-area of social policy. Thus, in terms of temporal explanations, the 'social dimension' was not a concern of European policy until the 1980s because until the 1970s economic crises welfare states could expand in an era of strong economic growth. However, unemployment, welfare strain and continued economic integration raised the question of issue linkage in the 1980s, when debates around social dumping appeared. By then, however, institutional diversity as a result of enlargement made harmonization problematic, if not impossible, as governments expanded, embedded and legitimized their social welfare roles over the course of decades. Spatially, the organization of welfare states also reflects their function of ensuring national cohesion, and this association with national identities renders transnational integration difficult. More widely, populations look to their domestic government to ensure improving standards of living through well-adapted labour market and social policies, which thus become an element of national competitiveness. Again, functional considerations dovetail with spatial ones.

Indeed, the characteristics of the functional specificities of social policy provide powerful explanations for the lack of integration in this area. Institutional diversity, complexity, policy interdependencies and opposition to change render harmonization problematic. In addition, centripetal effects in the area of social policy are weak, not only for the above reasons, but also because of the free-rider problem.

This was the case with the UK 'opt-out' from the Social Protocol in the beginning of the 1990s. There was then a fear (be it real or just an excuse) that the UK would benefit at the expense of other Member States from not being bound by common social regulations. In that sense, the explanation of the lack of social Europe does not arise from a rational-choice approach which sees poorer countries choosing to exploit their comparative social advantage. On the contrary, it arises from a careful reading of national attitudes; ideological and political reasons better explain the less developed countries' positions. Socialist governments in Spain and Portugal, for example, were in favour of developing social Europe because the European legal approach (which was not about wage convergence but about minimum standards) had little impact on southern countries, which already had highly developed legal social systems, partly inherited from periods of authoritarian government.

This variant of the social dumping argument explains the increasingly perceived need for policy coordination as a substitute for the Community method of legal regulation, and the development from the late 1990s of the OMC and social dialogue as a means of bringing about convergence in the area of social policy. Here we have argued that, through these processes of policy sharing, normative integration is a possibility, but it is not one that appears to be overcoming national interests at present.

Furthermore, whether such normative integration, if it should occur, will lead to integration in practice is open to question. The development of the social dimension through soft coordination and the social dialogue is a function of the incapacity of the EU to carry out reforms in the social sphere to accompany market-making reforms due to blockage at this level and/or the fact that social policy remains, by and large, in the hands of Member States and is characterized by a diversity of national institutional arrangements. Hence the processes of OMC and participation in the EES and National Action Plans (itself variable across states) represent a form of soft regulation, aimed at increasing employment and growth. However, it can result in considerable divergence in processes and outcomes at the national level within a minimalist framework. Such potentialities take on increasing importance when one considers the increased diversity of social provision and labour-market arrangements following the 2004 and 2007 enlargements. Indeed, concerns over social dumping returned during the 2005 French referendum campaign on the Constitutional Treaty. The emblematic figure of the 'Polish plumber' undercutting French wages became a symbol of the threat to the 'French social model' from an integration process that was seen as producing an EU that threatened social and labour-market protections. These concerns were influential in the victory of the 'No' campaign (Startin, 2008). The French rejection of the Constitutional Treaty amply demonstrates how a lack of integration in the functional realm of social policy as a counterweight to economic integration has the potential to undermine the legitimacy of the European project among a significant part of the population, weaken one of the main drivers of European integration and, ultimately, to stall and even derail the whole process.

18

'Green' Europe: Differentiation in Environmental Policies

Rüdiger K. W. Wurzel and Anthony R. Zito

Introduction

Early EU environmental policy showed less differentiation than many other EU policies. There have not been the opt-outs seen, for example, in monetary and in social policies, for three main reasons. First, many environmental problems (such as climate change) are trans-national problems that states cannot resolve in isolation. Environmental protection requires common public policies to safeguard public goods (such as clean air) from the use of which no one can be excluded. Free-riding is therefore salient for EU environmental policy (see Chapter 3 by Kölliker in this volume). Second, as explained below, national environmental product standards pose a serious threat to the unitary functioning of the internal market and therefore must be harmonized on the EU level. Third, environmental policy has been one of the most popular areas for European integration (Eurobarometer, 2005–2009). Whilst in the early 1990s certain actors pushed the concept of subsidiarity as signifying that the most appropriate level of action should occur at the national (or sub-national) level, the Commission, supported by the European Parliament (EP) and the Environmental Council, has managed to defend the need for EU environmental action.

Although environmental policy has been popular in all Member States, there are significant territorial differences (see Chapter 4 by Keating in this volume). The wealthier Northern Member States generally show a higher degree of public environmental awareness (particularly for long-term global environmental problems like climate change) than the poorer Southern and Central/Eastern Member States (where visible local environmental problems, such as water pollution, are of higher public concern). Despite the public support for EU environmental policy, and the need to harmonize environmental product standards to ensure a functioning internal market, differentiated integration is growing in importance in EU environmental policy (Holzinger and Knoepfel, 2000; Knill and Liefferink, 2007: 219–22).

EU environmental policy has allowed Member States some flexibility to adapt common environmental policy measures to national contexts during the implementation phase. However, short-term temporal differentiation (different national implementation timescales) and more permanent territorial differentiation (namely that the peculiar national environmental conditions resulted in special rules) were severely constrained by the adoption of uniform emission limits. These limits featured prominently in early EU environmental policy. Only since the 1990s has differentiation played a more prominent role in EU environmental policy.

The next section provides an overview of the theoretical concepts. Section three examines the justifications for EU environmental policy, showing the dynamics of functional and territorial differentiation. Section four examines more closely some of the functional aspects of EU environmental legislation. Section five charts the temporal evolution of environmental policy to gauge how time and policy cycles have shaped differentiated environmental policy integration. The sixth section focuses on the differentiation of policy instruments. The final section contextualizes and analyses differentiation in terms of the three core questions addressed in this edited volume.

Theoretical overview

This chapter draws on institutional approaches to explain the differentiated temporal patterns and on ideationalist approaches to explain functional variation (see Chapter 3 by Kölliker and Chapter 5 by Goetz in this volume). Hall (1993) differentiates policy change into changes of style, content and structure (see also Jordan and Liefferink, 2004). Policy style focuses on standard operating procedures and action-guiding norms which inform EU environmental policy actors. Policy content involves three aspects: 1) the policy goals which are centred on ideas; 2) the instruments for achieving the policy goals; and 3) the precise instrument calibration. Finally, policy structure denotes the institutional and procedural structures to adopt and implement policies. Embedded in these structures are paradigms that inform decision-makers' actions (Hall, 1993: 278–9).

The Member States implement (often at the sub-national level either through state, regional or local authorities) EU environmental policy. In this multi-level environmental governance context, the four key EU institutions (Commission, Council of Ministers, EP and European Court of Justice, ECJ) all play significant roles, which vary between different EU environmental policy-making stages (agenda-setting, formulation, adoption, implementation and revision).

Using Lowi's typology, EU environmental policy is largely regulatory in nature (Lowi, 1964). The lack of significant common budgetary resources meant that the environmental policy's trajectory is the further development of the EU 'regulatory state' (Majone, 1996). There are very limited distributive environmental policy measures, such as the LIFE fund which made available €604m between 2000 and 2004 (Haigh, 2004: 12.1–4). More recently the EU made available moderate funds to save energy (SAVE funds) and to promote renewable energy (ALTENER funds). However, most of the cost burden of EU environmental policy falls on the regulated elements of society.

The supra-national EU institutions have tried to limit regulatory differentiation during the EU environmental policy implementation stage. Since the Amsterdam Treaty, Member States can be fined for failing to comply with ECJ judgements. In 2000, Greece became the first Member State to be fined for repeatedly breaching EU waste legislation. Importantly, the fines allow for considerable differentiation as they are dependent on: 1) the seriousness and duration of the environmental offence; 2) the size of the Member State in terms of population; and 3) the Member State's GDP. Small and/or poor Member States face lower fines for the same (or similar) offence than large and/or rich Member States. Paradoxically, therefore, the attempt to achieve greater harmonization of EU environmental laws during the implementation stage relies on a highly differentiated system of fines for persistent defectors.

Multi-level environmental governance and differentiation

International differentiation

Many environmental problems are trans-national (such as North Sea pollution) or global (such as climate change). EU multi-level environmental governance therefore often reaches outside its borders. Most international environmental treaties signed by the EU (and [some of] its Member States) move environmental governance responsibilities to a spatial level above the supra-national level. International treaties (such as the Aarhus Convention on access to environmental information and justice) have set key elements of the EU's environmental policy agenda (Haigh, 2004:11.5–4; Kellow and Zito, 2002; Zito, 2005). Some international environmental regimes pertain to Europe, such as the Baltic Sea and North Sea Conventions whilst others have a truly global dimension (such as the Kyoto climate change protocol). Listing all the relevant institutions and treaties would be inappropriate in this chapter. Table 18.1 provides only a sample of important international environmental treaties that have been signed and ratified by the EU.

Many international environmental treaties to which the EU has become a signatory have induced some form of functional, temporal and/or territorial differentiation to the EU environmental policy system. For example, only the respective riparian EU Member States became signatories of the Baltic Sea, North Sea and Barcelona Conventions (which were also ratified by non-EU states). As can be seen from Table 18.1, considerable time-lags often exist between the date on which the EU signed up to a particular international environmental treaty and its entry into force.

Early EU environmental policy consisted of a wide range of functionally specific water or air pollution control measures. For instance, there are EU laws that regulate bathing waters, drinking water and water for mussel breeding. However, all EU Member States are subject to the environmental *acquis communitaire;* they cannot opt out of, for example, particular EU water policy measures. EU environmental policy therefore allows for less territorial differentiation than most international environmental treaties. Proposals to create highly differentiated 'optimal regulatory units' (Holzinger, 2000) involving only certain Member States, and excluding others, were unacceptable to EU policy-makers who instead adopted EU-wide environmental standards to ensure a level playing field and to protect the unspoilt environment (Bungarten, 1978; Weale et al., 2000).

Given the single market's importance to European integration, EU membership in the World Trade Organisation (WTO) creates potentially important dynamics. WTO

Table 18.1   Examples of international environmental treaties with EU participation

Treaty	Year in which the EU became a Signatory	Year of Council Decision	Year in which Treaty entered into force in the EU
Barcelona Convention for the Protection of the Mediterranean Sea	1976	1977	1978
Helsinki Convention on the Protection of the Marine Environment of the Baltic Sea Area	1992	1994	2000
OSPAR Convention for the Protection of the Marine Environment of the North-East Atlantic	1992	1997	1998
Long range transboundary air pollution (LRTAP)	1979	1981	1983
Convention on the Protection of the Alps	1991	1996	1996
UN Framework Convention on Climate Change	1992	1993	1994
Kyoto Protocol	1998	2002	2005
Aarhus Convention on Access to Environmental Information, Public Participation in Environmental Decision-making and Access to Justice	1998	2005	2005
Convention on Persistent Organic Pollutants (POP Stockholm Convention)	2001	2004	2004

Source: Adapted from http://ec.europa.eu/environment/international_issues/pdf/agreements_en.pdf.

members can challenge EU environmental policy measures. This dynamic raises an important distinction between environmental product and process standards.

Product standards set emission limits for products (such as car emission limits), while process standards regulate production processes (such as the environmental pollution caused during the automobile production process). The EU has adopted both product and process standards, although agreement on the latter has been significantly more difficult (Scharpf, 1996). The harmonization of Member State environmental product standards has often been justified on the grounds that national environmental product standards create barriers to trade within the internal market. Political disagreement amongst EU Member States about environmental product standards occurred mainly about the stringency levels at which harmonization should occur – that of environmental leader states or the environmental laggard states? Demanding that 'outsiders' (that is, importers) comply with environmentally motivated EU product standards is legal under WTO rules. However, although EU internal process standards do not conflict with WTO rules, their extra-territorial application has been successfully challenged under international trade rules. Applying environmental process standards only on EU-based companies will impose extra costs on domestic firms and may put them at a short-term economic disadvantage *vis-á-vis* firms outside the EU. However, in the long term the more strictly regulated EU-based companies may develop environmental abatement technologies that can be exported, leading to a 'double dividend' in terms of both environmental and economic benefits (see Wurzel et al., 2003).

'High regulatory states' (Héritier et al., 1996), with high levels of environmental regulations, are keen to avoid adaptation costs and therefore try to 'upload' to the EU level their domestic environmental regulations (Börzel, 2002; Hèritier et al., 1996). Vogel (1995) has identified a 'trading-up' dynamic within the EU, which allows the rich, environmentally minded Northern Member States with large markets, such as Germany, to 'ratchet upwards' the EU's environmental product standards to their national level. Similarly, Sbragia (1996) has argued that a 'push–pull' dynamic allows environmental leader states to push for stringent EU environmental standards and pull laggards up to their level of stringency. Consequently, there is a strong linkage between environmental and Single Market policy.

Some EU rules and institutions apply directly to countries that are not Member States. Norway and other European Economic Area (EEA) members accept EU environmental laws, without being represented in its decision-making processes. The European Environmental Agency (EEA) has a membership base which reaches beyond the EU's territory. In addition to the current 27 EU Member States, Iceland, Liechtenstein, Norway, Switzerland and Turkey are full members of the EEA; many Balkan states enjoy cooperative status. However, the EEA's role is limited to the collection and dissemination of environmental information (Schout, 1999).

Differentiation according to policy styles, content and structures

Europeanization has had a differentiated effect on the styles, contents and structures of Member States' environmental policy systems (Jordan and Liefferink, 2004; Weale et al., 2000; Wurzel, 2003). It is widely accepted that the *content* of Member State environmental policies has been most affected by the EU, while national environmental regulatory *styles* and institutional *structures* have been impacted less strongly. However, EU environmental policy has affected significantly the structures of those Member States (such as the Southern and Central/Eastern states) that did not have in place well-developed institutional structures for environmental policy at the time they joined the EU (Laffan, 2004; Weale et al., 2000). Institutional dynamics thus had an intervening effect on differentiated integration.

There are important differences between Northern and Southern states. Southern states have long perceived the bulk of EU environmental legislation as reflecting Northern Member State priorities (Börzel, 2003, 1–2; Weale et al., 2000). They opposed, for example, ambitious uniform emission standards under the so-called Large Combustion Plant Directive; they demanded financial compensation (in the form of increased structural funds) for agreeing to the Single European Act and the Maastricht Treaty, both of which expanded the EU's environmental policy competences (Börzel, 2002, 203–6; Weale et al., 2000, 44–5). However, side payments are rarely used to secure Southern acceptance and implementation of EU environmental legislation. More common is the use of temporal differentiation (namely the granting of extended implementation deadlines) to prevent Southern states from vetoing proposals during the negotiations phase or from acting as free-riders during the implementation phase.

Southern Member States have often complained that their central concerns (such as desertification and water shortages) have a lower EU priority (Weale et al., 2000). Southern and Northern Member States dispute whether such perceptions are more apparent than real, but perceptions matter as they may help build identities that shape the path of differentiated EU integration. There is empirical evidence that some Northern Member States (such as Denmark and Sweden) have overall a better implementation record than some Southern Member States (such as Italy and Greece). However, there are also important differences *within* the groups of Northern and Southern Member States (Börzel et al., 2008). Both Weale and colleagues (2000) and Börzel (2003) have argued that labelling the Southern Member States as environmental laggards is problematic as all Member States have implementation problems.

The 2004 and 2007 enlargements have added a Central/Eastern and a Mediterranean dimension to EU environmental policy, further complicating the spatial divide. Some Central and Eastern accession states have a better record of transposing formally EU environmental Directives into national laws – partly because they had fewer domestic environmental policy measures in place originally. For instance, Slovenia and Estonia completed the transposition process of the Habitats Directive by 2004, while Hungary faced difficulties due to administrative problems (Laffan, 2004). Extended deadlines and transitional arrangements were granted to Central and Eastern states on many EU environmental laws. The EU made available considerable resources for environmental capacity-building to the accession countries, which, however, had to accept the environmental *acquis communitaire* in principle. Nevertheless, the 2004 and 2007 enlargements significantly increased temporal differentiation in EU environmental policy (Holzinger and Knoepfel, 2000; Laffan, 2004).

Environmental leaders and laggards

While acknowledging the above-mentioned limitations, the environmental leader–laggard dimension is a useful heuristic device for capturing territorial differentiation. Environmental leader states have long been identified as drivers behind EU environmental policy (Bungarten, 1978; Rehbinder and Stewart, 1985). There is widespread agreement that Denmark, Germany and the Netherlands composed a 'green trio', which was extended to a 'green sextet' when Austria, Finland and Sweden joined the EU in 1995 (Liefferink and Andersen, 1998; Veenman and Liefferink, 2005; Wurzel, 2008a). Environmental leader and laggard states both try to persuade 'swing' states to join their respective camps. However, Member States' classification as environmental leader, laggard and swing states can vary over time – or even from issue to issue. Environmental leader states are not immune from infringement proceedings (Wurzel, 2008a).

The group of environmental leader states can be differentiated into 'pushers' and 'forerunners' (Liefferink and Andersen, 1998; Veenman and Liefferink, 2005). A pusher will try to 'upload' to the EU level its domestic environmental standards and dominant regulatory philosophy; a forerunner aims to maximize the freedom to develop its national environmental policy. For example, Sweden often tries to set a 'good example' in environmental policy (Liefferink and Andersen, 1998: 74).

Austria, Finland, Sweden (and Norway) held coordination meetings prior to Environmental Council meetings during their accession negotiations. A so-called 'review process' allowed Austria, Finland and Sweden to keep nationally more stringent environmental standards for a period of four years when they joined in 1995. During this transitional period, the EU reviewed its supra-national standards with the aim of increasing them to the level of the three new Member States. This temporal differentiation aimed to facilitate EU accession (see Chapter 3 by Kölliker and Chapter 5 by Goetz in this volume). Eventually the EU raised its common standards to the level of the three new Member States, although it took longer than four years (see Chapter 3). Once Austria, Finland and Sweden had become full EU members, they discontinued their coordination meetings before Environmental Council meetings. They feared that semi-permanent coalitions between (some of) the environmental leader states might antagonize the less environmentally concerned states (Wurzel, 2008a). Sweden made a conscious effort to overcome entrenched positions between environmental leaders and laggards through closer informal contacts with Southern Member States. However, even without formal cooperation arrangements, the six 'green' Member States – Austria, Denmark, Finland, Germany, the Netherlands and Sweden – often adopt similar positions in Environmental Council negotiations.

Semi-permanent coalitions of environmental leaders across a wide range of environmental issues do not exist on the EU level (Rehbinder and Stewart, 1985: 263; Wurzel, 2008a). Instead, 'they have to be formed on an issue-by-issue basis and remain liable to defection' (Liefferink and Andersen, 1998: 262; Veenman and Liefferink, 2005). One reason for the lack of a coherent environmental 'core group' is that EU's environmental leader states exhibit different preferences in terms of environmental regulatory philosophies and policy instruments (Andersen and Liefferink, 1997). For example, Germany has long held a preference for uniform emission limits derived from the best available technology (BAT) principle (Weale, 1992; Wurzel, 2002). Until the mid-1990s, the Netherlands and Sweden also favoured BAT-derived uniform emission limits. However, more recently Dutch and Swedish governments have emphasized the need for more cost-effective policy instruments. As explained below, Germany (together with Austria) initially opposed the EU emissions trading scheme for reducing greenhouse gas emissions (GHGE); Denmark, the Netherlands and Sweden (as well as Britain) strongly pushed for the adoption of this novel market-based policy instrument on cost-effectiveness grounds.

The Nice Treaty introduced the possibility of enhanced cooperation, which would allow the formal introduction of differentiated European integration

(Holzinger, 2000). However, enhanced cooperation has not been applied to environmental policy for the following two main reasons. First, many EU environmental policy measures are based on the internal market Treaty provisions which allow only for limited differentiation. During the accession negotiations the Finnish and Swedish governments argued that the internal market Treaty provisions contain an 'environmental guarantee', enabling environmental leader states to retain and/or adopt more stringent domestic standards (Liefferink and Andersen, 1998). However, the ECJ has set narrow parameters (such as proportionality) for justifying more stringent national standards on the basis of the internal market provisions. Second, more stringent national environmental standards usually impose higher costs on the forerunners, at least in the short term. Governments in environmental leader states with significant industrial interests (such as Germany) were therefore often faced with influential corporate actors. These interests opposed the unilateral adoption of more ambitious environmental standards while demanding a level playing field, namely ambitious uniform EU-wide emission limits.

The EU's failure to adopt a supra-national carbon dioxide/energy tax, which the Commission had formally proposed in 1992 (Zito, 2000), led like-minded Member States (and some non-EU states) to arrange informal meetings between Environmental and Finance Ministry officials and Ministers during the period 1994–8. Most of the pro-eco-tax Member States involved favoured adopting an EU-wide eco-tax over the introduction of coordinated national eco-taxes: the former solution would have avoided concentrating the costs in the forerunner group while allowing other states to free-ride. The momentum behind the eco-tax group dissipated over time, particularly when the EU adopted measures to set a floor for Member State taxes on energy products.

Functional dynamics and policy justifications

As mentioned above, one important justification of the EU's early environmental activism was that different national product standards threatened the internal market's functioning, while trans-national environmental problems often created negative externalities. Polluter states often externalized the cost for pollution abatement technologies: an example is Britain's high-chimney policy, which minimized local pollution but triggered pollution in other countries (Weale, 1992). From the early 1970s onwards, environmental leader states such as Germany and the Netherlands (but also others such as France, which was a high regulatory state that adopted a large number of relatively modest environmental measures) started to adopt an increasing number of national environmental laws; these triggered Commission harmonization proposals (Héritier et al., 1996; Rehbinder and Stewart, 1985; Wurzel, 2008a).

Environmental regulatory competition has been a major driver for adopting EU environmental legislation (Héritier et al., 1996). Within the Environmental Council, environmental pioneers often took the lead on a given issue while pushing for a Commission proposal and Council decision (Liefferink and Andersen, 1998).

Environmental pusher states tried to export their national standards to the EU level, in order to minimize adjustment costs and to impose similar regulatory costs on fellow Member States (Börzel, 2002; Héritier et al., 1996; Knill, 2001).

The economic 'level playing field' argument (advanced by 'high regulatory' states) also partly drove the adoption of harmonized environmental process standards (Héritier et al,, 1996). It is nevertheless surprising that EU Member States adopted unanimously more than 100 environmental policy measures prior to the 1987 SEA, which created the first explicit Treaty base for a common environmental policy (Haigh, 2004).

Temporal evolution

Wurzel (2008a) (adapting Hildebrand, 1992) identified five distinctive EU environmental policy phases: 1) 1958–72: Infancy; 2) 1972–87: Adolescence; 3) 1987–92: Maturity; 4) 1992–2005: Sedateness; 5) 2005 onwards: Selective Activism. The early phases consisted of narrowly focused, detailed environmental legislation, which had a strong harmonization effect on Member States (Haigh, 2004). These policy measures imposed substantial costs on Member States but also achieved significant, discernible environmental benefits. The problems of achieving a consensus between diverging Member State interests led to differentiation in early common environmental legislation, which was riddled with exemptions, extended deadlines and vague obligations that were wide open to interpretation (Holzinger, 2000; Wurzel, 2008a). Moreover, there was considerable differentiation during the implementation stage. Holzinger (2000: 81) has therefore argued that early EU environmental policy was characterized by 'harmonization illusion'. However, greater differentiation (in terms of policy content, style and instruments) has been introduced into EU environmental policy only since the early 1990s. This reflects the temporal changes in the environmental policy sector that follow an evolving sequential pattern and has an independent differentiation effect (see Chapter 5 by Goetz in this volume).

Before 1972, common environmental policy measures, such as the directive on dangerous substances, were adopted in an incidental manner (Bungarten, 1978). In 1969, a legally non-binding Information and Standstill Agreement (the 'Standstill Agreement') was adopted. It required member governments to inform the Commission about draft national legislation with a potential internal market impact.

EU environmental policy moved into its adolescence after it was sparked by the 1972 United Nations (UN) Stockholm conference on the environment (Bungarten, 1978). A few months after the UN conference, EU Member State environmental ministers agreed that common environmental policy proposals could be justified with reference to either: 1) the Standstill Agreement; 2) existing Treaty provisions (that is, mainly the internal market provisions that allowed for the harmonization of national standards which threatened the functioning of the internal market); and, 3) legally non-binding Environmental Action Programmes (EAPs). In 1973, the Standstill Agreement was amended to include draft national environmental laws. It induced a 'follow-the-leader' effect: 'Strongly environmentalist Member States were more or less able to set the pace and direction for Community action by unilaterally proposing strong national environmental legislation, which forced the Community to react with measures of its own' (Rehbinder and Stewart, 1985: 17).

The Rome Treaty included a (differentiation) provision allowing Member States to adopt more stringent environmental standards in cases of public emergencies/catastrophes. However, this provision has been interpreted very restrictively. In contrast, the Rome Treaty's internal market provision for harmonizing national laws became the most important legal base for EU environmental policy prior to the SEA. However, exemptions and extended deadlines were often hidden in footnotes or drafted in such a way that only 'insiders' could comprehend easily the implications for differentiated integration. More implicit differentiated integration was allowed through the use of vague terms that were wide open to interpretation during the implementation phase. For example, the bathing water directive (76/160/EEC) defined bathing waters as waters in which bathing is 'authorised or not prohibited and is traditionally practiced by a large number of bathers'. The British government interpreted the wording 'large number' in such a way that for several years Britain identified fewer bathing waters than landlocked Luxembourg (Wurzel, 2002: 208–9).

The 1987 SEA marked the beginning of the mature phase, introducing explicit environmental Treaty provisions and qualified majority voting (QMV) for the revised internal market harmonization provisions. The late 1980s also saw a growing ideational recognition that a serious implementation gap had occurred in EU environmental policy. The Commission, as the guardian of the Treaties, has had to rely substantially on environmental NGOs (ENGOs) as whistleblowers to find out about breaches. However, ENGO activity levels vary significantly across Member States (Mazey and Richardson, 1993; Wurzel, 2002: 146). In the early 1990s, British ENGOs issued the largest number of complaints about alleged EU environmental non-implementation.

The debate about the subsidiarity principle, which became important after the Danish 'no' to the Maastricht Treaty in 1992, marked the sedate stage. Britain and France composed a 'hit list' proposing the repatriation of more than 100 EU laws, including 24 environmental laws (Wurzel, 2002). The repatriation of such a high number of common environmental laws would have triggered a significantly higher degree of differentiation in EU environmental policy. Although the EU scrapped none of the environmental laws on the hit list, the Commission's Directorate General (DG) for Environment shifted its preference for ambitious detailed regulations that stipulate emission limits derived from the BAT principle towards more flexible framework directives, cost-effectiveness appraisals and procedural measures (Héritier et al., 1996; Knill and Lenschow, 2000; Knill, 2001; Wurzel, 2008a). The sedate phase therefore saw a shift in the Commission's preferred style, guiding norms and policy instruments. There was a move from detailed emission limits derived from the BAT principle towards environmental quality objectives (EQOs), cost-effectiveness considerations and procedural measures. The latter allowed greater Member State discretion, which coincided with EU environmental policy's transition from a mature phase into a defensive and reorientation phase. However, as explained below, there has been only a very moderate uptake of non-regulatory and/or market-based environmental policy instruments.

The most high-profile environmental issue and most important differentiated integration development during the selective activist phase is the EU adoption of a leadership position in international climate change politics (Zito, 2005). This role includes supporting a legally binding post-Kyoto Protocol agreement to reduce significantly GHGE. Partly to retain international leadership credibility, the EU had to adopt an emissions trading scheme initially opposed by certain Member States, including Germany. European Council meetings in 2007 and 2009 (under German and French EU Presidencies) reaffirmed the EU's leadership ambitions in international climate change policy, adopting ambitious GHGE reduction and renewable energy targets for 2020.

At the beginning of the Kyoto protocol negotiations the EU proposed a collective 15 per cent GHGE reduction (by 2012 compared to 1990 levels) conditional on its main economic competitors (that is, the USA and Japan) accepting similar goals. However, the EU eventually settled for an eight per cent GHGE reduction target by 2012. The 1997 Kyoto protocol endorsed the three flexible mechanisms: 1) emissions trading; 2) clean development mechanism (CDM), granting developed countries emission reduction units if they sponsor certified GHGE reduction projects in the developing world; and 3) joint implementation (JI) which allows certain countries jointly to implement GHGE projects. Some EU Member States (especially Germany) strongly opposed the flexible mechanisms and emissions trading in particular (Wurzel, 2008b). However, to keep the USA in the international climate change negotiations, the EU finally accepted the flexible mechanisms while insisting that at least half of each country's GHGE reduction target be achieved through domestic reduction measures.

To implement its collective eight per cent GHGE reduction target, the EU-15 Member States adopted a highly differentiated internal 'burden-sharing' agreement (later renamed 'effort-sharing' agreement) in June 1998. Table 18.2 shows the agreement's highly variable reduction targets, which allow the cohesion countries (Greece, Ireland, Portugal and Spain) significant increases in GHGE while Luxembourg, Denmark, Germany and the United Kingdom have to achieve major cuts.

In 2005 a decentralized EU emissions trading scheme became operational. It allocates emission allowances to companies, which can buy and sell the allowances on the market. As explained below, after a difficult start the EU emissions trading scheme sparked further differentiation concerning the attainment of the collective GHGE target.

Policy instruments

Changes in policy instrument usage reflect increased differentiation since the 1990s – a reality seen more broadly in EU legal integration (see Chapter 3 by Kölliker in this volume). Hall's (1993) distinction between the instrument and its calibration matters here. The EU has established a policy instrument mix, giving Member States (and their societal actors) varying degrees of flexibility in the attainment of environmental objectives. This chapter follows a widely used four-fold categorization of policy instruments: 1) traditional 'command-and-control'

Table 18.2   EU 'burden-sharing' agreement

Member State	Greenhouse gas emission reduction target in percentages under the EU burden-sharing agreement
Austria	−13
Belgium	−7.5
Denmark	−21
Finland	0
France	0
Germany	−21
Greece	+25
Ireland	+13
Luxembourg	−28
Netherlands	−6
Portugal	+27
Spain	+15
Sweden	+4
United Kingdom	−12.5

Note: All reduction targets refer to 1990 as base year.
Source: Adaped from www.eea.europa.eu/themes/climate.

regulation; 2) market-based instruments (such as emissions trading); 3) voluntary agreements; and 4) informational and self-organizing instruments, like eco-labels (Holzinger and Knill, 2003; Jordan et al., 2005, 2007).

One important example of market-based policy instrument differentiation is the EU emissions trading scheme. However, target differentiation was occasionally already adopted under command-and-control policy instruments. The Large Combustion Plant Directive set different sulphur dioxide emission reduction targets (Weale et al., 2000) while much of the early car emission legislation was optional (that is, it obliged Member States to allow the sale of cars which complied with the EU legislation without forcing them to adopt the common standards on the national level) and/or differentiated emission standards according to engine size (Wurzel, 2002).

The EU environmental policy bedrock is traditional legislation consisting of Regulations, Directives and Decisions. The most prevalent instrument, the Directive, is binding on Member States 'as to the result to be achieved' but leaves open the form of implementation. Member States are obliged to transpose Directives into national legislation and then implement them within a stipulated deadline. The EU has also agreed a number of Regulations, which are directly applicable without the need for further national laws. The same is true for Decisions, which are mainly utilized for implementing international environmental treaty obligations.

Since the sedate phase many EU environmental laws have become less detailed and prescriptive (Héritier et al., 1996). In 2002, the Commission explicitly asserted the need to 'avoid making its legislative proposals unwieldy, in accordance with the Protocol on the application of the principles of subsidiarity and proportionality' (CEC, 2002, 12). Consequently, framework directives (such as the water framework directive) and procedural measures (such as integrated pollution and prevention control) have featured increasingly.

EU-level demand for new environmental policy instruments (NEPIs), covering the market-based, voluntary and informational categories, has increased considerably, although the actual NEPI uptake has remained limited (Holzinger and Knill, 2003; Jordan et al., 2005, 2007). EU environmental policy comprises more than 1000 pieces of regulation, a dozen voluntary agreements, a flagging eco-label system, and a GHGE trading scheme. It has no common eco-taxes (Haigh, 2004; Jordan et al., 2005, 2007).

One important reason for the EU's particular policy instrument mix is institutional path dependency: the EU lacks the Treaty-based authority to adopt certain types of NEPIs (voluntary agreements) and/or requires unanimity in the face of continued Member State opposition (supra-national eco-taxes). Concerns about national environmental standards acting as trade barriers within the internal market, and the desire by high-regulatory Member States to create a level playing field, produced a relatively large number of EU environmental harmonization laws. Demands for market-based instruments have increased as cost-effectiveness considerations have become more important while EU environmental policy has matured.

Considerable differentiation exists between the Member States' environmental policy instrument mixes (Jordan et al., 2005, 2007). For example, voluntary agreements play a very important role only within the Dutch and German national environmental policy instrument mixes. However, while Dutch voluntary agreements usually constitute formally negotiated covenants that can be enforced through the courts, German (and Austrian) voluntary agreements are all non-binding although they are often adopted in the 'shadow of the law' (see Wurzel et al., 2003). Depending on the wider institutional context, there can be considerable differentiation in the use of the same type of policy instrument.

Conclusion

There has been a distinctive temporal differentiation in EU environmental policy. Early EU environmental policy phases were characterized by an attempt to achieve a relatively high degree of harmonization as regards environmental policy content and style, although Member States' environmental policy structures were affected to a much lesser degree. A moderate degree of differentiated integration occurred in the selection and calibration of policy instruments.

EU environmental policy was initially characterized by a relatively low degree of formally recognized differentiated integration because many of the early common environmental laws stipulated uniform emission limits and were based on market harmonization Treaty provisions. However, informal differentiation (in the form of exemptions, extended deadlines, vague obligations and incomplete implementation) was relatively common. Since the early 1990s, demands have increased for the formal recognition of a much greater degree of differentiation in EU environmental policy. The most important drivers for increased environmental integration include: 1) the maturing of EU environmental policy, which had led to diminishing margins of return in the use of traditional environmental regulation that had relied heavily on uniform emission limits; 2) the recognition of a serious implementation gap, which led to the adoption of a differentiated system of fines and a search for more flexible NEPIs and procedural measures in the hope that they might be more effective than traditional regulation; 3) the EU becoming a signatory of a growing number of highly differentiated international environmental treaties, some of which (such as the Kyoto climate change protocol) demanded the adoption of flexible instruments; 4) increased international economic competition, which triggered a search for more cost-effective environmental policy solutions; and 5) the various enlargements, which increased differentiation in terms of ecological diversity but also greater economic disparities and thus national abilities to pay for environmental protection. Short-term temporal environmental differentiation and EU-funded environment capacity-building has allowed Southern and Eastern accession states to accept the relatively ambitious environmental *acquis communitaire*. These differentiated policy measures have helped to reduce territorial differentiation (North versus South versus East) and allowed the EU to conduct successive rounds of accessions while maintaining relatively ambitious common environmental standards.

Neo-liberal ideology, which perceived environmental regulation mainly in terms of a cost burden to industry, became dominant in the 1990s. At a time when the principle of subsidiarity was in the ascendance, it pushed EU environmental policy onto the defensive. However, attempts to repatriate many EU environmental policy measures and thus allow for greater differentiation amongst Member State environmental policies largely failed because of concerns about 'environmental' barriers to trade within the internal market. Moreover, EU environmental policy has long been one of the most popular common policies. The popularity of EU environmental policy counteracts centrifugal tendencies and highly differentiated arrangements because ENGOs and European citizens often demand the same level of environmental protection across all Member States. It has allowed the EU to maintain a considerable number of regulatory tools despite concerns about costs and international competition. The strong public support for a common environmental policy has increased the EU's legitimacy, which helps to explain the EU's leadership ambitions in international environmental politics. In order to maintain its leadership position in international climate change politics, however, the EU had to adopt the world's first supra-national emissions trading scheme. This is a flagship policy instrument which will further increase differentiation in EU environmental policy.

19

The 'Area of Freedom, Security and Justice': 'Schengen' Europe, Opt-outs, Opt-ins and Associates*

Jörg Monar

The domain of EU justice and home affairs (JHA), which since the Treaty of Amsterdam has been regrouped under the treaty objective of creating an 'area of freedom, security and justice' (AFSJ),[1] is probably the most rapidly expanding EU policy-making area of this decade.[2] It is also one of the leading competitors for the doubtful distinction of having developed one of the highest degrees of differentiation. On the surface there is a similarity between differentiated integration in the JHA domain and in European economic governance (see Chapter 15 by Dyson in this volume). In both cases there is currently an inner core with lower degrees of participation surrounding it. Yet the forms that differentiation has taken in the JHA domain, its functions, and its space and time dimensions, are rather different. There are also particular dimensions of complexity.

Not only does the AFSJ cover six fairly distinct fields of policy-making – asylum, immigration, border controls, judicial cooperation in civil matters, police cooperation and judicial cooperation in criminal matters. Also, those fields are divided – and affected – by the artificial 'pillar divide' between the first four, which have been 'communitarized' in the framework of Title IV TEC, and the last two, which remain in the more 'intergovernmental' framework of Title VI TEU. To complicate matters further, the Schengen *acquis*, which grew out of compensatory measures for the abolition of controls at internal borders and still constitutes the inner core of the AFSJ, stretches well across the borderlines of the 'pillars', but comprises only part of the current JHA *acquis* under both of the 'pillars'.

The only slightly less complex aspect of differentiation in this policy-making domain is that of the actors. Mainly because responses to internal security and illegal immigration risks as well as the administration of justice have traditionally been exclusive preserves of central governments, there is so far no significant involvement of sub-national or non-governmental actors in the emergence and development of differentiation within the AFSJ. The AFSJ remains essentially a political space for governments and ministries – and for the EU institutions within the limits of their respective treaty assigned roles.

In order to provide a basis for the subsequent analysis of differentiation in the JHA domain, this chapter starts with a survey of the main forms of differentiation inside and outside of the AFSJ. It will then assess the 'deepening' and the 'widening' functions of this differentiation, proceed to an analysis of the space and time dimensions, and finish with an assessment of the impact of differentiation on the development of the AFSJ as a major integration project.

The different types of differentiation within the AFSJ

The 'opt-outs'

Three Member States have been granted opt-outs from substantial parts of the AFSJ on the basis of Protocols annexed to the EU and the EC Treaties by the Treaty of Amsterdam: the UK, Ireland and Denmark. Protocol No. 3[3] guarantees to the UK the continuation of its right to exercise controls on persons at its borders to other Member States and grants to the UK and Ireland a derogation from the Schengen *acquis* to continue the special arrangements between them for maintaining the 'Common travel area'. As a result Ireland and the UK are exempted from the Schengen *acquis* relating to the Schengen border control system and, in particular, the abolition of controls on persons at internal borders, arguably one of the most important principles of the AFSJ. Protocol No. 4[4] grants the two countries a complete opt-out also from the communitarized fields under Title IV EC. Protocol No. 5,[5] finally, grants Denmark a similar opt-out from Title IV TEC as the one of Ireland and the UK, but with specific provisions on opting-in possibilities which take into account the special position of Denmark as a Schengen member not wishing to be bound by 'communitarized' Schengen measures. As a result of the three Protocols, therefore, three Member States can in principle stay completely outside of the 'first pillar' part of the AFSJ. Yet such a complete self-exclusion could obviously deprive them from participating in measures of benefit to them, so that it was part of the 'Amsterdam deal' to provide for possibilities to opt-in (see below).

The Treaty of Lisbon marks in a sense the beginning of a second phase of opt-out evolution within the AFSJ as it not only fully maintains the existing opt-outs but extends the ones provided for by current Protocols (4) and (5) – with a number of procedural changes and slight variations[6] – from the current 'first pillar' JHA fields to the 'third pillar' fields of police and judicial cooperation in criminal matters. This concession had to be made to make Denmark, Ireland and the UK accept the 'communitarization' (in all but name) of the Title VI TEU fields within the framework of new Title V of Part 3 TFEU with the introduction of qualified majority voting and co-decision by the European Parliament.

The 'opt-in' possibilities

Article 3 of the aforementioned Protocol No. 4 gives Ireland and the UK an opt-in possibility as regards any measure proposed under Title IV TEC at the latest three months after it has been proposed. Even if they decide not to opt-in at this stage, they can do this later by virtue of Article 4, subject to the approval of the Commission. In addition, Article 8 of the same Protocol grants Ireland the possibility to opt-out from the entire Protocol – a sort of opt-out from the opt-out. Both Ireland and the UK have therefore an opt-out status from Title IV TEC which is combined with a selective opt-in possibility. Denmark has also been given an opt-in possibility, but the Danish case is more complicated because its status as a Schengen member means it normally has to adopt all Schengen-related measures under Title IV TEC. Article 5 of Protocol No. 5 deals with this problem by giving Denmark six months to decide whether it will implement any Council decision building on the Schengen *acquis* in its national law. Whenever Denmark does so, this decision only creates an obligation under international law between Denmark and the other Member States. This is one of the most peculiar arrangements of the whole EU legal system because it effectively gives Denmark an *opt-out* from the specific obligations of the EC legal order although the measures in question are EC legal acts.[7] The special arrangements for Denmark are completed by an *opt-out* from the *opt-out* possibility, similar to the Irish one. The Treaty of Lisbon extends all these *opt-in* possibilities to the new extension of the existing *opt-outs* to police and judicial cooperation in criminal matters.

The opting-in possibilities provide the opt-outs in practice with a high degree of flexibility in the respective areas. Not only can they decide to opt-in during the decision-making stage but also – if they change their mind – later after the other Member States have adopted the measure. While their votes are not counted if they have not decided to opt-in before the formal adoption in the Council, they fully count in case of a declared opt-in, and in any case they participate in all the Council deliberations irrespective of any opt-in decision. In practice this 'pick-and-choose' option has been extensively made use of, with the UK and Ireland, for instance, having opted into most proposals concerning asylum, illegal immigration and civil law, but only very few concerning visas, borders and legal migration.[8] In a sense the opting-in possibilities have a strong incentive side to them as the opt-outs have to ask themselves with every new legal measure coming up for adoption whether they would not be better off by opting-in, something which would not be the case with a simple complete opt-out. This can result in some complex domestic debates, as was recently shown in the case of UK participation in the 2008 'Rome I Regulation' (EC No 593/2008) on the law applicable to contractual obligations. In this case the British government first decided not to opt-in, then had second thoughts followed by a public consultation,[9] and finally opted-in after all.

The 'enhanced cooperation' possibilities

The existing *opt-outs* indicate that differences between the Member States over the nature and scope of the AFSJ as an integration project can be too substantial for them to agree on the basis of certain shared objectives. In order to prevent this from becoming an obstacle to further policy development in the AFSJ domain, the Amsterdam Treaty negotiations led to the introduction of 'enhanced cooperation' as an option for a group of Member States to go ahead with certain JHA measures. Articles 11 TEC and 40 EU enable such an 'avant-garde' group of Member States to establish an enhanced cooperation under both Title IV EC and Title VI TEU and to fully use EC/EU institutions and procedures in this context. Article 43 TEU, however, provides that such cooperation must be a) aimed at 'furthering the objectives of the EU'; b) respect the existing Treaty and institutional framework; and c) may only be undertaken as a measure 'of last resort'. There is a whole range of other conditions attached to it, such as a minimum of participating Member States, openness to all Member States and respect of the interests of those not participating. The Schengen system constitutes, formally, the first case of such a differentiated form of integration in the JHA domain,[10] although it was obviously established well before the Amsterdam Treaty (Papagianni, 2001). Otherwise this instrument has not been used so far, although its potential application has on a few occasions been used to put pressure on Member States. The Belgian Presidency of the second half of 2001, for instance, hinted at a potential use of enhanced cooperation in case the Italian government would not lift its isolated objections against elements of the Framework Decision on the European Arrest Warrant.

As in the case of the opt-outs, the Treaty of Lisbon not only maintains existing 'enhanced cooperation' possibilities (Articles 20 TEU–Lisbon and 326–334 TFEU) but further enhances their differentiation potential. The new Treaty provides in fact for a quasi 'automatic' establishment of 'enhanced cooperation' in the AFSJ in a number of cases. As regards the adoption of directives establishing minimum rules regarding criminal procedure (Article 82(3) TFEU), and establishing minimum rules concerning the definition of criminal offences (Article 83(3) TFEU), a Member State which considers that the draft directive act may affect fundamental aspects of its criminal justice system may request a suspension of the ordinary legislative procedure and the referral of this act to the European Council.[11] If the European Council does not reach an agreement within four months, a group of at least nine Member States can simply notify Council, Commission and the European Parliament (EP) that they intend to adopt it by way of an enhanced cooperation. Of equal significance are the new possibilities for a group of at least nine Member States to apply a similar procedure if unanimity cannot be reached with regard to the establishment of a European Public Prosecutor's Office (Article 86(1) TFEU) and with regard to measures relating to operational cooperation between police forces (Article 87(3) TFEU).[12] In both cases the 9+ group can refer the measure to the European Council. If the European Council fails to reach an agreement within four months, the group can again simply notify the institutions of their wish to proceed with the respective measure on the basis of enhanced cooperation.

In a sense the enhanced cooperation possibilities are just another – although potentially more constructive – variation of the logic of pursuing separate interests within the AFSJ which also forms the basis of the opt-outs: whereas in the case of the opt-outs certain Member States have reserved themselves the right to participate only in those (further) measures developing the AFSJ which they consider to be in their interest, enhanced cooperation offers groups of Member States the chance to propose[13] and proceed with certain common measures even if their interest in them is not shared by the others.

The Schengen 'Association' status

A special aspect of differentiation within the AFSJ is that three non-EU countries, Iceland, Norway and Switzerland, have concluded Association Agreements with the EU on their participation in the Schengen border control system which provide for the abolition of controls on persons at internal borders between them and the EU

Schengen Member States and the implementation by those countries of most of the Schengen *acquis*.[14] As a result Iceland and Norway have been part of the *Schengenland* area since 25 March 2001 and Switzerland has been fully part since 29 March 2009. By virtue of a Protocol signed on 28 February 2008 between the European Union, the European Community, Switzerland and the Principality of Liechtenstein,[15] the last is 'associated' with Switzerland's 'association' with the implementation, application and development of the Schengen *acquis*. As a result a substantial part of the *acquis* of the AFSJ has been extended to four non-Member States while two Member States, the UK and Ireland, still enjoy an opt-out from the core part of the *acquis*.

Iceland and Norway were included in the Schengen system as a result of the accession of Denmark, Finland and Sweden to Schengen in order not to disrupt the *Nordic* Passport Union between the Scandinavian countries. Also, both countries saw security and migration control advantages in their participation in the Schengen system. The same advantages played a key role in Switzerland's decision – followed by Liechtenstein – to seek a similar inclusion. There is, however, a political price which the 'associates' have to pay for their inclusion in the Schengen system without being members of the EU. As Schengen 'associates' they have to implement all the legal *acquis* of the Schengen system – including applicable financial requirements – without having formal decision-making powers in the Council of the EU. According to the formula of 'decision-shaping rather than decision-making' provided for by the Association Agreements, they can participate in those parts of the JHA Council meetings which deal with Schengen items (so-called 'mixed' agenda items) and express their views on proposed measures. However, if it comes to their formal adoption, only the EU Schengen Member States have voting rights (Cullen, 2001).

The complications generated by the Schengen 'association' status do not end here. Because of the Schengen opt-out of Ireland and the UK separate legal arrangements had to be negotiated on the rights and obligations between those two Member States and the 'associates'. These provide, in particular, for a special consultation of the 'associates' in case the opt-outs exercise their right to an opt-in resulting from the opt-out and the legal implications of any already existing or future British and Irish opt-in into Schengen measures.[16]

JHA-related differentiation outside of the AFSJ

Historically, one can almost speak about a 'tradition' of JHA-related differentiation outside of the framework of the EC/EU Treaties because that is where the all-important Schengen system – whose 'exile' ended in 1999 – came from (see below). This tradition has in recent years been revitalized by some Member States which – frustrated by the lack of progress on some issues and seeking a higher collective impact on the shaping of EU JHA policies – have formed groups outside of the EU/AFSJ legal and institutional framework to engage in closer cooperation with the objective of achieving progress with regard to general AFSJ objectives. There are in fact quite a few groupings of European countries in which JHA-related matters are more or less regularly discussed, but only two of those have systematically focused on the AFSJ agenda development:

The first is the so-called 'G6-Group' which originated in 2003 out of discussions between the British Home Secretary David Blunkett and French Interior Minister Nicolas Sarkozy to organize at regular intervals meetings between the interior ministers of the biggest Member States. The purpose was to exchange views on topical JHA issues and to develop common positions which could then be pursued more effectively inside of the EU framework. France, Germany, Italy and Spain formed the initial 'G5-Group', which became the 'G6' after the joining of Poland (which had resented its initial exclusion) in 2006. The Group is based on an informal arrangement between the interior ministries and not on any legally binding text or permanent institutional structure. The (normally) two annual meetings of the interior ministers held in the country of the (rotating) presiding minister tend to focus on cross-border law enforcement and illegal immigration issues of common concern.[17] Although substantial common positions have been rare, the informal discussions and their common conclusions have occasionally facilitated compromise-building on some EU measures in the EU Council because of the collective weight of the six Member States. Overall the impact of the Group has remained limited, not only because any real progress can only be obtained through the normal EU procedures, but also because the G6 has often disagreed on substantive issues.

The second of the 'outside' differentiation frameworks is the so-called 'Prüm Convention', which originated in 2004 with meetings at ministerial and senior official level aimed at establishing closer forms of cross-border cooperation between a group of Schengen countries. The Prüm Convention was signed on 27 May 2005 by Belgium, Germany, Spain, France, Luxembourg, the Netherlands and Austria with the declared objective of playing a 'pioneering role' in cross-border law enforcement cooperation, especially in the sphere of exchange of information for the purpose of combatting terrorism, cross-border crime and illegal migration.[18] In line with these objectives the Prüm Convention, which is open to all EU Member States, establishes rules for automated access to, and transfer of, DNA profiles, dactyloscopic data and certain national vehicle registration data, as well as for the supply of data in connection with major events with a cross-border dimension (such as sporting events) and the prevention of terrorist offences. It also introduces rules for stepping up cross-border police cooperation through joint patrols and other joint operations. While ratification of the Convention was under way, a steadily increasing number of other Member States, starting with Finland and Portugal in June 2006, declared their accession to the Convention. This political momentum of support was then effectively used by the 2007 German Presidency to secure political agreement in the Council in June 2007 on the incorporation of most of the Prüm Convention provision into the EU *acquis* by way of a special Council Decision which – after further delays – was adopted on 23 June 2008.[19]

Officially presented as a major breakthrough in a field where progress within the AFSJ is notoriously difficult because of the unanimity requirement in the Council, the Prüm Convention cooperation can in fact only be regarded as a qualified success as far as the AFSJ is concerned. Not all of the Prüm Convention provisions were accepted by the EU Member States in the Council,[20] the European Data Protection Supervisor identified serious shortcomings,[21] and the – at least initial – bypassing of the EU framework and its procedures has attracted severe criticism from various quarters[22]. In addition, the Prüm Group – 'diluted' by the joining of the other Member States – has not emerged as a 'core group' regarding any other JHA issues.

In terms of political and legal importance neither the G6 nor the Prüm Group are in any way comparable to the aforementioned forms of differentiated integration within the AFSJ. Such cooperation frameworks outside of the Treaties may well be able to play an occasional role in facilitating or – in favourable circumstances – even initiating developments within the AFSJ. However, as the formalization of any progress depends on the applicable EU-procedures and the political dynamics involving all Member States, such forms of differentiation can overall be regarded as a *quantité négligeable* in terms of their effective impact on the JHA domain.

Differentiation as an instrument of 'deepening'

The 'deepening' function of the Schengen differentiation

Differentiation was first brought into the JHA domain by the original five Schengen countries. With the signing of the Schengen Agreement on 14 June 1985 on the abolition of controls on persons at internal borders, France, Germany and the three Benelux countries took the decisive step towards implementing an objective which – with the support of the Commission and the European Parliament – they had tried in vain to achieve inside of the European Economic Community's free movement remit. The opposition of several Member States – most prominently by the UK – blocked the path to what the governments of the five countries regarded as an important progress for both political integration – the removal of physical borderlines between the peoples of Europe – and economic integration – the removal of the obstacles systematic border controls (with their queues) posed to the free movement of goods and services. Hence the Schengen founders clearly perceived themselves as the *avant-garde* of a 'deepening' of European integration in these respects, affirming on top of the Preamble to the 1985 Agreement that:

> the ever closer union of the peoples of the Member States of the European Communities should find its expression in the freedom to cross internal borders for all nationals of the Member States and in the free movement of goods and services.[23]

Right from the start the Schengen system was destined to be integrated into the European Community as soon as politically possible. The clearest indication can be found in the 1990 'Convention implementing the Schengen Agreement' (CISA), whose Preamble explicitly refers to the EC Treaty objective of an internal market without internal frontiers and which rules out any application incompatible with Community law (Article 134) and any non-Community Member State from becoming a party to the Convention (Article 140).[24]

There can therefore be no doubt that this first framework of differentiation in the JHA domain was driven by a forceful rationale of 'deepening', with the development of the Schengen system outside of the EC Treaty framework being regarded as a temporary device to make progress towards the 'deepening' objective of abolishing controls on persons at internal borders.

The 'spill-over' effect generated by the abolition of controls at internal borders played a major role in strengthening the Schengen system. During the 1990s the Schengen 'compensatory measures' developed a dynamic of their own, extending well beyond border control and surveillance aspects into asylum, immigration, visa, police and judicial cooperation issues and generating until the final incorporation of Schengen around 3000 pages of legal *acquis*.[25] This in turn increased the attractiveness of the Schengen system for non-participating Member States. If some of those were already attracted by the political (and economic) benefits of joining the 'border-free' Schengen zone, the laborious but eventually successful efforts of the Schengen group not only to achieve their objective but also to put into place measures of an interest well beyond the border control issue[26] served as an increasingly powerful magnet. As a result more and more of the other EC/EU Member States acceded to Schengen until, with the accession of Finland and Sweden on 19 December 1996, only Ireland and the UK remained outside.

The incontestable success of the Schengen group both in developing its cooperation and in expanding its membership increased the pressure on the British (and Irish) delegations in the Amsterdam Treaty negotiations in 1996–7 not to oppose any longer their countries' incorporation of the Schengen system. In the final phase of the negotiations the Blair government finally accepted its incorporation after having traded this concession for the rather advantageous 'opt-out/opt-in' arrangements described above (Best, 2002). The consequent 'Protocol integrating the Schengen acquis into the framework of the European Union'[27] required some structural and legal adjustments – such as the distribution of the Schengen *acquis* between the 'first' and 'third' pillar parts of the AFSJ[28] – and the sorting-out of the details of the above-described Schengen 'association' status. Yet in the end the Schengen group was finally able to vindicate the 'deepening' role that it had always claimed for itself with the full incorporation on 1 May 1999 of its *acquis* into the EC and EU Amsterdam Treaty framework. Not only was the original objective of abolishing controls at internal borders achieved, but through the range of 'compensatory' measures Schengen also generated a substantial *acquis* in a range of other JHA fields on which the development of the AFSJ continued to build. The current EU visa policy – which is essentially a 'Schengen policy' – is one of the foremost examples.[29]

Considering this success story one has to take into account, however, that Schengen benefited from a unique advantage. When it was launched in 1985, the Community had no real JHA dimension, so that Schengen could develop its substantial JHA *acquis* on the basis of a *tabula rasa*, not being hampered by an existing *acquis* and the constraints of an EU Treaty-based policy-making domain. Because of the massive political weight the Schengen group had acquired as a result of the extension of its membership, it could then – in 1999 – simply transfer the whole of this *acquis* into the EU without having to compromise on any part of it.

The 'deepening' function of differentiation within the AFSJ

The British and Irish 'opt-outs' from the abolition of controls on persons at internal borders, the Schengen 'association' status and the temporary enlargement-related 'waiting' status of new EU/Schengen members are all a consequence of the incorporation of Schengen. They all fulfil a certain 'deepening' function, although each in a rather different sense.

The granting of the *British and Irish border opt-outs* (see above) was simply a necessary condition for making those two countries accept the incorporation of the Schengen system in 1999 – and hence for securing the full 'deepening' effect of the Schengen system.

The *Schengen 'association' status* (see above) has a double 'deepening' function. The first is that its development was necessary in order not to break-up the Nordic Passport Union, the prospect of which would no doubt have caused a major conflict between the Nordic Member States (Denmark, Finland and Sweden) and the other Schengen members. The second is that the availability of this status is now facilitating the participation of other European non-Member States in the Schengen system, as the example of Switzerland and Liechtenstein shows, and in this sense the extension of important AFSJ integration elements beyond the EU's borders.

The *temporary enlargement-related Schengen 'waiting' status* (see above) has – apart from its 'widening' function to which we will return in the next section – also a 'deepening' function in the sense that it is an instrument of pressure at the disposal of the old Schengen members to force the new Schengen members to bring their JHA policies fully in line with the respective 'deepening' objectives and standards of the EU/Schengen *acquis*.

Yet as a political project the AFSJ goes much further than the Schengen system with its focus on the abolition of internal border controls and related 'compensatory measures'. Hence the other AFSJ-related forms of differentiation have deepening functions beyond the scope of the Schengen system.

The *British, Danish and Irish opt-outs and opt-in possibilities as regards the 'communitarized' JHA fields of Title IV TEC* (see above) were a necessary condition for making those three countries accept that the other Member States could proceed with development of JHA policies in these fields on the basis of Community legal instruments and principles as well as the use of the EU institutions and decision-making procedures, with the corresponding advantages from the perspective of a further 'deepening' of integration in those fields.

The *enhanced cooperation possibilities* (see above) have a 'deepening' function in so far as they allow a group of Member States to go ahead with cooperation on some JHA issues for the 'furthering of the objectives of the Union' (Article 43(1)(a) TEU), manifestly in situations in which not all Member States are willing to participate. Because of the broader scope of the objectives of the AFSJ – which includes, in particular, that of 'providing citizens with a high level of safety' (Article 29 TEU) – such enhanced cooperation can clearly extend well beyond the scope of the former

Schengen cooperation. There may also be a tactical 'deepening' effect of this possibility as its potential use may induce individual Member States obstructing progress under a matter subject to a unanimity requirement to agree to compromises.[30]

Differentiation as an instrument of 'widening'

The 'association' of (by 2009) four non-EU Member States with the Schengen system (see above) does not constitute a case of 'widening' of the EU, but arguably of a partial 'widening' of the AFSJ through its Schengen parts. The Schengen 'association' status thereby fulfils a rather special – even unorthodox – 'widening' function by permitting non-Member States to participate in and benefit from, although without formal decision-making powers, the development of a substantial part of AFSJ policies. At the same time it also instrumental in exporting parts of the AFSJ *acquis* to those non-Member States, extending effectively the reach of part of EU JHA policies, especially of the Schengen border control and internal security system, to the respective countries.

Otherwise none of the forms of differentiation described above can be regarded as instruments of 'widening'. The phased operational integration of new Schengen members into the Schengen zone – which means that external border controls between old and new Schengen members are maintained until it has been ascertained that they meet all capability requirements of the Schengen *acquis* – could be regarded as a special form of 'differentiation within the differentiation'. Yet this 'Schengen waiting room' – which is currently occupied by Bulgaria and Romania (because of capacity deficits) and Cyprus (because of the partition problem)[31] – has as its primary function the protection of good functioning of the Schengen system and not the facilitation of enlargement.

The space and time dimensions

Looking at the evolution of differentiation within the AFSJ in terms of space and time, the most significant evolution over time has clearly been that of the Schengen system, which since its inception has gone through two processes of geographical expansion:

1 The expansion from 1985 to 1996 of the original Schengen group from five to 13 members, prior to their incorporation into the EU in 1999.
2 The expansion of the Schengen system to the *associated* non-Member States since 1999, with a first stage completed in 2002 (Iceland and Norway) and a second stage in the process of completion (Switzerland and Liechtenstein).

From a spatial perspective this amounts to a continuous expansion of the original Schengen group of five Member States to now 25 'full' EU Schengen members and four 'associated' non-EU members (including Liechtenstein), with only two EU Member States (Ireland and the UK) still enjoying an opt-out in combination with a partial opt-in.

The Schengen differentiation and its evolution, having been absorbed within the AFSJ since its introduction in 1999, accounts for most of the differentiation currently related to the AFSJ. Yet the AFSJ has also shown a non-Schengen-related evolution of differentiation since 1999: one is that of the *opt-outs* combined with *opt-in* possibilities, which are related to the progressive 'communitarization' of the JHA fields. These opt-outs were introduced by the Amsterdam Treaty in 1999 and are going to be expanded to the remaining 'third pillar' JHA fields if the Treaty of Lisbon enters into force (see above). The other is the introduction, again by the Amsterdam Treaty, of *enhanced cooperation possibilities*. These have so far never been used, but are to be expanded if the Lisbon Treaty enters into force (see above). One can therefore say that EU treaty reforms – because of the link between communitarization and opt-outs deals – have so far been the key time-line markers for non-Schengen-related differentiation within the AFSJ.

The impact of differentiation on the development of the AFSJ

Overall differentiation within the JHA domain has emerged primarily in order to allow for the pursuit of a 'deepening' of integration in circumstances in which the full participation of some countries is not possible: This is certainly true with regard to the original objectives of the Schengen group to implement a single but major integration objective with huge consequences for the JHA domain, the abolition of controls at internal borders. Yet it is also true with regard to the currently existing forms of differentiation, which all have certain 'deepening' functions: the *opt-out and opt-in possibilities* – as they have rendered the incorporation of Schengen and the 'communitarization' of JHA fields possible; the *enhanced cooperation* possibilities – as they provide a safety-valve for '*avant-garde*' groups if agreement on progress of all Member States appears impossible; and the *Schengen 'associate' status* – as it allows for the effective partial integration of non-Member States in the AFSJ and has removed an obstacle to the incorporation of Schengen. There can also be no doubt that in the case of Schengen differentiation has cast a long 'shadow' over initially non-participating Member States (and even non-EU Member States), which were increasingly drawn into Schengen because of its success in meeting its objectives and the advantages it brought in terms of cross-border free movement and internal security cooperation. Although never formally used, the mere threat of an 'enhanced cooperation' also helped to bring Italy into line in the 2001 negotiations on the European Arrest Warrant.

By comparison, the 'widening' functions appear more limited: while it is true that the Schengen 'association' status has allowed widening of the Schengen part of the AFSJ to four non-Member States, this form of differentiation has emerged as a result of the incorporation of the integration-oriented Schengen system into the EU/AFSJ framework in 1999. It can therefore be regarded as ancillary to the 'integration' functions of the Schengen differentiation.

In terms of spatial evolution, the most significant evolution has been the expansion of the Schengen system from originally five to all Member States but two, and even to four non-Member States. As regards evolution over time, the

Amsterdam Treaty reforms of 1999 clearly mark the single most decisive change as they brought both the fulfilment of the objectives of the original Schengen differentiation and the introduction of new forms of differentiation within the AFSJ. The recent expansion of the *opt-outs* and *enhanced cooperation possibilities* in the Treaty of Lisbon indicates that differentiation within the AFSJ is increasing rather than decreasing – and that treaty changes remain a major pathway for this increase.

In comparison with Schengen other, more recent, forms of AFSJ-related differentiation – such as the Prüm Convention and the G6 cooperation – have had only a marginal impact on the development of the AFSJ. This can be explained because the abolition of controls at internal borders – by creating *de facto* a common internal security zone – radically changed the whole context of national justice and home affairs policies and forced Member States to adopt wide-ranging compensatory measures. Neither the G6 cooperation nor the Prüm Convention created any similar constraints to act for the sake of a major political objective, and Schengen also benefited from the fact that, with cooperation between the Member States in the JHA domain still in its inter-governmental infancy, it could pre-empt a still largely empty field.

The 'deepening' effects that differentiation has had in the JHA domain have come at a hefty price from a 'constitutional' perspective. The British and Irish opt-outs, as well as the Danish one from 'communitarization', mean that three Member States do not participate fully in what since 1999 has become a fundamental treaty and integration objective – the construction of the AFSJ with the fundamental public goods it is intended to deliver to EU citizens. The *enhanced cooperation possibilities* provide a further breaking-up potential for what this 'area' is intended to deliver. The AFSJ is already or – in regard to *enhanced cooperation* – potentially not the same for all Member States and consequently does also not 'offer' the same in terms of 'freedom, security and justice' to EU citizens.

Notes

*This chapter was finalized before the final adoption of the Lisbon Treaty and treaty articles quoted refer to pre-Lisbon numbering, unless specific reference is made to post-Lisbon articles.

1. Article 2 TEU.
2. In 2007 alone the Council adopted 144 new texts relating to the AFSJ (information provided by the DG H General Secretariat of the Council).
3. 'Protocol (3) on the application of certain aspects of Article 14 of the Treaty establishing the European Community to the UK and to Ireland'.
4. 'Protocol (4) on the position of the UK and Ireland'.
5. 'Protocol (5) on the position of Denmark'.
6. The Danish opt-out, for instance, will not apply to the laying down of the conditions and limitations under which national law enforcement authorities may operate in the territory of another Member State (Article 89 TFEU) which is anyway 'protected' by the unanimity requirement.
7. On the questions of legal coherence and 'constitutional' consistency this raises see Thym (2004), 103–7.

8. On opt-out/opt-in practice see Peers (2004), 1–9.
9. See UK Ministry of Justice, 'Rome I – Should the UK opt in?', Consultation Paper CP05/08, London, 2 April 2008.
10. Article 1 of 'Protocol (2) integrating the Schengen acquis into the framework of the European Union to the TEU and TEC' establishes Schengen formally as an 'enhanced cooperation' in the sense of the Treaties.
11. A procedure now often referred to as the 'emergency brake'.
12. This is one of the few changes introduced by the Treaty of Lisbon which were not already provided for by the Draft Constitutional Treaty.
13. As already mentioned, legislative initiatives in the respective fields can also be brought by a quarter (at least) of the Member States. This opens up the possibility of a 9+ group bringing in a legislative initiative which is right from the start designed to be rejected by the others simply in order to get the 'automatic' authorization to proceed with 'enhanced cooperation'.
14. Text of the agreements with Norway and Iceland: OJ L 176 of 10.07.1999. Text of the agreement with Switzerland which entered into force only on 1 March 2008: OJ L 53 of 27.02.2008.
15. 'Protocol between the European Union, the European Community, the Swiss Confederation and the Principality of Liechtenstein on the accession of the Principality of Liechtenstein to the Agreement [...] on the Swiss Confederation's association with the implementation, application and development of the Schengen acquis', Council document 16402/06 (sic) of 13 February 2008 and 7059/08 of 28 February 2008 (signature). The ratification process is not yet completed.
16. See Article 2 and 3 of the 'Agreement concluded by the Council of the European Union and the Republic of Iceland and the Kingdom of Norway on the establishment of rights and obligations between Ireland and the UK of Great Britain and Northern Ireland, on the one hand, and the Republic of Iceland and the Kingdom of Norway, on the other, in areas of the Schengen acquis which apply to these States', OJ L 15 of 20 January 2000.
17. For details on the origin, procedures and issues discussed, see House of Lords, European Union Committee (2006) *Behind Closed Doors: The Meeting of the G6 Interior Ministers at Heiligendamm, Report with Evidence, 40th Report 2005/2006* (London: The Stationery Office).
18. Text: 'Convention between the Kingdom of Belgium, the Federal Republic of Germany, the Kingdom of Spain, the French Republic, the Grand Duchy of Luxembourg, the Kingdom of the Netherlands and the Republic of Austria on the stepping up of cross-border cooperation, particularly in combating terrorism, cross-border crime and illegal migration'; Council document 16382/06 of 6 December 2006.
19. 'Council Decision 2008/615/JHA of 23 June 2008 on the stepping up of cross-border cooperation, particularly in combating terrorism and cross-border crime', OJ L 210, 6 August. On the Prüm process see Luif (2007), 8–15.
20. For instance, those on cross-border pursuit in cases of imminent danger and on the use of air marshals were not accepted.
21. 'Opinion of the European Data Protection Supervisor on the Initiative [...] with a view to adopting a Council Decision on the stepping up of cross-border cooperation, particularly in combating terrorism and cross-border crime', OJ C 167 of 21 July 2007.
22. See, for instance, House of Lords, European Union Committee (2007) *Prüm: An Effective Weapon against Terrorism and Crime?, House of Lords European Union Committee (Sub-Committee on Home Affairs), 18th Report of 2006/07* (London: The Stationary Office, 11–12; Balzacq et al. (2006), 2–4 and 17.
23. OJ L 239 of 22 September 2000, 13.
24. ibid., 19–62.
25. A good survey of the development of the Schengen system prior to its incorporation is provided by Hreblay (1998).

26. A key example here is the development of the Schengen Information System (SIS) which – originally established to help border guards at external borders to take decision on entry or refusal of entry on the basis of information available in all Schengen countries – has developed into the biggest and so far most sophisticated cross-border electronic law enforcement instrument in Europe.
27. Protocol (2) annexed to the EU and the EC Treaties by the Treaty of Amsterdam.
28. Rather elegantly called 'ventilation'.
29. For other examples, see Monar (2000), 22–6.
30. The above-mentioned case of the Belgian Presidency of the second half of 2001 successfully threatening a potential use of *enhanced cooperation* in order to get case the Italian Government to lift its isolated objections against the Framework Decision on the European Arrest Warrant is a case in point.
31. The other nine Member States of the 2004 enlargement were operationally fully integrated into the Schengen system in March 2008 pursuant to a Council Decision of 6 December 2007 (OJ L 323 of 8 December 2007) based on the fulfilment of all *acquis*-related conditions.

20
Bologna's Deepening Empire: Higher Education Policy in Europe

Paul Furlong

'Differentiated integration' is both a tautology and a paradox. It is tautological as a simple proposition, since integration must imply some degree of differentiation, unless by 'integration' we mean homogenization or assimilation, which is not usually the case. Integration has difference at its starting point: it is not usually understood to mean erasing of differences, but rather rendering them more coherent in some way. In this case, the emphasis is on the maintenance of difference or even on its development in the process of integration. On the other hand, in terms of how we understand it in practice, differentiated integration is paradoxical, in that there is a puzzle inherent in any concept requiring us to talk of two opposing trends in the same phrase. Though the term itself may be relatively new, this paradox is inherent in how studies have understood the processes of change inherent in European integration. One of the important features of the debate about differentiated integration is that it has focused our attention on core aspects of integration, especially on the point that integration may be as much about the elaboration of difference as about its disappearance.

If we think of differentiated integration as a guided process of change involving at its core a tension between differentiation, which separates, and integration, which unites, policies relating to the management of knowledge in Europe can be located at one end of the scale – more differentiated than integrated, and differentiated across a variety of dimensions.

In the case of higher education policy, the integration element is a process of agreeing that the participants share generic objectives and can achieve them by harmonizing policies around core standards and guidelines. To achieve this, they manage structures and processes that vary significantly in different countries, and that are specific to the policy sector. Differentiation occurs as participants find that seeking to achieve the common objectives requires them to adopt custom-built solutions. In doing so, they attach to the common objectives a penumbra of meanings. It is not only that they start at different baselines, move at different speeds, enter the process at different times and adopt separate institutional arrangements. They also refine the objectives, break them down to different component parts and rank them differently. How this happens in higher education

(HE) policy and why, what this may mean for relations between European states and for European integration, and for EU education policy, is the subject of this chapter.

We do not deal here with cultural policy, or in any detail with broader issues relating to, for example, the role of knowledge production and knowledge management in economic development, though these are touched on in discussion of the Lisbon Agenda. Because of the place of education in the *acquis*, much of the discussion centres on two related aspects of policy: on the one hand, the Commission's attempts to expand from its treaty-based involvement in vocational training and professional qualification to a wider role in education more broadly defined; and, on the other, the success of the Bologna Process as, whether despite or because of its lack of a treaty basis, it continues to deepen and widen. A key question that cannot be answered within the scope of this chapter is whether Bologna has succeeded in its longer-term goals related to the international competitiveness of European HE institutions; more attainable are answers on issues concerning how and why differentiation takes place in this policy sector, and what this means for our understanding of differentiated integration.

A successful education policy may be regarded as an excludable network good (to use Kölliker's taxonomy, discussed in Chapter 3 in this volume[1]); it is excludable, in the sense that participant countries could if they wish exclude non-participants by technical means from benefitting – free-riding is difficult. It may appear notionally possible for non-participants to transfer an educational policy such as the Bologna process by observation and copying, but in practice much of the material content of the policy is technical and difficult to adapt without support. There is evidence of high levels of collaboration and exchange of experience within the Bologna Group which non-participants need and may not have access to. It is a network good in that consumption by additional users is complementary; additional users are not rivals in consumption, on the contrary they may add to the benefits to existing users. This is because of the expected benefits of increasing scale within the European knowledge economy. The Bologna process is intended to contribute by enhancing mobility in research and teaching; also, increased competition between national variants improves practice across the group as a whole. The excludability is mitigated in practice by the objective of using the creation of the European Higher Education Area to promote the influence of what is referred to internationally as 'the European system' of HE.

As an excludable network good, the Bologna process is characterized by strong incentives to join a flexible voluntary arrangement. In theory it is highly centripetal. We would expect the Bologna process to continue to attract new participants, though after a certain point the extent and form of participation may be affected by factors such as diminishing commonality among new entrants of key factors such as institutional, cultural, economic and linguistic ties that gave Bologna its initial impetus.

This leads us to expect not only temporal differentiation resulting from the difference in time of entry, but also spatial differentiation resulting from the increasing strain of integrating larger numbers of actors. Some of the consequent limitations are already appearing. For example, in moving towards the wider Bologna goals related to employability and European economic performance, differentiation may result from factors that Bologna can do little about. The 2009 stock-taking report comments:

> The acceptance of graduates in the labour market varies significantly: countries that have had a bachelor-master system for a long time see no specific problems and some other countries report increasing acceptance of bachelor graduates in the labour market, but there is a third group of countries with no bachelor-master tradition where the labour market seems to completely reject bachelor graduates.
>
> It appears that the acceptability of bachelor degrees in the labour market can depend as much on the established custom and practice of different countries as on the effective implementation of the Bologna reforms.[2]

The effectiveness of the reforms in countries where they involve major change in recruitment practice may depend on the existence of 'custom and practice' in the labour market that accepts such change or may be disposed to do so. This is outside the remit of Bologna, but may be critical to its success.

We would also expect functional differentiation within the Bologna Process to gather pace. This is because of the divergence in the capacities, interests and resources of participants; Bologna is about deepening integration, but it is also about widening, and the widening of its membership is perhaps one of its most distinctive features, precisely because it is outside the *acquis*. As widening occurs, the incentives to participate increase, because the costs of exclusion may be assumed to increase, but the challenges of achieving genuine institutional compatibility within the Bologna framework also make themselves felt to an ever greater extent. The parameters of the differentiation are set, among other things, by the extent to which participant countries benefit from the advantages of harmonization and the extent to which this converges with other domestic motives for reform. This implies that in individual countries we can identify a variety of motivations for Bologna, of which mobility, compatibility and transparency, the core Bologna values, may not be the most important.

A separate question is why the process has attracted such widespread support and active participation, relative to some other forms of integration. The political usefulness of the Bologna process is one obvious answer: Bologna grows and changes because it enables political leaders in participant states to exercise a greater degree of control over how the consequences of other European or international policies impact domestically in education policy, or enables them to persuade domestic interests that flexible policy change in response to external factors is necessary and desirable. However, at a certain point in the development of Bologna, particularly at the 2003 Berlin meeting, the internal debate seen in the many policy documents emphasized a quite different aspect.

As the institutional structure of Bologna developed, some of the limitations of voluntarism became apparent. Concern was expressed that a degree of free-riding is taking place, in the sense that participants may claim to have undertaken reforms in pursuit of Bologna objectives when they have not done so, or have not implemented them effectively. The Bologna executive relies on the accuracy of national reporting. An informal 'Bologna status' is emerging as a form of accreditation that appears to entitle participants to privileged access to European networks in teaching and research, and perhaps other networks as well, such as those associated with international organizations such as the UN, the IMF and the WTO. The difficulty of maintaining standards within the group led the Berlin summit of 2003 to adopt prior vetting and application processes to prevent participants abusing membership. In terms of Kölliker's categories, if we regard Bologna membership itself as a benefit, because of the international recognition it brings, this aspect of the Bologna process, that is, the status associated with membership, began as a non-excludable network good. It is only since 2005 that the club began to restrict access to the cachet that membership brought.

Origins of the Bologna process

The Bologna process has a discrete set of structures, objectives and operations that to a great extent are formally independent of other European integration functions, especially those that depend directly on the European Union. To understand the factors that shape and constrain it, it is necessary first to explain briefly how it came to have its particular configuration. The founding document is the Bologna Declaration, agreed by ministers of 29 European countries at a meeting of what is now the European University Association in Bologna in June 1999. This was an elaboration of the Sorbonne Declaration, agreed at the equivalent meeting the year before in Paris by the Ministers for Higher Education of France, Germany, Italy and the United Kingdom. This in turn referred to the Lisbon Convention on the recognition of HE qualifications, agreed in 1997. It was the Sorbonne Declaration that effectively started the drive towards greater collaboration across HE in Europe; the key final paragraph commits the four signatories 'to encouraging a common frame of reference, aimed at improving external recognition and facilitating student mobility as well as employability ...'

The document also commits them to seek 'to create a European area of higher education', and calls on 'other Member States of the Union and other European countries to join us in this objective'.

Ten years later, at its biennial ministerial summit in Leuven, the Bologna process had 46 Member States. Its membership included all states within the Council of Europe that have an HE function. All its members are signatories to the European Cultural Convention and to the Lisbon Convention,[3] though not all have ratified these, and full implementation of the Lisbon Convention is one of the key current targets. The European Commission is an additional member, and there are eight consultative members, including the Council of Europe and UNESCO.

There is also significant interest from outside Europe. At the Leuven 2009 meeting a Bologna policy forum was held for the first time which was attended by Bologna ministers and delegates from 16 other countries, including Brazil, China, Japan and the USA. A good example of what Bologna means to others is the Australian statement to the 2009 Leuven meeting, which referred specifically to the importance of Bologna in providing Australia with improved global connections in HE research and teaching, and in developing policy initiatives from which Australia and others in its region could learn.[4]

Bologna has a secretariat provided by the country holding the presidency for the next two years, other administrative support provided by the European Commission, a Bologna Follow-up Group, a list of main objectives that amounts to 10 distinct items, and a programme of meetings and action plans that stretches to 2020. At the Leuven meeting, it was agreed that the presidency would be shared by the EU Member State holding the presidency for the six months, together with the next host (in 2011, Finland).

By most standards, this is an impressive example of institutionalization, albeit a rather unusual one. Perhaps even more striking is that this institutional change was associated with rapid and fundamental change in national policy in an area that had been vexing EU and national policy-makers for some time.

Issues and achievements

At the outset, the most important issue appears to have been the one that we see first in the Sorbonne Declaration – the harmonization of recognition of professional and academic qualifications.

However, targets such as this have been set within a wider set of objectives, which make it clear that the context and the motivation go beyond the traditional concerns of European HE. The Bologna Declaration, referring to the Sorbonne document, commits participants

> to engage in co-ordinating our policies to reach ... within the first decade of the new millennium, the following objectives, which we consider to be of primary relevance in order to establish the European area of higher education and to promote the European system of higher education world-wide.[5]

These two goals, the establishment of the European Area of Higher Education and the promotion of the 'European system' worldwide, are widely regarded as the key Bologna objectives.

Though the Bologna process is not formally an EU initiative, it has strong EU support, and the European Commission supports the development of specific reforms to help achieve the 'Europe of Knowledge'.[6] In the early years of the Bologna process, European Councils in Lisbon in 2000 and in Barcelona in 2002 supported these and other initiatives with decisions that emphasized the importance of the knowledge economy in promoting the goal of lasting change in the overall competitiveness of the European economy.

This particular emphasis on the role of HE in European economic reform is relatively new. As Corbett (2005) argues, the involvement of the EU in European HE is not new. Some of this involvement has generally been regarded as successful, for example the ERASMUS programme as a means of achieving student and staff mobility. Other efforts have been less successful, such as attempts to promote the goals of harmonization of degree qualification frameworks and reciprocal recognition, especially beyond the rather narrow remit of professional qualifications which are achieved outside formal HE institutions. The involvement of the EU institutions in policy relating to European HE is seen by the European Commission as a natural development of its role in promoting political and economic integration, and to some extent as a development of existing responsibilities with regard to training and with regard to the effectiveness of the labour market. Prior to Bologna, the European Commission had limited success in promoting this agenda, for reasons that relate partly to the lack of clear authority in EU treaties, but also to suspicion on the part of universities about attempts to compel them to adopt policies and practices that may be more concerned with market responsiveness than with traditional academic standards. This especially applies to issues such as curriculum content and quality assurance. Article 128 of the Treaty, on which the Commission's role relies, refers to guidelines for vocational training, not to education. Several cases heard by the European Court of Justice have dealt with related issues, among them the extent to which education may be regarded as a service and therefore covered by Single Market provisions. This has generally been answered in the negative.

Universities in many EU Member States are recruiting grounds for national political élites, have historical status as contributors to the development of national political identities, especially in the 19th century, and are powerful autonomous institutions within civil society. These factors make universities difficult for national politicians and bureaucracies to challenge. The problems facing a supra-national authority, appearing to take on entrenched and vocal national academic elites without a thoroughly-grounded Treaty authority, are even greater.

What is significant about Bologna, as Hackl observes, from this point of view, is that the process is inter-governmental, driven by the nation-states themselves. At the outset, it included university representatives in the directorate, though they have now been relegated to the role of consultative members (Hackl, 2001: 28; see also Goldsmith and Berndtson, 2002). The inter-governmentalism applies not only to those areas which are outside the Commission's usual remit, such as any that touch on academic autonomy, but also to the more limited objectives that relate to areas in which the European Commission is already active, or which it might take into its remit without major issues of principle being raised. Thus, Bologna may be seen as a new approach to an area of EU interest whose current configuration reflects the inconsistent experience of Commission initiatives since the Single European Act of 1986.

The Bologna process and its objectives

The Bologna process combines high-level strategy with detailed reform. The targets in the biennial stock-taking are policy instruments that are intended to achieve the European Higher Education Area. They are thus a means of enrolling the hitherto reluctant European HE cohorts into variants of integration, united by a common concern with the 'Europe of Knowledge'.

Within the overarching objectives of the European Higher Education Area and the European Research Area (competitiveness, adaptation to new labour-market conditions, reinforcing European citizenship, reinforcing shared values), the specific Bologna objectives are to coordinate national action on a range of policy issues of a highly technical character, focusing on key issues in the management of teaching.

After Berlin 2003, there was no substantive addition to this list of objectives, but the Leuven 2009 meeting acknowledged that with the experience gained in seeking to achieve these, and in view of the successes and remaining challenges, further progress was both possible and desirable. It was agreed to mandate the next meetings to refine long-term objectives so as to produce a realistic programme, taking Bologna beyond its original 2010 deadline to an enhanced set of goals and instruments for 2020.

The Berlin meeting also reaffirmed the importance of academic autonomy and the identity of European HE as a public good. At the European level, the Bologna process has already raised anxieties about the impact of increased mobility on the quality of learning, the difficulty of teaching a core disciplinary curriculum within the first three-year cycle, and the threat to relatively small disciplines from standardization pressures driven by representatives of larger disciplines. There are also those who argue that the Bologna process neglects some of the key issues facing European HE, most notably the declining unit of resource, the increasing pressure on academic research time and the increasing centralization of national processes infringing academic autonomy.

The institutional structures of the Bologna process achieved a high level of complexity in a relatively brief period. This was driven first by the French and German governments, and then increasingly by the European Commission. This resulted in two separate sets of dynamics: first, the national pressure to reform HE so as to improve international competitiveness, reduce costs and enhance the responsiveness of HE institutions to national policy concerns; second, the pressure at EU level to pursue long-term integration goals, especially the extension of the Single Market to the employment sector, in which obstacles to recognition of qualifications played an important role, and the range of concerns associated with the Lisbon Agenda, especially the development of a Europe-wide HE system as a competitor to the USA in the market for non-national students.

European and domestic policy-making

One of the key differences in the way the Bologna process works lies in how this combination of EU institutions, expert groups and lead organizations was able to achieve rapid progress on a range of issues that had been taxing the EU for a considerable time. This was the first time these issues had been dealt with as a single package, outside the formal EU structure, by an autonomous group of governments of individual states, and involving a broad range of stakeholders from the beginning. As a declaration agreed through *ad hoc* procedures by a number of governments, some of them unlikely to be EU Member States in the foreseeable future, the agreement is clearly not the product of EU institutions. Also, it is phrased in such general terms that it is difficult to envisage how in this form it could be enforced through national or international courts. The Bologna Declaration may be best regarded, in Hackl's phrase, as 'public international soft law' (2001: 28).

A central issue that we cannot consider here is the extent to which the soft law of the Bologna commitments could in future be incorporated into EU hard law, perhaps through EU directives that assume Bologna commitments as part of the *acquis communautaire*. This appears unlikely at present, not least because Bologna may be regarded as successful enough without such a step being needed. Nevertheless, it is possible to envisage that current non-binding inter-governmental commitments may acquire legal status in the EU. The public international soft law of Bologna could foreseeably become EU hard law, subject to its usual policy procedures. At present, however, if signatories may feel obliged for practical reasons to fall in with the coordination, the reasons for doing so are not directly related to legal compliance.

The administrative arrangements for the Bologna process are fluid, but the original impetus came from an inter-governmental agreement signed by the EU big four, who were given a major role through the follow-up group. At that point, the process appeared dominated by French and German concerns, and especially by French activism, which set the pattern in degree frameworks and in quality assurance. This helped explain why the adoption of a degree framework initially bearing some resemblance to Anglo-American models soon diverged from these.

The early objectives of the 'Sorbonne Four' were not uniform. The British were involved, it appears, partly because the initiative occurred at a propitious moment in UK–EU relations, when the new Labour government was willing and able to engage openly on issues of reform. But it was also because this was seen as a cost-free exercise for UK HE interests, since it seemed to involve recognition of many of the principles that UK HE had adopted over the previous 17 years. A further factor for the UK was the risk of exclusion, with the consequence that without UK involvement the process might result in the adoption of processes and standards that challenged British practice. It is not clear whether the UK government considered this aspect in any detail at the time, but it certainly did become a factor.

Possibly the most important single policy gain to the UK government from Bologna membership was the agreement at the London meeting of 2007, after lengthy debate and preparation, that quality assurance mechanisms in HE within Bologna should focus on learning outcomes and not on time spent in learning. This was also the position of a significant proportion of Northern European countries, but not initially of Germany, France and Italy. The significance of this lies in what it tells us about the advantages of inclusion in the voluntary association. This is one of the policy issues in the Bologna process that is so central that here the differentiation stops and the integration takes over. The adoption of the alternative approach would have entailed very significant costs for the UK – either dismantling existing structures that are the result of long and costly reform processes, or exiting Bologna and suffering the exclusion costs, especially in important international markets. The UK already had a defined position, the result of a long internal process of reform and investment based on a strategic choice in favour of flexibility and market-responsiveness. Exclusion could in the long run have brought into question the quality of UK degrees, the capacity of UK HE to compete in the market for international students and in the long run the quality of UK graduates. In other words, it could have undermined the goals of the reform process in the UK.

For the other three, the main concern seems to have been that European universities were falling behind the North Americans in teaching quality and in research. There was also the strong sense that the existing teaching system was expensive, inefficient and unresponsive. This was partly why Bologna focused initially on shortening the degree cycle. It was implicit that the improvements in competition resulting from the Bologna reforms would result in the emergence of an select group of top European universities. Funding for these would be released by the savings made in the national systems. This is a familiar Open Method of Co-ordination (OMC) sequence. Bologna was intended to stimulate a race to the top.

The process is now in the hands of educational administrators from individual Member States, supported by the European Commission, with a range of subcommittees and working groups on particular action lines. This may pose problems of harmonization, but it is not necessarily unwelcome at national level if it provides national policy-making elites with the opportunity to reform flexibly. Other changes, however, have obscured the competition aspects of the initial vision.

After Berlin in September 2003, the pace of change increased considerably. Both in national reform programmes and in the administrative coordination, OMC is now institutionalized through the monthly 'Bologna seminars', coordinated by the European Commission, which seek to promote the spread of best practice. A key actor in the Bologna dynamics is the ENQA – originally the European Network of Quality Assurance Agencies, now the European Association for Quality Assurance in Higher Education. This is a typical OMC institution in its structure and operations, in that it is primarily a grouping of national peak agencies supported by the European Commission for the purpose of driving national coordination in its policy area. The ENQA was mandated at the Berlin Conference 'to develop an agreed set of standards procedures and guidelines on quality assurance, [and] to explore ways of ensuring an adequate peer review system for quality assurance'.[7]

ENQA is a network of professional administrators in HE quality assurance. The centrality of quality assurance to the Bologna process, and its direct relevance for other target areas such as qualifications frameworks and degree structure and recognition, ensure that this is a key force within Bologna. According to the European Commission, ENQA 'has shown ... it is possible to evaluate study programmes across borders against sets of common criteria as long as the universities agree to take the common criteria as a starting point for evaluation', in other words that common curricula across Europe are possible.[8] ENQA is also directly responsible for the Standards and Guidelines for Quality Assurance in the European Higher Education Area (ESG), adopted in Bergen in 2005.

Patterns of convergence and divergence

Since 2005 the Bologna secretariat has been producing detailed reports and scorecards on the progress of individual participants towards the Bologna objectives.[9] These are primarily a management tool used to set targets, and do not pretend to be quantitatively precise. They are based on national responses, interpreted by the secretariat and by the Bologna groups after discussion with the national authorities.

The targets themselves change after each iteration. As specific objectives are met, the relevant targets may be adjusted to promote further development, or merged with other objectives where there is a clear operational relationship, or dropped entirely. They do not give us a consistent quantitative time-series of progress towards constant goals. The analysis below uses the scorecards to calculate aggregate ranking of individual states in each of the three years of the biennial meetings, and to identify contributing factors.

Most obviously, in the 2009 reports there are clear time-based clusters in the rankings. Though the process has been in operation for only about 10 years, its pace has been such that there seems to be a marked advantage gained by most of the original 29 entrants over the 17 later arrivals. In 2009, all but one of the states in the upper half of the ranking was a 1999 original member. The outlier was Georgia. In 2009 Georgia reported a major legislative reform programme that had been in action since 2007, listing a wide range of measures taken to remove legal obstacles on issues of degree accreditation and recognition, and to set up structures to provide Bologna-proof quality assurance mechanisms. The report includes the revealing comment:

> Future challenges include:
> limited time to implement the reforms (since 2005); lack of full understanding of the Bologna Process and low level of involvement of social partners and other stakeholders; lack of resources for implementation ... [10]

This is inherent in the Bologna process; for many of its participants, the gap between legislative action and full implementation is likely to be significant.

This differentiation by time seems to be the direct result of three separate factors: the early pace of change, the emphasis on continuing enhancement, and the existing conditions of HE in the early entrants. The pace of change and the continuing enhancement are integral to how Bologna works, and result from the deliberate practice of repeatedly adjusting targets upwards even though the slower states might not have made significant progress towards the original targets. Unlike the EU, Bologna does not demand a capacity to adopt an existing *acquis* immediately. It requires evidence that the new participant will be able to make progress towards the objectives, and that it has the administrative structure to enable it to join the Bologna process fully, including meeting the reporting requirements. Bologna does not proceed at the pace of the slowest.

We should not overstate the time factor. The existence of obvious anomalies in the rankings suggests that a range of territorial and policy-specific factors may have had a more important effect in differentiation.

Territorially, the Bologna process has the shape of the Council of Europe; politically, it is the European Union writ large. Its territorial differentiation matches that of the Council of Europe almost exactly, since of the 46 states participating in Bologna, only the Vatican is not also a member of the Council of Europe, and of the CE states, Monaco and San Marino are not part of Bologna. The last of the entrants,

Armenia, Azerbaijan, Georgia, Moldova and Ukraine, joined in 2005. In Keating's phrase (Chapter 4 this volume: 57), Bologna can be interpreted as an example of a 'hard border' that can include all prospective members without too heavy an entrance fee. This includes some countries, such as Turkey and Russia, whose European identity, culturally, economically and politically, is internally and externally disputed.

As Table 20.1 indicates, the time factor masks spatial and functional factors that may be more significant in the long run. As Goetz discusses in detail in Chapter 5 of this volume, there is an interaction between time factors, especially the relative timing of accession, and phases of integration of the entry states. The original Bologna states were central and western European, closely integrated into wider European/ international networks such as the Council of Europe, NATO and OECD. Within this group, the main territorial differentiation is between the smaller Northern states that dominate the top quartile on the Bologna rankings, the Central European group, mainly 2nd quartile, and the southern Europeans, mainly 3rd quartile.

In general, the clusters are distinguished by different types of policy issues. though states outside the first cluster all tend to have particular issues with the development of a national qualifications framework (under the organization of the degree systems), and recognition of prior learning (under the recognition heading). Apart from the UK, they also have a variety of policy implementation issues related to the emphasis on the learning outcomes approach and on issues of access and recognition.

The learning outcomes approach seems on its own to be held to justify an extended Bologna programme. The 2009 stocktaking reported that it

> ... clearly indicates that fully-fledged introduction of a learning outcomes-based culture across the EHEA still needs a lot of effort, and it will not be completed by 2010.[11]

The report finds that implementation of Quality Assurance provisions is also inconsistent, notwithstanding the passing of appropriate formal legislation:

> It is surprising that quality assurance agencies from only 22 countries are full members of ENQA. [...] This suggests that the standards and guidelines for external quality assurance and the work of QA agencies may not yet be fully implemented in some other countries.[12]

These functional factors result from the agreement by HE Ministers and the European Commission at the 2003 and 2005 meetings to give priority to the 'knowledge economy' issues. These examples of functional differentiation from the 2009 report could be expanded considerably. The explanation of the 2009 report is that:

> two significant factors have had an impact on the pace of progress: firstly, new action lines and activities have been added over the years, not least a change of paradigm with a shift to towards outcomes-based qualifications frameworks; secondly, countries have started the reform process at different times depending on when they joined the process.[13]

Table 20.1 Temporal, spatial and functional differentiation in the Bologna group (2009)

Cluster definition	Members	Typology	Outliers
1st quartile ranking	Belgium (Flemish), Denmark, Finland, Iceland, Ireland, Netherlands, UK (Scotland), Sweden	*Policy issues* – none outstanding	None
2nd quartile	Austria, Belgium (French), Bulgaria, Czech Republic, Estonia, Germany, Hungary, Latvia, Liechtenstein, Poland, Portugal, Romania, Switzerland, UK (EWNI)	*Policy issues* – Introduction of National Qualifications Framework, Recognition of prior learning (RPL)	Germany, UK (EWNI), Belgium (French), Portugal
3rd quartile	Croatia, Cyprus, France, Georgia, Greece, Italy, Lithuania, Luxembourg, Malta, Montenegro, Serbia, Slovakia, Slovenia, Turkey, Vatican	*Policy issues* – Introduction of National Qualifications Framework, RPL; also quality assurance measures	France, Georgia
4th quartile	Armenia, Albania, Andorra, Azerbaijan, Bosnia-Herzegovina, FYROM, Moldova, Russia, Spain, Ukraine	*Policy issues* – Introduction of National Qualifications Framework, RPL; also recognition measures generally	Spain and Andorra

Further research would be necessary to identify how this is patterned across the Bologna Group, and the interaction between the time factor and the impact of new action lines and activities, as specified by the 2009 report.

The questions of time, space and function are overlaid by a further factor, which at least at a superficial level seems to have a predominant effect: that is the question of size. The four signatories of the Sorbonne Declaration in 1998 – France, Germany, Italy and the UK – are not in the vanguard of Bologna implementation, with the exclusion of UK (Scotland), which is now treated separately.

The four largest countries in the group of first entrants seem to resist the particular temporal and territorial differentiations that configure the remainder. A similar observation may apply to Spain, which uniquely among the EU Member States finds itself in the last quartile in terms of Bologna performance. Russia, largest of the participants in terms of population size, makes up the sixth member of this group of outliers. Is it size that matters, or is this masking other factors such as political history and academic culture? The first aspect to note is that these countries all have highly developed university systems, some of considerable longevity. But they are not alone in this. The differences may lie in the scale, and in the extent to which because of recent history in central and eastern Europe the academic profession may be assumed to be more consistently supportive. In the six larger outliers referred to, this cannot be assumed, for various reasons. In the 'Sorbonne Four', and in Spain, there is academic opposition or indifference of a size and quality that cannot readily be ignored. The Sorbonne emphasis on the introduction of a two-cycle degree programme was significant not because it might imply the adoption of an Anglo-American HE structure, but because it implies more cost-effective management of the student learning process. This in turn entails the implementation of different forms of budget control and new forms of state involvement in how universities manage their teaching and research. In the countries referred to in this last group, it seems that size, institutional structure, cultural importance, and extent and type of relations between academics, politicians and civil servants make the reform process particularly complex. How this develops in the individual countries depends on the particular contexts, and is therefore a factor of further differentiation.

Conclusion

Bologna was established as a deliberately inter-governmental association. Participants can 'pick and choose' not only how to cooperate (at what pace, with what interpretation of common policy goals) but even whether to cooperate at all on individual issues, at least in the short and medium term. Generally, one of the main questions, from this point of view, is why the threat of exclusion exercised by cooperating groups does not generate enough negative externalities to motivate remaining outsiders to become insiders. Bologna is an extreme case of inter-governmentalism in this sense, in that effectively all potential members have now joined. We can assume the negative externalities outweigh the costs of membership in all cases.

This unusual result is possible, it seems, not because the costs of exclusion are high, but because the costs of membership are relatively low. Membership was initially a matter of choice on the part of the participants: only later did some of the existing members begin to question the capacities and motivations of their colleagues, and then introduced qualifying periods for prospective members. The benefits are, first, the international status that membership confers in an increasingly salient policy sector and, second, access to a large policy-learning network. Third, members can also influence how the Bologna group develops policy in this sector. This is limited by the factor referred to several times already, that non-compliance as such carries no direct costs to the state concerned. The capacity to affect policy in other countries through the Bologna network, to achieve harmonization that is in the interests of one particular member or group of members, is not its most important feature. Nevertheless, it does occur, as we saw in discussing the position of UK governments on quality assurance and learning outcomes.

The initial impetus behind the Bologna process was the concern of the four largest states in the EU about the quality of European HE and its capacity to compete within an increasingly global market. In this, they were supported by the European Commission, and by the emerging consensus at Member State level that led to the Lisbon Agenda of 2000. The emphasis on the creation of a wide inter-governmental European Higher Education Area enabled the 'Sorbonne Four' to begin the development of a vision of a European university system, acting outside the Treaty confines that had hampered previous efforts at EU-wide reform in this sector. The vision included the aim of improving internal competition among European universities so as to stimulate the emergence of a number of elite universities able to compete in teaching quality with the best, especially with those in the USA. The successful spread of the model to 46 countries, its increasing complexity, and the later prioritization of the social dimension, life-long learning and access issues, have significantly obscured this initial vision. As a result, the savings to be made by pruning the standard degree programme appear to have been mitigated by the increased costs of the reform process. Complex new demands on teaching performance and new assurance processes have been introduced, and quality-enhancement reforms have been introduced across the degree-awarding institutions. The release of savings to fund research and teaching selectively in the emerging elite of the best European universities does not appear to have occurred.

Differentiated integration is built into Bologna. The process now is multi-speed, and variable in format. Participants have agreed criteria in HE teaching standards, but they progress at different paces and in different ways depending on a variety of factors. What will be important in future developments in Bologna is how this differentiation relates to the aim the 'Sorbonne Four' shared at the outset, to use the approach to promote the emergence of a small number of world-class universities. It is not clear now to what extent Bologna can still help towards this aim. The differentiated integration achieved so far is not what was envisaged in 1999.

Notes

1. See also Kölliker (2006b); Cornes and Sandler (1996).
2. Bologna Process (2009), 8.
3. 'Convention on the Recognition of Qualifications Concerning Higher Education in the European Region', agreed Lisbon April 1997.
4. See the Statement by the Australian Delegation, at: http://ond.vlaanderen.be/hogeronder wijs/bologna/forum/Bologna_Policy_Forum_Australian_statement.pdf
5. 'Bologna Declaration: The European Higher Education Area, Joint Declaration of the European Ministers of Education, convened in Bologna 19 June 1999', 1.
6. See Corbett (2005).
7. Culture, Directorate-General (8 November 2003) 'From Berlin to Bergen: the EU Contribution' (Brussels European Commission), A2/DVPH. 2.
8. ibid., 4.
9. For the 2009 reports, see Bologna Process (2009).
10. Bologna Process (2009), Bologna Process Stocktaking Report, 6.
11. ibid., 8.
12. ibid., 9.
13. ibid., 12.

21
Foreign and Security Policies: 'Trilateral' Europe?

Angelos Sepos

Introduction

Much has been said about the global role of the EU (Whitman, 1998; Hill and Smith, 2005; Bretherton and Vogler, 2006; Elgstrom and Smith, 2006; Sjursen, 2007; Laidi, 2008; Telo, 2009) and the particular ineffectiveness of its CFSP/ESDP which has led to a 'capability-expectations gap' (Hill, 1993). This has been manifested into a rather unconvincing record in foreign and security matters which has undermined the international standing of the Union *vis-à-vis* other global powers (such as the USA, Russia and China). The distinct historical experiences, capabilities, identities and ambitions of Member States (MS) have contributed to this predicament. Ongoing tensions between 'allies' and 'neutrals', 'Atlanticists' and 'Europeanists', 'extroverts' and 'introverts', 'small' and 'large', 'old' and 'new' states have been highlighted to emphasize these distinct experiences. The utilization of differentiated integration in this policy area has frequently been seen as an effective way to manage this diversity. Historical figures in the integration process such as de Gaulle (1959),[1] Brandt (1974), Tindemans (1976), Schäuble and Lamers (1994), Kohl and Chirac (1995), Fischer (2000), Delors (2001) and Sarkozy (2005, 2007), have proposed various flexibility initiatives in the Union, the underlying assumption being that foreign and security[2] and matters would be among them. Debates in the public domain, the various IGC and the European Convention over the creation of a 'centre of gravity', 'pioneering' and 'avant-garde' groups that would further integration in this policy area have come to epitomize these tensions but may also be the potential remedy forthem – at least in the last resort when other means had failed.

It was not until the Treaty of Maastricht (1992) that flexibility was formally acknowledged and introduced into the Second Pillar with the 'opt-out' clauses in foreign and security policy. And while the Treaty of Amsterdam (1997) established the provision of 'closer cooperation'[3] it excluded it from the Second Pillar, providing instead for the use of another form of flexibility, namely, 'constructive abstention'.[4] The Treaty of Nice (2003) 'enhanced cooperation'[5] and extended it to foreign and security issues but not in the newly developed area of defence. The Constitutional and Lisbon Treaties further extended the use of enhanced cooperation in this Pillar as they established the provisions of 'permanent structured cooperation'[6] as well as the 'passarelle' clause.[7]

These various efforts to account for differentiation reflected

1 the determination of the majority of Member States to retain an intergovernmental approach in the Second Pillar given foreign and security policies' significance for the traditional nation-state;
2 the differing positions of Member States, not least within the UN system, with Britain and France holding permanent seats in the Security Council;
3 recognition that with NATO and WEU, differentiation already existed.

This chapter will analyse these developments and indicate that the existing and proposed flexibility initiatives in the area of foreign and security policies have been conditioned by the territorial and temporal dimensions of these actors and also from the particular functional characteristics of this policy area.

The positions of Member States on differentiated integration

While the positions and attitudes of Member States in Pillar Two have varied, sometimes on principle, sometimes over the nature of particular challenges or crises and how to deal with them, the original larger Member States have generally been in favour of extending those provisions in the treaties whereas small and new states have more often been generally in favour of maintaining the status quo. At the same time, variations have usually existed within such clusters. More specifically, there is a variation within the attitudes of the 'Big Three', where the UK was traditionally more in favour of the status quo, though since the trilateral meeting in 2003 is now in favour of these initiatives; within small states where the Benelux are more in favour of extending these provisions; and within new states, where Bulgaria has expressed more positive views on the issue.

The positions of these Member States were particularly clearly expressed during the negotiations of the Amsterdam Treaty. Among the 'Big Three', Germany was in favour of a model of differentiated integration which would not exclude any Member State from joining a hypothetical 'vanguard' group, while France proposed the introduction of 'a general clause on reinforced cooperation' and emphasized that any such initiatives should be 'confirmed by the Union as a whole'.[8] The UK's position was even more guarded in that it accepted that the EU needed a certain degree of flexibility or 'variable geometry' but was concerned that it should not fall 'into the trap of a two-speed Europe with a hard core centred on certain Member States or certain policies'.[9] It, too, stressed that these initiatives should be open to all Member States. Both Spain and Italy considered 'variable geometry' or differentiated integration in general as critical in resolving the dilemma between widening and deepening of the Union. While Spain saw it as a means of preventing an '*à la carte*' Europe, Italy emphasized the need for preserving the *acquis* and for any arrangement to be open to all Member States.[10]

There were variations among the smaller Member States, with, for example, Sweden arguing against an '*à la carte*', 'single' or 'multi-core' Europe, Denmark against the emergence of a 'class-based Europe', Ireland and Finland against a 'hard core' Europe, Portugal against 'variable geometry', and Greece against any form of integration that would destabilize 'the situation of unity and equality between MS'. All, though, insisted that should flexibility be used, it should be the 'exception to the rule', a 'last resort' and a 'traction effect' allowing others to eventually catch up. The Benelux, on the other hand, expressed their support for the principle of flexibility as 'an approach to European integration' but under certain conditions. They, too, argued against forms of flexibility such as '*à la carte*', 'single' or 'multi-core' Europe.[11]

Similar positions were also voiced during the negotiations of the Nice Treaty. In a joint position paper, Germany and Italy supported the use of enhanced cooperation as 'a gravitational force in order to allow the Union to achieve progress' and the establishment of 'an open, functional avant-garde' which would respect the common institutional framework while also rejecting the notion of '*à la carte*' Europe. The UK and France were also supportive of such flexibility initiatives. They also supported the Commission's proposal to lower the critical mass that might form a pioneering group from the majority to one-third of Member States[12] and also proposed the lowering of this threshold to five in areas of foreign, security and defence policy. Such measures were rejected by Finland, Ireland and Greece which insisted on maintaining the one-half majority threshold.[13] They were joined by candidate states such as Poland, the Czech Republic and Cyprus. In supporting the preservation of the Amsterdam regime on close cooperation, Poland emphasized the point that any extension should not lead to the exclusion of future Member States from participating, nor any form of 'second-class' membership or 'two-tier' Europe. Only Bulgaria expressed its support for an extension of enhanced cooperation, requesting, however, a stronger role for the Commission as a 'mediator' for this provision.[14] Here again, the Benelux were in favour of lowering the critical mass forming threshold to one-third arguing that such a provisions were necessary in light of the imminent enlargement.[15]

During the negotiations of the proposed Constitutional Treaty, there was concern not only on the majority threshold but also on the scope (that is, extension in CFSP; provision of 'permanent structured cooperation') and the decision-making framework (the 'passarelle' clause) of enhanced cooperation. France, Germany, the UK, Italy and Spain all supported such initiatives[16] while Finland, Ireland, Sweden and Greece as well as other small candidate states were against such proposals. Latvia, for example, warned that such provisions would lead to the creation of 'first and second class members differentiated by their military capabilities'; Slovenia warned against a 'policy of exclusion' in defence; Estonia emphasized that 'the Union can only be strong as are all the MS together'; Poland insisted on flexibility being 'inclusive, open and transparent'; while Romania and Malta argued for a 'solidarity clause' in enhanced cooperation which would be 'mediated and guaranteed by the Commission' so that 'no one falls behind unnecessarily'. The Benelux were again supportive of these provisions.[17]

During the short, intensive and mostly 'behind the scenes' negotiations of the Treaty of Lisbon led by the German and Portuguese Presidencies in the latter part of 2007, small Member States, with the exception of the Benelux, reiterated their concerns on these issues. They saw mixed success. For example, they were successful in ensuring that enhanced cooperation was not extended to common foreign and security policy while also ensuring that the entry criteria for enhanced cooperation in the area of defence (that is, permanent structured cooperation) were watered down to make participation in the EU Battle Groups easier. At the same time, the one-third majority threshold was maintained, QMV was introduced in initiatives of enhanced cooperation (the 'passarelle' clause) while the solidarity clause in enhanced cooperation was not adopted. Important in shaping this outcome was the support of the 'Big Three' as well as Spain and Italy for the Commission's proposals.

Territory, time and function as mediators of differentiated integration in foreign and security policies

In all these negotiation phases, territorial and temporal dimensions of Member States were critical in shaping attitudes, as well as the functional characteristics of the policy area. These variables have contributed to the diversity of Member State foreign policies and, in turn, have shaped the nature and scope of flexibility initiatives. Temporal or historical factors that have helped to shape the foreign policies of states include: the historical experiences of fascism, in the cases of Germany, Spain and Italy; communism in the cases of the central-eastern and Baltic states; colonialism in the cases of France, Britain, Portugal, Italy, the Netherlands and Belgium. The interaction between post-authoritarian, post-communist and post-colonial democratization with economic liberalization and modernization have been factors in the cases of Italy, Greece, Spain, Portugal, Ireland, Cyprus and Malta. The interplay of other historical and geo-political factors have helped to create and foster the distinction between 'Atlanticists', 'Europeanists' and 'Neutrals' as defined in relation to the role of the United States and NATO in the European security architecture – Britain, Germany, the Netherlands, Denmark, Portugal, the Visegrád and Baltic States are notable examples of the first group; France, Italy, Spain, Belgium, Cyprus (Greece is also shifting towards this group) are examples of the second group; and Ireland, Austria, Finland and Sweden are examples of the third group.

If empire created an 'extensive' network of external relations beyond the EU for Britain, France and to a lesser extent Spain and Portugal, Germany, Austria, Finland and Sweden might be said to have looked to an 'international' network of relations through international organizations such as the UN, NATO and the OSCE. Past ties have created and maintained various politico-economic and security relationships while other ethnic and cultural attributes (including shared memories such as war), have also sustained particular relationships, as in the case of France's relations with the Francophonie (mostly former colonies but with additional countries where French is widely spoken such as Quebec, Lebanon and, in addition, countries such as Romania and Moldova); Britain's relations with the Commonwealth as well as countries of the Gulf[18]; Spain's relations with its former empire in Latin America and North Africa, as well as over Gibraltar; Portugal's Lusophone relationships and so on. For Germany's part, there are special relationships with Israel, Turkey, Namibia, Tanzania, Cameroon as well as, too, with the USA; Italy with Libya, Somalia and Eritrea.

Within the EU and across its boundaries there are also particular groupings and special relationships, for example, the Franco-German relationship that has been critical to the development of the Union; the Nordics' relationship among themselves and with the Baltic states of the Union and with Russia, or Poland's relations with Germany and Russia; Greece's relations with Cyprus and both with Turkey. A key relationship for many Member States has been that with the United States, conceived differently say by the UK or France, or Germany or Poland, but one whether bilaterally and/or through NATO has been regarded as of critical importance.

Many of these relationships have meant that there have been 'special policy issues' which are 'ring-fenced' or excluded from the EU policy process by Member States because of national sensitivities (issues of a *domain privé*) (Manners and Whitman, 2000: 273). These might include issues such as the specific behaviour in certain international organizations with, for example, the British and French determined to retain their permanent seats in the UN Security Council, while others such as Germany and Ireland have looked to the UN for approval for any ESDP missions, particularly if they involve the use of armed forces in peace-keeping. For the UK and France, their status as nuclear powers has been a critical factor, while for other issues of neutrality and non-alignment have bulked large. One can therefore observe very different patterns in the role conceptions of Member States such as, for example, the Nordic promotion of peace, human rights, democracy and redistributive justice and poverty eradication in the developing world; the British, German, Dutch and central and eastern European promotion of the free market economy and liberalization; and the French and British preparedness for military intervention in areas of geo-strategic interest.

Finally, the functional characteristics of foreign and security policy has been another important factor in shaping differentiation. While CFSP within Pillar Two remains inter-governmental in principle – though working through a consensus has long been the working method (Nuttall, 2000) – many of the policy instruments of CFSP remain within Pillar One, that is, the EC. The EU's trade and development policy, as well as enlargement and neighbourhood policies, have been intertwined with the CFSP as evident, for example, in the relations of the EU with Africa, Latin America and South-East Asia as well as the immediate neighbourhood (such as former Soviet states and Turkey). Principles such as negative and positive conditionality, joint-ownership and reciprocity are civilian policy instruments though with clear foreign and security dimensions aimed at expanding the borders of the Union, opening markets, accessing energy and raw materials resources, but also, as stated by the EU institutions, preventing and transforming conflicts, rescuing and sustaining fragile and failing states, poverty eradication and inducing democratic reforms and good governance. These principles also complement others aimed at peace-keeping, peace-making and crisis-management. In these cases, cross-pillar policy-making has been critical and hence there has been a close collaboration between EU institutions such as the Council, the Commission and to a lesser extent the European Parliament. The Commission has been particularly involved in civilian military missions and past efforts, not least on the part of France to exclude the Commission, have now largely fallen away. In many instances, there has been a particularly close accord between the smaller states and the Commission in exchanging information and in Pillar One cases, for the Commission to act as a strong mediating factor between the Member States. To some extent within the framework of Pillar Two, the information role has been taken up by the High Representative, supported by the Policy Unit, the Joint Situation Centre (SitCen) and DG E in the Council Secretariat. In the past, it was also the case that Germany took the role of being 'a friend' to the smaller Member States though this has largely fallen by the wayside since the Schroeder Chancellorship and the appointment of the High Representative.

Nonetheless, despite of the changing nature foreign policy-making, the continued national sensitivities in ceding sovereignty in this area remain and this has also been reflected in the inter-governmental agreement regarding the provisions of enhanced cooperation in the Treaties. Accordingly, the institutional threshold for enhanced cooperation (that is, nine states in an EU-27) means that should the 'Big Three', along with the remaining large states of Italy, Spain and Poland, decide to proceed with an enhanced cooperation initiative in this policy area, they would need the agreement of only three small, potentially pioneering, states such as the Benelux to form a core. This, in theory, can leave 18 small states excluded and as mere observers of flexibility initiatives in this area. In addition, the scope of enhanced cooperation in Pillar Two whereby such initiatives can be initiated only for the implementation of joint actions or common positions and not in matters having military and defence implications[19] can induce the 'Big Three' and other large states to cooperate outside the *acquis* in order to realize their ambitions. This may have important implications for the excluded states as later entry would be particularly difficult as the institutional rules of the initiative would have been shaped by the participating states. It is in this sense that the perennial argument has been that greater enhanced cooperation in the area of foreign and security policies 'would militate against the emergence of a directorate, a recurrent directing coalition, more or less formal, whether within the EU or outside of it' (Wallace and de la Serre, 1997: 17).

Finally, foreign and security policy is an area which has clear characteristics of a 'public good' (that is, a non-excludable good with neutral consumption) where the costs of exclusion from such policies are low (that is, positive policy externalities) and the possibilities for free riding high. According to Kölliker (Chapter 3 in this volume), this creates weak centripetal effects and incentives to unwilling states eventually to join. At the same time, one observes that in many flexibility initiatives such as directorates states were eager to participate or join the bandwagon. Kölliker (2006: 237–40) indicates that alternative factors might explain why non-participating states in these initiatives declared their willingness to participate despite possibilities for free-riding. He argues that this might be explained by a change in the fundamental preferences of the countries concerned or that non-participating states may not have been 'initially unwilling' in the first place. This might explain why Member States which are not participating in foreign policy 'directorates' such as those from the 'Big Three' protest for their exclusion: either they were not unwilling in the first place but did not participate because they were not invited due to their political clout and capabilities, or they were initially unwilling but changed their preferences and position in regards to the whole notion a directorate in foreign and security policy.

Form and scope of differentiated integration in foreign and security policies

The most predominant form of differentiation in the area of foreign and security policies have been the various *directoires*[20] or directorates and other cooperation initiatives among the 'Big Three' but also other regional constellations. As early as 1977, a contact group consisting of the USA, the UK, Canada, the Federal Republic of Germany and France worked to negotiate an agreement on Namibian independence. In 1993, the 'Big Three', the USA and Russia aimed to halt the Bosnian conflict with their own 'Joint Action Plan' circumventing the EU-proposed 'Vance–Owen Plan'. The Franco-British St Malo initiative in 1998, followed by the Franco-German defence initiative in Tampere (1999), was also an example of a 'Big Three' directorate leading the way in of a more independent EU on foreign and security matters. Such directorates in the form of mini-summits or diplomatic missions were held repeatedly in regards to the wars in Afghanistan and Iraq, Iran's nuclear programme crisis, the Constitutional Treaty, the Lisbon Agenda, EU–NATO cooperation, Turkey's candidacy, the Middle East Peace Process, the Cyprus Problem and Kosovo's independence. And there are also reports of the existence of a secretive 'quint' (Lockwood, 1999; Gegout, 2002) consisting of the 'Big Three', Italy and a notable outsider – the USA – which discusses the relations of the EU with the rest of the world. The 'Big Three' have recently began to cooperate with the other three large states of the EU (that is, Italy, Spain and Poland) in the internal dimension of foreign policy, such as the fight against terrorism, illegal immigration and organized crime, and in February 2008, France and Spain fielded proposals for the creation of a 'Big Six' defence 'intervention force' envisioned to be realized after the ratification of the Lisbon Treaty.[21]

There are important reasons why the 'Big Three' and other large states are compelled to forge ahead with such flexibility initiatives in this policy area. In an enlarged Europe, where consensus has not always been easy, so that the EU Troika [22] has been unable to be effective on any consistent basis, the 'Big Three' with their financial strength, their position within the G8, in the French and British case, their military forces (they contribute over 60 per cent of defence spending in EU-27), permanent seats in the UN Security Council (excluding Germany),

NATO and the G8, and powerful defence industries pushing for cooperation, are more likely to 'surge alone' if their ambitions are not realized within the EU framework.[23] There are also more underlying strategic reasons for their cooperation. Germany has sought to escape the exclusive embrace of France and has often looked either to the UK, or possibly more often to the USA. For its part, the UK is keen to indicate its willingness to lead the European project in the light of domestic and European criticism for its unconditional Atlanticism over Iraq, while it also sees trilateralism as a means to keep in check the Franco-German locomotive. France is eager to further involve the UK in security and defence issues, as it perceives this to be critical for the strengthening of this policy arm, while it also hopes to use Britain's influence to put pressure on Poland and Spain on other important constitutional issues. The so-called Weimar Group of France, Germany and Poland has often dealt with foreign policy issues (Joskowiak, 2003).

The above are not to suggest that a 'Big Three' or 'Big Six' directorate is an institution in Europe. This is because there are still fundamental differences between these states that prevent them from formalizing it into a permanent structure. France, Germany and the UK have fundamental differences in their foreign, security and defence policies and view differently their moral and strategic role in the world. As opposed to Germany, France and the UK are permanent members of the UN Security Council, they are nuclear powers with military bases and troops in overseas territories and they have both the willingness and ability to intervene militarily outside their borders and accept the sacrifices. Their position is also specific as they evaluate international relations in more strategic terms than Germany which (like other MS) emphasizes more the moral dimension and the factor of legitimacy in its analysis of international relations (as evident from its different views on the need for a UN and OSCE mandate for EU actions). The 'Big Three' construct in different ways foreign policy space and have divergent external interests, ambitions and views in regards to the European security architecture, and particularly the role of the USA, NATO and the EU within this security architecture. Overall, Germany primarily sees itself and acts as a civilian power, France stands for the ambition to create an autonomous European defence, and the UK is characterized by its 'special relationship' with the USA and its 'semi-detachment' from the European project, its devotion to the NATO security architecture and opposition to a European army, as well as its more global outlook. Their distinct perceptions of international affairs were evident during the Yugoslav conflict, the Iraq War, the Israeli–Palestinian conflict, the Lisbon Treaty, Turkey's membership, the Georgian conflict, the Russian–Ukrainian gas crisis as well as overall relations with the USA, Russia and China, and were reflected within the EU framework, the WEU, the UN and NATO. In trade, aid and development policy one would be sceptical about the creation of a directorate in this area. This was evident, for example, in the common perceptions of France and the UK – as well as Spain and Italy – in the conclusion of preferential trade agreements (such as in the banana regime) with their former colonies in the ACP countries as opposed to Germany which emphasized that the current regime discriminated against Latin American producers – a disagreement which subsequently escalated within the WTO forum. Moreover, there are equally significant divergences in the capabilities, ambitions and interests between and among the 'Big Three' and the other three large states that might undermine the success of core initiatives. Italy and Spain have long been considered the 'poor relations' in the club of six, in terms of the power of their economy and their foreign policy impact across the globe, and this is even more so for Poland. They have long been frustrated for not being included in the overwhelming majority of informal large state directorates on a range of issues, even though they consider themselves to be major actors in the EU. For example, Italy was frustrated at not being a member of the Contact Group for Bosnia despite the fact that its territory was used as a forward base for NATO air strikes in the area and that it increasingly became a front-line country and actor (Keukeleire, 2001). The frustration of these countries of not being included in these initiatives has often evolved into an opposition to the whole notion of a directorate. Indicative were the sharp reactions of these states to the February 2004 'trirectoire' meeting in Berlin. Italian Prime Minister Silvio Berlusconi described the meeting as a 'big mess' and stressed that 'nobody needs a directorate in Europe', while Spanish foreign minister Ana Palacio argued that 'nobody should be allowed to kidnap the general interest in Europe'.[24] Wlodzimierz Cimoszewicz, the head of Polish diplomacy, simply stated that 'establishing a "directoire" by the three states would not serve the interests of the European Union'.[25] With the initiative of Spanish Prime Minister José Maria Aznar, a letter of discontent condemning 'Big Three' initiatives was signed by Poland, Italy, Netherlands, Portugal and Estonia and presented to Commission President Romano Prodi.[26] Eventually, German foreign minister Joschka Fischer was compelled to make a strong statement against core Europe, arguing that the idea is 'passé' and that 'he did not see France and Germany forging ahead' if disagreements continued on major EU issues.[27]

The opposition of these countries against any 'Big Three' directorate not only has to do with them being excluded from it but also with the fact that these countries no longer have blind faith in the direction that the Franco-German duo (in particular) is leading them. Many of these countries believe that, particularly in the past two years, the Franco-German partnership is becoming less of a motor and more of a brake on integration – as the two countries have united to block reforms rather than to promote new ideas – and that the initiatives of these two countries are geared more towards their self-interests than the interests of the Union as a whole (Grabbe and Guérot, 2004). This mistrust is not unfounded. In October 2002, Berlin and Paris united to block reductions in the size of the EU's agricultural budget after 2006, a deal very much in the interest of France, which benefits significantly from the Common Agricultural Policy. Also, when both countries failed to bring their budget deficits back in line with the limits of the Stability and Growth Pact, they teamed up to persuade their fellow Member States to suspend the Pact's sanction mechanism. The fact that many Member States no longer support the policy preferences of Berlin and Paris was evident during the Iraq crisis, when Franco-German opposition to US military action split the Union in two. Many concluded then that France and Germany should not be relied upon to shape the EU's relationship with the USA. Cole (Chapter 11 in this volume) also points out how time has altered the capacity of the Franco-German axis to exercise political leadership in the integration project, as the institutional, symbolic, economic and political leadership resources of the Franco-German relationship have diminished.

Spain, Italy and Poland also have divergent positions on major foreign policy issues and view differently European foreign and security policy and transatlantic relations. As a result of their distinct territorial and temporal dimensions, they have divergent interests and ambitions in areas such as the Balkans (Italy), Latin America and North Africa (Spain) and Russia and eastern Europe (Poland) and relations with the USA. In the Iraq war, for example, Poland and Italy sided with the Anglo-American position whereas Spain withdrew its support in the midst of the campaign, siding with the Franco-German position. In that sense, in the most major foreign policy challenge of the EU in the 21st century, the six largest countries of the Union were completely divided.

Even if the divergent interests and ambitions between 'Big Three' and 'Big Six' are surmounted, there are many reasons why any large state flexibility initiatives are likely to include smaller Member States. The changing and more complex nature of foreign policy-making has meant that large states are increasingly dependent on the special capabilities and resources of small states to be effective in the international arena. The manoeuvrability, entrepreneurship and flexibility in policy-making (Katzenstein, 1985) – as evident from their effective running of Council Presidencies (Quaglia and Moxon-Browne, 2006) – immaterial power assets such as credibility, diplomatic skills and expertise in civil crisis management, make small states indispensable partners for any large state ad hoc directorate or other initiative, which, in order to be effective, requires the combination of both civilian and military means. This has been evident, for example, in the key roles of Austria, Denmark, Belgium, Greece, Romania and Slovenia in the Italian-led 'Operation Alba' in Albania in 1998 (Missiroli, 1999: 13); the role of Austria, Finland and Sweden in the WEU mission in Mostar; the role of Sweden in the WEU de-mining operation in Croatia and peace-keeping mission in Somalia (Keukeleire, 2001, 2006); the role of Belgium in the crisis in Congo; Portugal in East Timor; Finland in the Baltic Sea Region; Lithuania in the Ukrainian Orange Revolution; and Cyprus and Norway in the Hezbollah/Israel conflict. The participation of these states in these initiatives has also been facilitated by the fact that these states have significantly adapted their views to that of large Member States (Wivel, 2005; Janning, 2005) as mostly evident in the toning down of the 'policy of neutrality' of the Nordic states (Rieker, 2005). In addition, the cross-pillar nature of foreign policy-making has meant that the Commission and the High Representative are increasingly involved in any ad hoc directorates, something that enhances the voice of smaller states.

Moreover, smaller states have also been known to pursue their own separate agenda from large states and flexibility initiatives in this policy area. The Benelux, building on their historical free trade agreement – for many a precursor of the European Community – have extended that cooperation on foreign policy issues related to the Union's enlargement, energy security and conflict-resolution with their role in the Israeli–Palestinian conflict (Janssen, 2006). They have also been known to hold directorate meetings before every important summit as evident in their joint memoranda in the IGCs of Amsterdam, Nice and the Constitutional Treaty (Bossaert and Vanhoonacker, 2000; Bunse et al., 2006). The Nordic states have been cooperating in the field of foreign, security and defence policy with the establishment of the peace-keeping brigade (Nordcaps), war crimes, civil defence and disaster response, peace-keeping and peace-making, nuclear power, air space, Arctic issues, maritime and cyber security as well as holding director- ate meetings before important summits (Herolf, 2000; Bailes et al., 2006). The Baltic States have been cooperating in foreign policy, particularly in relation to Russia and the 'Eastern Dimension' of the European Neighbourhood Policy (ENP), with emphasis on their relations with Moldova and Georgia (Galbreath and Lamoreaux, 2007), in regards to trade and in the defence sphere with the various peace-keeping (Baltbat), naval (Baltron) and air space (Baltnet) networks (Kasekamp, 2005). The Visegrád countries have been cooperating within the framework of the 'Eastern Dimension' of the ENP (Dangerfield, 2009) and on issues such as energy security, terrorism and organized crime while they have been holding regular foreign ministerial meetings in order to coordinate within the framework of the ESDP, NATO, OSCE and the WEU (Hamberger, 2006). In April 2007, the Ministers of Defence of these countries pledged to establish a Visegrád EU Battle group in the horizon beyond 2015.[28] Finally, in July 2007 a Balkan battle group (HELBROC) was created among Greece, Romania, Bulgaria and Cyprus focusing on crisis management missions in the Balkans and Eastern Mediterranean.

Cooperation among these regional groups has also taken place, more specifically with the Nordic–Baltic security cooperation on issues such as strategic planning, parliamentary control of the military, procurement processes, training, technology, research and public policy, as well as joint programmes supporting the building of the national defences of Ukraine, Moldova, Georgia and Armenia (Hakamies, 2007). The Baltic and Nordic countries have also been coordinating their positions on security issues before important summits, as well as within the framework of the Northern Dimension Initiative (NDI), giving rise to an emergent Nordic–Baltic sphere of Union which includes the establishment of the three + five framework comprising the Baltic Assembly and the Nordic Council of Ministers. In the case of these countries, non-state actors such as trade unions, voluntary organizations, local councils, choirs and churches have led to a 'localization of foreign policy' which is driving these initiatives (Bergman, 2006: 79). The most notable example of Visegrád–Nordic cooperation is the Polish–Swedish-led 'Eastern Dimension' initiative of the ENP which envisions enhanced partnership agreements with countries such as Armenia, Azerbaijan, Georgia, Belarus, Moldova and Ukraine, dealing with a variety of security issues and essentially ring-fencing these states for a potential future EU membership. The Visegrád and Baltic states have also been cooperating on energy security and defence issues from as early as 1991, focusing on common challenges in relation to the 'Eastern Dimension' of the ENP, Russia and NATO's expansion (Bleiere, 1997; Hamberger, 2006), while the Visegráds have also discussed potential projects with Ukraine, Croatia and Romania on issues of the security dimension of justice and home affairs (Dangerfield, 2009: 11). Moreover, the Council of Baltic Sea States (CBSS) which comprises the Nordic–Baltic cooperation as well as Russia, Germany and Poland has the potential to cover issues of common interest in security (such as energy, terrorism and organized crime). Other cross-regional cooperation structures include those between the two of the Nordic countries (Sweden, Finland) and an Alpine country (Austria) within WEU and NATO structures – in the former structure as observer countries and in the latter as participants in the Partnership for Peace (PfP), the Planning and Review Process (PARP) and the Euro-Atlantic Partnership Council (EAPC) (Ferreira-Pereira, 2006: 107); there are also informal directorates between the Finno-Ugrian countries (Hungary, Estonia and Finland) on the ENP and Russia (Hamberger, 2006: 98) and between Greece and Cyprus in regards to Turkey's accession negotiations.

Bargaining theory and coalitional analysis in the EU-27 also supports the existing pattern of flexibility initiatives among states. While studies have revealed coalitions among the Franco-German axis (Naurin, 2007) and other territorial constellations such as the Baltic, Visegrád and Nordic states (Hosli, 1996; Kaeding and Selck, 2005; Naurin, 2007), they have not revealed an all large state or small state coalition, or even a 'Big Three' alliance. Constellation theory also indicates that both small and large Member States co-exist in different constellation groups (Mouritzen and Wivel, 2005).

Conclusion

The increased cooperation in foreign and security policy between the 'Big Three' in the form of a directorate has caused reason for concern among other Member States, particularly small states, which fear that that they would be marginalized in this important and sensitive policy area. Evidence, however, indicates that there are important differences between the three large states in their territorial and temporal dimensions and that it would be difficult to institutionalize this directorate into a permanent structure. In addition, states such as Italy, Spain and Poland, which are named in a possible core, have important divergences with the 'Big Three' but also among them. Moreover, any core initiatives with any chance of long-term success would most likely need to involve states with distinct territorial and temporal dimensions, such as small states, whose special capabilities would be indispensable in light particularly of the changing nature of foreign policy-making. Furthermore, groups of states with similar territorial and temporal dimensions such as the Baltic, Nordic, Visegrád and Balkan states are not reactive actors and have indicated that they are also capable and willing to forge ahead their own flexibility initiatives. In that sense, flexibility in the foreign and security policies has not been expressed exclusively in the form of a trilateral axis but in the form of cooperation initiatives among a group of states with distinct territorial and temporal characteristics, such as small and large, new and old, northern and southern, and colonial and non-colonial. It remains to be seen whether the trilateral axis will at some point in the future be strong and cohesive enough in order to attract a large group of states to deepen integration within the CFSP, in the likes of the Eurozone or the Schengen initiative. At this point, one can argue that, unlike Pillar One and Pillar Three, in the CFSP the 'shadow of differentiation' most significantly expressed by the 'Big Three' directorate has acted as both a source of unity and division, sometimes drawing states to the trilateral core and in others alienating them and undermining prospects of deeper integration in the area.

Notes

1. See Stercken (1969).
2. The chapter adopts a broad definition of foreign and security policy which also encompasses the area of trade, aid and development.
3. According to Article 43, closer cooperation is aimed at furthering the objectives of the Union and at protecting and serving its interests; respects the principles of the Treaties and the single institutional framework of the Union; is only used as a last resort where the objectives of the Treaties could not be attained by applying the relevant procedures; concerns at least a majority of Member States; does not affect the *acquis communautaire* and the measures adopted under the other provision of the Treaties; does not affect the competences, rights, obligations and interests of those Member States which do not participate therein; is open to all Member States and allows them to become parties to the cooperation at any time, provided that they comply with the basic decision and with the decisions taken within that framework.
4. According to Article 23(1), constructive abstention allows Member States to abstain on a vote in the Council in foreign and security issues without blocking a unanimous decision. The clause is essentially a compromise between states that aimed for QMV and closer cooperation in CFSP matters and those that wished to hold on to the status quo of the Maastricht regime.
5. According to Articles 27a-e, enhanced cooperation may be used for joint actions or common positions, but not in matters having military or defence implications. At least nine Member States (in a EU-27) need to address a request to the European Council to authorize the cooperation. The Commission 'shall give its opinion particularly on whether the enhanced cooperation proposed is consistent with Union policies' (Article 27c). Otherwise, the Commission and the EP must only be informed about developments. Authorization to proceed with enhanced cooperation should be granted by a unanimous Council decision. Overall, enhanced cooperation should be used as a 'last resort', 'should serve the interests of the whole Union' and 'should respect the single institutional framework and the acquis'.
6. According to Articles 28 a-e, permanent structured cooperation enables those (unspecified) Member States 'whose military capabilities fulfill higher criteria and which have made more binding commitments to one another in this area with a view to the most demanding missions' to integrate further in the area of military capabilities, *within* the Union framework (Article 28e). Such cooperation is governed by Article 205 (3a) whereby it stipulates that any decisions for the establishment of such cooperation, the admission of a Member State to the cooperation and any suspension are submitted for a qualified majority vote. The participating states make their decisions on the basis of unanimity. In light of the difficulty of establishing enhanced cooperation in the second pillar – given the requirement of unanimity – permanent structured cooperation offers a viable alternative for states to integrate further in this policy area. It also institutionalizes the notion of the EU Battle Groups, initially established since the early 1990s, and brings them within the integrative structure.

7. The passarelle clause essentially allows, in certain cases, the replacement of unanimous voting in the Council with qualified majority voting (QMV) when initiating enhanced cooperation.
8. White Paper on the 1996 Intergovernmental Conference, Vol. II, 29 March 1996. Commission (2000) *Adapting the Institutions for Enlargement*, Commission Opinion on IGC 2000, 26 January.
9. Ibid.
10. Ibid.
11. Ibid.
12. Commission (2000) *Adapting the Institutions for Enlargement*, Commission Opinion on IGC 2000, 26 January.
13. CONFER 4723/00, CONFER 4719/00.
14. CONFER/VAR 3951/00; CONFER/VAR 3958/00; CONFER/VAR 3962/00.
15. CONFER 4765/00, CONFER 4720/00.
16. 'Joint Franco-German proposals in the European Convention in the field of European Security and Defence', Embassy of France in the US, 27 November 2002.
17. CONV 723/03; CONV 557/03.
18. United Arab Emirates, Bahrain, Kuwait, Oman and Qatar.
19. Articles 27a-e TEU.
20. The term *directoire* was initially used for the five directors who governed France after the post-revolutionary terror in the 1790s and has now become EU jargon suggesting intergovernmental cooperation outside the framework of the treaties.
21. The common rules envisioned among this six countries for this 'permanent structured cooperation' initiative are: the spending of a minimum two per cent of their GDP on defence, a common defence equipment market and provision of 10,000 troops for the intervention force. This elite group would also commit to carry out joint security anti-terrorism projects, as well as defence infrastructure programmes, such as missile defence and intelligence technology. Note that only the UK and France fulfill the criterion of minimum two per cent of their GDP contribution to defence (*EU Observer*, 15 February 2008).
22. The EU Troika consists of the Foreign Affairs Ministers of the Member States holding the Presidency of the Council of the EU; the Secretary General/High Representative for the Common Foreign and Security Policy; and the European Commissioner in charge of external relations and European Neighbourhood Policy.
23. The argument that these large states suffer from a 'lilliput-syndrome' where they view themselves as giants being held by a crowd of mini and small countries is often brought forth (Magnette and Nicolaidis, 2005: 87).
24. *EU Observer*, 18 February 2004.
25. *EU Business*, 19 February 2004.
26. *EU Observer*, 18 February 2004.
27. *EU Observer*, 1 March 2004.
28. Joint Communiqué of the Ministers of Defence of the Visegrád group countries, Bratislava, 12 April 2007.

22

Defence Policy: Temporal and Spatial Differentiation within Reformed Bandwagoning

Tom Dyson

Post-Cold War European cooperation in defence displays significant spatial differentiation. The borders of cooperation in matters of 'hard' security are defined by Russian power in the east.[1] At the same time, a diverse set of intergovernmental arrangements have arisen within these territorial boundaries (Tables 22.4 and 22.5). They include '*à la carte*', 'variable-geometry' and 'multiple-speed' initiatives in joint military capability procurement programmes and the cross-national generation of crisis-management forces. However, the main institutions of European security, the European Security and Defence Policy (ESDP) and NATO, display stronger complementarity in membership.[2] Apart from Austria, Cyprus, Finland, Ireland, Malta and Sweden, all EU states are members of NATO.[3] Of the 24 European NATO members, only Denmark,[4] Turkey and Norway are not full participants in ESDP (see Table 22.1).

Nevertheless, at first glace, there appears to be differentiation in preferences to route cooperation through NATO or ESDP. UK defence policy remains firmly anchored within NATO and committed to capability acquisition, ensuring interoperability with the USA, despite an incremental shift towards embeddedness within ESDP (Dover, 2007: 88; Farrell, 2008: 781–2; Jones, 2007: 223; Miskimmon, 2004). Contemporary French defence policy prioritizes ESDP and capability procurement, seeking an autonomous European capacity for military action (Brenner, 2003; Irondelle, 2003; Lungu, 2004b). It is, however, increasingly Atlanticized, symbolized by France's return to NATO's integrated military command in 2009 (Sutton, 2008: 307–11). The institutional forums of German defence policy cohere around a 'bridge' role, between British and French preferences and, until recently, Germany has been a relative laggard in the development of interoperable crisis-management capabilities (Dyson, 2005: 373–6). Similar differentiation is evident amongst Europe's smaller states. Whilst Finland and Sweden prefer to route defence cooperation through ESDP, Denmark, Norway, the Baltic States, east-central European (CEE) states, and Balkan states are more Atlanticist (Jones, 2007: 238; Lansford and Tashev, 2005).

This differentiation raises the question of what broader function these initiatives serve. Are European states moving towards common or divergent policy objectives through ESDP, NATO, and bi/plurilateral initiatives? Determining the level of

Table 22.1 Membership of the core institutions of European security

State	ESDP	EDA	ESA	ESC¹	WEU	OSCE	NATO
Austria	x	x	x	x	3	x	1
Belgium	x	x	x	x	x	x	x
Bulgaria	x	x		x	4	x	x
Cyprus	x	x		x		x	
Canada			1			x	x
Czech Republic	x	x	1	x	2	x	x
Denmark			x	x	3	x	x
Estonia	x	x		x	4	x	x
Finland	x	x	x	x	3	x	
France	x	x	x	x	x	x	x
Germany	x	x	x	x	x	x	x
Greece	x	x	x	x	x	x	x
Hungary	x	x	1	x	2	x	x
Iceland					2	x	x
Ireland	x	x	x	x	3	x	
Italy	x	x	x	x	x	x	x
Latvia	x	x		x	4	x	x
Lithuania	x	x		x	4	x	x
Luxembourg	x	x	x	x	x	x	x
Malta	x	x		x		x	
Netherlands	x	x	x	x	x	x	x
Norway		1	x		2	x	x
Poland	x	x	1	x	2	x	x
Portugal	x	x	x	x	x	x	x
Romania	x	x	1	x	4	x	x
Slovakia	x	x		x	4	x	x
Slovenia	x	x		x	4	x	x
Spain	x	x	x	x	x	x	x
Sweden	x	x	x	x	2	x	
Switzerland			x			x	
Turkey					2	x	x
UK	x	x		x	x	x	x
USA						x	x

KEY
1 = Cooperation Agreement
2 = Associate Members
3 = Observer Members
4 = Associate Partners

complementarity between these arrangements, particularly NATO and ESDP, is central in establishing the level and significance of differentiated cooperation.

This chapter will highlight how NATO and ESDP are converging around increasingly similar functions: a new form of 'forward defence' tackling threats to international instability at source (Ben-Ari, 2005; Kaitera and Ben-Ari, 2008; Farrell, 2008: 798–9). This convergence in function has been accompanied by spatial differentiation. ESDP focuses on Europe's geopolitical neighbourhood, whilst NATO increases emphasis on global instability. Consequently, NATO is increasingly acting as a forum for developing capabilities of benefit to ESDP. Likewise, the

European Defence Agency (EDA) and Headline Goals 2010 are fostering capability and doctrinal developments of use to Atlantic Alliance missions. The greatest divergence exists in the 'provision' or 'consumption' of security.

This chapter begins with an analysis of complementarity and differentiation in the function, territoriality and temporality of ESDP/NATO initiatives and other post-Cold War instances of defence cooperation. It then demonstrates the analytical leverage of neo-classical realism in explaining these patterns: that is, the powerful effects exerted by international structure, combined with the important intervening role of unit-level factors in shaping the temporality, territoriality and functional scope of cooperation.

Functional, spatial and temporal complementarity and differentiation: a case of duplication?

The EU's longer-term development as an increasingly militarized actor since the launch of ESDP in December 1999 appears to herald the development of a rival security organization to NATO (Art, 2004; Pape, 2005; Paul, 2005; Posen, 2006). Whilst NATO is an institution of collective defence, both institutions have emerged as forums for coordinating similar objectives: tackling threats to international instability at source, through low-intensity, expeditionary crisis-management operations.

The European Rapid Reaction Force was created in 1999, consisting of 60,000 troops deployable at 60 days' notice, sustainable for up to one year, capable of undertaking lower-intensity tasks and of sustaining one medium-to-high-intensity operation (Cornish and Edwards, 2005: 804–5). The December 1999 European Council also established three main institutions to support ESDP, reflecting NATO's intergovernmental political–military structures: the Political and Security Committee, the EU Military Committee, and the EU Military Staff. Since 2004 there has been a clear attempt to establish structures facilitating robust, higher-intensity tasks, notably the Headline Goal 2010 and the May 2004 Battlegroup Initiative that created up to 15 Battlegroups, each consisting of 1500 troops, deployable within 15 days (Cornish and Edwards, 2005: 804; Howorth, 2007: 107; Ulriksen, 2004: 469–70). This development has been accompanied by steps to ensure a 'comprehensive approach' to the planning and conduct of military operations, integrating civilian and military instruments.

NATO's development as a focal point for expeditionary operations began in earnest at the April 1999 Washington Summit, which resulted in an updated Strategic Concept outlining crisis-management as a core function. This concept was given concrete form at the November 2002 Prague Summit through the NATO Response Force (NRF): a high-readiness, technically advanced joint air, naval and infantry force of 21,000 troops, deployable within five to 30 days for up to three months, drawn predominantly from NATO's European members and designed to undertake high-intensity war-fighting tasks, disaster relief and peace-keeping (King, 2005: 331).

The November 2006 Riga Summit endorsed Comprehensive Political Guidance (CPG) that built upon the 1999 Strategic Concept by identifying the core threats to NATO as international terrorism, the proliferation of weapons of mass destruction (WMD), failed/failing states, regional crises, misuse of technologies and disruption of resource flows. The Riga Declaration is significant as it outlines the requirement for a shift in force structures and capabilities to permit simultaneous combat, stabilization, reconstruction, reconciliation and humanitarian missions; notably the strengthening of NATO's crisis-management instruments and cooperation with the UN, non-governmental organizations (NGOs) and local actors in the conduct and planning of military operations.[5]

Hence the EU is gradually developing the institutional mechanisms and instruments to facilitate more robust missions at the higher end of the conflict spectrum and appears to represent a growing competitor to NATO, which is at the inception of developing its peace-support capabilities (Kaitera and Ben-Ari, 2008: 7–8). This apparent functional duplication is evident in the December 2003 European Security Strategy, which outlines a similar set of challenges to CPG.[6]

This picture of competition is, however, misleading. It is more accurate to point to increasing complementarity and cooperation in military capacity, command facilities and force planning and to growing strategic coherence between NATO and ESDP (Mowle and Sacko, 2007: 597–618; Rynning, 2005: 155, 172; Ulriksen, 2004: 468). This is evident in the March 2003 Berlin-Plus Agreement, facilitating the inclusion of EU outsiders into ESDP structures and providing the EU with access to NATO operational planning, capabilities and assets. Furthermore, Berlin Plus included arrangements to facilitate mutually reinforcing capability acquisition, establishing the EU–NATO Capability Group in May 2003, supplemented by regular meetings between EU and NATO officials (Cornish and Edwards, 2005: 814–18). Moreover, in October 2005 a permanent NATO liaison within the EU Military Staff and a permanent EU planning cell at Supreme Headquarters Allied Powers Europe (SHAPE) were established (Cornish and Edwards, 2005: 812).

Whilst the EU is developing the capacity to undertake higher-intensity tasks, the NRF remains heavier, more rapidly deployable and more focused on full-spectrum tasks than the Battlegroups (Kaitera and Ben-Ari, 2008; Howorth, 2007: 14–15; Rynning, 2005: 157).[7] This functional difference is reflected in ESDP missions, which have largely been at the lower end of the conflict spectrum. Furthermore, NATO and the EU are emerging as organizations characterized by spatial differentiation. Although the strategic radius of EU operations has expanded significantly since 1999, ESDP missions are predominantly focused on the EU geo-strategic neighbourhood, whilst NATO's deployments have been ever more global (Jones, 2007: 216).

European capability initiatives and the gradual emergence of military isomorphism

It is possible to distinguish an increasingly distinct model of military convergence amongst Europe's Great Powers that is being reflected in capability cooperation: the development of joint, flexible, military forces capable of expeditionary missions on the full range of the conflict spectrum. Capability investment in Britain,

France, Germany[8] – and to a more limited extent in lesser-rank European states, particularly Finland, Italy, the Netherlands, Norway, Spain and Sweden – forms a partial and selective emulation of the US-led Revolution in Military Affairs (RMA) (Adams and Ben-Ari, 2006: 58–83; T. Dyson, 2008: 729–37; Flournoy and Smith, 2005: 91).

Crucially, European military isomorphism does not support the 'technological determinism' that has defined US reform (Reynolds, 2007). European states are in the process of undertaking a modest emulation of the core concepts underpinning US 'transformation' in the form of Network Enabled Capability (NEC) and the Effects-Based Approach to Operations (EBAO) (T. Dyson, 2008: 729–37).[9] Capability acquisition, not least of C4ISR (command, control, communications, computers, intelligence, surveillance, reconnaissance) and precision-guided munitions, reflects the desire to augment their capacity to undertake stand-off, high-intensity war-fighting operations against peer or near-peer competitors, alongside the USA and each other. At the same time convergence is focused on crisis-management operations of varying intensity and the limitations of technology. Reforms have also emphasized the effective integration of civilian and military instruments in low-medium intensity peace-support operations (the 'Comprehensive Approach') (Farrell, 2008: 793; Kaitera and Ben-Ari, 2008: 7). This isomorphism, led by Britain, France and, to a lesser extent, Germany, has been accompanied by the development of niche capabilities by smaller (largely west European) NATO/EU states, in support of low-high intensity crisis-management operations (Reynolds, 2007: 364).

ESDP capability procurement initiatives: from civilian crisis-management to C4ISR

European military isomorphism is increasingly reflected in ESDP initiatives. The Battlegroup Initiative was supplemented by the EDA's establishment in July 2004. Whilst inter-governmental and deficient in enforcement mechanisms, the EDA is an important step towards cross-European acquisition (Posen, 2006: 181; Reynolds 2007: 375).[10] It is the first EU-level agency charged with identifying European capability needs, promoting armaments cooperation, coordinating research on defence technology, and strengthening Europe's defence industry. The organization has taken responsibility for leading up the Headline Goals 2010, which outlined interoperability, sustainability and deployability as the core capabilities necessary to permit several simultaneous Battlegroup operations (Cornish and Edwards, 2005: 804; Howorth, 2007: 109).

Of particular note is the 2006 'Long-term Vision for European Defence Capability and Capacity Needs (LTV)', outlining the C4ISR capabilities required for ESDP, and forming the basis for a more detailed Capabilities Development Plan that is currently under negotiation.[11] The EDA's 'Comprehensive Capabilities Development Process' has also highlighted several areas of joint procurement required to facilitate Battlegroup missions.[12] Furthermore, the EDA has instigated numerous collaborative '*à la carte*' projects in R&T, including a Joint Investment

Programme on Force Protection (JIP-FP) beginning in January 2007, and resulting in eight C4ISR projects.[13] In May 2008 a second, two-year JIP was launched, investigating Innovative Concepts and Emerging Technologies (JIP–ICET) (see Table 22.2). An additional EDA R&T programme is the 'Miracle' Project on Micro-Satellite Cluster Technology (transferred from the West European Armaments Group in June 2007). Miracle investigated the technologies necessary for the use of SAR cluster (Synthetic Aperture Radar) and ELINT (Electronic Intelligence) satellites in military operations as a basis for European ISR (Intelligence, Surveillance and Reconnaissance) capabilities.[14]

Another important development within the EDA is the July 2006 Code of Conduct on Defence Procurement (CoC), establishing a European Defence Equipment Market

Table 22.2 Major 'multiple speed' capability initiative within the EDA

State	Software Defined Radio	21st Century Soldier Systems	JIP-FP	JIP-IECT	MIRACLE	Code of Conduct on Defence Procurement
Austria		X	X		X	X
Belgium			X		X	X
Bulgaria						X
Cyprus			X	X		X
Czech Republic			X		X	X
Estonia			X			X
Finland	X	X	X		X	X
France	X		X	X	X	X
Germany		X	X	X	X	X
Greece			X	X	X	X
Hungary			X	X	X	X
Iceland						
Ireland			X			X
Italy	X	X	X	X	X	X
Latvia						X
Lithuania						X
Luxembourg					X	X
Malta						X
Netherlands			X		X	X
Norway			X	X	X	
Poland	X		X	X	X	X
Portugal		X	X		X	X
Romania						
Slovakia			X	X		X
Slovenia			X	X		X
Spain	X		X	X	X	X
Sweden	X	X	X		X	X
Turkey					X	
UK					X	X

and Europe-wide tenders for defence contracts. Whilst voluntary, the CoC is an important step towards an internationally competitive European armaments market and builds upon progress during the 1990s in consolidating Europe's defence–industrial base. In 1990 the European defence industry was characterized by a plethora of small and medium-sized national firms. It is now possible to identify three major defence firms: BAE systems, Thales and EADS. However, when compared to the USA, whose industry is dominated by Lockheed Martin and Boeing, Europe's defence industry remains relatively fragmented (Guay and Callum, 2002: 763).

Furthermore, in November 2003 the European Space Agency (ESA) entered into a Framework Agreement with the European Commission's Directorate-General Transportation. A particularly important ESA initiative is the Galileo global navigation system that, by 2013, will enhance NEC in Battlegroup and NRF operations, having proceeded in close cooperation with the USA to ensure complementarity with the Global Positioning System. Cooperation in space policy is 'multiple speed', as ESA membership is dependent upon a state's space industry capacity and contribution to the ESA budget (see Howarth, Chapter 16 in this volume). Europe's space technology development has also been supported by the January 2002 incorporation of the European Satellite Centre (ESC) into the EU.

Finally, the December 2004 European Council established the Civilian Headline Goal (CHG) 2008 that improved EU civilian crisis-management capacity by developing rapid-response capabilities, including Civilian Response Teams, Integrated Police Teams and Formed Police Units.[15] In November 2007 CHG 2008 was re-launched as CHG 2010, outlining several new priority areas for crisis-management capability development.[16]

In short, capability investment programmes under the auspices of the EU have not only bolstered the civilian dimension of ESDP, but have also begun to foster interoperability in C4ISR and develop the foundations to equip the Battlegroups with the necessary capabilities for network-enabled 'robust' crisis-management operations.

NATO *à la carte* capability procurement initiatives: improving C4ISR and interoperability

Recent developments within NATO are increasingly centred on improving Europe's capacity to undertake full-spectrum operations (see Table 22.3). Although NATO does not yet enjoy a common C2 (command and control) capability, the Alliance instigated several important (largely *à la carte*) programmes during the 1990s that developed the building blocks for NEC.

Firstly, the Allied Command Europe Automated Command and Control Information System (ACCIS) facilitated a common operational picture, supported by the December 2000 NATO Command, Control and Communications NATO Technical Architecture Initiative (NC3TA), outlining the short-term technical requirements to enhance C3 interoperability (Adams and Ben-Ari, 2008: 87). Secondly, the Air Command and Control System (ACCS) of 1999 was integrated into national militaries in 2008. Thirdly, a NATO General Purpose Communications System

Table 22.3 Major post-Cold War capability initiatives within NATO

State	ACCIS	ACCS	NGCS	MIDS	CAESAR	CoE	SAIS	SAC	Sea lift	NH 90	AGS	MAJIIC	ALT BMD	Satcom	NM EC	RTO
Austria																
Belgium	x	x	x			x				x	x		x			x
Bulgaria	x	x	x					x			x		x			x
Cyprus								x								
Canada	x	x	x			x	x	x	x		x	x	x		x	x
Czech Republic	x	x	x			x	x	x			x		x			x
Denmark	x	x	x			x	x		x		x		x			x
Estonia	x	x	x			x		x			x		x			x
Finland								x		x						
France	x	x	x	x		x	x			x	x	x	x	x		x
Germany	x	x	x	x		x(3)	x			x	x	x	x		x	x
Greece	x	x	x							x	x		x		x	x
Hungary	x	x	x			x	x	x	x	x	x		x			x
Iceland	x	x	x								x		x			
Ireland											x		x			
Italy	x	x	x	x				x	x	x	x	x	x	x	x	x
Latvia	x	x	x					x			x		x			x
Lithuania	x	x	x					x			x		x			x
Luxembourg	x	x	x				x				x		x			
Malta	x	x	x								x		x			
Netherlands	x	x	x			x(2)	x	x	x	x	x	x	x		x	x
Norway	x	x	x			x	x	x	x	x	x	x	x		x	x
Poland	x	x	x				x	x			x		x			x
Portugal	x	x	x			x	x		x	x	x		x			x
Romania	x	x	x			x	x	x			x		x			x
Slovakia	x	x	x			x	x	x			x		x			x
Slovenia	x	x	x			x	x	x			x		x			x
Spain	x	x	x	x		x	x		x	x	x	x	x		x	x
Sweden										x						
Switzerland																
Turkey	x	x	x			x	x		x		x	x	x	x	x	x
UK	x	x	x						x			x	x	x	x	x
USA	x	x	x	x	x	x	x	x			x	x	x	x	x	x

(NGCS) permitted the communication of data and voice information. Finally, the Multifunctional Information Distribution System (MIDS), a 'multiple-speed' initiative, was initiated in 1991 and fostered cross-platform telecommunications interoperability.[17]

NATO also took strides to develop ISR (Intelligence, Surveillance and Reconnaissance) capabilities in the late 1990s. Since July 1996 the coordination of NATO's C4ISR initiatives has been facilitated by the NATO Consultation, Command and Control Agency (NC3A) (Flournoy and Smith, 2005: 65–6).[18] One particularly notable project within NC3A is the Coalition Aerial Surveillance and Reconnaissance (CAESAR) programme testing national and NATO air-and-space-based C4ISR systems with the aim of creating a single system (Adams and Ben-Ari, 2008: 91). National development of interoperable C4ISR technology and its application in crisis-management operations has also been facilitated by the 1998 establishment of the Research and Technology Organisation (RTO), providing an important forum for exchanging technical information and bolstering cooperation in the development and operationalization of defence technologies.

The November 2002 Prague Summit formed a landmark in the development of NEC. The ability of European states to furnish the NRF with strategic lift, logistical and C4ISR capabilities emerged as critical for the initiative's viability. In its streamlining of NATO Command Structures, the Prague Summit established a Strategic Command for Transformation (the US-based Allied Command Transformation [ACT]) tasked with improving training, capabilities and doctrine in EBAO and NEC. Subordinate structures are distributed across Europe, augmented by national and multi-nationally funded Centres of Excellence (CoE) dispersed across NATO's European members.[19]

The core function of ACT is to lead up the Prague Capabilities Commitment, which outlined specific commitments and timetables for the acquisition of capabilities necessary to deploy the NRF.[20] The main projects are Strategic Air and Sea Lift Capabilities, Alliance Ground Surveillance (AGS), and Theatre Missile Defence (TMD). Improvements in airlift have taken the form of two initiatives: the Strategic Airlift Interim Solution (SAIS) and acquisition of three Boeing C-17 transport aircraft to develop NATO's Strategic Airlift Capability (SAC). Sealift capabilities are being developed by a consortium led by Norway.

Improvements in airlift build upon developments during the 1990s such as the NH90 Naval and Tactical Helicopters, which entered production in June 2000 and came into service after 2006. The core NATO programme in ISR is AGS, involving the development of manned and unmanned radar platforms (Flournoy and Smith, 2005: 33).[21] ISR has also been supplemented by the Multi-Sensor Aerospace-Ground Joint ISR Interoperability Programme (MAJIIC), a five-year technology demonstrator launched in 2005.[22] The current NATO AWACS (Airborne Warning and Control System) fleet is also being updated (Adams and Ben-Ari, 2006: 91).

The PCC also included a commitment to TMD that will link with ACCIS to protect NATO troops on out-of-area deployments, taking the form of the Active Layered Theatre Ballistic Defence System (ALTBMD) a 'system of systems' with a range of 3000km. Furthermore, the Alliance's satellite communications capabilities have been updated through the Satcom Post-2000 Programme, initiated in May 2004 and operable from January 2005.[23] Finally, ACT has provided a forum for the NATO NEC Project (NMEC) launched in November 2003 and completed in 2005. This study examined the utility of NEC in the NRF and the implications for future NATO procurement, resulting in a 'roadmap' for NEC adopted by ACT as the basis for future capability acquisition.[24]

In summary, following the Prague Summit, European NATO members have made important strides to enhance capabilities and interoperability with the USA and each other in C4ISR. This process has been led by the USA, in tandem with a group of European NATO states (Britain, France, Germany, Italy, the Netherlands, Norway, Spain), which have assumed the responsibility to push ahead with capabilities to be put to the service of the Alliance as a whole (Adams and Ben-Ari, 2006: 105).

Defence procurement initiatives outside NATO and EU frameworks: *à la carte*, multiple-speed and variable-geometry cooperation

NATO and ESDP initiatives build upon the achievements of numerous sub-regional '*à la carte*' capability procurement programmes, improving the capacity of the west European Great Powers to undertake joint high-intensity expeditionary warfare.

The Eurofighter Typhoon, a project whose roots lie in the Cold War, involves the development of an air-to-surface, multi-role combat aircraft.[25] The Eurofighter's NEC capabilities have been enhanced through the Meteor radar-guided air-to-air missile that enters service in 2010 and the addition of automated laser-guided weaponry.[26] The PzH 2000 Armoured Howitzer has been under development since the early 1990s. The Howitzer's tactical mobility makes it suitable for high-intensity expeditionary crisis-management operations, illustrated by its deployment by the Dutch in NATO's International Security Assistance Force (ISAF) mission. However, the Howitzer's weight has created problems of strategic mobility, reflecting its original design for territorial defence.[27] Finally, the 'nEU-ROn' Unmanned Combat Aerial Vehicle is a demonstrator project, maintaining and developing European skills in strategic technologies. Originally launched by France as an autonomous project in 1999, nEUROn has, since 2005, involved the delegation of 50 per cent of work to European partners (see Table 22.4).

Established in November 1996, the Organization for Joint Armament Coordination (OCCAR) manages collaborative armaments programmes by Britain, France, Germany and Italy. Membership is open to other European NATO/EU members, who may also participate in a procurement programme under a cooperative agreement. OCCAR has coordinated several joint ventures, augmenting its participants' capacities to undertake crisis-management operations within NATO/ESDP: FSAF (the Future Surface-to-Air Anti-Missile Family); the A-400 M transport aircraft; the Tiger multi-role attack helicopter; the Boxer multi-role armoured utility vehicle; COBRA (Counter Battery Radar) and FREMM (multi-role frigate).[28]

Table 22.4 Major bi/pluri-lateral capability procurement initiatives outside EU/NATO frameworks

State	Eurofighter	nEUROn	PzH 2000	OCCAR	FSAF	A-400 M	Tiger	Boxer	COBRA	FREMM	LOI	Galileo	Pleiades
Austria	x											x	x
Belgium				x		x						x	x
Bulgaria													
Cyprus													
Canada												x	
Czech Republic												x	
Denmark												x	
Estonia												x	
Finland												x	
France		x		x	x	x	x		x	x	x	x	x
Germany	x		x	x		x	x	x		x	x	x	
Greece		x	x									x	
Hungary												x	
Iceland													
Ireland													
Italy	x	x	x	x	x	x			x	x	x	x	x
Latvia													
Lithuania													
Luxembourg				1		x						x	
Malta													
Netherlands			x	1				x				x	
Norway												x	
Poland												x	
Portugal												x	
Romania												x	
Slovakia													
Slovenia												x	
Spain	x	x		x		x	x				x	x	x
Sweden		x									x	x	x
Switzerland		x											
Turkey						x							
UK	x			1	2	x			x			x	
USA												x	

KEY

1 = Participation under cooperative agreement

2 = The UK is participating in the Principal Anti-Air Missile System (PAAMS)

The development of OCCAR has been supplemented by the signature of a letter of intent (LOI) in 1998 by Europe's major armament-producing states aimed at integrating Europe's defence market. This 'variable-geometry' initiative was followed by a 2001 Framework Agreement between LOI states on compatibility in defence supply, export control, security of information, military research and technology, technical information, military requirements and R&D (Adams and Ben-Ari, 2006: 114).

French leadership has also been evident in the development of Europe's space-based assets. These comprise three '*à la carte*' initiatives: the SAR-Lupe and the Pleiades programmes, and the 'Common Operational Requirements'. The Pleiades Programme is a civilian and military Optical and Radar Federated Earth Observation Satellite system initiated on 29 January 2001 by France and Italy (Flournoy and Smith, 2005: 91). Pleiades led to the launch of radar satellites in 2005 and high-resolution optical satellites in 2007 which have a global imaging capability and operate jointly with the French Helios 2 optical reconnaissance satellite and Italian COSMO-Skymed satellite system.[29] SAR Lupe is a German reconnaissance satellite project (operational from 2008), involving the development of five satellites and one ground segment providing worldwide, all-weather information, operating jointly with the Helios 2, Skymed and Pleiades satellites (Flournoy and Smith, 2005: 91). This pooling of space assets is being augmented through the French-led Common Operational Requirements, creating a group of data-providers and users responsible for gathering and disseminating satellite imaging (Adams and Ben-Ari, 2006: 129). Together, these multi-national arrangements form significant steps towards developing the space technology necessary to conduct networked operations.

À la carte, multiple-speed and variable-geometry force generation initiatives outside NATO/EU frameworks

Several French-led, sub-regional *à la carte* multinational initiatives arose during the 1990s, aimed at developing high-readiness joint forces capable of participation in both NATO and ESDP missions (see Table 20.5). They included the Franco-German Brigade (established 1987) and renamed EUROCORPS in 1992, reflecting EUROCORPS' openness to all European NATO/EU members. EUROCORPS formed an NRF headquarters, as well as contributing to an EU Battlegroup.[30] The EUROFORCES were established in 1995 by France, Italy, Portugal and Spain to facilitate troop contributions for the Petersburg tasks (humanitarian and rescue, peace-keeping and peace-making tasks set out at the Petersburg declaration of 1992), but now operate under the auspices of ESDP. They are composed of two components: EUROMARFOR (European naval force) and EUROFOR (the European Operational Rapid Force) capable of deploying up to a Light Division in support of Battlegroup operations. The same states created the European Gendarmerie Force (EGF) in September 2004, capable of robust policing missions under military command (up to 800 police deployable within 30 days). The EGF has not only bolstered the EU's civilian crisis-management functions, but has also contributed to NATO operations in the former Yugoslavia. The German-Netherlands Corps was activated in August 1995 and has been an NRF headquarters since 2004 (Adams and Ben-Ari, 2006: 53).

The European Amphibious Initiative (EAI), established in December 2000 (open to all European NATO members and EU Member States), is aimed at enhancing the interoperability of forces under both NRF and Battlegroup missions. The European Air Group, launched by Britain and France in June 1996, serves a similar function: the enhancement of interoperability between participating EU/NATO airforces.[31] The Sealift Coordination Centre (SCC) was initiated in June 2001 by members of NATO's High-Level Steering Group's Working Group on Strategic Sealift and formed a framework for the provision of strategic sealift assets (roll on/roll off ships) to NATO and the coordination of chartering of private/military ships to the EU, UN or *ad hoc* coalitions of NATO/EU states.[32] The European Airlift Centre (EAC) was a Franco-German initiative of 2001, designed to coordinate the military airlift of European NATO Member States and create a common European air fleet.[33] The work of the SCC and EAC were brought under one roof in July 2007 with the creation of the *à la carte* Movement Coordination Centre Europe (MCCE), supporting EU and NATO operations.[34]

The Multinational Interoperability Council (MIC) is an example of 'multiple-speed' cooperation that focuses on improving interoperability in doctrine, operational planning, NEC and C4ISR capabilities of 'vanguard' NATO Member States through working groups and the conduct of 'Multinational Experiments', including the annual 'Combined Endeavour' exercises (Adams and Ben-Ari, 2006: 100).[35] The May 2008 exercise included 40 partner states, as well as NATO and the Multinational Peace Force South (MPFSEE). Finally, the 'multiple-speed' Multilateral Interoperability Programme (MIP) was established in April 1998 to deal with interoperability issues relating to C2IS (command, control and information systems).[36]

It is also possible to identify three sub-regional institutions of 'variable geometry': NORDCAPS, Baltic Defence Cooperation and the MPFSEE. NORDCAPS (Nordic Coordinated Arrangement for Military Peace Support) was established in 1997.[37] It forms a mechanism for enhanced cooperation between Nordic nations in the planning and conduct of crisis-management missions. Baltic Defence Cooperation comprises four projects: BALTBEAT (a Baltic Battalion, established 1994); BALTRON (a Baltic Naval Squadron, established 1997); BALTNET (the Baltic Air Surveillance Network, established 1996) and BALTDEFCOL (the Baltic Defence College, established 1998).[38] These arrangements are primarily designed to enhance the ability of Estonia, Latvia and Lithuania to contribute to NATO-led expeditionary crisis-management operations by developing C2 capabilities and training. Finally, MPFSEE was initiated in August 1999. Although initially designed for deployment within the Balkans under the auspices of NATO, the EU, Organisation for Security and Cooperation in Europe (OSCE) or the UN, MPFSEE contributed to NATO's ISAF mission from February to October 2006.

Table 22.5 À *la carte*, multiple-speed and variable-geometry force generation initiatives outside EU/NATO

State	Battlegroup Initiative	Eurocorps	Euroforces	EGF	EAI	MMCE	MIC	MIP	BDC	NORDCAPS
Austria	x							1		
Belgium	x	x			x	x		1		
Bulgaria	x							1		
Cyprus	x									
Canada						x	x	1		
Czech Republic	x							1		
Denmark		x			x	x				x
Estonia	x					x			x	
Finland	x					x		1		x
France		x	x	x	x	x		x		
Germany		x				x	x	x		
Greece		x					x	1		
Hungary	x					x				
Iceland										x
Ireland	x									
Italy	x	x	x	x	x	x		x		
Latvia	x					x			x	
Lithuania	x							x	x	
Luxembourg	x	x				x				
Malta										
Netherlands	x				x	x		x		
Norway	x	x				x		1		x
Poland	x	x						1		
Portugal	x		x	x				1		
Romania	x							1		
Slovakia	x									
Slovenia	x					x		1		
Spain	x	x	x	x	x	x		x		
Sweden	x					x		1		x
Switzerland										
Turkey	x	x				x		x		
UK	x	x			x	x	x	x		
USA					x		x	x		

Key
1 = Observer Status

Functional complementarity combined with spatial and temporal differentiation

In summary, post-Cold War defence cooperation has taken a distinct territorial form. Its geographical scope to the East is shaped by Russian power, with the emergence of vanguard states within these territorial boundaries. During the mid-late 1990s and early 21st-century 'core' states (Britain, France and Germany) pushed ahead with developing non-excludable public goods through intergovernmental, non-binding institutional arrangements under ESDP/NATO and '*à la carte*', 'variable-geometry' or 'multiple-speed' initiatives outside NATO/EU frameworks. A group of smaller European states, particularly Denmark, Finland, the Netherlands, Norway, Italy, Spain and Sweden, coalesced around the ability to make 'niche contributions' to Battlegroup/NRF missions through '*à la carte*'/'variable-geometry' procurement projects and force-generation initiatives. Furthermore, ESDP and NATO are becoming ever more spatially distinct in function: ESDP is emerging as a mechanism for Europe to engage with threats from its geopolitical neighbourhood, NATO as a global actor in crisis management.

Whilst much national duplication continues to exist in armaments procurement, the above initiatives increasingly serve a common function. They represent significant steps towards generating crisis-management forces capable of operating alongside the USA and other European states (Howorth, 2007: 44–5; Ulriksen, 2004: 469–71). The emergence of a 'core' Europe in defence has, however, been characterized by differentiation in temporal sequencing. From 1994 France has most single-mindedly pursued the 'Europeanization' of its security and defence policies and the enhancement of Europe's C2/C4ISR capabilities (Howorth, 2007: 45). France was joined by the UK in strengthening European autonomy following the October 1998 St Malo Accord. These states have been joined by a third regional leader – Germany, Europe's third great power. Whilst Germany, since 2003, has been developing a military capable of enabling it to assume a leadership role, through the 1990s and early 21st century the Federal Republic played a more reactive role in European defence cooperation. Germany displayed temporal lag in the development of the forces necessary to contribute to European/Atlantic 'public goods' in low–high-intensity crisis-management operations (Adams and Ben-Ari, 2006: 47–58; 124; Dyson, 2005).

Neo-realism and differentiation

Neo-realism provides a compelling account of the structural factors determining these patterns of functional complementarity and spatially and temporally differentiated cooperation (Waltz, 1979: 88–93). According to Waltz (1979), the international system is characterized by insecurity and self-help and is therefore highly competitive. States, as rational actors, assess the costs and benefits of different strategies in maximizing their security. The propensity for conflict and cooperation within the international system is dependent upon the balance of capabilities. It is possible to outline four main distributions of power: unipolarity;

bipolarity,[39] balanced multipolarity and unbalanced multipolarity (Hyde-Price, 2007: 41–4). Under unipolarity, one state enjoys an overriding dominance in economic and military capabilities (Mearsheimer, 2001: 44–5). Multipolarity is a power configuration in which three or more great powers exist. It can take two forms: balanced (where these states enjoy relatively similar power capabilities) or unbalanced (inherently unstable, as one state has the potential to strive for regional hegemony).

Post-Cold War Europe: balanced multipolarity situated within offshore balancing

As Hyde-Price (2007: 83–6) and Mearsheimer (2001) demonstrate, the USA's increased willingness to employ pre-emptive unilateral military force presents compelling evidence of offensive unipolarity[40] (Posen, 2003: 5–6). Situated within this systemic context in which the USA acts as Europe's 'offshore balancer',[41] west and east-central Europe are also subject to a dynamic of 'balanced multipolarity', where a balance of power exists between Britain, France and Germany. Defence cooperation is also subject to the constraints imposed by Russian contestation of US authority in Eastern Europe. As the following section will demonstrate, this context creates a powerful incentive for the development of European defence cooperation on terms that are increasingly complementary with NATO, yet subject to spatial and temporal differentiation.

Explaining complementarity in function: European security cooperation as reformed bandwagoning

Neo-realism suggests that four responses to unipolarity are possible: balancing,[42] buck-passing,[43] aggression,[44] and bandwagoning. Bandwagoning is defined by Schweller (1997: 928) as: 'Any attempt to side with the stronger, especially for opportunistic gain'. In Europe, 'reformed' bandwagoning is the dominant strategic response as European states strengthen their alliance with the USA in order to maximize their power, influence and, crucially, security (T. Dyson, 2008: 740–1; Schweller, 1998: 67; Walt, 1988). The fear of 'entrapment' into US policy in areas where strategic interests diverge, or 'abandonment' through the withdrawal of the US security guarantee, has incentivized policy leadership by Europe's Great Powers to pool European military resources (Press-Barnathan, 2006: 307–8). European security cooperation therefore represents a European attempt to develop a 'division of labour' strategy within the Atlantic Alliance following the failure of Europe's pursuit of a 'binding' strategy'[45] through NATO during the 2003 Iraq crisis (Brooks and Wohlforth, 2005; Press-Barnathan, 2006; Rynning, 2005: 170–5).

Reformed bandwagoning has taken place through a diverse set of initiatives. Firstly, the 'Europeanization' of NATO and creation of the NRF granted increased influence in Washington and access to global high-intensity capabilities. Secondly, the simultaneous development of an increasingly militarized ESDP permitted autonomous European action and collective 'milieu-shaping' in cases of US disinterest (Hyde-Price, 2007: 88–90; Jones, 2007: 219; King, 2005: 331; Posen, 2006: 180;

Reynolds, 2007: 361; Rynning, 2005: 151, 157). Finally, the development of *à la carte*, multiple-speed and variable-geometry initiatives outside the EU/NATO, led by the European Great Powers, sought to enhance national capacity to contribute to NATO and EU-led crisis-management operations.

The form and temporality of 'clustered convergence': resource constraints, systemic uncertainty and alliance options

Whilst neo-realism provides a compelling explanation of the increasingly complementary function of the core European institutions of 'hard' security, it also delivers substantial, though incomplete, analytical leverage in capturing the processes that determine differentiation in the functional scope, territoriality and temporality of reformed bandwagoning.

International structure acts as a selection mechanism on the basis of 'competitive effectiveness': the extent to which a state's defence policy allows it to maximize its power and influence and ensure its survival, autonomy and prosperity (Resende-Santos, 2007: 63). This systemic pressure leads to a dynamic and clustered military convergence: dynamic because it is consequent upon the constant competition that characterizes international relations, and clustered due to the variegated intensity of competition between particular states and to regional differentiation in the intensity of the security dilemma (Resende-Santos, 2007: 78; Taliaferro, 2006: 478). States are faced with three choices following a significant shift in the balance of capabilities: to emulate 'best practice'; to innovate in military practices; or to maintain policy stasis (T. Dyson, 2008: 738–9). The central criterion determining what is perceived as 'best practice' and the attractiveness of emulation is proven success in Great Power war (Resende-Santos, 2007: 81–2).

Neo-realism points to three factors determining the form and temporality of post-Cold War 'clustered convergence' in European military isomorphism. Firstly, in the context of the relative absence of Great Power war and the diverse nature of post-Cold War conflict, it has been difficult for European states to define 'best practice'. Whilst the 1991 Gulf War, the 1999 Kosovo Conflict, the 2001 attack on Afghanistan and the 2003 attack on Iraq highlighted the utility of technological prowess in high-intensity war-fighting and the success of the RMA, the Iraq conflict post-2003, the NATO ISAF mission and US/European involvement in the former Yugoslavia and Africa during the 1990s demonstrated the dangers inherent in reliance on C4ISR in peace-keeping, post-conflict reconstruction and counter-insurgency operations (Betz, 2006: 507; Cohen, 2004: 402–3; Posen, 2003: 30–6). Hence the emergence of an increasingly concrete model of military emulation is an important factor determining the pace of European capability procurement initiatives within ESDP and NATO (Cohen, 2004: 396–7; T. Dyson, 2008; Sperling, 2004: 456–9).

Secondly, the nature of European states as 'second- and third-rank' powers constrains their resource-technological capacity to copy the RMA and magnifies the risks associated with emulation (Resende-Santos, 2007: 73). Emulation of the RMA is most evident in areas of lower cost and risk: the reorganization of military structures and the creation of Joint Reaction Forces in the mid-to-late 1990s in Britain and France and in the early 21st century in Germany. Consequently, the European Great Powers emerge as the leaders of the process of reformed bandwagoning in these specific functional areas. 'Third-rank', smaller states are net consumers, by virtue of their material capability differential.

The final factor is the presence of alliance options. The threat of abandonment by the USA became particularly evident in the run-up to the Kosovo conflict, which clarified the post-Cold War systemic imperative of the pursuit of a policy of reformed bandwagoning. This explains the timing of the October 1998 St Malo Accord and forms a crucial additional factor determining the recent acceleration of European C4ISR procurement through the EDA and NATO.

The temporality and scope of cooperation: variance in external vulnerability and the alliance security dilemma

Significant divergence exists in the temporal dimension of the commitment of European states to the process of reformed bandwagoning, with leaders and lag-gards evident in ESDP and NATO initiatives (Adams and Ben-Ari, 2006: 21–58). A systemic explanation of this divergence relies upon attention to variation in the 'external vulnerability' of European states, a concept that encompasses territorial size, geographical location and productive capacity (Posen, 2006: 152; Taliaferro, 2006: 467, 479).

For example, in order to understand the comparatively early temporal location of the Europeanization of French defence policy, a focus on France's geographi-cal position is critical. The 'Europeanization' agenda outlined by Prime Minister Edouard Balladur in the 1994 Defence White Paper was not only a response to unipolarity but also a means to ensure French influence within its regional milieu as German power and influence increased through European monetary union (Brenner, 2003: 198-99; Howorth, 1998: 139–51; Menon, 1995: 27). This 'Europeanization without the European Union' reflects long-standing French concerns about relative power within the EU and attempts to exert leadership in European defence cooperation, helping explain the routing of France's response to the RMA through ESDP (Brenner, 2003: 198; Irondelle, 2003; Lungu, 2004b: 58–62; Menon, 1995: 22; Utley, 2000: 185). The French-led 'defence circle' would balance the German-led 'monetary circle'.

Variance in external vulnerability also provides a powerful motivation for the emergence of French leadership on sub-regional bi/plurilateral initiatives in the mid-1990s and for French efforts to improve Europe's defence-industrial base. Nevertheless, in line with the predictions of neo-realism, the threat of abandon-ment by the USA has led to increased willingness by France to ensure comple-mentarity between ESDP and NATO. By virtue of its geographical position, Britain was less acutely concerned with the regional power balance in the immediate post-Cold War era and emerged as a co-leader of reformed bandwagoning after the October 1998 St Malo initiative, only once the threat of abandonment by the USA became acutely pressing (T. Dyson, 2008: 765–71).

There continues, however, to be a high level of duplication in capability acquisi-tion. On average, 70 per cent of European land forces remain focused on territorial defence, and the relative fragmentation of European defence industries acts as a further barrier to an economy of scale that would foster greater defence spending efficiency (Whitney, 2008: 7). This reticence to specialize derives from the 'alliance security dilemma' within the EU and NATO that acts as an impediment to integration (Snyder, 1984; Siedschlag, 2006). Whilst facing an incentive to pool resources, European states cannot be certain that others will not renege on their promises, promoting the retention of a substantial territorial-defence capacity and capability duplication, in order to guard against the potential loss of power and influence that the non-compliance of other states could cause.

This problem is compounded for central and east European (CEE) states. They face the contradictory imperatives of developing networked, interoperable, expeditionary capabilities to enhance their credibility as Alliance partners, whilst sustaining national defence capabilities to respond to the heightened threat to their territorial integrity posed by Russia (Whitney, 2008: 24). Defence cooperation is therefore focused on demonstrating solidarity with the USA, making CEE states unwilling to champion arrangements that the USA views as threatening to NATO. Consequently, the development of regional initiatives by states at Europe's eastern borders was initially a means with which to prove the worth and loyalty of these states to NATO. However, as ESDP and NATO have become increasingly complementary in function, these structures have also acted as a forum in which to facilitate 'niche' contributions to Battlegroup missions (Whitney, 2008: 28–9).

The fear of strategic miscalculation, the variance in external vulnerability, and the alliance security dilemma mean that, despite increasing convergence in European defence policy objectives under systemic unipolarity and regional balanced multipolarity, the duplication of capabilities and the relatively limited cooperation between national defence industries remain inherent problems in European defence cooperation.

Spatial and temporal differentiation in the provision of non-excludable public goods: variance in external vulnerability and executive autonomy

Structural realism provides a persuasive account of the functional, territorial and temporal dimensions of differentiation in post-Cold War European defence cooperation. Russian contestation of US power in eastern Europe creates a strong incentive for using '*directoire*' differentiation in cases such as Georgia and Ukraine and restricting their cooperation to OSCE, Partnership for Peace, and European–Atlantic Partnership Council membership (Hyde-Price, 2007: 156–61). However, in western and central Europe the presence of the USA as an 'offshore balancer', combined with regionally balanced multipolarity, acts as a powerful force driving isomorphism in defence policy objectives and in the function of NATO and ESDP as institutional forums for 'reformed' bandwagoning on US power. At the same time, a common pattern of defence reform is beginning to emerge in Europe: a partial and selective emulation of the RMA.

This convergence in the objectives, instruments and institutional forums of defence policy is evidenced by the increasing willingness of states such as France, Finland and Sweden to contribute to the strengthening of NATO's expeditionary capabilities and its 'Europeanization' via the NRF. On the other hand, traditional Atlanticists, like the UK, have increasingly provided the impetus behind the development of ESDP. Consequently, ESDP, NATO and other bi/plurilateral initiatives are acting as institutional venues for the development of increasingly complementary military capability procurement, relating to strategic sea/airlift, C4ISR and other military hardware, and permitting the conduct of low–high-intensity crisis-management operations. Both ESDP and NATO also display an increasing focus on a 'comprehensive approach' to the conduct of military operations that more effectively integrates the civilian and military dimensions of crisis-management missions.

There is an important role for time as an independent variable shaping this growing functional complementarity. States are in a constant process of 'strategic learning' about how best to respond to structural imperatives in order to maximize their power and influence. Following significant power shifts, a temporal lag in responding to systemic imperatives is likely as statesmen require time to become more familiar with their new strategic environment. Far-reaching changes (such as the end of the Cold War) create particular informational uncertainty and flux, requiring the readjustment and fine-tuning of strategy to the new configuration of constraints and opportunities. As Rathburn (2008: 316) notes, 'learning does not proceed smoothly in response to a changing systemic environment, but rather in a manner of fits and starts ... power calculation is a complicated business'.

Differentiation in the territoriality and temporality of defence cooperation (time as the dependent variable) can be partly explained through recourse to variation in external vulnerability. Consequently, the states of greatest capability (Britain, France and Germany) emerge as 'core states' in the provision of 'public goods' (military forces and capabilities) (Whitney, 2008: 59–64). Variance in external vulnerability also provides a powerful explanation for the differentiated temporality of leadership in reformed bandwagoning, as the case of France illustrates. Germany, where domestic material power relations narrow the autonomy of the core executive in defence policy, also demonstrates the limitations of a focus on the systemic level of analysis. The example of the Federal Republic points to the utility of neoclassical realism that focuses on the intervening role played by unit-level variables in delaying conformity to the dictates of international structure (T. Dyson, 2008: 725–74). These restrictions in German executive autonomy derive from the linkages between budgetary, defence and social policy subsystems and the impact of the Federal state on the politics of base closures (T. Dyson, 2005, 2008: 749–58). The core executive also faces great difficulty in constructing new policy narratives in support of radical changes to defence policy as a consequence of the regularity of important *Land* (state) elections, which increase the sensitivity of the governing coalition to public opinion. Consequently German policy leaders have sought to engage in the temporal management of reformed bandwagoning (T. Dyson, 2008: 749–58).

A group of smaller west European/Nordic states emerged as niche contributors of troops and capabilities to the NRF/Battlegroups, notably Finland, the Netherlands, Norway, Sweden, Italy and Spain (Whitney, 2008: 28). Although 'public goods' in defence are non-excludable, creating a strong potential for free-riding, contributions to reformed bandwagoning are roughly equivalent to European states' relative power. Hence, whilst Kölliker notes in this volume (Chapter 3) that non-excludable public goods create only weak centripetal effects, there is a more complex and contradictory dynamic at work in defence. It reflects a trade-off between power maximization, variance in external vulnerability, and the alliance–security dilemma. Whilst centripetal effects are generated by states' concern with maximizing their power and influence within NATO/ESDP, amongst Europe's 'third-rank' states leaders and laggards exist in the contribution of 'niche capabilities'. Even within the favourable context of regional balanced multipolarity, the alliance security dilemma, combined with the threat posed by Russia to east European states, impedes the pooling of capabilities. These factors have led to the retention of a strong focus on territorial defence amongst east European states and capability duplication.

We should, therefore, be prudent in our expectations of the scope for cooperation in defence and recognize the significance of the steps already taken. Force-generation and capability procurement initiatives are likely to remain intergovernmental and differentiated, allowing the retention of a high degree of national autonomy: either *à la carte'* (to enable the participation of outsiders, particularly within force-generation initiatives and capability procurement projects within/outside ESDP/NATO); 'multiple-speed' (to encourage burden-sharing by making membership of 'vanguard' organizations, such as the ESA, MIC and MIP, dependent upon the development of national C4ISR capabilities/space technology), or 'variable-geometry' (in cases of sub-regional force-generation initiatives).

Notes

1. The Partnership for Peace (PfP) and European Atlantic Partnership Council permit case-by-case cooperation with non-NATO states in eastern Europe, the Caucasus region, Central Asia, Scandinavia and the Mediterranean region.
2. The WEU's capabilities and functions have been largely incorporated into the EU. The OSCE deals with 'softer' security issues, providing a forum for pan-European dialogue and is consequently characterized by broader membership than NATO/the EU.
3. Sweden and Finland have recently announced their intention to contribute to the NRF.
4. Denmark secured an opt-out on security and defence at the December 1992 European Council.
5. 'Comprehensive Political Guidance', 29 November 2006, pt. 6.
6. 'A Secure Europe in a Better World: ESS', 12 December 2003: 1–5.
7. The Battlegroups lack dedicated airborne and maritime capabilities; the NRF also focuses on collective defence (Kaitera and Ben-Ari, 2008: 7).
8. Whilst Germany lags behind Britain and France in EBAO doctrine and investment in high-technology weapons systems (Sperling, 2004: 457; Lungu, 2004b) it has, since 2003, made significant headway in C4ISR (Adams and Ben-Ari, 2006: 16–17, 53).
9. On NEC and EBAO see Farrell (2008).
10. Input into EDA project decision-making is determined by a state's financial contribution to an initiative. This '*à la carte*' differentiation helps overcome the problems encountered

by NATO's Research and Technology Organization (RTO) that operates on the principle of the equality of nations, thereby disincentivizing Great Power leadership.

11. 'An Initial Long Term Vision for European Defence Capability and Capacity Needs', EDA, October 2006, 25–8.
12. Project areas include Software Defined Radio; Network Enabled Capability; Chemical, Biological, Radiological and Nuclear ordnance disposal; Maritime Surveillance; 21st Century Soldier System and the development of a European Air Transport Fleet.
13. On JIP-FR projects, see: www.eda.europa.eu/genericitem.aspx?id=370
14. NEC Pre-Study, Public Executive Summary, 12 June 2006; Miracle Project Final Report, 12 July 2007.
15. 'Final Report on the CHG 2008', 2.
16. On CHG priority areas see 'CHG 2010', Section III Objectives, 3–5.
17. www.nato.int/issues/accs/index.html
18. www.nc3a.nato.int/organization/index.html
19. http://transnet.act.nato.int/WISE/TNCC/CentresofE
20. 'The Prague Summit and NATO's Transformation: A Reader's Guide', NATO, 2002, 11.
21. www.nato.int/issues/ags/practice.html
22. 'MAJIC Introduction', NATO C3 Agency, October 2006.
23. www.nato.int/issues/satcom/index.html
24. MAJIC Press Release October 2006, at: www.nato.int/docu/update/2007/pdf/majic.pdf.
25. www.eurofighter.com/news/chapter132.asp
26. Meteor is compatible with the Rafale, JAS-39 Gripen and Joint Strike Fighter.
27. www.kmweg.de/frame.php?page=19
28. www.occar-ea.org/view.php?nid=72
29. http://smsc.cnes.fr/PLEIADES/
30. www.eurocorps.org/history/eurocorps_history/
31. www.euroairgroup.org/history.htm
32. The SCC held quarterly coordination boards including representatives of the NATO HQs, NATO Planning Boards and the EUMS. See www.nosu.no/sealift/
33. www.defence.gouv.fr/defence_uk/enjeux_defence/la_defence_dans_l_europe/les_euroforces/cellule_europeenne_de_coordination_aerienne/cellule_europeenne_de_coordination_aerienne_eacc
34. www.mcce-mil.com/
35. www.jcs.mil/j3/mic/
36. 'Statement of Intent for the MIP, 01 October 2001', at: www.mip-site.org/01-Atccis/mip_doc/MIP_SOI.doc
37. www.nordcaps.org/?id=81
38. www.mod.gov.ee/static/sisu/files/baltic_co_2002.pdf
39. Bipolarity is the most stable distribution of power, where two superpowers enjoy equality in capabilities.
40. Offensive realism predicts that the dominant power in a unipolar system will attempt to grasp the opportunity to maximize its power by expanding its influence in areas of strategic importance and eschew cooperation to achieve its ends (Mearsheimer, 2001).
41. An 'offshore balancer' intervenes only to prevent the rise of challengers to its position and protect its vital strategic interests (Hyde-Price, 2007: 45; Layne, 1997; Walt, 2005: 18–19).
42. Defined by Pape (2005: 15) as: 'rearmament or accelerated economic growth to support eventual rearmament'.
43. Buckpassing refers to a situation in which a great power passes the responsibility for balancing to other states.
44. A state can counter a rising hegemon though aggressive, preventative war.
45. 'Binding' refers to the ability of smaller alliance partners to use existing institutional ties to restrain a larger alliance partner (Schweller, 1998: 70–1).

23
Conclusions: Generalizations and Patterns

Kenneth Dyson and Angelos Sepos

Differentiation and ideological space: moderate and polarized pluralism

The tension between differentiated and unitary integration has come to be one of the defining characteristics of contemporary Europe both at the macro-continental level (in which the EU is 'core' Europe) and within the EU itself. At the macro level EU enlargement (alongside NATO and Council of Europe enlargement) has served to reduce differentiation, though often by reconfiguration of relationships in terms of graduated membership around the EU (and NATO) as continent-wide poles of attraction. This change at the macro-European level reflects the narrowing of ideological space consequent on the end of the Cold War and the associated division of Europe into rival blocs. Broad acceptance of the principles of liberal democracy and of the market economy made the EU in particular the sole pole of attraction.

At the EU level, especially against the background of the broadened policy scope and thus *acquis communautaire*, enlargement has increased differentiation. It has produced a more fragmented EU in terms of constituent territories, economic structures and development, and geo-strategic interests. In consequence, the EU is more pluralistic in its composition. A more pluralistic structure increases the *scope* for differentiated integration. It does not in itself change the *character* of differentiated integration, which *ceteris paribus* would remain short-term and provisional, consistent with multi-speed Europe. The change in character of the pluralistic structure stems from the coupling of EU enlargement with the broadening of policy scope and with deepening in institutions and procedures. The result has been politicization of the EU with increased ideological space, consequent on greater potential for disagreements not just about policies but also about principles and fundamentals of integration. Increasing ideological distance around pro-integration versus pro-sovereignty principles and pro-market versus pro-social Europe suggests an underlying shift from moderate pluralism to a more polarized pluralism within the EU. In the emerging 'two-tier' Europe, a set of pro-integration states form a deeper *de facto* community through their participation across a range of differentiated integration projects.

'Multi-speed' integration remains an option across a range of policies, above all the traditional core. In this sense, 'moderate' pluralism is still in evidence within the integration process. However, in many new policy areas the increased resort to more polarized forms of 'variable geometry' and '*à la carte*' integration is producing a *de facto* 'two-tier' Europe.

Hence, depending on the level of analysis, differentiation is being simultaneously reduced, increased and reconfigured. Ideological space is being both narrowed and enlarged; ideological distance is being both moderated and sharpened. At the macro-European level centripetal drives have been most prevalent; at the EU level centrifugal drives have gained strength.

Differentiation: motor of integration or bridge?

In the context of this change in the scope and the character of differentiated integration – both more moderate and more polarized differentiation, European politicians face fundamental choice about their role in Europe. This choice is encapsulated in the two metaphors of 'motor' and 'bridge' in European integration and in the debate over 'core' Europe. The Franco-German relationship has typically been cast as the 'motor', driving the larger integration process and forming the basis for a 'core' Europe or 'avant-garde'. This view has resonated strongly amongst French politicians and officials, including Jacques Chirac (2000), Jacques Delors (2000, 2001) and Valéry Giscard d'Estaing (Giscard d'Estaing and Schmidt, 2000). It has also found support in the German political establishment, notably from former German Federal Chancellor Helmut Schmidt (Giscard d'Estaing and Schmidt, 2000) and Foreign Minister Joschka Fischer (2000), though later Fischer (2004) disavowed the 'core Europe' idea. In fact, two key re-launches of the 'core Europe' concept that stimulated Europe-wide debates had strong German imprints: Schäuble and Lamers (1994) and Derrida and Habermas (2003). Nevertheless, the main impulse has come from within the French establishment: in part, to project and secure French power in an expanding and changing Europe; and in part to redefine Europe as a 'counter-weight' to American power and its unilateral use in a multi-polar world.

In contrast, despite exceptions, German figures have tended to gravitate more towards the 'bridge' metaphor. The 'bridge' metaphor retained attractions. In geo-strategic terms, with the rise of China and India, a smaller 'core' Europe lacked the critical mass to project power at the global level and to give a political steer to globalization. Also, German unification and eastern enlargement highlighted the strategic importance of continuing a policy focused on European reconciliation in which Germany would enjoy security on all its many borders. Economically, even after monetary union, the mutual gains from continent-wide trade and from coordinating Europe-wide economic reforms to open markets trumped building a smaller 'core' Europe around 'Euro-Europe' (Fischer, 2004). In short, conserving and developing the central sectors of unitary integration, especially the single market, served to constrain differentiated integration.

Also, positing a 'core Europe' in terms that identified it with the 'old Europe' against the 'new Europe' and the United States risked cementing deep divisions within Europe, destroying the historic post-Cold War achievement of pan-European unification, and making EU enlargement into a hollow and failed project (Zielonka, 2000). The second Iraq War could be seen as a division within the West, not between Europe and the USA. Bridge-building in Europe was bound together with bridge-building in trans-Atlantic relations. It also accorded with the strategic reality of structural dependency on the United States for collective defence and an underlying preference for 'bandwagoning' on US power (see Chapter 22 by Tom Dyson in this volume).

For these various reasons 'core Europe' has had fitful intellectual and political support, even from initial advocates like Fischer and Wolfgang Schäuble. Its strategic attraction rested on the value of implied threat. *Potential* polarized differentiation might serve as an incentive to the reluctant to take the process of integration more seriously in order to avoid exclusion. The question was whether 'core Europe' was ever a credible threat.

More fundamentally, the shift to more polarized pluralism within the EU increased the attractions for a core state like Germany to seek to play the 'bridge' role. In playing the 'centre' role within this changing context the stress is more on *positioning* in order to mediate within the more polarized EU and less on strong *advocacy* of a particular agenda on integration.

Towards graduated membership

The growth of differentiated integration underlines the emergence of a pattern of graduated membership in the European Union. There remains a solid unitary core to integration, represented by the commitments to democracy and rights and to the single-market principles of freedom of movement of people, goods, services and capital. Policies to promote sustainable development also have the potential to become core to unitary integration. However, outside this core of unitary integration, differentiated participation is becoming a central feature of EU membership, not just for newer Member States but also for many older Member States (notably Denmark and the UK). As Přibáň notes in Chapter 2 of this volume, legal pluralism has begun to challenge the traditional principle of EU legal unity based on the supremacy of EU law.

Conversely, the case studies of differentiated integration in this volume suggest that *de facto* a deeper core community of Member States has evolved. They participate systematically in a range of projects in differentiated integration, notably the Euro Area, Schengen, social policy, the Charter of Fundamental Rights, and ESDP and defence-related projects. There is a *de facto*, though not *de jure*, core Europe that has sprung up in an *ad hoc* manner. It comprises France, Germany, the Benelux States and Austria. Italy is a more passive and ambivalent part of this core. On the other hand, some east-central European states (Slovakia and Slovenia, for example) seem to be entering this core, though they lack the institutional capacity and resources to be main players. Moreover, a comparative examination of different policy sectors suggests that Franco-German leadership has been central in differentiated integration: notably, monetary union, Schengen, various CFSP initiatives, ESDP, the Bologna process and industrial policy.

Finally, differentiated integration, in the form of graduated membership and 'special relationships', may be a useful political tool to accommodate diverging interests. It has a particular relevance for states whose EU candidacy has stirred controversy and tensions with existing Member States (like Turkey in relation to Cyprus, Macedonia to Greece, and Croatia to Slovenia); for states whose politico-economic institutions are still deemed too weak for EU candidacy (like Albania, Serbia, and Bosnia and Herzegovina); and for those states whose mere possibility of EU candidacy (like Morocco, Ukraine, and Georgia) is met with strong resistance from EU and foreign circles due to geo-political and cultural factors.

Implications of differentiation for the politics of European integration

The proliferation and sheer confusion of various types of differentiated integration illustrates the extent to which the EU increasingly lacks the fundamental attributes of a polity. There is little coherence between authority, function and identity (Bartolini, 2007). Differentiated integration compounds problems of institutional 'fuzziness', making the EU in most cases an 'arena' rather than an actor and blurring responsibilities and accountability. The normative foundations of differentiated integration are weak because it represents an addiction to giving momentum to the integration process and to expanding EU competences and budgets over principles governing the final shape and nature of the EU (Majone, 2009).

The triumph of *ad hoc*-ery over principle?

Both the scale and character of differentiated integration have major implications for how European integration operates and how we can best understand it. On the one hand, it has proliferated as the integration process has broadened in policy scope, deepened in institutional and procedural terms, and widened through successive waves of enlargement. On the other, much of this differentiation represents 'integration by stealth' (Majone, 2005) and is the outcome of complex strategic and tactical manoeuvrings (Walker, 1998). In short, differentiated integration has gathered pace in an *ad hoc* and pragmatic manner.

This *ad hoc*-ery and primacy to its use as a strategic tool poses the threat of destructive fragmentation. In addition to the core unitary policy areas of the customs union, external trade policy, the Single Market and competition policy, the EU is held together by a set of general principles. They include: the Copenhagen criteria; the duty of loyal cooperation in Article 10 EC; the reference in the Lisbon Treaty Article 4(3) to 'full mutual respect between and amongst the EU and Member States'; and the protection of the principles of legal unity, solidarity and certainty by the European Court of Justice. However, differentiated integration has put these principles under increasing strain, especially as national courts and academic commentators have begun to challenge legal unity.

The triumph of elite collusion over democratic values

Differentiated integration has compounded rather than proved a palliative to the EU problems of voter indifference and increasing impatience with the integration process. It has contributed to institutional 'fuzziness' and lack of transparency about who does what and who can be held to account; it is linked to a Europe of permeable and flexible borders that generates insecurity; it has failed to deliver on expectations that relative decline in productivity, output and incomes could be reversed; and, in consequence, it has been associated with the widespread perception that the EU is unable to deal with everyday matters of concern to citizens – notably sustainable prosperity and security. The strengthening of differentiated integration correlates with the weakening of the 'permissive consensus' about European integration (see Majone, 2009).

Differentiated integration offers insights into two facets of the integration process. They share an elite-driven approach. First, in its most visible historical manifestations – like ESDP and monetary union – differentiated integration has been associated with the political ambitions of Member State governments to fashion Europe in their own image and in the process to project or at least defend national power. Thus France has sought to lead in aerospace, defence and industrial policy projects; Germany has shaped 'monetary' Europe. This strategic state-based dimension, and the underlying Realist approach, was exhibited most clearly in French Prime Minister Edouard Balladur's advocacy of a Europe based on different 'circles': a 'defence' circle', led by France, and a 'monetary' circle, led by Germany. Balladur (1994) was articulating a 'balance-of-power' notion of differentiated integration. The support for 'monetary' Europe was further linked to German interest in appeasing European neighbours about German unification in 1989–90; to French interest in wresting monetary power away from the German Bundesbank; and to Mediterranean states like Italy, Greece and Portugal seeking to reduce the high costs of servicing their high public debts by 'borrowing' financial credibility. In short, differentiated integration exemplified the resilience of the Member States as 'the masters' of the integration process and their acute attention to relative power.

Secondly, and especially in the murkier areas of differentiated integration, far removed from the eyes of the general public, projects sprang from and were shaped by technical elites. Differentiated integration is not just about strategic manoeuvring for power. It is also highly technocratic and depoliticized, far removed from the language and values of democratic politics. Above all, it follows the logic of 'integration by stealth' (Majone, 2005).

Implications for integration theory

The overall emphasis in integration theory has been to explain unitary integration. As this book makes clear, the intellectual challenge is to explain differentiated integration and how it intersects with unitary integration in so many complex, different and changing ways. The very statement of the challenge, including the varied form of differentiation, suggests that we can hope for little more than an imperfect understanding.

What we have are not so much theories of differentiated integration as frameworks for its analysis. The most intellectually elegant is the typology of public goods inherited from economic theory, and elucidated in this book by Kölliker (Chapter 3). This typology is elaborate, with 'public' goods, 'private' goods, 'toll' goods and 'excludable network' goods and so on. The classification rests on two important attributes: whether costs and gains are distributed asymmetrically or are shared, and whether incentives exist for 'free-riding' or arrangements can be designed to inhibit this behaviour. Its strength is in underlining the influence of these systemic properties on processes of differentiation. Policy drives the politics of differentiation. The functional properties of policies are conceived as independent variables, constraining and even directing preferences for differentiation. It has had the intellectual advantage of being the main typology in the field and bearing the stamp of logic associated with its origins in academic economics. Public goods theory remains the sharpest and most precise intellectual tool in studies of differentiated integration, whatever its limitations.

However, the case studies in this book raise some questions about the discriminating capacity and utility of the public goods typology, reflected in the difficulties that authors had in applying it. The problem of the independent variable remains intractable. What is the direction of causality between policy and politics in differentiation? Policy and politics interact in differentiation. The typology has two main political weaknesses. First, it overlooks the political attribute of ideological closeness or distance with respect to two dimensions: integration/sovereignty issues (pro- or anti-integration) and market/social policy issues (conventionally but not accurately termed Left/Right). There is a fundamental sense in which politics drives the policy of differentiation. Ideological positions yield partial and contending judgements on such matters as euro entry, based on views about sovereignty and markets as the criteria for policy choices about participation/non-participation. Issues of integration/sovereignty and market/society are capable of generating ideological intensity of the type – 'if they must do it, not with us'.

Secondly, processes of differentiated integration interact with the strategic use of other instruments in the integration process. Issue-linkage and side payments are ways of providing incentives to participate in/support differentiation or to deter differentiation. Side payments are classically used to help gain support of potential alienated 'outs' for differentiated integration, like the establishment of the Cohesion Fund at the Maastricht Council to boost support for EMU from economically weaker EU states like Greece, Portugal and Spain. Conversely, issue-linkage can be used to inhibit differentiation. A classic example is how linkage to the Single Market constrains differentiation around the Euro Area, for instance in access to euro payment and settlement systems. Similar issue-linkages play a key role in differentiation in defence. Side payments and issue-linkages erode the neat distinctions of public goods theory.

The chapters on space and time do not yield the same precise typologies of differentiated integration as public goods theory. They suggest certain logics at work but ones that are more qualitative in character. European integration takes place in a context of spatial rescaling. Structural changes in markets and in technologies, along with geo-strategic changes with the post-Cold War period, open up new opportunities for differentiated integration. The consequent dissociation of function, space, and authority introduce new complexities into European integration in ways that make it more like a loosely textured traditional continental Empire of differentiated integration. In terms of temporal rhythms, European integration is bound up in the uncoordinated 'timescapes' of EU and domestic governance. The tight and obtrusive constraints of domestic electoral cycles shape and constrain the politics of differentiated integration, shifting calculations of whether and when to participate.

At the same time differentiated integration is shaped by the strategic use that domestic and European actors make of space and time. Spaces are invented and imagined for various political purposes, negatively in the case of Balkan identity, positively in Baltic or Central European identity. The Anglosphere serves as a distancing mechanism from Europe. Similarly, time is an instrument in differentiated integration, deployed to speed up or delay participation (for instance in monetary union, state-aid rules, freedom of work). In choosing early entry into the Euro Area, Finland and Slovakia broke ranks with their fellow Nordic and Visegrád Member States.

The case studies in this volume underline the complex politics of differentiated integration. Its politics is bound up with changes in ideological space (its closeness/distance); with strategic use of related instruments of issue-linkage and side payments to induce or deter differentiation; with processes of spatial invention and spatial imagination; and with the strategic use of time. Seen in this broader, more inclusive framework, the 'logic' of collective action that public goods theory attributes to differentiated integration gives way to the 'puzzle' of collective action.

Implications for regional identity formation

The empirical evidence in this volume suggests that there has been variation in the use of differentiated integration as a tool to promote regional identities and, more generally, to promote European integration. In some cases, differentiated integration has been used to strengthen regional identity (the Baltic, for instance); in others, it has weakened regional identity, creating tensions amongst the states in the same territorial grouping (for example, Central Europe); whilst in the Balkans the negative connotations associated with regional identity have made the use of differentiated integration an unattractive tool for regional elites. On a more general level, however, one can conclude that differentiated integration has served as a tool to ease the pressures from European integration on territorial groupings.

Rescuing states and the EU?

Finally, the evidence in this book offers a mixed picture of the contribution of differentiated integration to strengthening the 'output' legitimacy of the EU by improving its performance. On the one hand, differentiated integration has in many cases 'rescued' both states and the EU from the pressures and demands of European integration and globalization respectively. Thus transitional arrangements and temporary derogations have diffused the pressures for reform on domestic systems and allowed governments to promote EU membership to sceptical publics. Also, the various 'grand' differentiated integration projects such as the euro and the Schengen schemes have provided solutions to major challenges stemming from globalization such as shelter from financial crisis and from illegal immigration. Similarly, it might be argued that differentiated integration initiatives like 'Big Three' *directoires* in foreign policy may have 'rescued' or salvaged the global status and image of the EU when the latter was expected to act and make its voice heard in major security crisis (such as in relation to Iran or Iraq) and when consensus was difficult to reach.

On the other hand, the creation of the Euro Area has not reversed the relative economic decline of the EU *vis-à-vis* the United States and has deprived its Member States of the exchange rate and the interest rate as domestic adjustment mechanisms. As a consequence, they have to fall back on politically painful wage adjustments to regain lost competitiveness, creating potentially serious internal strains. Also, in foreign policy, it can be argued that differentiated integration has led to 'disintegration' and weakened support for European integration. Proposals for core Europe and *directoire* initiatives alienated (and polarized) many Member States and created fears of marginalization and exclusion in the purported unified and solidarity-based European project.

References

Aalto, P. (2006) *European Union and the Making of a Wider Northern Europe* (London: Routledge).

Aalto, P. (2004) 'European Integration and the Declining Project of Building a Baltic Sea Region', in J.H. Stampehl, A. Bannwart, D. Brekenfeld and U. Palth (eds), *Perceptions of Loss, Decline and Doom in the Baltic Sea Region* (Berlin: Berlliner Wissenschafts Verlag).

Adam, B. (2004) *Time* (Cambridge: Polity Press).

Adams, G. and G. Ben-Ari (2006) *Transforming European Militaries: Coalition Operations and the Technology Gap* (Abingdon: Routledge).

Agapiou-Josephides, K. (2003) 'The Political System of Cyprus at the Threshold of the European Union: Patterns of Continuity, Change and Adaptation', in Peter G. Xuereb (ed.), *Euro-Med Integration and the 'Ring of Friends': The Mediterranean's European Challenge*, Vol. IV (University of Malta: European Documentation and Research Centre), 237–52.

Alesina, A. (1987) 'Macroeconomic Policy in a Two-Party System as a Repeated Game', *Quarterly Journal of Economics*, 102 (2), 651–78.

Allemand, F. (2005) 'The Impact of the EU Enlargement on Economic and Monetary Union: What Lessons Can Be Learnt from the Differentiated Integration Mechanisms in an Enlarged Europe?', *European Law Journal*, 11 (5), 586–617.

Almond, G. and S. Verba (1963) *The Civic Culture: Political Attitudes and Democracy in Five Nations* (Princeton: Princeton University Press).

Amirah Fernández, H. and R. Youngs (eds) (2006) *The Barcelona Process: An Assessment of a Decade of the Euro-Mediterranean Partnership*, Royal Institute Elcano paper ARI 137/2006, at: www.realinstitutoelcano.org/publicaciones/libros/Barcelona10_eng.pdf

Andersen, S.S. (2001) 'Energy Policy: Interest Articulation and Supranational Authority', in S.S. Andersen and K.A. Eliassen (eds), *Making Policy in Europe* (London: Sage).

Andersen, M.S. and D. Liefferink (eds) (1997) *European Environmental Policy. The Pioneers* (Manchester: Manchester University Press).

Andersen, S.S. and Sitter, N. (2006) 'Differentiated Integration: What Is It and How Much Can the EU Accommodate?', *Journal of European Integration*, 28 (4), 313–30.

Apap, J. et al. (2001) *Friendly Schengen Borderland Policy on the New Borders of an Enlarged EU and Its Neighbours*, CEPS Justice and Home Affairs Policy Brief 7, November 2001.

Archer, C. (2005) *Norway Outside the European Union* (London: Routledge).

Armstrong, K. (1998) 'Legal Integration: Theorizing the Legal Dimension of European Integration', *Journal of Common Market Studies*, 36 (2), 155–74.

Armstrong, K. and Bulmer, S. (1998) *The Governance of the Single European Market* (Manchester: Manchester University Press).

Art, R. (2004) 'Europe Hedges its Security Bets', in T.V. Paul, J.J. Wirtz and M. Fortmann (eds), *Balance of Power: Theory and Practice in the Twenty-First Century* (Stanford: Stanford University Press), 179–213.

Art, R., S. Brooks, W. Wohlforth, K. Lieber and G. Alexander (2005) 'Correspondence: Striking the Balance', *International Security* 30 (3), 177–96.

Aydin, S. and E. Fuat Keyman (2004) *European Integration and the Transformation of Turkish Democracy*, CEPS EU–Turkey Working Papers, No. 2, 1 August (Brussels: CEPS)

Avery, G. (2009) 'Uses of Time in the EU's Enlargement Process', *Journal of European Public Policy*, 16 (2), 256–69.

Badie, Bertrand (1995) *La fin des territories. Essai sur le désordre international et sur l'utilité social du respect* (Paris: Fayard).

Bailes, A., G. Herolf and B. Sundelius (eds) (2006) *The Nordic Countries and the European Security and Defence Policy* (Oxford: Oxford University Press).

Baker, D. and D. Seawright (eds) (1998) *Britain For and Against Europe: British Politics and the Question of European Integration* (Oxford: Oxford University Press).

Baldwin, R. (2006a) *The Euro's Trade Effects*, ECB Working Chapter 594, Frankfurt am Main, March.

Baldwin, R. (2006b) *In or Out: Does It Matter? An Evidence-Based Analysis of the Euro's Trade Effects* (London: Centre for Economic Policy Research).

Balfour, R. (2007) *Promoting Democracy and Human Rights in the EU's Neighbourhood: Tools, Strategies And Dilemmas*, European Policy Centre, Issue paper 54, June.

Balladur, E. (1994a) Interview, *Le Monde*, 30 November.

Balladur, E. (1994b) 'Édouard Balladur: notre politique étrangère', interview, *Le Figaro*, 30 August, 5–6.

Balzacq, T. (ed.) (2007a) 'Construire le voisin. Pratiques européennes', *Cultures et conflits*, 66 (été), at: www.conflits.org/index2391.html

Balzacq, T. (2007b) 'La politique européenne de voisinage, un complexe de sécurité à géométrie variable', *Cultures et conflits*, 66 (été), 31–59.

Balzacq, T., D. Bigo, S. Carrera and E. Guild (2006) 'Security and the Two-Level Game: The Treaty of Prüm, the EU and the Management of Threats', CEPS Working Document No. 234 (Brussels: CEPS), 2–4, 17.

Banchoff, T. and M.P. Smith (1999) *Legitimacy and the European Union: the Contested Polity* (London: Routledge).

Bangemann, M. (1992) *Meeting the Global Challenge: Establishing a Successful European Industrial Policy* (London: Kogan Page).

Barbé, Esther and Edward Soler I Lecha (2005) 'Barcelona + 10: Spain's Relaunch of the Euro-Mediterranean Partnership', *The International Spectator*, 2/2005, 85–98.

Barber, N.W. (2006) 'Legal Pluralism and the European Union', *European Law Journal* 12 (3), 306–29.

Barbier, J.-C. and N. Samba Sylla (2001) *Stratégie européenne pour l'emploi: les représentations des acteurs en France*, Rapport pour la DARES et la Délégation à l'emploi du ministère du Travail et de l'Emploi, Paris.

Barbier, J.-C. with N. Samba Sylla and A. Eydoux (2006) *Analyse comparative de l'activation de la protection sociale en France, Grande-Bretagne, Allemagne et Danemark, dans le cadre des lignes directrices de la stratégie européenne pour l'emploi*, Rapport pour la DARES (ministère du Travail) (Brussels: CEE).

Barroso, José Manuel Durão (2007) *Shared Challenges, Shared Futures: Taking the Neighbourhood Policy Forward*, Speech at the European Neighbourhood Policy Conference Brussels, 3 September, at: http://europa.eu/rapid/pressReleasesAction.do?reference=SPEECH/07/502&format=HTML&aged=0&language=EN&guiLanguage=en

Barroso, José Manuel Durão (2008) 'EU Strategy for the Baltic Sea Region', *Baltic Rim Economies*, 5/2008.

Bartolini, S. (2002) 'Institutional Democratization and Political Structuring in the EU: Lessons from the Nation-State Development', in H. Cavanna (ed.), *Governance, Globalization, and the European Union. Which Europe for Tomorrow?* (Dublin: Four Courts Press), 129–88.

Bartolini, S. (2007) *Restructuring Europe: Centre Formation, System Building and Political Structuring Between the Nation State and the European Union* (Oxford: Oxford University Press).

Batt, J. (2003) '"Fuzzy Statehood" versus Hard Borders: The Impact of EU Enlargement on Romania and Yugoslavia', in M. Keating and J. Hughes (eds), *The Regional Challenge in Central and Eastern Europe: Territorial Restructuring and European Integration* (Brussels: P.I.E.-Peter Lang), 161–82.

Baun, M. (1996) *An Imperfect Union. The Maastricht Treaty and the New Politics of European Integration* (Boulder: Westview).

Beaumont, P. and N. Walker (eds) (1999) *Legal Framework of the Single European Currency* (Oxford: Hart Publishing).

Beazley, C. (2007) 'The EU-Strategy for the Baltic Sea Region: Making a Success of the 2004 Enlargement', *Baltic Rim Economies*, 6/2007.

Bechev, D. and K. Nicolaïdis (2007) *Integration Without Accession: The EU's Special Relationship With the Countries in Its Neighbourhood*, Report to the European Parliament, October, at: www.sant.ox.ac.uk/esc/ramses/ramsespaperDBKN.pdf

Bellamy, R. and Castiglione, D. (1997) 'Building the Union: The Nature of Sovereignty in the Political Architecture of Europe', *Law and Philosophy*, 16 (4), 421–45.

Bell, D. (2007) *The Idea of Greater Britain: Empire and the Future of World Order 1860-1900* (Princeton: Princeton University Press).

Ben-Ari, G. (2005) 'C3 Interoperability in Europe: The Challenge Ahead', *Eurofutur*, Winter, 1–4.

Bennett, James (2004) *The Anglosphere Challenge: Why the English-Speaking Countries Will Lead the Way in the Twenty-First Century* (Lanham: Rowman & Littlefield).

Bergman, Annika (2006) 'Adjacent Internationalism: The Concept of Solidarity and Post-Cold War Nordic-Baltic Relations', *Cooperation and Conflict*, 41 (1), 73–97.

Best, E. (2002) 'The UK: From Isolation Towards Influence?', in F. Laursen (ed.), *The Amsterdam Treaty. National Preference Formation, Interstate Bargaining and Outcome* (Odense: Odense University Press), 366–9.

Betz, D. (2007) 'Redesigning Land Forces for Wars amongst the People', *Contemporary Security Policy*, 28 (2), 221–43.

Betz, H.-G. (1998) 'Introduction', in H.-G. Betz and S. Immerfall (eds), *The New Politics of the Right: Neo-Populist Parties and Movements in Established Democracies* (Basingstoke: Macmillan).

Betz, H.-G. (2005) 'Mobilising Resentment in the Alps: The Swiss SVP, the Italian Lega Nord, and the Austrian FPÖ', in D. Caramani and Y. Mény (eds), *Challenges to Consensual Politics: Democracy, Identity, and Populist Protest in the Alpine Region* (Brussels: P.I.E.-Peter Lang), 147–66.

Bibó, I. (1986) 'A kelet európai kisállamok nyomorúsága' ('The Misery of East European Small States'), in István Vida and Endre Nagy (eds), *Bibó István, Válogatott Tanulmányok* (Selected Studies) (Budapest: Magvetö Könyvkiadó), [46], Vol. II, 185–266.

Bicchi, F. (2006) '"Our Size Fits All": Normative Power in Europe and the Mediterranean', *Journal of European Public Policy*, 13 (2), 286–303.

Blanke, J. and A. Lopez-Claros (2004) *The Lisbon Review 2004: An Assessment of Policies and Reforms in Europe* (Geneva: World Economic Forum).

Bleiere, D. (1997) 'Cooperation of the Baltic States with the Visegrad Countries: Security Aspects', *NATO Fellowship Final Report*, 1–34.

Boening, A.B. (2007) 'Mediterranean Regional Security in the 21st Century: Regional Integration through Development and Its Security Impact on Euromed Partnership Members', *Jean Monnet/Robert Schuman Paper Series*, 7 (9), University of Miami, Florida.

Boening, A.B. (2008) 'Unequal Partners in the EU Southern Neighbourhood Strategy: Is Regional Integration Feasible?', *EUMA Papers*, 5 (4), University of Miami, Florida.

Bohle, D. (2006) 'Neoliberal Hegemony, Transnational Capital and the Terms of the EU's Eastward Expansion', *Capital and Class*, 88 (Spring), 57–86.

Bohle, D. and B. Greskovits (2007) 'Neoliberalism, Embedded Neoliberalism, and Neocorporatism: Towards Transnational Capitalism in Central-Eastern Europe', *West European Politics*, 30 (3), May, 443–66.

Bologna Process (2009) 'Towards the European Higher Education Area', Bologna Secretariat and Follow-up Group, at: http://ec.europa.eu/education/higher-education/doc1290_en.htm

Booker, C. and R. North (2005) *The Great Deception: Can the European Union Survive?* (London: Continuum).

Bornschier, S. (2010) *Cleavage Politics and the Populist Right. The New Cultural Conflict in Western Europe* (Philadelphia: Temple University Press).

Börzel, T.A. (1997) 'What's So Special about Policy Networks? – An Exploration of the Concept and Its Usefulness in Studying European Governance', *European Integration Online Papers* (EIoP), 1 (16).

Börzel, T.A. (2000) 'Why There Is No "Southern Problem": On Environmental Leaders and Laggards in the European Union', *Journal of European Public Policy*, 7 (1), 141–62.

Börzel, T.A. (2002a) *States and Regions in the European Union* (Cambridge: Cambridge University Press).

Börzel, T.A. (2002b) 'Pace-Setting, Foot-Dragging and Fence-Sitting. Member State Responses to Europeanization', *Journal of Common Market Studies*, 40 (2), 193–214.

Börzel, T.A. (2003) *Environmental Leaders and Laggards in Europe: Why There Is (Not) a 'Southern Problem'* (Aldershot: Ashgate).

Börzel, T.A. (2005) 'Coping with Accession – New Modes and EU Enlargement?, in G.F. Schuppert (ed.), *Europeanization of Governance? The Challenge of Accession*, Schriften zur Governance-Forschung (Baden-Baden: Nomos-Verlag), 613–41.

Börzel, T.A., T. Hofmann, D. Panke and C. Sprungk (2008) 'Recalcitrance and Inefficiency. Why Member States Do (Not) Comply with European Law', conference paper at the NEWGOV Workshop in Zeuthen, Germany, 25–26 June.

Bossaert, D. and S. Vanhoonacker (2000) 'Relaunch of the Benelux?', in A. Pijpers (ed.), *On Cores and Coalitions in the European Union: The Position of Some Smaller Member States* (The Hague: Netherlands Institute of International Relations, 'Clingendael').

Brandt, W. (1974) Speech given to the French Organization of the European Movement, 19 November.

Brenner, M. (2003) 'The CFSP Factor: A Comparison of United States and French Strategies', *Cooperation and Conflict*, 38 (3), 187–209.

Brenner, N., B. Jessop, M. Jones and G. Macleod (eds) (2003) *State/Space. A Reader* (Oxford: Blackwell).

Bretherton, C. and J. Vogler (2007) *The European Union as a Global Actor* (London: Routledge).

Brooks, S. and W. Wohlforth (2005) 'Hard Times for Soft Balancing', *International Security*, 30 (1), 76–8.

Browning, C.S. (2006) 'Small, Smart and Salient? Rethinking Identity in Small States Literature', *Cambridge Review of International Affairs*, 19 (4), 669–84.

Browning, C.S. (2007) 'Branding Nordicity: Models, Identity and the Decline of Exceptionalism', *Cooperation and Conflict*, 42 (1), 27–51.

Browning, C.S. and P. Joenniemi (2004) 'Regionality beyond Security? The Baltic Sea Region after Enlargement', *Cooperation and Conflict*, 39 (3), 233–53.

Browning, C.S. and P. Joenniemi (2007) 'Geostrategies of the European Neighbourhood Policy', Danish Institute for International Studies, *Working Papers*, 9/2007.

Browning C.S. and Lehti, M. (2007) 'Beyond East–West: Marginality and National Dignity in Finnish Identity Construction', *Nationalities Papers*, 35 (4), 691–716.

Brubaker, R. (1992) *Citizenship and Nationhood in France and Germany* (Cambridge: Cambridge University Press).

Brubaker, R. (1996) *Nationalism Reframed: Nationhood and the National Question in the New Europe* (Cambridge: Cambridge University Press).

Brunazzo, M. and V. Della Sala (2007) 'The Variable Geometry of Policy Styles: Italy from Weak to Stronger State?', paper given at the European Union Studies Association (EUSA) Biennial Conference, Montreal, Canada, 17–19 May.

Bugajski, J. and I. Teleki (2005) 'Washington's New European Allies: Durable or Conditional Partners?', *The Washington Quarterly*, 28 (2), 95–107.

Bull, M.J. and J.L. Newell (2009) 'Still the Anomalous Democracy? Politics and Institutions in Italy', *Government and Opposition*, 44 (1), 42–67.

Bulmer, S. (1998) 'New Institutionalism and the Governance of the Single European Market', *Journal of European Public Policy*, 5 (3), 365–86.

Bulmer, S. (2007) 'Theorizing Europeanization', in P. Graziano and M. Vink (eds), *Europeanization: New Research Agendas* (Basingstoke: Palgrave Macmillan), 46–58.

Bunce, V. (1998) 'The Visegrad Group. Regional Cooperation and European Integration in Post-Communist Europe', in Peter Katzenstein (ed.), *Mitteleuropa Between Europe and Germany* (Providence and Oxford: Berghahn Books), 240–84.

Bungarten, H.H. (1978) *Umweltpolitik in Westeuropa: EG, internationale Organisationen und nationale Umweltpolitiken* (Bonn: Europa Union).

Bunse, S., P. Magnette and K. Nicolaidis (2006) 'Big Versus Small: Shared Leadership in the EU and Power Politics in the Convention', in D. Beach and C. Mazzucelli (eds), *Leadership in the Big Bangs of Integration* (Basingstoke: Palgrave Macmillan).

Buti, M. and Pench, L. (2004) 'Why Do Large Countries Flout the Stability Pact? And What Can Be Done About It?', *Journal of Common Market Studies*, 42 (5), 1025–32.

Byrnes, T. and P.J. Katzenstein (eds) (2006) *Religion in an Expanding Europe* (Cambridge: Cambridge University Press).

Cameron, F. (2004) 'Widening and Deepening', in F. Cameron (ed.), *The Future of Europe: Integration and Enlargement* (London: Routledge), 1–17.

Caporaso, J., M.G. Cowles and T. Risse (eds) (2001) *Transforming Europe: Europeanization and Domestic Change* (Ithaca: Cornell University Press).

Caramani, D. (2002) 'L'Italie et l'Union Européenne', *Pouvoirs*, 103, 129–42.

Caramani, D. (2004) *The Nationalization of Politics: The Formation of National Electorates and Party Systems in Western Europe* (Cambridge: Cambridge University Press).

Caramani, D. (2005) 'Natural Cultures: The Alpine Political Culture and Its Relationship to the Nation-State and European Integration', in D. Caramani and Y. Mény (eds), *Challenges to Consensual Politics: Democracy, Identity, and Populist Protest in the Alpine Region* (Brussels: P.I.E.-Peter Lang), 83–110.

Caramani, D. and Y. Mény (eds) (2005) *Challenges to Consensual Politics: Democracy, Identity, and Populist Protest in the Alpine Region* (Brussels: P.I.E.-Peter Lang).

Carley, M. (1993) 'Social Dialogue', in M. Gold (ed.), *The Social Dimension: Employment Policy in the European Community* (London: Macmillan).

Castiglione, D. (2009) 'Political Identity in a Community of Strangers', in J.T. Checkel and P.J. Katzenstein (eds), *European Identity* (Cambridge: Cambridge University Press), 29–54.

Coron G. and B. Palier (2002) 'Changes in the Means of Financing Social Expenditure in France since 1945', in C. de la Porte and P. Pochet (eds), *Building Social Europe through the OMC* (Brussels: P.I.E.-Peter Lang).

Carlgren, A. (2008) 'The EU Strategy for the Baltic Sea Region as a Tool for Implementing the HELCOM Baltic Sea Action Plan', *Baltic Rim Economies*, 3/2008.

Carter, C. and A. Scott (1998) 'Legitimacy and Governance Beyond the European Nation State: Conceptualising Governance in the European Union', *European Law Journal*, 4 (4), 429–45.

Cassidy, M. (2002) 'The Irish Economy: Recent Experience and Prospects', in V. Munley, R. Thornton and R. Aronson (eds), *The Irish Economy in Transition: Successes, Problems, and Prospects* (Oxford: Elsevier), 5–32.

Castles, F. (1993) 'Introduction', in F. Castles (ed.), *Families of Nations: Patterns of Public Policy in Western Democracies* (Aldershot: Dartmouth).

CEC (2002) *Communication from the Commission. Action Plan 'Simplifying and Improving the Regulatory Environment', COM(2002)278 final of 05.06.2002* (Brussels: Commission of the European Communities).

Chang, M. (1999) 'Dual Hegemony: France, Germany and the Making of Monetary Union in Europe', paper presented to the European Community Studies Association conference, Pittsburgh, 2–5 June.

Chang, M. (2006) 'Reforming the Stability and Growth Pact: Size and Influence in EMU Policymaking', *Journal of European Integration*, 28 (1), 107–20.

Chari, R. and P. M. Heywood (2009) 'Analysing the Policy Process in Democratic Spain', *West European Politics*, 32 (1), 26–54.

Checkel, J. (1999) 'Norms, Institutions and National Identity in Contemporary Europe', *International Studies Quarterly*, 43 (1), 83–114.

Checkel, J.T. and P.J. Katzenstein (2009) *European Identity* (Cambridge: Cambridge University Press).

Chislett, W. (2008) *Spain. Going Places* (Madrid: Telefónica).

Chirac, J. (2000) 'Our Europe', speech to the German Bundestag, Berlin, 27 June.

Chizhov, V. (2009) cited by Tony Barber, FT.com Brusselsblog, 17 February, *Financial Times* at: http://blogs.ft.com/brusselsblog/2009/02/eu-prepares-to-launch-a-low-flying-eastern-partnership/

Christiansen, T., K. E. Jorgensen and A. Wiener (1999) 'The Social Construction of Europe', *Journal of European Public Policy*, 6 (4), 528–44.

Chryssochoou, D. N. (1994) 'Democracy and Symbiosis in the European Union: Towards a Confederal Consociation?', *West European Politics*, 17 (4), 1–14.

Chryssochoou, D. N. (2001) *Theorizing European Integration* (London: Sage).

Cianciara, A. K. (2008) *Eastern Partnership – Opening a New Chapter of Polish Eastern Policy and the European Neighbourhood Policy?* Opinions 4, Institute of Public Affairs, Warsaw, June.

Cini, M. (2001) 'The Europeanization of Malta: Adaptation, Identity and Party Politics', in K. Featherstone and G. Kazamias (eds), *Europeanization and the Southern Periphery* (London: Frank Cass), 26–76.

Clarke, J. (2005) 'Reconstituting Europe: Governing a European People?', in J. Newman (ed.), *Remaking Governance: Peoples, Politics and the Public Sphere* (Bristol: Policy Press), 17–37.

Closa, C. and P. M. Heywood (2004) *Spain and the European Union* (Basingstoke: Palgrave Macmillan).

Coates, David (2000) *Models of Capitalism* (Cambridge: Polity).

Cohen, E. (2004) 'Change and Transformation in Military Affairs', *Journal of Strategic Studies*, 27 (3), 395–407.

Cole, A. (2001) *Franco-German Relations* (London: Longman).

Colomer, J. (2006) *Grandes imperios, pequeñas naciones* (Barcelona: Anagrama).

Commission (of the European Communities) (2003) 'Wider Europe – Neighbourhood: A New Framework for Relations with our Eastern and Southern Neighbours', COM(2003) 104 Final, at: http://ec.europa.eu/world/enp/pdf/com03_104_en.pdf

Commission (of the European Communities) (2004a) 'European Neighbourhood Policy Strategy Paper', COM(2004) 373 final, at: http://ec.europa.eu/world/enp/pdf/strategy/strategy_paper_en.pdf

Commission (of the European Communities) (2004b) 'Commission Communication on Proposals for Action Plans under the ENP', 9 December 2004, COM(2004) 795 Final, at: http://eur-lex.europa.eu/LexUriServ/LexUriServ.do?uri=COM:2004:0795:FIN:EN:PDF

Commission (of the European Communities) (2007) *Turkey 2007 Progress Report* (Brussels: European Commission), at: http://ec.europa.eu/enlargement/pdf/key_documents/2007/nov/turkey_progress_reports_en.pdf

Commission (of the European Communities) (2008a) *Report on the Implementation of the European Social Partners' Framework Agreement on Telework*, Commission Staff Working Paper SEC (2008) 2178 (Brussels: European Commission).

Commission (of the European Communities) (2008b) Communication from the Commission to the Council, the European Parliament, the European Economic and Social Committee, the Committee of the Regions and the European Central Bank on 'The Introduction of the Euro in Cyprus and Malta', 18 April.

Commission (of the European Communities) (2008c) *Eurobarometer 69: Public Opinion in the European Union*, First Results, at: http://ec.europa.eu/public_opinion/archives/eb/eb69/eb_69_first_en.pdf

Commission (of the European Communities) (various years) Economic and Financial Affairs website, at: http://ec.europa.eu/economy_finance/the_euro/index_en.htm?cs_mid=2946

Commission, DG ECOFIN (2007) *Annual Report on the Euro-area – June 2007* (SEC(2007)550), at: http://ec.europa.eu/economy_finance/publications/european_economy/2007/ero_area2007_en.htm

Commission, DG RELEX (n.d.), Euro-Med webpage, at: http://ec.europa.eu/external_relations/euromed/index_en.htm

Conceição-Heldt, E. (2009) 'On the Time Dimension of International Trade Negotiations', paper presented at the EU CONSENT Workshop on Political Science and Political Time, University of Potsdam, 2–3 April 2009.

Consolidated Version of the Treaty on European Union (2008) *Official Journal of the European Union*, 9 May, C115.

Cooke, P. and K. Morgan (1998) *The Associational Economy: Firms, Regions and Innovation* (Oxford: Oxford University Press).

Cooper, R. (2003) *The Breaking of Nations: Order and Chaos in the Twenty-first Century* (London: Atlantic Books).

Corbett, A. (2005) *Universities and the Europe of Knowledge – Ideas, Institutions and Policy Entrepreneurship in European Union Higher Education 1955–2005* (Basingstoke: Palgrave Macmillan).

Cornes, R. and T. Sandler (1996) *The Theory of Externalities, Public Goods, and Club Goods* (Cambridge: Cambridge University Press).

Cornish, P. and G. Edwards (2005) 'The Strategic Culture of the EU: A Progress Report', *International Affairs*, 81 (4), 801–20.

Council of the European Union (2003) *A Secure Europe in a Better World European Security Strategy*, 12 December 2003, at: www.consilium.europa.eu/uedocs/cmsUpload/78367.pdf

Council of the European Union (2005) Council Secretariat note (10900/05) on the Prüm Convention, 7 July, at: http://register.consilium.europa.eu/pdf/en/05/st10/st10900.en05.pdf

Council of the European Union (2009) *Joint Declaration of the Prague Eastern Partnership Summit*, 7 May 2009, Prague, at: www.consilium.europa.eu/uedocs/cms_Data/docs/press data/en/er/107589.pdf

Craig, P. and C. Harlow (eds) (1998) *Lawmaking in the European Union* (Dordrecht: Kluwer).

Cram, L. (1994) 'The European Commission as a Multi-Organization: Social Policy and IT in the EU', *Journal of European Public Policy*, 1 (2), 383–402.

Cremona, M. and C. Hillion (2006) *L'Union fait la force? Potential and Limitations of the European Neighbourhood Policy as an Integrated EU Foreign and Security Policy*, EUI Working Paper LAW, 2006/39 (Florence: EUI).

Cremona, M. and J. Rijpma (2007) *The Extra-Territorialisation of EU Migration Policies and the Rule of Law*, EUI Working Paper LAW 2007/1 (Florence: EUI).

Crouch, C., P. Le Galès, C. Trigilia and H. Voelzkow (2001) *Local Production Systems in Europe. Rise or Demise?* (Oxford: Oxford University Press).

Cullen, P. (2001) 'The Schengen Agreement with Iceland and Norway: Its Main Features', *ERA-Forum: scripta iuris europaei*, 2 (4), 71–5.

Curia (2007) 'Proceedings of the Court of Justice 2007' at: http://curia.europa.eu/en/instit/presentationfr/rapport/stat/07_cour_stat.pdf

Curtin, D. (1993) 'The Constitutional Structure of the Union: A Europe of Bits and Pieces', *Common Market Law Review*, 30 (1), 17–69.

Curtin, D. (1995) 'The Shaping of a European Constitution and the 1996 IGC: Flexibility as a Key Paradigm?', *Außenwirtschaft*, 50, 237–52.

Czada, R. (2003) 'Der Begriff der Verhandlungsdemokratie und die vergleichende Policy-Forschung', in R. Mayntz and W. Streeck (eds), *Die Reformierbarkeit der Demokratie* (Frankfurt-am-Main: Campus).

Dahl, R. (1994) 'A Democratic Dilemma: System Effectiveness and Citizen Participation', *Political Science Quarterly*, 109 (2), 23–34.

Defrance, C. and U. Pfeil (eds) (2005) *Le Traité de Élysée et les relations franco-allemandes, 1945, 1963, 2003* (Paris: CNRS Editions).

Dahrendorf, R. (1979) 'A Third Europe?', Jean Monnet Lecture at the European University Institute, Florence, 26 November.

Dalgaard-Nielsen, A. (2006) *Germany, Pacifism and Peace-Enforcement* (Manchester: Manchester University Press).

Damsgaard, O. (2008) 'Disparities and Potentials in the BSR', *Baltic Rim Economies*, 4/2008.

Davies, N. (1999) *The Isles: A History* (London, Macmillan).

de Búrca, G. (2001) 'Legal Principles as an Instrument of Differentiation? The Principles of Proportionality and Subsidiarity', in B. De Witte, D. Hanf and E. Vos (eds), *The Many Faces of Differentiation in EU Law* (Antwerp: Intersentia), 131–44.

de Búrca, G. and J. Scott (eds) (2000) *Constitutional Change in the EU: From Uniformity to Flexibility?* (Oxford: Hart Publishing).

Delanty, G. and C. Rumford (2005) *Rethinking Europe. Social Theory of the Implications of Europeanization* (London and New York: Routledge).

de Larosière (2009) *The High Level Group on Financial Supervision in the EU: Report (The de Larosière Report)*, Brussels, 25 February, at: http://ec.europa.eu/internal_market/finances/docs/de_larosiere_report_en.pdf

Delevic, M. (2007) 'Regional Cooperation in the Western Balkans', Chaillot Paper No. 104 (Paris: Institute for Security Studies).

Delhey, J. (2007) 'Do Enlargements Make the European Union Less Cohesive? An Analysis of Trust between EU Nationalities', *Journal of Common Market Studies*, 45 (2), 253–79.

Delors, J. (2000) 'Europe Needs an Avant-Garde, But …', Centre for Economic Reform, *CER Bulletin*, 14, October–November.

Delors, J. (2001) 'An "Avant-Garde" Driving the European Unification Process Forward', speech to the International Bertelsmann Forum, Berlin, 19–20 January (Paris: Notre Europe).

Delpla, J. and C. Wyplosz (2007) *La Fin des Privileges* (Paris: Hachette).

Del Sarto, R. A. and T. Schumacher (2005) 'From EMP to ENP: What's at Stake with the European Neighbourhood Policy towards the Southern Mediterranean' *European Foreign Affairs* Review, 10 (17), 17–38.

Del Sarto, R., T. Schumacher, E. Lannon and A. Driss (2006) *Benchmarking Democratic Development in the Euro-Mediterranean Area: Conceptualising Ends, Means, and Strategies*, A EuroMeSCo Report, at: www.euromesco.net/images/hr%20benchmarking%20draft%20final.pdf

Den Boer, M., A. Guggenhühl and S. Vanhoonacker (eds) (1998) *Coping with Flexibility and Legitimacy after Amsterdam* (Maastricht: European Institute of Public Administration).

De Neve, J.-E. (2007) 'The European Onion? How Differentiated Integration is Reshaping the EU', *Journal of European Integration*, 29 (4), 503–21.

Deporte, A. (1991) 'The Foreign Policy of the Fifth Republic', in J. Hollifield (ed.), *Searching for the New France* (London: Routledge), 250–74.

Derrida, J. and J. Habermas (2003) 'Unsere Erneuerung – Nach Dem Krieg: Die Wiedergeburt Europas', *Frankfurter Allgemeine Zeitung*, 31 May.

De Schutter, O. (2005) 'Anchoring the European Union to the European Social Charter: the Case for Accession', in G. de Búrca, B. De Witte and L. Ogertschnig (eds), *Social Rights in Europe* (Oxford: Oxford University Press), 111–52.

Deutsch, K. W. (1957) *Political Community and the North Atlantic Area: International Organization in the Light of Historical Experience* (Princeton: Princeton University Press).

Deutsch, K. W. (1966) *Nationalism and Social Communication. An Inquiry into the Foundations of Nationality,* second edition (Cambridge, MA: MIT Press).

Dewatripont, M., J. Giavazzi, I. von Hagen, T. Harden, T. Persson, G. Roland et al. (1995) *Flexible Integration: Towards a More Effective and Democratic Europe* (London: Centre for Economic Research).

De Witte, B. (2005) 'Future Path of Flexibility: Enhanced Cooperation, Partial Agreements and Pioneer Groups', in J. W. de Zwaan, J. H. Jans, F. A. Nelissen and S. Blockmans (eds), *The European Union: An Ongoing Process of Integration* (Cambridge: Cambridge University Press), 141–52.

Dimitrov, V., K. H. Goetz and H. Wollmann (2006) *Governing after Communism: Institutions and Policymaking* (Lanham: Rowman & Littlefield).

Dimitrova, G. (1999) *The Limited Effectivenes of Transitory Regional Trade Arrangements in East-Central Europe: The Case of CEFTA*, Unpublished MA dissertation (Budapest: Central European University, Department of International Relations and European Studies).

Dimitrova, G. (2008) *From Bright Light to Blackout: The Influence of the Europeanization Paradigm on Bulgarian Foreign Policy and Transport and Energy Infrastructure Policy*. Unpublished PhD dissertation (Budapest: Department of International Relations and European Studies, Central European University).

Di Palma, G. (1977) *Surviving Without Governing: The Italian Parties in Parliament* (Berkeley: University of California Press).

Directorate-General for Education and Culture (2003) *From Berlin to Bergen: the EU Contribution*, Brussels: European Commission, A2/DVPH, 8 November.

Djelic, M.L. and K. Sahlin-Andersson (eds) (2006) *Transnational Governance: Institutional Dynamics of Regulation* (Cambridge: Cambridge University Press).

Dover, R. (2005) 'The Prime Minister and the Core Executive: A Liberal Intergovernmentalist Reading of UK Defence Policy Formulation 1997–2000', *British Journal of Politics and International Relations*, 7 (4), 508–21.

Drazen, Allan (2001) 'The Political Business Cycle after 25 Years', *NBER Macroeconomics Annual 2000* (Boston, MA: MIT Press).

Duffield, J. (1999) 'Political Culture and State Behaviour: Why Germany Confounds Neo-Realism', *International* Organization, 53 (4), 765–803.

Duke, Simon (2008) 'The Future of EU–NATO Relations: A Case of Mutual Irrelevance Through Competition?', *Journal of European Integration*, 30 (1), 27–43.

Dumbrell, John (2001) *A Special Relationship: Anglo-American Relations in the Cold War and After* (London: Macmillan).

Durkheim, E. (1964) *The Division of Labour in Society* (New York: Free Press).

Duval, R. and J. Elmeskov (2006) *The Effects of EMU on Structural Reforms in Labour and Product Markets*, Frankfurt am Main: ECB Working Chapter 596, March.

Dyson, K. (1994) *Elusive Union: The Process of Economic and Monetary Union in Europe* (London: Longman).

Dyson, K. (2000) *The Politics of the Euro Zone* (Oxford: Oxford University Press).

Dyson, K. (ed.) (2006) *Enlarging the Euro Area: External Empowerment and Domestic Transformation in East Central Europe* (Oxford: Oxford University Press).

Dyson, K. (2008) 'The European Central Bank: Enlargement as Institutional Affirmation and Differentiation', in E. Best, T. Christiansen and P. Settembri (eds), *The Institutions of the Enlarged European Union: Continuity and Change* (Cheltenham: Edward Elgar), 120–39.

Dyson, K. (2009a) 'The Evolving Timescapes of European Economic Governance: Contesting and Using Time', *Journal of European Public Policy*, 16 (2), 286–306.

Dyson, K. (2009b) '50 Years of Economic and Monetary Union: A Hard and Thorny Journey', in D. Phinnemore and A. Warleigh-Lack (eds), *Reflections on European Integration* (Basingstoke: Palgrave Macmillan), 143–71.

Dyson, K. (2009c) 'Europeanization, Power and Convergence in Central Banking: Historical and International Context', in K. Dyson and M. Marcussen (eds), *Central Banks in the Age of the Euro: Europeanization, Convergence and Power* (Oxford: Oxford University Press).

Dyson, K. and K. Featherstone (1999) *The Road to Maastricht: Negotiating Economic and Monetary Union* (Oxford: Oxford University Press).

Dyson, K. and K. Goetz (eds) (2003a) *Germany, Europe and the Politics of Constraint* (Oxford: Oxford University Press).

Dyson, K. and K. Goetz (2003b) 'Europeanization Compared: The Shrinking Core and the Decline of "Soft" Power', in K. Dyson and K. Goetz (eds), *Germany, Europe and the Politics of Constraint* (Oxford: Oxford University Press), 349–76.

Dyson, K. and M. Marcussen (2010) 'Transverse Integration in European Economic Governance: Between Unitary and Differentiated Integration', *Journal of European Integration*, 32 (1), 17–39.

Dyson, K. and L. Quaglia (2008) 'Committee Governance in Economic and Monetary Union: Policy Experts and their Images of Europe', in *Communities of Experts in the European Union: Final Report*, EU INTUNE, Department of Politics, University of Exeter.

Dyson, K. and L. Quaglia (2010) *European Economic Governance: Commentary on Key Documents, Volume 1: History* (Oxford: Oxford University Press).

Dyson, T. (2005) 'German Military Reform 1998–2004: Leadership and the Triumph of Domestic Constraint over International Opportunity', *European Security*, 14 (3), 361– 86.

Dyson, T. (2007) *The Politics of German Defence and Security: Policy Leadership and Military Reform in the Post-Cold War Era* (New York: Berghahn).

Dyson, T. (2008) 'Convergence and Divergence in Post-Cold War British, French and German Military Reforms: Between International Structure and Executive Autonomy', *Security* Studies, 17 (4), 725–74.

Economides, S. (1992) *The Balkan Agenda: Security and Regionalism in the New Europe*, London Defence Studies 10 (London: Brassey's/Centre for Defence Studies).

Economist, The (2008) 'Mamma Mia. The Return of Silvio Berlusconi', 17 April.

Economist, The (2006) 'Sailing Apart?', 13 September.

Eder, K. (2004) 'The Two Faces of Europeanization: Synchronizing a Europe Moving at Varying Speeds', *Time and Society*, 13 (1), 89–107.

Edwards, G. (2008) 'The Construction of Ambiguity and the Limits of Attraction: Europe and Its Neighbourhood Policy', *Journal of European Integration*, 30 (1), 45–62.

Edwards, G. and E. Philippart (1997) 'Flexibility and the Treaty of Amsterdam: Europe's New Byzantium?', Occasional Paper No. 3 (University of Cambridge: Centre for European Legal Studies), 1–23.

Eder, K. (2004) 'The Two Faces of Europeanization: Synchronizing a Europe Moving at Varying Speeds', *Time & Society*, 13 (1), 89–107.

EGAS (2006), *La Dimension Européenne des Politiques Sociales* (Paris: La Documentation Française).

Egeberg, M. (2005) 'The EU and the Nordic Countries: Organizing Domestic Diversity?', in S. Bulmer and C. Lequesne (eds), *The Member States of the European Union* (Oxford: Oxford University Press).

Egeberg, M. and J. Trondal (1999) 'Differentiated Integration in Europe: The Case of EEA Country, Norway', *Journal of Common Market Studies*, 37 (1), 133–42.

Ehlermann, C.D. (1984) 'How Flexible Is Community Law? An Unusual Approach to the Concept of "Two Speeds"', *Michigan Law Journal*, 4 (3), 246–70.

Ehlermann, C.D. (1998) *Differentiation, Flexibility, Closer Cooperation: The New Provisions of the Amsterdam Treaty* (Florence: European University Institute).

Eichengreen, B. (2007) 'The Euro: Love It or Leave It?', *Vox*, 19 November, at: www. voxeu. org/ index.php?q=node/729

Eising, R. and B. Kohler-Koch (1999) 'Governance in the European Union: A Comparative Assessment', in R. Eising and B. Kohler-Koch (eds), *The Transformation of Governance in the European Union* (London: Routledge).

Ekengren, M. (2002) *The Time of European Governance* (Manchester: Manchester University Press).

Elgstrom, O. and M. Smith (2006) *The European Union's Role in International Politics: Concepts and Analysis* (London: Routledge).

Elman, C. (1996) 'Horses for Courses: Why *Not* Neorealist Theories of Foreign Policies?', *Security Studies*, 6 (1), 7–53.

Elveren, A.Y. and M. Kar (2005) 'Turkey's Economic Integration into the EU: Challenges and Opportunities', paper given at the European Union Studies Association (EUSA) Biennial Conference, 31 March–2 April, Austin, Texas.

Emerson, Michael, et al. (2007) *European Neighbourhood Policy Two Years On: Time Indeed for an 'ENP Plus'*, CEPS Policy Brief 126, March (Brussels: CEPS).

Emerson, Michael (2008a) *The EU's New Black Sea Policy: What Kind of Regionalism Is This?* CEPS Working Document 297/July (Brussels: CEPS).

Emerson, Michael (2008b) *Making Sense of Sarkozy's Union for the Mediterranean*, CEPS Policy Brief 155/2008 (Brussels: CEPS).

Emmanouilidis, J. (2008) *Conceptualizing a Differentiated Europe*, ELIAMEP Policy Paper 3, 2008 (Athens: ELIAMEP).

Eralp, Atila (1993) 'Turkey and the EC in a Changing Post-War International System', in C. Balkir and A.M. Williams (eds), *Turkey and Europe* (London and New York: Pinter).

Erhel, C., L. Mandin and B. Palier (2005) 'The Leverage Effect. The Open Method of Co-ordination in France', in J. Zeitlin and P. Pochet (eds), with L. Magnusson, *The Open*

Method of Coordination in Action. The European Employment and Social Inclusion Strategies (Brussels: P.I.E.-Peter Lang), 217–48.

Erler, Gernot (2007) 'Towards a New EU Ostpolitik? – Russia, Eastern Europe and Central Asia', Speech, 7 February, at: www.auswaertiges-amt.de/diplo/en/Infoservice/Presse/ Reden/2007/070207-Erler-EUOstpolitik.html.

Eriksen, E.O. and J.E. Fossum (2007) 'Europe in Transformation; How to Reconstitute Democracy?', RECON Online Working Paper 01 (Oslo: Centre for European Studies) at: www.reconproject.eu/main.php/RECON_wp_0701.pdf?fileitem=5456091

Esping-Andersen, Gosta (1990) *The Three Worlds of Welfare Capitalism* (Cambridge: Polity).

EUObserver (2008) 'EU Leaders Agree to Weakened Mediterranean Union Plan', 14 March, at: http://euobserver.com/9/25835

EURActiv (2008) 'Summit Approves "Union for the Mediterranean"', 14 March, at: www. euractiv.com/en/enlargement/summit-union-mediterranean/artcle-170976

Eurobarometer (various years), Public opinion surveys (Brussels: Commission of the European Communities), at: http://ec.europa.eu/public_opinion/index_en.htm

European Central Bank (2004) *The Monetary Policy of the ECB* (Frankfurt-am-Main: ECB).

European Council (2008) Presidency Conclusions June 2008, at: www.consilium.europa. eu/ueDocs/cms_Data/docs/pressData/en/ec/101346.pdf

European Parliament (2001) 'European Parliament Resolution on Malta's Application for Membership of the European Union, and the State of Negotiations' (A5–0262/2001).

European Supply Agency (2008) *Annual Report 2007* (Luxembourg: Commission of the Eropean Communities), at: http://ec.europa.eu/euratom/ar/last.pdf (accessed 13 January 2009).

EUROSTAT (n.d.) accessed at http://epp.eurostat.ec.europa.eu

EU-Turkey Negotiating Framework (2005), at: http://trade.ec.europa.eu/doclib/docs/2007/ september/tradoc_135916.pdf

Eyre, S. and M. Lodge (2000) 'National Tunes and a European Melody? Competition Law Reform in the UK and Germany', *Journal of European Public Policy*, 7 (1), 63–79.

Eyre, S. and N. Sitter (1999) 'From PTT to NRA: Towards a New Regulatory Regime', in K. A. Eliassen and M. Sjøvaag (eds), *European Telecommunications Liberalization: Too Good to be True?* (London: Routledge), 39–52.

Falkner, G., O. Treib, M. Hartlapp and S. Leiber (2005) *Complying with Europe* (Cambridge: Cambridge University Press).

Falkner, G., O. Treib and E. Holzleithner (2008) *Compliance in the Enlarged European Union* (Aldershot: Ashgate).

Farrell, H. and A. Héritier (eds) (2007) *Contested Competences in Europe: Incomplete Contracts and Interstitial Institutional Change*, special issue of *West European Politics*, 30 (2).

Farrell, T. (2008) 'The Dynamics of British Military Transformation', *International Affairs*, 84 (4), 777–807.

Faure, M., J. Vervaele and A. Wael (1994) *Environmental Standards in the EU in an Interdisciplinary Framework* (Antwerp: Maklu).

Featherstone, K. and C. Radaelli (2003) *The Politics of Europeanization* (Oxford: Oxford University Press).

Ferrera, M. (2006) *The New Boundaries of Welfare* (Oxford: Oxford University Press).

Ferreira-Pereira, L. (2006) 'Inside the Fence but Outside the Walls: Austria, Finland and Sweden in the Post-War Security Architecture', *Cooperation and Conflict*, 41 (1), 99–122.

Ferrero-Waldner, Benita (2006) 'The EU's Role in Tackling Current International Challenges', speech to the World Jewish Congress Governing Board, 12 November, at: http:// europa.eu/rapid/pressReleasesAction.do?reference=SPEECH/06/678&type=HTML &aged=0&language=EN&guiLanguage=en

Fischer, J. (2000) 'From Confederacy to Federation: Thoughts on the Finality of European Integration', speech at the Humboldt University of Berlin, 12 May.

Fischer, J. (2004) 'Klein-europäische Vorstellungen funktionieren einfach nicht mehr', interview with Foreign Minister Fischer, *Berliner Zeitung*, 28 February.

Fischer-Lescano, A. and G. Teubner (2004) 'Regime-Collisions: The Vain Search for Legal Unity in the Fragmentation of Global Law', *Michigan Journal of International Law*, 25 (4), 999–1046.

Flora, P. (ed.) (1999) *State Formation, Nation-Building and Mass Politics in Europe. The Theory of Stein Rokkan* (Oxford: Oxford University Press).

Flournoy, M. and J. Smith (2005) *European Defense Integration: Bridging the Gap Between Strategy and Capabilities* (Washington, DC: Centre for Strategic and International Studies).

Fossum, J. E. (2001) 'Identity-politics in the European Union', ARENA Working Paper 17 (Oslo: Centre for European Studies).

France 24 (2007) Mediterranean Union broadcast report, at: www.france24.com/france 24Public/en/archives/news/world/20071220-europe-sarkozy-prodi-zapatero-mediterranean-union-plan.php

Friis, L. and A. Murphy (2000) '"Turbo-charged Negotiations": The EU and the Stability Pact for South Eastern Europe', *Journal of European Public Policy*, 7 (5), 767–86.

Fry, Michael (2006) 'Scotland Alone', *Prospect*, 29 December.

Furlong, P. (2005) 'British Higher Education and the Bologna Process: An Interim Assessment', *Politics*, 25 (1), 53–61.

Gaja, G. (1998) 'How Flexible is Flexibility under the Amsterdam Treaty?' *Common Market Law Review*, 35, 855–70.

Galbreath, D. and J. Lamoreaux (2007) 'Bastion, Beacon or Bridge? Conceptualizing the Baltic Logic of the EU's Neighbourhood', *Geopolitics*, 12 (1), 109–32.

Galli, F. (2008) *The Legal and Political Implications of the Securitisation of Counter-Terrorism Measures across the Mediterranean*, EuroMeSCo Paper 71, at: www.euromesco.com.pt/images/paper71eng.pdf

Gamble, Andrew (2003) *Between Europe and America: The Future of British Politics* (London: Palgrave Macmillan).

Gamble, A. and G. Kelly (2002) 'Britain and EMU', in K. Dyson (ed) *European States and the Euro* (Oxford: Oxford University Press), 97–119.

Garcia, M. and N. Karakatsanis (2006) 'Social Policy, Democracy and Citizenship in Southern Europe', in R. Gunther, P. N. Diamantouros and D. Sotiropoulos (eds), *Democracy and the State in the New Southern Europe* (Oxford: Oxford University Press), 87–138.

Garton-Ash, T. (1994) *In Europe's Name. Germany and the Divided Continent* (London: Vintage).

Geddes, Andrew (2002) *The Politics of Migration and Immigration in Europe* (London: Sage).

Gegout, C. (2002) 'The Quint: Acknowledging the Existence of a Big Four–US *Directoire* at the Heart of the European Union's Foreign Policy Decision-Making Process', *Journal of Common Market Studies*, 40 (2), 331–44.

George, Stephen (1994) *An Awkward Partner: Britain in the European Community* (Oxford: Oxford University Press).

Gerber, D. (1998) *Law and Competition in the Twentieth Century: Protecting Prometheus* (Oxford, Clarendon Press).

Giavazzi, F. and M. Pagano (1988) 'The Advantage of Tying One's Hands: EMS Discipline and Central Bank Credibility', *European Economic Review*, 32 (5), 1055–82.

Girotto, Dimitri (2007). 'Parliamentary Procedures in Italy Concerning EU Drafts and Community Law Implementation', European Commission for Democracy through Law Report, 4 October, at: http://www.venice.coe.int/docs/2007/CDL-UDT (2007)013-e.pdf

Giscard d'Estaing, V. and H. Schmidt (2000) 'Time to Slow Down and Consolidate Around "Euro-Europe"', *International Herald Tribune*, 11 April.

Giuliani, M. (1999) 'Europeanization and Italy', paper prepared for the Annual Conference of the European Community Studies Association, Pittsburgh, 2–5 June.

Giuliani, M. and S. Piattoni (2006) 'Italy: Back to the Future or Steps Toward Normality?', in E. E. Zeff and E. B. Pirro (eds), *The European Union and the Member States* (Boulder: Lynne Rienner).

Glasner, C. (1994) 'Realists as Optimists: Cooperation as Self-Help', *International Security* 19 (3), 50–90.

Glenny, M. (1993) *The Fall of Yugoslavia: The Third Balkan War* (London: Penguin).

Goble, P. A. (2005) 'Redefining Estonian's National Security', in A. Kasekamp (ed.), *The Estonian Foreign Policy Yearbook 2005* (Tallinn: Estonian Foreign Policy Institute),

Goetschel, L (ed.) (1998) *Small States Inside and Outside the European Union* (Dordrecht: Kluwer Academic Publishers).

Goetz, K. H. (2005) 'The New Member States and the EU', in S. Bulmer and C. Lequesne (eds), *Member States and the European Union* (Oxford: Oxford University Press), 254–80.

Goetz, K. H. (2006) *Territory, Temporality and Clustered Europeanization*, Reihe Polikwissen- schaft/Political Science Series Papers, 109 (Vienna: Institute of Advanced Studies), at: www.ihs.ac.at/publications/pol/pw_109.pdf

Goetz, K. H. (2007a) 'The EU Timescape: An Emergent Temporal Order', paper presented at the conference 'Institutional Dynamics and the Transformation of Executive Politics in Europe' organised by CONNEX research group 1, Barcelona, 7–9 June.

Goetz, K. H. (2007b) 'Territory', in P. Graziano and M. Vink (eds.), *Europeanization: New Research Agendas* (Basingstoke: Palgrave Macmillan), 73–87.

Goetz, K. H. (2009) 'How Does the EU Tick? Five Propositions on Political Time', *Journal of European Public Policy*, 16 (2), 202–20.

Goetz, K. H. and S. Hix (eds) (2000) *Europeanized Politics? European Integration and National Political Systems* (London: Frank Cass).

Goetz, K. H. and J.-H. Meyer-Sahling, J. (2008) 'The Europeanization of National Political Systems: Parliaments and Executives', *Living Reviews in European Governance*, 3 (2), at: http://europeangovernance.livingreviews.org

Goetz, K. H. and J.-H. Meyer-Sahling (2009) 'Political Time in the EU: Dimensions, Perspectives, Theories', *Journal of European Public Policy*, 16 (2), 180–201.

Golden, M. A. (2000) 'Political Patronage, Bureaucracy and Corruption in Postwar Italy', paper given to the Russell Sage Foundation, New York, 22 September, at: www.russellsage. org/publications/workingpapers/Political%20Patronage%20Bureaucracy%20and%20Corr uption%20in%20Postwar%20Italy/document

Goldmann, K. (2001) *Transforming the European Nation-State* (New York: Sage).

Gow, J. and C. Carmichael (2000) *Slovenia and the Slovenes: A Small State and the New Europe* (London: Hurst & Company).

Grabbe, H. and U. Guérot (2004) 'The Not-So-Big Three', *Wall Street Journal online*, 26 February 2004, at: www.cer.org.uk/articles/grabbe_wsj_26feb04.html

Grabitz, Eberhard (ed.) (1984) *Abgestufte Integration: Eine Alternative zum herkömmlichen Integrationskonzept?* (Kehl am Rhein/Strasbourg: N. P. Engel Verlag).

Grant, Charles (2006) *Europe's Blurred Boundaries: Rethinking Enlargement and Neighbourhood Policy*, October (London: CER).

Greskovits, Béla (2005) 'Leading Sectors and the Varieties of Capitalism in Eastern Europe', *Actes de Gerpisa*, 39: 113–28.

Griffiths, R. T. and H. Pharo (1995) *Small States and European Integration*, ARENA Paper No. 19 (Oslo: Advanced Research on the Europeanization of the Nation State).

Griller, S., D. P. Droutsas, G. Falkner, K. Forgo and M. Nentwich (2000) *The Treaty of Amsterdam: Facts, Analysis, Prospects* (Vienna: Springer Verlag).

Gros, D. and A. Steinherr (2004) *Economic Transition in Central and Eastern Europe: Planting the Seeds* (Cambridge: Cambridge University Press).

Gstöhl, S. (2002) *Reluctant Europeans: Norway, Sweden and Switzerland in the Process of European Integration* (London: Lynne Rienner).

Gstöhl, S. (2000) 'The European Union after Amsterdam: Towards a Theoretical Approach to (Differentiated) Integration', in M. G. Cowles and M. Smith (eds), *The State of the European Union Vol. 5: Risks, Reform, Resistance, and Revival* (Oxford: Oxford University Press), 42–63.

Guay, T. and R. Callum (2002) 'The Transformation and Prospects for Europe's Defence Industry', *International Affairs*, 78 (4), 757–76.

Gunther, R., P. N. Diamantouros and D. Sotiropoulos (2006) *Democracy and the State in the New Southern Europe* (Oxford: Oxford University Press).